Idaho

for the curious

a guide

Cort Conley

First Edition

Backeddy Books
Box 301
Cambridge, Idaho 83610

Other titles available from Backeddy Books:
The Middle Fork and the Sheepeater War (1977).
River of No Return (1978).
Snake River of Hells Canyon (1979).

Library of Congress Cataloging in Publication Data

Conley, Cort, 1944-
   Idaho for the curious.

   Includes index.
   1. Historic sites – Idaho – Guide-books. 2. Idaho – Description
and travel – 1981-   – Guide-books. 3. Idaho – History,
Local. 4. Automobiles – Road guides – Idaho. I. Title.
F747.C66   016.91796'0433   82-1706
ISBN 0-903566-3-0   AACR2

The whole object of travel
is not to set foot on foreign land,
it is at last to set foot on one's own country
as foreign land.

G. K. Chesterton

To Johnny and Pearl Carrey:
the kind of persons whose generosity,
compassion, and humor make Idaho
such a special place.

Table of Contents

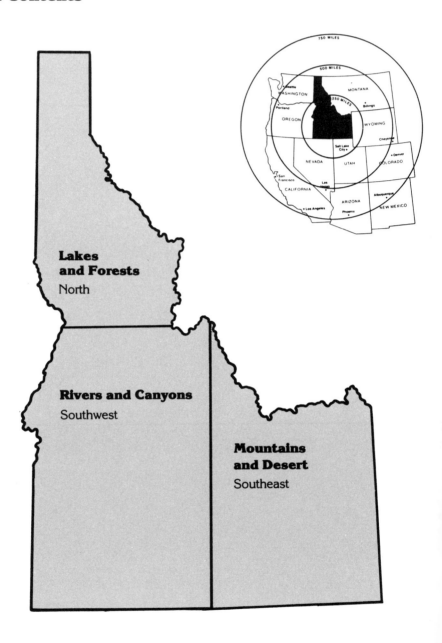

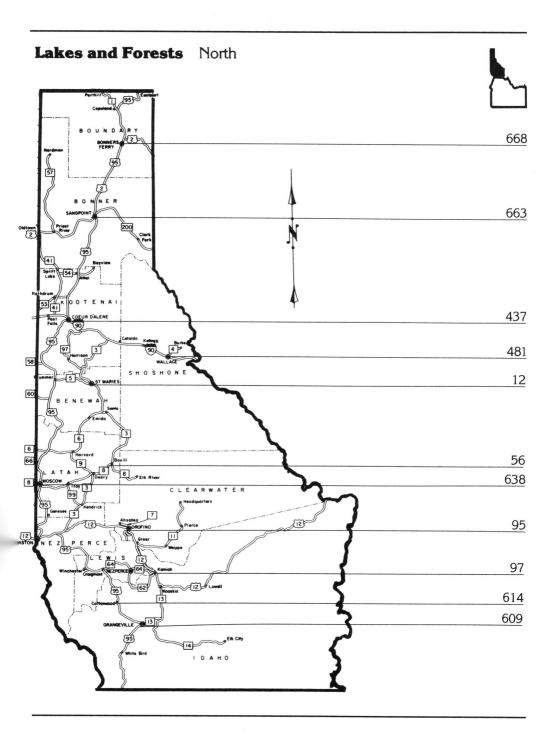

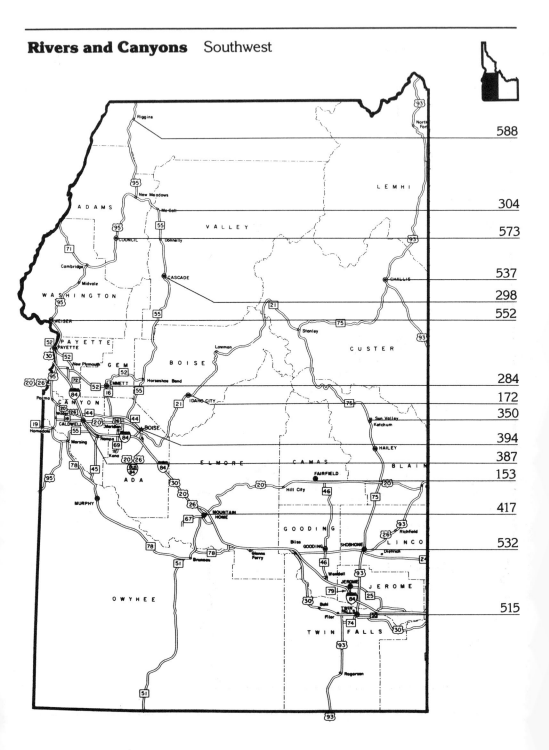

588

304
573

537
298
552

284
172
350

394
387
153

417

532

515

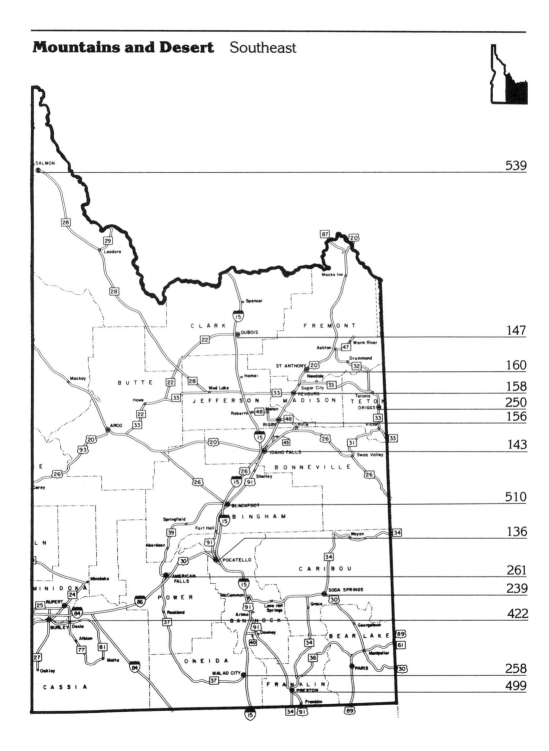

539

147

160

158

250

156

143

510

136

261

239

422

258

499

Acknowledgments

This guide is almsman to historians who worked for many years; without their efforts, in fact, it could not have been written.

A special debt to one of these historians, Dr. Merle Wells, is hereby acknowledged. No one can long trace Idaho history without discovering paths cut earlier by him, or without being deeply grateful that he clearly marked so many trails.

Other authors whose commentaries are too invaluable to go unmentioned include J. Meredith Neil, Fritz Kramer, John Carrey, Sr. Alfreda Elsensohn, John Fahey, Brigham Madsen, Grace Bartlett, Jim Huntley, Pearl Oberg, Esther Yarber, Richard Magnuson, J. Patrick Wilde, Patricia Wright, Ralph Space, Dorice Taylor, Rafe Gibbs, John Miller, Layne Spencer, Bert Russell, Sandra Crowell, David Asleson, Lisa Reitzes, Don Hibbard, Lloyd Byrne, and Mildretta Adams.

In addition I am indebted to the following.

To the expert staff of the Idaho Historical Society, especially to Larry Jones, Judy Austin, Arthur Hart, Karin Ford, Marje Williams, Gary Bettis, Elizabeth Jacox, and Guila Ford.

To Dr. John Conley, Robert and Mary Lee Conley, and Dr. Earl Perry for indispensible editorial help.

To Gerry and Fran Conley for the "Roanoke Chair," and to Mike and Kathy Doolittle, Roger and Julie Sliker, Keith and Ruth Gilmore, Charlie and Gretchen Clelland, and Jinny Hopfenbeck, my gratitude is equal.

For assistance of other kinds, to Jo and Harold Soules; Clyde, Mildred, and Dean Snell; Henry and Sherry Starr; Gary and Annie Clevidence; Jim Campbell, Jean Wilson, John and Karen Little; Bob and Joann Richel; Boyd and Barb Norton; Ann Strawn, Dorine Goertzen, Wallace and Mary Stegner; Stan Shephard, Rick Ripley, Jan Sevy, Bob and Marcia Beckwith; George Mancini, Karen Hopfenbeck, Julie Gorton, Nancy Goodman, Rolly and Mary Megorden, Peter and Carmela Alexander, Ginnie and Gordy Watts, Art Schoenfeldt, Bob and Virginia Hughes; Jerry Holes, Spud Dahler, Jim Woods, Max Pavesic, Bob Jarvis, Jim Cooney, Mike Stamper, Dave Kokot, Ray Chapman, Marie Driscoll, Paul Filer, Fred and Edna Shiefer; Mary Bokides, Fay Morris, Marvin Webb, Paul Fritz, Bill Vanluchene, John Powell, David Perkins, and Larry Adkins.

Jack Gruber of Potlatch Corp., Art Selin, Cliff Blake, Cort Sims, Jo Moltzen, and Fred Zensen of the U.S. Forest Service, Len Stears of the BLM, Ruth Kassens and Merl Mews of the Idaho Department of Parks and Recreation were very helpful.

Thanks also go to the following organizations: Idaho Department of Commerce and Development, Idaho Transportation Department, Idaho Air National Guard, *Idaho Statesman,* Weyerhaeuser Timber Co., and Oregon Historical Society.

Appreciative recognition is given to the photographic skills of Duane Garrett, Larry Hill, Ernie Day, and Media Specialties.

Special permission to reprint the following items is acknowledged:

Page 149 Lucullus McWhorter, *Yellow Wolf,* © 1940 Caxton Printers.

Page 244 *Oregon Trail,* Loren Eiseley, *Notes of an Alchemist.* © 1972 by Loren Eiseley. Reprinted with the permission of Charles Scribner's Sons.

Page 344 *The River Merchant's Wife: A Letter,* Ezra Pound, *Personae.* © 1926 by Ezra Pound. Reprinted by permission of New Directions.

Page 352 *At the Hemingway Memorial,* David Wagoner, *Collected Poems.* © 1980 by Indiana University Press.

Page 689 from *String Too Short To Be Saved* by Donald Hall. © 1978 by Donald Hall. Reprinted by permission of David R. Godine, Pub.

This is the first guidebook about Idaho in forty-odd years. The last one, *Idaho: A Guide in Word and Picture,* was done in 1937 by Vardis Fisher and his clerical helpers as part of the Federal Writers' Project under the New Deal. Since then, large tracts of Idaho's history have been surveyed, platted, and recorded.

The book is essentially a guide to history in a geographical context, to history both natural and human; it is *not* a guide to restaurants, motels and campgrounds. In the belief that any guidebook that resorts to "ask locally for directions" is unworthy of publication, throughout the directions are specific: where, when, how. The book deals with sights accessible by passenger car along 14,000 miles of Idaho roads, and always it answers questions for the incurably curious, such as the following. Where is the longest road without services in the country? When is the best time to visit the Birds of Prey Natural Area? How many persons have gone over Shoshone Falls? What is the meaning of Coeur d'Alene? Owyhee? Lapwai? Why is there a statue of Frank Steunenberg in front of the state capitol? Who was Pocatello? Tendoy? Limhi? Where is the finest mineral collection in the state? What parts of Idaho retain evidence of the worst floods on earth? Which is the queen of Idaho's ghost towns? How did the dredge at Yankee Fork operate? What town receives the least rain? the most snow? Where can one see the route of Lewis and Clark or the ruts of the Oregon Trail? What poet was born in Hailey? Who was William Craig? Fern Hobbs? Charlie Sampson? What Idaho lake is used to test Navy submarines? Where can one mine star garnets? Why did the state's white pine forests disappear? Where is the most impressive log building? the largest barn? the most mysterious mansion?

Material has been arranged according to highway number: south-north highways have odd numbers; west-east highways are evenly numbered. (With few exceptions, the numbers begin in the north with 1 and increase in size as the traveler moves south.) The system used here allows any visitor to pursue his itinerary simply by following the proper sequence of numbers through the book. Side trips of interest are introduced in the text at the point where the detour leaves the main road.

Since most visitors arrive in Idaho from the west, and from the south, the narrative follows even-numbered highways west to east, and odd-numbered highways south to north. Directions, however, are given according to compass point, thus anyone traveling in a counter-direction will still find the guide useful.

Because much of Idaho's history is the history of its villages, general information about each town is included, beginning with the derivation of its name, for, as Wallace Stegner has said, "the names contain our history as the seed contains the tree." In the larger towns a tour is suggested.

Most of the photographs in the book are historical, used with the assumption that travelers enjoy comparisons between past and present. Although some contemporary views are included, towns and sites are largely shown as they once looked – the present is apparent; the past beguiles.

Probably this guide sins by inclusion, rather than by exclusion, but should a reader detect gaps (or errors), a note to the publisher will be welcome.

Idaho, the last state to be discovered by white explorers, was largely ignored by non-Indians for over fifty years after Lewis and Clark groped their way across its convoluted terrain. Known as the Oregon country, its only visitors were fur hunters from the North West and Hudson's Bay Companies, Presbyterian and Catholic missionaries, and westering emigrants who followed the Oregon Trail.

By 1853 the area north of the Columbia River and west of the Cascades was sufficiently settled to establish Washington Territory, which encompassed all of present-day Idaho in 1859, when Oregon was admitted to the Union.

Unlike other western states, Idaho was eventually settled by a reverse migration eastward, when gold was discovered in the Clearwater and Salmon River canyons.

The sudden shift in population caused the Washington legislature to become sorely concerned that the territorial capital in Olympia might also shift east. Abetted by the citizens of Lewiston, the politicians managed to lop the mining country into a new Territory.

The word "Idaho" was coined in 1860 by a promoter for the Colorado mines of the Pikes Peak district. Changed to "Colorado" by the U.S. Senate, the word persisted in the name of the mining camp, Idaho Springs.

Later that same year, a friend of the promoter named his steamboat on the Columbia River the *Idaho,* and since it carried miners bound for the diggings of the Clearwater and Salmon Rivers, their destination became known as the "Idaho" mines. In 1863 Senator Henry Wilson of Massachusetts persuaded his colleagues to christen the new Territory "Idaho."

Before its borders were finally established, the shape of Idaho was modified in 1864 by the creation of Montana (a change unanimously requested by the Idaho legislature), and again in 1868 with the formation of Wyoming.

Over the next two decades, Idaho mining activity came and went like a swamp light; the greatest development occurred, however, after 1890.

As settlers overspread aboriginal lands with a thoroughness that must have made the natives wish Columbus had discovered some other country, the Territory experienced three Indian wars (1877-1879), prefigured, perhaps, by the Battle Creek slaughter in 1860, the bloodiest of all Indian engagements fought in the U.S.

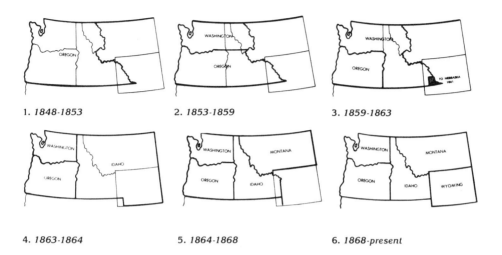

1. *1848-1853*　　　2. *1853-1859*　　　3. *1859-1863*

4. *1863-1864*　　　5. *1864-1868*　　　6. *1868-present*

Extensive railroad construction within the state from 1878 to 1884 gave birth to new towns, along with markets for their crops, livestock, lumber, and mineral wealth.

On July 3, 1890, after decades of a north-south sectional rivalry, and stormy attempts to divide the Territory between Washington and Nevada, thwarted only by presidential veto, Idaho was finally admitted to statehood.

The Carey Act of 1894, and the Reclamation Act of 1902, opened to irrigated farming a large area of the Great American Desert in south Idaho. Where earlier there had been only tall sage and rabbitbrush, now reservoirs and canals successfully converted 2 million acres to productive cropland.

From 1900 to 1920 thick stands of white pine, Douglas fir, and ponderosa pine were exploited. Despite disastrous fires in 1910 and 1919, and the advantage given Pacific Coast sawmills by the completion of the Panama Canal, the lumber industry of the state became second only to agriculture in economic importance.

Gold mining enjoyed a brief resurgence during the Depression of the 1930s, and Idaho was also the beneficiary of the largest share of Civilian Conservation Corps projects.

In 1938 the first paved highway (U.S. 95) linked the north and south areas of the forty-third state. At that time, the state system contained only 2,000 miles of asphalt roads; it now includes over 5,000 miles.

As elsewhere, World War II had a major effect on the region. Airbases were established in Boise, Pocatello, and Mountain Home; a large naval training center was opened on Lake Pend Oreille, a naval ordinance plant was erected in Pocatello and a Japanese relocation center at Hunt.

Post-war growth has been linked to the development of agriculture, as well as forestry, phosphate mines, hydroelectric projects, and nuclear engineering.

Although Idaho was the last state to be discovered, little time was lost in catching up with its neighbors, and no skywriter is needed now to spell the changes that have occurred in the last decade, when the population increased by more than 30 percent.

Many of the transformations have been regrettable, but "If the changes that we fear be thus irresistible," as Samuel Johnson observed, "it remains that we can retard what we cannot repel, and palliate what we cannot cure." In this light, some aspects of Idaho's heritage must be regarded as more important than corporate enterprise or legislative parsimony – aspects such as rivers, mountains, and parks; libraries, museums, and universities.

State Highway No. 1 from a junction on U.S. 95 southeast of Copeland northwesterly to the International Boundary near Porthill. Route length: 11.1 miles.

Highways 1 and 95 divide like a dowsing rod fifteen miles north of Bonners Ferry. A ten-mile drive north on 1 ends at **Porthill**: port-on-a-hill at the International Boundary.

The Idaho Continental mine, on the crest of the Selkirk Range, six miles from this community, produced 850,000 ounces of silver and 44 million pounds of lead for the Bunker Hill and Sullivan Company between 1915-1924. Other mines near Porthill added $1 million to the production of the area from 1940 to 1950.

For an inviting side trip, leave Highway 1 a mile from its intersection with U.S. 95. Take the paved road on the left, which points west; then after one mile, take the left fork across the bridge over the **Kootenai River**.

The waters of this 464-mile river, that drain 19,000 square miles, visit the U.S. twice: the source is in British Columbia, the river flows south into Montana, turns west into Idaho, and then flows northwest back into Canada, where it joins the Columbia, which in turn enters the U.S. in Washington. One can row or motor-boat the Kootenai from Montana to the Kootenay Lake in British Columbia.

Large areas of farmland along the Kootenai River in the Bonners Ferry area have been reclaimed from the river's flood plain. The project began in 1936, when the Public Works Administration funded eight contracts for diking irrigation districts along the river. The work was done by Morrison-Knudsen Company, though not without difficulty. Ice five to thirteen inches thick had to be broken in order to move the draglines along the frozen river.

After crossing the bridge, continue 1.5 miles to the Road 417 intersection. Turn right on 417 and drive eight miles northwest, traveling between the Kootenai River and the foot of the Selkirks.

Watch for a concrete bridge over Smith Creek – there is no sign. The pull-off on the shoulder can accommodate one vehicle. For a look at **Smith Falls**, take a brief walk along the viewpoint trail on the south side of the creek, to the upper bridge. The falls are on private property, and proceeding past the bridge without permission would be an unwarranted intrusion.

After a visit to the falls, it is possible to continue up Road 417, where a five-mile climb up the apron of the Selkirks provides a raven's eye view of the Kootenai River: gray-blue coils impressed on the glacially sedimented valley have cut the classic meander patterns of an ancient river – the best oxbows in the state.

Smith Falls on Smith Creek.

U.S. Highway No. 2 from the Idaho-Washington state line in Oldtown easterly via Priest River, Sandpoint, Bonners Ferry and Moyie Springs to the Idaho-Montana state line. (Overlaps U.S. 95 from Sandpoint to Bonners Ferry, 36 miles not included.) Route length: 44.3 miles.

Highway 2 enters Idaho from Newport, Washington, a town that was named in anticipation of steamboat traffic up the Pend Oreille River.

Two miles east of Newport, on the south side of Highway 2, is **Albeni Falls Dam**. A short exit road ends at an overlook area with an information building, restrooms and drinking fountain.

Albeni Poirier, a French-Canadian from Quebec, and one of thirteen children, came to north Idaho on the first Northern Pacific passenger train. He ran a cattle ranch with his brother until 1892, then moved to the land at Albeni Falls with his wife, Mary.

The dam was authorized, funded, designed, and under construction in less than a year – another of the Korean War era dams justified under the guise of the National Defense Program – though the war was fought to a stalemate without it, since the first generators did not begin to spin until two years after the war had been concluded, and none of the transmission lines went to defense plants.

Albeni Falls, looking north before the dam (left).

Albeni Falls, winter view.

Albeni Falls Dam was built as a U.S. Corps of Engineers project in 1951 at a cost of $33 million. It uses Pend Oreille Lake as a reservoir and coordinates water release with dams on the Columbia River system. The hydroelectric facilities are interconnected with the plants of other Northwest Power Pool members. Spillway length: 400 feet, gate height: forty feet.

The **Pend Oreille River** (now slackwater) which parallels the road from this point to the fringes of Sandpoint, drains most of the Idaho panhandle. In Idaho, only the Snake River has a larger mean annual flow. Pend Oreille River leaves the lake to flow westward twenty-five miles through Idaho, then northward through Washington and British Columbia to its confluence with the Columbia River. It drains an area of 25,000 square miles.

Many of the farms in this valley lie on a fertile mantle of alluvial and glacial deposits that well-drilling reveals are at least 470 feet deep.

The **town of Priest River** on Highway 2 is located at the confluence of that river with the impounded Pend Oreille. When Jim Hill's Great Northern Railroad came west from Montana and then south from Kootenai to Rathdrum in 1891-1892, the company advertised for laborers. Italian immigrants responded, and when track construction was completed, many of them remained in the area and filed on homesteads. As soon as money could be saved for their fares, wives and relatives also immigrated. Hence numerous residents of this community have Italian surnames.

Each spring, beginning in 1901 and for thirty years thereafter, millions of feet of white pine, ponderosa, and cedar logs from the slopes of Priest Lake country were rafted down the Priest River to Pend Oreille Lake, and on down to Newport, Washington. The third weekend in July commemorates the skills of these "river pigs" and "bankbeaver" with a logger's celebration in town. The festivities include championship log birling and lumberjack contests.

The community also has docks, where vacationers can launch their boats and travel twenty-five miles up the Pend Oreille River before entering Pend Oreille Lake. Campsites are available en route.

On the south side of the river, about eight miles east of Priest River, at the mouth of Hoodoo Creek, was **Seneacquoteen**, for a half-century one of the best-known settlements in Idaho. The word is from the Kalispell or Pend Oreille Indians and means crossing.

There were luxuriant meadows along the river here, and Indians often camped at the site while following a trail from the Spokane River, over the Rathdrum Prairie, to this ford across the Pend Oreille. The trail continued northward to a Kootenai River crossing near later Bonners Ferry.

North West Company trappers began to use the trail in 1810 – the explorer David Thompson camped here; American trappers from Astor's Pacific Fur Company arrived at the location in the spring, 1813.

In 1859 the International Boundary survey party had a base camp at Seneacquoteen, and a year later the first log building and ferry were established by Thomas Forde. Four years later, the Kootenay gold rush brought mining traffic, and the name "Wild Horse Trail" was attached to the pack route from the ferry to the Wild Horse mines in British Columbia. Men, and mules loaded with

4

freight, headed for the Alder Gulch mines in Helena, Montana, along this route because the Mullan Road had fallen into disrepair. Miles Moore, who became governor of Washington, kept a trading post here. The settlement at the crossing was named seat of Kootenai County by the second Territorial Legislature because, at the time, it was the most populated post in northern Idaho, but nothing came of the designation because fifty people could not be found to qualify the spot for a county government. However, the first school in the county opened here and served the site for fifty years.

Surveyors used Seneacquoteen as a campsite while they laid out the line for the Northern Pacific Railway in 1881, but railroads diminished the location's importance: the Northern Pacific crossed the river to the east of it and ten years later the Great Northern crossed west of it. With the first wagon bridge at Sandpoint in 1910, the old crossing lost what significance had remained. Seneacquoteen guttered out, like a campfire in the rain. The only clue that it ever existed is the cemetery on the hillside.

Laclede, across the river from Seneacquoteen, was founded in 1891, as the Great Northern was being built, and was named for an engineer on the railroad. The train brought supplies and mail to the new community, and a large sawmill offered more stability and employment than did the trading post across the water.

(At Sandpoint, U.S. Highway 2 merges with U.S. 95 to Bonners Ferry. See U.S. Highway 95, Sandpoint.)

U.S. Highway 2 resumes its eastward path three miles north of Bonners Ferry. Eight miles from that intersection is the **Moyie Bridge**, suspended 450 feet over the Moyie River Canyon. This impressive steel truss bridge is 1,223 feet long and was a two year project completed in 1964 at a cost of $1.4 million. It is the second-highest span in Idaho.

A steel tower was erected on each side of the canyon with a highline suspended between them. A "traveler" carried loads back and forth over the site. The first time it was used, the cable pulled one of the towers over as it collapsed into the canyon – the first of many problems for Northern Imperial Construction, a Seattle firm that dissolved after this contract.

The old bridge, built in 1923, can best be seen from a parking area at the east end of the new bridge, on the south side of the highway. From this location it is also possible to see the 212-foot Moyie Dam, built by the city of Bonners Ferry in 1949 to replace a dam twenty-eight years older. In the spring, **Moyie Falls** is worth a side trip. Drive down the road which leaves U.S. 2 just west of the bridge, at the community of **Moyie Springs**. Take the paved road south; it curves north beneath the new bridge. This road will allow the visitor to walk over to the cascades below the reservoir and overlook the falls as it plunges into the pool by the power plant.

Highway 2 reaches the Montana border nine miles southeast of the new bridge.

Upper Moyie Falls (left) and Lower Moyie Falls.

A scenic twenty-mile drive on a decent gravel road can be made alongside the waters of the **Moyie River**. The river is initially concealed in a forested canyon east of the road but gradually reveals itself as a thread that quilts together meadows and glades.

To reach the Moyie River Road 211, head north on the last road before the west abutment of the Moyie Bridge, on the north side of Highway 2.

This drive rambles past abandoned homesteads, orchards, and hayfields. After six miles the road forks – keep to the right and that road crosses the Moyie River after 0.4 miles. The road travels north against the grain of the descending river and both avenues are paralleled by the rail route of the **Spokane International**. This railroad has a tale worth unfolding.

At the turn of the century, Spokane businessmen felt the Northern Pacific and Great Northern were taking unfair advantage with their high freight rates. Canadian Pacific charges were much more reasonable, set on the theory that "pigs get fat and hogs get butchered." Shippers in Washington wanted out of the hog pen.

6

A competing railroad appeared feasible at the time because north Idaho was beginning to market its resources. Weyerhaeuser was buying timber lands. Farms were being irrigated, and some mines looked promising. In 1905, D. C. Corbin, who had earlier developed the narrow-gauge Coeur d'Alene Railroad in the Silver Valley, incorporated the Spokane International Railway Company. It was organized in close cooperation with the Canadian Pacific, which agreed to finance part of the construction in return for an option to purchase the line by 1917.

Corbin began laying track in February, 1906, and the job was completed nine months later at Spokane. The 140-mile line cost him $3,634,000.

The new railroad opened with 11 locomotives, 200 new freight cars, and 12 passenger cars. The coaches were meretricious: crimson and gold, trimmed in green, and upholstered with burgundy silk plush.

The company enjoyed a brisk business. It added branch lines to Lakes Pend Oreille and Coeur d'Alene, carried passengers, lumber and agricultural products. In 1916 Corbin sold to the Canadian Pacific for "a satisfactory price." He was eighty-four.

Canadian Pacific controlled the S. I. until the Depression, when the Spokane, unable to meet bond interest charges and other fixed debts, petitioned for reorganization. The railroad was reorganized as an independent company. Then in 1956 the Interstate Commerce Commission set aside objections by other major railroads, including the Canadian Pacific, which wanted to regain control of the S. I., and authorized merger of the Spokane International with the Union Pacific system.

Follow the Moyie River Road north to U.S. 95; it is possible to drive 5.5 miles farther and view **Copper Creek Falls**. (See U.S. 95, Copper Creek Falls)

State Highway No. 3 from a junction on U.S. 12 at Arrow northerly via Juliaetta, Kendrick, Deary, Bovill and St. Maries to a junction with I-90 north of Rose Lake. (Overlaps Highway 8 for 9.9 miles.) Route length: 117.8 miles.

State Highway 3 begins eight miles east of Lewiston at U.S. Highway 12. **Juliaetta** is nine miles north of the Highway 12 junction.

3

This town is located on a homestead filed in 1878; the first postmaster named the settlement after his two daughters.

After abandoning its attempt to reach Lewiston from Genesee (because of Lewiston Hill), the Northern Pacific made another attempt to come south from Moscow by way of the Potlatch River canyon. Work halted in late 1890 at Juliaetta because permission had not been obtained to cross the Nez Perce reservation. While lawyers litigated, Lewiston merchants raised $75,000 and purchased most of the right-of-way from the reservation to the city, but the Panic of 1893 delayed construction another six years. (The railroad is now part of Burlington Northern).

Juliaetta had a flour mill in 1882 and an 8,000-cans-per-day cannery in 1911.

In 1902 Juliaetta Institute, later known as the Foster School of Healing, opened its doors, and Professor Robert Foster taught magnetic and suggestive healing, which brought a certain notoriety and consequential affluence to a fraction of the town.

The community's museum is located in a cement-block mansion one block west of the highway, known locally as the "Castle." The castle was built about 1906, by Abram A. Adams, a stonemason from New York. He poured the eight-inch-thick concrete blocks himself, and made the main interior wall eighteen inches thick. The house had nine rooms, embossed metal ceilings, central heating and carbide lights. Adams lived in the "castle" with his five children; his wife had died in Minnesota.

The castle-turned-museum contains enough items and photographs to merit a visit. One curious story, revealed by a display, involves a Canada goose that Mr. Adams shot in 1909, in Canada. He found whole grains of wheat in its craw, which he planted in Idaho. The mature grain developed heads five inches long and almost two inches wide. He applied for a patent, and for two years marketed his "Alaska Wheat" in small quantities as seed grain. It produced seventy bushels per acre.

Two other items are worth remarking: a leather, six-inch-long steamboat ticket for the *Mountain Gem* (a vessel which plied the Snake River from 1904 to 1905), and a stunning five-foot model of a Case threshing machine made many years ago by a grandfather for his grandson.

Kendrick is 3.4 miles north of Juliaetta. The town, founded in 1889, was first called Latah, but when the Northern Pacific established its station, it named the depot after its chief engineer.

8

Ties for the railroad were cut along Big Bear Creek, which parallels the tracks southeast of Troy, and were floated down to the work crews. A railroad bridge was built in Kendrick in 1898 and guided down the Potlatch River to its abutments on the Clearwater.

The settlement was virtually destroyed by fire in 1904; most of the buildings on Main St. are later than that. The brick fraternal temple on the corner of Main and Seventh was built in 1905 as a joint venture by the Knights of Pythias, the Masons and the Oddfellows. It is now shared by the Masons, Eastern Star and the Grange.

Highway 3 travels 16.8 miles along the west side of Big Bear Ridge, to State Highway 8 at Deary. Highway 8 is superimposed on Highway 3 northeast to Bovill for ten miles (see State Highway 8).

Clarkia is located on Highway 3 about 15.5 miles north of Bovill.

From a point five miles south of the village, to an area five miles north of it, the traveler drives through a region occupied by a shallow lake 20 million years ago: **Miocene Lake Clarkia**. It formed quite rapidly after volcanic flows in the region of Santa dammed the precursor to the St. Maries River. Sedimentation also occurred with rapidity, assisted by volcanic ash, filling thirty feet in perhaps a few decades.

In the early 1970s a remarkable fossil legacy was recognized, revealed during construction of a race track near Clarkia. Fossil beds then discovered east and west of Clarkia presented an opportunity for cooperative scientific investigation at the University of Idaho.

The remains were abundant: a one-foot square, twenty-seven-foot column analyzed by layers revealed over 10,000 plant megafossils. More than 100 species of woody plants have been found. Many leaves were preserved as complete cellular impressions. Conifer shoots, cones, and moss, with the aid of acid baths, were removed as three-dimensional specimens.

Because the biota were deposited in water-saturated, unoxidized clays, leaves with autumnal colors and beetles with their metallic hues have been found. Some of the Clarkia insects represent rare Miocene records of their families or genera. Two types of fish and specimens of a snail and clam were also uncovered.

The fossils represent the complete life cycle of a Miocene lake. Undisturbed leaf chemistry was found in many of the specimens, providing an opportunity to explore questions concerning changes or differences among existing plants and their ancestors.

3

IDAHO

Investigations have revealed that the St. Maries River valley, in the foothills of the Northern Rockies, had a forest which could only exist in a warm, humid climate: hardwoods dominated by many genera that are now extinct in western North America. Among the plants represented in fossil form are redwood, magnolia, tupelo, persimmon, loblolly bay, bald cypress and hydrangea.

Rutledge Timber Company's railroad headquarters was located two miles south of Clarkia, on the eastern side of the highway. There were large barns to shelter logging horses during the winter, a railroad roundhouse and shop, cookhouse and bunkhouses. The site was known as the Rutledge Ranch.

Clarkia, called "Clarkie" by early residents, was a lumber-boom town. Witnesses say there were often several hundred horses along the main street during the rush for homesteads. While the white pine lasted, the community had its rough element, with saloons and gay ladies, even a bootlegger who hid his bronco-whiskey behind the altar of the Catholic Church. By 1928 Clarkia had acquired a more sedate atmosphere.

Clarkia, early view.

The turnoff for the **Emerald Creek Garnet Area** is on the west side of State Highway 3, about 5.5 miles north of Clarkia. Follow Road 447 southwest six miles up Emerald Creek to the only place in the world where the public is welcome to dig for star garnets.

Garnet is a mineral which normally forms in rocks subjected to high temperatures and pressure: 900 degrees F., and 70,000 psi. Elements required for formation include iron, magnesium, aluminum, silicon and oxygen.

Star garnets with four or six-ray stars are the collector's item. The star effect is called asterism, a phenomenon caused by light reflected from inclusions of titanium dioxide needles in the garnet crystal. The number of rays depends on whether the needles are oriented in two or three directions.

Garnets in alluvial deposits are normally found in a gravel and sand strata just above bedrock. (For this reason, the deeper one digs, the better his chance of success.) The only known deposits of star garnet are in Idaho and north India.

Through the efforts of Idaho Congressmen (the star garnet is the state gem), the Department of Interior's mineral regulations were expanded in 1973, authorizing the Forest Service to issue garnet-digging permits in the Emerald Creek area. The Forest Service administers the No Name Gulch location for watershed protection.

The garnet area is open from June through September. A USFS employee at the information center above the parking lot will explain the regulations and technique, exhibit sample garnets, and issue a permit for a nominal fee.

Garnet digging, like most mining, is hard, dirty work. However, if one has rubber boots, a shovel and bucket, a ¼-inch screen, and considerable determination, he has a fair chance of finding a garnet. In a typical season, 1,500 permits are issued and 2,000 pounds of gems are removed.

On the drive up Carpenter and Emerald Creeks, one can see evidence of one of the largest commercial garnet placer operations in the country. Emerald Creek Garnet, Inc. produces about 13,000 tons of finished garnet-sand a year. The product is used as an abrasive in sand-blasting and as a filtration medium.

Remnants of splash dams and a railroad trestle stand in the creek. In the 1920s Shay locomotives hauled white pine and cedar logs to the Milwaukee branch line from this drainage.

Fernwood, five miles north of the Emerald Creek turnoff, was originally Fennwood; a typographical error is responsible for the present spelling. Saturday nights in this town, between 1913 and 1930, were wild as a Santa Fe fiesta. Frank Blackwell's sawmill operated here during those years. Substantial logging camps were on all the nearby drainages, and weekends brought a torrent of lumberjacks into town, eager for booze, gambling and women.

Logs came down the St. Maries River from Clarkia and others spilled out of Emerald Creek. The drives on the St. Maries were not as large as those on the St. Joe, but they were still a colorful annual event.

From Fernwood, Highway 3 moves twenty miles north to St. Maries. The road crosses the St. Maries and St. Joe Rivers within a half-mile of each other as it travels through town.

St. Maries was the archetypal north-Idaho lumber town. More than most towns, it owes its existence to its location: the south bank of the St. Joe, just a few hundred yards west of the confluence with the St. Maries River.

The three Fisher brothers built the first sawmill in 1889. The St. Maries Land Co., owned by the directors of the Chicago, Milwaukee and Puget Sound (St. Paul) Railroad, subdivided lots on the site when an extension of the line arrived in 1909.

St. Maries, with float houses, on the St. Joe River.

By 1910, when the Great Idaho Fire skipped over the town, its "skid road" had already begun to acquire a dubious fame. There were saloons with girls and cribs upstairs; there were brawls and murders. In floathouses along the river, the belles of St. Maries – Molly and Giggles, and Josie and Nellie – made the world of the logger a little less hard, a little less solitary, and a little more expensive.

12

A large sawmill was opened by the St. Maries Lumber Co. in 1913. Fred Herrick owned the mill for seven years; his bankruptcy allowed Rogers Lumber Co. to buy it. Rogers survived the Depression, and a devastating flood in 1933, but a fire in the yard and sheds shut down the operation in 1940.

The mill was reopened by new owners in 1943 and was run successfully until 1961, when it was destroyed by fire. The St. Maries mill production is estimated to have exceeded 1 billion board feet; now a Potlatch plywood plant occupies the site.

The town of St. Maries became the seat of Benewah County in 1915, because of a prior arrangement with the voters of Kootenai County and Coeur d'Alene city.

St. Maries, from 1902-1915, was the location of John Porter White's shoe shop. J. P. White had skidded hardwood logs in West Virginia, and had learned to make calked boots from his father. He repaired shoes for the community and made one pair of boots each day by hand. He kept his customer's measurements on file. Thus began the most famous logging boot company in the west. White moved to Spokane in 1915, and after his death in 1939, J. P.'s son, Otto, ran the business until 1972. Men working in the shop became co-owners, and White's boots are still the standard against which others are measured.

As mentioned earlier, St. Maries River log drives were not as impressive as those of the St. Joe, but they were still significant. The river flow was supplemented by the water impounded behind an 18-foot high, 400-foot long log dam on Flat Creek, six miles northwest of Santa.

The railroad brought immense quantities of logs to St. Maries from 1918-1923; some trains had 150 loaded cars and each car weighed sixty tons.

In August, 1917, a redneck vendetta was directed against members of the IWW in the St. Maries area. The county fairgrounds, south of the St. Joe River, were converted to a barbwire stockade, and thirty-eight men were held, in violation of their constitutional rights, for selling IWW literature. Many of the townspeople sympathized with the goals of the Wobblies and managed to provide them with food while the men were detained. All charges were eventually dismissed. The IWW strikes served a purpose. As Oscar Blake has written:

At the time I'm writing about, lumberjacks and slough pigs carried their own blankets. There were terrible conditions in the logging camps; especially in the St. Joe area. Most of the bunkhouses had no floors; neither did the cook houses. The food

13

*was not too good. You took baths in the creeks. There were no
screens on the cook house windows or doors. Wobblies with their
strikes and sabotage corrected all of that.*

The rivers, which make the site of St. Maries a strategic one, also
caused the community considerable hardship. The effects of
several severe floods finally brought action by the Army Corps of
Engineers in the early 1940s. The Corps diked most of the industrial
and farm land along the southern bank of the St. Joe.

At the top of the hill on West Main Ave. at Twenty-first St. is the
Woodlawn Cemetery. Drive to the rear of the graveyard to see a
large, corner plot, where gravestones set in a ring constitute the Fire
Fighters' Circle. The fifty-seven corpses exhumed in the St. Joe
River drainage were reburied in this circle in 1912. In 1924 the USFS
appropriated $500 to mark the graves.

These men were killed while employed (for twenty-five cents an
hour) by the U.S. Forest Service as firefighters during the **Great
Idaho Fire of 1910**. (The sites where they died are mentioned,
where relevant, in this book.) A number of competent histories
concerning the fire have been assembled, but since the blaze had
national, as well as local, repercussions, it seems appropriate to
summarize the event. Only the briefest sketch is given here.

The snowfall in the winter of 1909 was normal, but summer
drought came early. July was hotter than a burned boot and crops
withered. The U.S. Forest Service was only five years old; it lacked
fire control appropriations, a reservoir of trained firefighters and
sufficient fire tool caches.

By August, the Bitterroot country, which included the Coeur
d'Alene and St. Joe Ranges, was as hot and dry as the back log of
hell. Several hundred fires simmered in the area. President Taft
authorized the use of Army troops to fight fire, and eight companies
were assigned to Region One.

Rangers were hopeful that the situation could be contained until a
break in the weather reduced the hazard. The likelihood of such an
event, according to Murphy, is always inversely proportional to its
desirability. The weather went awry.

A strong wind blew in from the southwest with hell hung on its
heels. Trees started burning like grass in a prairie fire. From the Nez
Perce National Forest in Salmon River country, north to the
Canadian border, fires conflated and flamed along many-mile fronts,
preheating their own fuel. On foot, on horseback, and on trains
people scurried to get out of the way – all but eighty-five did. The
fire destroyed small Montana towns on the east side of the
Bitterroots, and a third of Wallace, Idaho, burned. But many other

towns, such as Mullan, Murray, Burke, Gem, Avery, Elk City and St. Maries were spared by fate or backfire.

The fire on August 21 would not stop for God, man or wild horse. It raged along the Continental Divide, through the Blackfoot, Flathead, and Missoula National Forests. The central portion of the Coeur d'Alene Forest had a thirty-mile front that galloped sixty miles east into the Lolo National Forest, all the way to the Clark Fork River. Two other fires swept unhaltered north and east out of the Coeur d'Alene Mountains into the Cabinet National Forest. That fire then slammed into the Pend Oreille National Forest. The Kootenai and Kaniksu Forests also suffered destructive fires.

At the south end of the Coeur d'Alene National Forest, blazes on the headwaters of the St. Joe united with those on the North Fork of the Clearwater to desolate the northern end of the Clearwater National Forest. Township after township of the Lochsa and Selway River drainages burned quicker than hell can scorch a feather.

On August 23 increasing humidity and some precipitation began to retard the fire's advance; widespread rain snuffed the last flames at month's end.

When the smoke, which extended as far east as Denver, cleared, an inventory revealed about 3 million acres had burned – nearly 4,700 square miles in twenty-one National Forests. Estimates of the timber loss ran as high as 9 billion board feet: the equivalent of all the lumber cut in the eleven western states in 1910. The loss in erosion and stream damage was incalculable.

The fire produced other serious after-effects. Heavy stands of dead timber produced new fire hazards. Snags and downfall so clotted the country that they produced and fueled a whole cycle of subsequent fires: 1919, 1922, 1926, 1929. These fires reburned nearly 35 percent of the area involved.

In turn, pine bark beetles infested scorched trees, and as the pest grew in numbers it invaded green timber, too.

The Great Idaho Fire of 1910 did, however, spur the passage of the precedent-making Weeks Law in 1911, which established the basic pattern for federal-state cooperation in firefighting that has been followed ever since. The same year, Congress authorized deficit financing for fighting forest fires. This was over the objections of Idaho's Senator Weldon Heyburn, who insisted the fires were "inspired by divine providence to get the land ready for homesteaders."

Large-scale salvage logging operations began in 1911 and continued for several years. Though charcoal is a good barrier to fungus, burned timber still checks and blues; salvage profits decreased each year. (Loggers and horses worked in unimaginable dust and were black as the hair in Satan's beard most of the time.)

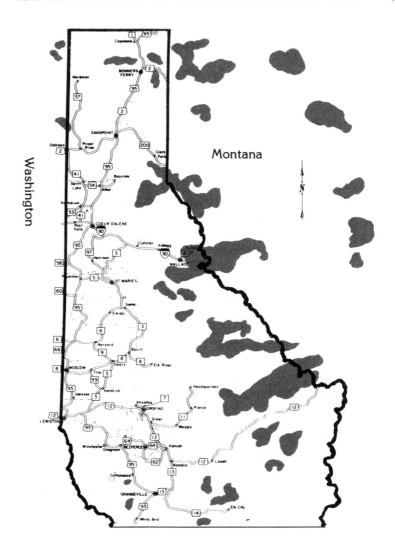

Areas affected by the Great Idaho Fire of 1910.

Mullan Trail Park is across West Main Ave. from the Woodlawn Cemetery. A three-spool, Willamette donkey engine is visible on one corner of the park. The donkey was used until 1928 on Hobo Creek above the St. Joe River. In 1958 it was skidded out to a lowboy and brought to town.

One block off Main Ave., at the corner of Ninth and Center, stands the Kootenai Inn, a three-story brick and stucco building erected by the Milwaukee Land Co. in 1910. The inn, which housed potential investors when they came to inspect the district's prospects, is a significant example of an early land development hotel. The ground floor has been renovated for a restaurant and cocktail lounge. The Kootenai Inn contains what may be the oldest piano in the Northwest, an instrument that was in Georgia during the Civil War, then at Fort Sherman in Coeur d'Alene, before being brought across the lake to St. Maries by the steamboat *Amelia Wheaton.*

St Joe River Road (East)

A loop drive up the **St. Joe River road** to Avery, then up Marble Creek over Hobo Pass and down to Clarkia at Highway 3, is one of the half-dozen more interesting historical-scenic drives to be made in Idaho. Route length: 77.7 miles.

Drive northeast out of St. Maries, up the St. Joe River. Fleets of cottonwoods forest the shoreline; the water tooling slowly through entangled reflections readily explains the phrase "the shadowy St. Joe." A visitor boating up the river in 1907 remarked that the cottonwoods were so dense their tops bridged the river, creating a canopy. Patriarchal white pines and cedar also grew along the shores.

At that time, the 120-mile river was one of the best trout fisheries left in America; many local newspaper accounts reported abundant catches of western cutthroat trout, with seven to nine-pound fish quite common. As the water quality deteriorated, and recreation pressure increased, the fishery was reduced to its present mediocre status.

In early July the upper thirty miles of the St. Joe offer challenging water for the experienced kayaker; the seventy-mile stretch from Avery down to Coeur d'Alene Lake provides a pleasant summer float for anyone with a boat and a lifejacket.

About 12.5 miles up the river from St. Maries, on the north side, between the road and the water, was the site of **Ferrell**. Its locator, William Ferrell, selected the piece of meadowland in 1883, and was in such a lather to reach it that, rather than await the thaw, he sledded his jonboat across the icy lake from Coeur d'Alene. Ferrell cut hay and boated it to Fort Coeur d'Alene (later Ft. Sherman). As prospectors and homesteaders became interested in the upper St.

17

Joe, the town's founder built the Ferrell Hotel on river pilings, opened a store, and began selling town lots.

This landing was the head of navigation for steamboats from Coeur d'Alene Lake. At 2,198 feet above sea level, the St. Joe is regarded as the highest navigable river in the world, and as such, was the destination of many excursion steamers.

As the population grew, two more hotels were added. By 1907 the town had Bill Dollar's Idaho Bank and Trust Co., a telephone office, drugstore, and ten saloons. Five steamboats a day moored at the landing. Word filtered through that the Chicago, Milwaukee and Puget Sound railroad had chosen the St. Joe corridor as part of its western extension from South Dakota to Seattle, and nearly a thousand people alighted on the area.

As the railroad surveyors established the right-of-way along the river, William Ferrell decided he would hold out (or up) for $100,000. Western railroads played hardball with people like Ferrell: the Milwaukee gave him nothing – it simply bridged the river east of his flat and came down the opposite (south) bank. Then the Milwaukee Land Co., a subsidiary of the railroad, purchased acreage across from Ferrell's town, platted a new townsite and sold lots. Farewell Ferrell. A ferry operated across the river until the new town, **St. Joe City**, overshadowed its rival. Within four years, William Ferrell was forced to move upriver to make a living. By 1925 only a school house marked the site of the town that had carried nis name. The empty field is a homily on "the vanity of human wishes."

St. Joe City.

18

St. Joe City rose on the gas of rising expectations. Dollar's bank switched riverbanks. Construction crews and all supplies for the railroad flowed to St. Joe's wharf and were unloaded for transportation over the tote road (some called it a "goat road") to Calder.

At the same time, many homesteaders were claiming magnificent white pine stands under the Timber and Stone Act of 1878, or the Forest Homestead Act of 1906. The former allowed any eligible person to file upon and acquire title to 160 acres of timber land in the public domain under provisions more liberal than the Homestead Act. The latter allowed one to file on 160 acres within the newly created Forest Reserves if the settler could show potential for agricultural development. After "proving-up," title could be acquired for $2.50 an acre under Timber and Stone, or $1.25 an acre under Forest Homestead. The law stipulated that the claimant could not have made "... directly or indirectly ... any agreement or contract, in any way or manner, with any persons whatsoever, by which the title ... should inure, in whole or in part, to the benefit of any person but himself."

Timber barons and speculators drooled at the prospect of acquiring the patented sections and obviously subverted the law by conspiring with homesteaders who had neither the knowledge nor the capital to log the land themselves. Claims sold briskly for $8,000-$10,000, depending on the quality of timber they contained.

Homesteaders and claim jumpers, loggers, gandy dancers, laborers of every nationality, saloon keepers and sporting ladies, grifters and drifters all eddied into St. Joe City.

A sawmill opened to cut ties for the railroad. The Milwaukee Land Co. bought and enlarged it. The railroad depot went up in 1907. A hospital and school were established. Early St. Joe was so favored, even the Great Idaho Fire of 1910 did not trouble it.

The Milwaukee mill operated until 1920, then it was sold to the Rose Lake Lumber Co., and that company cut white pine until 1926. The sawmill, which had produced nearly 500 million board feet, burned two years later. St. Joe's prospects were tied to timber, and as the trees dwindled, so did the town.

The townsite can be visited by driving across the river bridge at Bond Creek.

After 3.5 miles, the road crosses **Fall Creek** bridge. Thomas "Honey" Jones homesteaded the meadow by the creek in 1907. Jones had a beard so long he carried it coiled within his shirt front.

19

He developed secluded picnic areas along the creek where tourists could camp and enjoy the falls. He changed a $1.00 fee and supplemented this income by selling the honey his bees produced. Honey Jones put on the wooden overcoat at age 91, in 1927, and is buried on the hill that overlooks his meadow.

Fall Creek was considered the division point between the swiftwater of the upper river and the lethargic current of the lower. Well-paid boatmen poled svelte, elongated, shallow draft cedar or white pine canoes, loaded with freight, upriver from this point.

The road crosses railroad tracks after another mile. The tracks continue along the north side of the river to Avery, then climb the North Fork of the St. Joe and cross into Montana.

These are the rails of the Chicago, Milwaukee and Puget Sound, reorganized in 1927 as the Chicago, Milwaukee, and St. Paul. In the 1900s the C M & St. P was dependent upon its rivals, the Northern Pacific and Great Northern, for connections west of St. Paul. The railroad wanted its own access to the west coast, and in 1905 its board of directors authorized the construction of a 1,400-mile line from South Dakota to Seattle.

Since Standard Oil Co. was a major stockholder in the Milwaukee, and in the Montana mines, there was little doubt the route would come through Montana and northern Idaho, but the choice of the St. Joe canyon was a considerable surprise since the Lolo Pass was known to offer an easier passageway. The $77 million extension was completed in two years (1907-1909); however, the cost made the Milwaukee the most expensive of the transcontinental railroads. On its first freight haul from Tacoma, the train carried 500 tons of Japanese silk to the East Coast (see Avery).

The drive now enters an area that once contained a fair portion of the finest white pine forest in the world. When the forests of the Great Lakes had been skinned, the lumbermen moved west to Idaho. The timber folded in these mountains was wrestled to the river by rough, proud men. Their hard, dangerous work cut a brief, but significant channel in the historied bed of the St. Joe. There are several chronicles of logging; this is not the place for another. But unless their efforts are mentioned, the story here would be incomplete as a bob-tailed straight.

Loggers "rolled the round stuff" from the St. Joe and Clearwater Mountains with every device invented by their trade. As the easier sites were logged, plodding oxen were replaced with swifter horses. Much timber was hauled in the winter on go-devils or drays; sleighs were useful in flat, open areas such as a valley floor.

But the watery net that webs these hills was the key to transport. Sidestream strands of chutes fed mainstream splashdams and flumes that reached like filaments out from the web's center – the St. Joe River. If, to make a pun, Coeur d'Alene Lake was the "heart of all," then the St. Joe was the "vena cava" drawing logs from every capillary creek and rivulet in the region.

Hundreds of miles of chutes were constructed in the mountains. They were built with all the skill of a wooden pipeline, over difficult terrain, tapping remote areas of logging units. Chutes were dry, horizontal V-shaped troughs, fashioned from two logs, each with a smooth twelve-inch face on one side of the V. Logs could be horse-skidded or gravity fed down the gutter. In summer, some areas of high friction were greased with animal fat; in fall and winter slow sections could be iced. Finding a balance on the steep slopes was difficult: when logs traveled so fast that they smoked, or jumped the chute, iron "goosenecks" embedded in the trough would retard the logs by gouging them slightly; hot sand reduced the speed in icy spots.

Greasing a log chute in white pine country.

What furrows are to an irrigation ditch, so chutes were to flumes. Flumes required specialized contractors who provided their own teams of horses, and often a portable sawmill. Flumes were obviously built under more difficult constraints than chutes: water

21

grade, water tight, contoured and anchored on slopes steeper than the back of Paul Bunyan's head. Contractors charged $1.25-$2.00 a running-foot, which meant the finished product had to carry a large number of logs to justify the investment. Flume lumber was usually cut from low-value species like spruce and fir.

Logs were decked at the terminus of chutes, then rolled into the flumes. Often holding ponds and feeder flumes were constructed so that sufficient water could be collected overnight to flush the next day's cut. Great care had to be exercised not to let the logs outrun the water in the flume or a "maryann" would ensue that could be days in the untangling. (Incidentally, it was not uncommon for a 'jack to hitch a ride on a flume log if he was in a hurry to reach town.)

Loggers rolling white pine into a flume.

What irrigation ditches are to a canal, so the flumes were to driveable streams. Logs splashed out of the flumes into holding ponds that collected the creekwater behind a splashdam. Logs were driven down creeks to the St. Joe on the spring runoff, and on surge-releases from the dams during the drier season – as long as water conditions allowed.

Steam-powered donkey engines were skidded to the St. Joe country in about 1913. The upright steam boiler, that resembles a large can of stove polish, weighed many tons. The donkey had been developed in the coastal redwood forests to yard logs – by adapting a shipboard steam engine that had been used to sling cargo and weigh anchor. The donkey winched logs out of the woods with its steel spools by retrieving a cable, which was strung through snatch blocks.

22

Typical Idaho white pine stand.

23

At about the same period, railroads entered the St. Joe-Clearwater logging scene. Shay locomotives were used on short stretches to haul logs from decks to branch lines.

Once the timber reached the St. Joe from its tributaries, "river pigs," who had worked the logs down the creeks with pike pole and peavey, trailed them through the swiftwater. These men were burly as boulders, tough as a yard of latigo, working waist-deep in water cold enough to freeze a donkey's dong. They unsnarled jackstrawed jams and risked death daily, giving it no more thought than breathing. They had their own monikers, like "Moosehead" Hughes, "Mulligan" Hank, and "Dublin" Dan, and a language all their own, as well. They were nothing, if not colorful. Here is a hospitalized logger explaining his accident:

I was working on top, trompin' 'em down. The send-up man was a scissor-bill stubble-jumper that the startin' bar had sent out. He sent me up a swell-butted schoolmarm. It slewed cat-a-wampus and gunned. I told him to give 'er a Saginaw, but he give 'er a St. Croix and she gunned again. Broke four of my slats an' grounded me.

When the "stakey" loggers finally hit town, sometimes after six months in the "tall and uncut," they "blew 'er in" like the fur trappers, cowboys and miners before them. And like the white pine they cut, we will not see their like again.

Fitzgerald Creek, on the north side of the river, is reached after another mile along the road. It harbored a lengthy flume used to log the drainage in the late 1920s and early 1930s. The flume came beneath the railroad tracks, to the river.

Look above the road and note traces of the Milwaukee tote or "goat" road built in 1907-1908 from Little Falls through Calder to Goat Rock, near Spring Creek, about fourteen miles farther upriver. It was used by teams and wagons to haul freight, mail, and supplies to railroad construction crews.

At mile 25, the community of **Calder** can be seen on the north shore of the river. First called Elk Prairie, Calder was renamed when a railroad crew was stationed there. A homesteader had located on the meadow and opened a small store. The site escaped the 1910 fire and prospered somewhat when the Milwaukee Land Co. salvage-logged the burn to the north. It was further sustained by the Mica Creek logging show – there was even a sawmill in 1942.

24

Mica Creek flows in on the south after 2.7 miles more. Many Timber and Stone Act homesteads went to patent on the headwaters of this stream. A sawmill was built on the upper end in 1916 in order to cut lumber for an impressive flume which began floating logs out in 1917. St. Maries Lumber Co. operated with timber from Mica Creek from 1916-1920. Rose Lake Lumber Co. bought $100,000 worth of claims and ran a narrow-gauge railroad with a Shay locomotive in the drainage. Traces of the flume survive.

Another 1.5 miles brings the driver to Huckleberry Flat. Across the river, on the north bank, is the mouth of Big Creek, just below Herrick Flat.

The **Big Creek** drainage was scorched by the Great Idaho Fire of 1910: ten men were cremated on the middle fork of the stream and eighteen on the west fork – about seven miles from the river. Deadman Gulch and Cemetery Ridge commemorate the event.

Kokanee salmon were introduced to the St. Joe at the mouth of Big Creek in recent times and have established themselves as far as fifty miles upstream.

Fred Herrick built a logging camp on the flat at Big Creek after buying a large tract of white pine in the drainage. He began building a railroad up the east fork of the creek to bring the timber out. The 1910 fire destroyed his trees and track. He rebuilt sixteen miles of grade and conducted a salvage operation for several years.

Herrick was one of the most interesting figures of the Coeur d'Alene logging era. He came west from Wisconsin in 1909 (a "one-man migration" some called him), after he had already accumulated a sizeable fortune in the wood-products industry. Well past age fifty, he decided to form the Milwaukee Lumber Co. in Idaho. He treated his employees fairly, never truckled to the bigger outfits (Fred referred to the big game heads mounted on his office wall as his "board of directors") and was so successful that he became the largest independent lumber operator in the Inland Empire – worth about $12 million.

In the mid-1920s he won a contract-bid on an immense tract of National Forest timber in southeastern Oregon – a fifty-year supply for his operation. Development of a railroad and mill system required a multi-million dollar investment. Herrick borrowed heavily against his assets and then the Depression bankrupted him. He was seventy-five years old.

With public support, the Oregon congressional delegates succeeded in passing an act that returned $75,000 to Herrick from his Forest Service performance bond. He lived to be ninety-eight.

Herrick Flat was used for a CCC camp in the 1930s; about 200 men lived there. At that time it was not possible to travel from St. Joe to Avery except by boat or rail. There were nine CCC camps along the river, under control of the U.S. Army, but supervised by the Forest Service, which provided them with plans and equipment. The men received $30 a month and were expected to send $21 home. They built the road from St. Joe to Red Ives, several bridges, and did fire and flood control work as well. (The camp was badly flooded in 1933 and 1938.)

With the outbreak of World War II, the CCC came to an end. On V. J. Day in 1945, the two owners of the Herrick bar and their murderer were shot. The flat was abandoned.

Spring Creek, three miles farther up the river, marked the terminus of the tote road.

Two miles east on the river road is Marble Creek, and across the river is the mouth of Tank Creek, where the steam locomotives were rewatered. **Tank Creek** flows through a natural arch one-quarter mile above its confluence with the river. Before driving up Marble Creek, it is worth continuing upriver to Avery.

Slate Creek threads into the river from the north side, 5.5 miles from Marble Creek. This drainage burned in the 1910 fire. In the fall of that year, 3,500 pounds of hardwood seeds were planted on ninety acres by the Forest Service in an experiment to determine whether walnut, oak and hickory would grow in the area. Within a few years the seedlings had all frozen.

The McGoldrick Lumber Co. put a portable sawmill on the head of Slate Creek in 1915 and built trails, chutes, two splashdams and flumes to bring logs down the creek to the river. McGoldrick grappled 300 million board feet out of the Slate Creek basin, and those logs were towed across Coeur d'Alene Lake to the railroad that rolled them to the company mill in Spokane.

Hoyt Flat is six miles west of Avery. The U.S. Forest Service Avery Ranger District moved here from Avery in 1967 because more room was needed for housing regular and seasonal personnel. The railroad siding a mile above Hoyt was named Ethelton for John D. Rockefeller's grand-niece.

Storm Creek, one mile north of Ethelton, joins the St. Joe from the north side. Four miles up the creek, twenty-eight men were

26

incinerated by the Great Fire of 1910. Some of them were copper miners from Butte, Montana, who thought they knew better than the Forest Service when they were ordered to leave their meadow campsite for the town of Avery. For them, the fire arrived like the Battle Hymn's sword: terrible and swift.

When the district ranger and deputy sheriff arrived after the conflagration, they found most bodies burned beyond recognition. Watches, fused by the heat, fixed the time of death. One man, who had run up canyon, lived seven minutes longer than the others; the bodies were later buried at the St. Maries cemetery.

Four miles east: **Fishhook Creek** flows under the road and into the river. The creek is named for Fishhook Graham, a Southerner, who with his black friend, Brown Gravy Sam, ran a popular restaurant on this flat. They abandoned the enterprise when it was disrupted by the path of the railroad.

The 400-foot tunnel (four miles up the creek) and much of the road up Fishhook were completed by the CCC in 1939.

The creek, which once had a splashdam, was logged in the early Twenties.

Avery is situated two miles farther east along the river. Sam "49" Williams filed a claim and built a cabin on the site in 1894; his pards, Jake and Lee Setzer, settled nearby a few years later. The men did some trapping, and rafted logs downriver to Harrison.

The USFS cabin, which had been built three miles downstream, was moved to Avery when the railroad was staked. It was the railroad that established Avery, though "49" Williams founded it. Called "49" City and North Fork at times, the community became Avery in 1910, in honor of William Rockefeller's grandson. (Will was on the Milwaukee railroad's board of directors for forty years.) The settlement survived the 1910 fire because of backfires set along the edge of town.

Avery had a three-story hotel, then homes and a school. William Ferrell moved upriver after "49" Williams died and squatted on his claim. He built a store and a sawmill and feuded with the Forest Service, which filed trespass charges against him. At Ferrell's death in 1917, Avery had a population of 1,100 people, including a substantial Japanese colony.

The town was chosen as a transfer point by the C M & St. Paul railroad. The roundhouse established here employed 150 workers on three shifts. It must have been a noisy place as steam locomotives switched with electric engines to pull the cars over the North Fork stretch between Avery and Montana.

The railroad's expectations were diminished when the Panama Canal opened as an avenue to Oriental freight. The Milwaukee went into receivership in 1925, but emerged reorganized 1½ years later. The town's optimism was tempered, too. Trucks took much of the Milwaukee's business in later years. Steam locomotives were discontinued in 1957, and the Avery railroad car shop was closed in 1959. Passenger service ended two years later; in 1974 the division point was transferred to St. Maries. Diesel engines hauled more freight than ever in the 1970s, but the line had to file bankruptcy proceedings, and the last C M & St. P. engine came through in 1980. Faced with the "disappearin' railroad blues," Potlatch Corp. purchased the 115-mile section of the Milwaukee Road's Idaho lines for $4.5 million in May, 1980, and uses the St. Maries to Avery segment as a private line to haul timber.

The Milwaukee's roundhouse was dismantled for salvage, but the depot was converted to a community center and now includes a library and museum.

Electric locomotives of the Chicago, Milwaukee, & St. Paul Railroad.

Six early Forest Service structures remain in Avery. The log and frame, two-story, four room office with dove-tailed corners dates from 1909.

Avery may be unique among small Idaho communities. It has been visited by three Presidents: Taft Harding (a month before he died), and Truman (when he was Vice-President).

The road forks at the east end of Avery. The main road follows the St. Joe to **Red Ives** where the CCC built a Forest Service ranger station in 1935. The CCC also constructed a small dam half a mile up Ives Creek and laid a ten-inch wooden pipe down to a power plant by the river. The flow turned a waterwheel that was connected to a forty-amp direct-current generator. This power system provided lights for the ranger's station, warehouse and house for twenty-five years at a total maintenance cost of $500.

The north fork of the road past Avery travels up the **North Fork of the St. Joe** and over to Wallace; weather permitting, it is passable to passenger vehicles.

The stretch of the Milwaukee line that comes down the North Fork enters Idaho through the two-mile Taft tunnel at St. Paul Pass. The construction of the railroad for forty miles, from the Montana line down the North Fork and down the St. Joe cost $170,000 per mile, making it at the time "the largest cost ever paid by any railroad company in the world for a line of similar length." It required sixteen tunnels and twenty-one trestles. Two miles of flume were built to sluice fill down to the bridge sites. Crews worked on both sides of the Taft tunnel for six months – and that included one winter.

The railroad was opened to traffic in 1909. It evacuated several hundred people during the 1910 fire. Some were taken to Avery, others were hauled across burning trestles and into tunnels where they were able to survive. Ironically, the coal-burning engines were identified as the chief culprit for the start of the Great Idaho Fire of 1910.

The railroad lost fourteen bridges and several miles of rails and ties to the inferno. A crew of 325 bridge carpenters and 200 laborers worked a month to get the line reopened.

Forest Service regulations in the National Forests around Avery following the Great Fire forced the Milwaukee to switch from coal to fuel oil for its steam locomotives – an expensive change. This led to an interesting development on the rail system from Montana to Avery.

The Chicago, Milwaukee bought water rights to the St. Joe River, planning to build eleven dams for power to electrify the system. However, after consideration of seasonal flow variations, the board of directors was persuaded to buy electricity from Montana Power. (One of the board members was a major shareholder in Montana Power.) By 1917 400 miles of the line were electrified east of Avery. Cedar poles suspended copper wires above the tracks. It was the first such line in America – six times longer than any other in the world.

The railroad had a unique braking system that used the motors as generators while the train went down one side of the pass, in order to feed 40-60 percent of the power back into the system.

Electrification paid for itself in five years. The absence of steam boilers, which often froze during the winter, was an additional advantage. (President Harding called the electric section "... the most delightful ride I have ever known in my life.")

Curiously, the 200-mile gap from Avery to Washington was never electrified, so Avery was always busy, as steam engines switched with electric ones. Diesels replaced electricity in 1973, but not before the system was copied by many countries.

(From this point, return to Marble Creek.)

Road 321 (South)

The turnoff for **Marble Creek** is signed, just west of the bridge over the creek. It is a thirty-one mile drive from the river road over Hobo Pass and down to Clarkia on Highway 3. Drive this road as though a logging truck might be encountered along the way.

The Marble Creek drainage escaped the havoc of the 1910 fire, and every square yard of this ground has been gouged by a lumberjack's calks. An early trail up Marble Creek, in fact, was maintained by the county through funds withheld from loggers' paychecks.

The grave of the first logger to drown on Marble Creek, French Louie, was located on the bank, above the mouth. In the spring, as the 'jacks came by at the end of the drive down the stream, ready to start on the St. Joe, each man would drop a stone on Louie's grave – in tribute and thanks. (The grave's location has now been lost.)

Two and one-half miles up the road, on the west side of the creek, is a tunnel. It is the first of two such holes Fred Herrick's crew made while driving a railroad route up the stream to his white pine holdings. Rutledge Timber Co. refused Herrick a right-of-way, and ended the scheme. However, when Rutledge tried to build a flume through Herrick's holdings, Herrick filed suit and thereby evened the score. The two companies often clashed on St. Joe River log drives.

At **mile 5.3** there is an interpretive sign for the Camp 7 splashdam; the dam is located in the creek below the road. One of five Marble Creek dams, it was opened in sequence with the others to flush the timber to the St. Joe. When logs jammed in the stream, loggers had to go into the water in order to find the key log and make the jam "haul." Oscar Blake gave a first-hand account of such a jam on Marble Creek in *Timber Down the Hill:*

30

I had the donkey on the bank of the creek fifty feet higher than the jam, which was twenty-five feet above the creek bed. They were all sixteen-foot logs; some standing on end, with others piled on top of them, three or four deep.

I had the tail-block hanging in a tree on the other bank, so when the lines were tight they were fifty feet above the logs. I made it a practice never to send a man into a dangerous place where I wouldn't go, so I always hooked the key log myself. When I look back on the chances I used to take, it makes me shudder. I wouldn't go into places like that now for a quarter section of big white pine. However, my number just hadn't been called yet, I guess. I would take the end of a choker and crawl back under the face, sometimes fifty feet, and generally hook a log that was laying on the creek bed. The rest of the crew were always watching, some on the bank and some on top of the jam. If it started to haul, the engineer would blow the whistle and start raising the lines. When I heard the whistle, I wasn't long grabbing onto the cable. Then the engineer would raise me up and haul me to shore. I never went down under a jam unless Sycamore Slim was at the throttle.

This jam was a dilly, though. I had thought I had the key log hooked several times, but I had guessed wrong. I went down under to try again, but the water was rising all the time. I found a log that looked as though it might be the one, but lacked two feet of slack to hook the Peters hook. I was trying to get at it from another angle when I heard the whistle, "Toot! Toot!" fast and loud, and I knew this was it. I grabbed the line and one of the boys signaled Slim to pull me out fast. He sure did, with about three seconds to spare. Had I gotten the choker hooked, I never would have made it, as he couldn't have raised me and a seven-hundred foot log. But it was all in a day's work. That jam hauled about three and a half million feet.

I have seen log jams 'haul' when the creek was nearly dry in front of them. They were pushed along by the tremendous force of millions of feet behind them. They would start very slowly and the noise was terrific as the jam moved, logs grinding over rocks and crashing together. It went faster and faster as it unraveled, until a man couldn't have kept up with the logs, running his best. A movie camera, almost unknown at the time, would have recorded a sight few people today have ever seen.

As the logs went down, men generally worked the rear of the flood, "sacking" the drive by getting logs which had hung up or eddied out, back into the current.

The big Marble Creek drives took place from 1917-1927; the last drive occurred in 1930.

3
IDAHO

Obviously, "splashing" a creek with logs devastated the banks and the fishery, and while it would be unacceptable today, it was then considered the most efficient means available to get the "round stuff" to the river. In an interesting observation, Blake, who rolled wood with the best of them, wrote: "I have never seen trout fishing, from Canada to California, half as good as the fishing on Marble Creek before the log drives."

Donkey engine on Hobo Creek.

Remains of a Marble Creek splash dam (left).

At **mile 12.0** the road divides; stay on Road 321. There are fine views of Eagle Creek canyon to the west. A labyrinth of chutes and flumes wove its way to Eagle Creek.

A marked grave along the creek holds the remains of a claim jumper, Ed Boule (Boulette), murdered in 1904. Boule had been hired by one of the large timber companies to spook settlers off their homesteads. The fact that he was shot twenty-some times is beyond question; the circumstances, however, are unclear. One version says ten homesteaders met at night in a cabin – one black bean was dropped in a jar with nine white ones, and the lamp was blown out – each man drew a bean and left, so that none would know who had been compelled to resist evil with evil. When other settlers learned of Boule's death, they figured he was guilty as Cain and shed no tears.

Mile 13: A small roadside sign indicates the presence of an abandoned steam donkey and splashdam. The trail goes downhill through second growth timber about as far as you can shoot an arrow: the right fork leads to dam and donkey.

The donkeys were moved in during the winter so that snow could be used to provide the water necessary for the boiler. Their own cables were used to sled them.

32

Marble Creek district had about twenty donkey engines working
in various drainages. Eight came in from Clarkia in 1918. Only two
of the donkeys were Willamette long-liners, and one of these is still
on Cornwall Creek, not far from this site. The Willamette had 6,000
feet of two-inch cable on a mainline drum, 12,000 feet of ¾-inch
cable on a skidding drum and 12,000 feet of ⅝-inch cable on the
haulback drum – quite a machine!

Flags, and later a whistle-signal system powered by eight dry-cell
batteries, were the usual method of communicating with the
donkey puncher. On a good day a top-hole crew might haul
100,000 feet of timber and use two to four cords of wood firing the
boiler.

The donkey was tethered to the ground and an endless cable, fed
through snatch blocks and haulback blocks anchored to stumps
and trees, would bring the line in from, and back out to, the woods.
One observer wrote, "It is an awesome sight to see a log six feet
through and forty feet long bounding toward you as if the devil were
in it, breaking off some trees as if they were twigs."

Retrace the path and follow the other limb of the T down to a
creekside shelf of sand that contains a dozen log buildings. This was
Rutledge Timber Company's Camp 5. The roofs have vanished and
trees are rooted in the floors. It is a ghost town – a testament to a
vanished age: the bull of the woods has departed as surely as the
bison from the prairies.

Seated on a stump, it is possible to people the camp in one's
imagination, alive with lumberjacks: Seattle Red, Boomer Bloedel,
Eight-Day Wilson. They worked from starlight to starlight, returned
to this burg by the creek in time to wash their faces, wolf bread and
beans, sharpen their "misery whips," dry their boots, play a few
hands of seven-card stud – then out with the lamp and into the
soogan for a dreamless sleep.

The bunkhouse, going back to earth, was redolent with the odor
of tobacco and sweat, coal oil and drying wool. Cold dawns were
fractured by the clang of the gut-iron and the cry of "Daylight in the
swamp!" Sourdough pancakes and another ten-hour day. Months in
the woods, then a chance to "blow 'er in" at "Hollywood" by St.
Maries.

One day the virgin timber was gone. The chain saw, Caterpillar,
jammer and logging truck would get what was left – and what was
left was leavings. Now the loggers are house-broken, the timber
second-growth and the woods quiet as a stump. Sidehill Smith,
Sockless Johnson, Pig Iron Jack: gone to flowers, every one.

3
IDAHO

Nine miles farther up the road is a small sign indicating a spur that goes back two miles to the **Hobo Cedar Grove**. The 240-acre site was classified as a botanical area in 1969 by the regional forester. This pocket of western red cedars occupies steep slopes and has no access trail; consequently, it is not as impressive as some other cedar groves in the state. (Hobo is an abbreviation of a homesteader's name: Hobart.)

Cross **Hobo Pass** (4,525) and look west. Rutledge Timber Company's famous "**Incline Railroad**" was located about two miles from this point. It was built by Morrison-Knudsen Co. in 1922, so that Rutledge could expedite salvage logging of fire-killed timber that year. The two main lines came up Norton and Tole Creeks, and the railroad crossed the ridge and went down the west fork of Merry Creek to Clarkia.

The Incline was a half-mile long and the gradient was 70 percent. Shay locomotives hauled timber on the Bussel Creek side (north) to the base of the Incline, and a pair of donkey engines winched the cars to the top and down the other side. In five months the rail moved 21 million board feet.

The Incline was shut down in 1923 and remodeled so that one donkey, made from two Willamettes with joined boilers and 6,000 feet of spliced cables, could be used to make the pull. Cars were counterbalanced: a loaded car coming down the Clarkia side was offset by a loaded car coming up from Bussel Creek. Peak years for the Incline were 1929-1930, but the Depression brought its career to a close.

Shays hauled two loaded trains five miles to Clarkia each day. A trestle from the connecting railroad is still visible, two miles up the west fork of Merry Creek from its confluence with the Merry Creek road. The Incline rails and donkey were sold as scrap iron to Japan in the 1930s.

The road from Hobo Pass to Clarkia and Highway 3 follows the course of **Merry Creek** for about seven miles. A stretch of the old trestle, spanning the meadow near Clarkia, can be seen to the north of the road just before reaching State Highway 3. From Clarkia, logs were hauled by the Milwaukee to the St. Joe River.

Eight miles north of St. Maries, Highway 3 leaves the St. Joe River near its mouth on Coeur d'Alene Lake.

In 1902, F. J. Davies, of Rutledge Timber Co., interested various lumber companies in forming the St. Joe Boom Co., a self-supporting cooperative organization to sort and transport logs at the mouth of the St. Joe in order to keep them from floating out onto the lake.

Before they were rolled into the river, logs were branded several times on each end. The hammer-brand was registered with the state. As the logs came downriver, a permanent crew, housed by the company at the sorting gap, separated the logs into boomstick corrals for each outfit. (Boomsticks, chained end to end, were used to hold each company's logs.) Cables were stretched across the encircled logs to narrow them into brailes so that the timber could be towed downriver and onto the lake, where it was rounded into larger booms.

Company tug boats would tow the logs thirty miles to Coeur d'Alene, and the trip took thirty-six to forty-eight hours. Each boat had on board two pilots, a cook, fireman and lineman. A cordwood barge accompanied the tug because the steam engine could consume fifty-five cords of wood on the trip. The average tow was 8 million feet, about 1.5 miles long, and the rope stretched 1,200 feet between the stern and the logs in order to avoid throwing the prop-wash against the logs.

Eleven miles north of St. Maries is the junction with Highway 97, which leads to Harrison. The last twenty miles of Highway 3, that run north from the junction to U.S. Interstate 90, follow the lower Coeur d'Alene River. There are nine lakes linked to this stretch of the river, all accessible by boat. This marshy area was poisoned by mine slimes from the Silver Valley, but it is beginning to recover. It serves as wildlife habitat for muskrats, mink, beaver, Canada geese, whistling swans, osprey, herons, and the largest nesting population of wood ducks in the Northwest.

State Highway No. 4 from a junction with I-90 in Wallace, northeasterly to Burke. Route length: 6.4 miles.

An excellent view of minor geologic pressure-folds can be seen on the eastern outskirts of Wallace. Drive east on Bank St. 0.3 miles from downtown Wallace. Follow the curve left across the railroad tracks and onto the paved road that parallels the railroad and highway. Another 0.3 miles reveals folded rock exposures on the left side of the road. It is difficult to conceive of the enormous compression that squeezed these rocks while bending them in such intricate wrinkles.

A brief and oversimplified explanation of the Coeur d'Alene geology states that 2.5 billion years ago the region was part of an extensive shallow sea. Streams eroded massive nearby mountain ranges and deposited them as fine sand in a slowly sinking basin.

4

Deposition over hundreds of millions of years compacted the deeper layers into dense rocks called argillite and quartzite. These rocks, designated the Belt Series, were formed before the advent of life and therefore contain no fossils. Nearly five miles thick, they are among the oldest rocks in North America (radioactive isotope dating has revealed the rocks accumulated about 1.4-1.6 billion years ago). The bottom of the Belt Series is not exposed in the mining district.

The Belt Series was buried beneath younger rocks (which have since eroded) for several hundred million years more. Tectonic forces began to twist the layered rocks sideways. Under such pressure, the rocks were folded into high arches and low troughs called anticlines and synclines – the folds measure in miles. But many smaller drag folds, like those exposed here, which accompanied the larger ones, are clearly visible in the region.

The Coeur d'Alene mining district is aligned along the Osburn fault zone, which extends northwest from Montana to the north end of Coeur d'Alene Lake, where it plunges beneath volcanic rocks and gravel. The fault travels along the north side of Highway 90 from Mullan to a point three miles west of Wallace, where it crosses to the south side of the highway and runs through the Bunker Hill property.

Ore bodies in the Silver Valley are related to this fault, which probably developed in Precambrian times. Geologists estimate intermittent movement along the fault zone may have been as much as sixteen miles and perhaps continued to occur as recently as 70 million years ago, during the formation of the Rocky Mountains.

Because there are marked contrasts in the relative quantities of various minerals between ore bodies, it is thought that the district's mineralogy has been much influenced by these recurrent fault movements during the period of mineral deposition. In other words, this alteration of the "plumbing system" through which the ore fluids were traveling may have caused the differing mineral contents between ore bodies.

Burke Canyon is a seven mile drive from this point, and well worth the time. Avoid driving this route between 1:30 and 2:30 P.M., as the Hecla Star-Morning mine changes shifts, and traffic on the narrow road becomes temporarily congested. Canyon Creek, which flows alongside the highway, is an historic mining drainage where operations began in 1884. Within a half-dozen years, seven concentrators were working in this canyon.

Gem, 2.5 miles up the creek, was the location of the Gem of the Mountains mine. First called Davenport, Gem was a fifteen-minute train stop on the seven mile Wallace-Burke run – because the mayor here ran a saloon. The community, or what is left of it, was the site of one of the more famous disputes in the history of American labor. A sketch follows.

The price of silver by 1892 had suffered a catastrophic decline, and many commercial enterprises faced financial difficulties. The protective Mine Owners Association had shut down many of the Coeur d'Alene mines in order to conserve lead-silver ores while awaiting a better price, and in an attempt to gain rail rate and smelter charge concessions. When the railroads and smelters conceded, the companies offered to reopen if the miners would accept lower pay.

Union miners refused to take a pay cut. Theirs was a hazardous occupation, with frequent injuries and deaths from falls, blasts, cave-ins and gas. They worked ten hour days, six days a week, by candle light, for $3.50 a day. In many cases they had to room, board, and outfit at company concerns where one-third of their wages was recovered by the mine owners.

At the same time, mining was becoming more productive. Ingersoll power drills in 1892 reduced tunneling costs from $17.50 a foot to $2.30. Burleigh compressed-air drills required two men, but they could drill twelve to twenty holes a shift, when a hardrock miner with hand steel was expected to drill three or four.

When the mine owners received the miners' refusal, some of them imported immigrants from the Great Lake states and protected them with company guards. The Mine Owners Association hired a Pinkerton detective, Charlie Siringo, to infiltrate the union, where he served as secretary-informer. (His disguise was discovered, but not before he escaped by crawling under the Gem boardwalks to the edge of town and then taking to the hills.)

On the morning of July 11, 1892, union miners from Wallace, Mullan, and Burke gathered in Gem and marched up the hillsides around the nearby Frisco mine and mill. Company guards at the mill opened fire and union men returned their shots. While gunfire was exchanged, a charge of giant powder was sent down the flume into the mill, reducing the structure to kindling. One man was killed and seven injured. Surrounded, the seventy-five guards and non-union workers surrendered and were taken to the Gem union hall.

Frisco mill before and after the 1892 explosion.

Further trouble developed as the night and day shifts changed at the Gem mine. A non-union man was shot as he crossed the bridge over Canyon Creek. Company guards at the mine opened fire on the town. Volley after volley raked the community while women and children were evacuated to Wallace. Three union men were killed and several wounded. A conference was held under a white flag, but the non-union forces refused to surrender the mine.

About this time, the county sheriff, the district attorney, deputy U.S. marshals, and General Curtis (a former San Francisco police chief, appointed Brigadier General by President Johnson) of the state militia arrived. The truce was extended in order that the men on the Gem property could confer with the mine manager, A. L. Gross, who was in Wallace.

The non-union men were outnumbered and out-gunned. The union representative, Peter Breen, gave Gross twenty minutes to decide whether to surrender or lose the Gem mill. It was high noon. After twenty minutes, Breen pulled out his watch and said, "Time's up." Gross capitulated. The terms of the surrender were set out in a remarkable document:

Wallace, Shoshone Co., Idaho

The representatives of the Gem mine agree with Messrs. Breen and Bonner, representing the parties engaged in hostilities against the employes of the Gem mine, as follows:

The Gem employes are to surrender their arms to a committee of four citizens of Shoshone County, two of said committee to be chosen by Mr. Ed Kinney, of the Gem mine, and two to be chosen by the parties engaged in the hostilities. The employes of the Gem mine are to peacefully leave the mine and the town of Gem, and Messrs. Breen and Bonner, as such commissioners, guarantee said employes safe conduct and to protect said employes from any act of violence.

And Messrs. Breen and Bonner further agree that all the property of the Milwaukee Mining Company shall be fully protected and saved from harm of any kind.

    A. L. Gross,
       For Milwaukee Mining Company
    Chas. Bonner,
    Peter Breen,
       On behalf of citizens.
Dated July 11, 1892.

The non-union men from the Frisco were then released from the Gem union hall, and the deputy U.S. marshal took the guns and ammunition on a handcar to the bank vault in Wallace. Halfway there, he was stopped at gun point by a dozen men who seized the rifles and cartridges.

Union miners gathered in Wallace to bury their dead. Other miners went down to the Bunker Hill in Kellogg, where they placed blasting powder under the mill, thereby forcing management to discharge its non-union crews and vacate the premises. By nightfall, union men had returned to their homes, and the canyon was quiet as a crypt.

Reaction to the struggle was swift. Mine owners easily persuaded Governor Wiley (a mine superintendent from Warren, who had earlier vetoed a bill providing for a state mine inspector) to proclaim martial law. On July 13, the first of a thousand troops arrived: infantry companies from Fort Missoula and Fort Sherman, and three companies of the Idaho National Guard. There were 500 soldiers in Wardner, several companies stationed in Burke, and contingents between there and Wallace.

Colonel Curtis issued orders from Wallace on July 15th, that anyone destroying property was to be shot and that union men were to surrender. The Wallace schoolhouse on West Bank St. was converted to a guardhouse for arrested men. Over 400 miners, about two-thirds from Gem and Burke, had been taken into custody by July 22, but without positive identification or information on their activities, many had to be released. Charlie Siringo returned, with a gun to protect himself, in order to identify men in the guardhouse.

Newspaper reporters from San Francisco, Chicago, and New York were in town.

On July 25, twenty-five prisoners in custody of the National Guard were taken from Wallace to Boise for trial. The men all pleaded not guilty to a charge of violating a "non-interference" injunction that had been obtained by Bunker Hill and Sullivan Company. Ten of the men were found guilty of contempt of court and given jail sentences of up to eight months.

Sixteen prisoners were taken by a deputy U.S. marshal to Coeur d'Alene for a "conspiracy to violate the injunction" trial September 8. Siringo appeared to testify at the twenty-three-day trial. The jury returned guilty verdicts against four men – one was sentenced to two years. The other defendants were acquitted. The conspiracy convictions were later reversed by the U.S. Supreme Court because the defendants had been convicted of crimes against the state of Idaho – in a *federal* court that lacked jurisdiction. No one had brought state charges.

Martial law remained in effect until November 18. The last soldiers left a few days earlier. The Mine Owners Association now had a blacklist of 300 names, and hundreds of union miners left the area.

The Gem mine reopened on July 20 with 100 men, and was shipping ore at month-end. By August, Bunker Hill had 300 scabs from California at work – with no improvement in wages. The new Frisco mill began operating September 19.

A tense truce followed the Coeur d'Alene war of 1892, broken in 1899 by events mentioned in the section on Bunker Hill. The miners who were convicted and served sentences returned home to a hero's acclaim. While in jail, the union leaders decided to organize all miners under what became known as the Western Federation of Miners. Further, the unions organized politically, and in 1894 won all but two elective county offices and seated their candidate in the state senate.

As late as 1935, 1,700 persons lived and worked in Gem; the Northern Pacific picked up riders four times a day. The red stone building, now a storehouse for Hecla core-samples, was another of White and Bender's grocery markets. Across the creek and railroad tracks behind the old store, Hecla had a 1,000-ton mill

40

and another 300-ton mill was located just upstream from it. Twice a day, the trains brought ore down the canyon from the Hecla mine to be milled here. The area has now been largely usurped for tailing ponds.

Evidence of the old Frisco mill site can be seen on the hillside east of the creek, just before the road bridges the stream.

Mace was a small community that experienced a devastating snowslide in 1910, which killed forty miners and a mine superintendent. Temperatures in the canyon sometimes reached thirty-below, and twenty-foot snowpacks were not unusual. Consequently, spring floods down Canyon Creek were not uncommon either.

In August, 1923, a fire began at Mace when sparks from the Union Pacific train set fire to house roofs. The flames swept through the canyon and leveled the town of Burke. Residents evacuated, but many miners were trapped in the Hecla and Day mines while the surface workings burned above them.

The metal buildings near Mace on the northwest side of the road, by the railroad tracks, are the location of the Tamarack mine, part of the Day Mines Corp., which was acquired by Hecla in its 1981 merger.

Burke, so cramped it was once featured in Ripley's "Believe It Or Not," had its beginnings in May, 1884, when prospectors discovered the Tiger mine on the north side of Canyon Creek, and three days later the nearby Poorman mine. Within days, Colonel Wallace and some friends found the Oreornogo claim, which became part of the Hecla mine.

Thirty miners chose the name Burke for the community in 1885, and according to *An Illustrated History of North Idaho,* John Burke "thanked those present for the honor conferred upon him, and extended courtesies of a more substantial character to the miners." The perverse U.S. Postal Department attempted to alter the name to Bayard, but the switch did not assay with the miners.

Mining at Burke got off to a quick start: the Tiger had nearly 100 men at work in 1887, and the Poorman employed about seventy. Stephen Glidden built a shortline narrow-gauge from the Tiger down Canyon Creek to a connection with Corbin's railroad. Ore began moving by rail that year.

The Tiger built a four-story hotel for its employees, but the canyon is so enfolded that the building bestraddled the creek and the railroad tracks. A passageway for trains ran through the middle of the hotel and lodgers had to close their windows when the wood-burning locomotives steamed past. Outside, on the narrow street, a sign warned: "Beware of icicles falling from the eaves."

In August, 1889, Harry Day, whose father had come to Wardner to open a store, found the Hercules claim by the Murray trail at the head of Gorge Gulch – a north-running canyon half a mile above Burke. A brush fire had burned off the ground cover, and Day noticed an exposed outcrop as he was walking the trail. He and his two brothers worked at the mine, despite harassment by larger operators, for twelve years, to put it on a paying basis, and eventually the family became wealthy.

Tiger Hotel (center) and Hercules mill in Burke.

The Poorman mill was making the largest shipments of concentrates in the Coeur d'Alenes in 1891. It was also consuming a thousand cords of wood a month, and this expense and scarcity concerned the mine's owners. So $50,000 was spent to install the largest electrical mining plant in the world at that time. Water, dropping 800 feet in two miles, was flumed to a powerhouse above the mine. New experimental electric drills were introduced. Burke Canyon mines were wet (Bunker Hill mines were dry), and the new equipment made deep pumping feasible. The Poorman saved $30,000 in fuel costs the first year. It had, by then, paid $310,000 in dividends to stockholders.

The Tiger had its own concentrator and a 1,200-foot hoist. Nearly 600 men were on the Burke payrolls.

The Tiger-Poorman mines closed in 1908 – the first major mines of the Coeur d'Alenes to exhaust their ores. The death of those mines shocked many. It was too easy to forget that a mine, like a fire, consumes itself. Residents were reminded that extractive industries, unlike agriculture or tourism, have no future.

The present source of employment at Burke is the Star-Morning mine – actually two mines being run as one, by Hecla Mining Company. Hecla, established in 1891, owns 50 percent of the production, and the Bunker Hill Company owns the balance. Under terms of a 1961 agreement with ASARCO, ore from the adjoining Morning mine is being extracted by way of the Star. (There are

Hecla mine crew: working stiffs (left) and bosses (right).

more than sixty miles of tunnels within the two mines.)

The Star-Morning mine dates from 1889. Veins now worked are reached through the 2,000-foot level adit that travels south for over two miles from the surface plant at Burke to the No. 4 shaft. The shaft reaches to the 8,172-foot level, where production now occurs. This is the deepest lead-zinc ore body mined in the world.

A 2,500-h.p., direct current, double drum hoist, manufactured in Scotland, has been installed two miles below the mine's surface. (Double drum hoists are used to permit lifting in counterbalance.) The hoist will lift ten-ton skip loads of ore from the mine at better than 2,000 feet per minute.

The Star-Morning produces about 1,000 tons of ore a day. Trains pulled by diesel locomotives bring the ore along the 2,000-level tunnel from the shaft to the portal, and the cars dump their contents in a storage bin. The ore is then crushed, milled, ground, flotation separated and made into lead and zinc concentrates. The concentrates were sent in Union Pacific gondolas to the Bunker Hill smelter and electrolytic zinc plant at Kellogg for final refinement; now they are shipped to Montana. Much of the tailing material is pumped back into mined-out areas.

Most of the buildings from the earlier era were torn down by Hecla Mining to make room for parking areas. A Star mine crew razed the Burke hotel, with its train tunnel, in 1964.

Burke is only three air-miles north of Mullan, but it is thirteen miles by road.

State Highway No. 5 from a junction with U.S. 95 in Plummer, easterly via Heyburn State Park to a junction with Highway 3 in St. Maries. Route length: 19.1 miles.

Highway 5 is a serpentine road that travels 17.9 miles from Plummer to St. Maries. The principal attraction of the route, **Heyburn State Park**, occupies the middle six miles.

The park contains 5,505 acres of land and 2,333 acres of water. There are large stands of second-growth ponderosa pine, and the shrubbery includes syringa, ninebark and wildroses. Campsites, boatdocks and restrooms at Chatcolet, Plummer Point and Benewah are available.

Idaho's first state park includes three separate lakes (Chatcolet, Round and Benewah) that were essentially merged in 1906 by the backwaters of the Post Falls dam on the Spokane River. The St. Joe River, protected by its banks that form a natural levee, flows through the lakes to its influx at Coeur d'Alene Lake. It is ironic that this park carries the surname of Senator Weldon Heyburn.

The Senator was a fierce and often irrational foe of federal activities in Idaho. It is quite amusing that his amendment to a Department of Agriculture appropriation in 1907, providing "... hereafter no forest reserves shall be created within Idaho", impelled President Roosevelt to add 17 million acres of land to new forest reserves before he signed the appropriation bill.

W. B. Heyburn, described by a fellow Senator as having "an almost perverse spirit of opposition," nevertheless wanted one national park for Idaho. He did not want a state park, because in his words, "They are always a subject of embarrassment."

Since he lived in north Idaho, where he had mining interests, the lawyer-Senator chose Lake Chatcolet as the park site; he knew it was the favorite camping and picnicing area for many tourists. His vision of the park must have been rather myopic: the proposal did not include or even mention the site's most interesting feature, the St. Joe "river within a lake."

St. Joe River flowing through Lake Chatcolet.

At the time of his bill, the Senator felt some urgency regarding its passage. The land was part of the Coeur d'Alene Indian Reservation, and under the Dawe's allotment act, each Indian had to file for 160 acres of his own land, pending white expropriation of the balance. Heyburn realized that some Indians or eligible whites might file on tracts along the lake, and thus end any chance for park status.

The Senate passed their colleague's park proposal, but the matter died in the House. In the next Congress, Heyburn introduced a bill declaring that the area be "set apart as a public park or pleasuring ground for the benefit and enjoyment of the people." The park was to be under the control of the Secretary of the Interior. Again, the bill cleared the Senate but languished in the House.

In an attempt to solve the stalemate, Senate conferees suggested an amendment allowing the state of Idaho to buy the tract for use as a park. The alteration was not cleared with the Idaho Senator because he was out of town. The House conferees accepted the change.

Because Heyburn had run out of time when he learned of the switch (the Indians were to begin selecting their allotments within two weeks), he apparently accepted the change as interim protection until the area could be given the "national" status that he desired. President Taft signed the Indian Appropriations Act a few days later.

To Heyburn's amazement, chagrin and consternation, the Idaho legislature authorized spending $12,000 from the state's general fund to purchase the acreage around Lake Chatcolet in 1909, and established a commission to administer it. The Secretary of the Interior drew up a deed that required the land be used in perpetuity as a public park; Idaho completed the purchase in 1911 and named the park after the Senator.

Weldon Heyburn died in 1912, and was buried in Pennsylvania, where he was born. With him went Idaho's chance for a second-rate national park.

The State's vision of the park's purpose seems to have been as cloudy as the Senator's. The timber within the preserve was sold, and the Red Collar Line was permitted to dredge a channel into Chatcolet so that excursion steamers could reach docks constructed there.

Some time around 1920, Idaho began leasing summer homesites within the park. Automobile touring had replaced steamer excursions as a popular pastime; wealthy urbanites could afford to build vacation bungalows. The number of leased sites varied from 150 to 300.

During the 1970s pollution and garbage from summer homes and houseboats at leased sites inside the park became the focus of a strong public protest. Houses, houseboats and three resort developments were using septic systems in thin soil where seepage was contaminating shoreline water. In addition, shoreline leases paid an annual rental of $125, and those not on the waterfront paid only $94. The leases struck many as undemocratic and in violation of the terms of the federal deed. The Coeur d'Alene tribe also argued that the state had failed in its public obligation.

The Secretary of the Interior, in 1973, notified Idaho that there was reason to believe restrictions in the deed had been violated. The State Land Board announced it would not renew leases when they expired. Leaseholders were outraged. Litigation ensued. The federal government, with the Coeur d'Alene tribe as intervenor, was the plaintiff; the State of Idaho, with the leaseholders as intervenors, was the defendant. The court granted Idaho summary judgement; the Government and Indians appealed to the Ninth Circuit Court of Appeals; before oral arguments, the federal attorneys moved to dismiss their own appeal. The tribe persisted, but the case was remanded to the district level to determine whether the Indians had standing as plaintiffs, and the issue has not been decided at this time.

While the lawyers argue, the plans for improved sewage disposal have been shelved, and lessees have been exempted from payment of their token annual dues.

State Highway 5 merges with Highway 3 at St. Maries.

State Highway No. 6 from the Idaho-Washington state line easterly and northeasterly via Potlatch, Harvard and Emida to a junction with State Highway 3 west of Santa. (Overlaps U.S. 95 near Potlatch.) Route length: 40.5 miles.

Potlatch is eight miles east of Palouse, Washington, and one mile east of U.S. 95. The potlatch is a Northwest Indian ceremonial feast that involved the exchange of gifts in a rival display of wealth. The only potlatch here was nature's.

In 1905 Potlatch Lumber established this company town. All the land, houses, stores, hotels, church and school buildings belonged to the company.

William Deary purchased state timber, and other lands, in the Palouse-Clearwater drainages in 1901-1902 in the name of a Minnesota company. A year later, these holdings, along with those of a Wisconsin company, were sold to a Maine corporation: the Potlatch Lumber Company. The new firm had an authorized capitalization of $3 million; Charles Weyerhaeuser was president, Bill Deary was general manager.

The corporation planned to use a Moscow millsite because the railroad was there, but exorbitant right-of-way costs across farmland altered the decision in favor of the present Potlatch townsite, eighteen miles north of Moscow.

The lumber company built an enormous belt-driven mill at Potlatch, touted as the largest in the world. By 1907, when the Washington, Idaho and Montana railroad was completed, the town had 1,500 residents, 275 houses, and complete water, light and sewer systems. No saloons were permitted.

Located along the Palouse River, the mill had ample water for log storage. Loggers began to tap the extensive white pine forest of the Palouse basin. From 1908 to 1927 Potlatch milled 130 million board feet a year, but the company was a borderline enterprise because sawmill capacity exceeded demand, and transportation costs were greater than those in other regions.

In 1931 Potlatch Forests, Inc. (evolved from Potlatch Lumber) absorbed the properties of Clearwater Timber and Rutledge Timber. After another decade, the company became profitable. A large Potlatch Corp. sawmill is still located in town, but now less than 15 percent of the lumber is white pine.

The **Palouse River** parallels Highway 6, on the south side of the road, from Potlatch to Harvard. The river's name is Indian, and the meaning involves a rock formation at the mouth of the stream. Lewis and Clark labeled it Drewyer River, after George Drewyer (Drouillard), a member of their expedition. French Canadian trappers called it the Pavillon (in English, pavilion), though whose "flag," and where, is no longer certain. The Palouse Indians lived along the river in eastern Washington.

The Palouse drains 530 square miles of northwestern Idaho and 2,500 square miles of eastern Washington. It flows west and south for nearly 100 miles before entering the Snake River sixty miles west of Lewiston.

Midway between Princeton and Harvard, four miles north of Highway 6, is the **Gold Hill mining area,** where low-grade placer and quartz-lode claims were filed from 1870 to 1905. The district was so remote that all supplies arrived on pack stock. Interest in Gold Hill diminished when brighter discoveries were made at Alder Gulch, Montana.

Gold Hill yielded $500,000. In 1905 the Daisy mine, on Jerome Creek, east of Harvard, had sufficient production to justify a five-stamp mill.

Harvard is eight miles east of Potlatch, and along with **Princeton** and **Wellesley** to the west, is linked to a chain of university names given to railroad sidings on the forty-seven-mile

Washington, Idaho and Montana Railroad. Others southeast of Harvard are Yale, Stanford, Cornell, Vassar, and Purdue.

Since the railroad was owned by a subsidiary of Potlatch Lumber, and the parent corporation was owned by wealthy Midwest families, sons of those families were given summer jobs with the railroad during their college years. Rail work was easier and safer than logging. An engineer named a siding Purdue, after his alma mater, and the students quickly tagged the rest of the sidings with the names of their own universities.

In 1962 Milwaukee Land Co. (Chicago, Milwaukee and St. Paul R.R.) purchased the WI&MRR from Potlatch Corp. for $460,000, though the line still handles Potlatch freight. In 1981 after the Milwaukee Road had filed bankruptcy Burlington Northern bought the railroad.

Highway 6 leaves the grain fields along the Palouse River east of Harvard, and turns north through cedar and pine forests toward Emida. On the east side of the highway, 8.5 miles north of Harvard, is the USFS **Giant White Pine** campground. The tree for which the site is named grows on Mannering Creek, only thirty yards from the road. It is six feet in diameter, 188 feet high, and over 400 years old. White pines like this one are rarer than ten pound nuggets.

Western white pine was discovered by David Douglas, the Scotch botanist-explorer, in 1825, on the slopes of Mount St. Helens in present Washington. The species makes peerless softwood: light, even grained, slow to warp or shrink, prized for doors and window sash. When loggers in the Lake States exhausted its close relative, eastern white pine, they turned to the imposing stands of western white pine in Idaho. Homesteading was frequently used as a subterfuge to obtain the timber.

Principal demand for the lumber was from the matchwood industry. Before development of paper matches, pilot lights and cigarette lighters, Americans used 100 million wooden matches a day. White pines, averaging 60,000 board feet an acre, were cut into planks two inches thick, and cross-sawed into match-length blocks. Within a few decades, the western white pine forest was bare as a picked bone. Now white pines, with their silvery, cross-checked, scaly bark, their long stems and lofty crowns – pines that were once kings of the Inland Empire – grow only in the crevice of memory.

The U.S. Forest Service failed to preserve representative groves of virgin western white pine, but it was not simply logging and short-sighted Forest Service management that extinguished this extraordinary forest; another mistake compounded the blunder.

49

6

The White Pine King being felled near Pierce.

Reforestation began in the East from 1900 to 1910. A tariff on low-priced European nursery stock was removed, and millions of eastern white pines (a species not native to Europe) were imported, principally from France and Germany. They were cultivated in plantations throughout the Northeastern and Lake States. In 1909, white pine blister rust, a parasitic fungus, was discovered on eastern white pines in New York, introduced by European-grown seedlings.

The rust fungi alternates between conifers and currants or gooseberries called ribes. Wind-borne sporida from the ribes infect pine needles; within three years the pines develop blisters that

50

release new spores which can be blown hundreds of miles, infecting other ribes and renewing the cycle. As the branches of the pine are killed, the tree dies.

In September, 1921, the rust was detected in Vancouver, B.C., where it had arrived on a shipment of eastern white pines from France. Introduced in this manner, it spread rapidly throughout the white pine's western range. Blister rust became the most damaging and costly of conifer diseases; millions of dollars were spent in an unsuccessful attempt to eradicate the host ribes. At present, propagation of blister rust-resistant white pine seedlings offers a promising solution.

It is 9.8 miles from the Giant White Pine north to **Emida** on Highway 6. The town's name is a composite from three settlers: East, Miller, and Dawson.

State Highway 6 ends eight miles east of Emida, at Santa, on Highway 3.

State Highway No. 7 from Orofino to Ahsahka. Route length: 16.1 miles.

State Highway 7 goes west out of Orofino, on the north side of the Clearwater River, three miles to **Ashahka**, where an abbreviated road leads up to **Dworshak Dam**. The U.S. Army Corps of Engineers is responsible for erecting this structure across the North Fork of the Clearwater and naming it after Henry Dworshak, a Republican appointed to the U.S. Senate in 1949, where he served until his death in 1962.

Dworshak's memorial (begun in 1963 and completed in 1973) contains enough concrete to make two pyramids the size of the one at El Giza. Unfortunately, there have always been more politicians than suitable damsites. Building the highest straight axis gravity dam in the Western Hemisphere, on a river with a mean flow of 5,000 cubic feet per second, at a cost of $312 million, in the name of flood-control, is the second-funniest joke in Idaho. The funniest joke is inside the visitor center: a government sign entreats, "... help protect this delicate environment for future generations."

The North Fork of the Clearwater was an exceptional river with a preeminent run of steelhead trout, and the drainage contained thousands of elk and white-tail deer. Reports by the Bureau of Sport Fisheries and Wildlife and the Idaho Fish and Game Department indicated the fifty-four mile reservoir would seriously damage these resources. The Army Corps of Engineers proceeded to destroy the river, habitat, and fish; then acquired 5,000 acres for elk management and spent $21 million dollars to build the largest steelhead hatchery in the world, maintaining at a cost of $1 million a year what nature had provided for nothing.

The dam generates less than half the power it was designed to produce because peak loads would cause such a flood downstream that a second dam was needed at Lenore. But once the elephantine project was underway, enough people were dismayed by the Army Engineer's bogus objectives that the idea of a second dam was rejected as damnfoolish. The Corps, whose first responsibility had been clearing the snags and sandbars on the Ohio and Mississippi Rivers in 1824, had come a long way upstream to spawn its biggest-dam-ever. The visitor center should have a second sign: "Bureaucracy is a process of converting energy into solid waste." (In 1981 the Army Corps' civilian work staff numbered 28,000.)

Dworshak Dam under construction. For two decades (1905-1925) the Army Corps of Engineers argued that hydroelectric dams were an unconstitutional obstruction of navigable waters, and that reservoirs could not control floods.

In the auditorium on the second floor of the visitor's center it is possible to view two half-hour entrancing films: *The Last Log Drive* (Clearwater River) and *Construction of Dworshak Dam.* The center is open from 10:00 A.M. - 6:00 P.M. and the movies are shown on request.

Tours of the dam are given every hour during the summer, and at 1:00 and 2:30 P.M. in the winter. Boat cruises on the reservoir are available from May through September by making reservations with Dworshak Excursions in Orofino. Kokanee salmon and rainbow trout have been stocked in the impounded water; so fishing opportunities exist. (Concessions at Big Eddy are operated by the Nez Perce Tribal Council.)

Incidentally, the 717-foot high, 3,000-foot-long dam developed a leak through a 236-foot long crack on the reservoir-side in June, 1980. Water, 7,700 gallons per minute, was flumed past the powerhouse with sandbags and cement barricades and funneled down to the river.

The Corps' solution was to lower a plastic sheet over the crack. Prior to emplacement of the sheet, seventy diamond drill holes were bored to intercept the crack and to relieve pressure. The operation was partially successful; it cut the flow in half. Further repair, including a patch made of sawdust, cement, and volcanic ash was necessary. The repair bill exceeded $1 million.

The entrance to the **Dworshak National Fish Hatchery** is at the southeast end of the North Fork bridge at Ashahka below the dam.

Built by the Army Engineers and completed in 1968, this hatchery has been plagued by expensive problems. It is operated by the Department of the Interior's Fish and Wildlife Service.

Clearwater steelhead migrate over 500 miles from the Pacific Ocean, up the Columbia, Snake and Clearwater Rivers. They are captured in a collection system just below the dam, taken to the hatchery and stripped of their eggs or milt. Eggs are fertilized and incubated, and the fry gradually progress through various rearing areas. (Some fish come directly to the hatchery via fish ladders.)

The facility is open during daylight hours, and visitors can make a self-guided tour.

The wooden church, east of the main hatchery building, is the North Fork Presbyterian Church for the Nez Perce Indians, and was built in 1900. The lumber was rafted down the Clearwater to Ahsahka, and the building was completed after three years of labor. Rev. William Wheeler, a Nez Perce trained by the missionary Sue McBeth at Kamiah, was the first pastor. Mr. Wheeler translated his sermons into English for the white persons who attended services there.

Ashahka is reported to be a Nez Perce word that means "place where two rivers meet."

8
IDAHO

State Highway No. 8 from the Idaho-Washington state line easterly via Moscow, Troy, Deary and Bovill to Elk River. (Overlaps Highway 3 for 9.9 miles.) Route length: 52 miles.

It is three miles on State Highway 8 from the Washington border to Moscow. The **Appaloosa Horse Club and Museum** is located one mile west of Moscow on the north side of the highway. The museum deserves a visit.

The Appaloosa, a horse with a spotted coat, originated in China, and was noted among the Nez Perce. The Appaloosa Horse Club, a breed association, was incorporated in 1938. Ten years later, the first national Appaloosa horse show was held in Lewiston. The club outgrew its quarters three times, and in 1974 a new building, with 17,500 square feet, was erected on the Pullman-Moscow highway.

The west wing of the building houses the Appaloosa Museum. The collection traces the evolution of the Appaloosa breed and the historical aspects of the breed. The flight of the Nez Perce is traced on a large geophysical relief map; each year the horse club makes a trail ride over a different portion of the route. Other items displayed include Western art, saddles, photographs, Indian artifacts and beadwork.

(See U.S. Highway 95, Moscow.)

It is a 12.5 mile drive east from Moscow on Highway 8 to Troy. Crops grown along the road in this vicinity are mainly soft white winter wheats, peas, lentils and barley. Most of the wheat is exported to Asia and the Middle East, where it is used for noodles, cookies and pastry. The dry peas of the Palouse country constitute more than 90 percent of this nation's production, and the U.S. is the world's largest exporter of peas and lentils.

Seeds of the Austrian winter pea are exported for "An" paste in Japan and for "poor man's noodles" in the Middle East. The seeds are used domestically in the southern states to grow plants that fix nitrogen in the soil.

Barley is grown as feed grain for livestock and as a malting agent.

In 1890 **Troy** was simply Huff's Gulch. According to a Scandinavian settler at the time "It wasn't even a road, it wasn't even a town, it wasn't a horse even."

John Vollmer, an Idaho millionaire-banker and merchant, who had acquired much of his 32,000 acres through bank loan foreclosures, directed the path of the Northern Pacific to the gulch in 1890, and as the state agent for the company, made the first of two

54

unsuccessful attempts to name a town after himself (see Craigmont). Swedish homesteaders could only pronounce Vollmer with a "w," so after a tongue-in-cheek suggestion to switch the community's name to "Romeo" as a match for nearby Juliaetta, the citizens voted in 1897 to call their town Troy. It became a supply center for the region.

The most remarkable business in the community is the First Bank of Troy, chartered in 1905. The bank weathered the severe recessions of the early 1900s, and the Depression (it was closed for only one month) and still functions as an excellent local bank. Bank president, Frank Brocke, was once robbed of $4,000 by a hold-up man who was later captured and sentenced to the state penitentiary. When the convict was finally released, he returned to the bank and asked Brocke for an auto loan. After a little thought, the president approved his application.

Deary is 11.3 miles east of Troy at the confluence of Highway 3 and Highway 8. It began as a stop on the Washington, Idaho and Montana rail line. The town's name memorializes a burly Irish-Canadian who logged in the Great Lake country before coming to Moscow in 1899. Bill Deary became the first general manager of Potlatch Lumber Co. (He died in 1913, age sixty.)

The Deary Townsite Company was organized in 1908 and sold lots on what had been the Joe Blailock homestead. Numerous springs provided a handy water supply for the first houses that were built.

The town was dependent on farms and the forest. It quickly boasted an Idle Hour Pool Hall, a postmaster with the off-trail name of Mel Call, and a newspaper: the *Deary Enterprise.*

A fire in 1923 burned every building on the west side of Main St. except the bank.

The eminence north of town, that rises a thousand feet above its surroundings, is known as Potato Hill (elev. 4,017). It is a volcanic vent of undetermined age. Early residents called it Spud Hill, but since the *Enterprise* always referred to it as Mount Deary, the present name represents a compromise.

An area five miles north of Deary (about eight miles by road), at the head of Swartz Creek, was the location of several mica mines; the first discovery was made in 1881. Mica crystals on the slopes of **Mica Mountain** occur in giant pegmatite, and some of those removed measured two feet-by-three feet and weighed over 100 pounds.

Sporadic mining, some as late as World War II, produced marketable quantities of muscovite. There was even a sorting station in Deary, and others in Troy and Moscow.

Mica, also known as isinglass, is heat resistant and translucent. It was used in stove doors, and in window panels for horseless carriages ("... with isinglass curtains you can roll right down, in case there's a change in the weather.") and later, for electrical insulation.

Mica Mountain pegmatites, in seams, have in addition revealed spectacular crystals of black tourmaline eight feet long and a foot in diameter.

Highway 8 travels ten miles east from Deary to Bovill. About 1.5 miles west of Bovill, on the north side of the road, are Latah clay pits, which have been mined by Simplot Company. The clay is used for refractory bricks and as a filler in grades of quality paper.

Bovill was settled by a fascinating couple: Hugh and Charlotte Bovill. They purchased the Warren Meadows homestead in 1901.

Hugh, the youngest of sixteen children, was the son of an English Lord Chief Justice of the Common Pleas. After university graduation, Bovill toured the U.S. briefly, before going off to supervise the family tea plantation in Ceylon. But Hugh, deciding he preferred the American West, migrated to Colorado and set up a horse ranch with a chap named Lord Ogilvie. On a visit to the Sand Hills of Nebraska, Hugh met his wife, Charlotte. She was the daughter of an English clergyman who was also the Commissioner of Education to Queen Victoria. Charlotte had completed nurse's training in Denver. She and Hugh must have paired like belt and buckle.

Mr. Bovill drove some cattle and horses to Montana and Idaho and then took a train ride to Moscow. Taking a fancy to the country there, he went back to Nebraska and returned with Charlotte and their two daughters and began quilting a new life.

The Bovills ranched 580 acres on Warrens Meadows, but timber cruisers, homesteaders and sportsmen began moving into the area so the couple opened a lodge-hotel, then a store, and even a post office in 1907. That year the community of Bovill was incorporated.

At the same time, the tracks of the forty-seven mile Washington, Idaho and Montana railroad from Palouse reached Bovill. Three years later, this Potlatch Lumber line was connected to the Chicago, Milwaukee & St. Paul railroad at Bovill, when the Milwaukee extended a spur to Elk River.

56

Hotel Bovill.

Logging began north and west of town. The settlement became a bit more western than Westminster – with saloons and a house of the rising sun. When more sun worshippers arrived, a second house went up. Times had changed, and the Bovills decided to leave in 1911. (Hugh died in Oregon, in 1935; Charlotte in Santa Cruz, California, in 1947.)

The 1910 Idaho Fire burned a large area north of Bovill, but bypassed the town. The community became the railroad center and switch point for logs destined for the Potlatch sawmill. Crew bosses and family men built homes here. By 1914 it was the third-largest town in the county, and the woods superintendent for Potlatch Lumber was the mayor.

A fire on the Fourth of July, 1914, destroyed the lower west end of Bovill's Main Street. There were suspicions that arson had been used to conceal robbery and murder, because the remains of a man known to have withdrawn $1,450 from the town bank two days earlier were found in the ashes.

The mill in Bovill at this writing produces cedar shakes, power line poles and some lumber.

Half a mile south of Bovill, Highway 8 follows **Ruby Creek** briefly. Placer claims and a half-dozen lode mines, located on the north side of the creek, within a mile of the road, were discovered and worked from 1885-1910. Some gold was recovered and a lead-zinc vein was worked, but the claims were low-grade and nuggets were scarcer than raisins in a boarding house pudding.

57

The town of **Elk River** is thirteen miles east of Bovill. When the Milwaukee railroad completed its branch line from St. Maries to Elk River in 1909, there was nothing at the end of the spur except the Trumbull hunting and fishing lodge. But once the iron was laid, Potlatch commenced construction of an electrically-driven sawmill and the town grew up around it.

Elk River sawmill and planing mill.

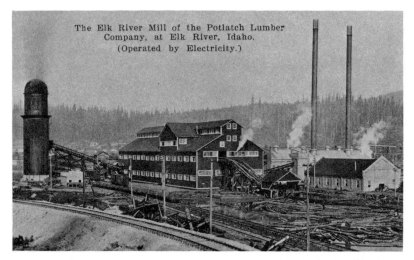

The Elk River Mill of the Potlatch Lumber Company, at Elk River, Idaho. (Operated by Electricity.)

Elk River Planing Mill, Dry Shed and Loading Platform. Potlatch Lumber Company, Potlatch, Idaho.

The mill and millpond were completed in 1911. The *Deary Enterprise* ran advertisements to attract millworkers – and subscribers.

58

The town in 1910 consisted of a cluster of log buildings, a few homestead cabins, a row of Potlatch houses, a company store and mess hall, and a large number of tents. Within five years, there were churches, a hospital, school, gymnasium, stores and numerous frame houses.

The mill operated for more than twenty years, but the larger Clearwater Timber sawmill built at Lewiston in 1927 spelled trouble in river city. The Elk River mill was phased out during the Depression.

The millpond can still be seen on the edge of town, and the handsome school and church, both built in 1912, still serve their purpose.

Elk Creek Falls.

Nearby **Elk Creek Falls** is certainly worth a visit. One mile west of town, turn south off the highway on a gravel road. Drive 1.4 miles to a spur on the left and park there. Walk 0.4 miles down the spur to a dead end, where the sound will serve as a guide. The path drops 100 yards into a semi-shaded gorge, where the cheerful cascade drops, pools, drops and pools again. (The creek drains into Dworshak Reservoir.)

State Highway No. 9 from a junction with Highway 6 west of Deary, northerly to a junction with Highway 6 west of Harvard. Route length : 13.5 miles.

This short road, which travels through farmland and second-growth forest, is Idaho's only unpaved state highway. According to local belief its condition reflects the state's effort to divert eastbound traffic to Highways 3 and 8 through Moscow.

State Highway No. 11 from a junction with U.S. 12 west of Greer, easterly and northerly via Greer, Weippe and Pierce to Headquarters. Route length: 42.4 miles.

State Highway 11 leaves U.S. 12 by way of a bridge over the Clearwater River to **Greer** on the east bank of the river.

At this location, in 1861, Colonel William Craig and Jacob Shultz constructed a ferry across the river to accommodate the miners and packers en route to Pierce. A ferry house was built so that travelers could spend the night. The tolls were: foot passenger 50¢, pack animal 75¢, horse and wagon $2.50.

John ("Jack") Greer and John Molly owned the ferry when the Nez Perce War swirled through the country in 1877, and the Indians on their way to Weippe Prairie cut the ferry adrift and burned the house, making it more difficult for the Army to pursue them.

Greer rebuilt his establishment, and in 1899, when the railroad came through, he platted a townsite with a partner, John Dunn. When Greer's health failed he turned the business over to Bill and Harry Gamble, who had it until 1914, when a bridge was built.

HISTORICAL SITE

The road bootlaces up the hill, providing a spectacular view of the Clearwater canyon, then levels out across the **Weippe Prairie**.

The Nez Perce meaning of the word "weippe" has been engulfed by time. The area is one of eight Registered National Landmarks in the state. Weippe has seen more history ride past than Holling C. Holling's *Tree in the Trail.* The Prairie was the west end, or commencement point, for eastern journeys over the Lolo Trail. It was a meeting place for Indian hunting parties intent on reaching the buffalo grounds of the Great Plains, and it was communal territory for Indians digging camas bulbs in the fall. All the Nez Perce bands gathered on the Prairie at that season; they settled their tipis in six camps circled over a two-mile area.

On September 20, 1805, Captain William Clark, of the Voyage of Discovery, came down Miles Creek to the Weippe Prairie and found two villages of Nez Perce. His men, and those of Lewis behind him, had just accomplished a difficult crossing of the Bitterroot Mountains and to survive had been reduced to a fare of horsemeat. The Indians gave them food. The soil, Sergeant Ordway observed, was "very rich and lays delightful for cultivation," notable prescience on his part.

When the Expedition returned from the Pacific to the Quamish Flats of Weippe June 11, 1806, they found the camas in full bloom and the blue-flowered landscape ". . . at a short distance resembles lakes of fine, clear water."

Miners who rushed to the placer strike in Pierce crossed the prairie in great numbers from 1861-1865. A few shelters were constructed where travelers could buy whiskey and a place to spread their blankets. Miners on the prairie in the spring and early winter were often snowblinded so severely as to be disabled – some of them froze.

The Nez Perce, who had treated Lewis and Clark with such generous hospitality, crossed the prairie in July, 1877, and times had changed. A band of 800 Indians, under Looking Glass, White Bird, Ollokot and Joseph had just fought an engagement with General Howard's troops on the Clearwater and were now en route across the Lolo to join their friends among the Flatheads and Crows in Montana (see White Bird Hill).

The area is still beautiful upland prairie, with ragged, dark ponderosas along its fringe. Camas bulbs bloom yet, in sequestered patches in the spring, but the soil so accurately gauged by Sgt. Ordway now meets his expectations with bountiful crops of wheat and grain.

The last active camas gathering spot for the Indian people of north Idaho is Musselshell Meadow, fifteen miles east of Weippe, along the USFS Lolo Trail Road.

The Lewis and Clark 1806 campsite was located approximately two miles southeast of the town of Weippe, between two branches of Jim Ford Creek. The site of the western-most of the two villages visited by the explorers in 1805 is about one mile southwest of the town; the other village was two miles farther south.

From Weippe, it is easy to make a rewarding twenty-mile drive past Musselshell Meadows to the Lewis and Clark Grove. Head east out of town on the paved road called Pierce St.; the pavement gives way to gravel at times. Cross Peterson Corners' bridge; when the road divides, take the Lolo Creek-Kamiah fork, indicated by a sign. Thirteen miles from Weippe, notice **Musselshell Meadows** on the north side of the road. The meadows are managed as a camas bulb harvest area for the Nez Perce Indians.

Follow the road toward Kamiah another 6.3 miles. Just before a bridge across El Dorado Creek, there is a signed intersection on the left that marks the start of USFS Road No. 500, which follows the Lolo Trail. (See U.S. 12, Kamiah, Lolo Trail Road.) Turn east (left) on Road No. 500 and follow it up El Dorado Creek 1.2 miles to the Cedar Creek sign. Turn left at that sign, and drive 1.5 miles to the small Clark Tree sign. This is the location of the **Lewis and Clark Cedar Grove.**

The remarkable tree, Clark's white pine, as well as the cedar grove, was saved from a timber sale through the vision and intervention of the Clearwater Forest Supervisor Ralph Space, and the district ranger, Jack Alley. We can be grateful for their sagacity. (For information about the western white pine, see Highway 6, Giant White Pine.)

On September 19, 1805, Captain William Clark, with an advance party of six men, camped on Cedar Creek in this vicinity. It was a warm day; they had come down the Lolo Trail, and overcome by hunger, had eaten horseflesh for breakfast and a pair of grouse for dinner. The next day the men found a Nez Perce village on Weippe Prairie.

(The road continues past the grove, and within four miles loops back into the Musselshell-Weippe Rd.)

The town of **Pierce** is found twelve miles north of Weippe; it has an important place in Idaho history.

It is a long way from Ireland to "placer land" in the Clearwater Mountains, particularly in 1860, and Elias Pierce, who made the journey, did not travel in a straight line. But he traveled. Much has been learned about his life through the recent discovery, in Dayton, Ohio, of a diary that Pierce dictated to a lady when he was in his seventies.

E. D. Pierce immigrated to Virginia when he was fifteen. He read law under the supervision of a lawyer and became a lawyer when his teacher let him "graduate." He practiced briefly in Indiana.

The Mexican-American War erupted in 1846, and Elias volunteered for service. After 9½ months he was released with the rank of Second Lieutenant. He returned to Indiana, where he met Rebecca Jones, to whom he became engaged.

However, Pierce decided to make his fortune before settling into married life; so he left with a wagon train from St. Joseph, Missouri, for the goldfields of California. En route, he was elected "captain" and used that title the rest of his life.

In California, Captain Pierce turned to trading as a more profitable business than mining. He acquired a partner in Yreka, California, who had been a Hudson's Bay man, and together they traveled north to Portland, then by boat up the Columbia to The Dalles, where a messenger sent to the Nez Perce persuaded those Indians to send a pack train from Lapwai for trade goods. Pierce and his partner spent the winter of 1852 at Lapwai and acquired 110 horses.

The following February they took part of the herd to California, made a profit on the sale, returned for the rest of the horses and brought them back to Yreka. For the next three years, the Captain worked on the eighty-mile Shasta River canal to bring water to the Dry Diggings of Yreka Flats. (The project was a failure.) He also became the first man to ascend Mt. Shasta, and represented Shasta County as a member of the Third Legislature of California.

Pierce left for Idaho again in 1856, with trading goods, but thinking of gold. Indian troubles in the area forced him to take up ranching in the Walla Walla country for four years, but one aborted prospecting trip had convinced Elias that mining opportunities existed on the Nez Perce lands. Despite warnings from the Indian agent and Colonel William Craig, Pierce stated he would go prospecting without crossing reservation lands. So the Captain's party of ten men left Walla Walla in August, 1860, for the Clearwater country, and en route acquired an Indian guide whose identity has long been a source of curiosity, since that person's actions, in a sense, betrayed the Nez Perce redoubt. Tradition indicates the guide was Jane Silcott – daughter of the Nez Perce Chief Timothy, and later wife of the Lewiston ferry owner – but Pierce's diary does not provide the name.

The men successfully penetrated the Indian's reserve and camped that fall on a meadow by Canal Gulch. When Wilbur Bassett gophered out a prospect hole and found color, days of fatigue were quickly dispelled. Since it was October, the men returned to Walla Walla for winter supplies.

The returning party had tripled in size. The miners notched eight cabins together and spent the winter building sluice boxes and flumes and staking their claims. They laid out a townsite and dubbed it Pierce City. The men also adopted mining laws and appointed a recorder for claims in expectation of the hordes that would arrive like geese in the spring.

The would-be miners alighted in May: several thousand of them. They flocked north from San Francisco, south from Victoria, up the Columbia past Portland, to Lewiston on the Snake. They followed the trail from Culdesac to Greer and across Weippe Prairie. The Washington territorial legislature appropriated funds for a wagon toll-road from Lewiston, and a ferry was built at Greer.

By June, 1,600 claims had been filed in the Pierce district. One miner wrote to relatives: "If you can stand more hard service and deprivation than a mule or cayuse pony, do come." Said another, "If all fools wore white hats, we should seem a flock of geese."

Cincinnatus Hiner Miller, a.k.a. Joaquin Miller, rode as pony expressman between Lewiston and Pierce for part of 1861 and left this somewhat more cheerful description of conditions in Pierce:

It was a brisk town, neatly laid out, built of hewn logs, brooks through the streets, pine trees here and there on the gently sloping hillside to the sun, with white tents all around and up and down the mountain of dark woods to the east, red-shirted men, mules, long lines of laden, braying mules, half-tame Indians with pack panniers, a few soldiers off duty, crowds of eager people coming and going – action, motion everywhere. The old days had come again, we all believed, and miners who had missed fortune in other lands and laid the blame upon themselves resolved not to miss her favors now, if work could win them.

(Miller later became a judge in Oregon, wrote reams of awful poetry, and was lionized in England as the "Poet of the Sierras" and "Byron of the Rockies," but his poetry was far worse than Byron's; most readers will recall "Sail on. Sail on. Sail on and on." from "Columbus.")

As the Pierce City boom gathered momentum, miners discovered the gold at Orofino Flat was six feet down, and sluices were required to recover it. Owners of adjoining claims formed companies of ten to twelve individuals and worked together on one claim at a time. By mid-August the district was producing about $60,000 a week.

But the ground played out before anyone could spit and holler howdy. Late-comers, who had arrived to find the diggings overcrowded, went off and discovered rich placers in Elk City, Florence and Warren. Their friends in Pierce and Orofino rushed to join them. Within two years, an 1863 census revealed only 525 people residing in Pierce. Some mining continued, particularly by Chinese. The most careful estimates place the amount of gold removed in the six-year period at $3.5 million. (The Nez Perce tribe was finally given a severance royalty on this gold in the 1970s.)

At the turn of the century, Pierce consisted of four stores, a couple of hotels and livery stables, blacksmith shops, a Chinese grocery, a sawmill on Canal Gulch, and a corner saloon that advertised:

A little whiskey now and then
Is relished by the best of men.
It smoothes the furrows off dull care
And makes ace high look like two pair.

64

The dredging of Orofino Creek, from Canal Gulch to Rhodes Creek, began in 1906. The first dredge was brought to Greer, then freighted overland by wagon. Electric dredging began in 1914, and diesel dredges gouged as late as the 1940s. The early dredges recovered countless bullets, razors, and Chinese coins in their trommel screens.

It was a strange twist, but the real wealth at Pierce lay in the timber that surrounded the community. When the government survey for the area was completed in 1903, another boom surged through the district, as settlers rushed to file claims under the Timber and Stone Act. Large-scale harvest did not occur until the Northern Pacific built its forty-mile spur from the Clearwater Timber Company's mill in Lewiston, through Pierce, to Headquarters in 1925-1927. The laborers spent their wages in the mining town; it must have been a nostalgic interlude for a few old-timers, who had heard the original ballyhoo bonanza tales first-hand. The forests eventually produced far more gold than the placer deposits.

Pierce waited longer than most Idaho towns for electricity. The first service, in 1932, was from a power plant that charged 12½¢ a kilowatt hour – which may have been the second-highest commercial rate in the world at the time. (The Idaho Power Co. rate was then 3½¢ per kwh.) Washington Water Power brought regular service to the area in the fall, 1947.

And what became of town-founder, Elias Davidson Pierce? In 1865-1866, he joined in a stage line venture from Sacramento to southwest Idaho, but Bannock Indian troubles ruined the enterprise. A few years later, he heard that a fellow was paying an inordinate amount of attention to his fiancee, Rebecca, whom he had not seen in twenty years. So Pierce went back to Indiana and married her. He then returned to California to look after some quartz-lode prospects that did not pan out. Finally, he retired to Pennville, his hometown in Indiana. Rebecca's youngest brother built the couple a cabin, and they survived on Captain Pierce's veteran's pension that amounted to $30 a month at the time of his death, in 1897. Rebecca outlived her husband by a few years. Their only child died at age six months.

One block east of Main St., at Court St. and First Ave. W., is the historic two-story Pierce courthouse, Idaho's oldest government building. When gold was discovered at Canal Gulch, the area was part of Washington Territory. Shoshone County was established in January, 1861, as an administrative convenience for the miners. That summer, the county cast the largest vote in Washington Territory for the congressional election. (The county initially included all of later southern Idaho and much of Wyoming.) In December, the legislature in Olympia, obviously alarmed by the shift in political power, reduced the Shoshone County lines so that little more than the Pierce mining district was included within its borders, but Pierce became the county seat.

In May, 1862, the county commissioners decided that a courthouse and jail were needed. The hewed-log building was completed within two months for $3,700; two small jail cells, each with a single forty-square-inch window, were constructed in the rear of the building.

The first marriage license was issued at the courthouse in 1875 – indicative of the perturbing scarcity of single women in the area.

When the county's population had shifted to the Coeur d'Alene mining district, the county seat moved with it – to Murray in 1884. At that time, the building was sold to a citizen for $50. In the 1920s the owner allowed groups in town to use the structure for meetings. One group made well-intentioned alterations that destroyed much of the interior's historical authenticity, including old newspapers used to chink the walls. A kitchen addition was made on the north side. However, Idaho's oldest courthouse was transferred to the state in 1972, and it is now administered by the State Historical Society.

The town's Chinese cemetery was located two blocks west of Main Street – it is now a corner park at Stover Dr. and Water St. Pierce's population was largely Chinese for about three decades. The transcontinental railroad was completed in 1869, and many Orientals sought other employment. They were legally prohibited from staking claims, but in Idaho, as elsewhere, insolvent claims abandoned by white miners were purchased or taken over by Chinese who toiled with great determination and patience to make them pay a second time. As elsewhere in the west, the Chinese in Idaho were subjected to virulent racial discrimination and harassment, and not infrequently, to murder. Their only crime in most cases was a language difference and their Oriental appearance. (The Idaho territorial legislature, in 1865, passed a $5-a-month Chinese miner's tax, which was collected by the county sheriff – proving once again that no man's life, liberty or property are safe while the legislature is in session.)

In September, 1885, Pierce merchant D. M. Fraser was the victim of a hatchet murder while asleep in the back of his store. His merchandise and safe were untouched. The only plausible motive advanced for the crime was jealousy or anger on the part of another storekeeper, Lee Kee Nam.

66

When word of the misdeed spread, a mounted posse of eighty men arrived from Lewiston and Weippe Prairie to encircle the town. A kangaroo court held session in the street. Accounts of the methods used to coerce a confession from several Chinese residents vary, but all agree a hangman's noose was used to accelerate matters. However, identification of guilt was apparently indefinite enough that a deputy sheriff decided to take five of the Chinese in a wagon to Murray for trial. Two miles outside of town, the deputy and the accused were halted by a masked band of vigilantes that kidnapped the prisoners and hanged all five on a nearby pole suspended between two trees.

The Chinese in Pierce paid a packer in town to bring the bodies to this cemetery (park) for burial.

This mass-murder, like the one that took the lives of thirty-one Chinese miners on Snake River sixty miles north of Lewiston only two years later, had international repercussions. The Chinese Consul in San Francisco, who learned of the event from newspaper accounts, sent a note of protest to the Chinese Minister, Chang Yen Hoon, in Washington, D.C. The Minister requested that Secretary of State Thomas Bayard order an investigation.

In April, 1886, Governor Edward Stevenson, who had been appointed to Idaho Territory a few months earlier, received a letter from the Secretary, requesting a full investigation. Stevenson promptly responded that he would take "the earliest opportunity" to visit Pierce and try to obtain the facts connected "... with that disgraceful outrage." The Governor had earlier taken a firm stand against the Boise Anti-Chinese League, but he seems to have found the Pierce road impassable for three months.

Then in mid-July Stevenson rode across Weippe Prairie with a letter of introduction, obtained from a Lewiston attorney, that stated in part, "The Governor does not want names as to parties who took part in the hanging but the cause ... Therefore, have a full investigation, and let it clearly appear the Chinamen who were hung were the real murderers ... and that they were hung for that only." With those instructions, the inquest was a charade.

Upon his return to Boise, Governor Stevenson wrote the Secretary of State that the Chinese hanged were the ones who "so cruelly, shockingly and brutally murdered, without the least provocation (except jealousy) one of the best citizens of Idaho." The Governor's position was clarified by further remarks in his letter concerning the Chinese "and their low filthy habits, their highbinder piratical societies ... their dens of infamy and opium smoking" and concluded with the wish of his fellow citizens that "the day is not far distant when Congress will relieve us of their presence."

11
IDAHO

At the time of the atrocity, Pierce had about 150 Chinese residents and 15-20 whites. The Orientals began leaving town in 1912 because a federal law required that they become citizens or leave the country. Since almost no Chinese could enter the country legally after the 1882 Exclusion Act, natural attrition and aging were also factors in diminishing the Oriental population.

Agents of the Chinese Six Companies in San Francisco collected the bones of deceased Orientals from the cemetery and shipped them back to China for reburial. Rural Chinese came from lineage villages, and it was important to them that they be buried in the village where they were born because relatives there would perpetuate their memory, a kind of immortality.

The site of the lynching is 1.5 miles southwest of the town; there is a sign alongside the road, about 120 yards from the place where the incident occurred.

Pierce courthouse in 1920.

Early view of Pierce.

Logging bateau in Pierce.

On the west side of Main Street, next to the library, is a screened display that contains a bateau used on Clearwater River log drives. This boat, used by crews behind the drive to assist "river pigs" or "bank beaver," is an heirloom worthy of careful inspection. (As far as the writer has been able to determine, not more than four survive in Idaho, and only this one is protected.)

The drive boat's origin can be traced to an Ottawa, Canada, wood carver, John Cockburn. He designed the "pointers" to "float on a heavy dew" – five inches of draft when loaded. In a small workshop beside the Ottawa River, three generations of Cockburns crafted V-bottomed bateaux with pine tongue-and-groove planking and cedar ribs, finished with a coating of oil and jeweler's rouge. The brick color became traditional.

The craft was constructed upside down. Posts were set to a string line, and two ribs were framed near the stern and one near the bow before the boards were curved around the knees. In Idaho, bateaux were twenty to forty-four feet in length, double-ended and lap-stripped of one-inch cedar planking (Later models used plywood.) The proper bevel at bow and stern was crucial. The flat keel allowed a boat to ride up on a log jam, where the bowman could hold it while the oarsmen used their peaveys to unknit the jam – always alert for his call to reboard.

A full-sized boat had a crew of six or eight men. When a man had graduated to pulling an oar, he was a far cut above a "river pig" who had to work all day in water "ass-deep to a tall Swede." The head boatman stood braced in the bow, facing downriver, with a twelve-foot pike pole in his hands. He had wrists and forearms like an axle tree. His job was to read the water, call commands to the crew and assist steerage with deft thrusts of his pole.

Two (or three) oarsmen were on each side of the bateau at alternate stations (bowmen on the right and sternmen on the left), and a stern man with a nine-foot draw paddle.

The crew synchronized with rhythm and power; there was no margin for indecision or imprecision. At the head boatman's command "head boat" all four oars pulled in unison, at the command "easy oars" all blades were raised. Direction was changed by "head bow and easy stern" or vice versa. The craft could be reversed with a "head bow, backwater stern" order.

The experienced boatmen would have appreciated Wallace Stegner's remark: "And oh, how beautiful a thing it is to work with men who know their job."

Gold was discovered two miles south of Pierce City, at the mouth of Rhodes Creek on Orofino Creek. Take the French Mountain Road turnoff from Highway 11, at the south end of Pierce, and drive 0.5 miles up Orofino Creek.

The town, **Oro Fino**, that sprouted on this site, quickly shaded Pierce – in 1861 it had 1,500 residents, 400 cabin-houses, ten stores, and a Wells Fargo office. One correspondent at the time made the marvelous observation, "Fortunately, there are no lawyers yet." The jealous residents of Pierce referred to the new community as Muttonville.

The winter of 1861-1862 was cold enough to make a polar bear hunt cover. Men were in grievous need of supplies, and the merchants of Walla Walla and Lewiston were eager to send them. But nothing moved, save on foot. Grostein and Binnard ran a 100-mule string out of Lewiston that brought nearly nine tons of freight each trip. Charges ranged from forty cents to eighty cents a pound.

One of the principal cargoes hauled by freighters was whiskey – usually in barrels. It was customary for freighters to levy on their liquid lading. One freighter revealed the secret in the Spokane *Spokesman Review* years later:

... the barrel-heads carried a government stamp about the size of a $10 bill, which was glued and also had tacks in the corners. They would pull back the edge of the stamp and remove the tacks, then drill a hole into a barrel under the tack point just large enough to insert a straw. After we had our fill of refreshments we would plug the hole, replace the tack and glue the stamp back. The purchasers never figured it out.

Another packer wrote:

Our pack trains charge for packing gold out to Lewiston, $4 an ounce. We furnish the animals, saddles, food and guards. The renegades robbing people has made the packing of gold too dangerous. We do not pack it now. Looks like all the jail doors have been opened in the states and the bad men come here. Some found a way to put these varments on the right road and give the others a lesson to follow for respect for other people's property and law. Our own laws are square for an honest man and others are not worth burying.

As soon as the gold was gone, Oro Fino wilted. Building materials were removed to Pierce. By 1866 a fire had destroyed what remained.

(USFS Road 250 continues from this point 111 miles to Superior, Montana, by way of the North Fork of the Clearwater and across the Bitterroots at Hoodoo Pass. There are no services.)

Rhodes Creek, which ventures into Orofino Creek from the east shore, enshrines a man worth remarking: William "Black Bill" Rhodes, a Missouri mulatto who arrived with the first group of miners in Pierce. Billy took more than $80,000 from the creek in one year. He was altruistic and good-humored to a fault, prodigal with his earnings, giving to anyone in need.

Rhodes had prospected in Scott Valley, near the Marble Mountains of California, before coming to Pierce. On leaving Oro Fino, he went to Arizona and discovered a promising quartz-gold mine, which he sold for $75,000. Bill returned to the Clearwater region, where John Silcott grubstaked him to a prospecting trip in the Bitterroot Range. There he found another likely claim (based on ore samples) but died by the mine during the winter.

His Lewiston friends traveled to Blacklead Mountain (fifty miles east of Pierce, and north of the Lolo Highway) in the summer and gave Bill a proper burial. Rhodes Peak (7,900 ft.) near the Idaho-Montana border, not far from his grave, serves as an additional memorial.

Jaype, 4.1 miles north of Pierce, is simply the location of an impressive Potlatch Corporation plywood plant that began production in 1967. The mill, which roofs seven acres, has the capability of producing 150 million square feet of sheathing-grade plywood each year. The site was given its name from the first initials of one-time Potlatch president, John Phillip Weyerhaeuser, Jr.

Headquarters is located twelve miles north of Pierce and is the terminus of the railroad extended from Orofino by the Northern Pacific. The rails were laid to this point in 1925-1927 at a cost of $4

Aerial view of Headquarters, 1940.

million – one ten-mile stretch required fifty bridges, and much of the grade required blasting work. The line is now part of the Camas Prairie Railroad.

Headquarters is a company logging town, and the company is now Potlatch Corporation. Logging in the region anticipated the railroad by about a year. At the peak of horse-logging, there were nearly a thousand men working out of fifteen camps, and each camp had twenty teams of horses. Hay was hauled by train to Headquarters and sledded to the camps. Logs were skidded from the camps to the railroad and loaded on cars by stiff-boom jammers powered by steam and horses. The last horses were used in January, 1942.

In 1936 Vardis Fisher wrote, "(the town) is unusual in the arrangement of the houses: they stand in a circle after the manner of early wagon trains when attacked by Indians; and are built to facilitate movement and communication in winter months when the snow lies from twelve to fifteen feet in depth."

The old town was rather self-sufficient. It had its own power-plant, school, community hall, store, dairy, and blacksmith shop. High voltage and telephone lines did not arrive until 1947. Today, loggers still rent housing from the company, but most of them commute to their homes on weekends.

The Forest Service Road 247, that travels north from Headquarters, is paved all the way to the North Fork of the Clearwater. Two sights of historical interest are reached from this road before it meets the river.

To visit the location of the first forest fire lookout tower in the U.S., drive 8.6 miles on the paved road north from Headquarters. Turn left onto a dirt road, and after 0.5 miles there is a **Bertha Hill** sign. Keep to the right and travel uphill 3.4 miles; ignore the spur roads. Make a sharp curve to the right, and the present lookout tower is reached after another 1.0 miles. (The original Little Bertha Hill lookout site is fifty yards off the dirt road 0.6 miles before the present tower is reached.)

In 1902 cruisers for the Clearwater Timber Co. (absorbed by Potlatch) built a ladder to a wooden roost atop a snag on 5,520-foot Bertha Hill. A man was left to watch for fires from his island in the sky. If he spotted smoke, he rode to the nearest timber crew or homestead.

Conscious that its assets could literally "go up in smoke," the company also organized the Clearwater Timber Protective Association in 1905, the first cooperative organization of its type in the nation. Timberland owners pooled their resources to make a more effective firefighting force. The Clearwater TPA merged with the Potlatch TPA in 1966 to provide an efficient industry safeguard on private lands.

The U.S. Forest Service began to budget money for lookout towers in 1909. From that time until 1953, when the number peaked at 5,060, federal, state and private towers were constructed.

W. E. Boeing, president of the Northwest Aero Club, made a prophetic observation in 1915, when he said, "There is no question in my mind but what the airplane will practically do away with some of the observation towers." He was right; airplane surveillance twice a day, or immediately following a storm, has proved to be a cheaper and more effective method of patrolling the forests. During fire weather, many back-country pilots attach a heat sensing device to their plane's wing that will automatically alert them to even a small ground fire. At present, there are fewer than 1,300 manned towers, and less than one-third of the fires detected are reported by lookouts.

The Clearwater Potlatch Timber Protective Association staffs the sixty-foot steel tower that now stands on Bertha Hill. It was built in 1959, and the fence guards around the catwalk are a precaution added after a lookout fell to her death in 1962. Bertha Hill has been added to the National Register of Historic Places. Visitors are welcome.

Back on the paved road, at the turnoff for Bertha Hill, continue north toward the North Fork of the Clearwater. About 15.5 miles from the turnoff, the road parallels Beaver Creek, which flows along the west shoulder.

Park where there is room to pull off the road, and look down across the creek. Traces of the **Beaver Creek flume** can be spotted among the trees and grass. The twenty-mile flume was used from 1930 to 1942 by Potlatch Corp. Its construction required 4 million board feet, but it served to bring about 170 million board feet out of the drainage. The flume was abandoned during World War II.

From Headquarters it is possible to make a drive ten miles northeast to the site of **Brown's Rock**. Take Road 246 past the Potlatch shops, and continue 5.2 miles to the Brown's Rock sign. Turn left. Since heavy trucks may be on the road, use caution. Drive past "A" and "B" Roads. After 1.8 miles the road enters Walker's Woods (timber companies avoid the word "park"), an old-growth cedar forest.

Another 3.7 miles reveals an abandoned spur road on the right. (If one misses this spur, the road suddenly frays into three strands; the one on the right ends at a quarry with a view of Bertha Hill.) Walk up the spur to the knoll covered with second-growth trees and brush. This is the location of Brown's Rock, though the stone itself is lost. On this eminence began an event as famous among timbermen as Christ's temptation by the Devil on a mountain top is among Christians.

73

Charles O. Brown, age fifty-nine, timber representative for Fred Weyerhaeuser and John Humbird, stood on this hill August 13, 1900, looking at the finest white pine forest left in the world. With him was his twenty-five year-old son, Nat, and Wallace Felter, a trapper who had guided them to the area for $20. Brown had been seeking more timber for his employers, and from this spot he saw what they wanted: the Beaver Creek drainage to the north supported "the choicest block of timber in the Clearwater country."

Brown returned to his office in Moscow, wrote a report to his superiors, and certain they would approve his choice, assembled a crew of six men. He promptly received "go at once" instructions, and within days the men were cutting trail into Beaver Creek Meadows.

From a base camp there, the team worked like birddogs in tall oats, cruising timber and laying out sections. None of the timber could be filed on until survey descriptions were obtained, but the urgency of their efforts was dictated by the knowledge that ahead o them a man named W. E. McCord, rather than wait for the government surveyor, had a crew in the area who were running a survey line north from Pierce. Both parties knew they were competing for the same prize.

Brown's men took advantage of McCord's survey line, and on September 9, Brown headed for Lewiston, where one of his bosses, John Glover, met him and filed railroad script on 30,000 acres of the best timberground in the Clearwater region. McCord arrived at the land office the next day – only hours too late.

Since Weyerhaeuser, Humbird and Glover wanted at least anothe 20,000 acres, Brown returned to the camp after making arrangements for fresh supplies. A chagrined McCord was also back in the woods. Both crews worked feverishly, nipping at each others flanks. Charles, out riding one afternoon, learned from a casual remark by one member of the rival crew that McCord had left to file a claim in Lewiston three hours earlier.

Brown burned a hole in the wind galloping back to camp, where he dispatched his resourceful and indefatigable son, Nat, to Orofino to telegraph land descriptions to Glover in Lewiston. Nat had a spirited horse and rode all night. He finally overtook his unsuspecting adversary at a rest cabin, and while the heedless McCord ate a meal inside, Brown silently took the fresh mount intended for his rival and turned both spent horses loose.

The young man rode into Orofino about daybreak, and at the livery stable, being mistaken for McCord, was handed a letter. He found the contents instructed the train engineer to take the bearer to Lewiston without delay. So Nat Brown, impersonating McCord, went to the Orofino depot, roused the engineer and arrived in Lewiston at 7:00 A.M. on McCord's chartered train. Glover met him, and the two men were still filing their claims at the land office when W. E. McCord arrived – mad as a fresh-cut bull. But legality has never been a synonym for morality, and the Weyerhaeusers, like the pine bark beetle, were now firmly entrenched in the Idaho woods.

It is possible to return to Orofino from Brown's Rock by way of the Grangemont Road, just north of Jaype, rather than going back through Pierce.

U.S. Highway No. 12 from the Idaho-Washington state line in Lewiston via Orofino, Kamiah and Lowell to the Idaho-Montana state line at Lolo Pass. (Overlaps U.S. 95 from Lewiston to Spalding.) Route length: 175.5 miles.

U.S. Highway 12 approaches Idaho on the west from Clarkston, Washington, via a bridge across the Snake River. The eastern end of the bridge rests in **Lewiston**. This city missed, by a few months, being the first permanent settlement in Idaho, but it was the first town to incorporate in the state. It has the lowest elevation of any community in Idaho (739 feet), and though it is on the same latitude as Bangor, Maine, its climate often provides shirt-sleeve weather in February.

Because of bridges and rivers, the emplacement of Lewiston can confuse a visitor. The Snake River flowing north, makes a sharp westward bend at Lewiston. The Clearwater, flowing west, meets the Snake at the bend and completes the top of a T. The town of Lewiston lies under the east limb of the T and along the eastern shore of the Snake, where it forms the stem of the T. So the Clearwater flows north of Lewiston, and the Snake slides along the western edge of the city.

Lewiston was established at the confluence of the Snake and the Clearwater Rivers as a result of Captain E. D. Pierce's gold discovery in 1860, about 75 miles east of the present city. Portland newspapers promoted the strike and the easiest route to the Pierce placer mines from the coast was up the Columbia, Snake and Clearwater Rivers. Since the shallow bed of the Clearwater was an obstacle to steamboat traffic, Lewiston was the natural choice for a supply center at the head of navigation.

At the time of the gold discovery the land where Pierce and Lewiston would be located was still part of the Nez Perce

US 12

reservation. Indian agent, A. J. Cain, warned the settlers that he would tear down any permanent buildings; so framed canvas tents were used as dwellings. This worked a hardship on the early fortune seekers as the winter of 1861-1862 was the most severe recorded in Idaho. Spring floodwaters followed.

The Fort Lapwai Army wagon master, Tom Beall, gave this account of how the town was named:

The way we came to name it Lewiston was when on May 19, 1861, there were five or six of us sitting on a log where Trevitt had his tent (Lewiston's first merchantile establishment). Several names were suggested by our party (the others present were Mr. Dutro, Mr. Carr and Dr. Buker). John (Silcott) suggested we name it after some Indian Chief. During our talk about the matter, Trevitt came out of the tent and said: 'Gentlemen, why not name this place Lewiston after Lewis and Clark' and the suggestion was accepted by us at once. It turned out later that Trevitt didn't have Lewis so much in mind as Lewiston, Maine, his former place of residence.

Since a biographical sketch of Trevitt indicates he was from New Hampshire, however, and moved to Ohio at an early age, he may have had Captain Meriwether Lewis in mind after all.

John Silcott established a ferry across the Snake River in 1861, about seven miles west of Lewiston. The following year, he built a ferry across the Clearwater River, thereby making it possible for travelers to avoid the hills on the old wagon road west of the townsite. His was a lucrative transport business: with one charge of $5.00 (horse and wagon) for both ferries, he sometimes reaped $400 a day.

The settlers were squatters on the Indian land, but they nevertheless staked, claimed, sold and bought lots, adopted the laws of a mining camp, elected a surveyor and recorded their claims in a record book. A number of permanent buildings appeared.

Most of the Indians agreed to a new treaty in 1863, and the site of Lewiston was ceded to the United States. However, Congress did not ratify the treaty for four years.

During this period, Lewiston was a sight to see, and then try to forget. There were 2,000 persons living on the flat, so many of them in tents that "Ragtown" became a popular nickname. There were twenty-five saloons and twenty houses of tolerance. Several murders were committed; three men were lynched and three more were legally hanged. (Lewiston's last lynching occurred in 1893.) The Lewiston Protective Association, a false-front for vigilantes, met weekly at the Pioneer Hotel. Henry Plummer, secret leader of an outlaw gang called "The Innocents," ran a gambling parlor in town. The Civil War had begun, and anyone who flew Old Glory was likely to find it aerified with bullet holes.

Political events, always material for a soap opera, now rose to the art of vaudeville theatre:

Act One: The same year the new treaty was accepted by the Nez Perce, Congress organized the Territory of Idaho, which until that time had been part of Washington Territory. President Lincoln appointed William Wallace as first governor and Wallace selected Lewiston as the territorial capital. Within a month, the governor had himself elected territorial delegate, resigned his position and departed for the nation's capital.

Gold discoveries in the Boise Basin in 1862 had caused a wild exodus from the Clearwater camps for southern Idaho. Lewiston's population had plummeted from 10,000 to about 375 by the time the first legislature came to town. Southern Idaho residents outnumbered those in the north nearly seven to one. Caleb Lyon, a charlatan from New York, was appointed the second governor in 1864. It was eight months before he arrived to fill his post. At the first meeting of the legislature under his tenure, southern legislators succeeded in passing a bill which moved the capital to Boise City. Furious Lewiston residents responded by placing the territorial seal and archives under twenty-four hour guard to prevent their removal, and kept a watchful eye on the new governor. Lyons decided to go duck hunting on the Snake River. Southern Idaho friends rowed him across the river and put him on a stage that would have eventually taken him to Boise. Instead, the governor went to San Francisco and then East for ten months. He visited Idaho once for a short spell, then went East again. In Washington, D.C. he complained that $47,000 had been stolen from his money belt while he slept on the train. The sum was apparently federal money, and under suspicion he retired to New York, where he died.

Act Two: March, 1865. Enter C. Dewitt Smith, newly-appointed territorial secretary. The citizens of Lewiston welcomed Smith and plied him with tanglefoot and popskull, but in the back of his mind he was figuring a way to move the state records to Boise.

Dewitt rode over to Ft. Lapwai one morning, and as acting governor, convinced the commander that he was entitled to assistance from the U.S. Army. That afternoon Smith rode into town accompanied by regular troops under Lt. Hammer.

Lewiston lawyers had the assistant U.S. Marshal attempt to serve C. D. Smith with an injunction notice. Service was resisted, while the secretary and soldiers seized the Idaho seal, records and treasury – then Smith went south to Boise, where he arrived in mid-April. A few months later he died of alcoholism.

*Lewiston,
Washington
Territory, late 1862.*

Act Three: Horace Gilson, Smith's assistant, took over as acting secretary-governor. Gilson left Idaho in 1861, stopped at the U.S. Depository in Oregon City and picked up $41,000 in territorial funds, then sailed for Hong Kong.

The denouement: The territorial district court ruled, in 1865, that the legislature had acted illegally and that the capital was still in Lewiston. On appeal, the territorial Supreme Court reversed the district court. But the decision was not published (it was only entered in a journal); so for several years Lewiston continued to argue the most lost of causes. As Mark Twain observed, "There isn't a parallel of latitude but thinks it would have been the equator had it had its rights."

In 1872 daily mail service began from Lewiston to Walla Walla (ninety-eight miles west). Steamboats hauled mail and freight via the river-road. Stage lines operated to Pierce and Mount Idaho.

The four-mile Lewiston ditch, dug by Chinese, brought water from the Clearwater, east of town, along the hem of the hill south of Main St. and then channeled it down to the Snake near the present Clarkston bridge. The ditch water powered two mills enroute and irrigated rows of poplar trees planted along the dirt streets.

In the 1880s Lewiston grew like its poplars. It began to recoup some of the population lost to Boise. There was a school, sawmill, telephone office, and there were flour mills and bakeries. So many churches crowded the intersection of Eleventh and Main that it was known as "Piety Corner." And despite a challenge from Moscow, the community managed to remain the seat of Nez Perce County.

During this span, the city became the center of a serious campaign aimed at having Washington State annex north Idaho.

78

The move had nearly unanimous support among the residents of
northern Idaho (Nez Perce County voted 1,675-28 in favor, in 1886;
five other counties gave similar margins of approval), and the Idaho
territorial legislature was sympathetic to the separatist movement.
Though northern Idaho held only about 20 percent of the territory's
votes, candidates for Congress invariably promised to support the
annexation.

The north-Idaho annexation bill introduced in Congress in 1886
passed the House, and the Senate in 1887, and was sent to President
Cleveland for his signature as Congress adjourned. (Nevada had
provided crucial help, because that state, having lost much of its
population when the Comstock lode played out, wanted to annex
southern Idaho.) However, the Idaho Governor, Edward Stevenson,
was a Democratic appointee of President Cleveland, and his
telegraphed objection to the separation persuaded the President to
exercise a pocket veto.

In the next Congress, Idaho delegate Fred Dubois, who came from
an Illinois Republican family and had influential friends in the Coeur
d'Alene mining district, succeeded in frustrating Nevada's designs
and north Idaho's aspirations. By 1888 the Boise ring in southern
Idaho decided it did not want to let the northern region depart, and
Moscow had been neutralized with the promise of the university.
Statehood in 1890 settled the matter, though the issue has surfaced
in three elections since 1907.

The 1890s were busy years for the Snake River city. For the third
time, a major fire devoured a portion of the business district. For the
fourth time, floodwaters ran through the streets. But not all events

79

were redundant. In 1893 the Lewiston Normal School was opened on the hill behind the commercial district. It was a two-year teacher's college, which was expanded to a four-year institution in 1947, and was designated Lewis and Clark State College in 1971. It still specializes in teacher education. (The college is located at the head of Fifth St.)

Other "grand openings" marked the life of Lewiston in that active decade. The Nez Perce reservation was hashed into 160-acre pieces for members of the tribe, and the larger portion of the Camas Prairie (540,000 acres) was bestowed upon covetous homesteaders, several thousand of whom rushed out from Lewiston at the noon

Lewiston in 1899.

First Idaho Territorial Capitol on Third St., Lewiston (left).

Lewiston, Main St., 1890.

report of a cannon on November 18, 1895.

The first railroad tracks reached an impatient citizenry in September, 1898 – years after other towns of similar size in the state had received such service. The Oregon Railroad and

80

Navigation Co. train (a.k.a. Union Pacific) had been so long in coming that even the governor was on hand to greet it. The event called for a three-day celebration.

A toll bridge was completed across the Snake River the following year. But it was thirteen years more before the city managed to construct a bridge across the Clearwater. At that time, the Snake River bridge was purchased jointly by the states of Idaho and Washington, and the toll gate was removed.

The commerce of the town shifted gradually from mining supplies to agriculture and forest products. The Lewiston Land and Water Co. and the Lewiston Sweetwater Co. conceived a 9,000-acre irrigation project on the plateau southeast of town, known as the Lewiston Orchards, which would be developed by tapping the Craig Mountain watershed. Land was divided into five-acre tracts, and prospective purchasers from as far away as Minnesota were offered free train rides to Lewiston if they bought a parcel. Most people took 10 years to pay. Promoted and propagated from 1912-1930, the area supported farms and orchards, but did not meet early, exaggerated expectations. By 1927 water cost $12.50 an acre. Cherries, apples and wine grapes were successful crops until the cherry fly and codling moth became serious pests in the late 1920s. By the time rotenone and lead arsenate proved effective, many of the orchards were gone. Roger Dahljelm, one of the chief promoters, left to start the Farmers' Market in Los Angeles. The land became more valuable as lots; houses and shops replaced the acres of fruit trees.

The Palouse country, on the plateau north and west of the Lewiston North Hills, became one of the best dry land wheat growing areas in the United States. Steamboats hauled harvests to Portland. The ships were an important part of Lewiston's commercial transportation, particularly after 1915, when the Celilo Canal on the Columbia River permitted a bypass of the railroad portage around Celilo Falls. However, government-built dams, begun on the Columbia in the late 1930s, grounded the romantic saga of Snake River steamboats in 1940.

Corporate interests then organized under the Inland Empire Waterways Association and began to promote a system of locks on the Columbia and Snake Rivers. "Any cat will drink milk if it is put in front of him." The Army Corps of Engineers began lapping the first appropriation, for four dams on the lower Snake, in 1955. Since Lewiston is only 739 feet above sea level, the project was quite feasible – given $350 million. Slackwater reached the city in 1975.

At 470 miles from the ocean, Lewiston became the most distant inland seaport in the west. Vessels drawing less than fourteen feet and weighing up to 12,000 tons can travel from the mouth of the Columbia to the mouth of the Clearwater. The port cost $6.5 million. It has two grain terminals and a stiff-leg derrick equipped to handle forty-foot containers. By 1977 the wheat tonnage handled by the port was so great that Lewiston qualified for listing as a "major port" in the National Register of Ports – shipments had already tripled the twenty-five-year tonnage projection. Expansion of the facility is planned. Most of the grain and forest products from the Inland Empire move down the waterway in barges towed by economical and efficient tug boats. (Access to the port is via Sixth Avenue North.)

Captain Peaney's ferry from Clarkston to Lewiston.

Camas Prairie Railroad depot in about 1915.

Lewiston has numerous buildings worthy of an extended inspection. The Camas Prairie railroad depot, built in 1908-1909, is located on Main St. at Thirteenth. The structure was designed by the Northern Pacific's engineering department after the Northern Pacific reached a compromise with Union Pacific that specified joint operation of the line to Grangeville. An old flour mill on the site was razed in order to make room for the new building.

Like most stations of its era, the Camas Prairie depot had a large general waiting room, a smoking area for men, and a lady's comfort room. The ticket office on the main floor was located in the trackside bay, allowing the agents a view of approaching trains. The telegraph office occupied the upstairs bay. Offices of the roadmaster, superintendent, and clerks absorbed the remaining upstairs space.

The long one-story wings of pressed brick were used as baggage and freight storage areas. One wing was originally left open for parking baggage carts.

The Hotel Lewis-Clark dominates the block of First and Main, on the west end of town. It was designed by a Spokane architect, Kirkland Cutter, and constructed at a cost of $350,000 in 1922. Built in the California Mission style, with a simplicity of form popular during the period, the hotel has 144 rooms, a large Italian-style lobby and three dining rooms. The hotel was saved by the Ponderosa Inn chain in 1972; it was given a million-dollar renovation. Visitors who stay at the Lewis-Clark not only have pleasant quarters, they also support a laudable effort at historic preservation.

The Luna building, at Third and C Sts., contains the county museum with its modest displays. It is on the location of an 1862 log building, which was owned by Hill Beachey. He had a parlor, kitchen and dining room on the first floor and twenty sleeping rooms upstairs. Legislators and territorial officials stayed at the house when Lewiston was the territorial capital in 1863-1864.

To view some of the better turn-of-the-century residences on Normal Hill, take the Ninth Street grade south from Main St. Ninth St. becomes Eighth St. by the time it travels five blocks to Fifth Ave. Turn right on Fifth Ave.

The houses opposite each other at the corner of Fifth Ave. and Eighth St. are those of the banker, Frank Kettenbach (southwest corner), and R. C. Beach, a Lewiston merchant (northwest corner). The Kettenbach house, with its sandstone retaining wall, was built for $11,500 in 1912. In 1916 the Beach dwelling was constructed for about $19,000, on the most expensive residential lot in Lewiston at the time.

Continue west on Fifth Ave. On the left, at 720 Fifth Ave., note the handsome Queen Anne house built in 1904, at a cost of $4,500, for Edwin Thomas.

On Fifth Ave., mid-block between Seventh and Sixth St., is St. Stanislaus Catholic Church. The parish was founded in 1867-1868 by Fr. Joseph Cataldo, S. J. The original frame structure was replaced by the present stone church in 1905.

St. Stanislaus was designed by James Nave, a Lewiston architect who had emigrated from Kansas. It is a Gothic-style building with an octagonal, forty-eight-foot bell tower, and the basalt was probably quarried at Swallow's Nest Rock, across the Snake River.

At 502 Fifth Ave. at Fifth St., Almos Butterfield's house is located. This is another outstanding Queen Anne-style dwelling with a curved porch and fish-scale shingles. The house was built in 1900.

A short detour can be made north on Fifth St. to Second Ave., to the entrance of Pioneer Park. The park affords an excellent view of the Snake-Clearwater confluence. It is also the location of the city's Carnegie library, a Renaissance Revival building erected in 1904 with a $10,000 grant. (The library has been altered substantially.)

Just southwest of the library is an 1862 squared-log house; it is representative of the first "permanent" houses in Lewiston. At one time, the park also contained the city's fire bell tower, a bandstand, and a fountain with a large statue of Sacajewea.

Return to Fifth Ave., continue west three blocks to Prospect Ave., and turn right. There are a number of elegant old houses along this west rim of Normal Hill, along with a pleasant view of the Snake River.

The structure at 312 Prospect was erected as a weather station in 1904. A combination of flags and pennants, flown from a pole there, conveyed the weather forecast to steamboat pilots on the river below.

The Curtis Thatcher residence, built in 1899, at 204 Prospect Ave., is worth noting. Across the street from the house is the footing for a staircase that was built by neighborhood subscription and provided a shortcut to the river front.

Another impressive house, built in 1901, stands at 113 Prospect. It was designed by I. J. Galbraith and belonged to Eben Mounce, a U.S. Marshal who lived in Lewiston.

Prospect Ave. is not a through street. Turn around, and at Third Ave. and Prospect, drive northwest two blocks down the Snake River Grade to the intersection with Snake River Ave. At the first opportunity, turn south on Snake River Ave.

A four-mile drive on Snake River Avenue, along the east shore of the river, leads to **Hells Gate State Park**. The 960-acre park is open year-round and the visitor center, on a knoll behind the marina, has a display of Snake and Clearwater history.

South of the visitor center is a campground, with vehicle hookups and picnic facilities. The day-use area can be used by swimmers, and there are short trails for bicyclists, runners and hikers.

Moored at the marina, a short distance north of the camp loops, is the sternwheel steamboat, *Jean*. The *Jean* was built in 1938 by Commercial Iron Works of Portland for the Western Transportation Co. of that city. She is 168 feet long and draws eight feet. Oil fired two steam boilers; they drove four pistons connected to the paddlewheel.

The steamboat was not well-designed for river work; she towed log rafts until she was decommissioned in the 1950s. Then Western Transportation gave a gift deed to the ship to Lewis and Clark State College and the Luna House Society, and berthed her at Lewiston in 1975.

After a number of misadventures, including the near loss of the ship when she rolled over on her side, the *Jean* was transferred to the Idaho State Historical Society. Plans are still being formulated which will give the *Jean,* the last sternwheeler on the Snake, a snug harbor.

The Hellsgate Marina is the meeting place for boat excursion trips up the Snake River to **Hells Canyon**. It is possible to ride the mail boat upriver seventy miles and stay overnight in the canyon. Boats go twice a week during the summer. Other outfitters offer day trips. Reservations are advisable. Look in the yellow pages of the Lewiston telephone directory under "river trips."

If one does not have time to boat the Snake, it is still possible to drive upriver thirty miles to the mouth of the Grande Ronde River. Cross the bridge over the Snake River at the west edge of Lewiston, turn south through Clarkston, and follow the paved road south upriver along the west shore. The pavement eventually gives way to gravel.

The enormous, distinctive basalt outcrop on the west side of the road (across the river from Hells Gate marina) is known as **Swallow's Rock** because cliff swallows return from Argentina and Chile each spring to build their gourd-shaped, mud nests against the stone face. This rock, and others seen along the west side of the river, consists of basalt from the Columbia River flows which began approximately 20 million years ago. The basalt in this area erupted from fissures and dikes (rather than central vents) in the Wallowa Mountains and Grande Ronde River valley in Oregon. In places along the river, the basalt has formed striking hexagonal columns as it cooled and crystalized.

Indian pictographs can be seen on a large roadside boulder (on the river-side of the road) about fourteen miles south of Asotin, at Buffalo Eddy.

Two miles farther south, on the west side of the river, across from and just below the mouth of Captain John Creek, are ten ancient Nez Perce fishing walls along a 300 yard stretch of beach. They were used well into the twentieth century. During high water in the spring they are submerged, but as the water drops during the summer, they can be observed easily. To disturb these walls in any manner would be senseless, and a violation of state and federal statutes.

Numerous white sand beaches are found along this stretch of the river during the summer; they can be seen from the road, on the drive to **Heller Bar** at the mouth of the Grande Ronde. Such

US 12

beaches existed in Hells Canyon, above the mouth of the Salmon
River, but surge releases and sediment entrapment by Idaho Power
Company dams have destroyed them.

Heller Bar offers meals, as well as jet-boat trips upriver.

The most memorable tour in Lewiston, and the most remarkable
display of technology to be viewed in north Idaho, is available on
the east end of town at the **Potlatch Corporation** complex. The
plant is situated on the south side of the Clearwater River and can
be seen from U.S. Highway 12, just east of the city.

Plant tours are conducted weekdays at 9:00 A.M. and 1:00 P.M.
June through August and at 1:00 P.M. weekdays the rest of the year.
The visit, which requires two hours, is not recommended for
children under eight years of age. Take the time to walk through
this operation – some of the machines are more wonderful than
prize hogs at a state fair.

A tour guide gives competent and thorough explanations of the
manufacturing processes, but some historical information about the
company may be useful.

In 1903 Northland Pine Co., a Minnesota firm, and Wisconsin Log
and Lumber Co. sold their newly acquired Idaho timber holdings to
a firm incorporated in Maine: Potlatch Lumber Co., which planted
its roots in an authorized capitalization of $3 million. Investors were
wealthy timber families from Minnesota, Wisconsin, Indiana and
Iowa. Frederick Weyerhaeuser, a German immigrant who had been
in the lumber business since 1856, and his brother-in-law, F. C.
Denkman, were among the founders. Frederick's son, Charles, was
the company's first president.

In 1906 Potlatch began to produce lumber at its sawmill eighteen
miles north of Moscow (see Potlatch, town). Over the next twenty
years, the company milled 2.5 billion board feet there, but
investment in timberlands, mill, and rails was so great that in the
same period the corporate net income was less than $5 million.

Pinched by the Depression, a number of the stockholder families
decided they might curb their losses and stimulate Potlatch Lumber
by merging it with two other losers: Clearwater Timber Co. (a
Washington corporation, owned by Fred Weyerhaeuser and John
Humbird, which had an electric sawmill at the Lewiston site linked
by railroad to 5 billion feet of timber in the Clearwater drainage) and
the Edward Rutledge Timber Co. (Rutledge was from Wisconsin and
a lifelong friend of Fred Weyerhaeuser, who invested in the old
company). In January, 1931, Potlatch Forests, Inc., as the new
company was called, began business with $26.5 million in capital

stock. John Philip Weyerhaeuser, Jr., grandson of Fred Weyerhaeuser, was the first president.

Recent changes in the tax system encouraged the company to begin selective logging and sustained yield operations, opening an era of more enlightened forest management practices. Utilization of a broad species of trees began. After ten years, war demands and rising prices brought the company out of the red in 1940, and dividends flowed like annual tides. The war was followed by ten years of corporate expansion that converted PFI from an Idaho lumber company to a nationally integrated forest products

Potlatch Corp. mill. Note dam (upper left), and log pond now occupied by the aeration plant. The county fairgrounds were located on the site before the mill was built in 1926.

operation. Potlatch tripled its net worth in twenty-five years.

The company extended its wood products business in 1950 when it completed Idaho's first (and only) bleached pulp and paperboard mill, using waste wood chips as its raw material. The mill was made possible by new technology that allowed quality bleached paperboard to be made from a mixture of wood chips from different species of coniferous trees.

In the 1950s and 1960s five wood product companies were acquired in Arkansas and two pulp and paper mills in Minnesota. The company completed a five-year, $380 million investment program in 1977 and shortly thereafter embarked on a second five-year capital plan that involved expenditures of $600 million. These efforts gave Potlatch three timber bases totaling 1.4 million acres, and production capability involving not only lumber, pulp and paperboard, but also printing and business papers, milk containers and food packaging, and consumer products such as tissue and paper towels.

PFI became Potlatch Corporation in 1973. The company owns 614,000 acres in Idaho – 960 square miles. The predominant wood species on those timberlands, in order of their harvest quantities, are white fir, red cedar, white pine, Douglas fir, and larch. In Idaho, the company normally purchases one-half of its saw timber needs and one-half of its chip and sawdust requirements annually. Most purchased wood comes from U.S. Forest Service and Idaho state sales.

In 1982 there were five Potlatch sawmills, three plywood plants and one particleboard plant within the state. The company employs about 5,000 people in Idaho, 3,000 of them in the Lewiston area. (The figure does not include indirect employment: nearly half of the logging is done by gyppo operators.)

For highway travelers who pass Potlatch Corporation, unable to stop, here is a capsule description of the processing area visible from U.S. 12.

The large buildings closest to the highway, on the north side of the site along the river, are the pulping and paperboard processing plants. Logs arrive by truck or Camas Prairie railroad car (200 million board feet a year) and are sorted by species: 65 percent for lumber, 25 percent for plywood, and 10 percent for pulp. (Logs that are not suitable for lumber or plywood veneer are chipped for pulp.) The sawmill is the building farthest south of the pulping plant and the plywood division is between the two. When running three shifts the sawmill can produce enough lumber for about 105 houses in twenty-four hours.

The chip pile can be seen near the river, east of the buildings. Large chips (2½-inches) are refined to produce a center layer or "core" for some plywood. Small chips (⅝-inch) and sawdust are the raw materials for pulp. Large chips are derived from logs; smaller ones come from mill waste.

In the pulping building, chips and sawdust are cooked, separately, with steam and chemicals, to separate cellulose fibers in the wood. The pulp is then washed and bleached to make paperboard and tissue products. Cooking chemicals and washwater are reused. It is the process of recovering these chemicals that is responsible for the odor in Lewiston. Most of the smell is exuded when the "black liquor" is burned in order to obtain the chemical residue that is recycled.

The cement building between the river and the chip pile is the tissue plant. Here fiber is blended, refined, and vacuum pressed to make jumbo rolls of paper for facial tissue, toilet paper, paper towels, and napkins.

In 1974 Potlatch completed $14 million worth of primary and secondary wastewater treatment facilities on the site. The secondary system, on the east end, features a 103-acre, 500-million-gallon capacity aeration lagoon capable of treating 50 million gallons of effluent a day. Sixteen agitators mix oxygen with the water, breaking down the wood sugar, so that the water returned to the river will meet established standards. The treated water passes through four miles of forty-two-inch pipe to an outlet at the confluence of the Clearwater and the Snake.

Potlatch has invested millions of dollars at the Lewiston plant to reduce its dependence on outside energy. The company recently completed a large wastewood-burning power boiler connected to an electric generator. More than half of the energy needs for the bleached pulp and paperboard operations are obtained by burning pulp wastes. Natural gas, primarily from Canadian sources, is the major purchased fuel at Lewiston.

On the flat, east of the plant operations, a row of greenhouses is visible. This facility is intended to produce 2.5 million seedlings annually for reforestation of Potlatch timberlands. The seedlings are primarily Douglas fir and white pine, and an effort is being made to produce genetically superior trees.

Sprinkling systems regulate water, fertilizers and fungicides; photo-period lights produce optimal growing conditions. Seedlings with root development and height that requires about three years under natural conditions can be grown here in six months.

The executive offices for Potlatch Corporation are in San Francisco, and since 1969 the company has been listed on the New York Exchange.

Lake Waha can be the object of another interesting sidetrip from Lewiston; it requires about a twenty-mile drive.

Take "G" St. to Twenty-first St. and drive south on Twenty-first 1.0 miles. Just past Nineteenth Ave., leave Twenty-first and curve left on Thain Grade (which becomes Thain Rd.) for 3.1 miles. Thain merges with Fourteenth St. Continue in the same direction on Fourteenth 0.4 miles, then turn left on Ripon Ave. After 1.0 miles, curve right, off Ripon onto P-2, which is also NP-505, and eventually Tammany Creek Rd. Follow P-2/NP-505 for 2.5 miles, turn right (south) on NP-505 1.5 miles farther. At the Y, take the Tammany Creek Rd. that makes a slight jog to the right. Drive another 7.9 miles and the **21 Ranch** will come into view along the right side of the road.

The ranch house is a 2½-story Queen Anne-style residence built in 1888 by the one-time ranch foreman, Frank Ward. The lower story has been sided with aluminum, but the upper stories retain their fancy shingles.

The ranch dates from the 1860s; the barn was built in 1921; the old building uphill from the house was used for storage when the ranch had an apple orchard.

John Siers and Joseph Schissler formed a partnership in the 1870s and irrigated the pasture land with water from Lake Waha. Schissler died in 1886, and Siers took the stock and his share of the land, and left the balance to Schissler's heirs.

Siers then leased his land to the foreman, Ward, who married the daughter of Mrs. Goddard, a rancher with whom the partners had often quarrelled. When Siers returned from the east in 1894, he terminated his agreement with Ward, but allowed the foreman, his wife, and her mother to continue occupying the new house. It became the scene of the "Waha Feud" in 1895.

Frank Ward claimed Siers owed him $1000 and sued him for it; Schissler's heirs also sued Siers to make him abide by the terms of the lease. The property was placed in the hands of a receiver, pending litigation, and the receiver leased it to Mrs. Goddard.

Siers obtained a written order from the receiver allowing him to recover some personal items which the woman refused to surrender. He stopped at the house, with three of his employees, on an errand. Frank Ward came out on the porch with a pistol in his hand and began to rooster Siers; Mrs. Goddard then came out and badgered him some more. Siers turned to go about his business, and Ward shot him twice. As the rancher fell, he drew his pistol and returned the fire, at which point Mrs. Goddard unloaded in his back.

Siers' hired hands moved toward the house with their rifles, and Mrs. Goddard's thirteen-year-old son appeared in the doorway and ordered them to halt. Ignoring the kid, Siers' man, Elmer Shorthill, raised his rifle and gave Frank Ward his everlasting and Mrs. Goddard a bullet in her shoulder.

Mrs. Goddard and her son were charged with Siers' murder but were acquitted by a jury. Shorthill was tried for Ward's death and was also found not guilty.

The house is now a local landmark.

The Waha ice cave saloon and store are located on a bend in the road, 1.2 miles south of the ranch, on the right side.

The Waha store/post office/saloon was built for Charles Faunce in 1892 and served as the first stop on the stage route from Lewiston to Cottonwood. The Faunce family had owned the Lake House resort hotel at the north end of Lake Waha ten years before they moved to this site.

The stone-and-log ice cave saloon is an enclosure constructed over a small, natural ice cave.

Follow the gravel road from the store 0.7 miles to a stop sign. Turn right, and the dirt road leads 0.5 miles down to the rocky shore and green lakewaters at Kiwanis Park. The ponderosa forest is remarkably cooler than nearby Lewiston.

Lake Waha was used as a natural reservoir to irrigate the Lewiston Orchards development in the early 1900s. Pumps, along with a gasoline engine and electric motors, were placed on a platform in the lake. A pipe, twelve inches in diameter, was laid up the hill and down the other side, to an electrical generating plant. The gasoline engine was used to start a siphon through the line. Once the water was flowing downhill, the electricity produced at the generator was returned to the motors on the lake. The gas engine was shut off and pump operations were handled by the electric motors.

U.S. Highway 12, east of Lewiston, follows the route of Lewis and Clark, along the Clearwater River to Orofino. Eight miles from Lewiston, on the left, just past the bridge that joins U.S. 95 to U.S. 12, is an inconspicuous rock arch above the road-cut, visible from the highway. This is the basalt figure of **Ant and Yellow jacket**, the source of a Nez Perce myth.

The fable relates that ants and yellow jackets lived harmoniously until their respective chiefs quarrelled. Yellowjacket was eating a piece of dried salmon on a tablerock, and Ant, spotting him, became jealous. Ant informed Yellow jacket that he should have requested permission to feed there. Tempers flared, and the two insects, standing on their hind legs, became locked in combat.

Coyote passed along the riverbank and saw his two subjects engaged in battle. He yelled at them to cease their fighting, but they ignored his warnings; his magic transformed them to this allegory in stone.

About 2.5 miles from Ant and Yellow jacket, the highway crosses to the south side of the Clearwater. The mouth of the **Potlatch River** can be seen on the north shore.

Arrow Beach archeological site is located at this junction, on the north side of the river. The Arrow site was excavated in 1967, and artifact materials were carbon dated to 2,800 years before white contact. This determination gave the location the earliest dated house in the southern Columbia plateau. The last phases of occupation (1500-1850 A.D.) represent Nez Perce residency.

Lewis and Clark named the Potlatch River "Colter Creek" after their splendid companion, John Colter, the discoverer of Yellowstone. It is unfortunate that the name was changed.

When excavations were made at the mouth of Colter Creek for the Northern Pacific railroad, one of Lewis and Clark's medals, wrapped in many thicknesses of buffalo hide, was uncovered. It is believed to have been the medal given to the friendly Nez Perce chief, Twisted Hair – perhaps he buried it for safe-keeping.

The Corps of Discovery had some problems at the head of an island 1.5 miles below Colter Creek. Private Joseph Whitehouse's journal gives the best account of the incident:

As we were descending a rocky rapids at the foot of an island, on which some Indians were camped, one of the canoes struck a rock and wheeled around, then struck again and cracked the canoe and was near splitting her in two. Threw the steerman (Gass) overboard, who with difficulty got to the canoe again. She soon filled with water and hung on the rocks in a doleful situation. Some of the men on board could not swim, and those that could had no chance for the waves and rocks.

An Indian went out in a small canoe to their assistance. Our little canoe went out also and took out some of the load and carried it to shore. We unloaded one of the other canoes and went into the rapid and took all of the load out of the canoe which was stove. All got to shore below the rapid and camped at dark. Found everything wet which was in the canoe that was stove. Some small articles lost.

Lenore is twenty-six miles east of Lewiston. A series of grain elevators built from 1934-1959 are visible from the highway. They are owned by the Lewiston Grain Growers. The "elevator" on the east end is actually a plant for cleaning seed in preparation for planting.

The Lenore archeological site is 0.4 miles below the town, on the south bank of the Clearwater, on Rattlesnake Point at Big Eddy. Professional excavations conducted between 1967-1971 provided a number of valuable conclusions about the prehistoric inhabitants of the area.

A relatively rich array of specimens indicated occupation went back 10,000 years, which makes it the earliest site in Nez Perce territory and gives it the longest sequence of prehistoric occupation in the region.

The eastern Intermountain region was initially occupied by peoples of a big-game hunting tradition. Changes in type and availability of game during a dry period (7000-5500 B.C.) brought a decline in the big-game hunting tradition. Tools and occupation patterns changed.

The Lenore site had an unusual village of large oval pithouses occupied from about 900 B.C. to 1300 A.D. This makes it one of the oldest and longest-used villages in the Columbia Plateau.

Big Eddy, the large meander around Rattlesnake Point, was an obstacle for loggers, and for steamboats. The Oregon Steam and Navigation Co., that monopolized the Columbia River passenger and freight service from 1860-1880, sent the *Colonel Wright* up to what would later be Lenore, in May, 1861.

The O.S.N. wanted to accommodate the rush to the Nez Perce mines that spring. The ship selected had been built at the Deschutes above Celilo, Oregon, in 1859, and named for the commandant of the military post at the Dalles. The *Wright* was the first steamer to run the rapids of the upper Columbia and the first to reach Lewiston. She was 110 feet in length and carried a mast rigged with a supplemental square sail.

The ship was under the command of Captain Len White, and the pilot was Eph Baughman. She carried passengers and freight, and they were discharged just above the eddy. Seth Slater, a Portland merchant, rigged a tarp over his stock in trade and announced that Slaterville was in business.

The *Colonel Wright* snapped a towline in Big Eddy on the second trip, a week later, because the river had risen. The O.S.N. decided to move the navigation terminal down to the mouth of the Clearwater, so Lewiston was born and Slaterville collapsed like a stricken tent. (Another steamboat, the *Okanagan,* managed to reach Slater's hamlet June 1, but that was the last attempt for many years.) Seth moved his goods to Lewiston.

The Clearwater River from Lewiston to Orofino is a template for the shape of the highway. The river itself served as a road for Potlatch Corp. to bring its logs to the Lewiston mill from 1930-1971.

The log drives began on the upper reaches of the North Fork, about ninety miles from the sawmill. Logs were corded in mile-long stacks until spring high water reached a level sufficient to flush them down without serious impediment. Key logs were pulled and the decks began spilling into the river like water through a sluice gate. The drive could last from a week to two months, depending on the water.

Thirty-some rivermen followed the logs, watching for strays and jams, like cowboys trailing a herd of cattle to the corral. Bateaux crews "sacked" the rear of the drive. The oar-powered "pointers" were eventually squared at the stern for a twenty-two h.p. engine; then aluminum river pigs (jet boats) replaced the bateaux altogether.

The drives were accompanied by a wanigan – originally a wooden raft with cookhouse aboard and sweeps at each end. ("Wangan" was an eastern Indian word for a wooden box or container of odds and ends that was usually found in the logging camp clerk's shack.) In later years, the wanigan was fashioned from war surplus pontoon rafts. The kitchen occupied the middle raft, and bunkhouses for sixteen men each were located on the fore and aft raft. Eating counted a great deal on those drives; the wanigan would moor ahead of the men for lunch and dinner – the river pigs worked just a little harder if they were "leaning toward the sawmill" as the expression went.

Wanigan on North Fork of Clearwater.

Dworshak Dam brought the log drives to an end, though for several years during the construction period logs were sent through the diversion tunnel at the dam site.

About 50 million board feet a year were moved down the Clearwater. Now the colorful wanigan and its crew that camped on the riverbank each evening like a carnival and moved on in the morning, has moved on forever.

Three boatmen were drowned in an accident just below Lenore on the 1951 drive.

Twelve miles east of Lenore, on the south bank of the Clearwater, 100 feet to the left of the highway, is a marker honoring **Lewis and Clark's canoe camp**.

The Voyage of Discovery camped here, between the highway and the river, from September 26 to October 7, 1805. The men observed "fine timber for canoes" (probably red cedars) and spent days gouging and burning out five canoes for the river journey down the Clearwater, Snake and Columbia.

Clark branded their thirty-eight horses and left the herd with the Indians to be retrieved when his party returned. The expedition dug caches at night, buried saddles, a cannister of powder, and a bag of musket balls. On October 7, the Corps embarked at 3:00 P.M.; they made frequent mention of the rapids encountered over the next three days between this point and the Snake River.

Bateau crew unknits a jam on the Clearwater log drive.

Orofino is located along a creek of the same name; the stream is a tributary of the Clearwater. The traveler enters town from Highway 12 by turning northeast across a bridge over the river. The first such bridge was built in 1911.

The origins of Orofino are sometimes confused historically with those of Oro Fino, established two miles south of Pierce City in 1861, and now a ghost town; but Orofino-on-the-Clearwater is still astir.

When the Nez Perce reservation opened to settlers in 1895, Clifford Fuller filed a homestead on the site and set up a modest trading post. He organized the Clearwater Improvement Co. that founded the town a year later, and in 1898 he installed a ferry. The Northern Pacific completed its line from Lewiston the following year. That track and the extension to Headquarters built in 1925-1927 are now part of the Camas Prairie Railroad.

Orofino in 1907.

Orofino (looking north up Johnson Ave.).

Four newspapers attempted to establish a subsistence circulation before one succeeded in 1912: the *Clearwater Tribune,* which is still published.

One amusing scrap of local lore concerning the first schoolhouse endures. Some of the folks on Orofino Creek felt that their children had to walk too far to school. Finally, one sunrise revealed the classroom had grown legs during the night and tiptoed a mile upstream.

Like other early Idaho towns, Orofino's Main St. was cleared by a fire, in 1906, and brick buildings replaced the wooden ones. Today, the town is largely a lumber-industry and tourist-trade community that also serves as the seat of Clearwater County.

Orofino has the highest annual mean temperature of any town in Idaho: 51.9 degrees F. The town also holds an unusual record, the highest temperature recorded in the state: 118 degrees F., July 8, 1934.

The **Clearwater County Museum** is located in Orofino, in a brick house on the corner of "A" and College Sts. It is open afternoons, Tues.-Sat.

There is a fascinating object on display in the lobby of the Clearwater National Forest district office, 0.5 miles west of town on State Highway 7. It is a section cut from a tree, found on the North Fork of the Clearwater, one mile above the Bungalow Ranger Station (twenty-one miles northeast of Pierce) in 1939 by Millard Evenson. The wood bears tiny, delicately carved Chinese ideograms. A translation of the writing revealed the following message:

The ninth day of the fifth month of the third year of the reign of Kuang Hsii.

I have gone into the wilderness 100 miles by water to wait for someone. This stream is halfway.

The date is therefore 1876, and Lewiston is 100 miles by water from the location, but all else about the inscription is mystery.

The **Clearwater River** that flows past Orofino drains 9,600 square miles, all within Idaho. It flows west from the Bitterroots into the Snake at Lewiston. Granitic and metamorphosed sedimentary rocks underlie the basin.

Kamiah is twenty-three miles south of Orofino on Highway 12. The origin of the town's name is uncertain. Meriwether Lewis referred to present Lawyers Creek, across the river from Kamiah, as Commearp Creek. The name may be derived from the kame hemp

US 12

(dogbane) collected by Indians in the area when they desired material for ropes or mats. The discarded outer bark was called "kamiah."

About 1.3 miles northwest of the Kamiah bridge, on the east bank of the river, Lewis and Clark's Corps of Discovery camped for four weeks (May 14-June 9) in 1806, on their journey back to St. Louis.

The men had wintered at Fort Clatsop, on the south shore at the mouth of the Columbia, and in all their time there, only twelve days were free of rain. Understandably, they had cabin fever and began their eastern return earlier than was prudent. As the expedition approached the foothills of the Rockies, the Indians informed the crew, in Lewis' words:

... that the snow is yet so deep on the mountains that we shall not be able to pass them until the next full moon or about the first of June; others set the time at still a more distant period. This is unwelcome intelligence to men confined to a diet of horsebeef and roots, and who are as anxious as we are to return to the fat plains of the Missouri and thence to our native homes.

This proved to be the third-longest camp on the Voyage of Discovery – only the winter encampments at the Mandan Village and Fort Clatsop were longer. Almost all of the horses left the previous year were recovered from Twisted Hair and Cut Nose.

The men exhausted their trading supplies by June 1. While Clark played medicine man to the Indians, Peter Cruzzatte played fiddler. Sergeant Ordway and Privates Frazier and Wiser were sent from this spot to the Snake River (down Corral Creek to Wild Goose Rapid) to get salmon from the Indians because the food was necessary for their journey across the Continental Divide. By the time the men returned to camp, most of the fish had spoiled.

While bivouacked at **Long Camp**, Lewis discovered a member of the primrose family, the lovely pink and white Clarkia. At this site he also gave us the earliest description of the sego lily and the western tanager.

(The expedition discovered 24 Indian tribes, 178 plants, and 122 animals then unknown to the world. All the tribes [except the Blackfeet], two-thirds of the plants, and over half of the animals were found west of the Rocky Mountains – and most of these were noted on the return from Fort Clatsop to Lemhi Pass.)

Lewis and Clark left the Clearwater for Weippe Prairie on June 10, and succeeded in crossing the snow-swathed Bitterroots only with the aid of three Nez Perce, who were given two rifles as compensation (see Lolo Trail).

The Long Camp site is accessible by a secondary road that takes off at the east end of the Kamiah bridge. Turn left on the paved road, immediately after crossing the bridge, and drive 1.3 miles to the Kamiah Unit sawmill of Potlatch Corp. The camp was located on this flat.

The Indians recommended that Lewis and Clark pitch camp on the thickly timbered spot because grass was plentiful for horses and game was available nearby. The men appropriated an "ancient" circular Indian house-pit area about thirty feet across and four feet deep as a defensible place to store their baggage and then erected their brush shelters around the circumference.

On a visit to the site in 1902, the historian Olin Wheeler could still see the sunken ring where the camp was established but the site has been destroyed by the Potlatch mill that now occupies it.

Along the river here, in July, 1877, when the non-treaty Nez Perce had left the Clearwater battlefield and crossed the river to the northeast, some soldiers rode down the hill on the west side of the river, in pursuit. In General O. O. Howard's words:

As Perry's and Whipple's cavalry neared the enemies' crossing and were passing the flank of a high bluff, which was situated just beyond the river, a brisk fire from Indian rifles was suddenly opened upon them. It created a great panic and disorder; our men jumped from their horses and ran to the fences. Little damage resulted, except the shame to us and a fierce delight to the foe.

In May, 1896, Captain H. G. Baughman left Lewiston at 2:00 A.M. with the steamboat *Lewiston,* for a voyage to Kamiah. A year earlier, the captain had removed obstructions to navigation between Greer's ferry and Kamiah. On board was a party of Union Pacific railroad officials; the U.P. owned the Oregon River and Navigation Company. The O R & N hoped to prove river transportation to the Kamiah valley was feasible for at least six months of the year.

The *Lewiston* made headway slowly. She was lined through rapids with the steam capstan four times; it required an hour to navigate a one-mile stretch. The ship finally reached Kamiah at noon. After a three-hour stay, she headed back to Lewiston, having proved the route was possible, but impractical.

The **Lolo Trail,** now known as the **Lolo Road** or Lolo Motorway, is a significant route in Western history; in 1963 it was registered as one of Idaho's eight National Historic Landmarks.

The trail can be reached from Kamiah, through Glenwood to the Bradford bridge, 23.1 miles; or it can be approached from Weippe, via Highway 11 and USFS Rd. No. 100 (see Highway 11, Weippe).

At the southeast outskirts of Kamiah, at the east end of the Clearwater bridge, take the road that travels downriver along the Clearwater's east bank. After a mile, the road swings east, away from the entrance to the Potlatch sawmill. Follow this main access road 11.7 miles to Glenwood. The USFS Pierce District ranger station is located in Glenwood. Obtain a Clearwater National Forest map there. Continue northeast from Glenwood 11.4 miles on USFS Road No. 100 to the Bradford bridge intersection with USFS Road No. 500. As indicated by the information sign at the junction, the Lolo Road begins at this spot.

A brief chronology of the trail-road's use is included here, but the more studious traveler will benefit from a copy of Ralph Space's *The Lolo Trail,* available in Idaho bookstores and libraries, and John Peeble's *Lewis and Clark in Idaho,* published by the Idaho Historical Society in Boise.

The Lolo Trail received its heaviest Indian traffic after the Nez Perce obtained horses in the early 1700s. It was a main route from the camas beds of Weippe Prairie to the buffalo plains of Montana. Lolo is a Chinook word for "carry."

Captains Lewis and Clark found the trail the most wearisome portion of their transcontinental expedition. On September 14, 1805 having crossed the Lolo summit, Clark stated that the mountains were "excessively bad and thickly strowed with falling timber and pine Spruce fur Hackmatak and Tamerack, Steep and Stoney our men and horses much fatigued." So it went – coming and going.

Fur trappers, forewarned by the expedition's tale, found little reason to use the trail. It was habitat for hawks, not beaver. In the fall, 1831, John Work's Snake River expedition passed over portions of the route. The Hudson's Bay Company party had sixty members, including Work's wife and three daughters. They suffered snowstorms, lost horses, and exhaustion.

More than twenty years later, Lieutenant John Mullan examined the trail in the course of his survey for a military road from Fort Benton, Montana, to Walla Walla, Washington. Said Mullan, "This route I found the most difficult of all examined. After eleven days of severe struggle with climate and country, we emerged into the more open region where Oro Fino now stands, glad to leave behind us so difficult a bed of mountains." He chose a route farther north, now followed by I-90.

100

The discovery of gold at Alder Gulch, Montana, in the 1860s, aroused interest among Idaho merchants in a route from Lewiston to the Montana placer mines. Congress approved $50,000 to develop a road over Lolo Pass that would shorten by 160 miles the distance between Walla Walla and Fort Benton.

An Iowa engineer, Wellington Bird, was hired as chief engineer for the road. In May, 1866, he left Lewiston with Major Sewell Truax, Colonel William Craig, and sixty other men. The group carried road building equipment in wagons, along with a six-month supply of food and medicine. The outfit consumed 40 percent of the crew's appropriation.

Since Bird found the snow six feet deep in the mountains, he settled for a survey to Lolo Creek in Montana. Then in mid-July he returned to the construction crew.

The men spent August and September improving the Lolo Trail. They moved the route out of several drainages, up onto the ridgetops, and though the grade still traveled between peaks separated by deep saddles, it did travel less steeply than before. But when Bird and the Idaho legislature sought additional funds from Congress to finish the job, they were refused.

The trail was utilized in 1877 by General O. O. Howard, and by the Nez Perce Indians as they fled to Montana from the war in Idaho. The Lolo was conjested with fallen timber, but the Indians and their horse herd managed to wedge through. General Howard, however, had a crew of fifty-two axe men to clear the lodgepole for his pack trains and artillery. He wrote: "Conceive this climbing ridge after ridge, in the wildest wilderness, with the only possible pathway filled with timber, small and large, crossed and criss-crossed; and now, while the horses and mules are feeding on unnutritious wire grass, you will not wonder at only sixteen miles a day." Decades later cannonballs were found at several spots along the trail.

In 1925 the USFS began road construction from Lolo Hot Springs in Montana and reached Powell in 1928. The Service began to replace the Lolo Trail with a single-lane road in 1930; crews worked on the trail from the Idaho and Montana ends during the summer. In 1934 the crews finally met in celebration at Indian Grave.

The dirt road has a gravel surface only as far as Canyon Junction, near Mexican Mountain. The Lolo is generally open from July 15 to September 15. It is suitable for passenger cars, provided they are not towing a trailer. Though it can be driven in one day, it is worth taking two. Campsites are available.

Not all of Lewis and Clark's campsites are signed. The mileage given for the locations that follow is taken from the junction at the

Bradford bridge. These distances will help the traveler locate the Lewis and Cark sites marked on the USFS Clearwater National Forest map.

Mile 12.0: **Canyon Junction.** The gravel ends as the road kinks north past Mexican Mountain (elevation 5,050).

Mile 22.7: **Pete Forks.** Forest Service campground.

Mile 24.3: **Gass Creek.** Named for Patrick Gass, chief carpenter and boatbuilder for the Voyage of Discovery. Gass kept a journal on the expedition. Afterwards, he reenlisted in the Army and served in the War of 1812. He lived to be ninety-nine – the last member of the expedition to die.

Mile 28.9: **Weitas Butte Road.** The name is a play on "wet ass."

Mile 34.2: **Deep Saddle.** The saddle is at the head of Doubt Creek, a name that reveals the travails of the Lewis and Clark party here.

Mile 37.7: **Sherman Saddle.** Also known as Horse Sweat Pass, the area was probably named by Major Truax while working on the Lolo Trail for Wellington Bird.

Mile 45.0: **Sherman Creek.** Nice view from Spirit Revival Ridge, elevation 6,000 feet. It is a little less than a mile from this point to a Lewis and Clark information sign.

Mile 45.5: **Bald Mountain** and **Greensward Camp.** Elevation 6,526 feet. On their eastern journey, June 26, 1806, Lewis and Clark camped here. They had traveled along the ridge dividing the North Fork of the Clearwater and the Lochsa. Captain Lewis: "late in the evening ... we arrived at the desired spot and encamped on the steep side of a mountain (Bald Mtn.) convenient to a good spring. There we found an abundance of fine grass for our horses. This situation was the side of an untimbered mountain with a fair southern aspect ... and had much the appearance of greensward."

Mile 51.9: **Indian Grave.** On the spur road is the grave of a fourteen-year-old Indian boy, buried in 1894. He apparently died from poisoning.

Mile 53.9: Lewis and Clark trail information sign.

Mile 58.2: **Devil's Chair.** A curious rock formation that juts up along the east side of the road.

Mile 60.4: **Howard's Camp.** General Howard camped at this spot, north of the road, August 4, 1877, in pursuit of the Nez Perce. Cannon balls were found here.

Mile 65.2: **Indian Post Office.** This is the highest point on the trail: 7,035 feet. Two rock cairns of unknown origin mark the site. Lewis and Clark's Lonesome Cove camp of September 16, 1805, is just north of the post office. Wet, cold and hungry, they were camped in thick timber at the bottom of a draw. "Lonesome cove" was Pvt. Whitehouse's description. The Bears Oil and Roots camp is midway between this point and Cayuse Junction.

Mile 74.0: **Cayuse Junction.** The road begins to drop, past Snowbank camp to Papoose Saddle, but it still follows the approximate trail of Lewis and Clark.

Mile 88.6: **Papoose Saddle.** The saddle is just north of the expedition's Thirteen Mile Camp of June 28, 1806.

Mile 89.6: **Powell Junction.** The road leaves the Lewis and Clark trail. Take the west fork seven miles down to U.S. 12 at Powell.

About 1.7 miles southeast of Kamiah, within 200 feet of the west edge of Highway 12 and visible from there, is an extrusion of volcanic stone known to the Nez Perce as **The Heart of the Monster**: "Ilts Wau Tsik." A sign indicates parking space.

This stone mound is the focus of the Nez Perce creation myth. The story relates that Coyote was informed by Meadowlark that a monster up the Clearwater was devouring all the other creatures. Coyote strapped on a pack that contained five knives and a flint fire-making set, along with some pitchwood, and trotted up the river.

When he suddenly encountered the monster, Coyote shouted a challenge. The monster promptly inhaled him. As he walked down into the monster's stomach, Coyote met some of the other animals and asked them to show him the creature's heart. They led him to the vital organ; he kindled a fire nearby. Then Coyote began slicing away at the heart. One by one his knives broke, but finally the heart came free, and as the monster's orifices opened, all the animals escaped.

Now Coyote butchered the monster and tossed the pieces to different parts of the country, creating a special tribe from each portion. But when he had finished, Fox pointed out that there was nothing left for the Clearwater-Salmon River region.

So Coyote washed his hands with water and sprinkled the bloody drops about him, thereby creating the Nu-me-poo: "the people" of the Nez Perce tribe. The heart and liver of the monster are preserved in the field, where the trickster left them.

Three miles southeast of Kamiah, on the east side of the highway, can be seen **Idaho's oldest Protestant church in continuous use**; it was built by the Nez Perce Indians in 1874.

Five remarkable women at one time labored for this church, which was organized on Christmas Day in 1871.

The earliest missionaries in the area were Asa and Sarah Smith, a pair of misdirected Congregationalists who arrived in 1837; they had quarrelled with the Whitmans and Spaldings, and Asa, a graduate of Yale Divinity School, had decided to move from the Whitman mission to Kamiah, where he would learn the Nez Perce language.

Heart of the Monster.

Presbyterian Church near Kamiah before it was renovated in 1890. Men sat on one side of the aisle, women on the other, and the most virtuous parishioners sat closest to the altar.

Chief Lawyer taught him, but the dissatisfied couple departed from their cedar cabin for Hawaii after two years; they were quickly and deservedly forgotten.

When President Grant placed the Indian tribes under the care of the Christian churches, another Congregational minister, Rev. H. T. Cowley, arrived in 1871 and began instruction of the Nez Perce at Kamiah. The church was erected with government funds and Indian labor.

After Cowley left, Henry Spalding, a Presbyterian missionary, moved up from Lapwai and began preparing young men for the ministry, but illness took his life a year later. Sue McBeth followed in his footsteps, though she had only five pupils in her first class.

McBeth was from Scotland, and had done missionary work among the Choctaws before coming to the Nez Perce tribe about a year prior to Spalding's death in 1874. She was a partial invalid, lame from an earlier illness and troubled by a lung condition. Her older sister, Kate, joined her teaching efforts six years later. The two sisters were the only white women in the Kamiah valley. At a later date, Sue taught boys at Mount Idaho, while Kate instructed girls at Kamiah.

When the Nez Perce War erupted in the summer, 1877, the Indian agent at Fort Lapwai ordered the women to the fort for protection. They crossed the river in canoes, and with Indian help, ferried the parts of a wagon across the water, reassembled them, and covered the sixty miles to Lapwai in a single day. After the war, the McBeths returned.

Alice Fletcher, holder of a fellowship at the Peabody Museum of American Archaeology at Harvard, and a pioneer in the ethnology and music of the American Indian, was influential in securing passage of the Dawes (Severalty) Act in 1887. In 1889 she was sent as the government's allotment agent to the Nez Perce. Alice brought an older, noted feminist companion with her: Jane Gay. The two women soon established an enthusiastic rapport with the McBeth sisters. They found their ideas and goals were similar.

Fletcher and Gay had shared a Washington, D.C. house with another friend, Mary Sibbet Copley of Pittsburgh. Miss Copley became the second wife of William Thaw, one-time owner of the Pennsylvania & Ohio Canal Line, with interests in over 150 steamboats, and later, director of the Pennsylvania Railroad Co. Thaw died of a heart attack in Paris in 1889. His estate was valued at $15 million. Mary, his widow, decided to sponsor the religious efforts of the women in Kamiah. Accordingly, she financed the restoration of the church, which had become dilapidated. New foundation logs and a shake roof were installed and the women furnished their native helpers with paint, wallpaper, glass and carpet.

Mary also donated funds to build a three-room cottage for Kate, to replace the "converted potato shed" she had called home. Additional Thaw contributions bought furnishings, including a much needed wood stove. Kate lived in Thaw Cottage until her death in 1915. It still stands, across the road from the church.

Fletcher and Gay left Idaho in 1892, when the allotment process was completed. Alice became vice-president of the American Association for the Advancement of Science and president of the American Anthropological Society. She contributed forty-six monographs to American ethnology, including the authoritative and monumental work *The Omaha Tribe* . At the time of her death in 1934, she held a chair at Harvard.

Sue McBeth died at Mt. Idaho in 1893, and is buried with her sister in the cemetery behind the Kamiah church (The Nez Perce leader, Chief Lawyer, is also buried there.)

Selway Falls.

U.S. Highway 12 swings east just north of Kooskia, about four miles from the church, and travels up the Middle Fork of the Clearwater River, which is formed by the confluence of the Lochsa and Selway Rivers at Lowell.

Lowell is twenty-six miles east of Kooskia. Here it is possible to turn southeast off Highway 12, across a bridge, and follow the **Selway River** nineteen miles to **Selway Falls**. (Sel-wah means "smooth water.") The cascade is more impressive in spring than in fall, but the paved (six miles) and oiled road is a lovely fern-edged, shade-splashed drive.

O'Hara Bar, six miles up the road, once had eleven buildings. An early 1½-story Forest Service log cabin still stands on the flat. The building is made from squared logs with saddle-and-rider joints. In the rear is a log cellar, and a vertical-log storage shelter that predates the cabin. The cabin, built in 1910, was thirty-two miles from the nearest road at the time, and all supplies were brought in on pack stock. The last CCC camp in the Clearwater area closed here in July, 1942.

106

The Selway Falls guard station is thirteen miles farther up the road, just past the falls. It is a log structure, built in 1912; the ranger was given a horse and $75 a month to patrol for fires. The road ends at a campground within a mile of this cabin.

The take-out point for Selway River trips is on the left bank just upstream from the bridge, which is located within a pistol shot of the guard station. The Selway is classified as a National Wild and Scenic River and in high water has some of the more difficult rapids on any western river. Four professional outfitters are licensed to run one trip a week during the comparatively short float season. The river cannot be run without a permit from the Forest Service; limitations on use have preserved the wilderness character of the stream. Peak flow almost invariably occurs during the first two weeks of June. A trail follows the river, from Paradise Guard Station, sixty miles upstream, down to Selway Falls.

The first documented run of the river from Paradise to the falls was in mid-July, 1960, by a four-man American Whitewater Affiliation party led by Oscar Hawksley. The men used a neoprene ten-man war surplus raft and a decked, fifteen-foot Grumman canoe.

The canoe was upset twice and had to be lined at times. Hawksley rafted all the rapids. The trip required five days, and the boatmen reported splendid cutthroat trout fishing.

A sign on U.S. 12, just east of Lowell, warns, "No Gas 84 Miles." This is the road Idahoans call the "**Lewis and Clark Highway**." It was the first east-west highway across central Idaho, and the fact that it was not completed until 1962 conveys a sense of the convoluted topography. Residents had urged its construction for forty years.

The Northern Pacific and Union Pacific began railroad surveys along the Lochsa River from Kooskia to Lolo, Montana, in 1908 and even completed some grades, but in 1909 they mutually agreed to abandon the project.

Canyon Creek enters the Clearwater from the northwest side about seven miles from Lowell, just west of the Forest Service Apgar recreation site.

A federal prison work camp was established here in 1935, only the second of its kind in the country. It housed up to 170 prisoners, who worked eight hours a day on construction of the roadway.

They completed eight miles in the first three years. By 1943, 1,250 prisoners had been assigned to the Lochsa Federal Prison Camp, and all of seventeen escapees had been apprehended.

In 1943 the camp was converted into an internment center for Japanese who were forcibly relocated, because of war hysteria, by order of President Roosevelt. The camp was used by 135 internees, who worked on the road until spring, 1945.

The Major Fenn Forest Service recreation site is 4.5 miles from Apgar. Fenn was the first supervisor for the Clearwater National Forest. A Pacific dogwood tree is growing in this campground, a rare species for an inland area.

Four miles east of the Fenn site, at Split Creek, Highway 12 enters the region of the **Idaho batholith**: an area of approximately 14,000 square miles (much of it in the central Idaho wilderness) which is underlain by a body of granite intruded as magma about 80 million years ago. It is one of the largest bodies of granite in the world, but visible from only three highways.

For the next forty-five miles, U.S. 12 cuts across the northern end of the batholith, along what is known as the Bitterroot lobe. Many of the road-cuts reveal striking displays of igneous and metamorphic rock. This stretch of the river is known as Black Canyon.

Nine miles farther up the Lochsa (24.3 miles from Lowell), on the left side of the highway, a small sign indicates the **Lochsa Historical Ranger Station**. There is an off-road parking area.

The Lochsa District Ranger Station of the U.S. Forest Service, built of logs in the early 1920s, was converted to a museum in 1976. This is undoubtedly the finest display of U.S. Forest Service historical materials in the western states. It is open to the public from Memorial Day to Labor Day. It is staffed and maintained by volunteers. (The present Lochsa district ranger's office was transferred to Kooskia in 1956.)

Highway 12, from the Lochsa Station to a point fifty miles east, is paralleled on the ridge four miles to the north by the Lolo Trail, used by Indians and by Lewis and Clark (see Lolo Trail Road).

Travelers who are not interested in covering the 100 miles of the **Lolo Trail Road**, but would like to drive a portion of it, will find it possible to make a scenic thirty-mile loop off Highway 12, up to the Lolo and along the ridge for nearly ten miles, and back down to the highway.

The departure point for this excursion is 18.6 miles east of the historic Lochsa ranger station. This loop is generally passable between July 15 and September 15; weather should be considered. Take the Saddle Camp Road No. 107 on the north side of the highway. At the saddle, turn northeast along the dirt motorway and visit the Devil's Chair, Indian Post Office, and Lonesome Cove camp, before descending on the Jerry Johnson/Doe Creek Rd. No. 566 nine miles back to U.S. 12. In addition to the historical sites, which are signed, the trip provides splendid views of the Selway-Bitterroot Wilderness and a wealth of wildflowers alongside the access roads.

Colgate Licks are 36.9 miles from the old Lochsa Station, or 8.3 miles east of the Saddle Camp Rd. There are two warm springs on the north side of the highway, and deer, elk, and sheep are attracted to the trace elements deposited by the water. A nature trail begins at the parking area and loops two-thirds of a mile around the springs.

George Colgate's grave is just east of the parking lot, about twenty feet below the road. The manner of his death is discussed in the next section.

Jerry Johnson campground is located along the highway, 2.3 miles past Colgate Licks.

Johnson was born in Prussia; he immigrated to New Zealand as a young man, became interested in mining and drifted about the world prospecting. He spent fifteen years working the "chlorides of assessment" in the Cascades and Rockies. At times he worked as a guide, packer, and trapper. He was sixty years old when he and a partner built a cabin on the flat by the river, in the fall of 1893. That October the men became involved in a now-famous saga of the Clearwater country, the ordeal of the Carlin hunting party.

The hunting party was organized by Will Carlin, the son of a Brigadier General stationed at Ft. Sherman, Idaho. Will was a passionate hunter, and passion is often accompanied by disaster.

Carlin's friend, Abe Himmelwright, was a civil engineer who had been employed by the Northern Pacific in the location of the rail route through Idaho, before he began to design industrial plants in Connecticut.

John Pierce was Carlin's brother-in-law; he had suffered from malaria for a year and came west to join the hunting expedition, partly in an effort to improve his health. The men were all in their twenties.

Martin Spencer, a knowledgeable guide who lived in Spokane, and had previously hunted with Carlin, was engaged to assist the party. Another former hunting companion, George Colgate, age fifty-two, was hired as camp cook. He lived in Post Falls, Idaho, where he served as justice of the peace. Spencer felt Colgate was too old for the trip, but George could not be dissuaded.

After meeting in Spokane, they traveled to Kendrick by rail, in order to begin their trip across the Lolo Trail to the Lochsa. They had ten horses, four dogs, a pair of cameras, and guns.

The men left Kendrick on September 18. Eight days later they branched off the Lolo down a trail to the Lochsa River and camped on the present Jerry Johnson flat. They were surprised to find two men already there; Jerry Johnson, and his partner from Missoula, Ben Keeley, had built a cabin and planned to spend the winter trapping.

In camp, the hunters discovered that Colgate was suffering from swelling in his limbs. Persistent questioning revealed that George had been under a doctor's supervision for twenty years because of chronic inflammation of the bladder and an enlarged prostate. He had intentionally left his catheters in Spokane because he thought he could get by without them.

Foul weather, which had plagued the party most of the trip, continued. Carlin and Himmelwright, not overly concerned about the cook's problem, began their hunt. In general, it consisted of approaching the nearby licks (now named for Colgate) at dawn or evening with the hope of surprising some game. The men were either poorly armed or aimed poorly. Carlin did bag an elk with rocking chair antlers after half-a-dozen shots, but much game was missed or wounded, including a grizzly bear with two cubs. They also hunted at Jerry Johnson hot springs across the river, where a fusillade by Abe brought down another elk.

By the second of October, it was obvious Colgate's condition was deteriorating. Snow was falling like feathers, and Spencer felt a shiver of apprehension. He remarked that the group might get snowed in, and that given George's situation, it was probably a good idea to pull out for Kendrick. Will and Abe apparently demurred.

But within another four days, Colgate's legs had swollen to twice their normal size. He was suffering from uremic poisoning. Spencer and Pierce urged a prompt retreat. Abe and Will, who in their own words, "had not yet had enough hunting to satisfy them" offered to follow after several more days. Since Colgate preferred that the group stay together, nothing was done until the tenth of October.

The Carlin party:
(left to right) Pierce,
Keeley, Carlin,
Spencer,
Himmelwright.

The party then attempted to return to Kendrick via the Lolo Trail but it was too late. Winter had pitched her tent atop three feet of snow on the ridge. Colgate could not walk, and even on snowshoes the others could never carry him through soft drifts with only eight day's provisions. They turned reluctantly back to the flat by the river.

It was suggested that the water route might offer a stellar solution. Spencer was dubious. He knew it would take a couple of weeks to build the necessary rafts and that there were some ungentle rapids in the canyon. However, with no other course evident, they adopted the plan. Will bought Ben Keeley's grub and assistance for $250. He agreed to accompany the men down the

111

river. Keeley was a valuable addition; he was a skilled woodsman, and he had rafted logs in Minnesota and Wisconsin.

Abe, an engineer, used a fish scales to weigh a small block of dry cedar and calculated the cubic feet necessary to float their supplies on two rafts.

Dead cedars were felled and rolled to the river. The only tools available were two axes, two hatchets, a broken cross-cut saw and a one-inch auger. Since there were no nails or bolts, the five by twenty-six foot rafts, each consisting of three large logs, were fastened together by key-wedged crosspieces. A sweep was installed at the stern.

Himmelwright, a graduate of Rensselaer Polytechnic Institute of New York, made this drawing of the raft.

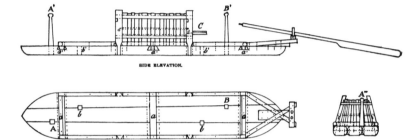

SIDE ELEVATION.

PLAN OF DECK.

END ELEVATION.

THE "CARLIN" RAFT.

Constructed entirely of wood. Dimensions: 26′ 0″ × 4′ 2″; *a a a, a′a′a′,* cross-pieces, dovetailed and wedged in the logs; *b b, b′b′,* vertical keys; *A A′ A′, B B′,* posts to hold to in rough water; *C,* seat for Colgate. The enclosed box in the middle portion afforded a safe receptacle for carrying the provisions, etc. Scale, 6 ft. =1 in. Designed in camp by Mr. Himmelwright.

The rigs, *Clearwater* and *Carlin,* were finished on the second of November. By then, Colgate was deteriorating rapidly. Fluid had collected in his lungs; he had to maintain a seated posture. The swelling in one of his legs burst, giving him only slight temporary relief; though he never complained, he was helpless.

The men left their horses and much of their equipment (but not their elk antlers!) with Johnson, and bid the prospector farewell as they pushed off. Spencer and Keeley took the lead. Miscues came early and fast. As with any sweep craft, landing was a major problem. Within a couple of miles, the *Carlin* stamped against some boulders and Colgate, who was seated by the cargo, was washed beneath the raft, then rescued. After an hour of transferring gear and pulling on ropes, everyone got ashore.

The water was cold as a snowdrift and George suffered greatly. Despite a warming fire, he was unable to move. The men lightened their loads and Keeley made a front sweep for the *Clearwater.*

Over the next nine days, every member of the party nearly left this sinful world on several occasions. The river was torn by rocks and so were the rafts. When they reached Holly Creek, about thirty miles downriver, they encountered such a rock garden above some severe rapids, that they pulled over for the night and scouted ahead in the morning.

Carlin, who kept a diary, wrote:

Saturday, November 11th. – It is still cold and clear. We went down the river a long way this morning, and were horrified to find that we were absolutely "stuck." Half a mile below camp is a ledge of rocks, and a rapid through which we cannot take a raft. Below this are two more places still worse. Every one gave his opinion of his own accord, that we could not get our rafts farther down the river. Our position is as follows: We have barely one week's short allowance of flour left. All our other provisions, except a few pounds of cornmeal and beans, and a handful of salt each, are exhausted. The shores of the river are a mass of irregular rocks. Numerous ledges or cliffs, some of them hundreds of feet high, rise vertically above the river and project into it. The hill-sides adjacent are steep and rocky, and covered with dense brush. Many of the ledges are so precipitous that it is all an able-bodied man can do to hang to bushes and climb around them on narrow clefts or steps in the rock. Most of us are considerably weakened from exposure, and are not in a fit condition to walk. Owing to the character of the country and our enfeebled condition, we cannot hope to accomplish more than four or five miles a day on foot. As nearly as we can estimate, we are fifty or fifty-five miles from civilization (Wilson's ranch, twenty miles below the forks). We know nothing whatever of the river ahead of us, of the obstructions we will meet with, or even if we can get through at all by this route. The dreaded Black Canyon is yet before us. Worst of all is the fact that Colgate cannot possibly walk, and it is absolutely impossible to help or carry him around the bad places along the river. His condition grows worse hourly. His legs are in a frightful condition, and the odor that comes from them is almost unendurable. He is perceptibly weaker than he was yesterday, and his mind is so far gone that he has lately appreciated no efforts that have been made to make him comfortable. On our return to camp, at half-past two P.M., we drew to one side and discussed every plan that could be thought of – not a stone was left unturned. If we stay with him, we can do nothing but ease his last moments and bury him, because it is impossible for him ever to get well again. His sickness is, besides, of such a character that he may linger in a stupor or semi-conscious condition for several days, during which a large portion of our remaining provisions will be consumed. We cannot even take him back and leave him with Jerry Johnson, while some of us go out on snowshoes for assistance. With no sign of game in the neighborhood, and the river full of floating ice so that the fish will not rise, were we to leave half our provisions here and one man to care for Colgate, he would probably starve before succor could reach him, while such a drain on the meagre supplies would render the chances considerably less of the others ever reaching civilization. We all feel that it is clearly a case of trying to save five lives, or sacrificing them in order to perform the last sad rites for poor Colgate. To remain longer with Colgate is to jeopardize to the very doors of folly all our lives – not in the cause of humanity, for Colgate is beyond any appreciation of such kindness – but for sentiment solely. We have exhausted every resource, and feel that we have gone to the extreme limit of duty toward Colgate in our endeavors to get him back to civilization. Our own families and friends have now a just claim upon us, and we must save ourselves if possible. We therefore have decided to strike down the river, and, with good luck, some of us may get through, unless we encounter a bad snow-storm. Every one feels very much dispirited at having to leave Colgate. There was hardly a word spoken by any one to-night.

The group now arranged their remaining provisions in packs for the overland journey. They spent most of the next day getting a raft across to the north side of the river. Then they cut the craft loose to verify their judgment – when it accelerated downstream and wrapped around some rocks near the middle of the river they felt their decision was vindicated. That evening Carlin wrote:

Colgate is very badly off to-night. He has great difficulty in breathing. It would not surprise me at all to see him collapse at any moment. I told him to-day that we could raft no farther and would have to walk, but it seemed to make no impression whatever upon him.

In the morning, they set off. As for George Colgate? "Poor Colgate," Carlin said,

Poor Colgate was so far gone that he could not remember his family, nor did he make any remarks or request concerning them. We made him as comfortable as we could, left him what necessaries we thought he might require in the brief period he had yet to live, and, shouldering our packs, we started sadly down the river. Although Colgate's head was turned toward us, he made no motion or outcry as he saw us disappear, one by one, around the bend.

114

The first three days the men averaged about four miles a day, often climbing in and out of drainages: Bald Mountain, Noseeum, Boulder. The exertion tolled their resources, and game was scanter than bee tracks in a blizzard. Their hiking dwindled to less than a mile and a half a day. Hunger was an unwelcome guest. November 17 they ate one of their dogs. At times, loss of coordination caused them to stagger and fall. It snowed two inches during the night of November 21; in the morning they considered eating another dog and fashioning a raft from driftwood. Inasmuch as they had noticed that the height of the hills had declined and that the river was more composed, they were certain the mouth of the South Fork was not very far, but their food was gone.

Near noon, Abe and Will were stumbling along, watching for hawberries on the river bank. In Carlin's words:

On turning the next point, we saw two men hurrying toward us. Thinking they were of our party I said, "I wonder what's the matter? Perhaps they have seen a deer and want us to shoot it!" but he replied, "I am afraid some one has fallen into the river." As they approached nearer, we saw they were not of our party, and a moment later Abe recognized our old-time shooting chum, Sergt. Guy Norton, of the Fourth Cavalry. With him was Lieut. Charles P. Elliott. It expresses it mildly to say we were overjoyed to see them.

Lt. Elliott's rescue party had been dispatched from Vancouver Barracks, Washington as the result of a letter written by a concerned guide-friend of Spencer's in Missoula. The recipient in Spokane gave the letter to Captain Merriam there, who telegraphed General Carlin on November 7. The General stated he would pay all expenses, and relief parties were dispatched from Fort Missoula, Spokane, and Vancouver Barracks. Captain Andrew's party attempted to penetrate the area from the east, Lt. Overton pushed up toward the Lolo Trail on the west and Lt. Elliott came by horse to Kamiah, then borrowed skiffs, which he loaded with provisions, and headed up the Clearwater.

Elliott took the Carlin group by boat to Ahsahka, and by horse to Kendrick, where General Carlin was waiting to greet them with an appropriate Thanksgiving Day dinner.

The next day, the entire party left for Spokane. There they met Mrs. Colgate, and Will spent three hours explaining the circumstances of her husband's death. George Colgate's physician was located, and on request, he composed the following statement:

Mr. Colgate came to me from Post Falls last summer and I placed him in the Sacred Heart Hospital, where he remained about three weeks, and then returned to Idaho. Early last fall he again came to

US 12

me to be examined and said, if he was well enough, he would start on a hunting-trip as cook. Mr. Colgate was troubled with an enlarged prostate and chronic inflammation of the bladder, and had been for twenty years compelled to use catheters to relieve the bladder. I told him he could make the trip, but to continue the use of the catheters; and from the history of the case and symptoms described by the Carlin party, I am satisfied Colgate's illness would have resulted fatally under any circumstances, and when he was left behind in the condition described, he could not have survived twenty-four hours.
W. Q. Webb.
Spokane, Wash., December 4th, 1893.

When the citizenry learned that Colgate had been abandoned, a waterfall of criticism thundered down upon the survivors. They had violated a code of the American wilderness that went back at least to the time Tom "Broken Hand" Fitzpatrick and young Jim Bridger disgraced themselves by leaving Hugh "Lord Grizzly" Glass to die on the Missouri plains after he was mauled by a bear. On the other hand, Colgate had broken an established wilderness principle too, by going there with infirmities that could cause troubles for others. "Judge not ..." but history has affixed a certain shame to the Carlin Party name.

In any event, the episode produced some curious backwash:

The Carlins paid Mrs. Colgate $25. She had seven children; so the community of Post Falls and the Masonic Lodge assisted her financially.

Ben Keeley filed for the rescuer's reward that had been offered by General Carlin, and threatened to file a civil suit if it was not paid.

Spencer and a friend were hired by Carlin to search for Colgate's body in June. They approached the area from the Missoula side and found that although Johnson had made it through the winter, the horses had starved. They discovered Colgate's blankets rolled up in a river driftwood pile, but failed to locate his remains.

A military party, led by Lt. Elliott, in mid-summer did find Colgate's remains about eight miles below the spot where he was abandoned. It appeared spring high-water had washed his body down from the campsite. They buried his bones at Colgate Licks.

The following year, Abe Himmelwright published a book about their experience titled *In the Heart of the Bitter-root Mountains*. It is interesting, but peculiar, reading. He used the pseudonymn "Heclawa." The account seems self-serving and defensive at times. The Appendix includes biographies of the hunters, a piece called "A few hints on suitable arms for big game shooting," and a digression on "Phenomenal precipitation of rain and snowfall in 1893."

A bottle, with a note purportedly written by Colgate, was recovered from the Snake River.

But perhaps no aftermath incident was stranger than the following item reported in a New York newspaper:

GEORGE COLGATE FOUND.

He Bitterly Denounces the Carlin Party for Deserting Him.

(Special to The World.)

MISSOULA, Mon., Dec. 15.—It is reported here to-day that George Colgate, who was the cook for the Carlin party which narrowly escaped death in the hills, has been found. John Mack, a railroad brakeman on the Northern Pacific road, is responsible for the story.

Mack says that Colgate was found by two trappers wandering through the mountains in a heavy snowstorm and almost dead. They took him to a cabin they had erected, and later to Lewiston, where he is now being cared for.

Mack says that Colgate was bitter in his denunciations of the other members of the Carlin party, who, he said, left him to starve and freeze to death.

He says they deserted him because he was unable to walk any longer. After he had rested he started to follow the party, got lost and wandered about the mountains for three weeks with scarcely anything to eat and no shelter. Then he was found by the two trappers.

The other members of the Carlin party are not inclined to believe the story, and insist that when they left Colgate he was barely alive and could live but a few hours.

Trapper Keely denounces the action of the Carlin party as most inhuman. He says that he wished to leave Colgate some food, but they would not permit it, saying that they had purchased the eatables and had not enough for themselves.

Trapper Keely is suing Gen. Cathn for the reward for finding the party.

Jerry Johnson Hot Springs are located two miles from the Johnson campground: one mile east on U.S. 12, and a mile south from the road by trail. A foot bridge, which crosses the Lochsa River on the south side of the highway, gives access to a mile-long trail up Warm Springs Creek to the pools.

The Bitterroot lobe of the Idaho batholith terminates near Badger Creek, four miles east of the hot springs.

A distance of 2.5 miles more brings one to Wendover campground. From this point to White Sands site six miles east the road follows the trail of Lewis and Clark. The explorers were traveling west in 1805 and turned north from here, up Wendover Ridge, on September 15; it was while going up that ridge that one of the pack horses slipped and rolled downhill into a tree, destroying Captain Clark's portable desk.

The Whitehouse campground is named for Private Joseph Whitehouse, who wrote one of the five journals kept on the Voyage of Discovery. The pond he mentioned passing here is within view of the north side of the road.

Powell Ranger Station is just south of Powell Junction, and the exit, 3.4 miles east of Whitehouse, is marked by a sign. Follow the gravel road down past the administrative office to the residential parking area.

The Lewis and Clark Expedition camped here on September 14, 1805, "all wet and cold" from rain, snow and hail. The men's bellies were rubbing their backbones, their food was exhausted and they had to kill a colt for dinner. William Clark named the stream, a mile east of the station, "Colt Killed Creek." That evocative name has been denatured to White Sand Creek.

To see the island in the river that Clark noted in his journal was used by the Expedition to graze its horses, walk beyond the helicopter landing pad to the riverbank which overlooks the island.

Highway 12 swings northeast up Crooked Fork. This stream and White Sand Creek form the Lochsa. Loch-sah is a Flathead word for "rough water."

The **DeVoto Memorial Grove** occupies the flat on the river-side of the highway 2.9 miles east of the Powell Junction. This impressive grove of cedars has been set aside as tribute to a man of impressive accomplishments: Bernard "Benny" DeVoto. A bronze plaque on a boulder in the grove notes he was "conservationist and historian of the west," and gives the dates, 1897-1955, but it seems apropos to add some words here about one who wrote so many in defense of the western landscape.

DeVoto was born in a "gopher hole of a Utah town," but he often wished he had been born in Idaho. He was the son of a freight agent

118

for the Union Pacific, but he graduated Phi Beta Kappa from Harvard. While living in the effete East, he began to read omnivorously – as a defense of sorts – about the West that was his home.

DeVoto served as a rifle instructor in World War I, taught English at Northwestern shortly thereafter, and published *Mark Twain's America* in 1932, which he called "an essay in the correction of ideas." The years 1929-1936 were spent as an English teacher at Harvard.

Three years later, Bernard DeVoto became editor of the "Easy Chair" at *Harpers Magazine* – a column his biographer, Wallace Stegner, has said might more suitably have been called "Fire Alarm." A year later, he also became the editor of the *Saturday Review of Literature.* He used his double forum as advocate and cultural critic: he took stands on issues of importance; he became the nation's environmental conscience and the West's most comprehensive historian.

In 1943 this eminent writer produced *The Year of Decision – 1846.* Then he won the Pulitzer Prize in history for *Across the Wide Missouri* in 1948, and the National Book Award four years later, for *The Course of Empire.* This trilogy, which has been called "history as literature," earned him a place on the shelf with Prescott, Bancroft and Parkman.

In addition, DeVoto edited Lewis and Clark's journals, wrote novels, scores of essays and several literary criticisms. Bernard died suddenly, one evening in November, 1955, from a heart attack.

A humorous accolade by the editors of *Harpers,* written shortly before DeVoto's death, said in part, (he was) ". . . as resolute in his approvals as in his dislikes, partisan of sound sense and adversary of cant, friend of the public lands and enemy of the lukewarm martini . . ."

The historian Samuel Eliot Morrison wrote, "Benny's conversation was sparkling; his writing whether essays or history was lively and vivid; his erudition in western history and American literature was amazing; his friendship warm and responsive."

Bernard DeVoto had asked that his ashes be scattered over a National Forest, and one of his close friends chose the Clearwater. So Chet Olsen of the Forest Service chartered a plane from Johnson Flying Service in Missoula, and DeVoto's ashes were sifted along the Lochsa over the Bitterroot wilderness.

There was an effort to change the name of the Clearwater Forest to the DeVoto National Forest, but opposition by parties who had never read his books or appreciated his efforts on behalf of the "plundered province" of the West, thwarted that testimonial. The cedar grove was dedicated in 1962; Senator Lee Metcalf attended and President Kennedy sent a written message. Though DeVoto's death left an inestimable void, his work stubbornly endures.

DeVoto Memorial Grove.

Lolo Pass is 9.3 miles up the highway from the DeVoto Grove. Lolo is a Chinook word for carry, but there is reason to believe that the name, which occurs as early as 1831, is that of a trapper.

A visitor center is located atop the 5,233-foot pass. Turn east on the gravel road that runs past the center and drive one mile to the clearing marked **Packer Meadows.** Lewis and Clark passed through these meadows September 13, 1805, late in the afternoon.

The campsite they used that night can be seen by driving south 1.5 miles down the first logging road east of the visitor center. The road follows Glade Creek, now called Pack Creek, and the campsite is on the east side of the road. The Expedition's meal that evening consisted of a mule deer and four Franklin grouse shot that morning. The next eight days were "starvin' times."

Lolo Pass marks the border with Montana; a border that was not surveyed until 1904-1906, so the two states got along without a boundary for forty years.

120

U.S. Highway 12 drops down the west fork of Lolo Creek 17.6 miles to **Lolo Hot Springs**. Though the traveler is now in Montana, brief notes are added along the most direct routes back into Idaho.

Lolo Hot Springs is a commercial development with indoor and outdoor pools. The water flows from the ground at 140 degrees F.

The Lewis and Clark Expedition visited the springs on their way west in 1805, and again on their trip eastward in 1806. On the return trip, the men took their first hot bath in at least nine months. Captain Lewis, June 29, 1806:

... after dinner we continued our march seven miles further to the warm springs [Lolo Hot Springs] ... situated ... near the bank of travellers rest creek which at that place is about 10 yards wide ... the principal spring is about the temperature of the warmest baths used at the hot springs in Virginia. In this bath which had been prepared by the Indians by stoping the run with stone and gravel, I bathed and remained in 19 minutes, it was with dificulty I could remain thus long and it caused a profuse sweat ... both the men and indians amused themselves with the use of a bath this evening. I observed that the indians after remaining in the hot bath as long as they could bear it ran and plunged themselves into the creek the water of which is now as cold as ice can make it; after remaining here a few minutes they returned again to the warm bath, repeating this transision several times but always ending with the warm bath.

An historic site sign, twenty-one miles east of Lolo Hot Springs, directs the driver's attention to the location of **Fort Fizzle** on the north side of the highway.

On July 22, 1877, scouts sent out by Captain Charles Rawn, commander of Post Missoula, returned with word that Nez Perce warriors were coming down the Lolo Trail into the Bitterroot Valley (see White Bird battlefield). Rawn telegraphed the news to Fort Shaw and was ordered to intercept and hold the Indians at the base of the trail.

Two days later, Captain Rawn, with a force of five commissioned officers and thirty enlisted men from the Seventh Infantry, along with about 200 citizen volunteers, began constructing a barricade from fallen trees at this site.

When the Nez Perce spotted the construction – which they called a "corral" – the chiefs had a parley with Rawn and requested permission to pass. The Captain had his orders and refused the Indians' request. Since the Nez Perce promised they would harm no one, many of the volunteers returned to their homesteads.

The Indians then came down the canyon on the morning of July 28, turned up a north gulch about half a mile distant from the "fort," and crossed to the east high on the mountainside before descending to the Bitterroot Valley. Outflanked, Rawn's troops returned to Missoula.

The last logs of Fort Fizzle, as some frontier humorist dubbed it, were consumed by a brush fire in 1934.

U.S. 12 intersects U.S. Highway 93 at a point 4.6 miles east of the "fort's" location. **Missoula** is eleven miles north of the intersection. From that city, it is 108 miles via Interstate 90 back into Idaho over **Lookout Pass** (4,726 feet), just east of Mullan (see Mullan, town).

A south turn on U.S. 93 at its junction with Highway 12 will take the driver eighty-four miles to **Lost Trail Pass** on the Idaho-Montana border. The southern route has a number of interesting sites, which are noted by mileage from this intersection.

Mile 1.0: **Travellers Rest** site is on the east side of the highway, in an open field. Lewis and Clark reached this camp on June 30, 1806, at sunset. They had used the spot on their way west, as well.

The men paused here, as Lewis and Clark made arrangements to divide the party. The thirty-one soldiers and Sacajewea had been together for two years; they had shared hard times and high times; the planned separation of the group, even though temporary, brought depression to all its members. On July 3 the Expedition divided. Lewis, with nine men, rode east over Lewis and Clark's Pass to the Great Falls of the Missouri. From there they were to explore the headwaters of the Marias River to determine whether part of the Missouri River drainage extended as far north as Latitude 50, providing a possible access route to the fur country of Canada. Then they would rejoin Clark at the confluence of the Missouri and Yellowstone Rivers.

"I took leave of my worthy friend and companion Capt. Clark and the party that accompanyed him. I could not avoid feeling much concern on this occasion although I hoped this separation was only momentary," wrote Lewis.

Clark and the rest of the group proceeded up the Bitterroot Valley, across the Continental Divide, and over the 1805 route to the Yellowstone. (The Corps was reunited August 12.)

Mile 25: The **Bitterroot River**, which parallels the road on the east side, flows into the Clark Fork near Missoula.

Mile 58: **Trapper Peak** (10,130 feet) can be seen west of the highway – it is the highest peak in the Selway-Bitterroot Wilderness Area.

Mile 61: The **Nez Perce Trail Road** from Conner to Red River Ranger Station enters the highway here (see Nez Perce Road).

Mile 63.5: **Medicine Tree**. A stately ponderosa pine, noted by a sign, stands on the east edge of the highway. The tree was revered by generations of Salish and Sahapten people. A mountain sheep horn, its tip embedded in the trunk, about eight feet from the ground, gave the tree sacred meaning to the Indians. The Nez Perce, on their exodus from Idaho, passed this pine in 1877, and several warriors proclaimed their dream visions of an impending disaster. Some of the chiefs scoffed at these fears. Four days later, the Indians lost ninety members of their tribe in the Battle of Big Hole.

The ram's horn no longer adorns the tree – the story, perhaps apocryphal, is that a logger cut it out in order to hang it in a Hamilton, Montana, saloon.

Mile 72.5: At Sula, an "historic point" sign draws attention to the **"Valley of Troubles"** campsite. Alexander Ross, leader of a Hudson's Bay Company trapping brigade, which consisted of fifty-five Indian and white trappers, eighty-nine women and children and 392 horses, spent the month of mid-March to mid-April, 1824 trying to cross the snow from here into the Big Hole Valley.

Mile 86: Scars of the 1960 **Saddle Mountain fire** that burned 3,000 acres can be seen west of the highway.

Mile 87: **Lost Trail Pass** (6,990 feet) at the Idaho state line. It is twenty-five miles from the pass south to the settlement of North Fork.

From the summit one can drive east on Highway 43, sixteen miles to the **Big Hole Battlefield,** one of the more impressive battlefields in the West; a National Monument under supervision of the National Park Service and a site the beauty and poignance of which is disturbed only by the thoughtless location of the Park Service interpretive center.

State Highway No. 13 from a junction with U.S. 95 in Grangeville easterly and northerly via Harpster, Stites, and Kooskia to a junction with U.S. 12 north of Kooskia. Route length: 26.3 miles.

Highway 13 leaves Grangeville, and like a snake with colic, twists nine miles down to **Harpster** in the Clearwater Canyon.

In the early 1860s William Jackson built a small stage station, with a toll bridge across the South Fork of the Clearwater, and called his location Bridgeport. The station was burned in the Nez Perce War of 1877 and was never rebuilt.

Loyal Brown obtained land at the site and sold eighty acres in 1893 to the Clearwater Mining Co., which platted a town dubbed Brownsville. The *Idaho Free Press,* in a gush of myopic enthusiasm, wrote, "In after years, in looking over the map of the great state of Idaho, you will find Brownsville one of the most important towns of the state."

The town of Riverside existed just north of Bridgeport in the early 1900s, but the post office, which moved from Riverside to the latter community at that time, had already been named Harpster after Abraham Harpster, an early homesteader, who died on his place in 1891. The area retained his name.

Seven and one-half miles north of Harpster is the location of the **Clearwater battlefield**.

The Nez Perce Indians were camped on the west side of the river, at the mouth of Cottonwood Creek, 0.8 miles south of present Stites. The tipis were on the flat on the upriver side of the creek. The Indians had just been engaged in the skirmishes at Cottonwood on Camas Prairie (see Cottonwood, town). Chief Looking Glass had joined the encampment with forty warriors.

After the battle of Cottonwood, Col. Edward McConville had organized the volunteers from Lewiston, Grangeville, and Mount Idaho into a single eighty-man "regiment," and set off on the trail of the Nez Perce, having sent a message to General Howard, who was enroute from White Bird to Grangeville, that they would keep the Indians under surveillance until the Regulars could catch up.

The Indians spotted McConville's troops on a hill just west of the Clearwater Middle Fork-South Fork junction. The soldiers dug rifle pits and sent a messenger to General Howard urging alacrity.

On July 9, Nez Perce ringed McConville's position, and desultory rifle fire was exchanged over the next two days. There were no casualties, but the volunteers referred to their spot as Mt. Misery. By July 11, supplies had run low; with no word from Howard, McConville decided to retreat to Mount Idaho.

The Indians relaxed. There were five bands encamped along the Clearwater; they engaged in games, contests and camp chores. Their only interest in the conflict at this point was avoidance of the troops.

124

Howard's command, however, was marching from Grangeville; it included the cavalry of Perry and Whipple and numbered about 400 regulars and 150 civilians. A local scout led Howard's troops across the South Fork of the Clearwater well south, or upriver, of the Indian camp and they moved north on the high ground on the east side of the river. On July 11, just after McConville's men had retreated, one of Howard's scouts, who made a sortie out to the canyon rim, spotted the Nez Perce encamped along the opposite side of the river below.

The unconcerned Indians had little warning, as they expected Howard to arrive from the west. A howitzer and Gatling guns opened fire from the rim. The Nez Perce promptly broke camp. Three war parties crossed the river on horses and worked their way up ravines to stall the soldiers, while women, children and horses were moved north down the Clearwater. Although the Nez Perce warriors were outnumbered four to one, their dash to intercept the soldiers temporarily halted the attack and forced the cavalry to dismount.

The battle lasted the rest of the day; the Army suffered from lack of water, and Indian sharpshooters defended the only spring on the plateau; it was nightfall before the soldiers were able to relieve their thirst.

The next day, the Indians, who were not given to siege tactics, broke off the engagement in the afternoon, hastily crossed back to the west side of the river and headed north with their families. The cavalry and infantry then crossed the river and occupied the abandoned camp. The soldiers recovered large amounts of Indian equipment and supplies.

Howard's troops had suffered fifteen dead and twenty-five wounded; Nez Perce casualties may have been as high as ten. The General postponed pursuit until the following day – one of his more serious blunders during the war, because by morning the Nez Perce had crossed to the east side of the river and were off on the Lolo Trail to Montana. The next battle would be at Big Hole, on the eastern side of the Bitterroot Range.

When Howard later claimed victory at the Clearwater battle, Yellow Wolf, a warrior, responded:

We were not whipped! We held all soldiers off the first day, and having better rifle pits, we could still have held them back. Not until the last of us leaped away did soldiers make their charge. Some tepees, robes, clothing and food were left. The women, not knowing the warriors were disagreeing, quitting the fight, had no time to pack the camp. Chief Joseph did not reach them soon enough.

But we were not whipped! Had we been whipped, we could not have escaped from there with our lives.

The Indians charged Battle Ridge, on the eastern side of the highway, through Stites and Anderson Canyons. It is possible to visit the site of the battle if one drives up Stites Canyon Road, opposite and just north of Cottonwood Creek. Up on the rim, the spring, over which the Indians and soldiers fought, still flows, and those who know where to look can find the rock breastwork piled by Indian marksmen during the night, at the edge of Anderson Canyon.

Cottonwood Creek marks the limit of steamboat navigation on the Clearwater River. June 4, 1886, a large sternwheel steamer, the *D. S. Baker,* was brought upriver from Lewiston in six hours. Investors believed the Cottonwood drainage might serve as a railroad route to the upland prairie, and a steamboat landing with a warehouse at the mouth of the creek could function for several months of each year. Though the *Baker* reached her destination, the trip's difficulties discouraged the investors.

Stites is seven miles north of Harpster. The town is located on what was Indian land until the Nez Perce reservation was opened in 1895. Jacob Stites, a native of New Jersey, acquired a quarter-section in 1897; he sold sixty acres to a townsite company in 1900 and exercised the privilege of naming the settlement.

The location became the terminus of the Northern Pacific (now Camas Prairie) railroad line up the South Fork of the Clearwater.

Mr. N. B. Pettibone in 1943 recalled the original, and rather amusing, manner in which telephone service first reached Stites:

I think it was along in 1904 or 1905 that James Jump, Dr. E. E. Briley and myself decided that the Clearwater Country needed telephone connections with the outside world, so I was delegated to look after the construction of a telephone line from Stites to Grangeville, to connect up with the Bell system. I put in poles where there was no fence but where there was wire fence I would connect to the top barbed wire. I drew the staples, and wrapped some old rubber around the wire for insulation. Where there were gates, I would put a pole on each side, run a smooth wire over and connect at each side to the barbed fence wire. In the nineteen miles I had only about six miles overhead wire. I gave the farmers along the line free use for one year so they permitted me to use their fence wire. However most all of them told me I was crazy and that it wouldn't work – but it did, and gave the people of the Clearwater section

126

very good service with the outside world. Business grew so rapidly
over the line, that it was not long till the Bell system bought us out,
and they put in all overhead line. Ours was the pioneer phone line in
the entire Clearwater area.

Kooskia lies bracketed by the Middle and South Fork of the
Clearwater where they merge to form the main river, four miles
north of Stites.

The town's name is a contraction of the Nez Perce word
"kooskooskia" that appears in the journals of Captain's Lewis and
Clark. The explorers applied the name to the Clearwater River,
apparently as a result of an interpretive misunderstanding. The
Indians were attempting to explain that two large rivers flowed
through their country – kooskooske: "this the little one," and the
other, larger, Snake River.

The town of Kooskia was established in 1895, when the
government set aside 104 acres for townsite purposes as it opened
the expropriated Indian reservation lands for settlement. The town
was first named for James Stuart, a Nez Perce surveyor and
merchant, but the Northern Pacific arrived in 1899, and since that
railroad already served one community known as Stuart, it
furnished the station with this second name, which prevailed by
1902.

Kooskia was known among western horsemen, for several
decades during the 1900s, as the home of the Decker saddle. The
saddle was developed by Oliver P. Robinett, a blacksmith and
packer who moved to Kooskia in 1906. The Decker was easier and
more efficient to use than the old sawbucks, and the Decker
brothers, who were also packers, had no trouble selling the OPR's
all over the West. Robinett, who died in 1945, also invented the
Pulaski – a mattock-axe tool that is now standard equipment for
forest fire crews.

The **Kooskia National Fish Hatchery** can be visited if one
turns east at the north end of town and follows the paved road on
the south side of the Middle Fork of the Clearwater for one mile.

The federal hatchery, open 8:00 A.M. to 5:00 P.M., raises 1.2 million
spring chinook salmon annually. There are instructive displays of
the five phases of Pacific salmon and a visual presentation of the
chinook's life cycle.

The road past the hatchery goes up Clear Creek, a tributary of
the Clearwater. The creek drains the territory of Chief Looking
Glass' band. During the War of 1877, his village, while attempting to

remain neutral under a white flag, was subjected to a reprehensible attack on July 1 by troops commanded by Captain Stephen Whipple.

Peopeo Tholekt, a warrior of the Looking Glass band, later told L. V. McWhorter:

Gardens had been plowed, planted, and everything growing when we were attacked. We had plenty for our living. One man had ten milk cows, and others had cows and beef cattle. All, everything was lost. Only about twenty men and boys – some boys small – had guns; part of them shotguns and light rifles. None of us wanted war; nobody expected war.

Looking Glass was not captured, but he was sufficiently angered to join the non-treaty Nez Perce and assume the duties of war chief. General Howard in retrospect admitted that Whipple's attack accomplished nothing except to "stir up another hornet's nest."

Highway 13, which was completed from Grangeville to Kooskia in 1934, terminates across the Middle Fork of the Clearwater at Highway 12, just north of Kooskia.

State Highway No. 14 from a junction with Highway 13 south of Harpster, southerly and easterly via Golden to Elk City. Route length: 49.5 miles.

To reach State Highway 14, leave Highway 13 three miles south of Harpster. (Drivers using the approach from Grangeville must kink to the right at the bottom of the canyon grade rather than cross the bridge that leads to Harpster.) The shortest route to Highway 14 from Grangeville goes through Mount Idaho. Highway 14 advances up the **South Fork of the Clearwater** 46.8 miles to Elk City. The first road to Elk City from Grangeville was completed in 1907, but went by way of Newsome, which is north of the South Fork.

The settlement of **Golden** is reached after a twenty-nine mile drive. One-half mile west of Golden, a squat, cement structure can be observed on the south bank of the river. Water was flumed out of Ten Mile Creek down to this power house, where electricity was produced for the Miller mine, located about a mile below Golden. The Miller operated through the late 1930s.

Golden came into being in 1899, when claims were staked 2½ miles south of the river. A trail was completed up the South Fork in 1910, and Golden moved down to its present location at the mouth of Ten Mile Creek. The existing highway followed that trail and arrived at Golden in 1929.

128

Elk City: eighteen miles from Golden. A party of fifty-two prospectors from Pierce, violating federal law and an agreement with the Nez Perce, explored up the South Fork of the Clearwater in 1861 and found color at American River. By the end of July, they had founded Elk City, and news of the strike drew miners from Pierce like filings to a magnet. At August-end there were 800 miners working the streams and slopes, and at least twenty log buildings had been squared and roofed.

Dr. Merle Wells is authority for the statement that gold recovered here was valued at $16.28 an ounce, which made it the richest found in the early northern Idaho mines.

Spring highwater in the creeks and river, and lack of water in the gulches and on the hills in the summer, caused problems in Elk City that were resolved by a special miners' meeting. It was decided that every miner could hold two claims, as long as each was a different class – thus with a spring high claim and a summer low one, miners would be able to work a longer season.

In October stories of richer ground in Florence knocked the antlers off Elk City while they were still in velvet. All but about seventy-five miners headed over the hill to yellower pastures.

Over the next three years, the miners who stayed expended considerable labor on ditches in order to water hillside claims. Ditches ranged from three to seventeen miles in length. About 200 men returned from Florence, but their earnings here averaged only $3.50 a day. Evenutally, hydraulic giants were introduced to speed the sluicing operations.

Chinese miners, "the very Quakers of industry," leased the ditches from 1872-1884 and worked the claims. At one point there were about 1,500 Orientals and only a dozen whites at the Elk City placers. (In 1870, of the 6,579 men classed as miners in Idaho, 3,853 were Chinese.) But by the late 1880s mistreatment of Chinese was so common that they were often forced to hire white guards while they worked. A judge ruled aliens could not hold mining ground under the U.S. mining laws after 1887, and a Chinese exodus began in 1889. (Aliens who leased from citizens prior to 1887 were allowed to retain their leases.)

Quartz lode operations began in 1902, and total production for the area may have reached $5 million. Elk City's gold rush, brief as it may seem, lasted longer than that of most other placer districts in northern Idaho.

The dredging era began in 1935, shortly after the completion of the South Fork road. Several dragline dredges and two bucketline dredges recovered almost a million dollars.

In later years, Elk City was the "mountain metropolis" for most Salmon River settlers on the north side of the river. The town's most frequent foe was fire: the Great Idaho Fire of 1910 burned the outskirts, a 1930 fire burned most of Main Street, and the last hotel was reduced to ashes in 1939.

Red River-Dixie-Orofino Loop (South)

The **Red River Road** leaves Highway 14, 2.7 miles southwest of Elk City. This loop trip of approximately sixty-five miles travels through country pocked and furrowed with evidence of the mining era; the road to Dixie is paved, the gravel road from Dixie up Big Creek and down Crooked River to Orogrande traverses uniform stands of evergreens, broken by occasional meadows and a few ridge-top views. The loop ends back at Highway 14, three miles west of the starting point. The road is quite acceptable for sedan traffic.

The **Red River Hot Springs** road is reached fourteen miles from Highway 14, on the Red River road. The springs are a commercial development, eleven miles up the gravel road from this turnoff. The road is generally open to vehicles April-December, and to snowmobiles during the winter. There is a heated outdoor swimming pool (seventy-two to ninety-five degrees) and four indoor pools with private rooms. Lodging and a restaurant are available on the premises. (See Nez Perce Trail Road for information about the road that goes east, just past the Red River Ranger Station.)

Dixie is 15.2 miles farther south from the Red River Ranger Station.

A few miners looked at prospects in Dixie in 1861, but no claims of consequence were filed until 1884. The first road was hewed by miners and freighters; the Forest Service, with CCC labor, opened an improved road in 1938.

There were dragline placer operations during the Depression; the area is estimated to have yielded $500,000 in gold.

In recent years, Dixie has become a summer-cabin settlement and a winter focus for snowmobilers. The town received telephone and power lines in 1980; its seventy-year-old store burned in 1982.

On the lower end of the main street, across the creek, is the cemetery where several Salmon River pioneers, such as Sam Myers, are buried.

The road from Dixie down to **Mackay Bar** is passable to four-wheel drive vehicles. Reservations are required at Mackay Bar Ranch.

Orogrande is twenty-four miles north of Dixie. The settlement was a trading center for the Buffalo Hump mining district at the turn of the century; there were about fifty residents in 1915.

14
IDAHO

James Penman relocated some gold claims here in 1905 and sold them to the Homestake Mining Co. The same property was mined by the Penman Mines Corp. in the 1930s and 1940s. The open-pit Orogrande Frisco mine also operated through the 1930s.

At the time, there were three two-story hotels in the town. The Yellow Dog had been reconstructed from materials hauled down from Callender in the "Hump." Miners lodged in the buildings.

Driving north from Orogrande, dredge scars become increasingly evident. Watch for the **Mount Vernon dredge**, in a pit on the right side of the road, about two miles from town. Dave Henderson, the owner, was from Mount Vernon, Washington. The diesel-powered machine ran from the 1930s until 1941. The area had been sample-tested for two summers before operations got under way. Orogrande placer gold, mined and dredged, amounted to $750,000.

Mount Vernon dredge.

Nez Perce Trail Road from the Red River Ranger Station east to Conner, Montana. Route length: 113 miles.

SCENIC AREA

The Nez Perce Trail road to Montana begins one mile past the USFS Red River ranger station. As far as the author has been able to determine, this is the longest unpaved road without services left in the western states: 113 miles. It is a splendid drive, a wide-angle lens

131

drive, but the distance requires foresight beyond "spare tire and gas" precautions. The road bisects as rough a piece of country as ever lay outdoors, but the route itself is not difficult – it is single lane, second gear, with a few miles where the rocks have been fertilized. Weather, however, can make the trip difficult: the road is generally not open before mid-July, and can close in late September with a heavy snowstorm. Better weatherwise than otherwise. A weekly patrol by the Forest Service is dependent upon the annual budget.

The Forest Service recommends eight hours for the trip; it can be done in six, but care must be used in stretches with blind curves. Stock trucks and hunters will be encountered in the fall.

To avoid missing some spectacular views, begin the drive by noon. There are campsites for those who decide to take more than a day.

As the Forest Service sign indicates, the trail was a major path for travelers to and from the upper Bitterroot Valley and the buffalo country of Montana. The missionary Rev. Samuel Parker who traveled the trail from Montana in 1835, took a shot at the future as he wrote in his journal:

Frequently between mountains there is space enough for a rushing stream of the purest water, the bank on one side of which terminates the descent of one mountain and the other bank commences the ascent of another. Can this section of the country ever be inhabited, unless these mountains shall be brought low and these valleys exalted? But they may be designed to perpetuate a supply of lumber for the widespread prairies, or they may contain mines of treasures which when wrought will need these forests for fuel and these rushing streams for power. Roads may be constructed running north and south so that transportation may be made south to the Salmon River and north to the Lochsa.

John Mullan considered the route for his military road, but rejected it as too expensive (see I-90, Mullan Tree). Major Sewell Truax, a surveyor, along with an engineer and a Nez Perce guide, made a hasty inspection of the trail (eight days from Fort Owen, Montana to Elk City) in July, 1866, and decided it would be easier to improve the Lolo Trail. He was looking for a wagon route from Lewiston to Helena, Montana.

In 1936 the Forest Service opened the present road, using CCC labor from both ends. The trail and road run close to the divide between the Clearwater and Salmon Rivers, but the road does not follow the old trail except in a general way.

132

Points of interest in route:

Mile 5: Large areas on the slopes to the south have been given a Dakota haircut by logging companies; the clearcut scalps will probably fur over within a couple of decades.

Mile 23.5: **Poet Creek-Bargamin Creek.** Bargamin Creek flows to the Salmon River, fifteen miles south of here. It was named for Vic Bargamin, a homesteader who ran a winter trapline between the Salmon and the Clearwater. During the summer he used a burro pack train to supply his trapping cabins.

Mile 35: **Sabe Saddle** and **Vista Point.** This extraordinary view looks south to the River of No Return Wilderness, 2.2 million acres set aside in 1980 after years of effort by conservationists who were aided by Idaho's Senator Frank Church. Sabe Creek, which flows into the Salmon ten miles from this point, is the divide for the Bitterroot and Nez Perce National Forests.

The blue ridges that recede in scalloped layers, dark, less dark, dim, until they collapse into the canyon, recall a stanza by Robert Penn Warren:

> *From this high place all things flow:*
> *Land of divided streams, of water spilled*
> *Eastward, westward without memento;*
> *Land where the morning mist is curled*
> *Like smoke about the ridgepole of the world.*
> *The mist is furled.*

Mile 50: **Gold Pan Lake Vista.** Worth the sixty-yard walk.

Mile 52: The **Magruder Murder** sign: The Forest Service explanatory sign, indicating the direction of the massacre site, is so brief, because of limited space, that it does little more than raise questions for the curious. The outline that follows has some answers.

Lloyd Magruder was a native of Maryland, the son of wealthy parents. He came west to scrape the green off his horns. By the time he was thirty-eight, he was running a successful freight business from Lewiston, polishing his seat on saddle leather from dawn to dark.

In October, 1863, he left Lewiston with a sixty-mule pack string, headed across the Nez Perce Trail for Virginia City, Montana, to sell supplies to miners in Alder Gulch.

A friend of the freighter, Hill Beachy, who ran the Luna House hostelry in Lewiston, noticed a gang of seven men leave Lewiston minutes after Magruder, and he was apprehensive about their intentions.

The group overtook Magruder a few miles from Bannack City, Montana. They struck up an acquaintance, accompanied him to Virginia City, and helped him sell his goods. Magruder cleared $25,000 from the sale. When he prepared to return to Lewiston, the group of men agreed to join up as guards on his trip home. A second group, of four men, approached Magruder and asked to join the party. Believing there was strength in numbers, he consented.

The night the party camped on the Little Clearwater, a tributary of the Selway (six miles north of Gold Pan Lake), the men who had accompanied Magruder to Virginia City committed mass murder. The freighters and two of the latecomers they killed with an axe; the other latecomers, with a knife and a shotgun. After dumping the bodies off a cliff, they erased the camp, herded the pack stock into a ravine and shot every animal. They then headed for Lewiston, avoiding the trail as much as possible. Fresh snow disguised their crime.

The murderers had planned to bypass Lewiston, but the Clearwater and Snake Rivers were too cold to ford. Using assumed names, they went to the Luna House and bought tickets for the stage. Hill Beachy was there. His suspicions flared. He had recently suffered a nightmare, so vivid he had discussed it with his wife, in which his missing friend was murdered. Now he went looking for the stock that the strangers had used to reach town. He found the animals at a nearby ranch – Magruder's horse and saddle were there. It was all the proof he needed. The villains were gone, but Beachy intended to apprehend them.

He obtained a commission as deputy sheriff and found a fellow bold enough to accompany him. They left for Walla Walla, Washington, where they learned the fugitives had gone on to Portland four days earlier.

Beachy and his pard used charter and regular boats to reach Portland, but found the criminals had left on a steamboat for San Francisco. No new departure was scheduled for ten days; the nearest telegraph line to San Francisco was in Yreka, 400 miles south. So Hill and his pard rode almost non-stop by horseback and buckboard to Yreka. There they telegraphed a warrant for the murderers, giving names and aliases. The men were arrested as they disembarked.

Beachy went on to San Francisco, obtained custody of the prisoners, and brought them back to Lewiston. They were lodged on the second floor of the Luna House and were guarded carefully. Eventually, three of the men made confessions.

134

The grand jury returned indictments in January, 1864, and the killers were tried, convicted, and sentenced to hang in March. They died on gallows built on Normal Hill behind the town.

During the summer, Beachy and some of his friends brought the victims' remains back to Lewiston for burial. He also located $17,000 of the gold taken by the robbers and returned it to Magruder's widow; the Territorial Legislature voted $6,200 to reimburse Beachy for expenses he had incurred.

A mountain, stream, and ranger station perpetuate Magruder's name; fortitude and tenacity perpetuate Beachy's. Hill Beachy died in Elko, Nevada in 1874. "A friend may well be reckoned the masterpiece of nature."

Mile 73: **Selway River** headwaters. The Magruder ranger station is 0.5 miles south, up the Selway River. The Paradise guard station, 12.1 miles north, is the launch point for Selway River trips. Drive east, up Deep Creek 10.2 miles, and pavement resumes at Scimitar Creek. The road gradually ascends to Nez Perce Pass.

Mile 87: **Nez Perce Pass.** The pass, elevation 6,587 feet, straddles the Montana-Idaho border. The exposed, square-topped peak east of the road is Castle Rock, 7,722 feet.

Once across the pass, the driver is in Montana. Without backtracking, he has three routes back into Idaho: 1) Turn north on U.S. 93 at Conner for Lolo (see U.S.93, U.S. 12). 2) Turn south on U.S. 93 at Conner for Lost Trail Pass (see U.S. 93). 3) Turn south on the paved and gravel road past Painted Rocks Lake to the Salmon River Road at Shoup, then east eighteen miles to North Fork at U.S. 93. This choice assumes sufficient time and gas, as it adds almost fifty miles without services to Shoup.

Interstate 15 from the Utah-Idaho state line south of Malad via Pocatello, Blackfoot, Idaho Falls and Dubois to the Idaho-Montana border at Monida Pass. Route length: 196 miles.

Interstate 15 travels north from the Utah border 10.6 miles to Malad (see Highway 37, Malad), then 11.8 miles farther, over Malad Summit (5,615 elev.), and 22.4 miles to the McCammon Exit to **Indian Rocks State Park.**

The elongated, 3,500-acre park of lava rock, sage, and Utah juniper is simply a convenient area with fifty campsites for travelers. It is open Memorial Day to Labor Day.

Inkom, on the east side of the highway 9.5 miles north of the park, has long been the location of the only cement producer in the state. Lime is mined next to the plant.

I-15 enters **Pocatello,** the second-largest city in Idaho, 8.7 miles northwest of Inkom.

Po-ca-ta-ro (whose meaning has eluded etymological bloodhounds) was chief of a northwestern Shoshone band of about 300 persons that ranged between the Bear Lake settlements in Utah, and Fort Hall, Idaho. Twice arrested by Army officers on charges of harassing emigrant wagons in southeastern Idaho, and twice released, Pocatello signed the Treaty of Box Elder in 1863 and eventually settled on the Fort Hall reservation. He died in 1884 and was buried in a spring that is now covered by the waters of American Falls reservoir.

Pocatello in 1889.

Pocatello Junction was built by the railroad industry. When the Utah and Northern narrow-gauge, which operated from Salt Lake City to Franklin, Idaho, was acquired by the Union Pacific in 1878, the tracks were extended north to the mines in Butte, Montana (see Highway 91, Utah Northern). Seventy miles of the railroad traversed the Fort Hall Indian Reservation, and though the rails were completed to Butte by 1881, the railroad did not obtain a lawful right-of-way until 1886, when it paid the Indians $6,000. Since the future Pocatello townsite was within the reservation, the Union Pacific chose Eagle Rock (now Idaho Falls) as its administrative and maintenance headquarters.

The **Oregon Short Line Railway,** a subsidiary of U.P., laid its track west from Wyoming, across Idaho, to Oregon in 1881-1884; the rails intersected those of the Utah and Northern at Pocatello Junction, which the railroad decided to use as its Idaho division point.

136

In an arrangement approved by Congress, the company purchased forty acres from the Bannock-Shoshone tribes. By 1866, however, the U.P. requested another 1,600 acres to accommodate the demands of a growing settlement; in 1887 the Indians agreed to sell the land for $8.00 an acre; and Congressional approval came within a year. Soon after the railroad moved its Eagle Rock facilities south to Pocatello, almost a thousand buildings were under construction, though the location was still being surveyed into lots for sale at an auction. In 1893 the site became the seat of Bannock County.

The Dawes Severalty Act was used as a lever to pry the young

Pocatello in 1896.

townsite outside of the reservation, and in 1898 the Shoshone-Bannock tribes agreed to sell 418,000 acres on the south end of the reservation for $600,000 (see Highway 91, Fort Hall). The arrangement was ratified by Congress two years later.

On June 17, 1902, "The Day of the Run," the land was opened to "sagebrush sooners," however, lands within a five-mile limit of Pocatello were sold in forty-acre tracts at public auction.

The railroad division point emerged as the principal townsite of southeastern Idaho. Its streets were laid out parallel and perpendicular to the U.P. tracks; Center St. became the chief business thoroughfare. Building stone was quarried nearby, and a brick factory provided the material for many of the commercial structures in the downtown district.

By 1920 with a population of 15,000 Pocatello qualified under state law as a city of the first-class. A large wholesale and manufacturing business was attracted to the area; during World War II more than 4,500 railroad cars passed through the city's yards daily. At present Union Pacific, Bucyrus-Erie, Garrett Freightlines, J. R. Simplot Co., FMC, and Idaho State Univ. are the area's major employers.

Pocatello, Front St., 1899.

Replica of Fort Hall, exterior and interior views.

Pocatello has a wide variety of architectural styles; the tour suggested here is representative, rather than inclusive.

Begin at the **replica of Fort Hall in Ross Park** on the southeast end of town at Exit 67 from I-15.

Fort Hall was established by Nathaniel Wyeth in 1834 on the east bank of the Snake River about fifteen miles northwest of this site (see Highway 91, Fort Hall). In 1963 the Bannock County centennial committee decided to recreate the old fort from the Hudson's Bay Company plans. (Even the whitewashed walls are an authentic particular.)

138

The replica is open afternoons in April and May, and during daylight hours from June to mid-September; it draws about 15,000 visitors yearly. Displays on the ground floor of the main log building are devoted to the history of the fort; Indian artifacts are exhibited upstairs.

Idaho State Univ. (Academy), 1910.

Tourist park; registration fee: 50¢.

From Ross Park travel northwest on So. Fifth Ave. 0.5 miles to the Mountain View Cemetery on the right side of the Avenue, opposite Logan St. The Gothic, gray, stone mausoleum facing the street is the most elaborate in Idaho; it held the ashes of James Brady, state governor (1909-1910) and U.S. Senator (1913-1918), but because of repeated vandalism to the door and stained glass windows, Brady's ashes were reburied outside, behind the crypt. The interior contains an alcove with a memorial plaque.

Follow So. Fifth Ave. for seven blocks past **Idaho State Univ.** The 790-acre campus was established as the Academy of Idaho by the legislature in 1910 – only three students enrolled the first day. It was essentially a high school; after three years a faculty of six had 122 students. In 1915 the name was changed to Idaho Technical Institute (a junior college), then renamed Southern Branch of the Univ. of Idaho in 1927, and, finally, Idaho State College (a four-year institution) in 1947. In 1963 it became Idaho State Univ.

The university offers graduate degrees in liberal arts, pharmacy, education, business, and engineering. It has one of the finer libraries in the state and a mediocre museum of natural history.

Turn right off So. Fifth Ave. onto East Halliday St.; drive two blocks to So. Seventh Ave. The Colonial revival house on the northwest corner, at 554 South Fifth, belonged to John Hood, who operated a chain of Golden Rule stories in Idaho and Utah. In 1977 the I.S.U. Alumni Assoc. purchased the house.

Follow So. Seventh Ave. southwest two blocks to East Whitman St., where the Xaivier Serval house is located on the northwest corner. Built in 1917, the three-story house with round-roofed dormers, has been the residence of University presidents since 1951.

Drive southwest four more blocks to Clark St., turn left (southwest) five blocks; follow the curve beneath an overpass and emerge on Center St. Turn right (northwest) on Main St. The Chief Theatre is visible on the left in mid-block. When the movie house (with 1,300 seats) opened in January, 1938, it featured the premiere of Wallace Beery's film *The Badmen of Brimstone.* The owner of the theater, which cost $250,000, invited President Roosevelt and all forty-eight state governors to its opening. The building still serves as a theater, but its interior murals were recently painted over.

Continue northwest five blocks to Bridge St., turn left two blocks to 648 No. Garfield, site of the **Stanrod mansion,** the finest example of Victorian architecture in the state and material for an essay by Thorstein Veblen on "the imputations of superiority."

Drew Stanrod built the mansion in 1899-1901. He had studied law in Kentucky before coming to Malad, Idaho, where he was elected judge of the Fifth Judicial District, a post he kept until he entered private practice in Pocatello. He had interests in eleven different banks in the state, and ran unsuccessfully for state governor and the U.S. Senate.

Stanrod mansion before restoration. Interior view.

The twelve-room, 3,200 square-foot mansion was designed by a San Francisco architect, and cost $12,000. Stone was quarried at nearby McCammon, hauled by wagon to the site, and dressed by masons in the backyard. A basement coal furnace provided central heating, and the library was wired with the first residential electric outlet in town.

In 1974 the city bought the mansion, undertook restoration, and opened it to public use. Visitors are welcome.

Turn southeast two blocks to 506 No. Garfield at No. Wyeth. This unusual house was built in the 1930s by Mr. Nichols, owner of a local dance hall, who was a mason. The exterior is made from rejected cinder bricks that he obtained in Wyoming; the interior has a rock fireplace and an extraordinary finish of jagged stucco.

Go one block southwest on Wyeth to 435 No. Hayes to see St. Joseph's Catholic Church, with a steeple of sheeted copper, built in 1897.

Return to No. Garfield and drive two more blocks southeast to West Lander St., where one can see the stone First Congregational Church that dates from 1904; then continue another two blocks to the **Bannock County Historical Museum** in the old Carnegie library at 100 No. Garfield and West Center St. This pressed-brick building with its sandstone trim was built in 1907, its cruciform plan resembles that of a Palladian villa.

The museum contains a number of photographs that will interest railroad buffs. Among other memorabilia is a sign from the paymaster tree, where the train stopped to deliver checks to railroad employees in Beaver Canyon (near Spencer).

Pocatello railroad roundhouse and maintenance shops.

Union Pacific coaling station in Pocatello.

Proceed southeast to 441 So. Garfield St. to view the Kinney house, built in about 1900 by a prominent Pocatello sheep rancher; then turn northeast on Benton St. for two blocks and left onto Main St. Two blocks farther, make a right turn on Bonneville St., which ends within a half-block at the **Oregon Short Line depot.**

It is worth the brief walk to view the interior of this three-story passenger depot, opened in 1915 at a cost of $325,000. Former President William Taft attended the dedication.

Across the street from the depot is the Yellowstone Hotel, patronized by train passengers. The four-story building of maroon bricks with elaborate terra-cotta trim was built in 1916 for Messrs. Stanrod and Daniels.

Return to Main St. and continue northwest five blocks to Fremont St.; turn left one block to No. Arthur St., and drive southeast one block to Lander St. The first stone Episcopal church in Idaho is located on the southeast corner. Built in 1897-1899 of rock from Ross Fork on the Fort Hall reservation, it has oak furnishings, stained glass from Ireland, and embossed tin panels on the ceiling.

Follow No. Arthur two blocks more and turn northeast on Center St.; follow Center about twenty blocks to a connection with I-15, and continue north twenty miles to Blackfoot (see Highway 91, Blackfoot).

Interstate 15 continues northeast, 26.2 miles to **Idaho Falls,** through lava slag and scattered junipers, where a rattlesnake would be ashamed to meet his mother. (This stretch had the first paved roadway in the state.) To enter the city take Exit 118 east onto Broadway.

In 1864 James "Matt" Taylor was working on a branch of Ben Halliday's Overland Stage line between Salt Lake and Virginia City, Montana. About eight miles south of the Eagle Rock ferry crossing, while riding along the rim of the Snake River canyon, he noticed a spot where the gap was scarcely wider than a snowball toss. Aware that a bridge would be more expedient than the ferry, Matt continued north to Montana, where he persuaded Ed Morgan and Bill Bartlett to join him in a construction project. The trio hauled logs from Beaver Canyon, eighty miles south across the treeless plains, to Black Rock Canyon. Then Taylor went farther south and obtained a bridge and ferry franchise for the site from the Territorial Legislature.

The Oneida Road, Bridge, and Ferry Co. began work in January, 1865, when river ice allowed the partners to work on both sides of the rift. They built a Queen-truss span nearly sixty feet long; in old photographs, it recalls Vincent Van Gogh's painting of the drawbridge at Arles.

The bridge acquired the name of the Eagle Rock ferry upstream, and the settlement that collected at its east abutment also shared the name. As a business venture, Matt Taylor's bridge was a conspicuous success: he charged $4.00 for a team and wagon, and 19 million pounds of freight crossed its planks in 1867, from which Taylor and his pards realized $3,000 a month.

In 1872, when Taylor heard rumors of a Northern Pacific railroad expansion into Montana, he sold his bridge to the Anderson brothers, who were local merchants. Instead of the Northern Pacific, the Utah and Northern came north from Franklin in 1879 and bridged the river 150 feet downstream from Taylor's bridge. The Andersons gave the railroad 104 acres in Eagle Rock for an administrative site, and by 1882 the population of the settlement had grown to 670. (The bridge toll discouraged settlers and merchants from taking land on the west side of the canyon.)

Oregon Short Line bridge at Eagle Rock (note Taylor's bridge immediately behind it).

Five years later a major shift clouded the town's future. The U.P. moved its headquarters south to Pocatello – at least partly in reaction to Eagle Rock's sympathy with a local railroad strike – and in a single day converted 262 miles of the narrow-gauge line to standard rails, which made the town's repair shops for narrow-gauge equipment obsolete. The population declined; those who remained turned to agriculture.

In 1891 Chicago developers persuaded the citizenry to change the name of the village to Idaho Falls; no falls existed on the river at the time, but in 1911 the city built a diversion weir for a power plant and created a twenty-foot falls that validated the name. Incorporated in

144

1900, Idaho Falls became the seat of Bonneville County and the third-largest city in the state – two of the town's mayors became Idaho governors.

Begin a tour of the city from Broadway and Capital Ave. The city library, opened in 1977, has the highest per-capita circulation rate in the state; it is also the state's most attractive library. A parking area is located behind the building.

From the library walk west across Capital Ave. to see the bulb-turbine power installation located in the river canyon. It is one of three bulb-turbines operated by the city, and the only such municipally owned installation in the country.

In 1978, by an almost unanimous vote, the citizens of Idaho Falls

Idaho Falls in 1908.

approved a $48 million bond issue to replace city-owned Kaplan turbines with three bulb-turbines having an efficiency rating of 92 percent. The plants produce seven megawatts each and provide about 30 percent of the city's electrical needs. A new 1,800-foot diversion weir has been constructed, and a flow just sufficient to wet its face keeps the "falls" in Idaho Falls.

The lava rock abutments for Taylor's bridge can still be seen downriver from the new turbine plant. Utah and Northern's railroad bridge has been lost to a steel one, and the iron Broadway bridge, which was built when Taylor's became unsafe, has been replaced twice, most recently in 1982.

From the library, drive one block west on Broadway, and turn north alongside the river on Memorial Drive for six blocks, then curve left on Riverside Dr., jog left on Jackson St. and right on Fremont Ave. Follow Fremont beneath an overpass and four blocks farther to Keiffer Office Park on the left, where the three-story office building for EG&G Idaho, Inc., is located.

EG&G Idaho is a prime contractor for the Idaho National Engineering Laboratory (see Highway 20, EBR1). Designed by an architectural firm in New Mexico, this structure, which in 1980 won the Owens-Corning energy-conservation award, is the most energy-efficient office building in the country.

Employees in the building produce about 540,000 BTU's an hour. This heat, along with that from lights, is collected by ceiling ducts and transferred to buried storage tanks filled with 200,000 gallons of water. Divided into four compartments, the tanks can be used 50 percent for heating and 50 percent for cooling, or in any other combination for either function, and the heat provided maintains a comfortable interior temperature down to outside readings of minus six degrees F.

Lighting is provided by high pressure sodium lamps that require only 40 percent of the energy needed by conventional fluorescent lights. Additional illumination is furnished by a 5,900 square-foot skylight and by sunlight, which is reflected from downward-sloped, stainless-steel window sills, through windows set at a complementary angle, up to white ceilings.

Although EG&G's office space was increased by 300 percent, its energy costs were reduced by 33 percent, and, as engineers are quick to point out, no new principles were involved.

To visit a more traditional area of the city, return to Broadway and Capital Ave. Continue east on Broadway three blocks, cross the railroad tracks, turn left on No. Eastern Ave. two blocks to Cedar St., and east on Cedar to No. Ridge Ave.

The brown brick mansion at 371 No. Ridge was built in 1909 for Gilbert Wright, a millionaire who owned a flour and grain mill on the west side of the river. He later managed Consolidated Wagon and Machine Co. on Broadway at Capital. Wright's home is in a prestigious district, where many of the city fathers resided.

Turn south one block to 288 No. Ridge at Ash St. This two-story brick residence built in 1908 belonged to Minnie Hitt, cashier for Anderson Brothers Bank, and perhaps the first female teller in the U.S. The house is now a halfway home for children.

Two doors farther south, at the corner of No. Ridge and Elm, stands the Palladian-styled First Presbyterian Church, built in 1918 for $90,000.

Follow Elm St. east two blocks to South Blvd., turn left two blocks to Eighth St. and right one block to Eighth and Lee Ave. The house on the southeast corner, bracketed by rock walls, dates from about 1868, and was built by a Welsh mason as a stage stop on the Salt Lake-Butte, Montana, run; at that time what is now the front of the house was its rear. According to colorful tales that linger within its walls, it was once the city poorhouse as well as a bootlegger's supply point.

(Return to I-15 via Broadway).

I-15 travels north of Idaho Falls 13.3 miles past Roberts and after another eight miles passes a junction with Highway 33.

Six and one-half miles north of the Highway 33 junction is Exit 150 at **Hamer,** which leads four miles northwest to **Camas National Wildlife Refuge.**

The 10,000-acre site is an oasis in an otherwise bleak landscape, and its exuberance amid such solitude conveys an impression unlike that of any other refuge in the state. From spring through fall arrowheads of geese soar overhead, and ducks descend in sudden showers. Herons, egrets, cranes and swans nest here; raptors can be readily observed, and mule deer, antelope, beaver and muskrats frequent the area. The refuge is open dawn to dusk.

The railroad siding of **Camas** is five miles north of Hamer; in the 1880s it was the principal depot for lead bullion from the Birch Creek mines and had a population of 3,000 – the largest shipping point on the railroad between Ogden, Utah, and Butte, Montana. It is no longer even a whistle stop.

Dubois, 12.5 miles north of Camas, was named for Fred Dubois, Idaho's Senator from 1891-1897 and 1901-1907.

The town is the seat of Clark County, which has the smallest population of any county in the state; the area's history, some of which has been collected in the **Dubois Heritage Hall,** is that of livestock ranchers.

Five miles north of Dubois, at Exit 172, a road travels two miles east to the **U.S. Sheep Experiment Station,** visible from the highway. Visitors are welcome, but since research projects crowd

147

the calendar, tours must be arranged in advance.

To improve the production and quality of lamb meat and wool, the Sheep Experiment Station was established in 1916 by the USDA for research with range sheep. Programs are operated in cooperation with the Idaho Agricultural Station and with several other western states.

Approximately 6,000 Rambouillet, Targhee, Columbia, Polypay, and Finn Crossbred sheep are involved in the study. Areas of investigation include crossbreeding, nutrition, range improvement, wool preparation, disease control, and coyote eradication. The flocks use forty-four square miles surrounding the station for spring and fall range, then summer on 23,000 acres of Targhee National Forest to the north, and winter on feedlots in Mud Lake, south of the station.

A sale occurs here annually in September when high-quality breeding rams, ewes, and lambs from the experimental flocks are auctioned to ranchers concerned with improving their own flocks.

I-15 continues north 8.4 miles to **Spencer,** named for an OSL railroad official.

To visit the **Spencer opal mine,** take Exit 184, and after 200 yards turn north into the hamlet. A permit to dig at the mine, which is run by the Mark Stetler family, can be obtained at the gas station, along with directions to the digging area. The open pit mine is seven miles from Spencer, on a south-facing slope (elev. 7,000) above the dirt road to Kilgore.

Discovered by deer hunters in 1948, the deposit is well-known among rockhounds for the quality of its precious star opal, colored fiery red, green, yellow, pink, and blue. Equipment may be rented or purchased at the site, and washing water is available.

The **Camas Meadows battle sites** of the 1877 Nez Perce War are reached from the Spencer-Kilgore gravel road. Drive east-northeast, past the opal mine turn-off, eighteen miles to Kilgore.

To see the first battle ground, that of the soldiers' encampment attacked by the Indians, drive due south from Kilgore four miles to Idmon. Continue south on Red Road one mile farther, turn east 0.5 miles and cross Camas Creek. The camp was on the flat between Camas and Spring Creeks. General Howard's tent was pitched on the elevation forty feet above the meadow.

During the night of August 19, 1877, Looking Glass, Toohoolhollzote, and Ollokot lead a force of twenty-eight warriors back to the Army camp, where they arrived after moon-set at 4:00

148

A.M., intent on stealing the military's horse herd. A sentry called, "Who are you there?," a rifle went off, and the camp roused to an unceremonious reveille. In the pandemonium the Indians fled with the horses. Yellow Wolf recounted:

After travelling a little way, driving our captured horses, sun broke. We could begin to see our prize. Getting more light, we looked. Eeh! Nothing but mules – all mules! Only my three horses among them. I did not know, did not understand why the Indians could not know the mules. Why they did not get the cavalry horses. That was the object the chiefs had in mind – why the raid was made. The place where we took General Howard's mules is called Kamisnim Takin (Camas Meadows).

We looked back. Soldiers were coming! Some foot-running, others mounted. Then we divided our company. Some went ahead with the mules; others of us waited for the soldiers. Then we fought, shooting from anywhere we found hiding. A few warriors made a flank move, and from a low hill did good shooting. Peopeo Tholekt was one of those flankers. Soon those soldiers ran for a bunch of small timber not far away. They went fast. It was then we crept close and shot whenever we saw a soldier. What I saw of soldiers falling, I do not know. Earlier in the fight, a soldier with a bugle was shot from his horse at foot of small bluff and killed. Indians were on that bluff, protected behind rocks. It was a sharp fight for some time. After a while I heard the warriors calling to each other, 'Chiefs say do no more fighting!'

Then we quit the fight. No Indians was bad hurt, only one or two just grazed by bullets. We followed after the mule herd to camp. When we all reached there, the Indians made for those mules. Some took two or three, others took three or five. I did not know how many mules we got. All were kept for packing and riding, but the warriors did not ride them.

To see the bugler's grave, marked with a marble tombstone and surrounded by a metal fence, continue across Spring Creek 0.5 miles and turn north 0.5 miles; the grave is on the right.

Captain Randolph Norwood and L. Company, Second Cavalry, fought a four-hour battle with the retreating Indians later that morning (August 20). The easiest way to visit that location is to return to Kilgore and continue east on A2 Clarks County Rd. 5.8 miles to a cluster of ranch buildings on the left side of the road. Turn right, through a fence gate, and follow that dirt track 0.6 miles through several curves to a lava rock formation. The rifle pits on top of this formation can still be discerned.

(Return to I-15 or continue east through Targhee National Forest thirty-one miles to U.S. 20 in Island Park.)

Interstate 15 climbs north, past Forest Service campgrounds at Stoddard and Beaver Creeks, 15.5 miles to the Montana state line at **Monida Pass** (6,823 elev.). The name is a contraction of Montana and Idaho.

State Highway No. 16 from a junction with Highway 44 east of Star, northerly to a junction with Highway 52 south of Emmett. Route length: 13.9 miles.

Shortly after it leaves Highway 44, Highway 16 crosses a half-dozen irrigation canals carrying water from the Boise River.

Eight miles north of the Farmers Union Canal, the road tops **Freezeout Hill.** In 1862 Tim Goodale (see Highway 71) led a train of wagons down a steep ridge just west of the present highway, and across the Payette River near Emmett. His route became known on the Oregon Trail as Goodale's Cutoff. A remnant of the trail is still visible on the hill.

In the 1870s John Basye built the first grade over Freezeout. For many years the hill was known for its spring view of the Emmett mesa orchard blossoms.

Highway 16 intersects Highway 52, 0.8 miles south of Emmett's Main St.

State Highway No. 19 from the Idaho-Oregon state line west of Homedale, easterly via Homedale and Greenleaf to a junction with U.S. 30 in Caldwell. (Overlaps U.S. 95 for 4.2 miles.) Route length: 16.9 miles.

Highway 19 passes through farmland growing row crops and hops. (See U.S. 95, Homedale, Wilder.)

Greenleaf, midway between Wilder and Caldwell, was a Quaker community named for the poet John Greenleaf Whittier. Though less than half the town's population is now Quaker, it is still the site of Greenleaf Friends Academy, founded in 1908. In 1972 Greenleaf incorporated.

U.S. Highway No. 20 from the Idaho-Oregon state line near Nyssa, Oregon, easterly via Notus, Boise, Mountain Home, Fairfield, Arco, Idaho Falls, Rigby, Rexburg, St. Anthony and Ashton to the Idaho-Montana border near West Yellowstone. (Overlaps I-84 from Boise to Mountain Home for 39.7 miles and U.S. 93 from Carey to Arco for 44.2 miles.) Route length: 392.9 miles.

U.S. Highway 20 travels east 1.6 miles from the Oregon border to an intersection with U.S. 95, then south 5.6 miles to Parma (see U.S. 95, Parma).

Notus is 8.1 miles southeast of Parma, on the Boise River. The town's name is another of the anonymous-Indian railroad names; somewhere Notus is supposed to mean (cum grano salis), "It is all right." Until the OSL arrived in 1883 and erected a water tank on the site alongside its railroad tracks, the area was known as Lower Boise.

In 1886-1887 Howard and N. B. Sebree excavated an irrigation ditch, later known as the Farmers' Cooperative Canal, which put farming on a more reliable basis. The Black Canyon Dam in 1921, and the second unit of that reclamation project begun in 1940, gave Notus sufficient population to call itself a town.

The highway continues southeast 5.6 miles to an intersection with I-84 near Caldwell; it overlaps the Interstate 2.8 miles, then exits at southeast Caldwell, to resume its easterly course. After 2.2 miles, the highway passes just south of the Ward Massacre site on Middleton Road (see Highway 44, Middleton).

After 17.6 miles more, U.S. 20 enters Boise via Garden City, divagates four miles through town to I-84, travels southeast with the Interstate thirty-five miles to Mountain Home, and from Exit 95 resumes its course in a northeast direction.

Seven miles northeast of the exit, the highway meets the Oregon Trail and the junction of the old Kelton (Utah)-Boise stage road, as well as the Boise-Rocky Bar toll road. The junction was known as **Rattlesnake Station** and is marked by a state sign.

(To see the site of the Teapot Dome hot springs which were visited by emigrants on the trail and noted in 1843 by John C. Fremont, turn southeast three miles on the gravel road opposite the historical sign on the west side of the highway.)

Kelton road traffic was initiated in 1863 by John Hailey; his teams, traveling between nineteen stations established at intervals, could make the Kelton-Boise run in forty-two hours.

In the 1870s Commodore Jackson purchased the station at Rattlesnake Springs and used it as a ranch, then moved south to a 160-acre homestead on the site now known as Mountain Home when the OSL railroad arrived in 1883.

Fourteen miles north of Rattlesnake Station a road exits from the west side of the highway and leads five miles to **Anderson Ranch**

Dam on the South Fork of the Boise River. Completed in 1950 by the Bureau of Reclamation, the dam was built to supplement the Boise Irrigation Project. It is an earth-fill structure, 456 feet high, and 1,350 feet long.

Castle Rock Road leaves U.S. 20 five miles northeast of the Anderson Dam Road on the west side of the highway. It leads into an enchanting area of stone sculptures, at least one of which must have been the inspiration for Constantin Brancusi's *The Kiss.*

Follow Castle Rock Road 2.4 miles, then look left of the road at the large boulder just beyond the fence, where light lettering can be traced on the rock: PIANOS SAMPSON BOISE.

Charlie Sampson arrived in Boise from Oregon in 1906, penniless. He began selling Gramophones, and before long opened the Sampson Music Company on South Tenth St. in Boise – the business grew to a chain of seven stores.

One afternoon in 1914, while out trying to make a delivery in the sagebrush south of town, Charlie lost his way. The experience annoyed him, and on his return to Boise he suggested to city officials that the roads should be signed. When no one responded he decided to mark the main routes to Boise for himself; he carried a bucket of orange paint on his travels and striped rocks, poles, fences, bridges, barns, and old wagons – thus **Sampson Trails** were born. The task became a consuming hobby; nineteen orange trails, with black arrows, converged on Boise from as far away as Oregon, Montana, Utah, and Wyoming. The larger signs carried an ad for Sampson's company, but he enjoyed providing a service to an appreciative public, and tourists sent him thank-you letters from all over the country. During the summer he had a three-man paint crew out on the roads retouching signs, and spent several thousand dollars on his unusual "travelers' aid."

In 1933 the Department of Works, and the Bureau of Highways, with questionable motives objected to Sampson's efforts on the ground that he was defacing the landscape. The state legislature responded by passing a resolution "in recognition of a service rendered to the public" and granted Charlie "the right and privilege of marking and maintaining the Sampson trail on state and federal highways."

Sampson died in Boise in 1935 and was buried in Ohio, where he was born. The Idaho *Statesman* editorialized, "...it is a bit difficult to imagine the city without him; his death leaves a kind of void which will be apparent for a long time. Yes, we'll miss Charlie Sampson."

U.S. Highway 20 continues east over Cat Creek Summit (5,527 elev.), 16.2 miles to **Hill City** – in 1911 the terminus of the Oregon Short Line branch that came northwest across the Camas Prairie from Richland.

The road travels east 13.7 miles farther to **Fairfield,** the corm of Camas Prairie.

In 1967 the finest Clovis projectile points excavated in North America were found about six miles east of Fairfield, evidence the area served as an Indian gathering ground for nearly 11,000 years. Bannock-Shoshone bands used the region for harvest of camas bulbs until as late as 1940.

The **camas** *(Camassia quamish)* is a blue-flowered lilly with a succulent bulb; it was a staple of the Idaho Indian diet. The bulbs have considerable protein but no starch, and when baked their non-reducible sugar increases to 25 percent.

White encroachment on these camas beds, with herds of hogs that rooted out the bulbs, was the principal cause of the Bannock War of 1878 (see Highway 91, Fort Hall Reservation).

Once the Indians were safely confined to the reservation, small villages began to sprout on the prairie; it became the chief route from Boise to the Wood River mines at Bellevue and Hailey. The town of Soldier began in 1884, but the OSL branch passed two miles to the south in 1911, and New Soldier developed alongside the tracks. The name was soon changed to Fairfield; in 1917 it became the seat of Camas County.

Visit the **Camas County Historical Society Museum** by turning south into Fairfield two blocks on Soldier Road to the railroad depot building on Camas Ave.

On Highway 20, 3.0 miles east of Fairfield, turn east 1.9 miles on a gravel road to the **Minard School monument** on the west shoulder of the road.

The triangular, shingled plywood roof shelters a testimonial to the Minard teachers who educated the children of this area for almost forty years.

Jack Frostenson, with assistance from his father, built the memorial when he was a sophomore studying architecture at the Univ. of Idaho. He never attended the elementary school, but his father, uncle, aunts, cousins, brother and sister did. His grandfather had been a school trustee for nine years, his father was on the school board for twenty years, his mother and two aunts taught at Minard.

The unusual monument contains the school bell (which can be rung), the old pitcher pump, a niche with the names of the teachers from 1909 to 1948, and bricks from the school chimney preserved in the walkway. (The school itself can be seen one mile southwest of the memorial).

U.S. 20 travels east nineteen miles around the north end of Magic Reservoir (a Carey Act reclamation project built in 1907) to an intersection with Highway 75, then continues east 18.9 miles through **Picabo** and **Carey** to a junction with U.S. 26. The two highways overlap as they move northeasterly past Craters of the Moon 42.3 miles to Arco (see U.S. 26, Craters of the Moon, and U.S. 93, Arco).

The **only natural arch in Idaho** is located six miles from Arco, and if one is willing to hike a mile, he will find that the sight more than recompenses the effort. (Photographers will need a wide-angle lens.)

Frank Church Natural Arch. Front view (left), rear view (right).

At the main intersection in Arco, turn southeast on U.S. 20-26, 0.3 miles to South Front St. Turn east across the railroad tracks onto South Front and follow the curve to the left on the gravel road for 1.0 miles. Turn left (north) under the Utah Power and Light lines and follow the road 3.7 miles to the Godfrey ranch. Immediately after crossing the cattle guard into Godfrey's spread, make a right turn east and proceed 1.3 miles to a break in the fence line, where another road leads due north toward the mountains on the left side of the road. Follow this lane, fenced on both sides, 1.6 miles to a gate; open and close the gate. After another 0.8 miles veer left in

154

front of the log and hogwire corral. Take an odometer reading, and at 0.8 miles swing right on the sketchy road that angles off to the base of the mountain. In mid-summer the grass on this road is hood-high. The arch is clearly visible on the shoulder of the mountain ahead. Proceed slowly 1.2 miles to a dead end. From this point follow the trail uphill a mile to the base of the limestone arch, which is about seventy feet wide and sixty feet high.

Douglas fir, juniper, mountain mahogany, sage and rabbitbrush add color to a sweeping view of the Snake River Plains.

From Arco U.S. 20 continues south-southeast in the direction of Idaho Falls. Eighteen miles from Arco a sign on the south side of the highway indicates the turnoff for the **EBR-1 site,** a National Historic Landmark. Whether one is an advocate of nuclear power or an anti-nuke zealot, the facility deserves a visit. The red brick

Experimental Breeder Reactor – 1, now a National Historic Landmark.

building contains the inoperative Experimental Breeder Reactor-1, which on December 20, 1951, became the first power plant to produce electricity by using atomic energy. It is two miles from the highway, and open mid-June to mid-September, seven days a week. Admission is free.

The self-guided tour through the reactor explains in a non-technical manner a great deal about its workings. One can see the reactor, its fuel rods, the turbine, control room, rod farm, remote handling devices, and the hot cell with thirty-four layers of oil-separated glass used for inspection and repair of radioactive materials. In addition, three films on aspects of nuclear energy can be viewed.

The EBR-1 site is 51.3 miles west of Idaho Falls. As the highway proceeds east, it travels for about twenty miles through the 900-square-mile location of the **Idaho National Engineering Laboratory.**

The Reactor Testing Station, as it was once more clearly called, was established in 1949 by the Atomic Energy Commission. An Idaho Operations Office in Idaho Falls administers the INEL, which consists of nine different operation areas run by four contractors doing experimental work for the government. The operation areas engage in light-water safety reactor research, naval propulsion reactor development and training for atomic submarines, fuels and materials testing for light-water reactors, and nuclear waste-management research.

Since 1964 the University of Chicago's **Argonne Laboratory-West** has operated **Experimental Breeder Reactor II** here, but it can be visited only by prior arrangement. The reactor now tests fuels and materials needed for the next generation of breeder reactors, and it is the nation's only fast-reactor test facility.

Three other major facilities occupy the laboratory. The hot-fuel examination complex tests remote handling, examination and destruction of nucear fuels and material; the transient reactor facility does safety-tests in support of the breeder reactor program; and the zero-power plutonium reactor provides experimental data for the design of large fast-breeder reactor plants. (Because there is no power, the plutonium reactor can be cooled by a simpler forced-air system and operates to check calculations used by reactor designers.)

U.S. 20 extends east forty-nine miles to Idaho Falls where the highway interchanges with I-15, jogs north 0.5 miles and recommences northeasterly 12.7 miles to Rigby.

Rigby was settled in 1883-1884 by Mormons from the Cache Valley of Utah. The course of the Rigby canal was promptly surveyed because without water the land was useless. The Saints purchased the townsite for $20 and built a church; a few years later another settler jumped the land because there had been no compliance with the townsite law, and the citizens bought the site a second time for $250. Named for William Rigby, an LDS leader in nearby Driggs, the village was incorporated in 1903.

Rigby has the notable distinction of being the place where the cathode-ray tube (later known as the dissector tube) for television was invented.

Its inventor, Philo Farnsworth, born in Utah in 1906, moved with his parents to a farm four miles from Rigby when he was twelve. The farm had an electric generator, power hoists for the haybarn, and mechanical equipment with which the boy loved to tinker. He assumed responsibility for all motors on the place, and even wound an armature and field coils in order to make an electric motor for his mother's washing machine.

Philo rode a horse to the Rigby school, where his desire and ability admitted him to senior chemistry classes. The boy attended high school for only two years, but while there, he read a magazine account of television experiments and figured out how to produce an electrical counterpart of an optical image. Experimenters were using mechanical whirling disks to scan images; Farnsworth decided that would never work because it was too slow. One could focus an image through a camera lens onto a sensitized surface, he reasoned, then control, transmit and reassemble the electrons, which moved at the speed of light, to reproduce, without moving parts, a distant image.

Philo's teacher offered encouragement, and one afternoon after school, the youth spent a couple of hours drawing his concept of an image dissector on the blackboard. When his teacher walked in, the two of them studied the theory and discussed it. Both realized the student had surpassed his teacher.

Two years later the Farnsworth family moved to Provo, Utah. Though he had not finished high school, Philo took special extension courses in electronics at Brigham Young University.

At age nineteen he met two California businessmen who decided to help him; they took Farnsworth to Los Angeles and set up a lab in his apartment. A patent attorney from MIT, and an electro-physicist from Cal Tech, after meeting with the young inventor, declared his theories "scientifically sound, startlingly original and staggering in their implications."

When Philo Farnsworth obtained financing from San Francisco bankers, he applied for patents on his plans and set about learning metallurgy, optics, photography and glass blowing. He blew and formed the cathode-ray tube that received the first image ever transmitted by electronic television. Though eventually replaced by a tube 100 times brighter, Farnsworth's invention set the course of modern television.

In 1934 he signed a patent lease agreement with Baird Television in London, where spectators watched a fashion show, horse show and boxing match all televised from ten miles away. Germany leased his system next, and in 1939, after cross-licensing agreements were signed with Philco and RCA, Farnsworth's invention enabled NBC (a subsidiary of RCA) to transmit America's first television program from the New York World Fair.

As a director of nuclear research at the time of his death in 1971, Farnsworth had obtained over 300 patents for television, radar, and electronics, and had been awarded an honorary doctorate by Brigham Young Univ., as well as the first medal of the Television Broadcasters Assn.

Rexburg is 11.6 miles northeast of Rigby. In 1883, in a foot of snow, the townsite was surveyed into lots at the direction of William Preston, president of the Cache Valley Stake, and Thomas Ricks, who had been ordained bishop of the new Bannock Ward. Preston gave the Mormon colony the Latin root of Rick's surname.

Rexburg began with thirteen settlers, but by May of 1884 there were 875 persons and 1,600 plowed acres. Bannock Ward became

Rexburg, looking toward Ricks College (center), Bigler's Pharmacy (left) and State Bank (right).

Bannock Stake, and Rexburg became the seat of Madison County.

Ricks College, on the hill at the end of South Center St., two blocks off Main St., was established in November, 1888, at the recommendation of the LDS Commissioner of Education in Salt Lake City. The Saints had been disenfranchised by the anti-Mormon Idaho Test Oath, and the new Bannock Stake Academy was intended to educate children under the wings of their Church. School began with sixty students and three teachers in two rooms

158

of the First Ward meeting house. It was both grammar and high school, but the grade school was dropped in 1901, and the name was changed to Rick's Academy.

By 1916 two years of college were offered, and twenty years later the institution was given state accreditation. The LDS Church tried three times to give the school to Idaho as a junior college, but the bills were defeated in the state senate.

In 1949 Ricks became a four-year college; five years later it reverted to a junior college at the order of the Church President in Salt Lake City.

A fierce effort, sanctioned by the Church, to move the college to Idaho Falls was initiated in 1957, and 160 acres were purchased in Idaho Falls for the new campus. Through vehement local objections the decision was reversed in 1961.

In 1976, when the Teton Dam flood flattened the Upper Snake valley like a wet leaf, Ricks College served as a relief center for

Interior of Bigler's Pharmacy, 1920.

persons who practiced the Ninth Beatitude: "Blessed are they who clean up."

Unquestionably, the architectural attraction of Rexburg is its tabernacle at 17 No. Center St., one block off Main St. The gray stone church, with its twin towers, was begun in 1911; its cost of $33,000 was paid in one year by local contributions. Volunteers quarried the rock at a spot four miles southeast of town. The design is Italianate, but the undulating false gables reflect the Mission-style, also popular at the time. Seating capacity was 1,400.

159

In 1972 the tabernacle was added to the National Register of Historic Places, and since the area's stakes had outgrown the building, it was sold to the city in 1978 for $50,000 as a museum and meeting hall.

The city's portion was paid by a grant from the Preservation Office of the Department of the Interior. In 1976 extensive flood damage was done to the basement, which has now been converted to the **Upper Snake River Valley Historical Museum.**

The new city library is next door to the tabernacle. In 1960 Rexburg had completed the library at a cost of $35,000; destroyed by the flood, it was replaced with this $500,000 facility.

Another building worth seeing is the Brenner house at 51 So. First St. West, one-half block off West Main, behind the Safeway store. Brenner was a blacksmith, and his sandstone house with its corner turret, built in 1901, is a local landmark.

The highway doglegs 4.3 miles northeast to **Sugar City,** a town begun in 1903 by the Sugar City Townsite Co. of Salt Lake, which purchased 320 acres for a workers' community alongside a new beet sugar factory. (Lots were sold with restrictive covenants against the sale of liquor).

The factory was also a Salt Lake enterprise, controlled by Mormons who organized the Fremont County Sugar Company.

In 1904 the four-story plant, which cost nearly $1 million, was the largest beet sugar factory in the U.S.; a six-mile pipeline carried beet juice from the beet cutting plant in Parker to the Sugar City refinery. Beginning with a capacity of 700 tons per day, the factory grew to peak production of 43 million pounds of sugar in 1933. In 1942 labor shortages and acreage limitations under the Sugar Act caused the factory to close; beets were shipped to a refinery in Idaho Falls.

In 1976 Sugar City was devastated by the Teton Dam failure (see Highway 33, Teton Dam).

Northeast 7.2 miles from central Sugar City is **St. Anthony,** bisected by Henrys Fork of the Snake River and so named because an early settler found the rapids carried a faraway resemblance to the Falls of St. Anthony on the Mississippi at Minneapolis.

To visit the **highest sand dunes** in the state (perhaps the highest in the country, since they surpass those of Death Valley), follow No. Bridge St., 0.7 miles north through town to Fourth St. North; turn west on Fourth St., drive 3.7 miles, then instead of curving south to Parker, continue west one mile more and veer

160

north on Red Road three miles to **St. Anthony Dunes,** visible west of the road.

The dunes cover an area about thirty-five miles long and up to five miles wide. They consist of quartz sand deposited over perhaps a million years by the prevailing winds of the Snake River Plain; since the grains are not volcanic, they must have been carried from the mountains as alluvial deposits by the Henrys Fork, Teton and Snake Rivers. A 1979 USGS report states that the younger, transverse dunes range from 75 to 400 meters in height.

St. Anthony dunes.

Fred Coleman's taxidermy shop, St. Anthony, 1909.

From the sand dunes area one can easily visit the site of the first American fur post west of the Rocky Mountains, **Fort Henry.**

Return south on Red Road to the intersection with Fourth St. North extension. Continue across the extension road south three miles, and immediately after crossing Henrys Fork, note the monument on the east side of the road. Erected in 1937 by local Boy Scouts, it is approximately 1,700 feet west of the actual site.

Andrew Henry arrived at this location in July, 1810. Along with Captain William Clark, Manuel Lisa, and the Chouteaus, he was a partner in the St. Louis Missouri Fur Co. In charge of a trapping expedition of nearly 400 men, who had left St. Louis in 1809, he chose to winter in this area because his men had suffered multiple attacks from the Blackfeet on the eastern side of the Rockies.

Several log buildings were erected here along the river that bears his name, and a difficult winter was passed; the men were forced to eat their horses in order to survive. (A century later a stone was found on the site, with the inscription, "Al the cook but nothing to cook.")

In the spring Henry's party divided into three groups, and it is thought that Henry made his way northeast and down the Yellowstone River with forty packs of beaver, which he delivered to Lisa at the Mandan villages.

Andrew Henry remained intermittently active in the fur trade until 1824; he died in Missouri eight years later.

The Wilson Price Hunt expedition was guided to Fort Henry in October, 1811, by one of Henry's trapping parties. It was here Hunt's voyageurs constructed cottonwood canoes and took to the river, with disastrous consequences. (Read *Astoria,* by Washington Irving.)

(Return from this point to U.S. 20 via St. Anthony.)

Follow Highway 20, 13.9 miles northeast to **Ashton.** The town owes its existence to the Oregon Short Line, which shifted its tracks two miles west of Marysville to avoid being gouged by land speculators who set a high price on the right-of-way there. The first train arrived in January, 1906, and the village incorporated the next month. (In 1907 the railroad was completed to West Yellowstone.)

The settlement was named for chief engineer of the OSL, Bill Ashton, who homesteaded on the site along with his son.

Seven miles south of Ashton the highway ascends Big Bend Ridge, then a mile farther on the right encounters Road No. 164, which leads eight miles east into Anderson Mill Canyon and ends one-quarter mile from Lower Mesa Falls, a spectacular 114-foot cataract on Henrys Fork (see Highway 47, Lower Mesa Falls).

Exactly nine miles north of Ashton, Road No. 163 leaves the east side of the highway for **Sheep Falls** on Henrys Fork. Follow the main road 2.5 miles, then turn left on a fork that dead ends after 0.2 miles. Hike down one-quarter mile to the river and walk fifty yards downstream to a ten-foot cascade that drops over basalt ledges in the narrow canyon. Note the potholes cut in the rocks by high water.

Scrivner's Stage Line, Ashton to Pocatello.

As U.S. 20 travels north for the next twenty miles, it traverses the **world's largest recognized caldera,** the Island Park, which is roughly eighteen by twenty-three miles in diameter and which was first remarked by geologists in 1939.

A large shield volcano, with a gently sloping circular cone, occupied this area in Pleistocene time (an epoch that covers the last one million years); the best exposure of its pink rhyolite tuff is visible in the highway cuts three miles north Ashton.

As the large rhyolite ash flows erupted, perhaps one-half million years ago, the roof of the volcano's magma chamber collapsed to form the caldera. Vents within the crater flooded the floor with rhyolite, then a mixture of rhyolite and basalt, and finally, basalt alone. Late in the collapse period rhyolite domes were extruded in the west and south area of the rim.

The clearest evidence of the caldera is visible as a 1,200-foot scarp on the south and west rims – the highway climbs the scarp at Big Bend Ridge. The eastern semicircle on the right is buried beneath younger rhyolite flows from the Yellowstone Plateau and is therefore difficult to see.

US 20

Green Canyon Road is on the west side of the highway nine miles north of Sheep Falls Road No. 163. It leads 2.5 miles west-northwest to **Harriman State Park,** Idaho's newest park, located on the old 10,700-acre Railroad Ranch. In 1880 three controlling shareholders of the Oregon Short Line bought the land from homesteaders, and it became known locally as the Railroad Ranch. The owners incorporated as the Island Park Land and Cattle Co., but sold to the Guggenheim brothers in the early 1900s.

By 1911 Solomon Guggenheim, and the Union Pacific president E. H. Harriman had become joint owners.

Harriman died without ever visiting the ranch and left his share to his sons, Roland and Averell. In 1954 Solomon Guggenheim sold his interest to Roland Harriman and to Charles Jones, president of Atlantic Richfield Corporation; the Harrimans later acquired Jones' share.

About 3,000 head of steers and heifers were ranged on the ranch and adjacent Forest Service allotments; the stock was wintered on a second ranch in Lima, Montana, and on feed lots at Roberts, Idaho. In the 1940s horses were raised here for use at Sun Valley, a Union Pacific resort.

In a generous gesture, the Harrimans decided to give the ranch to the people of Idaho; in 1963, the state legislature accepted the gift, given with the stipulation that the welfare of wildlife is always to be the park's first consideration. Deeds were signed in 1977.

The donation was made, Roland Harriman said, "Because we all felt such lasting gratitude for our many years of a full life at the Railroad Ranch and because we just could not face the prospect of its becoming nothing more than an uncontrolled real estate development with hot dog stands and cheap honky-tonks and because we could foresee the necessity for preserving such property for the enjoyment of future generations."

The State Parks and Recreation Department developed a careful and reasonable plan for controlled use of the park, which was opened in 1982. The ranch contained thirty-one buildings, seventeen of which will be maintained. Hiking and fishing are permitted where they do not interfere with the management plan.

Elk, reintroduced into Island Park by the Harrimans in the 1930s, still frequent the ranch. Beaver and muskrat signs are evident; at least fifty pairs of sandhill cranes use the meadowlands, and trumpeter swans nest on Silver and Golden Lakes. (Henrys Fork River within Harriman State Park is the most important wintering area for trumpeter swans outside Red Rock Wildlife Refuge in Montana.)

164

Note: In July the mosquitoes and biting flies at the Railroad Ranch will win one's undivided attention.

Harriman State Park, Henrys Fork in foreground. The land was valued at $10 million.

North of Harriman 14.4 miles is an area on the Henrys Fork known as **Island Park.** Gilman Sawtell was the first settler here; he started a ranch near Henrys Lake in 1868, but the mosquitoes and horseflies drove his operation off its hinges. He then switched to lake fishing – netting and salting trout, which he sold to the miners in Virginia City, Montana. Sawtell Peak (9,866 ft.), visible seven miles northeast of Island Park, bears his name.

From 1919 to 1930 about 1,500 persons in the region were employed making ties for the Union Pacific railroad; a good tie-hack earned $20 a day.

The road to **Big Springs** resort area exits to the east just south of the bridge across Henrys Fork. It travels four miles to a spot that provides about half of the Henrys Fork water; the springs percolate west from the volcanic aquifer of the Yellowstone Plateau.

Henrys Lake State Park is 9.7 miles north of the Island Park Bridge. The west turnoff, indicated by a sign, travels two miles to the 586-acre park on the southern shore of the lake.

Henrys Lake was formed in the late Pleistocene by glacial action; it was enlarged in 1922 by a dam built on Henrys Fork, two miles from its source at the south end of the lake.

The site has seen its share of history: Major Andrew Henry's expedition discovered it in 1810; Jim Bridger camped on its shores with trappers and Flatheads in the fall of 1835, and again in the summer of 1838. In 1877 the Nez Perce bands of Chiefs Joseph, White Bird and Looking Glass built their fires on the southwest side of the lake twelve suns after the Battle of Big Hole; General Howard in pursuit of the Nez Perce arrived just behind them, and rested for three days here while fresh mounts and supplies were brought from Virginia City.

The state park was established in 1965; it is used primarily by trout fishermen, from Memorial Day until the end of October.

U.S. Highway 20 enters Montana at the summit of **Targhee Pass** (7,072 elev.) 5.2 miles north of Henrys Lake.

The Pass honors Tahgee, head chief of all the Bannocks; in an effort to maintain peace between the whites and his tribe, he met with the governor of Utah in 1863 and the governor of Idaho in 1867. Tahgee died in 1871.

The epic flight of the Nez Perce crossed this pass on August 22, 1877, going northeast to Yellowstone (see Highway 95, White Bird Canyon). Lieutenant George Bacon had been sent to guard the summit, but deciding the Indians must have gone over Teton Pass into Jackson Hole, left his post. General Howard arrived a day later, only to find his quarry had eluded him once again.

The pass also served the Fort Hall Shoshone as an access route on their annual migrations to the buffalo hunting area between the Musselshell and Yellowstone Rivers.

State Highway No. 21 from a junction with I-84 at Boise northeasterly via Idaho City, Lowman, and Stanley to a junction with Highway 75 at Stanley. Route length: 130 miles.

Highway 21 can be reached from Boise by driving southeast on Warm Springs Ave., or from I-84 at the Gowen Road Interchange, northeasterly via Gowen Rd., Federal Way, East Amity and So. Eckert Rd.

As it leaves the Boise Valley, Highway 21 follows the northeast shore of the **Boise River.** The 190-mile river drains 4,000 square miles of west central Idaho. It flows westward from the Sawtooth Mountains into the Snake River at a point twenty miles northwest of Caldwell.

On the southeast outskirts of Boise, Highway 21 intersects with the Barber Dam Rd., 4.3 miles from downtown Boise. The Barber Dam State Park is 0.5 miles southeast of the highway. It is a popular summer launch site for inner-tube float trips down the Boise River to Ann Morrison Park. Tubes for the two-hour float can be rented at the park, and a shuttle bus returns from Morrison to Barber at regular intervals.

From Highway 21, two miles southeast of the Barber Dam Rd., it is possible to see scars left by the **Oregon Trail.** Look south across the river, toward the mesa; the trail is visible as it angles down to the Boise Valley from the rimrock.

The mesa, Bonneville Point, is the location from which Bonneville's party in 1833 sighted and named the Riviere Boise: "Les bois, les bois, voyez les bois!" (the woods, the woods, see the woods!)

Less than a mile farther up the highway, is the **Boise Diversion Dam** at the head of the **New York Canal,** on the south side of the road. The dam and canal were a federal answer to a state prayer.

Settlers began to farm the Boise Valley in the 1860s because the gold miners in Boise Basin (thirty-five miles northeast of the valley) provided a market for crops. Irrigation from the Boise River was limited to short, direct ditches.

In the 1880s farms occupied 80,000 acres in the valley, but agricultural growth was hampered by lack of comprehensive irrigation systems. Recognizing the opportunity, New York investors incorporated as the Idaho Mining and Irrigation Company in June, 1882, with plans to develop a major canal from the Boise River to the Boise Valley. They knew the arrival of the Oregon Short Line, within a year or two, would remove a major obstacle from the path of regional development. There would be farmers eager to buy irrigated desert land, and a rail system willing to transport their crops. Some investors even believed surplus water could be used to placer mine the fine gold from Snake River sand, and thereby repay the cost of the canal.

The New York Canal was an ambitious proposition. The proposal called for a ditch, seventeen feet deep and forty-seven feet wide at the lip, that would flow for seventy-five miles and feed 5,000 miles of laterals, in order to irrigate 500,000 acres. The main ditch would be completed in five years, and project costs would not exceed $1.5 million.

Boise Diversion Dam and New York Canal, looking west down the Boise River.

In 1883 Arthur DeWint Foote, the company engineer, surveyed the main ditch and laterals in order to draw the scheme's promotional map. Foote planned to begin the canal in the river canyon three miles above the present headgate; he estimated the first three miles would cost $225,000, but those three miles would give the ditch its highest practical contour. The first canal was a smaller model intended to attract the Eastern capital necessary to build the full-scale version.

Construction of the canal became a most complicated endeavor. The venture was harassed by financial panics, competition, lawsuits and bankruptcy. At times Foote was so beleaguered by creditors he could do no more than maintain appropriation rights by keeping a four-man crew busy with wheelbarrows.

168

In 1890 W. C. Bradbury, owner of a Denver-based construction firm, contracted with the Idaho Mining and Irrigation Co. to extend the Phyllis Canal from the Nampa region into the western end of the New York Canal tract. Bradbury put thirty-five miles of that system into operation by 1891, and then began building the New York ditch, two years after its projected completion. He had several hundred men, and 250 teams of horses at work on the canal in March, 1891, with "every convenience in machinery that was possible," when a dispute between New York and British bondholders dried up Idaho

Repairs on the New York Canal.

Mining Co. funds.

For another four months Bradbury pushed ahead with his own funds. He had fourteen miles under construction, but less than half completed, when he had to halt. He had spent $386,000, and the canal was still three miles from Boise. In 1892 Foote withdrew from the endeavor, discouraged. Then came the Panic of 1893. The Phyllis Canal went into receivership.

Bradbury hired William Borah as counsel in 1894, and filed a mechanic's lien for $208,000 against Idaho Mining and Irrigation. The lawyer acquired all of the New York and Phyllis property for his client at a sheriff's sale.

Because assessment work lapsed, water rights to the New York Canal expired. Valley farmers decided to complete the ditch themselves; they organized as the Farmers' Canal Company and jumped the New York claim. They did agree, however, to purchase Bradbury's interest. All too soon they found themselves, like Pogo, "surrounded by insurmountable opportunities."

After litigation involving another enterprise, which in 1896 filed appropriation rights a mile upstream from the proposed New York diversion, Charles Fifer merged the competitors in 1899 into a new organization – The New York Canal Co. Stockholders were given water in proportion to their share holdings. The new company spent $125,000 and managed to get twenty-five miles of main ditch and laterals flowing by June, 1900. Ditch widths varied, however, and the flow never exceeded 240 cfs. By 1905 only 10,000 acres were under irrigation. Additionally, the rubble diversion dam had to be torn out and replaced each season.

Finally, the U.S. Reclamation Service (organized in 1902) undertook the Boise Project with funds to be repaid by water users under a low-cost, long-term loan program. The Service enlarged and extended the New York Canal and built the present sixty-eight-foot high diversion dam, which bypassed the difficult upriver stretch of canal. (It was on this canal project that Harry Morrison and Morris Knudsen met as foremen and forged a friendship that produced M-K Co., the internationally-known engineering firm in Boise.)

In February of 1909, 3,000 persons gathered at the dam to watch the New York Canal headgates open. Federal industry had succeeded where private enterprise had failed. The Boise Project now irrigates about 300,000 acres. (The canal ends at Lake Lowell near Nampa.)

The power plant on the south side of the dam was installed in 1912. Three generators produce a total of 1,500 k.w., and the energy was originally used for construction of Arrowrock Dam, fourteen miles upriver. The power was sold to the city of Boise when Arrowrock was completed.

Diversion Dam is one of the oldest federal power plants in the Northwest and still provides electricity for irrigation pumps on divisions of the Boise Project. The plant is listed on the National Register of Historic Places, and is open to the public from spring through Labor Day, 9:00 A.M. to 9:00 P.M.

Three miles southeast of the Boise Diversion Dam is the **Lucky Peak Dam** viewpoint, overlooking Discovery State Park. A road extends along the crest of the 2,340-foot-long, earth-fill dam.

Construction of Lucky Peak by the Army Corps of Engineers began in 1949 and was finished in 1955. The dam is 340 feet high

170

and cost $19 million. It has six flip-bucket discharge gates, which deflect water upward in a spectacular plume. The water at the gates is traveling about seventy mph; the release method reduces downstream erosion. (Idaho Power has plans to install turbines for power generators that will modify the plume.)

This dam serves irrigation, flood control, and recreational interests. During the summer, the reservoir is popular with boaters, swimmers, and fishermen, and prolongs the flow of the Boise River.

The **Arrowrock Dam** turnoff is on the east side of Highway 21, 6.1 miles from the Lucky Peak viewpoint. Turn right and follow the gravel road 5.8 miles to the base of the dam.

Although every effort was made to trench the New York Canal along the hip of the Boise Valley, its proponents were aware that the project would never fulfill its promise without a substantial reservoir upstream.

Arrowrock Dam under construction, 351 feet high.

Following passage of the 1902 Reclamation Act, farmers along the Boise River petitioned the Reclamation Service to build a large dam in order to extend the duration of their irrigation season.

In 1910 Reclamation drilled test holes at the Arrowrock location. On the basis of engineers' findings and geologists' confirmations, the site was chosen for the world's highest dam.

Elaborate preparatory work was required. The Service established a seventeen-mile, standard-gauge railroad to Barberton, Idaho, a sawmill fourteen miles above the damsite, a construction camp for 1,500 men, a power plant at the Boise Diversion Dam to run machinery, and ran fifty-four miles of telephone line connecting worksites with the project office in Boise.

In 1911 construction began. The principal task was emplacement of 600,000 cubic yards of concrete. Every two hours, a sixteen-car train arrived at the damsite from the gravel pit thirteen miles away. Aggregate and cement were combined and delivered through three-inch pipes by compressed air to mixers that prepared a two-ton batch every minute. The concrete was carried in small electric cars through a tunnel to the distribution tower. A cable-way carried buckets from the tower to hoppers above the forms; they operated sixteen hours a day during the week. The dam was a four-year project, and all engineers and laborers were on the federal payroll.

The completion of Arrowrock Dam was a landmark in the history of irrigation. The reservoir surface is 3,100 acres.

Idaho City is 21.4 winding miles northeast of Boise on State Highway 21. It lies west of the road.

About five miles south of Idaho City, one begins to encounter the extensive despoliation left by dredges – dredges that gave the land, to use John McPhee's phrase, "a century's fouling and the century isn't over yet."

Dredging began in 1898 and continued, with a few belches, until 1952. The largest dredge to work the area belonged to Colonel Winthrop Estabrook, an engineer from Boston, with a Harvard degree. The Estabrook dredge was the world's largest. Each year it worked day and night until winter froze the bucket line.

Fred Baumhoff's smaller Mickey Mouse dredge also worked the creeks, until it was dismantled and shipped to Bolivia where it was never reassembled.

A road sign points to Idaho City. This sleepy little town, with its grid four blocks by four, was once larger than Portland. It was, in fact, the largest town in the Pacific Northwest.

In August, 1862, a prospecting party with Moses Splawn, Dave Fogus and George Grimes discovered placer gold about seven miles northwest of what is now Idaho City. Grimes was shot, perhaps by Indians, and the party returned to Walla Walla. Their news made the area, known as Boise Basin (eighteen miles square), the scene of the biggest gold rush since California's Mother Lode.

172

The party returned from "the two Wallies" in October, and founded Pioneer City (Pioneerville), known to latecomers as Hogem. Three other camps soon studded the creekbanks: Placerville, Centerville, and Bannock City, which was renamed Idaho City by the Territorial Legislature.

The Basin was part of Washington Territory in 1862; the mines were in Idaho County. In 1863 the Washington legislature established Boise County because the Idaho County seat at Florence was too distant for Boise miners. (At that time only six states in the Union were as large as the new county.) When Idaho became a Territory, separated from Montana in 1864, Boise County still contained 80 percent of the Territorial population.

Idaho City, at the confluence of Elk and More's Creeks, had a more plentiful water supply than the other camps and consequently outgrew them. Among the 200 usual businesses (three dozen saloons, two dozen law offices) were a few unusual ones: two bowling alleys, a mattress factory, a bookstore, a painter's shop, a photographer's gallery, two jewelry stores, and a hospital of sorts. The two main streets were described as each a half-mile long. A census reveals that among the town's 6,200 residents there were 360 women and 224 children.

On Sundays, a correspondent recorded, "the miners swarm into town from their camps, and render the day exceedingly lively, especially as they purchase most of their supplies then, and do up their drinking for the week."

Another visitor made this wry observation: "... the dirtiest men I ever saw, living in cabins with dirt floors and seldom washing, and all showing high water marks under their chins and jaws, below which water never touched."

In 1864 the *Boise News* described the camp at night:

A night scene in the Boise mines is as brilliant and magnificent as any similar spectacle to be met on the green earth. We counted more than thirty mining fires on Tuesday evening from a single standpoint in front of our office door. The ringing of shovels as the auriferous gravel slides from the blade, is distinctly audible above the murmur of the water in the sluices, conspiring with the haze and smoke through which the mountains beyond are dimly visible to render the scene most interesting and lovely.

All the fires viewed at Idaho City were not so picturesque. Lamps, candles, and woodstoves frequently caused extensive damage. Idaho City burned four times: 1865, 1867, 1868, 1871. Losses from the first fire were estimated at $1 million.

By 1870 most readily worked streams had surrendered their treasure. Water ditches several miles long were developed to wash placer deposits at higher elevations. Hydraulic giants hosed cliffs of aggregate down into sluice boxes. The Chinese began to arrive in Idaho City at this time, and eventually accounted for half the population.

A few quartz-lode claims were discovered, and along with reworked placer diggings, carried the camp through ebb tide for another decade. Boise Basin, including dredge operations, produced about 30 million ounces of gold.

Idaho City Stage.

Idaho City Stage

Tour Idaho City by driving north on Montgomery St., one block west of Main St. Drive north three blocks, past the old houses, to Wall St. Turn west on Wall. On the left is the white, two-story Masonic Temple, Idaho Lodge No. 1 AF & AM. The lodge received its charter in 1864, and the building was erected in 1865, after an earlier one burned. The lodge organization moved to Boise in 1920, but meets here in June each year. It is the **oldest Masonic hall west of the Mississippi** still in use.

The Ancient Free and Accepted Masons is a fraternal order descended from the guilds of European stoneworkers who labored on cathedrals. The Lutheran Reformation dampened cathedral construction, and the guilds (or lodges) became partly social. Membership was opened to non-tradesmen.

In 1717 the first four fraternal lodges were united under the Grand Lodge of England – the beginning of the society. The order spread rapidly to other countries. The first American lodge was chartered in Boston in 1733, and the order followed the covered wagons westward; about half of the grand lodges in the western states were formed before the states themselves. Membership reached 4 million, but has now declined.

Freemasonry is intended to promote brotherhood and morality among its members. The society does not solicit candidates. Membership requires belief in a Supreme Being – "The Great Architect of the Universe" – and good moral character. The secret symbols and rituals are based on the practices of the building

Idaho City pack train in 1910 loaded with supplies for the sheep camps.

trades. Members earn degrees by learning moral lessons and participating in ceremonies which illustrate them.

Masons spend millions of dollars annually for hospitals, and homes for the aged, for charitable relief, and for scholarships.

West of the lodge, on the same side of the street, is the Idaho Territorial Penitentiary. Built in 1864 for $10,000, the jail at that time was surrounded by a board fence and served both Idaho Territory and Boise County.

Before being superseded by the Boise penitentiary, this prison received 106 convicts. Twenty-six were discharged or paroled, and seventeen escaped and were never recaptured. (There was one guard per twelve-hour shift.)

The log building was moved from a site west of the city in 1930, then moved to the present location in 1953 by the Sons and Daughters of Idaho Pioneers.

Return to Montgomery St. The brick building with iron shutters, at the southwest corner of the intersection, is the **Boise Basin Museum.** It is housed in the James Pinney bookstore and post office (Central News Depot), built in 1867 to replace a post office destroyed by fire.

Turn north on Montgomery. The small, gap-boarded structure next to the park, at 511 Montgomery, was built in 1870. It was the Idaho City fire station, and served as the Boise County jail from 1920 to 1930.

At the north end of Montgomery St., turn right and then drive south on Main St. The white, three-story clapboard building on the west side of the street was originally the town's schoolhouse. A new

First penitentiary, Idaho City.

school was built in 1962; the old one serves as city hall and community church.

At Main and Wall Sts. the county recorder and auditor's offices are in the brick structure on the left; the building once contained a saloon and the Miner's Exchange. Miners traded their gold dust for legal tender.

Across the street is the county assessor's office and the district's courtroom. The building was originally a general store, then a hotel, before becoming county courthouse in 1909.

One block south, at the corner of Main and Commercial, on the east side of the street, is a building that was quarters for the *Idaho World* from 1867 to 1918.

The one-story brick structure with four arched doorways, on the west side of the intersection, harbored the Boise Basin Mercantile – among Idaho's oldest general stores.

Turn east on Walulla St., drive past High St. two blocks, uphill, and curve left to the white, wooden church. St. Joseph's Catholic Church was built in thirty days, after the 1867 town fire.

Two doors north of the church is the Independent Order of Odd Fellows hall. Established in 1864, the two-story, board and batten building is Pioneer Lodge No. 1, the **oldest Odd Fellow shrine west of the Mississippi.**

Hydraulic mining at Idaho City.

The origin of the society and the source of its name can no longer be traced. The society began in England during the eighteenth century, and at that time almost rivaled the Masonic fraternity. The Odd Fellows were first mentioned by name in 1778.

The American order was founded in 1819, and was affiliated with the Manchester Unity of Odd Fellows until 1842, when it established the Independent Order of Odd Fellows.

The IOOF is a self-governed, secret, benevolent and provident fraternity. It has stated weekly and funeral benefits, and a policy of payments to members who become disabled. Every grand lodge sponsors one or more homes for the aged.

21
IDAHO

HISTORICAL
SITE

Return to Main St. and drive north to see the gashed landscape left by the miners. Travel Main St. until it becomes Elk Creek Road; follow Elk Cr. Rd. 0.5 miles to its end at the base of bluffs skinned by hydraulic nozzles. Boulders, washed free of the gravel, rest in piles; a few pieces of riveted pipe are evident.

Drive back to the north end of Main St., and turn west on the Centerville Road. The road branches just after it crosses Elk Creek; take the left limb 0.4 miles uphill to Pioneer Cemetery. There are about 200 graves here; many are enclosed by elaborate wooden or iron fences.

Idaho City dredge in 1900.

Return to the Centerville Rd. Travelers interested in seeing the other mining camps of Boise Basin can continue northwest on dirt roads to Placerville (13.1 mi.), Quartzburg (16.2 mi.), Centerville (10.2 mi.) Pioneerville (17.3 mi.), and over Grimes Pass down across the South Fork of the Payette to Garden Valley (26 mi.). The Garden Valley Rd. leads west, ten miles to Banks on Highway 55, or east twenty-three miles on gravel road to Lowman at Highway 21.

Those who make this drive will find that the towns which are described below are only embers now.

New Centerville: 7.0 miles from Idaho City. This location was the terminus of the **Intermountain Railway.** In 1914 the Boise Payette lumber company obtained timber rights to 12,000 acres of state land in this area, and owned in fee an additional 200,000 acres of forest land. The company built a railroad in 1915 from Arrowrock Junction on the Boise River (where the U.S. Reclamation Service

178

track served the Arrowrock damsite) to New Centerville. The line
cost $317,000. Until 1926 logs were hauled by train from New
Centerville to the Barber mill, six miles southeast of Boise. After the
closing of the Barber mill in 1934, the railway was liquidated. (In
1957 Boise Payette became Boise Cascade.)

Placerville: 6.1 miles northwest of New Centerville. This was
the first camp encountered by miners and freighters who entered
the Boise Basin via the Payette River and Harris Creek. Because of
its advantageous location, the settlement grew rapidly – to 3,200 by
September, 1863.

*Placerville, late
1880s.*

During some years, lack of water stymied the miners at
Placerville. In 1869, however, ditches and flumes accommodated
twenty hydraulic giants which all operated within a mile of the
camp. Granite Creek ran thick enough to plow.

Gradually, Placerville's fortunes diminished. The population at
present would not fill a jury box. The Magnolia Saloon, once a fancy
bar, contains the **Henrietta Penrod Museum.** Summer homes
have been built within sight of the old Emmanuel Episcopal
Church, the Boise Basin Mercantile, and a post office-store.

The community cemetery is one mile south of Placerville. It
shelters a grave with a stout yellow pine growing at each corner.
The small concrete slab carries this inscription: "Fiddlers murdered
in Ophir Creek." Here is the story.

Two fiddlers played for a dance at Placerville; the next day they walked toward Centerville to fiddle at that camp's dance. En route they apparently stumbled upon the murder of a miner who had been carrying gold. The murderer then killed the fiddlers.

When the three bodies were discovered, the whole Basin was outraged. John Williams and two of his cronies were arrested for horse theft. On the basis of a conversation overheard in a flophouse, Williams was charged with the murders. Though the evidence was meager, the public was inflamed. The district court found the suspect not guilty.

Then a special grand jury charged Williams with assault and robbery. Williams' lawyers argued that their client had not committed a crime because in 1863 Idaho had no criminal law. In the Organic Act of Idaho Territory, Congress had failed to specify continuation of the old Washington Territorial code, or to legalize existing laws in the newly established Territory of Idaho. Idaho therefore had no criminal code until the Territorial Legislature passed the Criminal Practices Act one year later. The Idaho Chief Justice had to discharge the prisoner.

Once Williams was released, he disappeared like a tomcat with his tail on fire. No one was ever indicted for the murder of the "three" fiddlers.

Quartzburg: 3.0 miles northwest of the Placerville intersection at Ophir and Granite Creeks. In 1864 W. W. Raymond set up a ten-stamp mill on Granite Creek and developed the Gold Hill claim. This mine propped the camp for several decades. A forest fire in 1931 destroyed all but one building. Quartzburg is dead as last year's leaves among the tailing dumps.

Centerville: 3.2 miles north of New Centerville. The camp was midway between Idaho City and Pioneerville. Located on Grimes Creek, it was described as the most attractive of the Basin towns – a curious judgment amid the gash and gouge of the miners' frontier.

The settlement was founded in 1862, and swiftly acquired 3,000 residents. Five years later a large ditch was completed from Grimes Pass to the town, and placer mining hit fourth gear.

The Centerville graveyards are half a mile west of town, on the old Placerville road. "After the game the king and the pawn go in the same box" – but the Protestants are buried on the hill to the south of the road, and the Catholics on the hill to the north.

Pioneerville: 7.1 miles north of Centerville. Only a half-dozen buildings survive in this town, which once had 2,700 residents. Pioneerville was the "discovery" camp. In 1862 members of the

Splawn-Grimes party staked claims while their pards went to Walla Walla for supplies. When other miners arrived and found the ground staked, they dubbed the location Fort Hogem.

Pioneerville had the first post office in Boise Basin.

Pioneerville in 1902. Miner is using a hydraulic "giant."

The road climbs to **Grimes Pass** (5,099 elev.). George Grime's memorial is here, on a path 200 feet from the road. Traces of a flume can also be detected. The summit gives a good view of the Payette River's southern drainage. Below the pass, the road drops steeply to the South Fork, crosses the river, and arrives in Garden Valley.

From Idaho City, Highway 21 follows More's Creek, and the evidence of miners' ditches up to More's Creek Summit (6,117 elev.), where the evidence frays out. Five miles north of the summit, USFS Road No. 384 leads east forty-one miles to **Atlanta.**

HISTORICAL SITE

The road is hardpan, acceptable for passenger vehicles, and can be followed from Atlanta twelve miles south to Rocky Bar, then twenty-eight miles farther south, through Featherville and Pine, to State Highway 20, near Hill City. The details follow.

USFS Road No. 384 is well-signed. It travels past dredge combings up Crooked River and Willow Creek, then descends Little Owl Creek to the North Fork of the Boise River.

Turn left at the T, onto USFS Road No. 327, and go east up the North Fork and south down Swanholm Creek to an intersection with the Middle Fork of the Boise River.

About eight miles west of this point the old **Goodrich Trail** from Idaho City to Rocky Bar crossed the North and Middle Forks. In 1865 a traveler on horseback took this swipe at the trail:

... The North Fork is crossed on a very good bridge, the owner of which receives toll for both rivers, whereas the Middle Fork you must cross the best you can, at risk of life of man and beast; and yet you are charged toll. Oregon, Washington, and Idaho Territories are famed for their toll-bridges and toll-gates; you travel for hours over hard and dangerous roads, and come to a patch of ground sufficiently level for the erection of a gate and a small cabin, where you pay toll and proceed 100 yards only to find a road similar to the one ridden over; but two or three times in the course of a day you will come to another 'clearing,' another cabin and gate, and by this means you are enabled to remember the level parts of the country.

Follow the Middle Fork east upstream seventeen miles on USFS Road No. 268. About 1.5 miles west of Atlanta, on the south side of the road, is a log-crib dam, forty-six feet high. The dam and power plant (on the Middle Fork of the Boise) were built in 1906 for $100,000 by the Atlanta Mines Co. The plant was used to power the company's 150-ton stamp mill, and to operate the Monarch mine's air compressor and hoist. In 1907 the company provided the town with its first electricity, and the plant still lights Atlanta. The 550 h.p. plant has horizontal turbines and generators, a design which disappeared in the early 1900s.

The road bridges the Yuba River just east of the dam. **Greylock Mountain** (9,317 feet), which is inside the Sawtooth Wilderness, can be seen to the northeast. The mountain's name is reportedly a modification of Greyrock, adopted from Chinese miners who pronounced *l* more readily than *r*.

Development of the lode at **Atlanta** was slower than the Second Coming. In the summer of 1863 (possibly 1864) a party led by John Stanley, for whom Stanley Basin is named, found encouraging color on the Yuba River, two miles west of what is now Atlanta, and organized a mining district there. By mid-October a hundred miners were at work.

In November an extensive quartz-gold deposit, 1½ miles long and about twenty feet wide, called the Atlanta lode, was discovered just east of the Yuba River, and though claims were staked, winter prevented further assessment.

The name was given by Confederate miners to celebrate General Hood's victory over General Sherman at Atlanta; the news proved to be inverted rumor, but the name stuck.

When winter thinned away and miners emerged like groundhogs, further discoveries were made, but it became obvious development of the claims would depend on stamp mills. However, there were Gordian complications. The lode was far larger than the veins at Rocky Bar, but more inaccessible. Though miners tried to determine the extent and value of the ore, no suitable recovery process had yet been invented. Atlanta ore was high in silver, but the few mills hauled into the area, although capable of capturing gold from highgrade ore, lost three-quarters of the values when the silver was allowed to pass through the amalgamator like straw through a horse.

In 1868 British investors risked $800,000 on the Lucy Phillips mine in Atlanta. The Monarch Mining Co., with Indiana investors, purchased 775 feet of the Atlanta lode for $275,000. A summer road was pushed through from Rocky Bar, and several small mills were assembled. Even without reduction of the silver, the ore paid $60 a ton, but a better process was needed. The Lucy Phillips went belly-up.

Promoters and their ballyhoo did not help matters. In 1871 a resident griped:

This country has been infested with a set of "bilks" as trifling as ever cursed any quartz country. They play themselves off on the hard working miners as capitalists who have, or control large sums of money, and bum their way into some wild cat, bogus quartz, then get a little provisions and tools, and leave the boys to work for them on jawbone, which is mighty current in this camp. They go on to New York and London, and try to foist their bogus stuff off on the market. These bilks bring our real resources into disrepute, and they have been a great drawback on the camp. Thank God, they have none of the good ledges in this camp, and they will not get them unless they can show something more substantial than jawbone . . .

Surface work stuttered along through the 1870s. Some ore was shipped to Salt Lake and Omaha for more effective treatment, but lack of transportation and technology continued to halter development. In 1874 New York investors acquired a portion of the lode that was called the Buffalo, and financed a mill that went into operation three years later. (It handled ore from Yankee Fork mines, as well.) The Monarch was leased, and in 1878 the lessees began to process high-grade ore. Atlanta's population swelled to 500, and there was a flurry of mining from 1878 to 1884. But once the high-grade ore had been quarried, activity tapered. There was simply no economical way to work the large, low-grade deposit.

183

In 1891 the major Atlanta claims were merged and sold to London capitalists for $3.5 million. The new owners encountered the old recovery problem and were unable to solve it.

Finally, the St. Joseph Lead Company purchased the claims, and in 1932 began to operate an amalgamation-flotation concentrator. This method severed the knot of the Atlanta lode. In 1936 a road from Boise resolved transportation difficulties.

The Atlanta Mining District became Idaho's leading gold producer from 1932 to 1936. After World War II the Talache (one mile from Atlanta) became the state's principal gold mine. When it closed in 1953 Atlanta's mineral production had reached $16 million. (The town also processed $330,000 worth of antimony from 1947 to 1953.)

Freight sleds arrive in Atlanta.

Atlanta (date unknown).

184

Drive east through the town of Atlanta, and continue for a short distance to the Power Plant recreation road. Follow the road one mile to several undeveloped hot spring pools at the edge of the road, available for bathing. After a bath return to the Power Plant-Atlanta road intersection and turn left, on the gravel road that goes 0.8 miles uphill to the **Talache mine** and mill. The operation shut down in 1953.

Rocky Bar can be reached from Atlanta by the longer and easier USFS Road No. 156 that travels south from the intersection on USFS Road No. 268, seventeen miles west of Atlanta. However, the shorter and more interesting drive begins 0.2 miles east of the previously mentioned log-crib dam.

This is the old Boiler Grade Pass road; the first three miles are a bit like the Rock Island Line: "You got to ride it like you find it." James Creek Summit (7,543 elev.) is reached after six miles, then the road descends another six miles along Boiler Creek to Rocky Bar.

Prospectors from Boise Basin traced colors up the Feather River, and then in 1863 filed quartz-lode claims in the Rocky Bar region. About 100 miners worked the area around Bear and Steel Creeks that fall.

The 1863 census reveals South Boise mines had a population of 560, which made the region only slightly less important than Warren's diggings and Silver City, but of more consequence than Elk City, Pierce, or Florence.

The geology of the Rocky Bar basin (South Boise) was misunderstood; as a result claims were staked improperly and as always, lawyers skilled in circumvention of the law, profited.

The remoteness of the camp hindered Rocky Bar's development, but the South Boise Wagon Road Co. began building a toll road to the Bar from the South Fork of the Boise River, near Featherville, and completed it in September, 1864. Six stamp mills were hauled in that fall, one was freighted from St. Joseph, Missouri at a cost of $8,400; another came from Portland in forty-five wagons for $40,000.

No one took the trouble to block out the ore at Rocky Bar. A few rich surface pockets had been milled in arrastres (a circular pit in which a horse or mule drags a stone over broken ore and pulverizes it). Ore sent out to San Francisco and Portland assayed favorably, but the samples were not characteristic nor was the depth of the vein known.

Mills were in production by late 1864, and by spring, 1866, South Boise had more stamp mill capacity than any other Idaho district. There were, however, difficulties brought on by over-promotion and under-production. The largest mine, the Elmore, partly owned by Henry Comstock, required pumps to keep its shafts from flooding. Shallow deposits played out and created consternation among mining speculators. Investors pulled the pin. By 1870 a lot of miners had given up on Rocky Bar, and though the town kept the county seat until 1882, Lazarus had a stronger pulse.

Then in 1885 its pulse revived. British capital and more advanced techniques solved the problems of economical, large-scale production. The Elmore's best years were 1886 to 1892. Approximately $6 million was recovered from the area. In 1892 a fire swept the Bar. Within a couple of decades the town was as empty as a hog trough at sunrise.

Rocky Bar was for a time the home of Peg Leg Annie McInyre. In May, 1896, Annie and a friend, Emma "Dutch Em" von Losch, left Atlanta on foot for Rocky Bar. A blizzard ambushed them en route. When the storm abated after two days, a search party was organized. Annie was found deranged and crawling on the snow. Her friend Em was found, swathed in Annie's spare garments, frozen.

Dr. M. Newkirk came eighty miles from Mountain Home to help. He had to amputate Annie's feet.

Peg Leg Annie lived at Rocky Bar for several years. She supported herself by doing laundry and selling whiskey. She died in 1934, and is buried at Morris Hill in Boise. Her cabin still stands.

The gravel road from Rocky Bar travels ten miles south to **Featherville.** Featherville, also known as Junction Bar, was a stage station on the road to Rocky Bar. The area was dredged from 1922 to 1927.

The road is paved from Featherville through **Pine,** around to the east edge of Anderson Ranch Reservoir, then graded the last miles to the intersection with State Highway 20.

Lowman is 33.8 miles northeast of Idaho City on Highway 21. Nathaniel Lowman was the area's first homesteader.

The town did not receive telephone service until 1982. Long distance calls are transmitted via microwave to the Cambridge Telephone Co. relay station at Mesa, Idaho.

During the winter, Highway 21 is closed north of Lowman to Stanley. The road is usually opened on Memorial Day.

*Early travelers
(1923) on the Idaho
City - Lowman
road repair a flat
tire.*

Kirkham Hot Springs is a USFS campground on the south
side of the highway, four miles east of Lowman. There are rock
pools along the south bank of the South Fork of the Payette, as well
as four tubs with piped hot water in a campground shelter. The tubs
are free; they represent the last bargain available from the Forest
Service in the West.

The **Grandjean** turnoff is indicated by a sign on the east side of
the highway, eighteen miles from Kirkham. A five-mile drive down
the gravel road brings the traveler to a series of hot spring pools on
the south side of the road.

The **Sawtooth Lodge** is another mile east on the same road. It
has a hot spring, along with a restaurant, RV hookups, and log
cabins for summer guests and fall hunters.

The Grandjean area is named for Emil Charley Grandjean, who
was born in Copenhagen, and whose father was Chamber Councilor
of Forestry to the King of Denmark. Emil immigrated to Nebraska in
1884, then to the Wood River Valley, near Hailey, Idaho. In order to
live as a fur trapper, in the 1890s he moved to the spot that bears
his name. He became Idaho state supervisor of forestry and
supervisor of the Boise National Forest. Emil Grandjean died in
1961.

About fifteen miles north of the Grandjean Rd., there is a sign on
the west side of the highway for the road to **Dagger Falls.** The
gravel road, through Bear Valley, flows across wide meadows of

wildflowers twenty-three miles to the headwaters of the Middle Fork of the Salmon, a National Wild River.

The road to Dagger Falls was cleared in 1958-1959 for construction-crew access to a fish ladder built along the edge of the falls. Though salmon had migrated up the Middle Fork to Bear Valley for over a thousand years, the U.S. Fish and Wildlife Service decided the fifteen-foot drop at the falls was an obstacle to fish migration, and spent $181,000 to "improve" the passage. Army Corp of Engineer and Bureau of Reclamation dams, which *are* an obstacle to fish migration on the Columbia and Snake Rivers, have devastated the chinook salmon runs, but sometimes in early July it is still possible to see an occasional salmon lunging homeward up the falls, back from years at sea and an 800-mile journey up four rivers.

Stanley is on Highway 21, twenty-four miles southeast of the Dagger Falls road. Five miles before one reaches the town, the **Sawtooth Mountains,** like the rakers and gullets of a Great American felling saw, are visible along the south side of the highway. Beneath this ragged granite wave, Stanley looks like an Albert Bierstadt painting, or at very least, a "Come to Idaho" poster.

Stanley on a summer Saturday night is as wild as the mountain scenery. A roisterous western band draws boatmen, cowboys, loggers, hay-buckers, dudes, and anyone else who happens along, to town for the Stanley stomp. Saloons, stores, and a hotel front on an unpaved main street called Ace of Diamonds. Stanley has been profiled by the *New York Times* and front-covered by the *National Geographic.* Its raffish character is written on its face.

In 1824 fur trappers under Alexander Ross of the Hudson's Bay Company discovered **Stanley Basin.** The scarcity of beaver caused other trappers to avoid the area until 1831, when William Ferris marched up the Salmon River and camped in the Basin for ten days. He clubbed salmon in the streams for food, but found the same streams more bereft of beaver than when Ross' party waded through. The Ferris brigade left the area with the remark that their "visit to this now interesting country was a complete failure ..."

John Work brought his Snake River trapping expedition through Bear Valley and Stanley Basin in 1832, and the same year, Captain Benjamin Bonneville spent Christmas Day with a band of fourteen trappers, and Nez Perce Indians, feasting on elk and mountain sheep. Washington Irving wrote in his account:

Here, then, there was a cessation from toil, from hunger, and alarm. Past ills and dangers were forgotten. The hunt, the game, the song, the story, the rough though good-humored joke, made time pass joyously away, and plenty and security reigned throughout the camp.

Captain John Stanley, a Civil War veteran, was the patriarch of a twenty-three man prospecting party that traveled from Warren's diggings through Bear Valley and Cape Horn to Stanley Basin in the summer, 1863 (possibly 1864). The prospectors saw evidence of Indians, but none were met. The placer gold they found in the streams was insignificant; they moved over to the Middle Fork of the Boise River and discovered the Atlanta lode. The party's leader, however, left his name in Stanley Basin.

Upper Stanley, along the banks of Valley Creek on Highway 21, was first occupied in 1890 by Arthur and Della McGown and their two children. They built a log cabin, ran a store selling beef to miners and packers, and operated a saloon and post office until 1895.

The site was not considered a town until November, 1919, when Bartlett Falls surveyed and recorded lots and streets. The place was often referred to as "Dogtown" because the Niece family kept so many hounds. In the 1970s, Harrah's Reno and Lake Tahoe became the major corporate land holder in the community.

Highway 21 meets Highway 93 along the Salmon River, immediately east of town.

State Highway No. 22 from a junction with U.S. 26 east of Arco, northeasterly via Howe to Dubois. (Overlaps Highway 33 from beginning to junction east of Howe.) Route length: 68.8 miles.

Highway 22 begins 7.5 miles east of Arco, at U.S. 26. The road curves northeast around the southern spur of the **Lost River Range** and after 15.9 miles arrives in **Howe.**

The town was named in 1884 for its first settler, E. R. Hawley, but the Post Office Department decided Hawley was too similar to Hailey, Idaho, and contrived the present name.

(At Howe, a partially paved road heads northwest up the Little Lost River Valley, sixty-two miles to U.S. 93, north of Challis, Idaho.)

The highway continues northeasterly, along the bare Mongolian flanks of the Lemhi Range, across sage-splashed flats 8.7 miles to an intersection with the Mud Lake road.

Proceed 13.5 miles northeast, cross Highway 28, and follow the road east another 30.3 miles to Dubois.

Highway 22 from Howe to Highway 28 travels through the Idaho National Engineering Laboratory reserve (atomic energy) along the northwestern edge of the Lost River Sinks. This lava lowland is an immense sponge that absorbs completely the flows of Big and Little Lost Rivers and Birch Creek. The water feeds the Snake River aquifer which emerges at Thousand Springs, near Hagerman, Idaho.

Though the exact depth of the lava is unknown, it has been drilled to 1,400 feet, and electrical resistance data indicates it may extend an additional 4,500 feet.

State Highway No. 24 from a junction with U.S. 93 in Shoshone easterly via Kimama and Minidoka then southwest via Acequia and Rupert to a junction with I-84. Route length: 67.2 miles.

Highway 24 begins from U.S. Highway 93, 0.5 miles south of Shoshone. It travels east for ten miles through farmland irrigated by canals fed by the Big Wood and Snake Rivers. Dietrich, just north of the highway, was named for the federal district court judge Frank Dietrich, a popular critic of the Reclamation Service.

The road parallels the Union Pacific railroad, and names of stations such as Kimama and Minidoka are allegedly Shoshone Indian words given by the chief engineer of the Oregon Short Line in the early 1880s.

The area from Kimama to Minidoka was opened to homesteaders by the federal government under the desert land General Revised Act of 1891. Settlers could acquire 320 acres provided they cultivated one-eighth of the land within three years. Because of the Reclamation Act, it appeared that the region would eventually be irrigated. Though this area was north of the Minidoka Irrigation Project, homesteaders filed on it in the belief that they could dry-farm until the canals arrived.

Between 1912 and 1930 about 325 claims were filed in the area. The farmers cleared sage and boulders, disk plowed and planted Turkey Red hard winter wheat in early fall for harvest the following summer.

The first few years were encouraging; then came dry years and the trials of Job: late frosts, wind and dust storms, coyotes, rattlesnakes, jack rabbits, ground squirrels, and woodticks.

One woman who arrived at a siding between Kimama and Minidoka recollected:

I hurried to the end of the coach with my children as the brakeman opened the heavy door to let us out. My heart sank when I got a view of the outdoors; nothing but a wide expanse of greenish grey sagebrush. Not a building, not a tree, not a living thing was in sight.

I brushed back some tears as we waited. Had I given up my spacious house with its friendly trees, its green lawn, and its bright flowers for this desolate country?

The new home did little to lift my spirits. It was an unpainted frame building in a clearing in the sagebrush, no grass, no walks, not a growing thing but bunchgrass. It was a barren desert, plain and simple.

What was there in or about this life and this country that appealed to us? I do not know for sure. I can only name some of the things that helped:

There was the wide open space that stretched for miles to the distant mountains or the far horizon, and with it the absence of all the close-in, crowding things that take so much of your time and attention in other places.

There was the sky, the sunset, the clouds and the view of the stars at night that you noticed because there was nothing much else to look at.

And, I remember the penetrating stillness of the long evenings, and the impressiveness of the sounds that broke the stillness, the far away cry of the coyote, the reassuring noise of the trains as they emerged from the distance and died away in the opposite direction reminding us that the "other world" was still there.

Another homesteader furnished a clear description of the rabbit problem:

The jack rabbits came to the green wheat fields about sundown. They came from the lavas and the uncleared sagebrush fields where they "shaded up" during the daytime. They came in hordes so thick that it looked as though the ground was moving. Guns were useless against them, for though you could drop what you hit the rest kept right on coming.

The water from Minidoka Dam never arrived, and the settlers discovered labor alone would not conquer an arid climate. One by one they left. The windmills rasped to a halt. Jim Hill mustard, June grass, Russian thistles, and finally, sage, reclaimed the fields.

In 1946 deep wells with diesel pumps that fed ditches, and later, electric pumps with underground pipes and overhead sprinklers, resuscitated the land.

191

Minidoka is 50.2 miles east of U.S. 93. In 1880-1882 it was a railroad construction camp for the Oregon Short Line. The name reportedly means "broad expanse," which is appropriate.

Highway 24 elbows southwest at Minidoka and reaches **Acequia** after eight miles. Acequia means "irrigation ditch" in Spanish.

Take County Highway 400 North from Acequia to **Minidoka Dam and Wildlife Refuge.** The road travels due east for six miles to **Lake Walcott.**

Walcott was a Reclamation engineer, and Minidoka Dam, an earth-fill dam eighty-six feet high and nearly a mile long, was the first Reclamation Service project in Idaho. Construction began in 1904; most of the canals and laterals were finished by 1906. Costs far exceeded estimates.

Gravity irrigation served the farms on the north side of the river, but pumps were needed to water the higher ground on the south side of the river. Hydroelectricity was a cheap, available source of power, and during 1908-1909 the first federal power plant in the Northwest was installed at the dam. Most of the power from the five generators was used for three pumps that carried water to 50,000 acres on the south-side. By 1909 expenses on the Minidoka canal project reached $5.8 million.

Under the federal Town Site Act, surplus power generated on Reclamation projects could be leased for ten years provided the sale did not impair irrigation projects. Farmers and nearby townspeople formed cooperative utility companies, built their own distribution systems, contracted with the Service for power, and sold it to themselves. Minidoka farmers had electricity long before other rural areas. Senator George Norris of Nebraska used the area as an example to justify establishment of the REA.

Two generators have since been added to the Minidoka plant, giving it a capability of 13,000 k.w. In 1974 the dam and power plant were placed on the National Register of Historic Places. The power house is open to the public on weekdays as well as weekends during the summer.

Walcott Park, close to the dam, is a popular picnic area.

Headquarters for the Minidoka National Wildlife Refuge is adjacent to the park. The 25,000-acre refuge, which includes Lake Walcott, was established in 1909 by President Theodore Roosevelt. It is administered by the Fish and Wildlife Service.

The Minidoka refuge is open from sunrise to sunset; the best times to visit are spring and fall. A bird list is available from headquarters.

192

Rupert in 1909.

In the spring it is possible to see migrating whistling swans at the refuge. Colonies of great blue herons, black-crowned night herons, snowy egrets, and double-crested cormorants nest on Bird Island. The white-faced ibis has recently become a nesting species. In the fall 250,000 ducks and geese are present. Bald eagles are seen in the winter, and golden eagles year-round.

The highway enters **Rupert** 5.2 miles southwest of Acequia.

Rupert, the seat of Minidoka County, is one of three townsites platted by the Reclamation Service in 1905, and is the center of the North Side Minidoka Tract. The plat established a town square, which the Service had to defend against merchant trespassers – now the square gives Rupert its principal charm. The town was named for its surveyor.

Rupert was a base camp for POW's during World War II.

Highway 24 ends 3.4 miles south of Rupert at I-84.

State Highway No. 25 from a junction with I-84 west of Jerome easterly via Jerome, Eden, Hazelton, Paul and Rupert to a junction with I-84 and Highway 77 north of Declo. Route length: 50.9 miles.

Jerome, little more than a mile from I-84, was established in 1907 by the Kuhn brothers of Pittsburgh, as part of the North Side

Jerome about 1915, looking west on Main St.

Main St. with power lines; Northside Inn in the background.

LAND
OFFICE

Twin Falls Canal Co. It carries the name of Jerome Hill, one of the investors in the project, and a brother-in-law of W. S. Kuhn.

The town serves farms and farmers, in a region that produces sugar beets, wheat, beans, potatoes, and hay. Jerome is the seat of the next-to-last county formed in the state.

The Idaho Fish and Game **State Bird Farm** is located on the outskirts of Jerome. Ask locally for directions from town, or take Exit 168 from I-84, go 1.3 miles north, turn right at the state sign, and drive one mile east.

In 1931 the state purchased the forty-acre site for $5,000. Annual interest on the outstanding balance was paid by the Jerome Rod and Gun Club. Construction began in 1935 as a WPA project, and was completed in the spring of 1937.

The fish and game department raises 16,000 ring-neck pheasants and 1,200 chukkars at the site. After hatching in incubators, the chicks are placed in a brood house. The hen pheasants are released at ten to sixteen weeks of age; most chukkars are held for spring release, to nest in the wild. A small number of breeders are kept through the winter.

The public is welcome to visit the bird farm; the best time to see the chicks is in April and May. An interesting collection of cock pheasants is also caged on the grounds – about fifteen species.

From Highway 25, 12.7 miles east and southeast of Jerome, turn north to visit two unusual sites included on the National Register of Historic Places. (The road is 7.2 miles west of Eden, at the highway information sign titled "Prehistoric Man.")

Drive northeast 2.3 miles and stop just east of the bridge over the North Side Main Canal. A lava rock tower and a sign are on the south side of the road.

This is **Hunt,** the Post Office Department's name for the **Minidoka War Relocation Center.** What happened here deserves mention. In the words of the associate editor of the *Denver Post,* Bill Hosokawa, who was a prisoner at Hunt, "It's important to remember this chapter in American history. There are so many people who are completely unaware of what happened. We can set down the story of what happened, not out of bitterness, but to remind us, and to make damn sure it doesn't happen again."

At the time of World War II Japanese Americans had made notable contributions to the fabric of Idaho. Many had come to work on the Oregon Short Line in the 1890s, and remained to labor in the sugar beet fields around Idaho Falls and Nampa during the early 1900s. Gradually, they became successful independent farmers. In 1940 about 60 percent of Idaho's Japanese were native-born Americans, and with war imminent, the first man in Idaho to register under the new Selective Service Act was an American of Japanese descent.

In February, 1942, President Roosevelt issued an Executive order establishing the West Coast Defense Area, from which "any or all persons might be excluded at the discretion of the military commander." The War Relocation Authority held a meeting of Army and federal officials and western governors in April, 1942, and two weeks later announced plans to relocate Japanese Americans to ten guarded camps in the West. One of the camps was to be at Hunt, Idaho.

Idaho's governor, Chase Clark, was a bigoted supporter of the plan. In a Grangeville speech he said Japanese "lived, bred and acted like rats, and the solution is to send the rats back to Japan and sink the island." He denied that Japanese Americans had constitutional rights and thwarted their attempts to buy or lease land in the state. (Ignorance of the law, however, never hindered his legal career: when the Governor's term expired in 1942, he was appointed a federal district court judge.)

Farmers in the Magic Valley learned of the proposed camp and objected on grounds their water supply might be diminished. The American Legion and VFW in Twin Falls advocated deportation of all Japanese within six months after the war. The Idaho Grange asked that no Japanese be allowed to do agricultural work. Labor unions around the state passed resolutions prohibiting members from working on jobs with any Japanese. Over 100 Japanese homes in the Boise-Caldwell area were raided and searched. Only the FBI director J. Edgar Hoover, the U.S. Attorney for Idaho, and the state superintendent of public instruction spoke in their defense.

Relocation orders meant 110,000 persons of Japanese ancestry, two-thirds of them American citizens, had to move. With little notice, they had to dispose of their property.

Morrison-Knudsen Co. built the Idaho camp. It opened in August, 1942, on 946 acres of a 34,000-acre reserve. The camp housed 9,400 evacuees, making it the eighth-largest city in Idaho. There were barbed wire fences, towers, armed guards, and watch dogs. Prisoners were told they would be shot if they came within 3½ feet of the fence. Roll calls and mail censorship were routine.

There were thirty-five separate residential blocks, each with twelve barracks. The barracks were 120 feet long by twenty feet wide, with six apartments. Each block had a mess hall, laundry, bath house, social hall and recreation hall. Coal and water had to be carried to the apartments.

Despite hatred and discrimination encountered by the evacuees, they supported the war effort by performing agricultural labor on a work-release program. At first they were forced to accept Army wages of $12 to $19 a month, rather than the prevailing scale. Their labor saved Idaho's sugar beet crops.

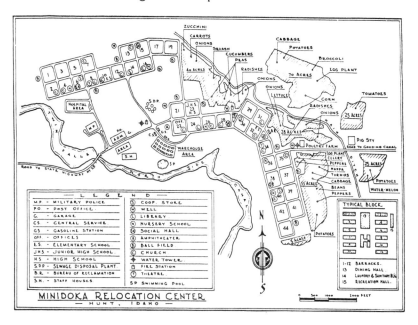

MINIDOKA RELOCATION CENTER
— HUNT, IDAHO —

Many of the persons who lived and worked in the Hunt camp did so while relatives in the Japanese American 442nd Regimental Combat Team fought in the Italian campaigns and became the most decorated unit in the war. About 800 residents of the camp also entered military service.

In January, 1945, the Japanese exclusion order was rescinded. Evacuees were given $25 and a train ticket to Portland. Many had no place to go. The last family left Hunt in October, 1945. Approximately 3,000 of the evacuees settled in Idaho, but only about one-third of these became permanent residents.

In 1952 new naturalization laws made Japanese aliens eligible for citizenship. Three years later Idaho Japanese obtained repeal of the 1923 Alien Land Law; in 1959 the anti-miscegenation statute was repealed, and in 1962 Idaho voters deleted a section from the state constitution that disqualified Japanese from full rights of citizenship.

The words of Norman Thomas are appropriate:

To struggle against demagoguery scarcely fits the St. George-against-the-dragon myth so popular in folklore. Our democratic St. George goes out rather reluctantly with armor awry. The struggle is confused; our knight wins by no clean thrust of lance or sword, but the dragon somehow poops out and decent democracy is victor.

Only six acres of the site are still public land; the rest was granted to war veterans under the Carey Act. The only barbed wire now visible keeps cattle from invading the farmland.

The Department of the Interior in 1979 held a public ceremony as the Minidoka site was added to the National Register.

Proceed north from the Minidoka center two miles to an intersection with stop signs on both sides. Turn west on the gravel road. After 3.7 miles the gravel ends and the dirt road scrapes its way through sage. (In wet weather this road is slicker than a greased watermelon, and the trip should be avoided.)

After two miles more the road crosses a wooden bridge over the North Side Canal. Note the piles of rock excavated from the canal at the time it was built. The water comes from Milner Dam.

The road curves slightly to the right. After another 0.6 miles a BLM sign points to **Wilson Butte Cave** 2 miles ⟶. At 2.1 miles, another sign points left, and the cave is 0.1 miles farther.

Wilson Butte Cave is a lava blister formed by gas expansion within the cooling lava during the early, or middle, Pleistocene. The top of the blister gives an unobstructed view of every point of the compass.

In the fall of 1958, Ruth Gruhn, a graduate student associated with the Peabody Museum at Harvard, came to Idaho State Univ. at Pocatello in search of an archaeological problem suitable for a doctoral dissertation. She chose Wilson Butte Cave, which had been located that year by ISU field archaeologists working under a National Park Service contract.

The Peabody Museum financed the excavation, and ISU provided support and guidance. Work began at the cave during the summer of 1959, and was completed the following summer. In 1961 Miss Gruhn's dissertation was published – the most comprehensive report ever written on a single archaeological site in Idaho.

The cave contained five major deposits. The lower three strata were water-laid, the upper two were deposited by wind. The lowest and oldest deposit contained bones of two extinct forms of camel and of one horse. The middle layer yielded bones of a modern form of bison, and the upper strata contained the bones of bison, deer and antelope, as well as some coarse pottery, arrowshafts, notched arrowheads, and a moccasin.

Study of the deposits and the types of animals associated with them allowed Gruhn to conclude that the climate was cooler and more moist 15,000 years ago than at present. The plains around the butte were grassland interspersed with marshes or lakes. About 6,800 years ago the climate began to grow warmer and drier, a phase that continues.

Artifacts from the lower middle stratum were radiocarbon dated at 14,500 years ago. This makes them "among the oldest definitely dated artifacts in the New World."

Wilson Butte Cave.

The late prehistoric artifacts indicate that the Shoshone peoples from the Great Basin had entered southern Idaho by 1300 A.D. The cave has become a benchmark in Idaho archaeology for comparing relationships between southern Idaho cultures and those of the Plateau, Great Basin, and Plains.

Though the cave has been spaded and painted by Boy Scout troops whose leaders should have known better, it still manages to retain an almost spiritual aura. "Men ... are images of clay, a race lightsome and without substance, creatures of a day, without wings."

Eden is 16.8 miles from Jerome. The town's name is a comment on the fertility of its soil.

East of Eden, Highway 25 travels 4.1 miles to **Hazelton** (named for the daughter of the village's founder), then 19.8 miles east to the farm town of **Paul.** The road continues five miles more to Rupert (see Highway 24) before turning south 5.5 miles to an intersection with I-84.

199

U.S. Highway No. 26 from the Idaho-Oregon state line near Nyssa, Oregon easterly via Notus, Caldwell, Boise, Mountain Home, Glenns Ferry, Gooding, Shoshone, Carey, Arco, Blackfoot, Idaho Falls and Swan Valley to the Idaho-Wyoming border near Alpine. (Overlaps U.S. 20, 30, 93, 95, I-84, and I-15 for 271.8 miles.) Route length without overlaps: 130.8 miles.

Only two significant stretches of U.S. 26 are not overlapped by other highways. Those two sections, Arco Junction southeast 51.8 miles to Blackfoot, and Idaho Falls southeast 70 miles to Palisades Reservoir, are treated here.

U.S. 20 and U.S. 26 part company at a fork 22.8 miles east of Arco. The turn-off for Atomic City and Big Southern Butte is on the south side of the road 6.8 miles from that junction. Atomic City is 1.3 miles from the highway.

Known as Midway (i.e. between Arco and Blackfoot), **Atomic City** adopted its new name in 1950 as the AEC expansion got underway with a $2 million improvement of Highway 26. The city was confident that its population would grow from thirty-five to 1000; it now looks like a town where first prize is one week in it, and second prize is two weeks in it.

The dirt pickup-road to Big Southern Butte begins at the southwest end of the townsite; passenger cars should not attempt the fifteen-mile drive. The road swings around to the northwest side of the butte and then climbs steeply to the lookout on the summit.

Big Southern Butte (7,576 ft.) stands out like Sirius Major over the sweep of space that forms the Snake River lava plain. A National Natural Landmark, it dominates the landscape for fifty miles in three directions. The Butte's almost-African appearance, and the Sandburg cloud that sometimes sits for hours on its peak, as well as the play of shadows along its wrinkled blue flanks, pleasure all who view them.

Big Southern Butte is a volcanic, rhyolitic dome, 300,000 years old. It consists of two coalesced domes that have lifted and tilted an older basaltic section which covers most of the northern slope.

Archaeological evidence suggests the Butte, with its springs and wildlife, formed the hub of an aboriginal culture for several thousand years. In more recent times, Frenchman Springs provided water for travelers on the Goodale Cutoff of the Oregon Trail and for freighters on Alexander Topance's Challis-Blackfoot stage line.

At present the BLM maintains a two-story fire lookout on Big Southern from June to October; the lookout has a battery radio system and reports fires as far away as the Burley district (eighty miles).

200

Big Southern Butte on the horizon; China Cup tephra cone in foreground.

Because of the abrupt 2,800-foot elevation, the Butte is often stropped by heavy weather. Winds in excess of eighty miles per hour have been measured; fifteen feet of snow in the winter is not uncommon. Battelle Laboratory of Washington twice erected 199-foot weather towers for NOAA on the Butte; both towers were lost to heavy ice, at a cost of $110,000. Two hang glider pilots who risked the temperamental winds have been killed.

The Butte, with help from BLM administrators and an advisory council, has withstood a surprising number of assaults on its profile. A forest fire burned most of its timber in the 1940s; in the 1960s the Navy tested sixteen-inch guns by firing them into the slopes from a railroad spur five miles away. In the 1970s commercial communication companies increased their efforts to obtain right-of-way for power lines and antennae on the Butte, a site they need like a hog needs a ruffled shirt. AMAX poses a more serious threat; the mining company has molybdenum claims on Big Southern and has drilled 1,400 feet of test holes.

On the north side of Highway 26, 3.7 miles northwest of the Atomic City exit, is **Middle Butte** (6,392 ft.); its age is the same as Big Southern's, but it is simply a block of basalt elevated by an intrusion of viscous magma.

If Big Southern Butte is Sirius Major, **East Butte** (6,572 ft.), 3.5 miles east of Middle Butte, is Sirius Minor. East Butte is 600,000 years old, a rhyolite dome formed from small magma chambers at a time of basaltic volcanism.

The Butte is quilled with antennae; the north ridge is subdivided into ten lots leased on a yearly basis, half for commercial use, half for government use. The southern peak is used by KID TV and radio transmitters.

U.S. 26 continues southwest 22.2 miles across the flatlands to Blackfoot, then 34.5 miles northeast in conjunction with I-15, to Idaho Falls.

U.S. Highway 26 resurfaces five miles northeast of Idaho Falls, and Iona Road is three miles northeast of the U.S. 26 junction with Highway 91.

Take Iona Road due south 2.8 miles to the Mormon town of **Iona,** settled in 1883. The name is reported to mean "the beautiful." Three unusual buildings grace the corners of Rockwood Ave. and Second St. The sandstone Iona Ward house was built in 1888 and enlarged six years later. It served as a school, social hall, and art gallery. Immediately behind the Ward House, on Rockwood Ave., is a smartly kept brick house of late Victorian style built by Bishop Charles Rockwood in 1905. On the corner, across Second St. from these buildings, is the old Sand Creek Store, constructed in 1897 by the same mason who built the Ward House.

From the Iona Road intersection, continue 10.9 miles northeast on U.S. 26 to the exit for **Heise Hot Springs,** on the north side of the highway. The commercial springs, with two outdoor swimming pools, are three miles from the road; this resort has operated out of the three-story log hotel since 1898.

Highway 26 continues 25 miles through wheat fields, lion-colored in mid-summer, to Swan Valley, and 11.9 miles farther southeast to **Palisades Dam** on the Snake River.

The dam was authorized in 1941, but was not completed until 1959. At a cost of $76 million, it was the largest earth dam yet built by the Bureau of Reclamation.

After 13.7 miles more, U.S. 26 reaches the Idaho-Wyoming border 2.4 miles west of Alpine Junction, Wyoming.

Palisades Dam under construction.

State Highway No. 27 from a junction with Main St. in Oakley, north via Burley to a junction with Highway 25 in Paul. Route length: 26.5 miles.

Oakley lies in a valley of the Goose Creek Mountains, 20.4 miles south of Burley. The location was selected by Mormon colonists from Tooele, Utah. The first family wintered in the valley in 1878; in 1880 the LDS Goose Creek Ward was founded. That year the first store was organized, the Oakley Cooperative Mercantile Association. Water rights were appropriated for the valley, and farmers grew wheat, barley and alfalfa. The town acquired its name from Thomas Oakley, who ran a stage station on the Kelton Road.

In 1911 the Oakley Dam on Goose Creek was begun. It was part of a reclamation scheme promoted by the Kuhn brothers of Pittsburgh. They gave water contracts in the Twin Falls Oakley Land and Water Project to the older settlers in exchange for their water rights. The plan was designed to irrigate 43,000 acres. When completed, the earth-fill dam was the largest in the world. However, the company that financed bonds worth $1.3 million failed in 1913, and the settlers had to complete the project, which they did by reducing it to 21,000 acres. Water from the dam feeds East Canal, which angles across Main St. through town.

The dam construction drew the Idaho Southern Short Line from Milner to Oakley. The railroad hauled the cement and timbers for the dam and the tons of coal required by the steam shovels on the job. Sheep and cattle ranchers began to ship their stock on the railroad.

The town's population declined between 1918 and 1935 when it became apparent that the amount of irrigable land had been overestimated. In addition, a fire destroyed much of the town's business district in 1923, and the Vipoint silver mine, twenty-eight

Oakley Co-op.

miles south of Oakley, which had operated since 1890, closed four years later.

Several quarries now operate within twenty miles of Oakley. The Oakley stone, Idaho quartzite, is shipped throughout the country and the world.

For its size, no town in Idaho has such a fascinating collection of old buildings. Oakley has been added to the National Register of Historic Places as an historic district.

Begin at Main and Center Sts. The two-story, stone Oakley Co-op building is on the southeast corner. Built in 1883, it is the oldest structure on Main St.

204

The building immediately east of the co-op, on Main, was the town's first bank. The exterior has a display of Idaho quartzite that is as variegated and colorful as a palette.

Drive west on Main from Center St. On the northeast corner at Main and Blaine Ave. is the **Daughters of Utah Pioneers Museum** inside the old Worthington Hotel.

South, across the street, at the rear of the city park is a jail cell which once held Diamondfield Jack Davis (see Highway 77, Albion).

The Farmers Bank occupies the southwest corner of the

Judge Benjamin Howell's house.

intersection. The brick building, with its decorative stone facade, was erected in 1910.

Continue west on Main St. to the railroad tracks, turn right and park at the U.P. depot. When the Idaho Southern began carrying supplies for the Oakley dam, it quickly attracted competition. The Oregon Short Line ran a spur south from Burley to Oakley and built a station at this site. The depot operated for forty years. Since closing, it has been occupied by Northern Stone Supply as a showroom for the company's quartzite. (The U.P. still brings freight cars south from Burley on request.)

Return to Main St., drive east four blocks to Blaine Ave. and turn north. In mid-block, on the east side of the street is the Oakley opera house. Proceed north to Poplar Ave.

The house on the northeast corner of the intersection (202 No. Blaine) is the most photographed building in town. It is the Judge Benjamin Howell's residence, built in 1909. With its turret, wrap-around porch, balcony and elaborate trim, it remains a local landmark.

Turn east on Poplar St., along the row of poplar trees, and observe the Jacob Dayley house, two doors east of Howell's, at 106 Poplar. The reddish gray stones bear the chisel marks of Joseph Beck, a mason's apprentice from Germany, who at age fourteen emigrated from Germany to America as a stowaway. He came by rail from New York to Minidoka, where he was adopted by an Oakley family. Other houses in town also reveal his craftsmanship. This one was built in 1898.

Swing south off Poplar St. onto Center St.; the Marcus Funk residence, in mid-block on the west side of the street, was built in 1895-1900. Local lore insists this house was built by a Mormon polygamist who planned one floor for each of his three wives. However, he sold it without ever living there, and for a time it was owned by the town's sheriff. The corner tower encloses a stairwell.

Continue south on Center St., past Main St. three blocks until the road curves to the left. The bungalow-style brick house on the south side of the street was built in 1912. The walls are three bricks thick.

Oakley had at least three brickyards at the turn of the century. The kilns were fired with aspen. Some of the local masons were LDS converts who had emigrated from Europe.

Retrace Center St. to Poplar Ave. and turn east on Poplar one block to Worthington Ave. On the southwest corner is the Cutler Worthington house which was built in 1905. The first story is stone and the frame second story encloses a balcony on each side of the center tower.

206

Across the street, on a northeast diagonal, is the striking Hector Haight house, which looks like a sister to the Funk residence on Center St.

Continue south on Poplar to Wilson Ave., turn south on Wilson Ave. one block to Main St. The unusual, two-story brick house on the northwest corner was built in 1900 by the mason Joseph Beck for his adoptive parents. Four other stone and brick houses of interest are a block farther south on Wilson Ave.

From Wilson Ave. turn west on Elm St. two blocks and south on Church St. to the town cemetery. Its white marble tombstones were quarried near Oakley, but the stone was too soft for commercial use.

A tall, simple gravestone is here, with the inscription: "Gobo Fango, Died Feb. 10, 1886, Aged 30 years." Before the Forest Reserves with their grazing allotments were established in 1905, sheep and cattle ranchers got along like hawks and crows. Gobo Fango, a Negro born in Africa, who was orphaned early, got caught in the middle.

He was smuggled to the U.S. by a sympathetic LDS family that raised and educated him in Layton, Utah. He worked as a sheepherder for a Mormon bishop, and eventually moved to the range north of the Oakley Basin with a partner, Walt Matthews. They leased a band of ewes.

On Feb. 10, while Fango was tending herd alone, someone shot him in the stomach. He plugged the wound with sage and crawled four miles to Matthews' house, where he died a few hours later. He left $400 to the LDS Church and $100 to the Grantsville Relief Society of Utah.

Daniel Cummings and John Wilson, two young sheepherders, are also buried here; Diamondfield Jack Davis was accused of the killing (see Highway 71, Albion).

One can reach the geological area City of Rocks by driving southeast from Oakley, up Birch Creek, but the trip is recommended only in dry weather – rain or snow transforms the road to a buffalo wallow. (For City of Rocks see Highway 77, Almo.)

Highway 27 travels north to Burley 20.4 miles through sprinkler-irrigated farmland. The road continues 2.8 miles north of Burley to Paul and a junction with Highway 25.

State Highway 28 from a junction with I-15 north of Roberts, northwesterly via Mud Lake, Leadore, and Lemhi to a junction with U.S. 93 in Salmon. (Overlaps Highway 33 from I-15 to a junction west of Mud Lake.) Route length: 135.5 miles.

Highway 28 begins at Sage Junction, west of I-15, 8.4 miles north of Roberts. It travels west 14.1 miles through Terreton to Mud Lake, then angles northwest for 16.4 miles to a junction with Highway 22. The road then continues northwest up the **Birch Creek Valley** between the Beaverhead Mountains of the Bitterroot Range on the east and the Lemhi Range on the west. The Bitterroot Range marks the Continental Divide; the Lemhi Range, with its 10,000-foot peaks, runs northwest for over seventy miles – the state's longest range unsevered by roads.

Thirteen and one-half miles northwest of the Highway 22 junction, on Highway 28, a small cement memorial is visible on the west shore of Birch Creek. It marks the site of five murders known as the **Birch Creek Massacre.**

On August 15, 1877, the Nez Perce bands of Looking Glass, Joseph, and White Bird were traveling southeast down Birch Creek Valley en route to Yellowstone and Montana. General Howard, on the other side of the Bitterroots, was in pursuit. The Indians surprised a party of freighters with eight wagons bound from Eagle Rock (near Idaho Falls) to Salmon with merchandise for George Shoup and Dave Wood. There were three teamsters, a herder, two miners, and two Chinese. The men shared lunch with the Indians, then, when it was discovered and demanded, gave them whiskey from the barrels in the wagon. It was the quart before the hearse.

The Indians began to get disorderly, then rampageous. The Chinese, sent to gather firewood, slipped away instead. The herder drifted back into the sage, then dived into the creek and hid beneath the willow bushes. Before long he heard shots and the sounds of a struggle. At midnight he left the stream and took to the mountains.

The Chinese fled to the settlement near Leadore. Col. Shoup, with a company of volunteers from Salmon, along with Tendoy's band of Shoshone, visited the freighter's lunch spot and found the wagons looted and burned and five men dead.

They buried the bodies but in early winter removed them to a grave in the Salmon cemetery. A marble marker there identifies the three freighters; the names of the two miners were never learned. (The herder who escaped was found after seven days and taken to Salmon.)

Two miles north of the massacre site, east of the road, archaeological excavations were conducted at the **Bison and Veratic rockshelters.** The excavations were part of the study conducted in Birch Creek Valley by Dr. Earl Swanson of Idaho State Univ., and financed by National Science Foundation grants from 1959 to 1972. Information from radio-carbon dates and artifact analysis indicates that the shelters were occupied continuously for almost 11,000 years and that Northern Shoshone cultural patterns existed in the valley for about 8,000 years. Periods of climatic variation influenced population levels and the amount of game.

Four phases of subsistence occurred in the Birch Creek Valley after the earliest occupation: the hunting pattern called the Bitterroot culture continued from 5200 to 1450 B.C., the Beaverhead culture from 1450 to 950 B.C., the Blue Dome culture from 950 B.C. to 1250 A.D., and, finally, the Lemhi culture from 1250 to 1850 A.D. Inhabitants of the valley pursued bighorn sheep in the mountains and bison at the lower elevations.

From the evidence gathered here, Birch Creek Valley has the most extensive record of bison hunting in North America.

The highway reaches Lone Pine 2.3 miles north of the rock-shelters. A second archaeological excavation, at **Jaguar Cave,** a few miles northeast of Lone Pine, revealed additional information about early inhabitants of Birch Creek. A hearth in the limestone cave yielded a carbon date of 11,580 years ago. Forty-four species of mammals were found in the faunal remains, including a Pleistocene lion, a dire wolf, a camel, and collared lemmings, a tundra species.

The most startling discovery was evidence that the Lemhi people 10,000 years ago had two breeds of domesticated dogs. At present it is the earliest record of such dogs. They probably served as pack animals for seasonal migrations.

The turnoff for the site of **Nicholia** and the **Viola lead mine** is 9.8 miles north of Lone Pine. Turn east on the unmarked dirt road that curves four miles northeast to Smelter Gulch.

In 1881, when William McKay was hunting lost horses, he stopped to pick up a piece of rock and noticed it was unusually heavy. Several months later he saw lead ore being loaded into railroad cars in Hailey and realized that it was the same mineral he had picked up in the Birch Creek Valley. Returning to the spot he staked a claim named the Viola. McKay sold the claim to Charles Rustin, who spent several thousand dollars developing it.

Ralph Nichols, a mining engineer from New York, was sent by the owners of the LaPlata Mining and Smelting Co. of Leadville, Colorado, to inspect the mine. Satisfied by his report, they bought the Viola for $117,000 and organized the Viola Mining and Smelting Co.

Between 1882 and 1885 high grade ore was hauled to the railroad near Dubois, Idaho, where it was shipped to Kansas City and Omaha smelters. A smelter was built on the flat below the mine, and ore was delivered by a 1½-mile tramway.

The smelter could process 100 tons of ore a day but required prodigious amounts of charcoal and coke. The coke was shipped by rail from Pennsylvania, and the charcoal was made in pits and kilns on the west side of the valley. Lead pigs were hauled in wagons to Dubois; on the return trip the wagons brought coke to the smelter. The Viola became the largest lead producer in the state, outside the Coeur d'Alene Valley.

A settlement called Nicholia took root at the mouth of Smelter Gulch; it was named for Ralph Nichols, who became manager of the Viola. By 1882 the town had over 400 residents, who supported the three-story company mercantile, a Woodmen of the World lodge, a skating rink, and ten saloons which sold drinks for 12½ cents each.

Lead poisoning from the smelter was a serious problem; it killed men who worked in the plant as well as the area's cats, dogs, horses, and cows.

In 1886, after the smelter was in operation, British capital of $5 million was invested in the Viola Co. Ltd. A year later Nichols found that the ore terminated at a faultline and advised the English company to distribute its profits and abandon the mine. The company rejected his advice, but lead prices collapsed, and a fire that destroyed the shaft, stulls and hoist forced the mine to close. The smelter was dismantled. British investors recovered one-third of their investment.

A pair of groggy, weathered buildings are the last in Nicholia. One can drive uphill from the site about four miles to the mine. There are a few cabins among the tailing mounds, but the real prize is the sweeping view of Birch Creek Valley and the Lemhi Range.

To visit the **charcoal kilns** that fueled the Viola smelter, return to Highway 28 and drive north 3.4 miles to the signed road on the west that leads six miles west up to the kilns.

"The success of a design is when there is nothing left to take away." Perhaps that maxim explains the beauty of the four kilns camped in the sage on the alluvial flat at the road end. Inside and out they have the quiet simplicity of a Greek tomb.

210

The kilns were built in 1883 by Warren King of Butte, Montana. The materials were made on the site.

Charcoal was produced here from 1883 to 1889. At that time about 300 immigrants – Irish, Italian, Chinese – lived on the flat around the spring and cut Douglas fir in the nearby canyons. The logs were hauled to the kilns and bucked into four-foot lengths.

Early photograph of the Nicholia charcoal kilns.

The kilns were loaded through the lower door; the wood was stacked on end as closely as possible; when the lower course was completed, an opening was made in the dome and the loading proceeded. Once the kiln was full, tinder in the base was ignited, the doors were sealed, and the draft vents in the base were carefully regulated.

The kilns are twenty feet high and twenty feet in diameter; their capacity was approximately thirty-five cords. As the moisture, noncombustible gases and tars were distilled, the wood was reduced to carbon with one-half its former volume and one-quarter of its weight. A cord of wood yielded about 500 pounds of charcoal. It took a week to load, fire, and unload a kiln. Wagons then carried the "coal" to the smelter across the valley.

There were sixteen kilns here at one time, but the bricks were salvaged by settlers. It is estimated the ovens burned 150,000 cords in seven years. When the Viola closed, forty acres of cordwood were stacked on the bench behind the kilns, and the owner could not even give it away.

Kilnmaster watched the color of the smoke to tell when the wood had been reduced to charcoal. Volatile gases sometimes blew the top off the kiln.

The 11,600-foot peak on the Lemhi crest, visible five miles south of the kilns, is **Bell Mountain.** It was named for Robert Bell, an Englishman who became Idaho's state mining inspector for seven years in the early 1900s. He lived in Lemhi County for twelve years and died in Boise in 1935.

Gilmore Summit (7,186 elev.) is on Highway 28, ten miles north of the kilns. About two miles north of the pass is a gravel road that leads west 1.5 miles to the ghost town of Gilmore, visible from the highway.

Turn left onto the road up to **Gilmore:** two dozen buildings no one wants to live in now.

The mining district in the Gilmore-Texas Creek area was organized in 1880, a year before the Viola mine discovery, but development of the lode was slower than a snail on a slick log. Transportation difficulties had to be overcome, and after the smelter at Nicolia closed, the Gilmore district had no outlet for its ore; so the mines grew whiskers for fourteen years.

In 1902 F. G. Laver of Pennsylvania acquired a major Gilmore property and interested fellow investors in its exploitation. Laver tried shipping the lead-silver ore in wagons of sixty-ton capacity, pulled by a huge steam tractor. Ore was hauled eighty-five miles to the railhead at Dubois; on the return trip the wagons carried coal, which was deposited at refueling stops for the steam engine. The cars were able to withstand only a dozen trips; their demise brought the experiment to an end.

Between 1902 and 1908 Gilmore shipped 6,700 tons of lead bullion and 325,000 ounces of silver. Further production demanded a railroad connection to the smelters at Butte, Montana.

The Gilmore and Pittsburgh Railroad was completed in 1910. A spur from Gilmore met the main line at Leadore and traveled north-northeast over Bannock Pass to the Oregon Short Line rail at Armstead, Montana.

Once the railroad was established, Gilmore's future was less problematic; merchants and miners gathered like flies around a milk pail; the camp's population grew to 500, and production was steady. The first year's rail shipments equalled the combined total of all previous years. The spot was finally named for John Gilmer, a partner in the local stage line.

The Gilmore lode was mined to a considerable depth, through four miles of tunnels, shafts and adits. The mines operated until 1929, when the combination of a power plant explosion and the Depression brought activities to a close. From 1903 to 1929 Gilmore was Idaho's largest lead-silver district outside the Coeur d'Alene Valley; production reached $11.5 million.

For the next seven miles, as the traveler drives northwest up the Birch Creek Valley, he can see traces of the old **Gilmore and Pittsburgh Railroad** bed, often only fifty yards beyond the fence on the east side of the highway.

The Gilmore and Pittsburgh investors in the mines, aware that although the area was Union Pacific territory, the Northern Pacific still coveted the Lemhi Valley trade, secretly and easily persuaded the Northern Pacific to finance the railroad for $4.8 million. The line was T-shaped: one limb ended in Salmon, the other in Gilmore; the trunk crossed Bannock Pass between Leadore and Armstead. The Northern Pacific used the U.P. connecting rail between Armstead and Dillion, Montana.

213

There were rumors of mysterious plans to extend the rail from Salmon through Challis to Boise, and from Salmon via the Salmon River canyon to Lewiston, but those plans were derailed by topographical reality.

Shortly after the railroad's completion in 1910, the Pittsburgh investors surrendered all the stock and promissory notes to the Northern Pacific.

Several factors doomed the G&P from its inception. It was always saddled with a heavy construction debt; closure of the mines ended its main source of revenue. Roads in the area were improved during the 1930s, and truckers undercut freight rates for farm products and livestock. The G&P never realized a profit. The last train ran in April, 1939; a year later the ICC granted a request to terminate service and the rails were removed for scrap iron.

Leadore (lead ore) marks the headwaters of the Lemhi River, a tributary of the Salmon. Leadore is 17.1 miles north of Gilmore on Highway 28, in the Lemhi Valley at the foot of the Bannock Pass grade (see Highway 29, Bannock Pass). The hamlet is a sequel to Junction, which was located slightly farther east, but was bypassed by the G&P Railroad.

Highway 28 continues north nineteen miles to Lemhi. The river increases in volume and wanders from one side of the road to the other, entwining itself like the serpents of the caduceus.

Lemhi was the site of a Salmon River outpost established by the Church of Jesus Christ of the Latter Day Saints. The twenty-seven missionaries left Salt Lake City in May, 1855, under directions from Brigham Young to settle among the Bannocks or Shoshone and "teach them the principles of citizenship."

The party, under the leadership of Thomas Smith, traveled north through what is now Pocatello, then west up the Birch Creek Valley, 333 miles from Ogden, according to an odometer attached to one of their thirteen wagons.

In June at this location they built a mud-walled fort called Limhi. A prominent King of a Nephite group in the *Book of Mormon,* Limhi was the son of King Noah, born in South America after the ocean voyage from Palestine. The American Indians are regarded as descendents of the Lamanite group who lapsed into idolatry in the *Book of Mormon,* and the LDS missionaries had come to lead their Lamanite brethren back to the righteous Nephite traditions.

Fort Limhi was constructed with a slip-form method for the rock and mud walls, which were two feet wide, seven feet high, and 265

214

ft. long. Initially, thirteen cabins were constructed inside the stockade; the number later doubled. Blacksmith shop, sawmill, and a well were added.

A garden was started, irrigated by a ditch that extended 300 yards upstream to the river. Crops were planted too late in the summer, so that half of the settlers were sent back to Salt Lake for more supplies.

Remains of the mud walls of Fort Limhi in 1903.

On his visit to the site in 1857 Brigham Young was encouraged by the missionaries' progress; they had baptized over 100 Indians. He urged the faithful to marry the native girls in order to increase the bonds of friendship. In addition, the Church president sent another fifty-eight adults from Utah to strengthen the colony.

The Shoshone and Bannock must have watched the colony's growth with some concern; in a valley which had never provided more than subsistence, 200 cattle were now pastured on the meadows, lumber was cut, salmon were smoked and shipped to Utah, and trade with the Nez Perce was encouraged.

In 1858 a distant, unexpected event brought matters to a conclusion. President Buchanan, at the urging of his Secretary of War, had dispatched 2,500 federal troops toward Utah Territory in 1857 to quell a possible Mormon secession. The troops wintered in Wyoming, and an Army detachment on the east side of the Bitterroots sought supplies for them.

The Indians realized that the Mormon cattle herd was of value to the Army, and they also realized that the soldiers would not punish them for harassing the Saints. In February, 1858, the Shoshone and

Bannocks raided the fort, killed two of its thirty-nine defenders, wounded five others, and absconded with the cattle.

Two LDS messengers after an eight-day ride to Salt Lake gave Brigham Young the news. He dispatched an armed legion of 150 men to bring the missionaries back to the Salt Lake Valley. The fort was abandoned.

A remnant of the fort's wall and part of the first irrigation ditch have survived on the Muleshoe ranch. The name of the Nephite king has fared better: though altered by a letter, it has been applied to a river, mountain range, village, and county.

The settlement of **Tendoy** is 6.3 miles north of Lemhi. Tendoy was named for the Northern Shoshone chief who lived in the Lemhi Valley from about 1857 to 1907. Aside from the activities of the Copper Queen mine (eight miles east), the area's principal business was forage for several thousand sheep, cattle and horses.

An engrossing historical sidetrip is available from Tendoy; it includes **Chief Tendoy's grave** and Lewis and Clark's route down Agency Creek from **Lemhi Pass,** which is a National Historic Landmark.

Turn east at the Tendoy post office, 0.1 miles to a T. Turn right, and after 0.2 miles turn left up Agency Creek. The right turn for Tendoy's grave is 1.5 miles up Agency Creek. Cross the cattle guard, drive 0.5 miles to a second cattle guard, continue straight, then follow the curve 0.2 miles west up to a knoll that overlooks the Lemhi Valley. The chief's grave is marked with a sandstone obelisk erected in 1924 by his white friends.

Tendoy was born in 1834 in the Boise River area, of a Bannock father and a Mountain Shoshone (Sheepeater) mother. He distinguished himself in battle against the Crows, Flatheads, and Sioux. According to Fort Hall Agency records he had three wives and a dozen children.

Tendoy became chief of the Lemhi band shortly after he moved to the valley, when the former chief, his uncle, was murdered in 1863 by a member of the Plummer gang. The Lemhi band was a mixture of Shoshone and Bannock and numbered about 500.

Since the chief recognized the folly of warfare with the whites, he worked hard to maintain a harmonious relationship with white settlers. In 1868 he journeyed to Virginia City, Montana, to sign a treaty that established the Lemhi reservation. But Congress failed to ratify the agreement, and the Lemhi, whose hunting grounds in Idaho and Montana had been disrupted by mining, were reduced, in the words of the Indian agent, to a "destitute and helpless" condition. They had neither the experience nor the equipment to grow their own food.

After several years, some federal money was finally appropriated for food, but when the Indian Commissioner recommended moving the Lemhi band to the Fort Hall reservation, Tendoy refused to go. Local residents, including George Shoup, expressed opposition to forcible relocation of the Lemhi. In 1875 President Grant established the Lemhi Reservation. It included 160 square miles along the Lemhi River.

Tendoy managed to dissuade his band from joining the Nez Perce War in 1877 and kept it out of the Bannock and Sheepeater wars as well. In 1880 he was taken to Washington, D.C. by the Interior Department to sign an agreement whereby the Lemhi band would move to the Fort Hall reserve and take up lands in severalty. The tribe would receive a $4,000-a-year annuity for twenty years. Tendoy signed the agreement, but reconsidered after he returned home, and refused to move.

The chief was amiable without being subservient. When the Lemhi Indian agent strung 1½ miles of fence-wire on the reservation without asking permission, Tendoy ordered it torn down. When the agent imprisoned some members of the band, the chief walked to the stockade and released them. On another occasion he fiercely resisted the agency's attempts to force his grandson to attend the reservation school.

In 1905 the Department of the Interior sent a federal agent to the reservation with an order that the Lemhi must move to the Fort Hall reservation. This time Tendoy made an impassioned speech, which persuaded the tribe to acquiesce. The removal took place in June, 1907, but Chief Tendoy did not suffer the humiliation – he died in May, 1907. Four hundred whites attended his funeral.

In 1971 the Indian Claims Commission allowed a final judgement of $4.5 million to the Lemhi tribe as payment for the loss of 5 million acres of aboriginal homeland.

From Tendoy's gravesite, resume the drive up Agency Creek, ten miles by narrow, dirt road to the top of the pass, elevation 7,373 feet.

Aside from the road, the only man-made distractions visible from the summit are a line of power poles in the canyon and the sawbuck fence that marks the Idaho-Montana border.

This is the Continental Divide, perhaps the most impressive pass in Idaho, and certainly the most important historically. It is a

National Landmark and the highest point on the Lewis and Clark trail. Looking west to the Salmon River Range and east across the Bitterroot National Forest, one feels like a hawk with wind under his wings.

The pass was created by a pair of valley glaciers that scoured in opposite directions, east and west, from the ridgeline. It is now a sub-alpine region of rolling grassland with islands of lodgepole and a few Douglas fir.

West view from the summit of Lemhi Pass.

Lemhi Pass was a major route for the Shoshone and Nez Perce, who used it for their annual fall migration to and from the buffalo grounds in Montana. The Blackfoot crossed it often enough (to reach the upper Snake River country) that Alexander Ross referred to the trail as the Blackfoot Road.

Capt. Meriwether Lewis, along with Drouillard, Shields, and McNeal, left the rest of the Voyage of Discovery on August 9, 1805, at the Beaverhead River (near Dillon, Mont.) and went ahead to reconnoiter for Shoshone Indians that might furnish horses to get

218

the Expedition's gear across the Bitterroot Range. Lewis and Clark had met no Indians since leaving the Mandan Village on the Missouri River (No. Dak.) in early April. They knew Shoshone inhabited the region because Sacajawea, who had grown up there, informed them.

The four men each carried a blanket, a rifle, and a pack with Indian trade goods. On the morning of August 12, standing on Lemhi Pass they realized that it was the Continental Divide – they had left the Missouri drainage and entered that of the Columbia; the first white men to cross the Divide south of Alberta and north of New Mexico, they had dispelled the dream of a water passage from the Missouri to the mouth of the Columbia. The portage had begun.

The party descended the steep canyon to the west, where Lewis drank from Horseshoe Creek and wrote, "Here I first tasted the waters of the great Columbia." That night they camped on the Lemhi River and the next afternoon encountered Chief Cameahwait's village north of Tendoy.

Capt. Lewis and Cameahwait returned with men and horses across Lemhi Pass and down to the Beaverhead, where the chief met his sister Sacajawea at Camp Fortunate (now flooded by Clark Canyon Dam).

Clark and eleven members of the Expedition, including Sacajawea, left with Cameahwait, recrossed the pass August 19, and descended to the Lemhi Valley to gather additional horses. Clark continued northwest to scout the Salmon River, while Cameahwait, Drouillard, and Sacajawea brought the additional pack stock back to Lewis at Camp Fortunate.

Lewis had cached some supplies, prepared the packs and saddles, and sunk the Expedition's canoes in a nearby pond for retrieval on the return journey. Lewis and the rest of the Expedition crossed Lemhi Pass for the last time on August 24. They did not use it on the return trip.

At the time of Lewis and Clark, Lemhi Pass was on the western boundary of the Louisiana Purchase. The Hudson's Bay Co. wanted the summit to serve as the division point between British and American interests in the Oregon Country, but the proposal was never accepted.

Rocky Mountain fur traders referred to Lemhi Pass as the North Pass, to differentiate it from the South Pass in Wyoming.

The route served the Red Rock stage line that carried passengers and freight between Salmon City and Red Rock, Montana, during the mining boom.

One can drive north along the road that parallels the border fence and descend Pattee and Warm Springs Creeks back to Tendoy and Highway 28.

The location of **Cameahwait's village** was five miles north of Tendoy, on the east side of the highway and river, at the mouth of Kenney Creek. This camp had moved south three miles between the time Capt. Lewis first entered it on August 14, and reentered it August 24. It served as the Expedition's base from August 20 to 29, while Capt. Clark examined the Salmon River to the north.

It was here that Capt. Clark gave ornithologists the first description of Clark's nutcracker, a crow-sized bird with flashing black, white and gray coloration, still frequently seen in the area.

It was also in this area, in 1823, that Finian MacDonald and his Hudson's Bay trappers set fire to the range in order to burn out a Blackfoot war party. The Indians lost ten warriors in the fray, but MacDonald said before he would again enter the region "the beaver will have a Gould skin."

Cameahwait's first village was located about 1.3 miles north of Kenney Creek, at the mouth of Sandy Creek, again on the east side of the road. Capt. Lewis and his three men were escorted to it by the chief and sixty of his warriors.

Though near starvation, the Indians fed the explorers and then lodged them in the only skin tipi in the village. When Lewis was given a piece of salmon, he said it "perfectly convinced me that we were on the waters of the Pacific Ocean." The men spent two days at this camp.

It is 4.5 miles farther to **Baker,** a town named in 1875 for its first settler.

Highway 28 continues northwest nine miles to its junction with Highway 93 in Salmon. Lewis and Clark noted conical willow wiers, twenty feet long, emplaced in the Lemhi to trap salmon along this stretch of the river.

State Highway No. 29 from a junction with Highway 28 in Leadore, northeast to the Idaho-Montana state line at Bannock Pass. Route length: 13.6 miles.

The pavement on the **Bannock Pass** highway ends after three miles. The dirt road climbs up the canyon along brushy Salt Creek.

In places the old Gilmore and Pittsburgh railroad bed can be glimpsed alongside the stream below the road (see Highway 28, Gilmore). After ten miles the leathered slopes are treeless. The view from the 7,672-foot summit, although attractive, is not spectacular.

This pass was used by the Nez Perce Indians after the Battle of Big Hole. They came south on Horse Prairie in Montana, then west across Bannock Pass on the morning of August 13, 1877, with their wounded in tow.

They went down Cruickshank Canyon and found the settlers near Leadore huddled in a stockade built a month earlier. Chief Tendoy of the Lemhi Shoshone had pledged his band would cooperate with the whites, and the Nez Perce Chiefs Looking Glass and White Bird advised the whites through a Shoshone interpreter that they would not be molested. The Nez Perce column then trailed southeast up the Lemhi, headed toward Yellowstone Park.

General Howard, in Montana, stayed east of Bannock Pass and crossed Monida Pass to the south, in the false expectation that his troops would intercept the Nez Perce.

U.S. Highway No. 30 from the Idaho-Oregon border east of Ontario, Oregon, easterly via Fruitland, New Plymouth, Caldwell, Nampa, Boise, Mountain Home, Bliss, Hagerman, Buhl, Filer, Twin Falls, Burley, Pocatello, McCammon, Lava Hot Springs, Soda Springs, and Montpelier to the Idaho-Wyoming state line near Border, Wyoming. (Overlaps I-84 from south of New Plymouth to Caldwell 18.1 miles, and from Nampa to Bliss 102.5 miles. Overlaps I-86 from Salt Lake interchange to Pocatello 68 miles, and I-15 from Pocatello to McCammon 19.6 miles) Route length: 424.3 miles.

U.S. 30 enters Idaho from the west, across the Snake River 0.4 miles from **Fruitland,** a town named at the turn of the century for its prolific apple and prune orchards.

The highway then extends south 4.4 miles in conjunction with U.S. 95 almost to I-84 before turning east another 4.7 miles into New Plymouth.

The streets of **New Plymouth** divulge a clue to its past: two boulevards curve in a horseshoe around the town's perimeter, and a trident of roads is superimposed on the toe of the shoe, which faces south.

As its name suggests, New Plymouth was a planned-community. In 1895 the newspaper writer William Smythe, a tenacious advocate

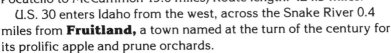

of land reclamation, chairman of the National Irrigation Congress, and later, Assistant Secretary of the Interior, visited Idaho and chose the area now known as New Plymouth for a model village of irrigated farms.

On returning to Chicago, Smythe called a public meeting to reveal his map and plans for the colony. Thirty-four members of the audience organized a seven-person committee to visit the location; their report was enthusiastic.

Aerial view of New Plymouth reveals its design.

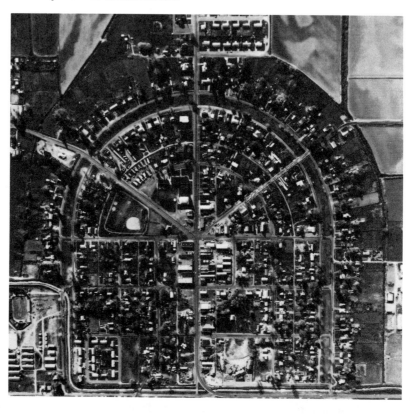

The Colony Company then sold each member twenty acres of irrigated land and twenty shares in the enterprise. Each investor was entitled to an acre on the "sole" of the horseshoe, which was reserved for the village site. Farmers were expected to reside in the village, within two miles of their crops. A covenant in the deeds provided for forfeiture of the land in the event that liquor was sold on the premises, "in order that there may be no inducement for men to be other than temperate." For forty years no alcohol was legally sold in the town.

222

"Every path has its puddle." The pilgrims of New Plymouth fought mud when it rained, and broken irrigation canals when it did not, but by 1896 over 1,000 acres had been cleared and planted. Gardens did well and fruit trees flourished. After its utopian ideals had been gradually abandoned, the company was purchased in 1901 by the town's farmers. By 1905 New Plymouth had grown to 200 persons.

Packing apples in New Plymouth, 1908.

New Plymouth cannery.

Orchards sustained the town until the Depression of the 1930s; at that time Payette County produced 40 percent of Idaho's fruit, and the area was served by the "Punkin Vine" railroad that extended from Emmett through Payette.

Though fruit is still an important crop, the region now supports a more diversified agriculture.

U.S. 30 travels south from New Plymouth five miles to a merger with I-84, then 17.9 miles to Caldwell (see Interstate 84, Caldwell), where it jogs 0.8 miles through town and parallels I-84 southeast 8.4 miles more to Nampa (see I-84, Nampa). There the highway slants north-northeast 3.1 miles and rejoins I-84.

U.S. 30 and I-84 are congruent for 11.1 miles east to Boise (see I-84, Boise) and for forty miles southeast to Mountain Home. They continue as one road for 4.9 miles around the northern outskirts of the city (see I-84, Mountain Home), then 25.5 miles to Glenns Ferry (see I-84, Glenns Ferry) and for 20.3 miles east to **Bliss.**

In 1878 David and Lydia Bliss and their three children moved to this site. Bliss arrived in the Hagerman Valley after the area around his ranches at Denver and Boise had become as crowded as seven men on a cot. He remained in the valley until his death in 1915, at age eighty.

In the early 1880s, when the Oregon Short Line built livestock pens and a loading chute at Bliss, sheep and cattle were driven south from Camas Prairie and north from the Three Forks country to the corrals and shearing sheds.

Ten years later Ben Mullins platted and surveyed a townsite and collected fees from settlers who had erected buildings near the siding; he eventually sold his rights.

Winters were longer than a Kansas well rope, and fuel was more precious than water. Lloyd Byrne recorded the tactic that some settlers adopted to survive the months of desert cold. At night a man would ride out to the middle of King Hill, west of town, and wait for an east-bound freight train. Boarding as it climbed the grade, he would hurl chunks of coal off a gondola until it reached the crest of the hill. The next morning he would bring his family with a wagon to collect the booty. If a train happened by, the husband would hide in the sagebrush; the railroad crew, thinking it was just a widow and her children retrieving a few lumps that had bounced off along the track, might even kick out a few extra pieces.

The highway continues south from Bliss 2.5 miles to an overlook of the Snake River on the west side of the road, with a sign that mentions "fossil beds."

The **Hagerman fossil beds** on the far side of the river, were discovered in 1928 by a valley resident; he notified the USGS. From 1930 to 1934 the Smithsonian Institution sent collecting expeditions to the site; 130 skulls and fifteen skeletons of a zebra-like horse, *Plesippus shoshonensis,* were recovered. (The animal was about the size of a modern horse.)

Lava flows, dated 3.5 million years ago by the potassium-argon method, blocked water-bourne sediments from the west and south and created a swampland. At the time, southwestern Idaho was a savannah or long-grass prairie region. Bones of zebras that died in the area were fossilized, and the Hagerman quarry, on state land, is considered one of the four major fossil deposits in North America.

A paved road on the right side of the highway 1.7 miles south of the fossil beds sign and immediately before the Malad River bridge, leads 1.5 miles north to the Archie Teater residence/studio – the only structure in Idaho designed by the architect Frank Lloyd Wright.

Wright never saw the stone building; the work was supervised by his son-in-law and a few apprentices. It is reported that after the original contractor Kent Hale, of Oakley, won a suit for delinquent payments, twenty-two different stonemasons were called to complete the job.

Hagerman is 3.5 miles south of the Malad River bridge; the town and valley are named for Stanley Hagerman, who established a post office for the area in 1892.

The town grew out of a village site by Lower Salmon Falls on the Snake River, where Shoshone Indians for centuries speared migrating salmon. The falls were the casualty of an Idaho Power Co. dam built in 1947.

South of Hagerman 3.5 miles, a sign indicates the turn-off for the state and national **Hagerman fish hatcheries.** The state hatchery covers thirty-five acres and produces about 1.7 million rainbow, steelhead and Kamloops trout. In addition, the six Oster Lakes and ten Anderson ponds are open to seasonal fishing.

The Hagerman National Fish Hatchery is on Riley Creek, two miles southeast of the state hatchery. Operated by the U.S. Fish and Wildlife Service since 1933, the facility raises about 3 million rainbow trout annually. Fish raised in the spring waters are transported by oxygenated tank trucks to streams in northern Nevada, eastern Oregon, and southern Idaho.

Just south of the fish hatcheries, U.S. 30 crosses the Snake River on the Gridley Bridge, and **Thousand Springs** can be seen flowing from the basalt bluff east of the highway and the river. (To reach the springs from Hagerman National Hatchery, drive north one mile to Vader Grade. Follow the Grade Rd. 1.5 miles east to the Idaho Power sign for the visitors center. The road travels four miles southeast through a half-dozen doglegs, and then turns west between a pair of fences down to a park next to the power plant.)

The springs were a landmark noted by emigrants on the Oregon

Thousand Springs before it was defaced. In the 1970s the National Park Service considered restoration of the springs as a National Monument. (Idaho Power Co. was willing to sell the power plant.)

Trail, who followed the south side of the river from Twin Falls to Upper Salmon Falls, near Hagerman. Discharged from the Snake River Plains aquifer, the springs are a feature of one of the larger ground-water systems in the world (see Highway 33), which is recharged by precipitation, percolation, and irrigation over an area of several thousand square miles. (The INEL, using tritium tracers, studied flow rates in the aquifer for seventeen years and found a maximum percolation of ten feet a day; the datum means some of the water emerging at Thousand Springs may have been underground for over 150 years.)

In 1911 the flow was amputated by the Thousand Springs Power Co. of Arizona when it built a concrete collecting flume 400 feet long along the upper face of the springs, and channeled the water to

226

electric turbines 165 feet below the canal. After purchasing the utility in 1917, Idaho Power Co. extended the diversion another 250 feet. From 1920 to 1945 the Thousand Springs plant produced about 20 percent of Idaho Power's electric load, and though it still supplies energy sufficient for about 6,000 homes, its overall contribution is no longer significant, a fact that has raised considerable discussion about restoration of the springs.

Concealed in a tangle of poison ivy and willows fifty yards north of the power plant, behind the fence and beyond the stream, rests a large steel tank and a few rusty lengths of riveted pipe (two feet in diameter) – relics of a brilliant idea: the **Priestly pneumatic water lift.**

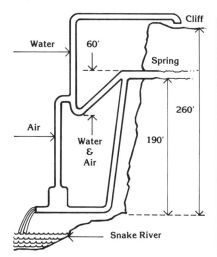

USGS photo of the Priestly lift.

In 1890 William Priestly wanted to irrigate the land on the bench 270 feet above the river, but his efforts to develop a well were frustrated by the basalt layer that underlies the topsoil. So Priestly conceived the idea of a hydraulic ram, powered by compressed air, to lift the flow from Thousand Springs onto the rim. Since the nearest railroad was seven miles away, the pipe had to be hauled by wagon, lowered over the rim and riveted in place. A water tank, about ten feet high, also built of ¼-inch steel, was assembled and riveted at the base of the springs.

Priestly aligned the mouth of the pipe with the largest spring; aerated water dropped 190 feet through one pipe to the reservoir tank, which drained through a lower pipe to the river. But the air, lighter than water, rose to the top of the tank and was carried up a

227

separate pipe joined to a second, shorter line that was also trained on the spring. The rising air met the flow from the second line and lifted its water, with seventy-five psi., sixty feet to the top of the cliff.

In 1894 the chief engineer on the Boise irrigation project A. D. Foote examined Priestly's invention and discussed it in a note added to the irrigation section of the 1911 *Encyclopaedia Britannica.* He described the arrangement as 70 percent efficient, and said Priestly, "had made a power, a transmission and a motor plant without a moving part."

In 1886 Dr. Julius Pohle patented a similar device in Arizona; Priestly, however, arrived at his discovery independently. The lift was copied in Canada and Connecticut, and it might have become popular had it not been for the rapid development of canal systems, along with more efficient steam and electrical pumps.

Priestly also designed a remarkable dredge to process fine gold from the Snake River at the base of the springs. The boat was twenty-four feet wide by sixty-five feet long, with sixteen mining tables powered by air pressure from the reservoir. It worked splendidly, but the fineness of the gold defied capture; the outfit was eventually auctioned at a sheriff's sale. Priestly apparently returned to farming. In 1972 the artifacts of his invention were added to the National Register.

U.S. 30 travels south three miles to the east turn-off for **Banbury Hot Springs.** The springs, on the riverbank 1.5 miles from the highway, were developed as a recreation site by an early rancher and feed a swimming pool and power plant. An RV park, picnic grounds, and boat ramp are on the grounds.

Buhl is ten miles southeast of the hot springs. The eastern capitalist Frank Buhl came west from Sharon, Pennsylvania, to Salt Lake City in 1901 to examine a mining property that interested him. On learning it had already been sold, he decided to investigate a proposed irrigation development in southern Idaho, the Twin Falls South Side Project.

I. B. Perrine met Mr. Buhl at the train depot in Shoshone and introduced him to Peter Kimberly and Stanley Milner. Buhl and Kimberly formed the corporation that accomplished the project. (See U.S. 93, Twin Falls.)

The townsite of Buhl was platted in 1905, and the Twin Falls Investment Co. sold lots at Broadway and Main Street for $1,750 each, in April, 1906. The location qualified as a village two years later; Buhl is now the second-largest town in Twin Falls County.

In 1927 a condensed milk company located here. Milk products still represent a major factor in the town's economy.

In 1928 Jack and Selma Tingey came north from Utah to start the area's first commercial trout farm at the springs north of the Snake River, six miles from Buhl. Tingey was the former commissioner of the Utah Fish and Game Department; his business was the forerunner of an enterprise that now employs local residents in the raising and processing of 25 milion pounds of trout annually.

Broadway St. in Buhl. (The repertoire of the local choir included the hymn "Bully for Beautiful Buhl.")

Commerical trout farm north of Buhl, on the Snake River.

One should visit three buildings in Buhl. On the southwest side of Broadway, as one enters town, the Mission-style Buhl city hall is evident. Built in 1919-1920 for $40,000, it included the fire department and city offices, and for farm families who visited town, restrooms, dressing rooms and a waiting lounge with writing tables.

On the same side of the street, one block south, is the Spanish-Moorish Ramona theater, remodeled in 1928 at a cost of $70,000, and named, in a local contest, for the heroine of Helen Hunt Jackson's novel. The theater has now been converted to a supper club.

One-half block northeast of Broadway on Maple St., one can view the United Methodist Church, built from 1920 to 1929; its construction was prolonged by the agricultural depression that struck the country in the early 1920s.

Balanced rock near Castleford.

A sixteen-mile side trip to the regionally-famous **Balanced Rock** can be made from Buhl; drive south from the south end of Broadway four miles toward **Castleford,** then west six miles to that town. At the outskirts turn north off Castleford Road onto 900 East Road one mile, then west on 3700 North Road four miles to an area where the road drops into a canyon of basalt formations which gave Castleford its name, and crosses Salmon Falls Creek. One-half mile west of the creek, the mushroom rock can be seen in silhouette against the northern skyline (the base of the forty-foot-high rock has been reinforced with concrete).

230

As U.S. 30 extends east from Buhl it passes three of the more **outstanding barns** left in the state. Those interested should turn south on the paved road exactly two miles east of Buhl. The large barn on the left 0.2 miles from the highway was built in 1910 by Henry Schick for Art Maxwell. The gambrel roof includes three shed dormers on each side, which illuminate the hayloft where local dances were held.

Henry Schick's own barn, identifiable by the onion-dome caps atop the barn ventilators and cement silo, is located 0.4 miles south of Maxwell's, on the west side of the road. The barn housed Schick's dairy herd.

One-tenth mile south of the Schick barn, across the intersection and on the east side of the road, stands the monumental Kunze barn, also built by Schick. Apparently it is the largest barn of its age in the state.

The structure was built in 1911 for Gustave Kunze, a Pennsylvania-German cheesemaker who had established a factory in Tillamook, Oregon, in 1891. His Idaho Clover Leaf Cheese factory was located in the wooden building, now used as a granary, visible east of the barn. Kunze had over 100 cows in his dairy herd; the large transept that extends behind the barn was built in 1916 when milk inspectors stipulated that horses must be stalled in quarters separate from those for dairy cows.

(Return to U.S. 30.)

Highway 30 continues southeast 5.8 miles to **Filer.** Established in 1906 at the end of the Oregon Short Line branch from Twin Falls, the town was named for the general manager of the Twin Falls Canal Company.

One and one-half miles east of Filer the road merges with U.S. 93 for 3.4 miles to Twin Falls (See U.S. 93, Twin Falls). Traveling three miles through Twin Falls, U.S. 30 emerges east of the town and continues three miles more before it doglegs one mile south into **Kimberly.** Peter Kimberly, as mentioned earlier, was one of the Pennsylvania financiers of the Twin Falls South Side Project. The town was founded in 1906.

Hansen, 2.4 miles east of Kimberly, bears the name of a pioneer merchant, John Hansen, who was also county superintendent of schools, recorder and probate judge, as well as commissioner of the U.S. Land Office.

The town is the starting point for a twenty-eight-mile drive to two sites of interest, one historical and the other scenic. After following County Road G 3 (Rock Creek Rd. or 3800 East Rd.) south from Hansen five miles, turn west on 3200 North Road one mile to a group of five buildings known as the **Rock Creek Stage Station,** or the Stricker store and homesite.

The station was established in 1865 on the Oregon Trail by James Bascom. Of necessity, it was a campground for emigrant wagons because Rock Creek was the first water reached after a trek of almost twenty miles from the Snake River. In 1869 it became a stop on Ben Halliday's stage and freight line, which ran trips three times a week from Kelton, Utah, to Boise.

Bascom's log store was purchased by Herman Stricker in 1875, and one of the Stricker descendents donated the building to the Daughters of Utah Pioneers. A rock root-cellar with a sod roof is located just north of the store. In 1979 the store and homesite were placed on the National Register of Historic Places.

From the stage station return to Road G 3, and continue south 9.1 miles into the Sawtooth National Forest and the **Rock Creek Canyon-Magic Mountain scenic area.** The road enters the gorge between spectacular basalt ramparts and gradually ascends the drainage for fourteen miles; typical desert flora of sage, rabbitbrush, cottonwoods, and juniper soon gives way to ponderosa, then lodgepole, and finally quaking aspen and subalpine fir at an elevation of 7,000 feet. The pavement ends at Magic Mountain Ski Area; however, during the summer one can drive thirty-two miles over dirt roads to Oakley. (Return to Hansen.)

South Side Canal, 1905 (left to right): Messrs Murtaugh, Kimberly, Buhl, Milner, McCollum, Liz Murtaugh, Mssrs. Filer, Perrine.

U.S. 30 heads east from Hansen for 4.3 miles, then south 4.7 miles, at which point it is one mile south of **Murtaugh,** a farm community named for the engineer and assistant manager of the Twin Falls Canal Co., Mark Murtaugh.

232

The site of **Caldron Linn** is two miles from Murtaugh. In 1811 an expedition of the Pacific Fur Company, owned by John Jacob Astor, and led by Wilson Price Hunt, abandoned its canoes on the Snake River at Caldron Linn and divided into three groups. They left the canyon in a westerly direction en route to Oregon.

Known as the Astorians, the men had departed St. Louis in 1810 and embarked in canoes on Henrys Fork of the Snake near Fort Henry (see Highway 20, St. Anthony) in October, 1811. At a point one mile below the site now occupied by Milner Dam, "an old experienced Canadian steersman named Antoine Clappine, one of the most valuable of the voyagers" overturned and was drowned; the other five persons aboard reached shore. After scouting downstream and seeing the Caldron, the expedition quit the river.

Almost all of the men, as well as the one woman, eventually reached the mouth of the Columbia, but they suffered severely along the way. A year later Robert Stuart returned to the site to retrieve supplies that had been cached there. Six of the caches had been opened and rifled. Looking at the bluffs downstream, Stuart wrote:

For the greater part nothing that walks the earth could possibly pass between them, & the water, which in such places is never more than 40 yds wide, rushing with irresistable force over a bed of such Rocks as makes the spray fly equal to the surf of the Ocean, breaking violently on a lee Shore, In particular spots the stream expands to the breadth of an hundred yards, but its general width for the 30 miles in question is from 35 to 40, and in one place, at the Caldron Linn the whole body of the River is confined between 2 ledges of Rock somewhat less than 40 feet apart & Here indeed its terrific appearance beggars all description – Hecate's caldron was never half so agitated when vomiting even the most diabolical spells, as is this Linn in a low stage of water & its bearing in idea such a proximity of resemblance to that or something more infernal, I think well authorizes it to retain the new name it has, more particularly as the tout ensemble of these 30 miles has been baptised the Devils Scuttle Hole.

In 1938 several rusty traps and guns were recovered two miles below Milner Dam; they were of the type carried by the Astorians and are believed to be from Clappine's canoe. The artifacts now rest in the State Historical Society museum in Boise.

To see Caldron Linn take 4500 East Rd. 1.2 miles into Murtaugh, turn east through town 0.4 miles, dogleg north at the Y and drive east 0.6 miles to a T. Take the right, or south, fork, that curves east 0.6 miles then straightens on 3425 North Rd., and drive 0.6 miles

233

farther. Park and walk north 100 yards to the rim where the Caldron can be seen in the canyon below. It is the most southern point on the entire Snake River.

Caldron Linn.

Highway 30 proceeds east past Murtaugh twenty-one miles to Burley (See I-84, Burley), follows Main St. 1.8 miles through town, then swings north across the Snake River 2.1 miles to Heyburn, and rejoins I-84.

234

Heyburn, though named for U.S. Senator Weldon Heyburn (1903-1912), should be better known as the birthplace of Donald Crabtree.

Born here in 1912, raised in Salmon, and a resident of Kimberly at the time of his death in 1980, Crabtree established an international reputation among archaeologists for his research into stone-tool technology.

In the 1930s he studied at the University of California under Charles Camp and Alfred Kroeber. Later he worked at the Ohio State Museum replicating stone tools found in the eastern U.S. Crabtree became the finest flintknapper (more familiarly, a maker of stone arrowheads, weapons and tools) in the world. His efforts were brought to the attention of Dr. Earl Swanson at Idaho State Univ., who was so impressed by the work that he was able to obtain a series of grants from the National Science Foundation to finance Crabtree's investigation of the techniques, and the consequences of techniques, used on glassy rocks to make flaked-stone tools.

Prior to Crabtree's work, stone tools were classified by shape or assumed function. Today classification requires consideration of the type of flake scars, features of the margins, and other technical characteristics previously unrecognized; in fact, it has been suggested Crabtree's contributions to archaeology and anthropology were significant enough to divide American archaeology into pre-Crabtree and post-Crabtree eras. In 1979 the flintknapper was granted an honorary Doctor of Science degree by the University of Idaho.

Though officially retired, Dr. Crabtree was still a lecturer and teacher with years of important scientific contributions to make when he died at age seventy-eight. On learning of his death, a colleague recalled William James' remark, "I have often said that the best argument I knew for an immortal life was the existence of a man who deserved one."

Interstate 84 overlaps U.S. 30 east of Heyburn for 10.8 miles to a junction with Interstate 86, where that highway, also overlapping U.S. 30, extends northeast 60.2 miles to the outskirts of Pocatello (see I-15, Pocatello).

U.S. 30 splits southeast from I-86, 4.7 miles west of the city, travels 3.9 miles through town and joins I-15 in a southerly direction 18.2 miles to McCammon, where it reestablishes itself at Exit 47.

In 1882 **McCammon** (named for a railroad official) was the junction of the Oregon Short Line and Utah and Northern railroads. Because the homesteader Henry Harkness refused to sell the railroad the land that it needed for facilities, the junction lost out to Pocatello as the major rail center for southeastern Idaho.

U.S. 30 travels east from McCammon up the **Portneuf River,** a stream that memorializes one of Peter Skene Ogden's trappers who was murdered by Indians along its banks.

Lava Hot Springs is 12.6 miles east of McCammon on the Portneuf River; it is one of Idaho's more popular resort areas.

The hot springs were a neutral gathering ground for several Indian tribes, including the Bannock and Shoshone. The first white settlement at the location (1880-1910) was known as Dempsey, after an Irish-born trapper who had camped in the area in 1860, before moving on to Montana.

Lava Hot Springs on the Portneuf River.

In 1883 the Oregon Short Line railroad came from Wyoming via Montpelier northwest through the valley, but the springs remained a flag stop until the OSL built a depot twenty years later.

After Congress ratified the Pocatello Cession Agreement in 1900, whereby the Bannock-Shoshone sold 418,000 acres off the southern end of their reservation, the U.S. government obtained the hot springs area and ceded 183 acres of it to the state of Idaho.

An English immigrant, John Hall, had homesteaded near the site,

236

and he filed a townsite plat in 1911. Four years later the lots he sold were incorporated as Lava Hot Springs village.

The Hot Springs themselves are on state land and are administered through state appropriations to the Lava Hot Springs Foundation. In 1911 a log structure was built over a portion of the springs, followed in 1920 by the State Natatorium, with mud baths and indoor-outdoor swimming pools.

The village had its own pool in the middle of town. Hotels and summer homes accommodated a thriving tourist business. In 1924 more 200,000 persons visited the resort.

In 1968 the state legislature appropriated $550,000 for construction of the modern swimming complex visible from the highway above town. The Olympic-sized pool is filled with mineral

Tourists at the hot springs.

water that flows from the springs at a rate of 6 million gallons a day, odor-free and 110 degrees F.

Lava Hot Springs is particularly suited for a walking tour of its historical buildings. Begin on West Main St. at the **town museum** in the Boyce Hotel, where early photographs provide a sense of the resort's milieu.

Walk east down Main St. one block to Center St. and south one block to Elm St. The small house on the corner behind the Royal

Hotel was built in 1910 by John Hall, the first house on the townsite. It was a log cabin that has since been enclosed by stucco.

Return to Main St. and continue east. In 1936 the block on the north side of the street between Center and East First Ave. was destroyed by fire.

The Whitestone Hotel, one of the two more imposing commercial buildings in town, occupies the block on the north side of Main St. at East Second Ave. Built by the Maranoni brothers from sandstone quarried southwest of town, it opened on the Fourth of July, 1919. Its style is Renaissance revival.

In addition to hotel rooms, the Whitestone contained a ballroom, cabaret and theater; free mineral baths in the basement were provided for guests. Both hotel and theater operated until the 1960s.

Walk north on East Second Ave. one block to the three-story Riverside Inn, a brick, Georgian Revival hotel, built in an L-shape facing the river.

The Inn dates from 1914. It was the property of William Godfrey, a local rancher who filed a claim for use of the hot springs water. Four large tubs in the basement are still available to hotel guests.

Considerable care has been devoted to the interior restoration of the Riverside Inn. A delightful place to stay, it is one of the better-kept secrets in Idaho.

To view the old State Natatorium, cross the footbridge over the Portneuf to the large building facing the Riverside. Though no longer open to the public, the natatorium contains a forty-five by ninety-foot pool with sixty-two dressing rooms around its edge, and a balcony on three sides that held 300 spectators. The roof is supported by elaborate wooden trusses. Recently the outside pool was filled in order to increase the size of the riverbank park.

Highway 30 continues 6.9 miles east from Lava Hot Springs to an intersection with a paved road that leads due north 4.9 miles to **Bancroft,** a small farming town named in 1905 for the vice-president of the OSL.

Ten miles north of Bancroft by paved road is the captivating settlement of **Chesterfield,** a Mormon settlement where the past stands still, like time in a watch unwound.

In 1879 Chester Call, and his nephew Christian Nelson, from Bountiful, Utah, entered the Portneuf Valley in search of grazing land for their horses. They found this area suited their needs and went home to persuade twelve families to join them in a new endeavor.

Local lore states that the town's name honored Chester Call, as

238

well as the English town native to some of the first settlers.

A traditional Mormon townsite grid was laid out over the hilly terrain: thirty-five ten-acre blocks, seven tiers north and south, and five east and west, every block square. The streets were ninety-nine feet wide. Though dimmed by age and agriculture, the pattern is still evident.

The LDS Chesterfield Ward was recognized in 1884, and the town's population eventually reached 400. Over 80 percent of the residents were lineal descendants, or married to descendants, of Cyril Call (1785-1873). The others were close friends of Call relatives before they moved to the area.

Apparently social changes in the 1900s reduced the site to its near-ghost town status: the opening of Carey Act lands in southwestern Idaho, World War I, the agricultural depression of the early 1920s, and the Great Depression of the 1930s.

At a century's remove the town now contains one of the better Mormon historical endowments left in the state. The entire site has been added to the National Register of Historic Places. Twenty-three of the original buildings still sprinkle the site; all but two were built before 1910. A variety of architectural styles and materials is represented.

Six homes, two stores, the church, school, and tithing office are made from orange bricks fired here. Some of the wood "slab" homes built of *vertical,* squared logs, chinked with batten strips are most unusual.

In 1960 after the ward closed, the Daughters of Utah Pioneers obtained permission from the LDS church to maintain the meeting house on the hill as a memorial and museum.

Local citizens formed the Chesterfield Foundation, Inc., in the 1970s and assumed responsibility for the protection and annotation of the buildings.

(Return to U.S. 30.)

Sheep Rock (now Soda Point), on the south side of Highway 30, eight miles east of the Bancroft Rd., was a noted landmark on the Oregon Trail. Here the main trail swings northwest, while the Bear River elbows south and gropes its way to the Great Salt Lake.

The highway continues east along the north side of Soda Point Reservoir 7.1 miles to **Soda Springs.** This town traces its origins to Utah and the Morrisite rebellion of 1862.

A Welshman named Joseph Morris received "revelations" that directed him to warn Brigham Young that he was "wandering from the right course." Rebuked severely, Morris moved to a site on the

Weber River thirty-five miles north of Salt Lake City, where his own group of believers gathered in a settlement called Kington Fort. When some of Morris's prophecies proved amiss, however, apostates departed with a portion of the communal grain. The remaining Morrisites then took the apostates hostage. Judge Kinney's writ for the release of the prisoners was defied, and Governor Harding dispatched a deputy marshal with the militia to enforce the order. A three-day battle resulted in the deaths of two militiamen and six Morrisites, Joseph Morris among them.

Camp Douglas, established in 1862 by General Patrick Connor, became a refuge for the Morrisites, and the following spring, Connor, intending to establish a post for the protection of the emigrants on the Oregon Trail, took 160 members of the sect, along with his troops, to Soda Springs. The journey required fifteen days.

After selecting a mile-square site for Camp Connor, the General surveyed a townsite adjacent to the camp, just west of present Soda Springs. By June the Morrisites had roofed twenty houses, and during the fall a detachment of sixty soldiers cleared a wagon road from Franklin to Soda Springs.

In 1865 General Connor ordered the camp abandoned. In the meantime, a number of soldiers had married Morrisite girls.

In 1870 Brigham Young and W. R. Hooper bought land immediately northeast of the village and built houses in the "upper town" for twelve families, who moved north from Utah. When the OSL arrived in 1882, its depot drew the settlers from the "lower town" to the new location. The waters of Soda Point Reservoir have partially flooded the old townsite. In 1919 Soda Springs became the seat of Caribou County; it remains the youngest county in the state. The region has been sustained by the development of phosphate beds a few miles east of town. (See Highway 34, Conda).

Monsanto Chemical Co. came to Soda Springs in 1951 and built a multi-million dollar plant 2.5 miles northeast of the city to produce elemental phosphorus.

Phosphate ore is strip-mined fifteen miles away and hauled by tandem-trailer rigs on a private road to the plant. The phosphorus is used to manufacture phosphates for detergents, fertilizer, food, and water treatment.

In 1963 Kerr-McGee Oil Industries opened a plant adjacent to Monsanto to recover vanadium compounds from a by-product of the phosphate plant. Most of the vanadium compounds are used as steel alloys and chemical catalysts.

One block north of U.S. 30, on Main St. in Soda Springs, one can see the site of the town's homemade geyser. In 1937, while

240

attempting to locate hot water for a community swimming pool, the drill crew struck a chamber of carbon dioxide. The geyser had to be capped because its mineral content discolored nearby buildings.

In the park across the street from the geyser, a Dinkey engine used in the construction of the Soda Point Reservoir is displayed. It was discovered when the reservoir was drained in 1977; U.P. restored it and gave it to the city.

Soda Springs geyser in city-center.

Early view of Soda Springs (top left).

Idanha Hotel at Soda Springs.

Hooper and **Steamboat** are two of the more **historic springs** that can still be seen in the Soda Springs area. Travel east from Main St. three bocks on First South and turn north on Third East for 1.5 miles. At the Y follow the curve to the west another 0.5 miles to the pavillion in the park. John C. Fremont visited Hooper springs in 1843, and William Henry Jackson was here in 1871.

Steamboat was a more famous spring, with a hot three-foot geyser. Its subterranean noise made it the subject of innumerable comments by emigrants on the Oregon Trail. Though inundated by the slack water of Soda Point Reservoir, its bubbles still dimple the surface of the water, and it can be observed on a calm day. To see it, drive west from town on U.S. 30 two miles to the country club; 0.4 miles west of the clubhouse turn south on a gravel road and follow it 0.4 miles to a point just past the Monsanto picnic pavilion. Walk to the knoll overlooking the reservoir, where the boil broaches the surface.

241

U.S. 30 resumes an easterly course from Soda Springs and after fourteen miles crosses Georgetown Summit (6,283 elev.), then drops 700 feet in four miles to **Georgetown.**

Settled in 1870 at the urging of Brigham Young, who instructed a band of Saints to establish a community somewhere between Soda Springs and Montpelier, the area was called Twin Creeks for two years, until Young visited the location and requested the name be changed to honor his companion, George Cannon.

Phosphate mining in nearby Georgetown Canyon was the major employment here from 1908 until the 1960s. Farming is now the principal occupation.

Bennington is six miles southeast of Georgetown; it was established in 1860, by an act of the Richland County court in Utah, before anyone knew the area was in Idaho Territory.

Named for the Vermont community where Brigham Young once lived, the town struggled to survive. Winters came early and lasted long; summers brought a dearth of water. In the 1930s a WPA project developed a more reliable water supply for the town.

Five miles farther south Highway 30 reaches **Montpelier.** In April, 1864, sixteen families moved from the west side of Bear Valley to the present townsite. A ferry was built at the Bear River crossing, two miles west of the settlement, and by mid-summer the number of families had doubled. Brigham Young suggested that the community be named after his birthplace in Vermont.

The arrival of the Oregon Short Line (from Wyoming in 1882) made Montpelier the shipping point for the valleys of Bear Lake, Thomas Fork and Star. Stockyards were built on the northwest side of town, and the OSL spent $100,000 on machine shops and a roundhouse for maintenance of trains. But the sudden increase in outsiders doing business here divided Montpelier into a Mormon "uptown" and a Gentile "downtown" – Washington Avenue connected the two. Infected with the village virus for twenty years, each district wished the Devil would swallow the other sideways.

In 1892 the town was recognized as a city of the second-class; by 1900, with a population of 1,400, it was the largest settlement in Bear Lake Valley. When the highway was rerouted westerly on Washington St., uptown businesses were compelled to move downtown, and differences were finally reconciled.

On August 13, 1896, the Montpelier bank was robbed of $7,165 by George Leroy Parker (alias Butch Cassidy), William McGinnis (alias Elza Lay), and Bob Meeks. The outlaws allegedly wanted the money to hire lawyers for their pard, Matt Warner, who was in the Ogden, Utah, jail awaiting trial on a murder charge. Only Meeks was ever apprehended. He was sentenced to thirty-five years in the state penitentiary at Boise, where he escaped twice; the second time a gunshot wound cost him one leg. Committed to the insane asylum at Blackfoot, he escaped again and managed to reach his brother's ranch in Fort Bridger, Wyoming, where the local sheriff left him in peace. (The bank has been incorporated into the Montgomery Ward office on the south side of Washington St., between Eighth and Ninth Sts.)

Montpelier as it looked in 1920.

Montpelier has three historic buildings worth a visit. The old tithing house of the Montpelier Stake is located at 430 Clay St., two doors from the corner of North Fourth St. Built in 1895, the house has been converted to the town's relic hall by the Daughters of Utah Pioneers. (The Latter Day Saints were expected to contribute one-tenth of their income and one-tenth of their labor to the Church.)

One block east of the tithing house, and two blocks south, at 155 Fifth St., stands the three-story John Bagley mansion.

Bagley, the state attorney general (1903-1904) built the Queen Anne-style house in 1890 for his wife. A tragic tale of a mother and daughter's suicide stains this otherwise resplendent structure.

The semi-circular LDS tabernacle, with ornate terra-cotta trim, is located at Washington and Sixth Sts. It was built in 1918 at a cost of

$50,000 by the same Salt Lake architectural firm that made the plans for a kindred tabernacle in Blackfoot.

Highway 30 continues southeast along the Bear River, 11.7 miles, then east to Border Summit (6,335 elev.).

An excellent view of an undisturbed reach of the Oregon Trail can be seen just north of Border Summit. Take the road immediately west of the summit, on the north side of the highway, and follow its north fork 0.6 miles. Look southwest down toward Thomas Fork and the trail can be seen angling northwest uphill from the valley. This is a good spot to sit and read Loren Eiseley's poem "Oregon Trail." With such a view, most history buffs can excuse the somewhat maudlin tone:

It is spring somewhere beyond Chimney Rock
on the old Oregon trail now.
I remember the time when the ruts of the wagons
could still be seen across a half mile
of unbroken short-grass prairie as though
in that high air they had just passed,
the rolling Conestoga wagons
heavy-freighted for the Sierras,
as though time was only yesterday,
as though, if one hurried, a fast horse with good wind
would bring you to the buckskinned outriders
and the lined brown women with sunbonnets,
the grandmothers, the fathers, children
who became the forest cutters, wheat raisers, gold seekers,
sharpshooters, range killers, users of
the first Colts in the cattle wars or at the gamblers' tables –
a time a fast horse might still catch up with almost anything.
I whirl my animal three times about
and bend over the tracks trampling uncertainly.
It is time to go home.
But the other time is there tempting just beyond the horizon.
I back off reluctantly and out of some shamed courtesy
slip my spectacles into my pocket and raise my hand
saying a wordless goodbye.

The highway travels east from the summit three miles to the Wyoming state line, 11.8 miles from Cokeville, Wyoming.

244

State Highway No. 31 from a junction with U.S. 26 in Swan Valley northeasterly to a junction with Highway 33 in Victor. Route length: 21 miles.

This highway rambles with delightful inefficiency north to Victor. It climbs fourteen miles up Pine Creek, through the Big Hole Mountains to Pine Creek Pass (6,764 elev.) Most of this stretch is within Targhee National Forest, where stands of fir and aspen are splotched with meadows. From the summit the road descends 6.1 miles to Victor in the Teton Basin.

State Highway No. 32 from a junction with Highway 33 northwest of Tetonia, northerly and northwesterly via Felt, Lamont and Drummond to a junction with U.S. 20 in Ashton. Route length: 29.3 miles.

Highway 32 travels straight as a section line, which it is, from the Tetonia area to a bridge across Bitch Creek. On a clear day, the Teton Range is visible to the east, like the toothed jaw of a bear.

From Bitch Creek the highway threads its way through farm country, and two hamlets with railroad depots attached, and 20.5 miles later reaches Ashton.

State Highway No. 33 from a junction with Highway 22 at Howe, easterly and southerly via Mud Lake, Rexburg, Teton, Newdale, Tetonia, Driggs and Victor, up Trail Creek canyon to the Idaho-Wyoming border. Route length: 99.9 miles.

Highway 33 begins at Howe and travels twenty-eight miles east and north to Mud Lake. It overlaps Highway 28 for 14.1 miles east between Mud Lake and I-15.

From I-15 the road continues due east, and after eleven miles the **Menan Buttes** can be seen three miles south of the highway.

The buttes are well-preserved cones of glassy olivine-basalt tuff 500 and 800 feet high, with 300-foot craters. Their unusual shape is the result of an eruption through the water-soaked flood plain of the Snake River. As the lava struck the water, extruded glass fragments, chilled to solidity, built the inner and outer walls of the craters. The explosive power of the eruption is indicated by basalt blocks, three to five feet in diameter, scattered around the crater rim. Prevailing winds elongated the cones northeastward.

Both cones may have been formed in a few months, probably within the last 30,000 years. Henrys Fork, which flowed where North Butte now stands, was diverted southward to its present course.

(The Buttes are a National Natural Landmark.)

245

Three miles farther, on the south side of the highway is **Beaver Dick Park,** on the bank of Henrys Fork. The graves of a mountain man's family are located here.

Beaver Dick Leigh was an English immigrant who became a western trapper. He came north from Utah to Idaho and Wyoming in the 1840s. Leigh married an Indian named Jenny, and the couple had five children. When the trapper guided F. V. Hayden's surveyors through Jackson Hole, the men named Leigh and Jenny Lakes for the couple; the lakes are now within Grand Teton National Park.

For many years, the Leighs lived on an island between meanders of the river near the present park. In 1876 the family traveled to Montana on a hunt. After they had stayed in a cabin, Jenny became ill and her husband brought the family back to Idaho. They had been infected by smallpox, and one by one they died – only Beaver Dick survived. He buried his wife and children not far from the riverbank, marked the graves, and left the area. The graves can still be seen.

Leigh later married again, and his wife, Susan Tadpole, bore him three children. The trapper died in 1899 and is buried on his place north of Newdale, Idaho.

Highway 33 crosses Henrys Fork of the Snake River and five miles farther enters Rexburg (see U.S. 20, Rexburg). The road veers northeast and overlaps U.S. 20 for 5.6 miles to Sugar City where it doglegs 1.2 miles northeast through town and then continues east 2.7 miles to **Teton,** and 2.3 miles farther to **Newdale,** a town established in 1914, one year before the railroad arrived and named it.

Three and one-quarter miles east of the center of Newdale, on the south side of Highway 33 is a small sign: **Teton Dam Site** ⟶. Turn north on the paved road opposite the sign one mile to the overlook. It offers one of the more bizarre scenes in the West: a deserted engineering lab, a parking lot with grass growing in the cracks, and in the chasm beyond the fence, the great pyramid of the Teton – all that remains of a 9.5 million-cubic-yard earth dam. The silence is that of the Empty Quarter. On nearby signs the Bureau of Reclamation pulls its own oar through explanations of why the dam failed, and what perks were thereby lost.

If foresight were as good as hindsight, we would all be better off by a damn sight. This was a dam that should never have been built. It was constructed on highly permeable, intensely jointed volcanic rocks, by a government agency that exaggerated the benefits and

246

downgraded the costs in order to serve its own ends and those of a special-interest group which was doing well without it. The project was opposed by the Environmental Protection Agency, the Bureau of Sports Fisheries, the Idaho Fish and Game Department, and the Idaho Conservation League.

In 1948 the Fremont Madison Irrigation District began lobbying the Bureau of Reclamation for a reservoir on the Teton River. Most of the flow had been claimed under prior appropriation rights, and only surplus water could be diverted from downstream users; in other words, if the Teton reservoir was filled, and American Falls reservoir downstream was not, the law would require upstream water be released. The Bureau, in collusion with the irrigation district, worked out a scheme for 100 wells downriver from the Teton Dam. The wells would pump groundwater into the Teton and Snake Rivers to meet downstream requirements in low-water years. The entire project was based on these wells, which would cost $3.6 million. Downstream well-water could be traded to persons with prior appropriation rights in return for water stored behind Teton Dam.

Floods are a penalty rivers periodically dish out to those foolish enough to build on a flood plain. Flood control, however, was used as a stalking horse to justify the dam. The Army Corps of Engineers had studied the river for a levee system, but was unable to find economic justification for the project. In 1972 the Corps estimated the flood benefits to be $146,000. To validate the Bureau of Reclamation's cost-benefit figure, a Teton flood equal in magnitude to the worst on record would have had to occur once every three years.

Irrigation claims were also fallacious. Three and one-half acre feet of water is sufficient to grow a crop. The Idaho Department of Water Administration will not authorize more than five acre feet unless additional need is proved. Yet 87,000 acres of the 111,000 that the Bureau stated were in need of supplemental irrigation already received an average of eleven acre feet.

Phase Two of the project intended to irrigate 37,000 additional acres with a thirty-mile pump canal and a twenty-eight-mile gravity canal. However, farms on that acreage along the Rexburg bench averaged 1,200 acres, which placed them outside the federal 320-acre eligibility limit. Additionally, by 1972, 20,000 acres of that land was already irrigated by private means.

Most of the 13,000 k.w. from the Teton Dam was to be used for irrigation pumping; excess power was to be marketed by the Bonneville Power Administration in other areas. Even under the

33
IDAHO

most optimistic projections by the Bureau of Reclamation, irrigators would pay only 13 percent of the project, while rate payers and taxpayers picked up the balance.

In 1964 the dam was approved by Congress. Construction began in 1972 under a $40 million contract awarded to Morrison-Knudsen Co. and Peter Kiewit Son's Co. It was scheduled for completion in 1976.

Up to 500 men worked on three shifts around the clock, though winter crews were reduced to about seventy-five men. A key trench was excavated 100 feet into the bedrock. All borrow areas were in the vicinity of the dam, and hopper towers loaded hauling units at each abutment. The finished structure was 305 feet high, 3,050 feet long, and 1,600 feet wide at the base.

Teton Dam three days after its collapse. If experience is proportional to the amount of equipment ruined, the Bureau of Reclamation is now a grizzled veteran.

View looking southwest, downstream.

On Saturday morning, June 5, 1976, the reservoir was nearly full. At 8:30 A.M. two leaks were reported: one on the north embankment 130 feet from the crest; the other at the downstream toe of the dam. At 10:00 A.M. another leak appeared near the crest. Crews with bulldozers were summoned to plug the gap; the machines were swallowed by the growing hole. Evacuation warnings were sent to the Fremont and Madison County sheriff's offices. At 11:15 A.M. an engineer warned four fishermen in a raft below the dam to get off the river. At 11:52 A.M. the dam split like a snake's back. Eighty billion gallons surged south.

248

"The sound was just like a roar," said a witness, "like we were standing at the bottom of a waterfall. The powerhouse disintegrated like it was made of cardboard. There was a beautiful grove of cottonwood trees and they bowed over like matchsticks. There was a strange odor. I guess it was just the fresh dirt."

The flood moved about fifteen miles per hour. It hit Wilford first, drowned six persons and destroyed 150 homes. It passed through Sugar City at 1:00 P.M., Rexburg at 2:30 P.M., then Idaho Falls, Shelley, Blackfoot, and finally, three days later, into the backwaters of the American Falls Reservoir.

Topsoil was stripped or buried on thousands of acres, 25,000 persons were driven from their homes, 18,000 head of stock were lost, and thirty-two miles of railroad. Damages amounted to $800 million.

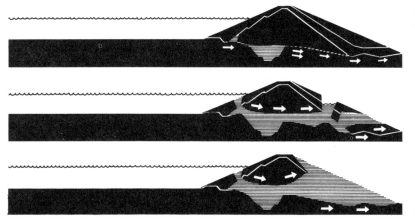

Mechanism of failure.

"Nature bats last."

An independent panel of nine prominent engineers and geologists was appointed to investigate the cause of the failure. Their 580-page report cited three principal reasons: 1.) The geological formation at the damsite allowed water to move with equal ease in most directions; open joints provided passages for egress of water. 2.) Clayey silts chosen for the key trench and core fill were highly erodable. 3.) Rock immediately beneath the grout cap was not adequately sealed. Leakage beneath the grout cap began piping in the key trench and eroded a tunnel across the base of the fill.

In order to prevent a recurrence of such a disaster, the Bureau of Reclamation agreed to a review of design and construction activities on any major dam by engineers outside the government.

The feelings of most Idahoans about the incident were summarized in a verse by a flood victim: "If I sound a little bitter, / it's for certain that I am / Because right now the Upper Valley / isn't worth a Teton Dam."

Continue east and southeast on Highway 33, 23.8 miles to
Tetonia. The town is on the northern end of the **Teton Valley,**
once known as **Pierre's Hole.** It is a basin thirty miles long and
fifteen wide, bounded on the west and south by the Big Hole
Mountains, and on the east by the Teton Range.

The valley was discovered in 1808 by John Colter, a mountain
man and trapper who had served with the Lewis and Clark
Expedition. The hole was named, however, for Pierre Tevanitagon,
who led a band of Canadian-Iroquois trappers into the area while
working for David Mackay and the North West Company of
Montreal. Pierre was killed in 1827 by Blackfoot on the head of the
Jefferson River in Montana.

The **Teton Range,** visible along the eastern horizon from
Tetonia to Victor, is less than ten million years old, the youngest
mountains in the Rockies. The range has been elevated on a
faultline that lies along its eastern base, and lift continues at the rate
of an inch every hundred years or so.

The peaks, which were glaciated as recently as 9,000 years ago,
consist of gneiss, schist, granite and pegmatite.

Driggs is 8.5 miles southeast of Tetonia. There were few settlers
in the Teton Valley in 1888 when two Mormons arrived from Salt
Lake City to look over the country. They were so impressed that
they staked claims, and persuaded their lawyer-friend, B. W. Driggs,
to journey north from Salt Lake and do likewise.

The favorable reports from these men caused a wagon train of
emigrants to depart from Temple Square in Salt Lake City in March,
1889, bound 400 miles for the Teton Valley. They found the climate
rigorous, but cut wild hay, dug canals, and established the first
farming town in the basin. In 1915 it became the seat of Teton
County.

The fur trade's uproarious **1832 rendezvous** (July 8-18) was
held about one mile south of Driggs, on the east side of the road,
just north of Teton Creek. Pierre's Hole was noisier than a calf corral
as over 200 mountain men joined 120 lodges of Nez Perce and 80
lodges of Flatheads to trade and frolic a thousand miles from
civilization.

The 1832 rendezvous was the best reported of all the mountain
gatherings; nine men who were present published accounts. The
Rocky Mountain Fur Company of Fitzpatrick, Sublette, and Bridger
was camped on the site with 100 trappers, and John Jacob Astor's
American Fur Company trappers were encamped three miles south,
up the valley. Most of the important figures of the fur era were here:

Warren Ferris, Bill and Milton Sublette, Robert Campbell, Nat Wyeth, Zenas Leonard, Joe Meek, Jim Bridger, Antoine Godin, Henry Fraeb, Jean Baptise Gervais, Alexander Sinclair, Capt. Bonneville, Henry Vanderburg, Andrew Dripps. There must have been many a blanket stretched and many a long bow pulled as the flames licked the logs of twenty campfires.

Washington Irving, working from Capt. Bonneville's journals, left this description:

In this valley was congregated the motley populace connected with the fur trade. Here two rival companies had their encampments, with their retainers of all kinds: traders, trappers, hunters, and half-breeds, assembled from all quarters, awaiting their yearly supplies, and their orders to start off in new directions .... There was, moreover, a band of fifteen free trappers, commanded by a gallant leader from Arkansas, named Sinclair, who held their encampment a little apart from the rest. Such was the wild and heterogeneous assemblage, amounting to several hundred men, civilized and savage, distributed in tents and lodges in the several camps.

The arrival of Captain Sublette with supplies put the Rocky Mountain Fur Company in full activity. The wares and merchandise were quickly opened, and as quickly disposed of to trappers and Indians; the usual excitement and revelry took place, after which all hands began to disperse to their several destinations.

Five and one-half miles south of Driggs is **Victor.** The most celebrated scrimmage against the mountain men occurred about 1.5 miles northwest of Victor, on Trail Creek. Though there is some local disagreement about the precise site, scholars who have examined the journals of participants place the location of the **Battle of Pierre's Hole** there.

The rendezvous was breaking up and on July 18, 1832, two brigades of the Rocky Mountain Fur Co., under Henry Fraeb and Milton Sublette were en route south to trap southern Idaho and the Wasatch Range. The parties had decided to travel together for protection from the Indians as far as Raft River. On the way, a band of 200 Indians was spotted traveling north from the Trail Creek route over Teton Pass. Fraeb sent Antoine Godin and a Flathead interpreter to learn the identity of the Indians.

The pair discovered the band was Blackfoot. A chief came forward with a peace pipe to greet them. Godin's father had been killed by the Blackfeet two years earlier; no tribe of Indians was considered more treacherous by the mountain men. Godin seized the chief's hand, while the Flathead shot him out of his saddle. They grabbed the chief's blanket and galloped back to the trappers.

When the pursuing Blackfeet realized they were outnumbered, they took refuge in a willow grove along the creek bottom and constructed an embrass of logs and sticks.

Bill Sublette's account of the ensuing battle, written to General Ashley two months later, is the best:

When we arrived at the spot we found the Blackfeet had taken possession of a point of woods surrounded by willows where they had formed a strong fort of fallen timber and had dug holes in the ground inside the fort where they could be secure from our fire. Finding them thus fortified and that we were exposed to their fire on the prairie without being able to injure them, I proposed entering the willows and approaching their fort where we could be on more equal footing. I was joined by about 30 whites and as many friendly Indians making our force nearly equal, to that of our enemy. We advanced to within paces of their fort and continued firing on them which they vigorously returned for some time. Discovering at length that they were too securely protected against our rifles we determined on burning their fort and when nearly prepared to apply fire to it, one of our friendly Indians who spoke the Blackfeet language and had held conversation with them during the engagement was told by them they were convinced we could kill them all, but that six or eight hundred warriors of their tribe were momentarily expected there who would give us enough of fighting. Owing to the misconstruction of the interpreter who communicated it to the whites he was understood to say that six or eight hundred warriors were then in the valley attacking our camp; consequently the fight was immediately discontinued and not until we got to the prairie was the matter properly explained. It was then deemed too late to renew the attack.

The Blackfeet departed during the night and took their wounded with them. In the morning Ferris Warren described the West's first recycling effort:

The trees both within and outside of the pen were covered with the marks of balls, or the axes successfully employed by our comrades, to exhume and save them; lead being very valuable in these remote regions where it is so extremely necessary, both to the purpose of defense and subsistence. Bones, of both men and animals, lay scattered about in and around the pen, bearing evident indication of having contributed their fleshy covering to the sustenance of wolves and ravens, who undoubtedly gratified their gastronomical propensities, after a protracted fast, for some days subsequent to the conflict.

252

Casualty figures included four trappers dead, four wounded; six Nez Perce dead, two wounded; and nine Blackfeet killed, along with two dozen of their horses.

Four years later, in a remarkable, if fitting, postscript to the story, Antoine Godin got his everlasting at Fort Hall. He was invited across the river by a small group of Gros Ventre to trade for some beaver plews. As Godin sat in a circle smoking the pipe with his customers, one of the Blackfeet shot him and peeled his scalp before he died. Then before the Indian rode off with the scalp, he cut the initials NJW (Nat J. Wyeth, Godin's employer) on the trapper's forehead.

Victor was established in the spring of 1899, shortly after the Mormon colony at Driggs. Emigrants from Cache Valley were advised by the Saints at Driggs to take the land south of them; the cabins scattered from the foot of Teton Pass to the base of Piney Pass were known as "the String." The LDS Church was the earliest governing body of the community until a townsite was granted by the federal government and platted in 1901.

Victor's main industry, hay ranches aside, was a lime quarry on Fox Creek, north of town, that operated from 1926 to 1970. The high-grade stone was quarried and hauled by wagons and sleighs to the OSL railroad spur, where it was loaded for the Utah and Idaho beet sugar plant in Idaho Falls. (The gas, released by the limestone in kilns, was used to purify the sugar.) The train came every other day to drop empty cars and collect loaded ones. Trucks eventually replaced the draft horses and wagons.

Victor was a waystop on the route to Yellowstone, and at one time had three hotels, including one with twenty-five rooms.

The town, first called Raymond, was renamed to honor Claud Victor, who, undeterred by the Bannock Indian scare of 1895, continued to carry the mail across Teton Pass.

Highway 33 turns southeast from Victor and goes 5.5 miles up Trail Creek to the Wyoming border. The drive up Trail Creek through groves of aspen and fir is lovely enough in its own right, but the view of **Jackson Hole** from **Teton Pass** (8,429 elev.) should not be missed.

In 1808 John Colter was the first white man to use the Indian trail over the pass; the Wilson Price Hunt expedition used it three years later.

In the early 1900s the Dunn Mining Co. scratched the first road through in order to get its equipment into Jackson Hole.

From 1913 to 1917 USFS crews used horse-drawn equipment to build a road that in many places parallels the present one, and the first car used the route in 1913.

In 1921 the Bureau of Public Roads assumed responsibility and highway funds were allocated to widen and gravel the Forest Service road.

State Highway No. 34 from the Idaho-Utah state line south of Preston, north to Preston, Grace, Soda Springs and Wayan, and east to the Idaho-Wyoming border north of Freedom. (Overlaps U.S. 30 for seven miles from a junction west of Soda Springs to Soda Springs.) Route length: 112.7 miles.

Highway 34 reaches **Fairview** one mile north of the Utah border. The name of this Mormon farm town, given in 1883, celebrated the view of the LDS Temple in Logan, Utah, visible on a clear day.

The highway travels north five miles to Preston (see Highway 91, Preston) and doglegs north and east through town two miles, then heads north across the Bear River after 4.5 miles and continues north another 20.7 miles to **Thatcher.**

From Thatcher it is 11.6 miles north to **Grace.** The large steel pipeline that angles southwest from the west side of the highway in Grace carries water four miles from the Grace Dam on Bear River to a Utah Power and Light Co. power plant in Black Canyon on the Bear River.

The road continues due north five miles to an intersection with U.S. 30 and follows that highway six miles east to Soda Springs. Highway 34 swings northeast two miles through town.

The exit for **Conda** is 3.8 miles north of the Soda Springs city limits. Take the paved road east 2.5 miles to view the Simplot phosphate mine and the remains of a company town.

Conda was established in 1916 by Anaconda Copper Co. as a base for employees at the phosphate mine. Since the site was isolated in the winter, the company built about seventy houses, as well as a church, school and store.

In 1959 J. R. Simplot Co. entered an operating agreement with Anaconda, and a year later Simplot purchased the plant and subleased the claims.

The mine contains thirteen miles of phosphate outcrop on patented ground. The phosphoric formation angles down from the surface and deposits only within 300 feet of the surface can be

254

exploited through open-pit mining. Electrically powered shovels strip the overburden during the winter and stockpile the ore to be shipped in the summer. To maintain a uniform grade of ore, the rock is sampled and blended as it is mined.

Phosphate rock mined at Conda is upgraded in beneficiating plants. Raw phosphate is soluble in water; as fertilizer it must be rendered soluble or roots cannot absorb it. This is accomplished by grinding the rock to powder and treating it with sulfuric acid. The phosphorous is transformed to water-soluble phosphoric acid; the acid is used on fresh phosphate ore and produces phosphorous oxide, or super-phosphate.

There are two beneficiating plants at Conda: one is operated by J. R. Simplot Co., and the other by Beker Industries, Inc. After Simplot ore is upgraded and calcined, it is shipped by rail to the company's fertilizer plant in Pocatello.

Beker Industries (formerly Agricultural Products Co.) uses ore mined at Maybe Canyon in the Caribou National Forest, eleven miles northeast of Conda. The rock is transported twenty-six miles by train to this site.

The Beker fertilizer plant at Conda was built in 1945 and was operated by El Paso Products until 1967. In 1972 Beker acquired it.

Continuing north-northeast, Highway 34 skirts the Blackfoot River reservoir, and after 28.4 miles reaches a junction at the south end of Grays Lake, 2.5 miles northwest of Wayan.

To visit the **Grays Lake Wildlife Refuge,** turn north at the junction 2.5 miles to the refuge headquarters on the east side of the road.

Grays Lake, known as Greys Hole, was named for the Hudson's Bay Co. trapper, John Grey, a half-Iroquois Canadian whose actual off-trail name was Ignace Hatchioraquasha. He discovered the lake between 1818 and 1820, while trapping for Donald McKenzie's Snake River brigade. (Grey was killed in 1844 at the site of Kansas City by an Indian woman who was an enemy of his family.)

In 1965 Grays Lake was set aside by Executive order as a national wildlife refuge. The U.S. Fish and Wildlife Service manages the 19,000 acres as a nesting area for Great Basin Canada geese and for the greater sandhill crane.

Sandhill cranes (200 pairs) nest in greater numbers at the marsh than anywhere else in the world. In September 4,000 or more cranes may be found in the valley preparing for their migration to the Bosque del Apache refuge in central New Mexico.

In 1975 a wildlife restoration project was begun at Grays Lake using sandhill cranes as foster parents to hatch and rear endangered whooping cranes. The plan envisions a separate flock of whooping cranes that would use the shorter and safer Pacific Flyway, instead of their more hazardous traditional route which is three times longer. During the first four years a total of thirteen birds fledged from forty-five eggs that were placed under foster parents. Only three of these birds were known to be alive at two years of age. Additionally, there is the possibility of cross breeding, but with only sixty whoopers left, the risk is acceptable.

Franklin's gulls nest in large colonies on the lake; some years the population reaches 40,000. Other common nesting species of interest are Forsters' terns, black terns, Wilson's phalarope American bitterns, snipe and willets. The bird list for the area contains 163 species.

Since the area is part of the Fort Hall Indian Reservation irrigation project, water levels in the lake are managed by the Bureau of Indian Affairs. An effort is being made to return the water to its traditional shoreline.

The best time to visit the refuge is from April to August. A viewing platform has been built on the hill, a short walk behind refuge headquarters.

Cariboo Mountain (9,800 ft.) is the peak visible five miles to the northeast of the headquarters. **Cariboo City** was located three miles northeast of the mountain; it was the scene of a minor gold rush in September, 1870. Tales told by the B. C. prospector Jesse Fairchilds gave the area the same name as the Fraser River mining district, where he had worked earlier.

William Clemens, a cousin of Mark Twain, was postmaster at Cariboo City for sixteen years, until the place folded. In 1874 Clemens also served in the Territorial Legislature.

Wayan is 2.5 miles southeast of Grays Lake; the name is a compound of Wayne and Ann (Nevils), who ran the post office. Without the post office-gas station there would no longer be anything on which to hang a name.

From Wayan Highway 34 flows 20.2 miles to the Wyoming border one mile north of **Freedom.** (Freedom's Main St. is the state line.)

State Highway No. 36 from a junction with Highway 34 north of Preston, northeasterly via Mink Creek and Liberty to a junction with U.S. 89 at Ovid. Route length: 33.9 miles.

Highway 36 leaves Highway 34 just north of a bridge across the Bear River. The drive from the river through Hay Valley for about ten miles has more grand-caliber wooden barns than any other road of comparable length in the state.

The community of **Mink Creek** is located just south of the highway, about eight miles from the Highway 34 junction.

In 1873 Mink Creek was established as a Mormon colony, 1½ years after Janus Keller and his three sons built a log cabin on nearby Strawberry Creek, just north of the present village. The Kellers scythed wild hay for their animals, then Janus left his two sons, ages twelve and fourteen, to look after the claim while he returned to family and chores in Utah, sixty miles away. The younger boy got homesick and hiked home; the older one spent the winter alone, looking after the place and the stock. In April his mother and the rest of the family arrived with the household goods.

Other Mormon families moved to the area. Grain was harvested with a scythe, bound by hand, and threshed with a flail. Bunchgrass was cut where the land was level enough for a mower.

The first post office was opened in 1878, two schools opened that fall, and a road was eventually scratched north from Franklin.

Though the population of Mink Creek once reached 500, it is one-tenth that now. Since 1965 students have been bused to Preston.

Six miles north of Mink Creek the highway enters Cache National Forest, an area known for its bear and deer populations. The road descends Emigration Creek through **Emigration Canyon** to Liberty, five miles northwest of Ovid.

Emigration Canyon was named so for the large companies of Saints who used the corridor to travel from the Cache Valley and Franklin to Bear Lake Valley in the mid-1860s.

At one time it appeared possible that a railroad would be built through the canyon to connect Bear Valley with Utah.

Liberty, at the mouth of the canyon, was settled in 1864 by Mormons who answered a call from their church. A townsite with thirty-six plots, of 1¼ acres each, was surveyed in 1866, and the Saints were given their choice in order of arrival.

The community was the first in Bear Lake Valley to adopt cooperative farming practices. An irrigation ditch from nearby Mill Creek watered the land.

Highway 36 ends at U.S. 89 in Ovid.

State Highway No. 37 from a junction with I-15 in Malad, westerly via Pleasantview and Holbrook, then northerly via Rockland to a junction with I-86 south of American Falls.

Malad is within earshot of I-15. The town's name is attributed to some trappers who had a close call with poisoned food on the Malad River. (The word means "sick" in French.)

The town grid overlies a hill; the houses have shirtfront lawns, and in what otherwise would be an arid landscape, trees splash the streets with shade.

In 1864 the first settler built his house on the site. Malad became a major stage and freight station on the Utah-Montana road. It was a community of unusual harmony – Mormons, Josephites, apostates, and Gentiles lived, worked and traded together. The town became the seat of Oneida County.

In 1906 the first train arrived on the Malad Valley Railroad that extended north from Garland, Utah. The rails gave valley ranchers and farmers access to the Utah market. At present a Union Pacific branch line from Ogden serves the town.

Tourists from I-15 enter Malad on Bannock St. The Co-op block, built in 1893 to 1911, is on the corner of Bannock and Main Sts.

The national anti-Mormon hysteria of the 1870s and 1880s caused the bishop of Malad to organize the Malad Cooperative, part of Brigham Young's United Order of Enoch. The cooperative was reorganized in 1882 by David Evans, a prominent Mormon businessman, but he did not allow the enterprise to become too closely identified with the LDS Church.

The building, which was erected over the original bishop's storehouse, has several sections. In addition to the general store, it housed a state bank, a bowling alley, and a meeting room-dance hall upstairs.

The David Evans, Sr. residence is located at the corner of N. Main and 200 North Sts.; it is an L-shaped, dark brick, bungalow-style house with an entry porch and walk set at an angle to the street. In 1915 it cost $8,000.

Evans was president of the J. N. Ireland Bank and the Evans' Co-op in Malad and served terms in the territorial and state legislatures (1888-1903). His son lived in the smaller house next door, which was designed by the same architect and built at the same time.

David Evans, Sr's. grandson, John Evans, was raised in the second house. In 1979 when Cecil Andrus was appointed Secretary of the Interior, John Evans became governor of Idaho.

The First Ward LDS chapel and recreation hall at Fourth North and Third West Sts. is worth seeing. The colonial style executed in maroon-colored bricks is striking.

The **Daughters of Pioneers museum** is located at 270 West 500 North St.

Highway 37 travels west from Malad 4.4 miles to **Pleasantview** – the view referred to is that of Malad Valley.

Drive south 2.5 miles from Pleasantview to Samaria, just north of the Samaria Mountains.

Samaria, named for the district in Palestine, was colonized in 1868 by Welsh Mormon converts. Irrigation canals were begun the following year. By 1870 there were nineteen families raising sheep and cattle, wheat and hay. A flour mill and a sawmill aided the area's economy. The town's population peaked in 1890 at about 800.

The settlement retains numerous time-stained log buildings and substantial brick homes among the fields of sage and sunflowers.

Hauling water from a spring in Samaria, 1905.

From Pleasantview, the road climbs to Holbrook Summit (6,104 feet), and pushes west 17.7 miles to **Holbrook,** another community established by Mormons. The post office opened here in 1902 was named for the local bishop, Heber Holbrook.

A mile northwest of Holbrook, the highway enters **Curlew National Grassland.** Most of this region now grazed was once plowed for dry-land grain production but the soil was unsatisfactory. The ground deteriorated, and the area's farmers had wolves whelping on their doorsteps. In the early 1930s Congress passed the Bankhead Jones Act, which allowed the federal government to purchase submarginal farms in the interest of soil conservation and agricultural stability.

The program required voluntary cooperation from the distressed landowners. The Resettlement Administration purchased the land and relocated the farmers on more productive ground. Curlew purchases involved 185,000 acres, and the farmers who accepted assistance moved to farms in the western Willamette Valley or to northern Idaho. For some there was a considerable adjustment from dry-land farms to irrigated dairy farms.

The resettlement project here involved range restoration. Fences were strung, reservoirs established, and reseeding, principally to crested wheat grass, was undertaken. Trespass by cattle and horses was eliminated, and a grazing season, April 15 to Nov. 15, was set. Livestock numbers were regulated.

The area was fenced into twenty-four pastures and leased to the Curlew Valley Horse and Cattle Association, comprised of fifty members, and the Pleasantview Association, which has about ninety members. Permitees are engaged in cow-calf operations, and most graze 50 percent of their cattle on the allotment.

The BLM administers most of the acreage. In 1954 the Soil Conservation Service transferred its 49,000 acres to the Forest Service for management. Some revegetation programs are still necessary, because without them sage and rabbitbrush would replace more desirable forage within fifteen years.

The road follows Rock Creek for ten miles to **Twin Springs,** in the sage flat just west of the road, ten miles from Holbrook. The springs site is accessible on a short sideroad.

Hudspeth's Cutoff from the Oregon Trail came past Twin Springs and the trail is still visible going up the hill west of the flat.

In 1849, when the Oregon Trail emigration consisted largely of gold seekers headed for California, speed was important. Some Missourians, led by Benoni Hudspeth and guided by John Myers, left the established route at Sheep Rock on Bear River in Idaho and took a shortcut west and southwest to rejoin the main trail where it turned west from Raft River near present-day Malta, Idaho. Until 1859 when the Lander Road opened, Hudspeth's Cutoff became the main route west.

Emigrants traveled west twenty-two miles without water until they reached Twin Springs. Some parties traveled at night to reduce the hardship. One goldseeker wrote of the spot: "I found several excellent and copious springs of pure water close to the creek ... two of which cannot be excelled."

From Twin Springs, Highway 37 continues through sage-fretted cattle range 23.3 miles north to **Rockland,** established in 1879 by Mormons, and then 13.0 miles more to its intersection with I-86 west of American Falls.

State Highway No. 39 from a junction with I-86 east of American Falls, westerly in American Falls, then northeasterly via Aberdeen, Springfield, and Riverside to a junction with U.S. 26 west of Blackfoot. Route length: 52.6 miles.

The town of **American Falls** was moved to its present location in 1925 when American Falls Dam was built and flooded the original townsite to the northeast. At low water, the bones of the old town – streets, sidewalks, a granary, the graveyard – are visible from the reservoir. (The brick United Methodist Church at Ft. Hall Ave. and Polk St. is an example of a building that was taken apart, moved, and reassembled.)

The falls on the Snake River were named for a party of American trappers whose boat was carried over the brink; one man survived to tell the story.

American Falls was an attraction for early travelers. The river compressed to a width of 200 yards and dropped about fifty feet in six-to-ten-foot pitches over basalt blocks. In October, 1811, the Wilson Price Hunt expedition camped for the night at the head of the cataract; John C. Fremont's party was here in 1843.

The Oregon Trail passed north of the present town, (through the reservoir) and then came south along the bluff above the Snake River south of the present dam. Leander Loomis, an emigrant who passed the falls in 1850, remarked, "... a grand sight. We all stopped our teams and went down to see them. At their foot was a continual rainbow while the sun was shining." Another wrote, "The sound of the falls was heard some time before reaching them ... The scene was truly magnificent. Here was an entire change in the face of the country as well as the river."

Beginning in 1901, three power plants were built along the falls: a west and an east-side plant, and another on a rock island in mid-stream. Supplies were rafted to the sites. Financing and floods

39 IDAHO

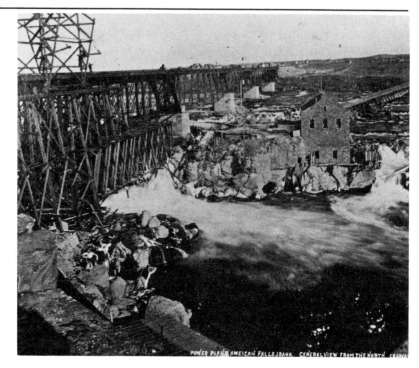

Early power plant at American Falls; the building still stands.

POWER PLANT AMERICAN FALLS, IDAHO. GENERAL VIEW FROM THE NORTH

Original town of American Falls; the site was flooded in 1927 by a Reclamation Service dam.

caused problems, but construction was finished in 1913. The American Falls Power, Light and Water Co. was then sold to the Kuhn brothers of Pittsburgh for $2 million. It provided 4,000 k.w. to the Minidoka area. When Idaho Power Co. was established in 1916, from the merger of five other companies, it acquired the plants. Idaho Power closed the west-side and island plants in the mid-1920s.

In 1927 the Bureau of Reclamation spent $3 million on a reinforced concrete dam for irrigation storage slightly upstream from the power plants and thereby obliterated the falls. By 1976 the dam had so deteriorated that the reservoir was reduced to two-thirds of its capacity. At that time Idaho Power contracted to build a new, larger dam of which half of the cost, or $23 million, was to be paid by a new generating plant with an output four times greater than the earlier one. The new dam, eighty-six feet high and 2,900 feet long, was completed in 1978. It is immediately downstream from the previous damsite.

From Fort Hall Ave. in downtown American Falls, travel west on Idaho St. and follow Highway 39 west across the crest of the American Falls Dam. The three intake gates are on the north side of the road, and eastbound traffic is on the adjacent, lower roadway. To see the old island and east-side power plants, turn left at the west end of the dam on the paved road by the west abutment. Turn left again, on the state fish and game hatchery road and keep left 0.5 miles down to the parking area below the dam. The abandoned power houses are visible across the river, and the U.P. railroad trestle can be seen upstream.

Highway 39 swings north from the dam, and after five miles it is possible to leave the highway for a side trip 28.2 miles to **Crystal Ice Cave** in the **Great Rift Natural Landmark.** The cave is open May through September, and operates under a special-use permit from the BLM. Users pay a small entrance fee for a guided tour that offers a most unusual and informative lesson in volcanic geology.

Turn west at the sign for Crystal Ice Cave, five miles north of American Falls Dam. The pavement gives way to gravel after six miles. Arrowed signs at the necessary turns will keep the driver on the proper course.

After arrival at the ice cave, before or after the tour, the visitor can walk 200 yards south from the parking lot and view the King's Bowl, a crater 150 feet deep and 100 feet wide, created by an explosion which blew ejecta blocks and ash out around the rim. It represents the youngest eruption on the rift.

Crystal Ice Cave is located in the King's Bowl fissure, part of the longest exposed rift in the U.S. The rift was the source of a lava lake about two miles square. As the lava poured back into the rift, spatter cones released trapped gas and created fissure caves. Burned sage recovered from beneath the flow carbon-dated the event at 2,130 years ago.

This cave may have been discovered as early as 1929, but it was not until 1956 that two local spelunkers made a reconnaissance and wrote a report about it. In 1961 Jim Papadakas made a more detailed exploration of the rift and began excavation of a tunnel parallel to the ice cave. After ten years he sold his interest to the present permit-holders.

King's Bowl in the Great Rift.

Ice formations in Crystal Ice Cave.

Visitors at Crystal Ice Cave descend 155 feet on a one-eighth mile path into a dormant volcano; the tunnel passes through three lava flows where the old soil horizon can be seen. Water trickles down through the fissure and freezes into ice formations. Visitors will want a jacket because lava is a good insulator, and glass doors and windows maintain an interior temperature of thirty-one degrees F.

In 1961 a blind beetle, previously unknown to science, was found inside the cave. Its scientific name, *Glacicavicola bathzscioides,* is longer than the insect itself, which does not exceed a quarter-inch. The beetle feeds on algae that grow on the ice.

264

After the tour, it is possible to visit other regional volcanic features, but the desert is a bramble of roads, and without topographic maps it is easy to become lost. Instructions to reach **Bear Trap Cave** and **Split Butte** are given here, but passenger vehicles should not attempt the roads except in dry weather. If the ground is wet the mud will bog a horse.

Leave the ice cave parking lot and after 0.9 miles turn left (northwest) on the road to Minidoka. Follow it 8.2 miles to a major junction. Turn left (southwest) toward Minidoka. After 0.1 miles note the mouth of Bear Trap Cave on the right, below the road.

The cave is an uncollapsed segment of a thirteen-mile-long lava tube that appears to have originated near the Idaho Rift System. It travels westward through a series of collapsed and uncollapsed sections until buried by lava flows from Craters of the Moon.

Lava tubes pipe lava away from vents, and form almost exclusively in pahoehoe – the gassiest type of lava, which is very fluid when extruded. The tubes can feed lava to a flow-front many miles from its source, with almost no drop in temperature.

A second, and better, uncollapsed tube is located 1.3 miles on the side road that parallels the axis of the first cave. After visiting the second lava tube, return to Bear Trap. Take an odometer reading.

Continue southwest on the Minidoka road. There is a branch road at 0.4 miles; ignore it, and stay on the main road. Split Butte (4,795 feet) becomes visible to the southeast. At 4.0 miles there is another junction; take the left fork, away from the Minidoka road. Ignore the branch road at 1.2 miles, but take the right fork at the junction 0.8 miles farther on. Turn left after another 0.5 miles and park.

Split Butte Crater has an outer tuff ring about 90 to 145 feet high and 1,800 feet in diameter. Its tephra ring enclosed a lake of lava formed when basaltic magma erupted through ground water. The magma withdrew, and as the lake subsided it created the crater pit.

From Split Butte, return to the main Minidoka road. It is shorter (about twenty miles), and easier, to reach I-84, I-86, by continuing toward Minidoka and using Highways 24 and 25 to I-84, rather than retracing the road to Crystal Ice Cave and Highway 39.

Aberdeen is on Highway 39, on the west side of the reservoir, 13.6 miles north of American Falls. The town was founded in 1908 by the American Falls Canal and Power Co. and named after Aberdeen, Scotland.

The American Falls Project, which includes the irrigated land along the reservoir's west side from the dam north through Aberdeen and Springfield, was Idaho's first Carey Act development.

Under the 1894 act, federal lands were given to the states provided they were irrigated within sixteen years. States contracted with private companies for the irrigation systems. The American Falls Canal and Power Co. signed such a contract with the State Lands Board to reclaim 57,000 acres at a cost of $250,000, but the costs were so grossly understated that the company went bankrupt.

The rights were purchased by a second company, and additional water was obtained from Jackson Lake on the headwaters of the Snake, through an agreement with the Bureau of Reclamation. The completed project has eighty-six miles of main canal and 100 miles of laterals and cost $886,000. The current operator is the Aberdeen-Springfield Canal Co. Owners hold assessed shares.

Springfield, seventeen miles north of Aberdeen, was probably named by Mormon settlers for Springfield, Illinois.

The highway continues northeast twenty-two miles to intersections with Highway 26 and I-15 near Blackfoot.

State Highway No. 41 from a junction with I-90 near Post Falls east city limits, northerly via Rathdrum, Spirit Lake and Blanchard to a junction with U.S. 2 in Oldtown. Route length: 39 miles.

State Highway 41 begins from U.S. Interstate 90, about 2.5 miles east of Post Falls. The road reaches the town of **Rathdrum** after traveling 6.5 miles north of the Interstate.

Rathdrum Prairie is located at the southern end of the western fork of the Purcell Trench. Enormous lobes of glacial ice rasped slowly down the trench from icefields in northern Canada. These icy projections advanced and retreated with climatic variations 30,000-80,000 years ago. Outwash of clay, silt, sand and gravel accumulated to depths of several hundred feet south of the glaciers' margins. Rathdrum Prairie is regarded by geologists as a remarkable example of a glacial plain.

The gravel deposit serves as an aquifer for the Spokane River, and an estimated 700,000 acre-feet of water from Lake Pend Oreille percolates through the prairie annually. In Idaho, only the Snake River plain has a larger aquifer.

The Wesley Wood family had a "little house on the prairie" in 1880, and the location had the customary meals-drinks-rooms establishment. When the post office was opened, Washington, D.C.

266

authorities complained that there were already too many Westwoods in the wooded west; so the suggestion was altered in favor of the Irish birthplace of an elderly resident.

Northern Pacific came through Westwood-Rathdrum in July, 1881, and Frederick Post, of Post Falls, had a sawmill and flour mill in operation here the following year. The mill produced ties for the railroad, and the settlement soon had the first shingle mill in the Coeur d'Alenes. Shingles were made from yellow pine because residents were dependent on rain barrels (cedar shingles stain the water).

The town's first newspaper had an illustrious title: *The Silver Blade of Rathdrum.*

Rathdrum in 1908, prairie in background.

Much of Rathdrum Prairie is now irrigated and produces wheat, peas, and seed grasses.

St. Stanislaus Catholic Church in Rathdrum is an exceptional example of the Gothic-style in brick. Though the tower is wooden, the building itself is the earliest brick Catholic church in the state. It was erected under the administration of Bishop Alphonsus Glorieux, who was appointed to the Idaho Territory in 1885. At that time, the Territory had two secular priests and eight frame churches.

Ten miles north of Rathdrum is the community of **Spirit Lake.** It was a company town, the company was Panhandle Lumber, and it was owned by its president, Frank Blackwell. He arrived in the Coeur d'Alene from Pennsylvania in 1902 and acquired 100,000 acres and 2.5 billion feet of timber for himself and a Pennsylvania lumber company. Four years later, Frank sold the holdings for $6

267

million, and the Pennsylvania company was dissolved without ever having owned or operated an Idaho sawmill.

Blackwell then acquired some new associates and another 100,000 acres of north Idaho timberland, about one-fourth of which was near Spirit Lake. He formed the Panhandle Lumber Co. and the Spirit Lake Land Co.

In 1907-1908 the lumber company built a large mill with double-cut band saws, planers and kilns, while the land company platted a townsite and sold lots. Blackwell provided water works, sewage system and cement sidewalks without charge. A year later the town is reported to have had 100 buildings and 1,000 residents.

Figuring he might as well go whole hog, since it cost no more than pork chops, Blackwell then built the Idaho and Washington Northern Railroad from Rathdrum through Spirit Lake and north to Newport and Metaline Falls, Washington. The machine shops and roundhouse in Spirit Lake cost $250,000 and were among the more modern in the country. (The railroad was acquired by the Chicago, Milwaukee and St. Paul at an auction in 1916 for $5 million.)

Much of the timber cut at the Panhandle mill came from Mount Spokane in Washington, ten miles east of Spirit Lake. Logs were flumed down Brickle Creek to the east end of the lake, then towed by tug to the mill.

A destructive forest fire sluiced down the slopes of Mt. Spokane in August, 1939, and reached the town of Spirit Lake. With great effort the sawmill was saved, but the railroad roundhouse, the lumberyard and 40 million board feet were burned. Faced with a $1,250,000 loss, Panhandle Lumber, a company that had produced over 1 billion board feet of lumber, had to close. Blackwell was not on hand; he died in 1922.

Spirit Lake today is a town of modest agriculture, logging and tourism, but Main St. presents a picturesque facade of frontier commercial architecture. The public square has setback corner lots at the principal intersection and fifteen buildings dated 1907-1910 line the streets. Most of them were built with simulated, concrete stone that could be manufactured and assembled more rapidly than brick or stone.

The Panhandle Hardware store at the crossroads has some local historical photographs on display.

State Highway 41 continues north nineteen miles, through Blanchard to Oldtown and intersects with U.S. Highway 2.

State Highway No. 44 from a junction with I-84 north of Caldwell, easterly via Middleton, Star, and Eagle to a junction with U.S. 20-26-30 in Boise at Twenty-third and Fairview. Route length: 27.3 miles.

Middleton is 3.9 miles east of I-84, on Highway 44. The Oregon Trail passed two miles south of the settlement, which was midway between Boise City and Keeney's ferry at the mouth of the Boise River.

A post office was established in 1866, followed by a grist mill and general store. Later the town was a depot on the Idaho Northern railroad.

Take the Middleton Rd. 2.1 miles south of Middleton to the **Ward Memorial State Park,** south of the Boise River, on the east side of the road. The names of eighteen persons who were killed here August 20, 1854, by Boise Shoshone Indians are graven on a granite cenotaph.

The Alexander Ward wagon train was en route to Oregon; the group was attacked while eating dinner. All of the men were killed, and women and children were taken captive; nine Indians died in the fight. Two of the Ward children survived their wounds: a nine year-old boy was found hiding in the brush, and his fourteen year-old brother walked to Fort Boise with an arrow through his lung. The victims were buried in a common grave on the site.

When news of the massacre reached The Dalles, Oregon, Major Rains dispatched Captain Haller and twenty-six enlisted men to punish the Indians. The troops were joined by Captain Olney and thirty volunteers. They found two small parties of Indians, shot three, and hung three others on gallows at the Ward site.

Highway 44 arrives at **Star,** 6.5 miles east of Middleton. The town, settled in 1863, was one of the earliest villages in the Boise Valley.

Eagle is located 5.3 miles east of Star, at the junction of Highway 44 and 55.

On the western outskirts of the town, on the north side of the highway, at the rear of a deep lot marked by an iron fence, stands the remarkable Oliver Short house.

The two-story, western colonial house, with its elaborate porch, was built in 1906. It is the largest river-rock house left in the state. It contained fifteen rooms, but the interior has been altered. The cobblestones came from the Boise River.

Oliver Short was from Kansas; his father, a government surveyor, was killed by Indians, and Oliver was sent to live with his uncle who had a homestead on Eagle Island (on the river south of Eagle). Short managed his uncle's ranch, and later purchased most of it.

The Eagle Flour Mill is located at the southwest corner of the Main St. intersection. It was built in the 1920s and operated until the 1960s, the last flour mill in the state.

Eagle Island State Park is reached from Eagle, by taking Linder Road, three miles west of the Main St. intersection with Highway 55, south 0.5 across a branch of the Boise River onto the island.

The island was a livestock ranch for many years. In 1930, 523 acres were purchased by the Department of Corrections for a prison honor-farm. It served the purpose until 1974, then the department removed its facilities and released the site to the state Department of Lands. In 1977 the Idaho legislature passed a resolution to sell the island property for funds to build a cell block at the new prison.

Governor John Evans felt the land could be better used for public recreation. A poll conducted by the *Idaho Statesman* revealed 80 percent of those who responded agreed with Evans. The State Land Board in 1978 voted to set aside the Eagle Island land as a state park. In 1980 the Department of the Interior granted $1.1 million for planning and development, which was matched by the state with the donated value of some eastern Idaho land.

The Idaho Parks and Recreation Department excavated a twelve-acre lake and developed thirty acres for day-use.

Highway 44 continues 8.3 miles east, inside the Boise city limits to Fairview Ave.

State Highway No. 45 from a junction with Highway 78 near Walters Ferry northerly to a junction with U.S. 30 in Nampa. Route length: 18.1 miles.

The south-alternate route of the Oregon Trail, for emigrants who did not cross the Snake at Three Island Crossing, passed along the south shore of the Snake River opposite present **Walters Ferry.**

The ferry became a viaduct on the most direct route between the Boise Basin mines to the north, and the Owyhee mines to the south. The overland route in the 1860s from San Francisco to Boise ran from Virginia City, Nevada, through DeLamar and Silver City, down

270

Reynolds Creek, across Walters Ferry, north through present Kuna to Boise City.

In 1863 John Fruit and a partner made the first oar-powered log ferry and began to shuttle customers here. The men paid $100 for a Territorial license to operate the only ferry along two miles of river front. Fees were $4.00 for a loaded wagon and $3.00 for an empty one, $1.00 for a man on horseback. Revenues, dependent on the fate of the mines, rose and fell like a fiddle bow; income from farmers and ranchers was steadier. In 1868 the partners sold their enterprise for $8,000.

The location had an adobe brick house and hotel, a saloon, blacksmith shop, barn, and extensive corrals. It acquired its present name in 1886, when Lewellyn and Augusta Walter bought the rights to the site for $4,000. The ferry at that time was ninety-feet long by thirty-feet wide, with a twenty-foot rudder. A windlass on the upstream side was connected to a two-inch rope that ran through pulleys to a steel cable that was anchored on each side of the river. Cranking the windlass canted the rudder against the current, and the current's vector shoved the boat across the river. The Walters sold their interest in 1901.

Walters Ferry operated until 1921, when a steel and concrete bridge replaced it. Over 2,000 persons showed up for the dedication. The old bridge still stands upstream, adjacent to its replacement. The old ferry landing can be seen on the downstream side of the new bridge.

The collection of buildings on the east shore of the river, just south of the bridge, comprise the **Cleo's Ferry Museum.** Dr. S. A. Swayne, and his wife, Cleo, worked fifteen years to assemble the collection housed in the stone buildings. The displays include a hundred old clocks, early medical instruments, music boxes, and other antiques. The museum, however, is opened only by appointment with Mrs. Swayne, who lives in Nampa.

Information inscribed on the monument opposite the museum entrance serves as a reminder that the West was not settled with blank cartridges.

Take an interesting seven-mile detour from Walters Ferry. Just north, uphill from the ferry store, turn right on Ferry Road. Follow this paved road two miles to a T. Turn right on Hill Road, which is also paved, and wind 4.2 miles to Sinker Rd. Make a right turn on Sinker, which has a gravelled surface. The road travels through fields of Melon gravel 2.8 miles to a dead end.

The double-arched iron bridge that spans the river at this point is the **Guffey railroad bridge,** built in 1897.

Colonel William Dewey, the mining promoter, organized the Boise, Nampa, and Owyhee Railroad, which was to operate from Nampa to Silver City. The rails got as far as Murphy, south of the river, and trains ran that far in 1899, but the track was never completed. It carried livestock from Murphy north to Guffey for a time.

The profusion of boulders along the benches above the river is **Melon gravel,** deposited by the colossal Bonneville Flood that roared through the Snake River canyon 30,000 years ago. Peak discharge through this area is estimated to have been 10 million c.f.s., which means the river was nearly 300 feet deep at this point. (See Highway 91, Red Rock Pass.)

Map Rock Road leaves the west side of Highway 45, 0.6 miles north of Walters Ferry. After 5.3 miles on the gravel road, a large, gap-boarded building that was the stage barn for **Bernard's Ferry** can be seen on the west side of the river.

James Bernard, a native of B. C., came to the area in 1864. He, and his wife, Ada, built a two-story, fourteen-room house near the river and raised nine children. Their place became the region's social center.

Bernard operated a fast-freight service between Caldwell and the Owyhee mines. His drivers could make the trip in twelve hours. The barn, which has lost its transept on the river side, served the freight teams.

In 1882 Bernard built a ferry to serve traffic on the Owyhee road. He had three different boats here – one, ninety feet long, with fancy railings, was called *Queen of the River.* Completion of the Walters Ferry bridge ended the ferry's usefulness, and James Bernard died that year, at age eighty-one.

The road travels four miles farther down the river to **Map Rock,** a large basalt boulder on the right side of the road. This stone displays numerous petroglyphs, including an extensive serpentine shape imagined by some to resemble the course of the river. The age and meaning of the glyphs are indeterminable; they may be artistic expressions or simply magical doodles.

Highway 45 continues north from the Map Rock road intersection, 17.1 miles to Nampa and U.S. 30.

*Map Rock on the
Snake River.*

State Highway No. 46 from a junction with I-84 south of Wendell, northerly via Wendell and Gooding to a junction with U.S. 20 east of Fairfield.

Wendell, the "Hub City of Magic Valley," is 0.5 miles north of I-84, and was named in 1907 by W. S. Kuhn for his son. The Kuhns were members of a wealthy Pittsburgh family that invested in three Carey Act irrigation projects in southern Idaho.

The town is located on the second segregation of the Twin Falls North Side Project, originally backed by the Kuhn brothers and the American Water Works and Guarantee Co. of Pittsburgh. W. S. Kuhn and his associates obtained the irrigation rights to the North Side from the developers of the Twin Falls South Side Project. Kuhn and American Water Works selected townsites, subdivided them, and sold the commercial lots, while retaining the new towns' utilities and transportation lines.

(American Water Works failed, and the project, with 100 miles of main canal and 800 miles of laterals, irrigating 125,000 acres, was completed in 1920 under a different arrangement.)

Drive one block west of Main St. to 210 North Idaho, between First and Second Aves. The three-story, Mission style Magic Valley

273

Manor located here is an outstanding example of the imposing hotels erected by irrigation development companies to impress prospective investors. This one was built by the North Side Land and Water Co. in 1909-1910 for $54,000. It is now a resthome.

Another unusual structure in Wendell is found east of the Magic Manor, at Main and Boise Sts. The adobe-colored Methodist Church was designed by a Methodist architect and built during a fourteen-year period (1934-1948) by the congregation.

The highway travels north, straight as the shortest distance between two points, 9.6 miles to **Gooding,** between the Big and Little Wood Rivers.

Main St. in Gooding.

The Oregon Short Line had a station at this location before Frank R. Gooding purchased a large tract, surveyed a townsite, and modestly named it Gooding. In 1913 the town became the seat of a new county, also called Gooding. Mr. Gooding was state governor (1905-1908) and a U.S. Senator from 1921 until his death in 1928.

The **State School for the Deaf and Blind** opened in Gooding in 1910; there are now fourteen buildings on the campus. In the late 1960s emphasis shifted from a resident-school to one which prepared students to attend their own public schools. The center aids young people with visual or aural handicaps until they are twenty-one.

274

State Highway 20 reaches Flat Top Butte (5,557 feet) 18.2 miles north of Gooding. To visit **Gooding City of Rocks** (not to be confused with City of Rocks near Almo) turn left, or west, on the gravel road at the Butte. An inconspicuous sign, set back from the highway, reads: City of Rocks 9 miles.

In wet weather this road is slicker than frog eggs. The gravel ends after three miles. Continue on the dirt road, and at two miles ignore the fork marked to Davis Mountain. One mile west the road forks again; take the southern branch 3.5 miles and the "city" comes into view.

The striated shale and sandstone formations appear primeval, as though some saurian might emerge in silhouette at any moment.

The Gooding "school bus."

There are enough gargoyles and hobgoblins to suggest a movie-set, and children can pretend they are movie-extras. Vardis Fisher described the location as "this acreage of eroded and lonely masterpieces of weather and wind."

It is 13.7 miles on Highway 46 from Flat Top Butte to an intersection with Highway 20, near Hill City. En route, the road provides an unbounded view of the Camas Prairie from Johnson Hill (5,678 elev.).

State Highway No. 47 from a junction with U.S. 20 in Ashton, east and northeast via Marysville and Warm River to the Bear Gulch Ski Area and north on USFS paved road back to U.S. 20. Route length: 38.8 miles.

Marysville is east of Ashton, two miles from U.S. 20. In 1893 a Mormon ward was organized and named for Mary Lucinda Baker, the first woman to settle here.

The area north and south of the town is irrigated by the Marysville Canal, which takes water from Falls River, thirteen miles to the east. Proposed in 1898, the canal project was the third Carey Act reclamation effort in the state. Early settlers who had already built some diversion works opposed the development.

Construction finally got underway in 1904, but it was plagued. A dam had to be rebuilt three times, the price of water contracts was doubled, and the State Land Board reversed its decision to transfer the canal works to the settlers. In 1917 the company went bankrupt, and it was 1921 before operation of the project was finally turned over to the farmers.

Highway 47 travels east-northeast from Marysville. After 4.2 miles there is a paved road (Green Timber Rd.), which soon gives way to gravel, that goes east nineteen miles to **Cave Falls** in the southwest corner of Yellowstone National Park. The drive is well worth the time.

Cave Falls (left).

Belcher Falls.

The pavement on Green Timber Road resumes three miles before Cave Falls. Osprey nest in the snags along the river, and there are picnic tables at the road-end.

Upstream, visible from the picnic area, Falls River breaks along its entire width in a lustrous, sheer sheet, then regathers itself and slides off downstream.

A gentle, fairly level trail leads from the parking area through lodgepole woods one mile to **Belcher Creek Falls** on Belcher River. The water there stumbles down a rocky stairs and scarcely

276

collects itself before being swept down Falls River for an encore. (Hikers can make an overnight trip from Belcher, eleven miles to **Union Falls**).

North of the road to Cave Falls, Highway 47 passes through Warm River (too small to call a town) and Bear Gulch Ski Area, and after 8.6 miles reaches Grandview campground, which is on the west side of the road.

Grandview is an overlook for **Lower Mesa Falls,** and is about seventy-five yards off the road. The cataract is a feature of Henrys Fork of the Snake. The river below is squeezed in a gorge where it drops sixty-five feet in a white froth that would fold a Campways raft like a bivalve, then turn it inside-out.

Lower Mesa Falls on Henrys Fork.

277

47

In 1981 this falls, and the one upstream, were the subject of a hydroelectric proposal from a consortium of Idaho Falls businessmen represented by a California lawyer who had never seen the site. The group applied to the Federal Energy Regulatory Commission for a preliminary permit for diversion studies above each falls. The Idaho Park and Recreation Board filed a petition to intervene against the permit and requested a minimum stream flow in Henrys Fork.

Upper and Lower Mesa Falls are the last undisturbed waterfalls of consequence in Idaho; the others – Twin, Shoshone, American, and Salmon – have been defaced or destroyed. It takes only three minutes thought to realize Mesa Falls should be left unfettered, but as A. E. Housman has observed, "thought is irksome, and three minutes is a long time."

To visit **Upper Mesa Falls,** return to the highway and drive north 0.6 miles to a gravel road on the west side of the highway, where a sign states "Not maintained for public use." (The upper falls is not on USFS land, and is therefore not marked.) Drive 0.9 miles down to a parking area at the brink of the 114-foot waterfall.

The visitor's view of the falls, from this western angle, allows him to see about one-third of its width. Nevertheless, it is an awesome sight.

In 1920 while auto-camping as a child with his parents, Wallace Stegner spent the night at this spot. Decades later he recollected in his euphonious style.

I gave my heart to the mountains the minute I stood beside this river with its spray in my face and watched it thunder into foam, smooth to green glass over sunken rocks, shatter to foam again. I was fascinated by how it sped by and yet was always there; its roar shook both the earth and me.

When the sun dropped over the rim the shadows chilled sharply; evening lingered until foam on water was ghostly and luminous in the near-dark. Alders caught in the current sawed like things alive, and the noise was louder. It was rare and comforting to waken late and hear the undiminished shouting of the water in the night. And at sunup it was still there, powerful and incessant, with the slant sun tangled in its rainbow spray, the grass blue with wetness, and the air heady as ether and scented with campfire smoke.

By such a river it is impossible to believe that one will ever be tired or old. Every sense applauds it. Taste it, feel its chill on the teeth: it is purity absolute. Watch its racing current, its steady renewal of force: it is transient and eternal. And listen again to its sounds: get far enough away so that the noise of falling tons of water does not stun the ears, and hear how much is going on underneath – a whole symphony of smaller sounds, hiss and splash and gurgle, the small talk of side channels, the whisper of blown and scattered spray gathering itself and beginning to flow again, secret and irresistible, among the wet rocks.

Upper Mesa Falls
(114 feet).

279

From Upper Mesa Falls the highway continues north through cut-over lodgepole forests, 23.4 miles to a reunion with U.S. 20, just south of Island Park.

State Highway No. 48 from a junction with I-15 west of Roberts, easterly via Roberts, Menan, Lewisville, and Rigby to a junction with U.S. 26 business loop in Ririe. Route length: 24.4 miles.

Roberts is 0.2 miles east of I-15. The town is at the southern end of the Market Lake slough, a waterfowl habitat area formed in 1863 by a Snake River flood.

In 1898 Market Lake became a railroad station, but according to Fritz Kramer, when the town was incorporated in 1910, the name was changed to honor H. A. Roberts, superintendent of the Union Pacific railroad.

Highway 48 travels east 6.2 miles to **Menan,** an agricultural area below the mouth of Henrys Fork, islanded by incised meanders of the Snake River. The land is irrigated by a tangle of sloughs and canals.

Menan is a Mormon settlement founded in 1879 and originally called Poole's Island. The present name is allegedly Indian; interpretations range from "island" to "many waters."

At Menan the highway turns south through **Lewisville,** 7.1 miles to Rigby (see U.S. 20) and continues 8.6 miles east and south to **Ririe.**

The Mormon settler David Ririe helped the Oregon Short Line secure right-of-way from the local farmers, and the depot's name was the railroad's requital.

Highway 20 meets a business loop of U.S. 26 in Ririe.

State Highway No. 50 from a junction with U.S. 30 north of Kimberly, northeast via Hansen Bridge to a junction with Highway 25 west of Eden. Route length: 8.1 miles.

Highway 50 begins 0.4 miles north of Kimberly and goes east and north four miles to the **Hansen Bridge** across the Snake River. There is a view area on the west side of the highway at the south end of the bridge.

Before there was a bridge at this location, travelers crossed the river by ferry above Shoshone Falls, or later, over a river-level steel bridge that I. B. Perrine built on his property at Blue Lakes, west of this site.

The first suspension bridge here cost $100,000, and opened on the Fourth of July, 1919. The present concrete span cost $1.4 million and was dedicated in 1966. It is 350 feet high and 762 feet long.

The name honors John and Lawrence Hansen; John was a pioneer merchant and probate judge; Lawrence was a prominent stockman and a member of the state legislature (1917-1918).

Highway 50 continues northeast of the bridge, 4.1 miles to a junction with Highway 25, three miles west of Eden.

State Highway No. 51 from the Idaho-Nevada state line south of Riddle northerly via Riddle, Grassmere, and Bruneau to a junction with I-84 and U.S. 20 in Mountain Home. Route length: 93.7 miles.

Highway 51 for the most part is as straight and level as an airport runway. It is the principal north-south road through Owyhee County, the first county to be established by the Idaho Territorial Legislature in 1863. The county encompasses 4.9 million acres.

The highway travels north from the Nevada border through the **Duck Valley Indian Reservation** for eleven miles. The reservation was established by Executive order in 1877 for the Western Shoshone. In 1886 a group of Northern Paiute also settled on the reservation by governor's order. The two groups were combined and organized into one tribe in 1938 under the Indian Reorganization Act. The tribal governing body is a business council composed of eight members elected to three-year terms.

The only source of tribal income is Mountain View Lake, built in 1969 on the west side of the road. Fishing permits for the trout-stocked reservoir are sold at the tribal office.

About 875 Indians live on the arid, 293,000-acre reservation. Unemployment usually exceeds 40 percent.

The Northern Paiute lived in an environment that was not compatible with the horse culture of the Great Plains; there was insufficient forage. Most of the Paiutes' energy was expended in pursuit of food: spring roots and salmon, summer currants, huckleberries, sage hens and deer, and fall rabbits and antelope.

The high desert (5,000 ft.) that extends for sixty miles from the reservation to the **Bruneau Valley,** was cattle and sheep range. Though the big sagebrush and native grasses have been largely destroyed by overgrazing in the late 1800s, the area still serves as livestock range.

51

Bruneau is two miles west of the Highway 51 intersection with Highway 78, 71.6 miles from the Nevada border.

The town's name is derived from that of the river, and the river's from French trappers (brun: brown), or possibly for an early hunter, Baptiste or Pierre Bruneau. The word first appears in the trapper John Work's journal in 1831.

By 1870 about forty ranches were established in the valley, where it was possible to grow lettuce, grain, corn, and even Chinese sugar cane. The first store opened in 1881, and the first steel bridge across the Bruneau River in 1910.

The Bruneau desert was good spring range, but the scarcity of water has always been a problem. Sheep men trucked 500-gallon tanks of water twenty miles to their flocks on the desert. Watering troughs were moved with the sheep camps. In the fall bands were driven to railheads in Murphy or Mountain Home; some stock was wintered in the Bruneau Valley.

The Air Force preempted much of the public land for aerial gunnery and bombing ranges, and that ended the sheepherder's era.

Since 1950 deep drilling (1,200-2,000 ft.) has produced artesian wells for irrigated farmland above the Bruneau Valley.

The most spectacular vertical-walled river gorge in Idaho, accessible by car, is nineteen miles from the town of Bruneau. It is the **Bruneau Canyon,** 800 feet deep and 1,300 feet wide, viewed from Bruneau Overlook.

From the center of Bruneau, take the paved road southeast off Highway 51, along the Buckaroo Ditch. It is the same road that leads to Indian Bathtub hot springs, though the springs have been so trashed they do not merit a visit. After eight miles, the road crosses the ditch and forks; stay left and avoid the branch that leads to the hot springs. The pavement ends and the road becomes a bit western, especially for drivers who have never ventured west of the Hudson. In wet weather it can be rougher than a rock quarry. Continue through the Saylor Creek Aerial Gunnery Range for eight miles, to a spur road on the right, with a sign pointing to the Bruneau Overlook. Take the spur three miles to a dead end at the Bruneau Canyon rim.

The canyon is incised upon the Bruneau-Jarbridge eruptive center, an area of numerous huge volcanic eruptions that began about 12 million years ago, according to potassium-argon dates. Volcanic activity lasted for several million years; it covered an area of about 1,800 square miles and amounted to several hundred cubic miles in volume.

The eruptive center was the source of about twenty major rhyolite flows before it formed a caldera, which was then covered by the basalt from at least forty volcanoes. Most of the vulcanism, in time and volume, consists of extruded rhyolite; it is a volcanic rock very similar to granite and characterized by a high content of silica, sodium and potassium. It was formed by a partial melting of portions of the earth's lower crust beneath the region.

In a distance of sixty miles, only two cattle trails cross the Bruneau Canyon.

Each weather-resistant layer exposed in the stepped canyon wall was formed from a series of immense eruptions spaced closely enough to cool into a single layer of dense rhyolite. Deposits of stream and lake sediments and volcanic ash occur between the rhyolite steps.

The Bruneau River, which heads in the Jarbridge Mountains sixty miles south, and joins the Snake twenty miles north, has cut this chasm in comparatively recent geological time.

Five miles north of Bruneau, at Highway 78, is the turnoff for Bruneau Dunes State Park (see Highway 78, Bruneau Dunes).

Highway 51 travels north twenty-one miles from Bruneau to a junction with U.S. 20 in Mountain Home.

State Highway No. 52 from the Idaho-Oregon boundary north of Payette southeasterly via Payette and Emmett to a junction with Highway 55 in Horseshoe Bend. Route length: 54.1 miles.

Highway 52 begins at the Snake River bridge in north Payette (see U.S. 95, Payette) and travels 2.8 miles through town, then follows the Payette River southeast 27.2 miles to the outskirts of **Emmett,** where it turns due-north one mile into the city's center.

In 1862 the mountain man Tim Goodale guided a train of sixty wagons down Freezeout Hill and across the Payette River where Emmett now stands. Part of the group was seeking a route to the mines in Florence Basin; the others were bound for Oregon.

Two years later Jonathan Smith and Nathaniel Martin, partners who had come west from Missouri, settled at present Emmett and built a roadhouse, feed barn, and ferry. Their livelihood was provided by the traffic en route to Boise Basin mines. The Martindale ferry, as it was called, charged $1.00 for a team and wagon and 25 cents for a man on foot.

In 1870 a lawyer from Missouri, Thomas Cahalan, was appointed postmaster at a location seven miles west of the ferry, and named the spot Emmettville in honor of his seven-year-old son. After six years Cahalan moved to Boise, and the post office was moved to the ferry crossing, which took the name Emmettville. At that time the location had two sawmills, which sold lumber to Boise Valley residents, who came over Freezeout Hill to buy it.

James Wardell decided it was time to organize the town; he purchased the Johnson homestead in 1883 for $1,000 and laid out the streets and lots. The following year a bridge was built across the

284

river to replace the ferry, the Rossi irrigation ditch was completed, and the number of buildings doubled.

In 1900 Emmettville incorporated and cropped its name to Emmett. Within two years the town welcomed the Idaho Northern branch of the OSL railroad from Nampa.

With railroad transportation, irrigation, fertile ground, and a moderate climate, Emmett was ripe for the silk hat promoters. In 1910 the Idaho Orchard Co. began to tout the area as a wonderland, where money figuratively grew on trees. The company brochure brayed:

Time was when the West meant hardship and danger. That day is past. There are no luxuries in the East not everyday commonplaces in the West. The West is at the front in school and church and social enjoyments. Wealth commands all things and in the West wealth comes so rapidly, so easily and so abundantly that the luxuries of life will follow all too quickly in its train.

Why the Payette Valley? Those who live here think it is going to be another Garden of Eden. It is full of sunshine, is the home of the Payette River and is genial the whole year through. People love to live here. Its orchards are the next thing to gold mines. Its Jonathan apple ranks the world both in beauty and price. Transcontinental trains stop in the Payette Valley to replenish their fruit.

In a word, Emmett Mesa is to occupy a radiant spot on the world's map. Its enormous money-making power will be forgotten. It will be spoken of and thought of as the beautiful fore-runner of the world's ORCHARD CITIES.

Emmett did grow and prosper. The populace was busier than a kingfisher at a fish hatchery. About 26,000 acres were brought under irrigation, and 40,000 trees were planted in the valley. Packing sheds prepared apples, cherries, peaches and apricots for market. By 1928, just before the Depression, the town had become the largest shipping point in Idaho on the U.P. line. Figures for that year show 4,300 boxcar loads originated in Emmett: including 2,400 of lumber, 540 of apples, 200 of prunes, and 100 of livestock.

The town was avalanched with wool; it was the distribution point for about 100,000 sheep that flowed through the streets every spring and fall.

Boise-Payette Lumber Co. had established a mill on the west edge of Emmett in 1916, and it employed two shifts totaling 400 men. It produced 400,000 board feet a day. (The site is now the location of a Boise Cascade mill and plywood plant – the largest in southern Idaho.)

Fruit, agriculture, and timber still support Emmett.

52

The town has inherited some notable architecture. In 1980 five churches were added to the National Register of Historic Places as a thematic group. To see them, turn east off Washington Ave. (part of Highway 52) onto East First St. The large, brick Methodist Episcopal Church is on the northeast corner at the intersection. Drive one block on East First to South Hayes, the site of the First Baptist Church. The Christ Church is one block south, on South Hayes at East Second St.; the First Southern Baptist Church one block east on East Second and one block south at South Wardell Ave. Then go north on South Wardell back to East First St., to the Episcopal Church of St. Mary the Virgin, founded in 1881.

Another unusual structure can be seen by continuing north on South Wardell to East Main. Turn east on Main St., and drive three blocks, past the city park, to 604 East Main at the corner of Johns St. The two-story residence on the northeast corner was built in 1903 for Frank DeClark. It has shingled columns, an octagonal tower, and Queen Anne glass. A sturdy hitching rock still squats by the curb.

Across the street, three doors east, is an interesting bungalow-style house with narrow dormers and an unusual river-rock porch.

Continue east on East Main to see **Picket's Corral,** a notorious outlaw redoubt in the 1860s. From East Main and Johns Sts. drive one mile to the Substation Rd. intersection. Turn north on Substation Rd. 2.2 miles and cross Frozen Dog Rd. (That wonderful name demands an explanation: "Colonel" William Hunter owned a ranch in this area in the late 1880s, before he moved to Kansas City, where as editor of an imaginary Idaho newspaper, *The Howling Wolf,* he wrote amusing tales about his Idaho experiences in a column titled "Tales of the Frozen Dog." In 1905 the stories were published in book form.)

Substation Rd. becomes Plaza Rd., and 1.5 miles north of Frozen Dog, lava cliffs can be seen east of the roadside orchards. The cliffs form a tight, watered box canyon, known as Picket's Corral.

The corral was used by horsethieves to hide stolen stock. It was not until William McConnell (later governor of Idaho) and other settlers confronted the corral gang in the 1860s, that the outlaws were finally herded out of the area.

Highway 52 leaves Emmett north across the Payette River and passes **Black Canyon Dam** and reservoir, 4.5 miles northeast of town. The dam was built by the Bureau of Reclamation in 1924 for $1.5 million as part of the Boise federal reclamation project. The concrete dam is 183 feet high, but eighty-six feet of the dam penetrates into bedrock. The U.P. railroad runs along the south side of the reservoir, and the tracks limited the water level to ninety-five feet. The reservoir holds the runoff from the north, south, and middle forks of the Payette. Pumps supply water to the Emmett Irrigation District.

Eight miles from the dam Squaw Creek flows into a lobe of Black Canyon reservoir, and one-half mile farther is a road intersection with Squaw Creek valley and Montour.

Turn north on the paved road 2.5 miles to visit **Sweet.** Stop en route, after a half-mile, at the Sweet-Montour cemetery. Just inside the front gate, on the left, is a grave site outlined with chain. The gravestones are those of Ezekial, Isabel, and Etta Sweet.

Zeke Sweet arrived in the Squaw Creek valley in 1877. Seven years later he opened the valley's second post office in his cabin. Since the Post Office Department objected to the length of the Squaw Creek name, Zeke advised, "Call it Sweet, that's short and sweet."

Zeke Sweet was from Ohio, the ninth son of ten children. He met Isabel when she came to visit her uncle, Andrew McQuade, the first settler in the valley. Zeke ran a general store, and in 1902 bought McQuade's holding. The couple had two children; Etta died at age two.

Drive north another two miles to the village. Sweet prospered in 1905, during the Thunder Mountain boom in Chamberlain Basin. There were a bank, hotel, church, flour mill, two lodge halls, three saloons, and a newspaper – the *Boise County Sentinel.* Today town is a courtesy title.

Turn south, back across Highway 52, and one mile south down across the Black Canyon backwaters to the townsite of **Montour.**

The town was established by William Dewey, Jr. in 1912, on the edge of the old Edson Marsh-John Ireton ranch, which had operated as a stage station during the 1860s for traffic headed to Placerville and Idaho City in the Boise Basin.

Dewey was building the Idaho Northern railroad up the Payette River from Emmett to McCall. The railroad company platted the town and Dewey's secretary is said to have suggested the name, which in French *(monture)* means setting or frame, because of its pleasant environment. Montour attracted farmers from Kansas and Nebraska. Grain was the principal crop, and supplied a flour mill here.

In 1924 the Bureau of Reclamation built Black Canyon Dam, and destroyed the Payette River salmon run. Sediment gradually filled the reservoir, and water began backing into the community. In 1973 thirty-six landowners decided to sue the government for $4 million. Two years later the Bureau of Reclamation began buying out the landowners. Building materials were sold for salvage.

From the Sweet-Montour intersection Highway 52 continues 9.4 miles to Highway 55 at Horseshoe Bend.

State Highway No. 53 from the Idaho-Washington border southwest of Hauser, northeast and east via Rathdrum to a junction with U.S. 95 south of Garwood. Route length: 13.5 miles.

Highway 53 angles northeast from the state line through the whistle-stop of **Hauser,** named for an owner of the Coeur d'Alene Railway and Navigation Co., and reaches Rathdrum after 8.3 miles (see Highway 41, Rathdrum).

The road turns east from Rathdrum and intersects U.S. 95, 5.2 miles farther.

State Highway No. 54 from a junction with State Highway 41 south of Spirit Lake, easterly via Athol to a local road junction in Bayview. Route length: 15.5 miles.

State Highway 54 travels seven miles east from Highway 41 to Athol and U.S. 95. Five miles east of Highway 95 the visitor enters **Farragut State Park,** a 2,700-acre preserve on the edge of Pend Oreille Lake. The park is open all year; it has facilities for swimming, boating, fishing, and roads for bicycles and snowmobiles. Though the park now quietly revegetates, it once held the largest city in Idaho.

Eleanor Roosevelt allegedly noticed Pend Oreille Lake on a flight from Washington, D.C. to Seattle, and aware of her husband's search for a secure inland naval training site, mentioned the location to him. President Franklin D. Roosevelt made a secret tour of the area.

In March, 1942, selection of Pend Oreille lakeshore as the site for the second-largest U.S. naval training center was announced in the Coeur d'Alene newspaper. The center was named for Civil War Admiral, David G. Farragut.

A contract for the $64 million project was awarded to Walter Butler Construction Co., and the builder broke ground a month

288

later. Since the only road in the area was the one to Bayview, new roads were graded and a rail extension was laid from the Northern Pacific track at Athol. Telephone and power lines were strung. Butler Construction employed 22,000 workers at Farragut.

Bayview and Farragut Peninsula from Capehorn Road in 1942, prior to construction of the Naval Training Base.

Farragut Naval Training Base in 1945.

Five months after the job began, the first boot camp, Camp Bennion, was commissioned. Captain Sowell, a 1912 Naval Academy graduate, with thirty years of Navy experience, arrived fresh from sea duty to assume command. The first ship's company men reported for duty. By September, 1942, Farragut Naval Training Center was the largest city in Idaho, with a peak population of 55,000. Recruits were being sent from induction centers throughout the country. Liberty trains ran from the base to Spokane three times a day.

In all, six separate camps, named after World War II naval heroes, were constructed. Each camp was self-contained, built in an oval around a large asphalt drill field that became known as "the grinder." The camps each trained 5,000 sailors in five to twelve-week sessions.

Every camp had twenty-two, two-story barracks and a drill hall that accommodated six basketball courts and a seventy-five-foot square swimming pool. Each had its own staff headquarters, chief petty officers quarters, service and requisition buildings, indoor rifle range, and a mess hall that could feed all the camp's recruits in an hour.

Quarters were heated by steam produced from 127,000 tons of coal, which arrived each year by rail. Eight wells were drilled on the base, and water was stored in concrete towers, one of which still serves the town of Bayview. Sewage was treated in a large plant near the edge of the lake – the outline of the holding tanks can still be seen.

The naval hospital was superior to any in the state. It consisted of almost 100 buildings connected by covered passageways; there were beds for 2,500 patients. The hospital was available to Navy, Marine Corps, and Coast Guard personnel and their dependents.

Though the training schedule varied from day to day, a certain routine prevailed. The barrack's guard yelled "hit the deck" at 5:30 A.M. Before breakfast the cleaning crew would swab the decks, and the task was repeated at noon and evening. Inspections were held on Saturdays. Recruits were given watch duty: two hours at night, four hours during the day. Rifle and small arms practice was required. Instruction included rigging, lifeboat rowing, abandon-ship drills, swimming, and the use of gas masks. The lake was used by motor launches and sailboats.

Fire-fighting school was taught by eighty-three instructors at special concrete bunkers north of Camp Hill. Oil and gasoline fires were ignited to demonstrate suppression techniques.

A school was built on the base for the children of ship's company personnel. It had sixteen classrooms; in the fall, 1944, there were 158 pupils. High school students went to Athol.

Approximately 850 German POWs at the center were employed as gardeners and maintenance men.

In fifteen months, 293,381 sailors were trained at Farragut. The last recruit graduated in March, 1945. The camp was decommissioned in June, 1946.

Because the camp's closure caused local economic hardship, nearby towns began an effort to convert the center to a two-year college, with emphasis on vocational and technical training. Since the Wartime Assets Administration was amenable to the proposal, a regional non-profit corporation was organized, and a fund drive began. Contributions were made by the businessmen of Silver Valley, and by the Coeur d'Alene VFW and Elks Club. A sixteen-page catalog publicized the college, and its nearby low-cost housing, to veterans.

Farragut College and Technical Institute opened in October, 1946, with 300 students from forty-three states, but only 175 found the campus the first day. Most of those who enrolled were veterans; only twelve were women.

By January, 1947, enrollment reached 900, and there were thirty-nine teachers on the staff. Administrative offices occupied the former hospital; classrooms were located in the service buildings of Camp Peterson. Forty percent of the students were married. Farragut Village rented 280 apartments to families, and 526 rooms to single persons.

Though the college charged tuition, finances were always a problem. Building maintenance was expensive, long-range planning was impossible, and the WAA sold those buildings not occupied by students. Enrollment slipped. Finally, in the fall, 1949, the administration announced that the college would not reopen.

The remaining buildings were sold by the WAA. In 1963 the GSA gave the state title to the land for one-half its fair market value. As its matching share, Idaho exchanged state land with the federal government. In 1964 the state legislature converted the 2,733 acres to Farragut State Park.

The year of its inauguration, the park was selected for the National Girl Scout Roundup. In 1967 it was chosen as the site of the World Boy Scout Jamboree. That summer the 17,000 Scouts built the attractive swimming area at Beaver Bay; they trucked the sand for the beach from Sandpoint. In 1969 and 1973 the park hosted the National Boy Scout Jamboree; the first gathering drew 42,000 participants.

The museum at park headquarters contains natural history exhibits, a gallery of Navy photographs, and rosters for each camp, where former recruits can find their names.

Camp roads have been linked in an agreeable bicycle circuit and the outdoor rifle range is now used by local gun clubs. The brig has been converted to a park maintenance building.

The Navy has not abandoned Pend Oreille Lake. Four barges anchored off Bayview are naval property and support the David W. Taylor research center, which tests small, electronically controlled submarines. The secret research is conducted here because the lake depth reaches 1,200 feet.

A drive down the park road to **Buttonhook Bay** group camp area brings one to the site of **Pend Oreille City.** Buttonhook is a lobe of Idlewild Bay; it is the southern extremity of the lake, and Pend Oreille City was located at the northwest edge of the hook. Only a small hollow that acted as a reservoir remains.

The settlement was founded by Zenas Leonard (who later became governor of Oregon) in 1865, making it among the earliest communities in northern Idaho. There were five houses, a hotel, pool hall, and store. The site was an overnight stop for miners and freighters using the Pend Oreille Lake – Clark Fork route to the Montana mines.

The hamlet was port for the first steamboat on the lake, the *Mary Moody,* built in 1866 by Mr. Moody, and named for his wife. The *Mary Moody* was 108 feet long, with a twenty foot beam. Construction required four months; she was planked with fir, and the upper two decks were built of white pine. The twenty h.p. engine was brought from Delaware, around the Horn, up the Columbia and Snake, then by wagon to Pend Oreille. On her maiden voyage, the *Mary Moody* carried fifty passengers, eighty-five mules, and 10,000 pounds of freight.

At the time, Portland merchants sent supplies up the Columbia with the Oregon Steam Navigation Co., then by trail to Pend Oreille, and the *Mary Moody* carried cargo across the lake to Clark Fork River, where after a portage around Cabinet Gorge, smaller packets hauled the freight to Jocko River, and then pack trains took it the last 120 miles to Helena. The route was open six months a year, the journey required seventeen days, and the charge was thirteen cents a pound.

The Oregon merchants captured most of the freight business because the eastern route up the Missouri River to Fort Benton was only open for six weeks, while the water level was sufficient. But in

1868 the St. Louis merchants built a fleet of sixty shallow-draft boats and thereby destroyed the Oregon competition. Pend Oreille City popped like a soap bubble; the *Mary Moody* was sold, then scrapped in 1876.

Highway 54 continues north from Farragut State Park three miles to **Bayview** on Idlewild Bay.

Bayview was established in 1891 as a logging town. Logs gathered in brails were towed across the lake by steamboats to the mills at Hope. (Hope was on the Northern Pacific railroad and was the main city on the lake until 1900.) Sternwheelers served the needs of miners and railroad contractors, then homesteaders, lumber companies, and finally, tourists. Although steamboat traffic on Lake Pend Oreille never developed like that on Coeur d'Alene Lake, about eighty tugs and steamers, such as the *Northern,* the *Defender,* and the *Western,* operated during the period. In time, propellers phased out the paddlewheels.

Lime kiln at Bayview.

54
IDAHO

Limestone deposits about 200 feet thick exist at Bayview, and across the lake at **Lakeview,** visible to the east from Bayview. The deposits are the remains of fossil invertebrates that lived in a Cambrian sea 550 million years ago. The Lakeview carbonate is richer than Bayview's; it was quarried from adits and barged to Hope for the Washington Brick and Lime Co.

In 1911 D. C. Corbin ran an extension from the Spokane International railroad to Bayview, at a cost of $514,000. Lumber and lime could then be transported directly to Spokane. Kilns, such as the five still visible along the Bayview shore, were operating as early as 1914, producing lime for the International Portland Cement Company's plant at Spokane.

Eventually the quality of Bayview-Lakeview lime deteriorated and Portland Cement raised its standards, forcing the quarries to close in the 1930s. In 1936 the railroad spur was abandoned.

A mail boat operated from 1912 to 1931 between Bayview and Sandpoint. Mail is still transported from Bayview to Lakeview, and to lakeshore residents, by the *La Seal.* The boat leaves the Bayview dock at noon and returns at 3:00 P.M. Passengers are accepted on a space-available basis.

55
IDAHO

State Highway No. 55 from a junction with U.S. 95 west of Marsing, easterly via Marsing, Nampa, Meridian, Eagle and Boise, then north via Horseshoe Bend, Cascade, Donnelly and McCall, then northwest to a junction with U.S. 95 in New Meadows. Route length: 142.4 miles.

Highway 55 travels 2.6 miles east from its junction with U.S. 95 to **Marsing,** a farm town named in 1920 for Henry Marsing, a resident who owned the townsite.

One-half mile east of Marsing the road crosses the Snake River, swings northeast 0.5 miles past Lizard Butte, and one mile farther forms the western boundary of Sunny Slope – 25,000 acres of orchard with a southern exposure, which was first planted in the early 1900s. The 1,100-acre **Symms Fruit Ranch** is located on the east side of the highway; it is part of the largest orchard and fruit packing operation in the state.

R. A. Symms arrived at Sunny Slope from Kansas in 1913 and bought an eighty-acre homestead. The following year he planted eight acres of apples, peaches and plums; in ten years he had a forty-acre orchard. During the 1930s Symm's sons went into a partnership with their father and expanded the acreage. R. A. Symms died in 1934.

294

The brothers added packing houses and cold storage in the 1950s; in the 1960s, as packing and storage capacity was further increased, their sons joined the enterprise. The ranch now processes 500,000 boxes of apples each year.

One-half mile farther north, turn right (east) on Lowell Road; after 0.4 miles the **Ste. Chapelle Vineyard** is visible on the north side of the road. At present this is Idaho's only commercial winery.

The winery began in Emmett, Idaho, in 1976; two years later it was moved to Sunny Slope, where the soil and climate are considered ideal for wine grapes. In 1975 Riesling, Chardonnay, Pinot Noir and Cabernet Sauvignon grapes were first harvested. The winery now grows six varieties of grapes to produce eight kinds of wines; eastern Washington vineyards supply additional grapes.

The name of the winery, and its building, is derived from a Paris chapel built by Louis XIV. The octagonal chapelle serves as a visitor center and tasting room, and its twenty-four-foot Gothic windows provide a view of the Sunny Slope orchards and the distant Owyhee Mountains.

Ste. Chapelle produces 60,000 cases of varietal wines a year. Its principal Idaho wines are Johannesberg Riesling, Chardonnay, and Gewurztraminer. The tasting and sales room are open daily, except Sunday.

Drive north two miles from Lowell Rd. on Highway 55 and then east seven miles to the intersection with Lake Ave. To visit **Deer Flat National Wildlife Refuge** take Lake Ave. three miles south to **Lake Lowell;** the refuge headquarters are at the west end of the frontage road at the foot of Lake Ave.

In 1907-1909 Deer Flat was converted to a reservoir by the Reclamation Service as a part of the Boise Project. Three huge earth embankments were constructed (one 36 ft. high, 7,200 ft. long; another 74 ft. high, 4,000 ft. long) to catch the overflow from the New York Canal which carries water south forty miles from the Boise River. Three Deer Flat canals are then fed from the Lake Lowell reservoir.

The wildlife refuge was established by Executive order in 1909, and encompasses the lake as well as eighty-six islands on the 110-miles of the Snake River from above Walters Ferry to Farewell Bend, Oregon.

The Boise Valley is a major wintering area for birds of the Pacific Flyway, and up to one-half million ducks and geese gather at the refuge in the fall. The waterfowl attract numerous bald eagles during the winter.

The shoreline serves as a nesting area for eared and western grebes, blue and black-crowned night herons, and a variety of ducks. Canada geese nest on the Snake River islands. The bird list for the refuge, available at headquarters, includes 180 species. Mid-September to March is the best time to visit the area.

Fishing for large and small mouth bass is permitted from motor boats during daylight from April 15 through September 30.

Continue east on Highway 55 from Lake Ave. 2.6 miles to U.S. 30. The merged highways jog southeast two miles, then Highway 55 turns north one mile to an interchange with I-84. Follow I-84 nine miles east to the **Meridian** exit and travel north and east 2.7 miles into town.

The first sizeable building at the location was an I.O.O.F. hall built in 1893. Since it was situated on the Boise Meridian, the prime north-south line from which all lands in Idaho are surveyed, it was known as the Meridian Lodge. Although the lodge burned in 1923, the city, incorporated in 1909, established itself as the center of southern Idaho's dairy industry. It claimed to have "more cows per acre" than any other place in the U.S., but Boise's suburban growth has made inroads on the farmland.

One mile past Meridian the highway turns north again for 5.2 miles, crosses the Boise River and Eagle Island, enters Eagle, then turns east 2.2 miles before veering north through Dry Creek Valley 12.6 miles to Spring Valley summit (4,242 ft.).

A dirt road leaves the west side of the highway on the summit; it leads 4.7 miles west to the old mining settlement of **Pearl,** where tailing piles, foundations, and a few dilapidated, gutted shacks are the only evidence of a district that produced $2 million in gold and lead.

Pearl began in 1867 when the proprietor of the Dry Creek ranch-station found a quartz prospect on Willow Creek. The area was worked after the Panic of 1893, and in 1903-1907 a dozen mines were active; their names are as colorful as those of racehorses: Checkmate, Easter, Black Pearl, Leviathan, Red Warrior, Middleman, Afterthought.

Ball mills, one of them with a 150-ton capacity, were steam-powered at first, then the Payette River Power Co. provided electricity. Supplies were furnished from Emmett.

Colonel William Dewey had five claims here and work was done on his mines as late as 1945.

One can follow the dirt road 10.6 miles west past Pearl to Highway 16 just south of Emmett.

After Highway 55 moves 2.2 miles from the summit a bit of natural whimsy, known as **Bread Loaf Rock,** can be seen 300 yards east, below the road. The highway continues five miles north, across the Payette River, into **Horseshoe Bend.**

Bread Loaf Rock.

The **Idaho Northern** railroad tracks (now the Union Pacific), on the west side of the road and the river, were extended from Emmett to McCall in 1914. The railroad was purchased for $2 million in 1911 by E. H. Harriman from the son of Col. W. H. Dewey. The road follows the eastern edge of the rails and river from Horseshoe Bend 14.2 miles to Banks.

Banks is situated at the confluence of the South and North Forks of the Payette. The road to **Garden Valley** and Lowman travels east from Banks up the inviting South Fork Canyon thirty-three miles to Highway 21. About half of the road is paved.

The drive north from Banks to Cascade alongside the **North Fork of the Payette** is a distracting one, especially in the spring. The river pummels its way south in a smoky white turmoil of haystacks and souse holes – it drops 1,700 feet in fifteen miles.

"That which is best left alone is not always what least allures." In 1978 Idaho Power Co. revealed plans for a run-of-the-river hydro-development that would produce slightly more than 100,000 k.w. most of the time. A license for the $220 million project was granted in 1982.

The plan requires a diversion dam fifteen miles north of Banks (three miles south of Smith's Ferry) with a headrace tunnel sixteen feet in diameter driven seven miles through the mountain on the east side of the road to an underground powerhouse four miles north of Banks. The water will drop from the tunnel through three generating units, then reenter the river briefly above a second dam that will divert it through a second tunnel on the west side of the river and carry it four miles to another underground powerhouse with three generating units, just north of Banks. From the turbines, a 570-foot tailrace will spew the river back into its bed at Banks. The southern stretch of the project will be built first. (Some residents have begun to feel that Idaho Power is a bit like the little girl who said she knew how to spell banana, but just didn't know when to stop.)

Cascade is 36.8 miles up the North Fork from Banks. The town is located one-half mile from Cascade Dam and reservoir on the Payette River; the rapids in the river suggested the name in 1912.

The Bureau of Reclamation built the **Cascade Dam** as part of the Black Canyon irrigation project. Construction began in 1942, was interrupted by World War II, resumed in 1946 and was completed two years later. The highway and railroad were relocated but three village sites were inundated.

Cascade occupies the southern end of **Long Valley,** which extends north to Payette Lake; the valley was a summer pasture for most of Boise Valley's livestock. The town, which has been the seat of Valley County since 1917, is dependent on agriculture, ranching and logging; the Boise-Cascade sawmill here often produces 30 million board feet a year.

SCENIC
AREA

There can be little doubt that the finest two-day backcountry drive in Idaho begins at the north end of Cascade. One can make a 170-mile loop from Cascade via Yellow Pine, Big Creek, and Warrens back to Highway 55 at McCall. The trip covers some of the roughest country God ever coughed up, over dirt roads with more curves than a case of muleshoes, but the drive is also beautiful, historied, and uncrowded.

Before attempting this excursion, check with the Payette National Forest office in McCall to learn whether it is possible to cross Elk Creek Summit (8,670 elev.) – snow can block the pass until the Fourth of July. Though gas is usually available in Yellow Pine, it is advisable to leave Cascade with a full tank.

From Cascade follow the paved road twenty-four miles east to **Warm Lake.** Warm Lake offers a choice of two routes to Yellow Pine: fifty miles down the South Fork-Poverty Flat road, or thirty-five miles east and north down Johnson Creek via Landmark. It is a jump ball; each has its own beauty.

In 1902 Al Behne, the first settler in **Yellow Pine Basin,** built a cabin on Johnson Creek. A few other homesteaders joined him during the Thunder Mountain boom (1902-1907), which occurred eighteen miles east of **Yellow Pine.** In 1907 a slide dammed Monumental Creek and flooded the mining settlement of Roosevelt; Thunder Mountain's boom diminished to an echo.

In the 1920s Bradley Mining Corp. began to develop mines at Stibnite, fourteen miles from Yellow Pine; about 125 men worked there during the Depression, and activity increased during World War II. The influx boosted Yellow Pine to the status of a town.

Continue east down the East Fork of the South Fork of the Salmon 4.5 miles to the Profile Gap – Stibnite junction.

Stibnite is 9.5 miles southeast of this fork. The mining center derived its name from the chief ore of the metal antimony. About 1913 Albert Hennessey discovered gold and antimony ore on Meadow Creek at Stibnite. Gold, antimony and cinnabar were mined between 1914 and 1918, before Hennessey sold his claims to United Mercury Mines Co. in 1921. In 1928 United Mercury leased the claims to Bradley Mining Co. and that company began an open-pit mine ten years later. Drill crews from the U.S. Bureau of Mines discovered high-grade tungsten at the site in 1940; from 1942 to 1945 the Yellow Pine mine at Monday Camp, two miles north of Stibnite, became the largest producer (50 percent) of tungsten in the U.S. The mine also produced 95 percent of the nation's antimony, a metal used in armor-piercing shells, aircraft carrier decks, and radar tubes. At the same time, the Cinnabar mine just east of Stibnite was the second-largest mercury producer in the country.

The Stibnite mines closed in 1952; yields for a twenty-year period were: antimony, $24 million; tungsten, $21 million; gold, $4 million; mercury, $3 million; silver $1 million. The Bureau of Mines estimates $50 million in antimony remains at the mine.

The last residents departed Stibnite in 1959; most of the houses were trucked to new locations. Bradley left nothing in its wake but a disordered watershed – and a telling argument for mining regulations.

In 1980 Canadian Superior Mining, Ltd., a subsidiary of Superior Oil of Texas, ran successful leach tests for gold in the antimony tailings. Sodium cyanide was sprayed over rock piles; it dissolved the gold from its matrix, and the solvent was pumped through charcoal filters to recover the metal for further processing. The company has not yet decided whether to pursue the project.

Stibnite mine and mill in 1948.

From Stibnite return up the East Fork of the South Fork to the Profile Gap road and drive up Profile Creek to **Profile Summit** (7,605 ft.). A memorial to the old prospector Profile Sam Wilson has been placed at the edge of the road. Profile Sam had secret mines in the area; he lived in a tiny cabin here until he committed suicide in 1935; his friends buried him in Yellow Pine.

The mountains visible 2½ miles west of the Gap are Big Creek Point (8,893 ft.) and Profile Peak (8,965 ft.).

The road drops from the summit 8.5 miles along Big Creek to **Edwardsburg,** now an area of summer homes.

In 1904 William Edwards, son of a Georgia judge, and a graduate of Emory College and Georgetown Univ. Law School, built a cabin here. Edward's health had failed after ten years in the Asst. Attorney General's Office in Washington, D.C.; he came west to Spokane, and then brought his wife Annie (Napier), and son Napier, to the Thunder Mountain boom. Annie was from an aristocratic Georgia family, an honors graduate of Wesleyan Univ., and was as out of place in the Idaho backcountry as a rabbit in a coyote's pen.

300

Mr. Edwards became convinced certain ore deposits on Logan Creek were very valuable and spent much of his life trying to promote them. By training he was a specialist in mining law. In 1928 he formed the Copper Camp Mining Co. and persuaded wealthy friends to invest in it. When the values proved illusory, he and his wife were broken. Annie gradually lost her mind, and died at the state asylum in Blackfoot. William died in Nampa.

Big Creek is just a hoot and a holler past Edwardsburg. It is a sportsman's outpost, with a lodge that rents rooms during the summer and fall. The log lodge was built in 1937 by Jim Carpenter, Joe Powell and Dick Cowman to serve the miners in the area.

Big Creek flows almost fifty miles from this point down to the Middle Fork of the Salmon River in Impassible Canyon.

From Edwardsburg the road forks west and gees and haws through tortuous switchbacks up Government Creek 7.5 miles to **Elk Creek Summit** (8,670 elev.). The view of Big Creek drainage and the **Big Horn Crags** across the void of the Middle Fork Canyon is unforgettable.

Elk Creek Summit to Warrens is thirty-two miles; the angular road that descends Elk Creek is steeper than a cow's face. It enters the crevice of the **South Fork of the Salmon,** an area pocked with mines; many of them had a half-life of six months; others, like the Werdenhoff and Marshall Mountain, lasted for years. Follow the South Fork north downstream, then climb through stands of ponderosa to Warren Summit (6,974 ft.) and proceed four miles to Warren's Meadows.

Warren, called **Warren's,** now looks like a settlement that cannot make up its mind whether it is coming or going but there was no such doubt when it held the seat of Idaho County from 1869 to 1875. Norman Willey, a Warren's miner, was elected second governor of the state in 1890.

In 1862 James Warren led a party of prospectors from Florence into the meadows here; word of their gold discovery spread like news of an assassination. Although the ground was not as rich as that at Florence, the diggings had more water, and by the following summer the camp had grown to 660.

Extensive dredge scars resulted from an effort that began with a wooden steamshovel in 1904, and continued with a pair of electric dredges from 1932 to 1942. Estimates place the dredge harvest at $4 million, and earlier mining efforts yielded a similar amount.

55
IDAHO

No graveyard is so handsome that one would like to be immediately buried there, but the one on the slope behind Warren's has a pleasant location and markers of interest.

Warren's diggings.

West of Warren's the road runs 14.2 miles to the Burgdorf junction. Turn two miles northwest to **Burgdorf Hot Springs.**

Fred Burgdorf was a German immigrant who came to the Warren's diggings in 1864 from San Francisco. He obtained rights to the springs in 1865 as payment on a promissory note; only a roadhouse and express station were there at the time. Fred was familiar with German spas and developed a twenty-room hotel, several cabins around the springs, and a barn. His hospitality, courtesy, and baronial meals filled the guest rooms for fifty-eight years. The Thunder Mountain boom in 1902 helped; so did Jeanette Foronsard, a singer from Denver, whom Fred married that year. She changed the name of the spot from Resort to Burgdorf. Jeanette died in 1923.

After his wife's death, Fred sold the place to Jim Harris and moved to Weiser, where he was buried in 1929.

Follow the paved road southwest from Burgdorf junction northwest up Summit Creek to **Secesh Summit** (6,434 ft.), named by southern miners during the Civil War. The road then drops 1,400 feet in 22.5 miles along the North Fork of the Payette to a junction with Highway 55, 1.2 miles north of McCall.

302

Highway 55 travels north up Long Valley 15.1 miles from Cascade to Donnelly. **Donnelly** emerged along the railroad tracks that bypassed Roseberry 1.5 miles to the east; it is the youngest town in the valley. In the 1930s the village was a shade rough: the Richmond & Samuel Pea Co. used migrant workers in their packing and shipping sheds; loggers lived in Boise-Payette's McGregor camp two miles south of town, and the CCC boys were drawn south from McCall by the pool room and dance hall. Bootleggers were busier than a man fighting bees.

The pea company and the CCC shut down during World War II;

Long Valley threshing outfit, 1935.

the logging camp moved to New Meadows in 1940, and Donnelly, in comparison, is now quiet as a wooden Indian.

The **Roseberry** church, 1.5 miles east of Donnelly, contains the **Valley County Museum.** It is open on weekend afternoons during the summer. The Methodist church was opened to any denomination that requested permission to hold services; the sexton used to say, "We're all spittin' at the same crack."

In the 1920s most of Roseberry's buildings were skidded across the snow to the railroad tracks at Donnelly (read Cynthia Pottenger: *My Roseberry).*

The road to **Gold Fork hot springs** is 1.5 miles south of Donnelly on the east side of the highway and leads five miles east to the springs on Gold Fork River.

Lake Fork is seven miles north of Donnelly; it was the location of a Finnish community whose members emigrated to the area from 1896 to 1910, one of two such settlements in the state. By 1915 eighty-five Finnish families lived on farms in the area.

Take the Farm-to-Market Road east from the highway 1.5 miles to the hilltop where the Finnish Evangelical Lutheran Church is located. This white, ship-lap structure was built in 1916-1917 for about $1900 by volunteers, on land donated by Uriel Kantola.

At present there is no Finnish minister in the valley and the Finnish Ladies Aid Society maintains the building. It is only used for weddings, funerals, and Bible-study classes. The church has been added to the National Register of Historic Places.

McCall is four miles north of Lake Fork. One of Idaho's three better-known resorts, its 5,000-foot elevation gives it the highest mean annual snowfall of any town in the state: 151 inches, but its summer climate, like Baby Bear's porridge, is just right.

In 1891 Tom McCall purchased squatter's rights to the first cabin on the site from Sam Devers for a team and a wagon. Tom was appointed postmaster in 1894.

McCall.

Lumber was produced on **Payette Lake** for almost eighty years. Warren Gold Dredge Co. built the first sawmill on the lake, and sold it to Tom McCall; he used it to cut wood for a hotel and several houses. When the mill burned, he built another, and a pattern for lakeside sawmills was established: they burned, rebuilt, and burned with the regularity of smoke signals, until Boise Cascade closed the last one in 1977.

The origins of McCall as a vacation-land can be traced to the first sailboat, made by Anneas "Jews Harp Jack" Wyatte to carry tourists around the lake. Its successor was a prop-driven steam vessel called the *Lydia.*

The arrival of the Idaho Northern Pacific Railroad in 1914 opened the lake to tourists seeking relief from the summer heat of the Boise Valley. In the 1920s the State Land Board began leasing vacation homesites along the lake. At present there are 252 leases: lakeside tenants pay $730 a year; others pay $422.

In 1938 McCall and Payette Lake were selected as the location for an MGM film, *Northwest Passage,* starring Spencer Tracy, Robert Young, and Walter Brennan. The script was based on a novel by Kenneth Roberts about Rogers' Rangers during the French and Indian War. The movie company employed 900 white persons and 360 Indians.

McCall is noted for events, as well as sights:

The Fourth of July is celebrated with a waterfront boat parade and evening fireworks over the lake.

Labor Day weekend attracts antique car buffs for a parade through town and a concourse at the Shore Lodge.

McCall and Payette Lake in about 1915.

The first weekend in February is Winter Carnival; the streets are lined with ice sculptures which are based on an announced theme. Prizes are awarded.

A U.S. Forest Service smokejumpers base in McCall is open to visitors during the summer. It is located on Mission St. across from McCall-Donnelly School. The base, which normally has sixty jumpers, has operated here since 1943.

Visitors are also welcome at the McCall summer chinook fish hatchery on Mather Rd. by the Payette River. The hatchery, jointly funded by the U.S. Fish and Wildlife Service and the state Fish and Game Department, was built to increase the regional chinook runs, especially that of the South Fork of the Salmon, which was destroyed by faulty logging practices on the Payette National Forest. The $4 million facility began operations in late 1979; its visitors center has written and pictorial explanations.

Ponderosa State Park is located on a peninsula 1.8 miles northeast of town. The first road through the 830-acre park was built by the CCC; the State Lands Board narrowly reversed their own decision to subdivide the area. It opened as a park in 1969, with 170 campsites, and beaches, trails, boat ramps, restrooms and showers.

Highway 55 goes west from McCall across the North Fork of the Payette River and through **Rocky Flat** on Goose Creek 2.2 miles from town. A few octahedron diamond crystals are alleged to have been recovered here, the only such site in Idaho. The find occasioned a tunnel and sluicing operations, abandoned long ago.

The **Packer John's Cabin State Park** (sixteen acres) 1.4 miles farther west on the north side of the road, is the site of a cabin built in 1862 by John Walsh and used for the first Democratic convention in the Territory. The present cabin is a reproduction of the original.

New Meadows and the junction with U.S. 95 are located three miles west of the state park.

State Highway No. 57 from a junction with U.S. 2 in Priest River northerly via Nordman to a junction with a local road north of Nordman. Route length: 37.2 miles.

The **Priest River** can be glimpsed in spots along the east side of Highway 57 as one drives north from Priest River town.

River trips with kayaks, canoes, or small rafts can be made on this stream, with access at five points. The source of the lower river (Outlet Bay on the south end of Priest Lake) is twenty-five miles from its mouth, but because of numerous meanders, it is a forty-four-mile float to the city of Priest River.

During late spring the water can be high and swift, and two rapids are regarded as hazardous at that stage. In the summer, the river is fairly torpid and the depth averages 2½-3 feet. Fall rains and storage release raise the water level in October. (A reference map is available from the U.S. Forest Service.)

Highway 57 travels nineteen miles north from Priest River to Dickensheet Junction, which at one time was headquarters for log drives on the river. Ten miles north of Priest River, on the west side of the road, grows the largest known larch tree, but no sign reveals its locale. This area is included in the Kaniksu National Forest, established in 1908 from the 650,000-acre Priest River Forest Reserve set aside in 1897 by President Cleveland's proclamation. This forest at present embraces an additional million acres, covers portions of three states, and borders Canada for nearly fifty miles.

At Dickensheet Junction the road bifurcates. Continue north on 57. (The Coolin-Indian Creek stretch is treated at the end of this section.)

Take the Outlet Bay turnoff, which is signed. A short road leads to the Bay, the source of the lower Priest River, and gives a view of Priest Lake.

Priest Lake.

Priest Lake is the least used of the three large north Idaho lakes. It reposes in a north-south valley glaciated a million years ago, but with evidence of glaciation as recent as 7,000 years ago. The Priest is actually two lakes: the upper 3½ mile lakelet is connected by a brief waterway to the lower 17½ miles. The lake has seventy miles of shoreline and a maximum known depth, according to the Fish and Game Department, of 369 feet.

Although the elevation of the lake is only 2,438 feet, some of the peaks along the eastern shore exceed 7,000 feet. The forest that shields this southern spur of the Selkirk Range consists of hemlock, cedar, Douglas and grand fir, ponderosa and white pine, lodgepole,

307

Engelmann spruce and larch. White birch and alder are sometimes seen. Huckleberries and mushrooms grow here, too. Mule and white-tail deer, black bear, moose, elk, mountain goats, and even an occasional mountain caribou are found within the boundaries of the forest.

Fish thrive in Priest Lake. The Idaho record Mackinaw trout (57½ lbs.) and the U.S. record kokanee salmon (6½ lbs.) were caught here. Mackinaw were introduced to Priest Lake in 1925; kokanee were released in 1942.

Mysis shrimp did well in the lake and provided food for the fish. The Idaho Department of Fish and Game went to Canada and collected mysis from Waterton and Kootenay Lakes and released them in Priest, but that mysis competed with other, smaller organisms in the lake which newly hatched kokanee fed upon. The kokanee fishery collapsed, and so did the Mackinaw, which feed on the kokanee. A massive hatchery program for kokanee followed.

Dolly Varden, cutthroat, and rainbow trout can also be taken by fishermen. The season runs from May through November, but spring and fall provide the best results.

Summer lakeside temperatures average seventy-five degrees, and the water in the sandy shallows is sometimes that warm. In the winter, the shores get about four feet of snow, and the lake often freezes.

Fr. Pierre De Smet, the Jesuit missionary, named this lake Roothan, for his Superior General in Rome. The Indian name, "Kaniksu" (black robe) may have referred to Roothan; their name was applied to the lake for almost forty years. Then the promoters of the Great Northern Railroad gave it the present name in 1890. Whatever the name, the beauty of this lake exceeds that of its more developed rivals: Tahoe, Chelan, and Kootenay.

Look east from this point, across Priest Lake, to 6,300-foot Sundance Mountain. The scarred slopes are the result of the Sundance Fire in 1967, which became the subject of a *National Geographic* article. This fire burned 56,000 acres in twelve hours. Scientists estimated at its height the flame-front released energy equivalent to that of a twenty-kiloton bomb exploding every two minutes. It sluiced down the face of this mountain for two hours, then turned back toward the ridge.

There is a resort at the bay with store, cafe, motel, cabins, rental boats and moorage. USFS campsites are established along the shore and on Kalispell Island.

North 4.5 miles farther on Highway 57 is an exit on the left for **Hanna Flat Cedar Grove**. Drive west one mile; the grove is on the north side of the parking area.

In 1926 an extremely destructive 80,000-acre fire burned through the Priest Lake area, but it missed this exceptional stand of old-growth cedar. Most of the trees are over 200 years old; some may be about 800. A quarter-mile interpretive trail has been built by the Forest Service through this sixteen acres that was set aside in 1955. The area averages eighty-nine inches of snow a year.

USFS Road 1338, on the east side of State Highway 57, travels less than a mile to **Kalispell Bay**, where Kalispell Island basks like a sleepy blue whale within easy reach of any boat, and the island shelters five campgrounds.

Drive along the shoreline 1.5 miles to the road end and inspect the Indian pictograph on the granite face about six feet above the water. It is four feet long and six to eight inches wide; no one now knows its meaning.

Roosevelt Memorial Cedar Grove.

The drive for the next four miles, north to Nordman on Highway 57, passes through dense stands of evergreen and deciduous trees, broken by tenuous meadows and small hayfields.

A right turn at **Nordman** takes one to **Reeder Bay**, the last commercial launch ramp that allows boats access to **Upper Priest Lake**. It is possible to follow the shoreline road about nine miles north to launch at Tule Bay-Beaver Creek, but it is not recommended. At the mouth of Beaver Creek there is a six-mile horse and foot trail to a campground on the north end of Upper Priest Lake. Priest Lake and Upper Priest Lake are connected by an easy-going, two-mile stretch of river called "The Thorofare."

Nordman is also the take-off point for a fine twelve-mile excursion (which enters Washington at the halfway mark) to the **Roosevelt Grove of Ancient Cedars**, an undisturbed stand of red cedars set aside in 1943. Many of the trees are several centuries old. **Granite Falls**, pitching down through a rocky fissure in this grove, is a delightful bonus. A USFS campground is nearby. nearby.

Dickensheet Junction (east, off Highway 57)

A right turn at **Dickensheet Junction** leads across the Priest River after a half-mile. A small state campground is located along the streambank at the east end and downstream side of the bridge.

Go north past **Coolin** and **Cavanaugh Bay**, where the graveled road skirts the shore of Priest Lake. At times the road climbs several hundred feet above the lake and grants extended views of the water and the Selkirk slopes. Pine and fir shadows lattice the road in early morning and late afternoon.

Indian Creek camping unit of **Priest Lake State Park** is located ten miles north of Coolin. The site includes a white, granular, crescent beach shaded by conifers, a view of water and islands blue as dolphins in the distance, and drumlin-mounded mountains softly shaped against the skyline.

Indian Creek contains park headquarters, a large campground with modern facilities and recreational vehicle hookups, inconspicuous gas and grocery service, and rental boats, launch and dock.

During 1940-1950, Diamond Match Company operated a log flume from the upper reaches of Indian Creek down to the lake, through the present campground. A company crew lived on the site, doing flume maintenance and binding logs into brailes that were towed by barge to Cavanaugh Bay, where they were trucked to a mill. The flume was abandoned when roads gave trucks access to the timber.

Chimney Rock stands at the head of the north and south forks of Indian Creek, about six miles to the east, and can be spotted in places from the road.

Another marvelous state beach can be reached by proceeding past Indian Creek twelve miles to **Lion Head** campsite. Limited facilities are available at this state unit.

This area, named for a lion-headed rock, was a movie location for actress Nell Shipman: silent screen star, novelist, and script-writer. Her movie camp, Lionhead Lodge, was located on a promontory now occupied by a boat ramp, and known today as Shipman Point. The movie crew of thirty persons headquartered in the lodge; the grounds served as corral for two dog teams, a herd of horses, and a menagerie. Most of the supplies and animals were brought across the lake from Coolin by steam barge. Dog sleds were used in the winter.

During the four-year production stay (1923-1926), the film company made several movies on location, among them, *White Water, The Grubstake, Trail of the North Wind, The Light on the Lookout,* and *Love Tree.*

Shipman's director got gangrene from frost-bitten toes, then suffered a mental breakdown. The creditors moved in. Nell had to kill the horses to feed her dogs and zoo animals. Finally the San Diego zoo agreed to take the surviving animals, and paid transportation costs.

The *Atlantic Monthly* serialized the story of the movie-making hardships in a May-July, 1925 series titled "The Movie That Could Not Be Screened." Nell Shipman died in 1970.

State Highway No. 62 from a junction with Highway 64 in Nez Perce south, east, and northwesterly to a junction with Highway 64 in Kamiah. Route length: 23.2 miles.

This road covers portions of the Camas Prairie wheat lands and Lawyers Canyon, before descending into the Clearwater Canyon. The region's geology, history, and agriculture are discussed along U.S. 95 from Grangeville to Spalding.

State Highway No. 64 from a junction with U.S. 95 in Craigmont easterly via Nezperce to a junction with U.S. 12 in Kamiah. Route length: 31.1 miles.

Highway 64 travels east from Craigmont, through Mohler sixteen miles to **Nezperce,** then twelve miles across the prairie and down into the Clearwater canyon to Kamiah.

Nezperce is the seat of Lewis County. It is linked to Craigmont and the Camas Prairie Railroad by an independent Class II fourteen-mile rail called the Nez Perce and Idaho. The railroad was built in 1909-1910 by Z. A. Johnson, with the help of local farmers.

The townsite of Nezperce was staked by government surveyors in anticipation of the land rush that accompanied the subdivision of the Nez Perce reservation under the Allotment Act. When lots were distributed on November 18, 1895, there were 5,000 people camped on the townsite. In 1911 the population was about 1,800 but it has never since approached that figure.

Newsworthy events on the prairie in those days must have been like angel visits, few and far between. The *Nezperce Herald* published the following request in 1908:

This paper is always glad to get the news. If you are dead or about to commit suicide, or if you have been arrested lately and want to bring the matter to the attention of the people; if you have eloped with another man's wife, if you are going away or coming back; if you or your wife or children or any of your relations have a party, delirium tremens, bone erysipelas, scarlet fever, money left you, a call to preach, smallpox, an idea, or anything of the sort, tell us about it. We must have news.

Nezperce is entitled to a certain fame as the home of the Camas Prairie Sage, York Herren. Herren wrote a column for the *Herald* for several years about his observations along Main St. His reply to the following letter, from a buckass Boise bureaucrat, rivals Mark Twain's letter to the gas company:

STATE OF IDAHO
DEPARTMENT OF FINANCE
BOISE

Mr. York Herren, Agent
Nezperce, Idaho

Dear Mr. Herren:

Enclosed find statement and check to Shoemaker's. I have noticed in these statements that the janitor there is constantly buying toilet paper, 25 cents to 35 cents at a time. How many of the offices does he keep suppled? The one in connection with the court room I should think would be all. Those fellows downstairs should supply their own. Please check this up and let me know. It may seem a small matter, but at the rate he has been buying lately, it would mean the cost of several cases in a year.

With kindest regards, I am

Your very truly,
E. SCOTT
General Liquidating Agent

Union State Bank
Nezperce, Idaho
March 8, 1929

Mr. M. E. Scott, General Liquidating Agent,
Department of Finance,
Boise, Idaho

Dear Mr. Scott:

I have your letter of March 4th relative to amount of toilet paper used in the building. We have two toilets upstairs here, one for the exclusive use of the ladies and the other for the balance of humanity. They are used by the County Officials and the other renters on this floor and by the public at large, which seems to assume that a County Court House should provide these luxuries. Particularly during cold weather we have regular customers who partake of our hospitality, among whom are a great many ladies.

Nezperce affords few comfortable retreats for the gentler sex, and many of them learn of the superiority of our service by being patients of the Doctor and Dentist, and a customer once acquired is rarely lost. Perhaps under these circumstances the visitors should "roll their own" and some of them may for all I know, for I must confess that this is a matter I have not given the careful and astute attention it seems to deserve.

I had rather assumed that the janitor held exclusive jurisdiction over all matters relating to toilet paper and that I could act only in an advisory capacity. In the pursuit of this theory, what goes on behind the door of ladies' toilet is a closed book to me. I am both married and modest and feel that undue inquisitiveness on my part might be misconstrued or might be deemed by the ladies as a violation of their privileges which might be justly resented.

In this section the use of toilet paper is strictly a private practice and its excessive use is a secret vice in which an addict is rarely apprehended in the pursuit of his passion. It is the custom of the country that when one sequesters himself to seek solace for his soul

*in solitary communion with nature, his meditations shall be
undisturbed.*

*One phase of the situation suggests to me a possible reason for
the apparent extravagance. Many of our county "Indigents" were
reared in the land of corn cobs and coarse brown paper. When these
people first come in contact with the caressing luxury of silk tissue
they are so fascinated by its soothing and sanitary influence that
they lose all restraint and indulge wastefully in the new found
delight.*

*At any rate, your agent will pursue his investigations assiduously
and energetically and will endeavor by both precept and example to
keep the use of paper within reasonable limits.*

Very truly yours,
YORK HERREN

Highway 67 extends from the northern boundary of the Mountain
Home Air Force Base northeasterly to a junction with Highway 51
west of Mountain Home. Route length: 8.9 miles.

Mountain Home Air Force Base, the only major military
installation in Idaho, was established in November, 1942. The
location was chosen for its low cost, its isolation, and its favorable
flying weather. By September, 1943, $13 million in construction had
been completed, and in October, 1944, the site was designated
Mountain Home Army Air Field. The 396th and 470th
Bombardment Groups (Heavy) were stationed at the base, which
became a replacement training school for B-24 crews. In October,
1945, shortly after the base was changed to a B-29 Superfortress
training school, it was deactivated.

In December, 1948, the base was reactivated for the 311th Air
Division, Reconnaissance (Strategic Air Command). Again
deactivated, from August, 1949 to February, 1951, it reopened
under the control of the Military Air Transport Service. SAC
returned in May, 1953 with the 9th Bombardment Wing, and three
Titan I missile sites with three missiles each were activated in 1963,
but have since been abandoned. SAC departed in late 1965; the 67th
Tactical Reconnaissance Wing arrived in January, 1966, and was
replaced in 1972 by the 366th Tactical Fighter Wing. The 366th flies
the General Dynamics F-111A, a long-range, mach 2.5 fighter
bomber with variable-sweep wings.

The 388th Electronic Combat Squadron at Mountain Home flies
the EF-111A, designed to provide electronic countermeasures in
support of fighter planes.

314

The primary mission of the 9th Bombardment Wing is to train and maintain fighter squadrons capable of destroying enemy targets with conventional and nuclear weapons.

The Wing's history goes back to the 1st Provisional Aero Squadron, which was activated in March, 1913, to assist the Second Division, then on guard along the Texas border. At that time the Air Force consisted of twenty-four pilots (military aviators). Their airplanes were the Wright B; it cruised at forty-nine mph, with a range of 125 miles.

Mountain Home AFB is part of the Tactical Air Command headquartered at Langley AFB, Virginia.

Other commands represented at Mountain Home are Military Airlift, Air Training, and Air Force Communications.

With notice, tours are available to the public. Open-house is an annual one-day affair, usually in mid-summer. Air Force Appreciation Day is also an annual event, celebrated in September in Mountain Home.

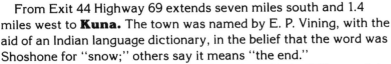

State Highway No. 69 from a junction with the eastbound off ramp at I-84 in Meridian south and west to Kuna, then by local road south to Birds of Prey Natural Area. Route length: 27.4 miles.

From Exit 44 Highway 69 extends seven miles south and 1.4 miles west to **Kuna.** The town was named by E. P. Vining, with the aid of an Indian language dictionary, in the belief that the word was Shoshone for "snow;" others say it means "the end."

In November, 1905, Mr. and Mrs. F. H. Teed filed a 200-acre claim under the Desert Land Act, where Kuna now stands. The site was on the freight road to Silver City, and along the OSL railroad. At the time, only one house was located between their shack and Walters Ferry, thirteen miles to the southwest.

Until wells were dug, water had to be hauled in barrels from the Snake River. The Teeds opened the Kuna post office in 1907; receipts for the first quarter amounted to 16¢.

To visit **Kuna Cave** and the **Birds of Prey Natural Area,** leave Highway 69 and travel south from Kuna across Indian Creek to Kuna Way. Follow Kuna Way due west 3.7 miles, turn south onto Robinson Blvd. for 4.5 miles, then turn due east 1.8 miles on a dirt road to a south-southeast fork. The cave is 1.1 miles down this spur, on the south side of Kuna Butte. Its entrance, like a rabbit hole, is not revealed until one is almost on top of it.

Kuna Cave is a lava tube, about 1,000 feet long. A thirty-five foot steel ladder, heavily vandalized, provides access. Since the interior is as dark as the inside of a cow, a flashlight is recommended.

When exploring the cave in 1911, General A. Utter found a human skeleton on a ledge. Claude Gibson, a Boise lawyer, said that he discovered the cave in 1890, and with a group of friends descended into it by means of a rope attached to the rear wheel of their wagon. They found rocks assembled in a pile beneath the opening, and bones nearby. The entrance was half its present size, and they assumed that an Indian had fallen through the opening, and then was unable to escape.

Interior of Kuna Cave in 1920.

To visit Birds of Prey Natural Area return to Robinson Rd., drive north 3.5 miles, turn due east on Bennett Rd. 4.0 miles, then south on the Swan Falls Rd.

After seven miles, a one-mile road on the east leads to **Initial Point** (3,240 elev.), chosen in 1867 as the Boise Meridian point from which all Idaho lands were surveyed.

Continue south five miles, east one mile, then southeasterly another five miles to the **Snake River Birds of Prey Natural Area,** established in 1971 on 26,000 acres by Secretary of the Interior Rogers Morton.

Containing the densest nesting population of raptors in the world, the area was recently the subject of thirteen research projects, most of them contracted to universities by the B.L.M. According to the findings the birds hunt areas up to fifteen miles from the canyon. In

1980, concerned with protecting the raptors' food supply, in addition to their nesting sites, Secretary of the Interior Cecil Andrus ordered the BLM to expand the Natural Area by about 480,000 acres.

The area in question represents a unique ecosystem. Hawks, eagles and owls nest in the fissures and ledges along the 300-foot cliffs above the Snake River. Their prey, however, is located on the shrub-grassland desert above the nests. This unusual reversal allows adult birds to rise easily out of the canyon on updrafts, hunt the desert flats, and descend to their nests with food – up light, down heavy.

The surrounding desert is covered with a mantle of deep silt loam; it supports sage, bluegrass, cheat-grass, winterfat, and shadscale. Soil and vegetation types combine to furnish superb habitat for Townsend ground squirrels, blacktailed jackrabbits, and badgers. Protection of this vegetation, and its concomitant rodent population, is regarded as essential to the welfare of the raptors.

Agricultural and mineral development of 110,000 acres of the area is also considered vital to the welfare of Atlantic Richfield Corp., Idaho Mining Assn., Idaho Farm Bureau Federation, and Idaho Water Users Assn. – these organizations, at least, are the ones that screamed like a mashed cat when expansion of the Natural Area was proposed. The Secretary's directive does not foreclose grazing permits or mineral leases; it does preclude farm withdrawals on public land within the area under the Desert Land and Carey Acts. It preserves, in other words, the sage-grassland for livestock and for raptor prey, while recognizing that farms are not compatible with either goal. (Corporate opposition to the directive recalls a line from Robinson Jeffers, "...(mans') needs and nature are no more changed in fact in ten thousand years than the beaks of eagles.")

The best time to visit the Natural Area is between February and June; May is considered "prime-time." Viewers can observe prairie falcons, red-tailed hawks, and golden eagles soaring like "kites without strings" above the canyon rim. The birds court, mate, and rear their young before the Townsend ground squirrels resume their hibernation in mid-June. At that time, the raptors move on.

Establishment of the Birds of Prey Natural Area protected a significant remnant of our wild heritage, a remnant that pleasures all given to noticing such things. As D. H. Lawrence put it, *Birds are the life of the skies, and when they fly they reveal the thoughts of the skies. The eagle flies nearest to the sun, no other bird flies so near. So he brings down the life of the sun, and the power of the sun, in his wings, and men who see him wheeling are filled with the elation of the sun.*

317

69
IDAHO

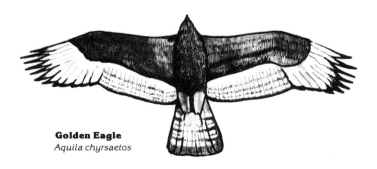

Golden Eagle
Aquila chyrsaetos

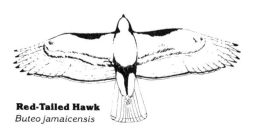

Red-Tailed Hawk
Buteo jamaicensis

318

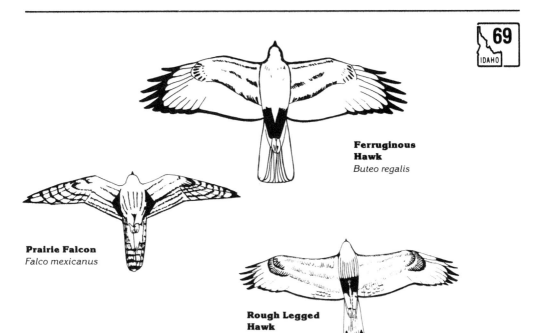

Ferruginous Hawk
Buteo regalis

Prairie Falcon
Falco mexicanus

Rough Legged Hawk
Buteo lagopus

Eagle at her nest in Natural Area. (Photo by Michael Kochert.)

319

69

Swan Falls Dam, visible where the road reaches the river, was built in 1900-1901 to provide power for the mining operations at Silver City, twenty-eight miles to the southwest.

The dam was designed for the Trade Dollar Consolidated by A. J. Wiley, a young Boise engineer. He took advantage of a rock shelf that crossed the river along a five-foot fall. Building a concrete dam twelve feet high and forty-five feet long on the east side of the river, the engineer closed the remaining 424 feet with a rock crib dam. The power plant was located atop the concrete section, and was equipped with four vertical turbines that turned a shaft belted to three generators. With a seventeen-foot head, each generator produced 300 k.w. at 500 volt alternating current.

Swan Falls Dam near completion.

The permanent 288-foot dam of concrete across the main channel also added a much larger powerhouse. Trade Dollar Consolidated wholesaled power to distributors, who ran a 4,400 volt line to the Interurban railway at Nampa and Caldwell.

In 1910 Trade Dollar investors organized the Swan Falls Power Co. and added two new generators. New spillways were built in 1914, along with two additional turbines and generators. Idaho Power acquired Swan Falls in 1916; at that time the dam had the largest generating capacity in the state. A new concrete dam replaced the wooden crib in 1920, and in 1936 the rocky outcrop on the east side of the river was excavated for an additional spillway and ten new gates. In 1983 Idaho Power replaced ten turbines with two efficient bulb turbines.

320

Swan Falls, the first dam on the Snake River, obliterated chinook salmon and steelhead runs above this point because it had inadequate fish passage.

A ferry worked the river about one-half mile above the dam and served the residents of Melba, Guffey and Murphy. Since slackwater in the reservoir deprived the boat of the current required by a cable ferry, the boat was fitted with sidewheels and electric motors, which made it the only motorized ferry on the river. Electricity was carried to the craft by an overhead line, and anyone on board could operate the boat by pressing a button.

State Highway No. 71 from a junction with U.S. 95 in Cambridge, northwesterly to the Idaho-Oregon state line at Brownlee Dam, then on paved, non-highway road to Hells Canyon Dam. Route length: 63.7 miles.

Highway 71 leads northwest from Cambridge, through the hay fields along Pine Creek.

In 1862 a train of sixty wagons camped near present-day Cambridge, before starting up Pine Creek, and down Brownlee Creek, to cross the Snake River. The party was guided by the mountain man Tim Goodale.

Goodale was a competent wilderness chaperon; he had come west as a trapper in 1839, hunted sheep and antelope in Colorado during the 1840s, drove horses to Fort Laramie with Kit Carson in 1850, and herded sheep from New Mexico to California a couple of years later. From 1854 to 1856 he operated an emigrant ferry on the Green River. Goodale had also piloted railroad and military survey parties through the mountains, including one with Major Berthoud and Jim Bridger that led to the discovery of Berthoud Pass in Colorado.

The Goodale party on Pine Creek in 1862 crossed the Snake at Brownlee's ferry and traveled through Pine Valley and up the Powder River to rejoin the Oregon Trail. Mr. Brownlee hauled the wagons and stock across the river without charge after the men agreed to clear a tread from Salubria Valley down to his ferry.

For several miles along Pine Creek, Highway 71 follows the old **Salmon River stock driveway.** The driveway was used by sheep ranchers from 1918 to 1958: herders prodded 80,000 ewes from their canyon winter range, past Cambridge, north to McCall, south through Long Valley, and east to summer range in the Landmark area.

On a clear day, about twenty miles west of Cambridge, just before the road skews down Brownlee grade into Hells Canyon, the traveler can see the broken world of the **Cornucopia** and **Wallowa Mountains** on the western skyline in Oregon.

After an eight-mile grade, the highway levels alongside Brownlee Reservoir.

Brownlee Dam, at 395 feet among the world's highest rock-fill dams, corks the river below the mouth of Brownlee Creek. The dam was built by Idaho Power Company, a corporation chartered in Maine in 1915. The company grew out of the bankruptcy of Idaho-Oregon Light and Power Company. I-OL&P had been organized to exploit the power potential at the Oxbow site downriver. Expenses exceeded estimates on that project and the company failed to meet its first mortgage bond. Electric Investment Company, an organization of I-OL&P bondholders, was successful bidder at the foreclosure. The company worked out a merger whereby five hydroelectric companies were consolidated, integrating potential markets and resources. The property and systems of the five were transferred to Idaho Power Company for operation and development as a combined system.

Because of the 1935 Federal Holding Act, Idaho Power became an independently owned utility. However, since Idahoans own less than 5 percent of the corporation's common stock, it remains an "Idaho company" in name only.

By 1941 Idaho Power had joined a power pool which included electric service companies in Oregon, Washington, Montana and Utah. The systems in five states were linked in order to exchange power loads, which vary with time and weather among the states. After World War II, the company quadrupled its generating capacity in six years. With eight dams on the Snake between Twin Falls and Mountain Home, Idaho Power eyed the energy possibilities in Hells Canyon.

The late 1940s were a time of fierce debate over the plans for the river's hydroelectric potential. The Army Corps of Engineers issued a report with a plan for a 600-foot dam in Hells Canyon at Hells Canyon Creek. The Interior Department's Bureau of Reclamation favored the idea and hoped to build the dam. Idaho Power still had ten years left on its federal site-withdrawal certificate, which had been issued to one of its predecessors in 1906 for a dam at Oxbow, downriver from Brownlee ferry. In 1947 the company filed for a preliminary permit with the Federal Power Commission to develop the Oxbow site, and thereby gave the Corps of Engineers notice of a prior claim to the area. The horse race was on.

The same year, Lewiston was the scene of hearings by the Corps of Engineers on its proposals. Support for a federal dam began to gather momentum as the Army Engineers and the Bureau of Reclamation reached an agreement in 1949 that gave the Bureau jurisdiction over projects above the mouth of the Salmon River and the Corps control over dams below the Salmon. Within a few months, Idaho Power counter-attacked by filing with the FPC for a final construction permit at Oxbow, and by suggesting four other projects it was prepared to build in the canyon which would use the same head as the high federal dam. Arguments like "cheap federal power" versus "tax giveaway" flew thick as seagulls over garbage.

The Truman administration backed the federal dam proposal, and legislation was actually introduced in both houses of Congress authorizing construction of the single high dam. But Dwight Eisenhower's election in 1952 initiated a policy that favored power development by private utilities. The FPC held hearings and Idaho Power filed two more construction applications: one for a low dam at Hells Canyon Creek, the other for a dam at Brownlee ferry. The FPC hearings on the tri-dam proposal lasted for a year. The examiner recommended a license be issued to Idaho Power solely for construction of a dam at Brownlee. Two months later the full board of the FPC overruled his recommendation and decided in favor of the three-dam complex. On August 4, 1955, the FPC issued a construction license to Idaho Power for all three dams, and within weeks company equipment was raising more hell along the river than a turtle when the tank goes dry.

Brownlee is a rock-fill dam with a clay core. The rock came from the excavation for the spillway and powerhouse. The clay, which is impervious to water, was taken from a hill on the Idaho side of the river above the dam site. A base was excavated 120 feet below the riverbed and the clay core (135 feet wide at the base) was sandwiched between layers of sand and gravel. Hydraulic nozzles watered the fill continually in order to increase its density.

At the height of the Brownlee-Oxbow scheme 3,400 workers were employed in shifts seven days a week. The dam was completed in 1959. It has a usable storage of a million acre-feet and a reservoir length of fifty-seven miles.

The FPC required that the dam be designed with space for two additional generators. In 1975 construction began on a fifth generating unit at Brownlee which was finished in 1979. The newest hydro turbine runner is the second largest in the country, and its output surpasses the peaking capacity of the entire power plant at Oxbow Dam. There is sufficient water to operate the turbine only in late spring, and energy produced at that time is traded to systems in other states in return for electricity they produce during the summer when Idaho Power incurs shortages caused by high agricultural demand.

Brownlee Dam under construction (looking south, up-river).

The FPC license to Idaho Power to develop three dams required a program to conserve the salmon and steelhead runs on the Snake River. The goal of the FPC was passage of the fish to their spawning grounds. One might as well hunt a horse thief in heaven as build a high dam compatible with anadromous fish runs. The dam was too high for fish ladders. Upstream, fish were to be trapped and trucked around the dam. To handle downstream migrants the company strung a net of plastic mesh across the reservoir a mile upriver from the dam. Barges with siphon pumps were anchored along the net to

324

capture the fingerlings. The net was plagued with problems: young fish went through it as though it were a cobweb. The director for the Oregon Fish Commission found that only a quarter of the million fingerlings that should have passed downstream made it through the turbines or over the spillway. In 1962 the net was scrapped, and fish runs above Brownlee, up the Weiser, Payette and Boise Rivers became a wonder of the past.

John Brownlee's ferry has been replaced by a bridge across the river below the dam. The west end of the bridge rests in Oregon at the end of Highway 71. It is possible to follow the pavement north twelve miles to Oxbow, Oregon, then twenty-three miles farther north to Hells Canyon Dam. Since this is a drive that will interest the curious, historical information about sites along the road has been included.

The earliest white explorers in this canyon were the members of Wilson Price Hunt's party in 1811. They were attempting to trace the route between the Snake and the Columbia for John Astor's Pacific Fur Company. The expedition of forty-two men and one woman entered the canyon in early December, with half of the group on each side of the river. They were starving, and one man drowned in a canoe while crossing the water to obtain some horse meat. After ten days they retreated, and found a more feasible route through the Blue Mountains to Umatilla Valley, which with slight variations became famous as the Oregon Trail.

In late March and early April of 1819, Donald McKenzie, a trapper for the North West Company, along with six French-Canadian boatmen, made a successful reverse passage of Hells Canyon, coming upstream from Fort Nez Perce at the confluence of the Snake and the Columbia. They found the river passable but not practicable; the overland trip through the Blue Mountains was far less perilous.

In the winter of 1833 the canyon blocked a second attempt at a downriver journey. The soldier-trapper Capt. Benjamin Bonneville set out from the area near present Pocatello with the intention of reconnoitering Hudson's Bay Company territory around Fort Walla Walla by riding horseback down the Snake River on ice. The plan melted with an unexpected thaw.

The Bonneville quartet reached a point somewhere between Oxbow and Hells Canyon Dam before being forced by snow and hunger to climb out near Post Office Saddle and flounder north into the Imnaha River canyon, where Nez Perce Indians rescued them.

Though the Snake River through Hells Canyon never served as a commercial road, the prows of two steamboats once creased its current. The *Shoshone,* a 136-foot long sternwheeler, was built by the Oregon Steam and Navigation Company at the mouth of the Boise River in 1866. The O.S.N. hoped to compete for traffic to the Boise Basin-Owyhee mines by making the longer, expensive Oregon route more comfortable than that from California. The plan failed because the river was not navigable above the mouth of the Bruneau, and there was a dearth of cordwood for the vessel's boilers. Completion of the Central Pacific railroad knocked the heart out of the experiment. The O.S.N. ordered the *Shoshone* brought down to the Columbia River, where she could be used.

Captain Sebastian Miller, in April, 1870, brought the ship through a froth of whitewater to Lewiston. It was an eventful seven-day trip, with a couple of wrecks that punched a few holes in the hull. Four years later the *Shoshone* sank on the Yamhill River in Oregon.

The second, and last, sternwheeler to go down the Snake was the 165-foot *Norma,* built at Huntington, Oregon, in 1891. Ore from the Seven Devils mines was brought down to the foot of Kleinschmidt Grade, where the *Norma* could load it for an upriver haul to the Oregon Short Line railhead at Huntington. The ship made two trips, but the Panic of 1893 discouraged development of the mines, and it is said that Kleinschmidt refused to pay for the steamer. In May, 1895, the owner sent Capt. William Gray to Huntington to bring the sternwheeler down to the Columbia.

Gray's week-long trip to Lewiston was beset by problems not unlike those of Capt. Miller, but he also succeeded in bringing his ship through the canyon. The *Norma* was leased to the O.R.N. for use on the lower Snake, then served on the Columbia as a ferry until she was dismantled in 1915.

Ten miles north of Brownlee it is possible to look northeast across the reservoir and see the crest of **Oxbow Dam.** (Though this is the only view of the dam site visible from the road, a discussion of the dam is given in the text after Oxbow Village, because a short road leads from the village to the dam's surge tanks and turbines.)

In the next two miles, the road ascends across the neck of Oxbow point and drops to Oxbow Village, once the site of notorious **Copperfield.**

Near the turn of the century, when copper was discovered at the Iron Dyke mine three miles north of this location, a railroad survey was made from Blake's Junction, east of Huntington, to the mine. In 1907 a northern extension was begun from Huntington.

Businessmen in Baker, Oregon, who learned of the plans for a railroad, as well as for a hydro power plant at the Oxbow, bought the 160-acre Copperfield Ranch and laid out a townsite. In two years they sold all their lots.

While the railroad was under construction, the Idaho-Oregon Light and Power Co. was working on acquisition of the Oxbow site for a powerhouse. In late 1906 the company established water rights to 8,000 cubic feet per second, and a month later obtained a federal power-site authorization. Within another year implementation of development plans was underway.

The power scheme involved exploitation of the Oxbow feature which occurs on the river upstream from Copperfield. The water swings in a single hairpin meander two miles around a point just above the village. In that distance the river drops over twenty feet. The plan was to drive a thousand-foot tunnel through the rocky point, and by drawing river water into the upstream opening of the diversion tunnel, power a turbine located at the exit on the downstream side.

Construction workers of every nationality began arriving in groups on foot from Baker. They were housed in tent camps at the mouth of Pine Creek. Since both railroad and dam projects involved extensive tunneling, there were ample powder monkeys, drillers, muckers, blacksmiths, and mechanics. They worked hard and recreated harder – tough men in a tough country.

Power for the two projects, as well as for a sawmill a couple of miles up Pine Creek, was provided by giant coal-fired steam engines brought in from Baker.

Pine Valley served as a major source of food for the new community. Beef, mutton, pork, eggs, fruit and vegetables were hauled by wagon twenty miles to the boom town.

Numerous wooden buildings fronted Copperfield's main and side streets. There were eleven saloons (most with whorehouses behind them), gambling halls, a post office-meat market, two boarding houses, a livery barn, barber shop, several stores, a couple of hotels, and eventually a railroad depot. The four-cell jail had an outside stairway to a second-floor meeting room.

At the height of the boom about 700 men were employed. Perhaps another 400 residents lived nearby. Many of these were family persons living respectable lives with permanent employment, innocent of Copperfield's night life, which was wild as a waterspout and rough as a rasp. Liquor flowed freely; large-scale

327

brawls were common as sawdust at a sawmill. Gambling and prostitution represented a release from hours of heavy labor, money changed hands faster then dice in a crap game.

Railroad tracks reached Copperfield in the fall of 1909. The whole town turned out for a celebration. Three times a week the train arrived with mail, supplies, and an occasional passenger.

The power company's diversion tunnel was completed, but the electricity produced was a pathetic return for the effort expended. In the face of bankruptcy, the grandiose 24,000 kw. had been scaled to a meager 600.

Though imperceptible at first, the town's fortune had begun to ebb. A slightly diminished population resulted from the departure of men whose work was finished. Competition stiffened between local businesses, then gradually became a cutthroat struggle for survival. A 1913 census counted the town's inhabitants at approximately 400.

Establishment owners and gamblers began to feud at this time. Arson occurred. The school teacher and fifty other residents sent the governor of Oregon a complaint about the town's gamblers, thugs, drunks, and prostitutes. Governor Oswald West issued an order to the county sheriff to clean up the community by Christmas or face state action. Sheriff Rand replied that Copperfield could handle its own problems.

The governor was a man dedicated to temperance. When he learned of a wild Christmas celebration in Copperfield following his notice, he decided to act.

West was discerning enough to send an intermediary, his secretary Fern Hobbs. Miss Hobbs was a woman of twenty-five; at 5'3" and 104 pounds hardly bigger than tiny. More important, she was obviously self-sufficient, having earned her own way since high school. She had learned stenography while acting as governess to the family of a Portland banker, and had studied law while working as secretary to the president of a title guarantee company. In 1913 she was admitted to the Oregon bar. Governor West hired her as chief stenographer, then promptly made her his private secretary.

And now she was on her way to cleanse what an Oregon minister had recently called "the poisonous toadstool of the badlands." Fern Hobbs boarded the train on New Year's Day, 1914. She carried resignations prepared for the signatures of the Copperfield councilmen and a formal proclamation of martial law. In addition, seven men, inconspicuous in civilian clothes were aboard the train: Lieutenant-Colonel B. K. Lawson and five soldiers of the Oregon National Guard, and Frank Snodgrass, chief of the penitentiary guards. All seven were veterans of the Philippine Insurrection.

Miss Hobbs wired the Copperfield mayor, saying she wished to meet with city officers and citizens at the city hall as soon as she arrived.

After the delegation had entrained, Governor West called a press conference and revealed what he had done. It was a western scenario whose drama was not lost on the press. National and even international attention was focused on the confrontation.

The news penetrated to Copperfield, where Mayor Stewart replied, "We are decorating the city with ribbons and we will try to have some flowers for Miss Hobbs."

When Os West learned the response, he observed that flowers were appropriate for funerals.

In the middle of a rain storm on January 2, Miss Hobbs arrived in Copperfield, wearing a blue suit, a black hat with two green feathers, and gold-rimmed glasses. She proceeded to the meeting hall above the jail; the room was packed.

She took the platform while the Colonel stood nearby. Two guards remained at the single doorway. Fern removed some papers from her briefcase and announced that they were official resignations for all of the city officers. The councilmen perused the documents and then refused to sign.

The governor's representative stood quietly for a moment, then withdrew another sheet from her briefcase and handed it to Colonel Lawson. Lawson read the proclamation of martial law to the audience.

The Colonel then arrested the mayor and councilmen. He quickly informed them that if they did not get their whiskey, bar fixtures and card tables out of town by the next afternoon, he would stack the tools of sin in the streets and burn them. The crowd was asked to check their firearms at the door and disperse quietly. As the assembly left, witnesses say about a dozen guns were left in the custody of the militiamen.

Outside the hall the townspeople discovered "closed" signs nailed on every saloon, whorehouse, and gambling den.

In less than an hour Fern Hobbs had returned to the waiting train and waved goodbye to a silent crowd. The six guardsmen remained behind to enforce the governor's proclamation.

The city officers promptly hired Baker attorneys to file suit on their behalf. Lawson ignored them, and when additional soldiers arrived, gathered faro tables, roulette wheels, birdcage games, and all the barrels of beer and whiskey they could locate and placed them on the train for shipment to a Baker warehouse, where all would be kept under state seal.

An injunction against the militiamen obtained in Baker was also ignored by Lawson, who continued his work until completed. He installed a provisional city council before leaving.

Twenty-seven indictments were returned against defendants. Some pleaded guilty and paid their fines; others filed actions that were taken to the State Supreme Court. Two of them received judgments that included damages and restoration of property at state expense.

But the governor accomplished his objective. Copperfield was a busted flush; only thirty-two voters were registered in 1914. Fires, in 1915 and 1935, destroyed major buildings.

Two I-OL&P houses, some faded photographs, and memories ever receding, like train tracks that converge in distance, are all that remain of a town once decried as "Gomorrah on the Snake."

There is a spur road, on the east side of the paved road coming into Oxbow, and just upriver from the village, that leads to the dam's surge tanks (take the right fork) and turbines (take the left fork.)

When construction of Brownlee Dam was well underway, concurrent work began at the Oxbow site. At the time the company received authorization for Oxbow, the old Idaho-Oregon Light and Power generator was still boosting the power in the line from Huntington to Homestead with its 600 kilowatts per hour.

Idaho Power used the old tunnel, which fed that generator's turbine, to divert the river, while constructing a new 205-foot rock-fill dam. **Oxbow Dam** is similar in design to Brownlee, but has half its generating capacity. Twin tunnels, thirty-six feet in diameter, were driven 900 feet through the rock point around which the river curves in its three-mile meander. When the gates of the dam closed in 1961, river water spilled through the tunnels into a pair of surge tanks, where it dropped 124 feet to power four turbines on the downstream end of the Oxbow.

The powerhouse is open to the public for an hour each afternoon, and the unusual features of this installation are worth viewing.

Fish losses at Brownlee were reenacted at Oxbow, with a variation. The Snake River is the second-largest producer of chinook salmon and steelhead in the world. About 25 percent of the fish entering the Snake passed the Oxbow en route to redds, some going as far as Swan Falls. The runs in the late 1950s ranged from 40,000-55,000 adult salmon annually. A cement fish trap for the salmonids going upriver had been placed at the mouth of the Oxbow diversion tunnel in 1958. Outwash turbulence caused the structure to fail. River flow was reduced at Brownlee, to 500 c.f.s. at one point, while emergency repairs were attempted. The fall run of chinook had just started up the Columbia. Despite efforts by Idaho Power and fishery personnel, repairs were not effected before the fish arrived. When a cofferdam, erected to dry the diversion tunnel while repairs were made, was breached, thousands of salmon were stranded in the splash pool below it and exhausted the oxygen in the stagnant water. Some fish were captured and transported above Brownlee, but before oxygen was pumped into the pool with a drilling compressor, at least 4,000 salmon died. The loss of this portion of the spawning run was a catastrophe. The fish count made at Oxbow showed a run of better than 20,000 fall chinook – five years later, when the migration loss was evident, the count tallied 945.

As compulsory mitigation for salmon and steelhead losses caused by its dams, Idaho Power has established a salmon hatchery on Rapid River, an adult steelhead trap and egg-taking station on the Pahsimeroi River, and a steelhead hatchery at Niagara Springs. The sites are in Idaho and are run by Idaho fish and game personnel. Part of the spring chinook salmon run has been successfully transferred to Rapid River, a tributary of the Salmon. Unfortunately, tributary habitat is not suitable for *fall* chinook. Historically, these salmon have only been found in the main Snake.

It is fair to say that the eight Army Corps of Engineer dams on the Columbia and lower Snake are equally responsible for Hells Canyon fish losses – though all of the federal dams are equipped with ladders. It is also fair to observe that Idaho Power is as concerned about fishery conservation as a utility can be, when its primary purpose is to make money from a national resource.

Cross east over the bridge at Oxbow, back into Idaho. After about three miles, **Homestead** is evident on the Oregon side of the reservoir.

In 1896 the Vaughn brothers were running cattle along the Snake River when they discovered a copper lode on the south wall of Irondyke Creek, about one-third of a mile from the river. Homestead residents gathered about the mine like midges around a lamp.

A smelter that had failed to operate properly for the Blue Jacket mine across the river on Indian Creek was purchased for use at the Iron Dyke. Relocated, it worked well.

Theron and Halsted Lindsay, from Colorado, bought the mine about 1914. They owned a mining concern in Canada called Ventures, Ltd. The Lindsays installed a flotation plant which, along with the smelter, gave Homestead the largest copper concentrator in the state in 1917. Copper was piped in a slurry down to the filter plant on a bench by the river, where it was dry-pressed. The concentrate was then shipped on the railroad, which had been extended from Huntington for that purpose.

The Lindsays erected the buildings on the sloping bench as quarters for the supervisors and miners. Approximately 150 men lived on the bar at the height of production. Homestead had two stores, a post office, meat market and gas station.

Production records for the Iron Dyke for the period of 1910-1934 show 34,000 ounces of gold, 256,000 ounces of silver and 14 million pounds of copper realized from the operation. There is no record of production after 1934, and the mine closed at the start of World War II. A request that twenty-six men be allowed to work at the mine was denied; output was considered unessential for the war effort. The Lindsays sold their interests to the Butler Ore Company of St. Paul, Minnesota, and that company was the owner in 1981 – though Texas Gulf is reported to have the claims under option. A report by Wallace Butler in 1944 states that estimated reserves above the 650-foot level in the mine total 148,000 tons containing 1.16 percent copper.

With the removal of the railroad tracks, and the start of dam construction at Oxbow, activity in Homestead slowed to a shuffle.

The Snake River canyon from Homestead to Lewiston was the axis of a twenty-year dream held by citizens of Clarkston and Lewiston, who hoped that the only north-south rail connection in the state between the east-west transcontinental routes would be built through the river corridor.

In 1911-1912, the ORN surveyed a route from Homestead to Clarkston and filed location maps with the General Land Office for right-of-way on public lands. Because the Department of Interior withheld approval of the maps, which conflicted with water power sites, the railroad withdrew its applications.

The Idaho legislature adopted resolutions in 1913 and 1919 urging construction of a line through Hells Canyon and directing the state utilities commission to seek ICC help for such a plan. Under the Transportation Act of 1920, the ICC could order railroad companies to build lines which were "in the interest of public convenience and necessity."

In 1927 Idaho's Governor Baldridge sought cooperation from Oregon and Washington for the new line, in the belief it would solve transportation problems and develop the Seven Devils mines. Utility commissions of the three states did a feasibility study, and the tri-state railroad commissions petitioned the ICC for an order requiring U.P. and N.P. to build the 119-mile railroad. Arguments by the petitioners asserted the route was vitally needed and could be completed in 2½ years for $16.5 million.

The railroad companies fiercely opposed the proposal on the grounds that it would divert revenue from the lines between Huntington and The Dalles, Oregon, would cost $29 million, and in such a remote area would never produce the freight necessary to justify the expense. The rail companies also noted that the river drops 1,300 feet between Homestead and Lewiston – more than a water-grade would tolerate.

The ICC reached a decision in January, 1930, that agreed with the railroad companies' position. Lewiston's dream was derailed.

The foot of the **Kleinschmidt Grade** reaches the Idaho road, on the east side, three miles north of Homestead. The grade was built from the Seven Devils to the river to handle ore wagons from the mines. (See U.S. 95, Council.)

Big Bar is located eight miles north of the Kleinschmidt Grade, between the road and the reservoir. **Big Bar** was the subject of archaeological investigation in 1963 by the Idaho State University museum in cooperation with the Smithsonian Institute, River Basin Surveys. Evidence unearthed indicated the bar was a village site. Several hundred classifiable artifacts were uncovered. The survey concluded that the bar had been intensely occupied for hunting use from A.D. 1600 to historic contact.

White men settled the bar, most of which is now covered by water, in the 1890s and farmed it for fruit and vegetables which were sold in mining camps in the Seven Devils.

Two marble gravestones, each protected by a log fence, are located on the bar. Early pioneers Arthur Ritchie and John Eckels are buried there. The land is owned by Idaho Power, but the Forest Service maintains the site.

Idaho Power used Big Bar as a trailer camp for employees working on Hells Canyon Dam in the 1960s. The terraces are a vestige of that period. The river edge of the bar served as the gravel source for the aggregate used in the dam's concrete.

Eagle Bar and the **Red Ledge mine** can be seen about seven miles north from Big Bar. Eagle Bar contains a few buildings on the west shoulder of the road; the Red Ledge is up the opposite slope, east of the bar.

Morrison-Knudsen Co. constructed a road to Eagle Bar from Ballard's Landing in 1926 for the Butler Ore Company. This road, which is now under water, was built to give the Butler interests access to a copper prospect about five miles above the road end, on the forks of Deep Creek. The prospect is known as the Red Ledge because oxidized pyrite colors the ore mass.

Tom Heady staked the first claims in 1894, at the time copper deposits were being worked near Landore and Helena. Heady eventually interested Robert Bell, Idaho's state mining inspector, in the property which he leased with some other men. World War I suspended all activity on the claims, though at least a thousand feet of diamond drilling had been done by that time.

In 1925 the Idaho Copper Corporation, controlled by George Rice, Dr. Walter Weed, and associates, took over the deposit. Three years later Rice and the corporation were convicted of "using the mails to defraud" in connection with their promotion of the property. The claims were then acquired by Cooley Butler and Butler's company is the owner at this time.

The Red Ledge consists of twenty-three patented claims and a large number of unpatented lode and millsite claims covering 1,500 acres. No ore has been produced, but 2,400 feet of underground work has been done and about 16,000 feet of diamond drilling, which brings the estimated amount expended on the ledge close to a million dollars.

Eagle Bar was used for trailer offices, tool shops, and a first-aid station by Idaho Power Co. during construction of Hells Canyon Dam.

Hells Canyon Dam is one mile north of Eagle Bar. Even before Oxbow Dam was completed, the final phase of the Hells Canyon development had commenced just above Deep Creek. The bridge, which was to retire the one at Ballard's Landing, had been strung across the river below the Oxbow. A twenty-three mile access highway was cut along the cliffs on the Idaho side of the river to the site of **Hells Canyon Dam.**

Once the road arrived, crews drilled and blasted a forty-foot-diameter tunnel 1,800 feet through the mountain on the east side of the river, and a moveable form lined its interior with concrete. An earthen weir was pushed across the river below the tunnel's intake in 1965 and the river was diverted through the tunnel, away from the location of the dam and powerhouse. Temporary cofferdams were then constructed to isolate the upstream and downstream reaches of the site.

334

Substream strata were excavated to a depth of 100 feet. Mass placement of concrete began in March, 1966. Pours continued around the clock, as 700,000 cubic yards, heated or cooled to suit the season, were placed by rail-mounted cranes operating over the dam. Engine-drawn shuttle cars delivered the buckets of concrete from the mixing plant at the Idaho-end of the trestle. A quarter-mile conveyor belt brought aggregate to the mixing plant. Aluminum tubing, with temperature sensors , circulated water through the dam in order to limit the curing heat of the concrete to seventy-five degrees F. – higher temperatures can cause slips and cracks.

Sand and gravel for the concrete were hauled from Big Bar upriver. Some sand from the mill tailings at the Cornucopia mines was used to reduce the amount of cement and lubrication needed in the mixing process. Tailings from the mercury mine at Weiser were also used. The tailings were ground fine as talcum powder and added to the cement in order to accelerate the curing reaction.

Eight hundred men labored on the 320-foot dam; four of them were killed on the project. The dam began withholding water in 1968. Its spillway, like those of Brownlee and Oxbow, is designed to handle 300,000 c.f.s.

Hells Canyon Dam has three generating units, with space for another. The short peak flow through an added turbine could be tolerated only if a reservoir below the dam absorbed the sudden release. Since Mountain Sheep Dam was never built, it is unlikely an additional turbine will be installed.

Hells Canyon Dam is an impressive edifice, and the tri-dam complex represents one response to energy demand. But the dams were built with a number of costs never computed by accountants or engineers, and such costs must be balanced against the benefits. On one hand, a peak generating capability in excess of a million kilowatts an hour, thirty-nine permanent jobs, some recreation facilities and flood control, and $10,000 a year in taxes for the state of Idaho. On the other hand, thousands of acres of ranch land and wildlife habitat were lost forever, as were a town, salmon and steelhead runs, archaeological sites, and singular whitewater recreation. In addition, sand entrapment and daily flow fluctuations destroyed beaches, waterfowl habitat and spawning beds for sixty miles of river below this dam – with no mitigation whatever.

A gravel road at the west end of the dam leads a half-mile down to the launch site for Hells Canyon river trips. The Hells Canyon National Recreation Area Act was signed by President Ford in 1976. River parties, under Forest Service permit, travel eighty miles down this "wild and scenic" stretch of the Snake to Heller Bar, above Lewiston. (See Lewiston, Snake River Road.)

Travelers interested in a seven-mile jet-boat trip from the dam, down to Wild Sheep Rapid and back, may call Jim Zanelli, Oxbow, Oregon; those parties interested in a three or six-day raft trip down the river may communicate with Hughes River Expeditions in nearby Cambridge, Idaho.

Rafting Granite Creek Rapid in Hells Canyon. (Hughes River Expeditions.)

State Highway No. 75 from a junction with U.S. 93 in Shoshone, northerly and easterly via Bellevue, Hailey, Ketchum, Stanley and Clayton to a junction with U.S. 93 south of Challis. (Spur road includes Sun Valley.) Route length: 170.6 miles.

After the route of the Oregon Short Line had been surveyed in 1883, a post office was established in **Shoshone.** The town later served as a supply center for the construction of Twin Falls.

Six miles north of this crossroads is **Mammoth Cave.** The access road travels 1.5 miles from the west side of the highway to the site of a one-quarter-mile-long lava tube discovered in 1902. During the 1950s it was used as a civil defense shelter and as a supply depot for 8,000 persons. A self-guided tour is available.

The A-frame adjacent to the cave entrance contains over 400 bird mounts, one of the largest displays of avian taxidermy in the country.

Shoshone Ice Cave, also on the west side of the highway, is ten miles north of Mammoth. It was discovered in 1880, and furnished ice for the town of Shoshone until 1900.

In the 1930s the cave was developed as part of a WPA project, but a second entrance caused the ice to melt faster than hog fat in a hot skillet, and the site was abandoned in 1938. In 1954 Russell Robinson's experiments with air currents succeeded in reestablishing ice formation. Prehistoric animal fossils found in the

Bellevue, Main St. before the fire.

cave are on display at the entrance.

Twelve miles farther north Highway 75 intersects U.S. 20. Maybelle Hill can be seen on the west side of the road 3.5 miles north of the intersection. Goodale's Cutoff from the Oregon Trail crossed Poverty Flat and ran north of the hill, then swung southwest toward Rock Creek.

The highway continues north nine miles into the Wood River Valley to the town of Bellevue.

Wood River was first explored in 1824 by Alexander Ross and his brigade of 140 trappers working for the Hudson's Bay Co.; they traveled north across Galena Summit into Stanley Basin and on to the Weiser River.

Bellevue began in May, 1880, with the discovery of several rich silver-lead mines such as the Queen of the Hills and the Minnie Moore, in the canyon west of town. Referred to as Gate City, the camp had a population of 600 by mid-summer. After the coming of the railroad in 1883, the Territorial Legislature granted the town a charter, one of three given in the state. Since Boise and Lewiston have relinquished theirs, Bellevue's is the only one left. The town does not operate under the State Municipal Code; elections are held in April instead of November, and the state legislature has to approve any changes in the charter, such as land annexation or withdrawal.

Bellevue was the seat of Logan County from 1890 until the county was abolished in 1895.

337

Henry Miller's mansion, built in the 1880s, can be seen on the west side of the highway 0.7 miles south of town. The two-story house, screened by trees, is set at an angle to the road.

Mr. Miller, a mining parvenu, owned the nearby Minnie Moore, which yielded half of the $12 million taken from the Bellevue mines. He sold the Minnie Moore in 1884 to a British firm for $500,000, but acquired other successful properties in Nevada and Utah.

Miller married Annie Gallagher, whose father owned a boarding house in Bellevue. The millionaire sent his bride to Europe for schooling; she returned to the finished mansion, with its five bedrooms, ballroom, library, and parquet floors.

In 1914 the house was moved from Bellevue more than two miles to this site. The method involved a single horse that cranked a winch bound to a post and the operation required several weeks; while the move was in progress the cook prepared meals in the kitchen as usual.

Mr. Miller died in a Salt Lake hospital in 1907 at age sixty-five; Annie, who remarried, was buried in 1941 at the Hailey cemetery.

Eleven ox teams haul a boiler to the Minnie Moore mine.

Hailey is 4.2 miles north of Bellevue. It was the center of Mineral Hill mining district, the most productive part of the Wood River region. When the Wood River boom began, John Hailey was running the Utah, Idaho, and Oregon Stage Company. In 1880 he bought 440 acres on the Wood River as a speculative investment and segregated several blocks for a townsite. He lived there only briefly, however, before selling to the Idaho-Oregon Land Improvement Co. and moving to Boise, where in 1881 he was elected to the Territorial Legislature. At the time of his departure the young town had eighteen saloons, twelve gambling parlors, and a row of cotes for the drabs on River St.

In the spring of 1881 an election was held to transfer the Logan County office from Rocky Bar to the Wood River Valley. Both Bellevue and Hailey coveted the honor of the county seat; the voters were stimulated half way to combustion. After considerable vituperation and a lengthy search for a ballot box that finally turned up in Mountain Home, Hailey was declared the winner by twenty votes. When Alturas and Logan Counties were dissolved in 1895, Hailey retained the seat of the new county, Blaine. The name honored James Blaine, unsuccessful presidential candidate who served as Secretary of State under three presidents. (The county's peculiar southern pipestem was gerrymandered to add the assessed valuation of the Oregon Short Line.)

With the arrival of the railroad in May, 1883, Hailey's fortunes continued to prosper. The railroad brought the telegraph; the first telephone system in the Territory was in operation five months later. Hailey also earned the distinction of the first electric light system (1889) in Idaho. For four years, in the 1880s, the town had three daily newspapers and two weeklies. The only calamities between 1883 and 1889 were two extensive fires that seared the business district.

During Hailey's hey years, 1881 to 1889, the Wood River was Idaho's leading mining area; it eventually produced about $60 million in lead, silver and gold. By the time the Panic of 1893 struck the district, the Salmon City newspaper reported, "the Wood River Mines Region is deader than a lime fossil."

In 1883, when the first bullion was loaded on the railroad, the Union Pacific manager predicted Hailey would become "the Denver of Idaho." Hailey failed – but given the appearance of Denver, it is just as well.

Hailey has a half-dozen elderly buildings worth a visit. The **Blaine County Historical Museum** occupies a brick building erected in 1882 on North Main at Galena St.

Drive south three blocks on Main St. to Croy and turn east one block to First Ave. So. The remains of the monumental Alturas Hotel, a victim of arson in the late 1970s, stand on the north corner. The brick structure was built in 1883-1886; almost half of the $35,000 cost was contributed by Thomas Mellon of Pittsburgh. With eighty-two rooms, each heated by a wood stove, it was considered the best hotel between Denver and the Pacific Coast. In 1913 it was sold to the Hiawatha Land and Water Co., which remodeled and enlarged it. A nearby hot springs was tapped for radiant heating and a swimming pool.

Across the street from the hotel is the three-story Blaine County courthouse, built of brick and stone in 1883.

Follow First Ave. south two blocks to Pine St. The Gothic-revival church on the northwest corner was St. Charles of the Valley, built by a Catholic congregation in 1913 for $7,200. It has been replaced by a newer church.

Turn north on Pine St. one block to Second Ave. So. The unassuming 1½-story frame building on the northeast corner is one of the more significant houses in the state.

The man who was born in this house, **Ezra Loomis Pound,** was a diversely-faceted genius; he was the most important and controversial poet of the twentieth century.

Pound's paternal grandfather was Lieutenant-governor of

Hailey, Main St., 1888.

Wisconsin and later a U.S. Congressman. Because he had silver claims in the Wood River Valley, he obtained a presidential appointment for his son, Homer, as the recorder for a new government land office in Hailey, where mine claims were filed. Homer came west with his wife, Isabel Weston, a distant relative of Henry Wadsworth Longfellow. They built the first house with plastered walls in the young town; Ezra, their only child, was born here October 30, 1885.

Because Isabel was troubled by the mile-high altitude of Hailey, the couple moved to Pennsylvania before their son was two years-old. Homer became the assistant assayer at the Philadelphia Mint; his son drank in stories of gold bricks and "Free Silver." When Grover Cleveland's administration called for a recount of the silver coinage, Ezra witnessed "the recount of four million in the Mint

340

vaults, the bags had rotted, and the men half-naked with open gas flares, shovelled it into the counting machines, with a gleam on tarnished discs."

A precocious student, who specialized in modern languages, he took a master's degree in Spanish at the Univ. of Pennsylvania and began to teach at Indiana's Wabash College. On a snowy evening, Pound went out to post a letter to his fiancee and found a young woman in distress. He offered her his bedroom, but the next morning the cleaning woman discovered his guest and reported the incident to the college. Wabash terminated Pound's contract for "Latin-quarter behavior."

In 1907 Ezra left for Europe to do doctoral research. A growing interest in creating poetry caused him to abandon the thesis in favor

Hailey, Main St., 1918.

of a life in London, and in 1908 his first book of verse was published, while he was still learning to support himself precariously as an editor, translator, critic, and anthologist.

"He attempted," as Earle Davis wrote in an essay about Pound, "to recreate in English the finest writing of the Greeks, the Latins, the Troubadors, the Chinese, Japanese, Italians, French, and Germans. He tried to make words beautiful and expressive of the highest sentiments and emotions possible to our language."

Filled with energetic magnaminity, he was a human geode to other writers. He influenced two great poets, William Butler Yeats and T. S. Eliot, and important American poets as well: William Carlos Williams, Marianne Moore, Hart Crane, E. E. Cummings, Archibald MacLeish. He helped Joyce find a publisher for *Ulysses;* he edited Hemingway's early manuscripts; he pushed Robert Frost into print; he encouraged D. H. Lawrence and Ford Madox Ford. Ford left a colorful description of the young poet at the time: "(he) would wear trousers made of green billiard cloth, a pink coat, a blue shirt, a tie hand-painted by a Japanese friend, an immense sombrero, a flaming beard cut to a point, and a single, large blue earring."

In 1920 Pound moved to Paris; five years later he settled in Rapallo, Italy. His poetry and his public statements gradually developed an anti-usury paranoia. The poet's childhood no doubt influenced his obsession with monetary matters, but additionally, he nurtured the idea of an epic poem that dealt with world history, and he believed an understanding of economics was a necessary complement. Always in favor of individualism, he rejected its antithesis, communism; he also rejected American capitalist democracy, which made money by manipulating money; he became, instead, an adherent of Mussolini, in the belief that the socialist capitalist state would pay men in relation to their productivity.

During World War II Pound remained in Italy, and in 1942 made nearly a hundred broadcasts espousing fascism and Nazi anti-Semitism. Most of the broadcasts, however, were very difficult to understand in any terms – several of them were explications of certain Cantos he had written. Nevertheless, in 1943 on this evidence the U.S. Grand Jury in Washington, D.C. indicted him for treason. Pound learned of his indictment on a B.B.C. broadcast and wrote the U.S. Attorney General, saying in part:

The ruin of markets, the perversions of trade routes, in fact all the matters on which my talks have been based is of importance to the American citizen; whom neither you nor I should betray either in time of war or peace. I may say in passing that I took out a life membership in the American Academy of Social and Political Science in the hope of obtaining fuller discussion of some of these issues, but did not find them ready for full and frank expression of certain vital elements in the case; this may in part have been due to their incomprehension of the nature of the case.

At any rate a man's duties increase with his knowledge. A war between the U.S. and Italy is monstrous and should not have occurred. And a peace without justice is no peace but merely a prelude to future wars. Someone must take count of these things. And having taken count must act on his knowledge; admitting that his knowledge is partial and his judgment subject to error.

When the Allies entered Italy in 1945, Pound surrendered to the first American soldier that he encountered. He was taken to an

Army Detention Training Center in Pisa, which was organized to punish criminals in the U.S. Armed Forces. Housed outdoors in a 6-by-6½-foot cage, he was allowed to keep a book of Confucius, a Bible, pencils and paper. Visitors and conversation were denied. Pound was sixty years-old; in three weeks he collapsed from claustrophobia, partial amnesia, and hysteria. He was moved to a tent in the medical compound.

It was three months before he recovered from his attack, and two months more before his wife was permitted to see him. A month later he was flown to the U.S. to stand trial. (One can surmise government officials had spent six month's attempting to decipher transcripts of Pound's broadcasts.)

At the Lunacy Inquisition in February, 1946, the judge entered a plea of "not guilty" for the mute poet. The jury, hearing testimony from a panel of psychiatrists, found the defendant of unsound mind, unfit to stand trial; he was committed to St. Eizabeth's Hospital for the criminally insane in Washington, D.C.

Pound spent thirteen years in St. Eizabeth's. In 1949 *The Pisan Cantos,* which he had written while imprisoned by the Army, was awarded the first Bollingen Prize for Poetry. The judges were the Fellows in American Letters of the Library of Congress; among them: T. S. Eliot, W. H. Auden, Allen Tate, Robert Penn Warren, Katherine Anne Porter, Robert Lowell. The award stirred a tempest – some critics felt that the political and moral content of the poetry vitiated its quality; others felt that the decision reaffirmed an American tradition of liberalism which Pound had sought to destroy.

In 1958, after indefatigable efforts by Archibald MacLeish and a few other artists, Thurman Arnold, counsel from a renowned Washington, D.C. law firm, introduced a motion to dismiss the indictment; the U.S. Attorney stated that the motion was in the interest of justice and should be granted. Judge Bolitha Laws concurred.

Ezra Pound departed for Italy with his wife. Though he continued to write and publish, he entered a ten-year period of public silence. Pound returned to the U.S. briefly in 1969. Among other things, he planned to visit his birthplace, but on deciding the journey would be too wearing, he left America for good.

Ezra Loomis Pound died in his sleep, two days after his eighty-seventh birthday. His coffin was carried by gondola to the island cemetery of San Michele, where Protestants are buried in Venice. He was buried alongside the composer Igor Stravinsky, who had died a year earlier, and whose funeral the poet had attended. There were few mourners present.

Not all of Pound's poetry is as incomprehensible as the general public believes. The following poem, from *Personae*, in the form of a dramatic epistle, is an illustration. It is original poetry, not translation.

THE RIVER-MERCHANT'S WIFE: A LETTER

While my hair was still cut straight across my forehead
I played about the front gate, pulling flowers.
You came by on bamboo stilts, playing horse,
You walked about my seat, playing with blue plums.
And we went on living in the village of Chokan:
Two small people, without dislike or suspicion.

At fourteen I married My Lord you.
I never laughed, being bashful.
Lowering my head, I looked at the wall.
Called to, a thousand times, I never looked back.

At fifteen I stopped scowling,
I desired my dust to be mingled with yours
Forever and forever and forever.
Why should I climb the lookout?

At sixteen you departed,
You went into far Ku-to-yen, by the river of swirling eddies,
And you have been gone five months.
The monkeys make sorrowful noise overhead.

You dragged your feet when you went out.
By the gate now, the moss is grown, the different mosses,
Too deep to clear them away!
The leaves fall early this autumn, in wind.
The paired butterflies are already yellow with August
Over the grass in the West garden;
They hurt me. I grow older.
If you are coming down through the narrows of the river Kiang,
Please let me know beforehand,
And I will come out to meet you
        As far as Cho-fu-Sa.

                                    By Rihaku

In recognition of this native son, the University of Idaho library has established a special collection of works related to Ezra Pound; it contains nearly 300 books.

Ezra Pound in 1970, two years before his death. Photograph by Henri Cartier Bresson.

Ezra Pound house.

Bullion City in 1885.

Travel north on Second Ave. three blocks to Bullion St. Built in 1885, the Emmanuel Episcopal Church on the southwest corner has a charming, narrow, arched belfry. The style is Gothic revival.

Turn south on Bullion to visit the location of Bullion City and the 1880's mines. Cross Main St. and continue on Bullion (which becomes Croy Creek Rd.) 4.3 miles along the stream until the

346

Triumph mill.

pavement ends at Rotarun Ski Area. Follow the gravel an additional 3.0 miles to Bullion Gulch on the right.

In 1882 three mines here, the Bullion, Mayflower, and Jay Gould, supported a town of 500 persons. Bullion City was described as "two-miles long and eighteen-inches wide."

The Red Elephant mine in the canyon north of Bullion produced $1.4 million between 1882-1898. Its ore bin can still be seen, perched on the hillside southwest of Bullion.

Follow Highway 75, 6.8 miles north to the east fork of Wood River, and take North Star Road northeast from the highway 5.6 miles to **Triumph.** The Independence lead-silver mine opened here in 1883 and the Triumph mine in 1884. Federal Mining and Smelting Company bought the Independence, drove a 1½-mile tunnel through the mountain to connect it with the North Star, and built a mill in Independence Gulch.

In February, 1917, an avalanche swept the North Star camp, destroyed buildings, killed seventeen miners and injured fifteen others.

Because of the refractory nature of the ore, it was 1927 before major production began. Until trucks made it obsolete, a tram line carried the concentrates six miles to the U.P. railroad cars at Gimlet. When the mill, supplied by both mines, burned in 1948, it was replaced by a steel, 200-ton flotation mill. The mine closed from 1931 to 1936, then reopened until 1957, when reserves were exhausted and it closed for good. At the time, 110 men were employed on a $10,000 payroll; the mine had earned $28 million in its last twenty years.

The gray mess in the creek bottom is the slimes pond, a common corollary of mining operations.

Highway 75 continues north from the east fork of the Wood River nine miles to **Ketchum** below Bald Mountain (9,151 ft.).

Ketchum, as the smelting center of the Warm Springs mining district, was another child of the Wood River mines. The town was tentatively called Leadville, but the Postal Department decided

Ketchum, early view.

Leadvilles were as common as sage out west and changed the name to Ketchum – for David Ketchum who had staked a claim in the basin one year earlier.

Once the boom had dissipated, Ketchum became a livestock center. From 1895 to 1930 the settlement grew into the largest sheep-shipping center in the West. Every fall reiterative tides of sheep flowed to the Ketchum Livestock Association corrals at the U.P. railhead.

The rest of the year, the site was simply a crossroads that looked like it might be a town one day; in winter, its only link to the outside world was a twice-weekly train from Shoshone. The arrival of the Sun Valley developers in 1936 was the biggest surprise since thunder; construction crews and families had to be housed in

348

boxcars. The nearby resort forever changed the face and future of Ketchum.

Although the townsite was established in 1880, as early as others in the valley, the community apparently maintained a sense of humor during the county-seat brouhaha between its neighbors to the south. The *Ketchum Keystone* suggested Hailey's name be changed to Hogum, and that of Bellevue to Skinum, and then the valley towns would be known as Ketchum, Hogum and Skinum.

As the site of the Philadelphia Smelter, much of the early ore in the valley was milled at Ketchum. Since the mill had efficient

Ketchum in the 1930s.

equipment and prices comparable to those at smelters outside the territory, it was utilized to capacity. The arrival of the railroad in 1884 was invaluable.

The Golden Rule Market, established in 1887 at the corner of Main St. and Second Ave., is the oldest continuously operated grocery store in Idaho.

The red brick building on the northeast corner of Main Street and Sun Valley Road was built in 1887 by Thomas Teague and Walt Clark as a general store. Known as the Lane Mercantile from 1916 to 1946, it has now been converted to a bank.

A side trip to Sun Valley, and to Copper Basin via Trail Creek, can be made by turning east from Main St. in Ketchum onto Sun Valley Road.

349

Sun Valley Ski resort was the construct of Averell Harriman, chairman of the board of directors of the U.P. Railroad. Harriman had observed European ski resorts and recognized the potential of the sport in America, particularly after the 1932 Winter Olympics at Lake Placid, New York. He persuaded Carl Gray, president of the railroad, to pay the expenses of a young Austrian, Count Felix Schaffgotsch, for a survey of possible ski areas in the west. Harriman wrote, "We should know whether we have an asset which would be worthwhile our following up. It is conceivable that it is possible to build up long-haul travel to a popular center."

The Count toured Mt. Rainier, Mt. Hood, Yosemite, the San Bernardino Mountains, Zion National Park, Rocky Mountain National Park, the Wasatch Mountains, Pocatello and Jackson Hole. In January, 1936, he was steered to Ketchum by the state director of highways and a Boise U.P. freight agent. One mile east of the town, the Count was as certain he had found the place he was looking for as Brother Brigham when he saw the Great Salt Lake valley.

Two weeks later, Averell Harriman arrived, and the U.P. bought a 3,888-acre ranch for $39,000. The Count picked the site for the lodge; Charlie Proctor, a member of the U.S. Olympic Ski Team, and ski coach for Harvard, selected the sites for the ski runs: Dollar Mountain and Proctor Mountain. (Bald Mountain was not developed until later, because few skiers in the country at that time were expert enough to handle its slopes and elevations.)

The first chair lifts were installed on Proctor Mountain and Dollar Mountain in 1936. They were invented by James Curran, a U.P. engineer, who had designed equipment to load bananas on fruit ships in the tropics. He simply replaced the hooks with chairs.

The X-shaped lodge was built of concrete poured inside rough-sawn forms. The wood grain was impressed on the concrete finish, which was then acid-stained to imitate wood. When the $1.5 million, 220-room lodge was opened in December, 1936, the Union Pacific was as proud as a grandmother at graduation. Steve Hannagan, the man who had puffed Miami Beach into a major resort, was hired by Harriman to do the same job for the new ski area. It was Hannagan who picked the name, and it was his public relations that soon gave Sun Valley "elephantiasis of the reputation."

Union Pacific sold Sun Valley Resort in 1964 to the Janss Corporation for about $2 million; Janss constructed the first condominiums in Idaho. In 1977 the Valley was sold again, to Earl Holding.

(Read: *Sun Valley:*, by Dorice Taylor).

Follow Sun Valley Road one mile east from Main St. in Ketchum. To visit the remains of the original chair lift, turn south from Sun Valley Road onto Dollar Road. Follow Dollar Road 0.7 miles to a four-way stop. Continue in the same direction 1.1 miles on Fairways Road. The lift on the right side of the road was reassembled from the cables and wooden towers of the first chair lift on Proctor

Sun Valley (summer).

Mountain, one mile east of Rudd Mountain. The Rudd Lift served the ski jump visible on the slope.

Return to Sun Valley Road and 0.2 miles farther east take the short loop-road on the right to see the original **Sun Valley Lodge** with concrete, "imitation wood" walls.

One and one-half miles east of the lodge, on the right side of Sun Valley Road, is a small sign for the **Hemingway Memorial.** A short path leads to a commemorative bust alongside Trail Creek. The Washington poet David Wagoner has written an elegiac poem about the spot that is worth sharing:

AT THE HEMINGWAY MEMORIAL

Ketchum, Idaho

The day's bone dry. I've come through Sun Valley
To sit beside your rock and your greening bust
Above the Big Lost River
Where sage and bitterbush and broom
Have held their own, where the cicadas
Chirr through the cottonwoods in the dead of summer.

The plaque says you're a part of this forever,
Especially the "high blue windless skies" of the Sawtooths,
And looking at big lost Papa's place,
I believe it. The road's as hard,
As shimmering, straight, and spare as early you.
The style is still the man when it deserts him:

By my foot, the husk of a cicada nymph
lies pale as straw – the nervelessly crouched legs,
The head hunched forward hunting for some way out,
The claws grown stiff defending the clenched hollow,
The back split open,
And nothing but nothing to be brave about.

Continue east on the Sun Valley Road; the pavement ends after another five miles, and the road begins to climb above the Trail Creek bottoms along the shoulder of a glaciated valley. In the 1880s wagons hauled ore from the Yankee Fork mines, via the East Fork of the Salmon and Big Lost River, down this grade to the smelters at Ketchum. **Trail Creek Summit** (7,896 elev.) is five miles farther. The road leaves Sawtooth National Forest and enters Challis

National Forest, a sub-alpine area of unclad mountains which convey an austere, Bedouin beauty.

Three miles northeast of Trail Creek Summit the road bridges **Big Fall Creek.** Turn here (not at Big Fall Creek Road) and drive 0.2 miles to a parking area. Follow the trail 200 yards up the creek to the falls that drop about thirty feet from a notch in the smooth stone.

Freight team comes down Trail Creek grade to Ketchum.

Hemingway memorial.

From Big Falls continue through the sage flats four miles to Kane Creek, where Phi Kappa (10,516 ft.) and Devil's Bedstead (11,051 ft.) of the Pioneer Mountains are visible to the south. Hyndman Peak, (12,078 ft.) four miles southeast of the Bedstead, is the third-highest mountain in Idaho.

Another 4.8 miles reveals the Mackay-Copper Basin Junction: the left fork leads fifteen miles to U.S. 93, sixteen miles northwest of Mackay; the right fork travels eighteen miles into **Copper Basin,** one of the better areas in central Idaho to observe the effects of glaciation. The Copper Basin (7,800 ft.) covers thirty-six miles of high, barren desert "where there is all and there is nothing." From the Basin loop, one can return to Sun Valley, or continue thirty-seven miles southeast over Antelope Pass, and northeast to U.S. 93, fifteen miles south of Mackay.

As Highway 75 goes north from Ketchum, it passes the town cemetery on the right. **Ernest Hemingway** is buried here beneath a simple, flat granite slab in the fore-center portion of the graveyard.

Ernest Hemingway first came to Ketchum in 1939, invited by Sun Valley's publicity director. He worked on a portion of *For Whom the Bell Tolls* while he was there, and corrected galley proofs in the Valley the following year.

Hemingway was "the man who lived it up to write it down" – he was hunter, fisherman, skier, boxer, soldier, reporter; his subjects were love, war, and sports, and more non-literary copy was written about him than any other American writer in this century.

Thomas Hardy wrote, "Though a good deal is too strange to be believed, nothing is too strange to have happened." It was so with Hemingway's life. He was born in 1899, in Oak Park, Illinois; upon graduation from high school, he went to work as a cub reporter for the Kansas City *Star.* Ruled 4-F because of an eye defect, he entered World War I as an ambulance driver for the Red Cross, and won his red badge of courage when wounded by machine gun bullets and shell fragments in Italy. He was decorated for bravery.

During the 1920s Hemingway joined American expatriates in Paris, where Gertrude Stein observed he was "very earnestly at work making himself a writer." In 1925 his first book, *In Our Time,* was published.

In the 1930s the author was a correspondent in Spain during the Spanish Civil War; he won a bronze star in World War II while he accompanied American troops to Normandy, to the Battle of the Bulge, and to the liberation of Paris.

After 1945 Hemingway settled in Cuba, where he married his fourth wife, Mary Welsh, a war correspondent for *Time.* He won the Pulitzer Prize in 1952 and the Nobel Prize four years later. Between prizes, he survived (with injuries) two light-plane crashes in Africa.

After moving to Ketchum from Cuba when Castro took power, the writer began to feel like an anthology of ailments. He made two trips to the Mayo Clinic for diagnosis of hypertension, possible diabetes, and pigmentary cirrhosis. Additionally, he underwent shock therapy. On July 2, 1961, two days after his last visit to the clinic, he committed suicide, as had his father.

Ernest Hemingway left eight novels, three works of nonfiction and more than fifty short stories. His literary impact, however, was far more extensive. "Prose is architecture, not interior decoration," insisted one of his characters, "and the day of the Baroque is over." Hemingway's terse style, his simple and deft control of themes, influenced a generation of modern prose writers.

Highway 75 moves north up the Wood River Valley past houses that appear to have been built with Frank Lloyd Wright's remark in mind: "Give me the luxuries of life, and I will gladly do without the necessities." – most of the garages could hold an eight-mule baggage wagon.

The USFS **Sawtooth National Recreation Area headquarters** is located in a handsome wood building on the east side of the highway seven miles north of Ketchum. (A cassette player can be obtained here with a milepost-tour of the highway north to Stanley Ranger Station, where the player is returned.)

It is thirty miles from Ketchum up the Big Wood River, between the Boulder Mountains on the east and the Smoky Mountains on the west, to Galena Summit (8,701 elev.). The **Boulder Mountains** are metamorphosed sedimentary rock originally deposited on the floor of an ancient sea, then gradually uplifted. The **Smoky Mountains** received their name from frequent forest fires in the 1880s.

Galena Summit marks the divide between the Wood River and Salmon River drainages. The **Sawtooth Range,** thirty miles long and fifteen miles wide, is visible from a view area on the southwest side of the highway one mile short of the summit. Much of the area visible from the overlook is included in the Sawtooth NRA, 754,000 acres set aside in 1972 to protect scenic, historical, pastoral and wildlife values.

The path over Galena Summit was the Sawtooth Grade toll road, built to serve Sawtooth mines; it was completed in 1881 by the New York-owned Columbia and Beaver Mining Company, at a cost of about $13,000. A new road was cut in 1918-1919, and the present route was completed in 1953.

The road drops into the **Sawtooth Valley.** The mountains are part of a 16,000-acre wilderness within the SNRA: forty-two of the peaks are over 10,000 feet.

Because the bedrock of the range belongs to the eastern part of the Idaho batholith, the rocks are largely granitic with metamorphosed patches. Uplift began about 100 million years ago; more recently, the range has been heavily glaciated. The glaciers extended into the Sawtooth Valley, which is now floored by detritus.

Five miles north of Galena Summit the highway meets Smiley Creek Road, which enters on the west side. The **Vienna** silver-lead mining district was located 7.5 miles up Smiley Canyon from the highway. The Vienna Consolidated, which had a twenty-stamp mill, was active from 1879 to 1885. In 1904 the Vienna claims were sold for taxes; no trace remains of more than 200 buildings.

Beaver Creek is 2.8 miles north of Levi Smiley's Creek; **Sawtooth City,** 2.5 miles west of Beaver Creek, now has only a single cabin. The mining camp was a boisterous place from 1880 to 1886 when $100,000 was spent on the toll road to Ketchum and a ten-stamp quartz mill. When the shaft, hoist, and pumps burned at the Silver King mine in 1892, large-scale mining in the Sawtooths was finished. Production amounted to $250,000.

The turn-off for **Alturas Lake** is 1.7 miles beyond Beaver Creek. Alturas is 2.5 miles west of the highway; campsites are available.

Four miles farther north, Highway 75 crosses the headwaters of the **Salmon River,** which flows from this point almost 400 miles to the Snake River, the longest river contained within one state outside of Alaska.

To the northwest, the **White Clouds Range** can be glimpsed, its name suggested by rocks nearly white with metamorphic silicates.

Seven miles farther north, 1.7 miles past Obsidian, a dirt road travels east from the highway to the **Idaho Rocky Mountain Ranch** on Gold Creek, perhaps the most outstanding log lodge in the state. Guests are welcome, but reservations are required for dinner.

The 1,000-acre Rocky Mountain Ranch was purchased in 1929 by Winston Paul, the president of Frigidaire. He used it as a private guest ranch for eastern friends.

In 1932 he sold IRMR to Joseph Lanz, founder of Lanz of Salzburg clothes. He operated the place in the same spirit as Mr. Paul. After eight years, Lanz sold to Edmund Bogert, an auto dealer from Pocatello; Bogert developed the spread as a cattle ranch for purebred Herefords. His daughter reopened the lodge to guests for a few years in the early 1950s, but it was not until Mr. Bogert's death in 1975 that his children decided "dudes winter easier than cattle," and reopened the ranch to the public.

The lodge was built by a construction crew of sixty men in the fall of 1929; it was finished in six months. The logs were brought from Gold Creek; hinges were fashioned from scrap metal, door handles were carved, furniture handmade, showers lined with Oakley stone. Imbued with the special warmth and honesty logs can convey, the lodge has guest rooms, private cabins, a fishing pond and a private hot-springs pool. It is a unique spot for a week-long vacation or simply a dinner.

Highway 75 cuts through a sizable glacial moraine 4.7 miles north of Gold Creek. Some of the two-foot boulders may have been transported from the upper end of the valley.

The turn-off for **Redfish Lake** is marked by a sign 0.8 miles north of the moraine, where a paved road travels 2.5 miles southwest, past the SNRA visitors center, to the lake, which was named for the sockeye salmon that spawn in its tributary streams in September and October. Maximum lake depth is 300 feet; the ridges on the east and west shores are also moraines.

Little Redfish Lake and north end of Sawtooths.

357

Redfish Lodge at the north end of the lake is open from Memorial Day weekend until October 15; it has a restaurant and store, cabins and room rentals, and operates an excursion boat to shuttle persons five miles across the lake.

Fisherman will find Dolly Varden and rainbow trout, Kokanee and sockeye salmon in the lake.

Stanley is 4.2 miles north of Red Fish Lake (see Highway 21, Stanley). The town is colder than a mausoleum in the winter; it holds the lowest recorded temperature in the state, minus fifty degrees F., and the lowest mean annual temperature, seventeen degrees; snowfall averages ninety-three inches.

Lower Stanley, along the Salmon River, two miles northeast of the junction with Highway 21, was the first spot to use Stanley's name, but it lost the post office and school to Upper Stanley.

Eleven miles east of Lower Stanley, the remains of the **Sunbeam Dam** can be seen in the river below the north shoulder of the road.

The dam was the only one ever built on the Salmon River. Poured from 300 tons of cement in 1909-1910, it was intended to produce power required by the Sunbeam mill on Jordan Creek, one mile north of Bonanza on the Yankee Fork. The site was chosen by the manager of the mining company in the hope that the water would not freeze during the winter because it was downriver from the Sunbeam hot springs.

The Sunbeam mine and mill operated almost one year on the electricity, but even free power could not subsidize ore that sometimes ran only $2.00 per ton. In 1911 the mine property was sold at a sheriff's auction. (Part of the dam was dynamited in 1934, but irreparable damage to the sockeye salmon runs had already occurred.)

Yankee Fork enters the Salmon River from the north at Sunbeam, a short distance past the dam. This stream has a fascinating mining history.

Prospectors from Loon Creek, a tributary of the Middle Fork of the Salmon, moved to the Yankee Fork in the early 1870s, when their Middle Fork claims played out. Yankee Fork mines got off to a slow start, then in the summer of 1875 William Norton discovered a high-grade vein with an exceptionally rich three-inch seam. It proved to be the answer to a prospector's prayer; he was able to hand mortar $11,500 worth of gold in thirty days. He called his mine

358

the Charles Dickens. The following summer, Jim Baxter, E. M. Dodge and Morgan McKeim discovered the General Custer. It was another prospector's dream. Since most of the vein was exposed on the surface, the miners could avoid expensive developmental work. They packed their ore to a Salt Lake City mill and realized $60,000 the first year, and subsequently sold their claims for $285,000.

Doubts were overcome in 1879 as thousands of miners began a belated rush. The mining towns of Bonanza City and Custer were established, using Challis as a supply center. To visit the old townsites, drive north eight miles up Yankee Fork, past the catenated dredge ponds, to **Bonanza.**

This townsite was laid out by Charles Franklin in 1878; in 1881 it had a peak population of 600. In 1889, and in 1897, fires destroyed much of Bonanza, and many merchants relocated in Custer.

Take the road west from Bonanza 0.5 miles to Boot Hill graveyard. Drive 0.2 miles past Boot Hill to an island of graves marked by a picket fence in a cluster of pines at the end of the road. Custer County's most intriguing mystery is draped about these three graves. Here is the story in stick-figure fashion.

Charles Franklin organized the townsite of Bonanza in 1878 and ran the Franklin House Hotel. That summer a young couple arrived from Bodie, California: Richard and Agnes Elizabeth King. Both were English immigrants, and Franklin befriended them.

While her husband prospected, Lizzie opened the Arcade Saloon, and Yankee Fork Dance Hall; the businesses prospered under her competent management; it is said she knew to the decimal point how her enterprises fared.

Then Richard King was gunned down in a saloon over an argument about a city lot. Franklin arranged his friend's funeral and helped Lizzie choose the burial site. Leaving room for their own graves, he fenced the plot.

As Franklin helped Lizzie mend her torn life, the two of them became more than friends; townspeople expected that they would be married in the summer of 1880. But a young man named Robert Hawthorne stepped off the Bonanza stage and plans were altered – Lizzie married Hawthorne that summer instead.

One week after the wedding, Lizzie and her new husband were found at mid-day shot to death in their log house on the north end of town. Neither murderer nor murder weapon were uncovered. A grief-stricken Franklin took charge of the funeral, and buried the couple in King's plot, with Lizzie in the middle. The headboards he carved never mentioned Agnes Elizabeth Hawthorne's new surname.

But the dead are the only ones who never die, and Lizzie must have slept in Franklin's heart like a bear in a cave. He grew increasingly moody, his business was neglected. After ten years Franklin left Bonanza for a placer claim on Stanley Creek and became a recluse.

Two years later a pair of prospectors stopped at Franklin's cabin and found his decomposed body on the bed in his cabin. Clutched in his hand was a locket with a picture of Elizabeth King. They buried him in an unmarked grave behind his place. (Read *Land of Yankee Fork,* by Esther Yarber).

Lizzie King's grave (center).

The Yankee Fork gold dredge rests in a rusty trance 0.3 miles north of Bonanza in a pit on the west side of the road. In 1938-1939 the Silas Mason Company of Louisiana tested several mining claims along the stream to ascertain dredge values. Results indicated about $16 million worth of gold was recoverable. The Company formed a subsidiary, the Salmon River Mining Company, and contracted with Bucyrus-Erie Company for a 1,110-ton dredge with seventy-two buckets of eight cubic-feet capacity each – a medium-sized dredge. The parts were trucked to the site and assembled here.

The company operated the dredge from 1940 to 1949, with an interruption for World War II; the dredge was then sold to J. R. Simplot and Fred Baumhoff, who ran it until 1952, when accessible ground was exhausted. Simplot attempted to move the dredge, as a museum, to Pocatello.

360

Dredges are complicated (but efficient) machines for assembly-line mining. A pair of steel spuds held by the stern gantry anchor the boat. The bucket line digs the gravel to a depth of thirty-five feet and discharges it into a hopper which spills onto a revolving trommel screen with ⅜ to one-inch perforations. The oversize from this screen is discharged by a conveyor belt at the stern; the undersize, which contains the gold, goes to thirty-two riffled sluices with mercury in them to catch the gold. Once a week the dredge is shut down, the riffles cleaned, and the gold and amalgam removed.

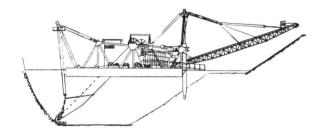

Profile of an eight-cubic-yard dredge. Shows bucket line down and spud pegged.

Yankee Fork dredge.

361

The dredge was powered by a pair of Ingersoll-Rand diesel engines, each with seven cylinders. The bucket line was driven by direct drive; diesel electric motors turned the trommel screen and the stacker. Under favorable conditions, the operation could move 4,000 cubic yards in twenty-four hours.

Winch cables, run through pulleys from the port and starboard bows to logs buried in land six feet deep, provided the method of pivoting the bow and bucket line. The rear stacker was stationary but swung with the barge – if it ever broke its bridle chains, it could upset the dredge.

The boat stepped ahead five feet at a time by use of a steel and wooden spud supported by the stern gantry. The dredge would pivot on the steel spud, drop the wooden one and move ahead on it, then drop the steel once again; the boat might make four steps in a shift.

A crew of four was required: a dredgemaster with the only key to the clean-up room, a winchman at the controls who decided when to move ahead, a deckhand who cleaned and swamped, and an oiler who tended the machinery.

Lights were mounted on the gantry so that the operation could continue round the clock, though in the winter work halted when the bucket line froze.

Custer is two miles north of Bonanza. The townsite was laid out in 1879, just below the General Custer mill; the thirty-stamps ran for a decade and produced $8 million. A second company used the same mill to work the Lucky Boy vein parallel to that of the Custer and turned out another million dollars before it halted operations in 1904. In April, 1911, with the closure of the Sunbeam mine, Custer's clock stopped.

The old schoolhouse in Custer contains the **McGown museum,** now run by the U.S. Forest Service.

Clayton, 20.5 miles east of Yankee Fork on Highway 75, was founded in 1881 when the Salmon River Mining and Smelting Company began operating a smelter here for the mines on Kinnikinic and State Creeks. It closed in 1904.

Clayton still has a number of active silver mines; the Clayton Silver mine, two miles up Kinnikinic, has operated since 1929 and employs about thirty-five persons. In 1979 a new shaft to the 1,100-foot level increased ore reserves by 400,000 tons.

Bayhorse Creek enters the Salmon on the left, 13.5 miles downriver from Clayton. The town known as **Bayhorse** was located about 2.5 miles up the creek from the present highway. Though a claim was filed as early as 1872, rich ore was not discovered on the creek until 1877. A mill with a smelter and charcoal kilns served silver-lead mines such as the Ramshorn, Skylark and Excelsior. The district closed in 1897 but was reborn from 1917 to 1925. Production amounted to $9 million.

The kilns are on USFS land and can be visited; the town is on private property.

Highway 75 meets U.S. 93 at a junction 10.5 miles north of Bayhorse. The sixty-foot cliff on the left side of the highway, 0.5 miles short of the junction, was a **Shoshone buffalo jump.** Bison grazing on the slopes behind the jump were herded along a driveway marked by small stone piles about five to ten yards apart. Hunters crouched by the piles and flicked their robes to move the herd along.

An archaeological excavation in 1971 uncovered nineteen glass beads among bones from approximately thirty buffalo; an historical archaeologist identified four of the beads as Cornaline d'Aleppo, produced from 1860 to 1880. This evidence was startling, since bison in the area were believed hunted to extinction by 1840. Over one hundred small projectile points were found as well as numerous hand-held skinning knives of the type used by the Shoshone after A.D. 1250. The buffalo jump has been added to the National Register of Historic Places.

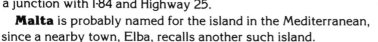

State Highway No. 77 from a junction with Highway 81 in Malta, westerly via Connor, then northwest via Albion and Declo to a junction with I-84 and Highway 25.

Malta is probably named for the island in the Mediterranean, since a nearby town, Elba, recalls another such island.

The Y, 7.8 miles west of Malta, where Highway 77 turns due north, is called **Connor.** The site is named for Col. Patrick Connor, who dispatched Major Edward McGarry into the City of Rocks area (south of Connor junction) in September, 1862, with orders to "...destroy every male Indian whom you may encounter in the vicinity of the late massacres. This course may seem harsh and severe, but I desire that the order may be rigidly enforced, as I am satisfied that in the end it will prove most merciful." McGarry found no Indians at City of Rocks, but he disarmed and killed twenty-four that were encountered along the Humboldt River in Nevada. Nothing like a satisfied mind.

77
IDAHO

For a twenty-three mile excursion to City of Rocks, leave Highway 77 at Connor and turn south on the paved road to Almo.

Elba, 4.5 miles south of Connor, was settled in 1873, and was first known as Beecherville. It is an agricultural community.

SCENIC
AREA

Driving south another 12.7 miles, the driver reaches **Almo.** The first emigrants arrived in this area in 1877. One settler opened a log cabin-store on the north side of Almo Creek; others grazed cattle in the region. In 1881 the name was given to the townsite, but its origin and meaning are now uncertain.

High wheat prices at the outbreak of World War I brought dry land farmers into nearby Circle Creek Basin, west of Almo. They cleared and fenced the land and planted grain, but drought and the agricultural depression plowed their hopes under in the early 1920s.

Almo is corraled by the Albion Mountains; sagebrush and runted junipers and pinyon pine stipple the burlap hills. This altogether satisfactory mountain hamlet has several log cabins, some red brick houses, a yellow brick, 1918 schoolhouse, and a Mormon church of orange brick, in need of a collection basket.

At the edge of the road, across the street from the gas station, is a monument erected in 1938 by the Sons and Daughters of Idaho Pioneers. It commemorates "those who lost their lives in a most horrible Indian massacre in 1861." "Of 300 emigrants," the marker states, "only five escaped." The leaves of this legend have withered before a winter of facts.

From 1860 to 1862 there were at least six skirmishes at City of Rocks between emigrant parties and a resident band of Shoshone Indians, but historical accounts reveal that no more than eight whites were killed.

HISTORICAL
SITE

In the **City of Rocks,** outside Almo, the marriage of baroque geology and western migration have created one of the more extraordinary locations in Idaho. In 1964 the site was listed as one of the state's eight National Historic Landmarks; in 1972 a National Park Service study recommended National Monument status for the site.

To reach the area, follow the signed, gravel road south out of Almo for six miles. (The gravel gives way to dirt, and in wet or snowy weather the ground becomes slick as a scalp.)

Few persons are prepared for the weird beauty of the City, a beauty not readily captured by photographs. Even the fatigued emigrants were taken aback: "We were so spellbound with the beauty and strangeness of it all, that no thought of Indians entered our head." "I have not time to write the hundredth part of the marvels of the valley of rocks ..." Nature's wit and plasticity here are reminiscent of the Doll's House in southern Utah, and the Alabama Hills of California.

An uncommon geology accounts for the bizarre, nude granite sculptures. The rocks are among the oldest known in western North America. A 2.5 billion-year-old basement of Precambrian crystalline rock was buried beneath 50,000 feet of Paleozoic and Mesozoic rocks, which created enormous pressure and temperature at great depths. The overburden was gradually uplifted, perhaps as much as ten miles, and the Precambrian rocks were eventually exposed by erosion in Circle Creek Basin.

The Albion Range, including the City of Rocks, is part of the Cassia batholith, which is a mantled gneiss dome that covers forty square miles. The gneiss, a metamorphic rock, has been split into thin layers here.

The dark caps on the formation are a harder granite than the light-colored stone beneath. Rain penetrates fractures in the granite and dissolves minerals that work their way to the surface through evaporation. On the rock's exterior, the minerals solidify within cracks and pores, cementing the surface to a depth of several inches. Additional water seeps down the sides of the formations, where granite with greater porosity allows deeper penetration. Since deeper absorption means less evaporation, frozen mineralized water causes expansion and decomposition along the sides and base of the formations, and creates the remarkable grottoes and alcoves.

The Albion Range, with its complex structure and thrust-fault patterns, makes an inviting study-area for geologists.

The City of Rocks was hub to several trails important to American migration. In 1862 at least 52,000 persons passed along the **California Trail** (sometimes called the Applegate Trail by settlers who used it to reach the Willamette Valley). Established in 1846 as a cutoff from the Oregon Trail, the route came south up the Raft River, west through City of Rocks, then south into Utah at nearby Granite Pass.

Hudspeth's Cutoff, begun in 1849 from the Oregon Trail at Sheep Rock near present Soda Springs, also funneled west into the California Trail at the rock city.

Additionally, the **Salt Lake Cutoff,** a major thoroughfare, came north from Salt Lake City through Emigrant Canyon, just south of Twin Sisters in City of Rocks, and connected with the California Trail. When the Idaho mines opened in the 1860s, freight from Utah settlements traveled over the Salt Lake Cutoff from Kelton, Utah, through City of Rocks, and north through Oakley's Goose Creek Valley.

Emigrants who camped in the City of Rocks were attacked by Shoshone Indians often enough to add an imaginative dimension to the castellated, movie-set landscape. Six attacks have been documented.

Of one, in 1862, the Virginia City *Territorial Enterprise* reported: "When our informant left Humboldt (Nevada) several wagons had just arrived whose sides and covers were transformed into magnified nutmeg-graters by Indian bullets."

By hiding in a willow thicket here for ten days John Comer survived an attack on his wagon train in September, 1862. He was found suffering, in bitter weather, from nine bullet wounds. The newspaper commented that insurance companies need not be afraid to take a risk on him.

Not all the attacks, however, were by Indians. In 1860 John Hagerty, victim of an ambushed wagon train at City of Rocks, reported to the *Deseret News:*

The Indians were all at the wagons immediately on their being abandoned by the emigrants, and without waiting to plunder them to any great extent, with much dexterity attached some of the oxen to them and drove off, taking one nearly a mile, the others a less distance, before rifling them of their contents. He is very confident that there were white men among the Indians in disguise. He positively saw one individual with short hair, who had on a pair of fine boots, and a pair of pants, but otherwise dressed and painted like an Indian, and when the attacking party were hitching the oxen to the wagons and driving them off, they spoke to the cattle in good English. He says that he was decidedly uneasy during the time he was compelled to remain in the brush, as the Indians were about him in every direction as thick as bees, and he did not know what ultimately might be his fate, neither what had become of those who had got away.

Evidence of the great migration is still abundant. At the first Y inside the basin, a large stone on the southeast side of the Y, called **Register Rock,** contains names daubed in axle grease by numerous emigrants. (Only someone with sagebrush for brains would deface this western ledger.)

Drive south from the Y, 1.4 miles, then west and southwest another mile to the **Twin Sisters.** The two granite pinnacles are of astonishingly different ages – one is 2.5 billion years-old, the other 25 million years.

The junction of the California Trail and the Salt Lake Cutoff is 1.5 miles south of the Twin Sisters. There is evidence of an old stage station. (The wagon ruts at Granite Pass are several miles southeast of this point.)

Return to the Y and drive northwest among stones with shapes analagous to their names – bath rock, two rock turtles, king on the throne – names so banal they deride nature's ingenuity. Provided the road is dry, it is possible to continue north on this road from City of Rocks twenty miles to Oakley, and follow Highway 27 north seventeen miles to Burley, just south of I-84 (see Highway 27, Oakley).

City of Rocks is an inviting spot for the traveler who likes to poke his campfire amid the ashes of the past. However, given the despoliation caused by grouse-brains who have ram-jammed their dirt bikes and four-wheel drive rigs through every pocket of the basin, it is unfortunate that the area was not accorded National Monument status. Though there was wide-spread support among local residents and ranchers for protection of the area, the private Park Service plan called for an end to grazing within twenty-five years, and for land acquisition through eminent domain. This private plan was contrary to public Park Service statements, and its discovery fractured the coalition which was working to establish the Monument.

At present 1,000 acres are under BLM management, 1,100 acres are administered by the USFS, 640 acres are state land, and the remaining 4,000 acres owned by local ranchers who use it for summer range.

Highway 77 runs north from Connor junction eleven miles to **Albion** – a name drawn out of a cowboy hat in 1879. (Albion is an archaic word for the island of Great Britain.)

As the road doglegs through Albion, there is a vest-pocket park on the right with an historical sign concerning **Diamondfield Jack.** Across the street from the park, on a diagonal, is the old Cassia County courthouse, where on the second floor, Diamondfield Jack was tried. (The Cassia County seat was located in Albion until 1918, when it was moved to Burley.) The knotted circumstances of the Diamondfield Jack case have made it Idaho's *Oxbow Incident* – with a different denouement.

Cassia County was lush rangeland from 1875 to 1885. By the 1890s hard winters and overcrowded range had eroded the cattle business and given a boost to sheepmen, whose stock could survive on the depleted ground, at least temporarily. Hard feelings existed between the two grazing interests, but in Cassia County a "gentlemen's agreement" kept the sheep east of Deadline Ridge (west of Oakley). Oakley, Albion, and the Raft River Valley were sheep country.

In 1895 when the woolgrowers expanded across Deadline onto the Shoe Sole ranch range west of Oakley, the cattle baron John Sparks hired Diamondfield Jack as a nightrider on "fighting wages."

Diamondfield Jackson Lee Davis was born in Virginia, and "succumbed to rumors of a diamond mine" as a young prospector, and thereby earned his nickname. He patrolled the Shoe Sole cattle range for Sparks that summer and got into wrangles with several sheepherders. The woolgrowers were given warnings. Finally, a confrontation ended in violence when Davis wounded a sheepherder. The range war had erupted. Diamondfield Jack trailed down to Nevada and pastured out of sight until tempers subsided.

Two months later he was back in Idaho. Within two weeks, a sheepherder found two fellow herders who had been shot and killed in their camp wagon. Word was sent to the sheriff at Albion, fifty miles to the northeast. The only clues the sheriff found were a corncob pipe and three empty .44 cartridges.

Public opinion pointed the finger at Diamondfield Jack. In March, 1896, a complaint was sworn against him and his partner, Fred Gleason. The sheepmen posted a reward and hired a young Boise lawyer, William Borah, as counsel.

Gleason was apprehended in Montana and extradited. Davis was found in the Yuma, Arizona, prison where he was serving a one-year sentence for complications that arose when he shot a dog that was harassing his horse.

Diamondfield Jack Davis was arraigned in the courthouse at Albion. John Sparks hired the best criminal lawyer in the West, James Hawley, to defend the gunman. (During Hawley's career, which spanned forty years, he was involved in over 300 murder cases.)

The trail that began in Albion in April, 1897, hacked a sinuous trail through the thickets of Idaho criminal law. It has been said that the criminal is prevented, by the very witnessing of the legal process, from regarding his deed as intrinsically evil. This case fit the remark. But Jack Davis had the additional misfortune of an old curse: "May you have a lawsuit in which you know you are in the right."

The state's case was wholly circumstantial, but like the trout in the milk, some of the circumstances were very strong. Hawley

368

based his defense on the theory that his client could not have ridden fifty-five miles round-trip in five hours from one of Spark's ranches to the murder site.

The trial lasted a week; the jury found Davis guilty of first-degree murder, and he was sentenced to hang a few weeks later.

Fred Gleason, tried separately for the same crime with the same evidence, was acquitted.

On the Hawley's appeal to the Idaho Supreme Court, the verdict in the Davis case was upheld.

In October, 1898, the general manager of the Spark's ranch, Jim Bower, appeared before the state pardon board and confessed that he and a pard, Jeff Gray, had gotten into an argument with the sheepherders and that Gray killed them in self-defense. Jim dropped his pipe at the scene. Gray corroborated the story. The pardon board, consisting of the governor, secretary of state, and attorney general, issued several reprieves, but finally denied Davis' pardon, and he was sentenced to hang in one week.

Hawley filed an appeal in the U.S. Circuit Court of Appeals. The court issued a restraining order the day before the hanging. Fearful that sheepmen would intercept the message, Hawley dispatched his law partner from Boise on the train to Minidoka with three copies of the reprieve. His partner met two riders there, and the three of them galloped separately twenty-five miles to Albion to give the documents to the sheriff.

While Hawley and Davis awaited the U.S. Circuit Court of Appeals decision, Jim Bower and Jeff Gray were tried for the murder of the two sheepherders, and were acquitted by the jury on grounds of self-defense.

In December, 1899, the U.S. Circuit Court of Appeals ruled that the issue raised by Hawley's appeal belonged in the U.S. Supreme Court and must proceed through the U.S. Circuit Court for Idaho. The lawyer filed for a writ and made other arguments against the conviction. Since the U.S. Circuit Court for Idaho denied the writ and arguments, Hawley succeeded in placing the case on the docket of the U.S. Supreme Court, but the high court confirmed the lower decision. After 3½ years, Diamondfield Jack's legal recourse was exhausted. Sparks had spent $50,000 on his defense.

The editor of the *Albion Times* had befriended Davis and called for his release. The sheriff described him as an ideal prisoner. William Borah and the *Idaho Statesman,* however, opposed his release.

In April, 1901, James Hawley moved for a new trial in the Cassia County district court, on the basis of new evidence, but the judge, who had once been Borah's law partner, denied the motion and resentenced Diamondfield Jack to hang June 21, 1901.

The composition of the pardon board had now changed. They agreed to review the case, and another date, July 3, was set for the hanging. On July 3 the board issued Davis his eighth stay of execution. Once again riders carried the news from Minidoka to a sympathetic sheriff who had prepared the gallows but held out for a late-afternoon hanging. The crowd dispersed.

Diamondfield Jack Davis.

370

On July 16, one day before his new hanging date, the pardon board commuted Davis' sentence to life imprisonment – on the basis of a ballistics experiment!

The indefatigable Hawley began planning another appeal to the state supreme court. Davis was moved to the penitentiary in Boise. On the day of his departure, the sheriff gave him a gold watch, and scores of residents stopped by the jail to say good-bye.

The state supreme court finally informed Hawley that the state constitution vested relief in the Board of Pardons for such cases. The lawyer went back to the pardons board.

On December 17, 1902, reacting to pressure from Hawley, and numerous public petitions, the Board of Pardons voted two-to-one for a pardon. William Borah and the *Statesman* were outraged.

Diamondfield Jack Davis walked out of the Idaho penitentiary the next day; he stopped at the Warm Springs Natatorium and had a few drinks with Boise's new mayor, James Hawley. Then he took a train to Tonapah, Nevada.

Hawley went on to become governor of Idaho, and Borah became the state's U.S. Senator – in fact, Hawley successfully defended Borah against federal grand jury charges of land fraud. John Sparks became governor of Nevada.

But the leading figure in this legal drama had one more scene to play. Davis discovered some first-rate mining claims near Tonapah. He became president of Diamondfield Triangle Gold Mining Co., capitalized at $1 million. Now wealthy and famous, with associates who were bankers and mining men, he gave shares in the company to the men who had ridden from Minidoka to Albion with his reprieve.

While in Goldfield, Nevada, Davis was involved in a couple of shootouts, and on one occasion interrupted a lynch party intent on hanging two men.

However, Diamondfield Jack Davis, the cowboy-miner, apparently squandered his wealth. He spent his later years adrift in the West, from California to Montana, aimless, begging grubstakes, until he died in 1949 from injuries inflicted by a Las Vegas taxicab. "O mortals blind in fate, who never know / To bear high fortune, or endure the low."

About three blocks northwest of the Albion city park, on the west side of Highway 77 stands the remains of **Magic Christian College:** depopulated, derelict, doleful.

Request permission from the city maintenance man to walk through the forty-acre campus. Rows of cottonwoods whisper above the weedy walks. There are a dozen large brick buildings with shingle roofs, including gymnasium, administration buildings, and student dorms. It is a forlorn campus – bare flagpole, empty benches, shattered lamplights.

In 1892 the people of Cassia County financed the building of Albion State Normal School, a two-story, three room structure. Col. J. E. Miller, state senator for Cassia and Owyhee Counties, donated five acres for the site. Four years later the state appropriated $37,500 for the school, and the main building was completed.

The school provided a two-year curriculum for teachers. In 1947 the program was increased to four years, and the normal school became Southern Idaho College of Education. Still a teachers' college, large numbers of veterans attended under the G.I. Bill. Between 1893 and 1951 it is estimated that the school trained 3,000 teachers.

The state legislature ended funding for SICE in March, 1951, on grounds the school duplicated services available from Idaho State Univ. at Pocatello. The campus turned quiet as a cloister.

Though no upkeep was done on the buildings, the state maintained the grounds at a cost of $10,000 a year for six years. Then in 1957 the legislature passed an act which allowed the Church of Christ to lease the college for ninety-nine years.

The Church of Christ has about 2 million members, most of them in the South and Southwest. The Church decided to reopen the school as Magic Christian College; it helped fund the school but did not administer it. After spending $190,000 to refurbish the institution, it was opened as a two-year college; there were 117 students the first year.

Enrollment grew, and in 1960 the college added two years to the curriculum, but in 1965, with only eighteen students, it reverted to a junior college granting A.A. degrees. Students paid $375 tuition a semester, and $306 for room and board. Their fees met half the operating cost; the other half came from donations.

In 1967, with an enrollment of eighty-two students, the school closed again. It never reopened. Magic Christian had been offered campus facilities at an airbase in Baker, Oregon. The New Jerusalem fell short of the dream; the Baker college closed after one year.

The town of Albion purchased the campus from the state of Idaho for $10.

372

State Highway 77 travels north nine miles from Albion to **Declo.** The farm town's name is a hybrid from the family names of Dethles and Cloughy.

The road intersects with I-84, 3.4 miles north of Declo.

State Highway No. 78 from a junction with Highway 55 in Marsing, southeasterly via Murphy, Grandview, Bruneau and Hammett to a junction with I-84 north of Hammett. (Overlaps Highway 52 for 8.6 miles near Bruneau.) Route length: 98.5 miles.

The road from Marsing to Grand View generally follows the south-alternate route of the Oregon Trail. Twelve miles from Marsing, along the south shore of the Snake, the highway reaches **Givens Hot Springs.**

Emigrants on the trail plugged a gully here and used the water for baths and washing clothes. In 1881 Milford and Martha Givens, who had seen the springs on their trip west, returned to settle here. Milford sold deer, antelope and sturgeon to the miners in Silver City. The couple divorced in 1898; in 1902 Martha's second husband built a pool lined with concrete. The hot springs, now part of a commercial campground, fill a large indoor pool and six private baths.

Archaeological excavations on the flat indicate the area was inhabited as early as 4,500 years ago.

Warms Springs ferry operated intermittently at this location between 1885 and 1921.

Walters Ferry is 7.8 miles east of Givens Hot Springs (see Highway 45, Walters Ferry).

Ten miles farther southeast is the town of **Murphy,** which became the seat of Owyhee County by four votes in 1934, at the expense of Silver City.

Owyhee County, with almost 5 million acres, has land the eagles have not yet flown over. Though it is the second-largest county in Idaho, from 1866 to 1966 its population only increased from 5,000 to 6,000.

Owyhee is the original spelling of Hawaii used by Captain Cook. Sandwich Islands, or Hawaiian, trappers were employed in 1818 by Donald Mackenzie in the Boise Basin. Several of them explored the region southwest of Boise that winter and failed to return in the spring. Their name was left on the land.

Murphy acquired its name through Col. William Dewey, who chose it to honor his friend, Con Murphy. The townsite was the terminal for the Boise, Nampa and Owyhee Railroad; Dewey's line intended for the Silver City mines.

The **Owyhee County Historical Museum** is one block southwest of the highway and the courthouse. The site includes the old Murphy schoolhouse and a homesteader's cabin; Indian artifacts and mining items are exhibited, as well as a reconstructed mine adit and a pioneer kitchen. A library of local lore is also available.

The **Otter Massacre,** the major tragedy on the Oregon Trail, occurred almost midway between Murphy and Grand View, three miles north of the highway, on Castle Creek.

On September 9, 1860, a band of Shoshone Indians attacked the Elijah Otter wagon train, and the seige lasted for two days. Eleven of the forty-four emigrants were killed in the battle, twenty-one more were killed or died after they left the scene. Most of the twelve survivors were rescued by a military party near the Owyhee River a few days later.

For sixty years the site was believed to have been three miles south and six miles east of Murphy, just west of Sinker Creek, but skeletal remains of the dead were noted in the emigrant diary of Henry Judson two years after the incident; he placed the site on Castle Creek near Castle Rock. In 1982 Larry Jones of the Idaho Historical Society detected the error revealed by Judson's journal.

Five miles south of Murphy the road to Silver City in the Owyhee Basin mining district leaves the west side of Highway 78. **Silver City** is an unrestored piece of American history; the queen of Idaho ghost towns, a trove of forty disheveled buildings. There are few places one can visit alone any longer, and Silver City in the summer is not one of them, but all who are curious about the past should make the trip at least once.

Although the road is usually open by May 1, after that date even St. Christopher himself could have problems getting over New York Summit if the surface is wet.

From Highway 78 the road travels twenty-three miles through sagebrush hills up Striker Creek Basin Gulch, then crosses Sinker Canyon (Sinker Creek disappears in places during the summer), and climbs Scotch Bob Creek (Bob Beaton built this stretch of road) to 6,676-foot New York Summit (named by promoters who peddled mining stock in the East), and descends to Silver City on Jordan Creek, between Florida Mountain (7,784 ft.) on the west and War Eagle Mountain (8,051 ft.) on the east.

374

In the spring of 1863 Michael Jordan led twenty-nine prospecters south from Placerville in Boise Basin to Jordan Creek in search of the placer diggings of the apocryphal Lost Blue Bucket. They discovered colors on the creek just above later De Lamar, about nine miles west of what is now Silver City. Each man took three claims along the stream before other miners arrived on the scene like flies around a honey pot.

Most of the placers were mined by 1864, but rich silver-gold lodes (the Oro Fino and the Morning Star) were discovered on War Eagle Mtn. to the east. The first assays reported values richer than those of Nevada's Comstock lode.

Ruby City, with streets that "looked like they were laid out by a blind cow," emerged on Jordan Creek, a mile north of later Silver City; the mills, however, were built a mile closer to the mines, and Ruby did not last as long as a pie at a picnic. All the structures which could be moved were pulled by ox teams up the creek to Silver City.

Because mining equipment and supplies were needed to develop the district, Silas Skinner, Col. W. H. Dewey, and Michael Jordan obtained a fifteen-year franchise from the Territorial Legislature for a toll road from Jordan Valley to Silver City and down Reynolds Creek to Boise City. The Skinner Road opened in May, 1866; freight from Chico, California, to Silver City arrived in four days.

Miners on War Eagle Mtn. were busier than chickens dibbling in a pie pan; they discovered over 300 ledges and filed on all of them. J. H. More and D. H. Fogus of Boise Basin collared the two best mines on opposite sides of mountain: the Oro Fino on the east, and the Morning Star on the west. Simon Reed and J. C. Ainsworth of the Oregon Steam and Navigation Co. also held important claims on the peak.

The first mills began to operate in the fall of 1864; More and Fogus made $1 million the first year. As New York capital flowed into the area, more mills went up along the creek. By 1866 eighty-two stamps, producing $70,000 a week, reverberated in the canyon.

Silver City became a town: there were six general stores, eight saloons and a brewery, a miner's union hospital, cotes for the soiled doves of Long Gulch, and all the other services required by such a settlement. It acquired the first telegraph service in the Territory – from Winnemucca to Boise City – and began publishing the *Idaho Avalanche,* the Territory's first daily paper.

Two major dust-ups occurred on War Eagle in the 1860s. Hays and Ray, who had eight claims on the mountain, excavated a shaft;

375

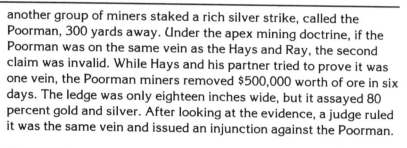

another group of miners staked a rich silver strike, called the Poorman, 300 yards away. Under the apex mining doctrine, if the Poorman was on the same vein as the Hays and Ray, the second claim was invalid. While Hays and his partner tried to prove it was one vein, the Poorman miners removed $500,000 worth of ore in six days. The ledge was only eighteen inches wide, but it assayed 80 percent gold and silver. After looking at the evidence, a judge ruled it was the same vein and issued an injunction against the Poorman.

Silver City in 1907. New York Summit (top right) and Morning Star mine (right center).

Production resumed in July, 1866, and in six months the Hays-Poorman returned $1 million.

In September, 1867, more discoveries were made on War Eagle, near the Oro Fino: D. H. Fogus and friends claimed the Ida Elmore mine, and Hill Beachy, who also ran a stage line from Silver City to Virginia City, Nevada, staked the Golden Chariot. The argument that developed between the two mines echoed the Hays-Poorman quarrel. In March, 1868, after the Golden Chariot miners had broken through to the Elmore's workings, a gunfight erupted between the factions. About 100 men were engaged in an underground war for three days; three were killed (including J. H. More) and several wounded.

Governor Ballard dispatched deputy marshal, Orlando Rube Robbins, to read a cease-and-desist proclamation. He arrived in six hours, corralled the company leaders and produced a formal agreement that ended the conflict. The governor also ordered

376

ninety-six soldiers from Fort Boise to Silver City as insurance. After four days they returned to Boise.

Once the "Owyhee War" was over, production resumed and shortly reached $200,000 a month. By the end of the year the mountain yielded $3 million.

In 1875 the failure of the Bank of California staggered the mining community. High-grade surface deposits had been worked out by that time, and future development of lower-grade ore required

Silver City today.

additional capital. About 75 percent of the Owyhee district's production came from these deposits, which were worked from 1885 to 1912.

Despite a flurry of activity during the Depression, by 1934 Silver City had gone so far downhill that voters moved the county seat to Murphy. Wartime mining restrictions spelled the end. Idaho Power Co. removed the electrical transmission lines from Swan Falls Dam and many of the old buildings were dismantled for their lumber. Records indicate that the district produced $40 million in gold and silver.

Silver City has two main streets, Jordan and Washington, parallel to each other on the east side of the creek. The Idaho Hotel on Jordan St., though showing signs of mutability, is perhaps the most interesting structure in town. It dates from the 1860s, and with its fifty rooms was among the finest hotels in the Territory. The remains of the Wells Fargo office are next door.

78 IDAHO

Silver City, Washington St.

Lippincott's daughter, Silver City.

Fifty yards past the hotel is the *Idaho* (Owyhee) *Avalanche* office. The newspaper was renowned for its pungent editorials. A sample is its taxonomy of drunkards in the town's saloons:

The first is ape-drunk. He leaps and sings and yells and dances, making all sorts of grimaces and cutting up all sorts of "monkey-shines" to excite the laughter of his fellows. The second is

378

tiger-drunk. He breaks the bottles, breaks the chairs, breaks the heads of fellow-carousers, and is full of blood and thunder. Of this sort are those who abuse their families. The third is hog-drunk. He rolls in the dirt on the floor, slobbers and grunts, and going into the streets makes his bed in the first ditch or filthy corner he may happen to fall into. He is heavy, lumpish and sleepy, and cries in a whining way for a little more drink. The fourth is puppy-drunk. He will weep for kindness, and whine his love and hug you in his arms, and kiss you with his slobbery lips, and proclaim how much he loves you. You are the best man he ever saw, and he will lay down his money or his life for you. The fifth is owl-drunk. He is wise in his own conceit. No man can differ with him, for his word is law. His arm is the strongest, his voice the sweetest, his horse the fleetest, his town the finest, of all in the room or land. The sixth and last animal of our drunken menagerie is the fox-drunk man. He is crafty and ready to trade horses and cheat if he can. Keen to strike a bargain, leering round with low cunning, peeping through cracks, listening under the eaves, watching for some suspicious thing, shy as a fox, sneaking as the wolf. He is the meanest drunkard of them all.

Walk east up the Morning Star Mill Rd., three doors past the Clyde Snell house to the two-story **Old Schoolhouse Museum.** The school was built in 1892 and is now leased from the Owyhee Cattlemens' Association. Beyond the museum stands an elaborate, two-story, T-shaped house that was built in 1870 for John Stoddard with lumber from his own mill. The interior has hand-grained woodwork. The Stoddard house, once the office of the Morning Star mine, is a durable testament to Otto Patocheck's carpentry skills.

On the knoll behind the museum is Our Lady of Tears Catholic Church. Silver City's first Catholic Church was built in 1869; the second was fashioned in 1882 out of a building purchased for $750. When that church collapsed under the weight of snow, the present Gothic revival structure was bought by the Catholics from the Episcopalians in 1933; it was erected in 1898.

From Silver City continue west down Jordan Creek five miles to the mouth of Bonneville Gulch, where Dewey was once located. The mine dumps are visible on the south side of the creek.

Limited mining occurred here until Col. William H. Dewey bought the major claims in 1896 and consolidated the Black Jack and Trade Dollar mines. (Dewey had lost most of his wealth while being defended in a murder trial, but after his acquittal, he crawled around Florida Mtn. on his hands and knees until he traced the source of gold float to a new discovery that restored his fortune.)

The Colonel built a twenty-stamp mill for the ore from the Florida Mtn. mines and established a small town next to it that was given his name. He built a three-story hotel that was much admired: the ground floor held offices, a bar, billiard and card rooms, a wash area, kitchen and dining rooms. The third floor was a dance hall. Electricity and steam heat were also provided. Across the street from the hotel was an elaborate, two-story house provided for the mine superintendent.

In 1895-1896 William Dewey was elected to the state senate to represent Owyhee and Cassia counties. He planned a railroad extension from Nampa to Silver City; the rails reached Murphy but were never laid farther west. Dewey sold his mining interests in 1900; he died in 1903, and the hotel burned in 1907. At the time of his death the site's production had surpassed the total yield of the War Eagle mines.

In the 1930s a fifty-ton ball mill was installed to rework the tailings.

Drive west another four miles down Jordan Creek to the **DeLamar** townsite. DeLamar Mountain, as well as the mine and tunnel, are on the south side of the road.

When Capt. Joseph R. DeLamar came to the Owyhee district in 1886 he could not afford a tie rope for a nightmare. Born in Amsterdam, Holland, he went to sea as a cabin boy and while still in his twenties settled at Martha's Vineyard where he was employed as a diver raising sunken ships.

In 1878, attracted to the silver strike in Leadville, Colorado, DeLamar decided to improve his chances as a prospector by studying chemistry and metallurgy in Chicago. He then returned to Colorado, where he went broke trying to develop the Star mine at Ilse.

The Captain slipped his moorings and drifted to Idaho. On what is now DeLamar Mountain he bought a group of claims and linked them with crosscut adits to make the Wilson mine. Christian and Louis Wahl of Chicago furnished most of the capital. In the fall of 1889 he succeeded in opening a large, efficient twenty-stamp mill on the site, which ended the need to haul ore up-creek to Silver City. The mill had a steel boiler fueled by coal from a deposit on Reynolds Creek and a 2,300-foot tram delivered the ore from the mine. DeLamar made $1.5 million in less than three years. He repaid his debts in Ilse fivefold.

Having proved the value of the mine, DeLamar sold it in 1891 to DeLamar Mining Co., Ltd. of London for $500,000 and a major share of the stock. The purchase was the only profitable British investment in the Idaho mines. The ore body was quarried through seven miles of adits; by 1896 the mine had produced $6 million in silver and gold.

The town of DeLamar roosted along both sides of the creek and had a population of 950 by 1896. A thirty-room hotel and a large bunkhouse for miners, along with nearly a hundred houses, occupied the site. Amenities included electric lights, water works, telephones, telegraph, and the *DeLamar Nugget* newspaper.

Captain J. R. DeLamar invested in highly successful mines in Bingham Canyon, Utah, and DeLamar, Nevada. His Nevada property was the leading gold mine in the state from 1892 to 1901 ($9.4 million).

The mining baron sold his mansion and moved to New York City; he returned two or three times a year to inspect his enterprise. In

Joseph R. DeLamar.

1893, at age fifty, he married Nellie Sands, the seventeen-year-old daughter of a New York druggist. The couple took his yacht, the *Fleetwing*, to Italy and Egypt, and settled in Paris for a time. A daughter, Alice Antoinette, was born there.

In 1895 Captain DeLamar filed for divorce and for custody of their child. He obtained both. The two of them returned to New York and lived in a mansion on Madison Ave., across from J. P. Morgan's residence. Joseph R. DeLamar died of pneumonia in 1918; his estate of $30 million made Alice one of the wealthiest girls in the U.S.

Alice DeLamar never married. She sold the New York mansion to the National Democratic Club for a headquarters and moved to a Park Ave. apartment. The peculiar events that life contrives for people caused her name to surface in an AP wireservice story on Christmas, 1979.

A retired Chicago businessman, whose hobby was tracing the whereabouts of lost stock certificates, had for years been trying to locate certificate No. 390 in the Texas Pacific Land Trust. The businessman had no idea of No. 390's location, but he knew its value. Transfers, mergers, and splits had converted the original shares into 83,000 shares worth $3.2 million. Additionally, $800,000 in dividends from the shares had been deposited in a custody account in a Dallas bank.

In 1979 an officer of the Wells Fargo Bank in San Francisco read a newspaper article in which the Chicago fellow speculated that the certificate was on the West Coast. He ordered a check of the bank's archives, and No. 390 was there. It had been sent to San Francisco when Wells Fargo's New York branch closed in 1904. Bank records showed the certificate belonged to Captain Joseph R. DeLamar.

Miss Alice DeLamar was located living in Palm Beach, Florida. She had two houses, lots of servants, and no living relatives. The find had little impact on her. When informed, she said, "It was not worth very much at the turn of the century. Yes, it seems very nice."

Earth Resources Co. began operating an open-pit silver mine in 1979 on the south side of DeLamar Mtn. The company mill can process 1,700 tons a day and in the first year it recovered 1.1 million ounces of silver and 18,000 ounces of gold. Maximum life for the new mine is estimated to be twenty years.

One can continue west down Jordan Creek another three miles to a junction, then drive northwest from the junction eleven miles to U.S. Highway 95, thirty-eight miles south of Marsing, Idaho.

DeLamar School.

Lower DeLamar, mine and mill in background.

Highway 78 continues southeast from the Silver City turnoff twenty-six miles to **Grand View.**

The exit for **C. J. Strike Dam** is 6.2 miles east of town, on the north side of the highway. The view area is one mile from the highway.

383

C. J. Strike is an earth-fill dam, named for a past-president of Idaho Power Co., and completed in 1952. It is located just below the confluence of the Bruneau with the Snake River.

A 582-foot bridge was built across the river to bring in the construction equipment. Core material amounting to 2.3 million cubic yards was excavated from the old river bed. Three welded penstocks, twenty-two feet in diameter and 400 feet long, carry water to the turbines that drive three 30,000 k.w. generators.

The highway extends east to Bruneau, twelve miles from the dam (see Highway 51, Bruneau). After sharing the roadbed with Highway 51 northeast for 6.6 miles, Highway 78 cleaves east. Two miles east of the junction with Highway 51 the access road to **Bruneau Dunes State Park** appears on the right.

Open year-round, Bruneau Dunes is the most unusual park in the state system; it was established in 1970 and covers 2,840 acres.

The site's major features are two large gray sand dunes that cover about 600 acres; the largest is 470 feet high. They occupy the Eagle Cove depression, an ancient meander scar of the Snake River. The sand, which was originally lava rock, began to collect in the cove 30,000 years ago, after the Bonneville Flood. It is blown off the plateau south of the depression and as the wind loses velocity over the cove, the heavier grains are dropped.

The two dunes have an unique crater between them, like a giant ant-lion trap, at the point where they merge. The reason for the pit is not completely understood; studies of the bimodal wind patterns (northwest-southeast) suggest that neither deposition nor a vortex motion occurs at the crater. The prevailing contrary winds do tend, however, to immobilize the dunes.

In 1952 the completion of the C. J. Strike Dam apparently raised the area's water table, and several handkerchief lakes appeared. The one at the base of the dunes will eventually destroy them through stabilization. Meanwhile, it has created an oasis for birds and small mammals.

The lake is a winter rest area for thousands of ducks; geese, teal, herons, blackbirds and muskrats are often seen along the shoreline. The sub-dune area is inhabited by coyotes, blacktail jackrabbits, white-tailed squirrels, and kangaroo rats.

Fishing from shore, or with paddle-boats, is permitted. The water has been stocked with bluegill sunfish, largemouth bass, and catfish.

Swimming is not recommended because of "swimmers' itch," caused by a microscopic larval parasite of a species of parasitic flat worm carried by waterfowl. It is a temporary discomfort, and the intrepid should simply towel vigorously after leaving the water, or shower promptly with water from another source.

The park has a small museum at the visitors center; tent and trailer sites are in the campground below the center. A five-mile hiking trail is also available.

Bruneau Dunes and lakelet.

Bruneau Dunes.

The highway continues east from the park ten miles to a bridge across the Snake River and 3.9 miles farther to **Hammett.**

Medbury, the precursor of Hammett, was laid out as an agricultural town by the Oregon Short Line; a depot and post office were established in 1883. In 1909 the site was renamed for Charles Hammett, one of the promoters of the King Hill irrigation project.

Highway 78 intersects I-84 two miles east of Hammett.

State Highway 81 from a junction with Highway 77 in Malta northerly and westerly via Declo to a junction with U.S. 30 in Burley. Route length: 33.9 miles.

Though Highway 81 begins at **Malta,** a paved road comes north from the Idaho-Utah stateline, through Bridge, to Malta. That road, and Highway 81, follow the Raft River Valley.

In the early 1800s the **Raft River** was a deep, muddy, swift stream that inconvenienced trappers and other, later travelers who had to cross it.

Peter Skene Ogden, John Work, and Milton Sublette were acquainted with the valley. John Work's trapping brigade spent a week in May, 1831, traveling up the river to its headwaters in the Raft River Mountains. On the the trip the men encountered a band of Blackfeet Indians and herds of bison.

The river intersected three trails of note and paralleled a fourth. The Oregon Trail crossed the mouth of the Raft River (now Lake Wolcott) along the Snake. The California Trail followed the west bank of the Raft to a point near later Malta; Benoni Hudspeth's Cutoff, established in 1849, forded the river near Malta; and a fourth route came northwest from Salt Lake City, down the Raft River Valley, and crossed the river near what is now Bridge, Idaho.

The highway travels 26.3 miles northwest from Malta to Declo, and joins U.S. 30 in Burley, 7.6 miles farther. There is an interchange to I-84.

386

Interstate 84 from the Oregon-Idaho state line southeast of Ontario, Oregon, via Caldwell, Nampa, Boise, and Mountain Home to the junction of I-86 east of Burley, then southeast to the Idaho-Utah border northeast of Snowville, Utah. Route length: 275.7 miles.

I-84 enters Idaho south of Fruitland, crosses the Snake River, and continues southeast 27.4 miles to Caldwell.

In 1883, when the tracks of the Oregon Short Line arrived, the site of **Caldwell** on the south shore of the Boise River was no more than an alkali flat daubed with sagebrush and greasewood.

The Idaho and Oregon Land Improvement Co., whose president, Alexander Caldwell, was an ex-U.S. Senator from Kansas, and whose vice-president was Robert "Pard" Strahorn, a publicity agent for the U.P. railroad, bought acreage along the tracks and sold lots for a townsite. The company also owned water rights to an irrigation ditch that was excavated south from the Boise River from 1887 to 1888.

Caldwell continued to grow. In January, 1890, the town was incorporated by order of the Ada County commissioners. Three years later the *Caldwell Tribune* slathered:

If you want a foothold in the coming town of Idaho, get into Caldwell as soon as possible. Come and see it and study the situation. Don't listen to anybody. Don't take anybody's word. Don't believe anything that you cannot see with your naked eye. Don't spend your money until you are convinced beyond doubt that the investment will pay. Caldwell is a straight business proposition. It is a cold-blooded, money-making consideration. You don't want to come here solely for your health and religion.

Good health doesn't sit well on an empty pocketbook, and salvation is accessible from every point of the compass, physically speaking. But your health will improve in Caldwell with the swelling of your assets, and salvation comes easier with prosperity.

In 1894 the town was voted seat of Canyon County, and within fifteen years the Interurban provided electric streetcar service between Caldwell and Boise. The trip required one hour and twenty minutes. (Service was discontinued in 1928.)

In 1908 completion of the Deer Flat dams and Lake Lowell six miles south of town provided irrigation for further agricultural development. The area became a farm-center for alfalfa and hybrid sweet-corn seed, sugar beets, beans, potatoes, onions, and hops. Canyon County, in fact, is one of the more productive agricultural counties in the U.S.

387

J. R. Simplot Co. began dehydrating onions in 1941 at a plant in Caldwell, then added potatoes during World War II. From this beginning the Food Division of Simplot Co. grew into one of the largest potato processing companies in the world. The division is headquartered in Caldwell; one plant produces frozen, dehydrofrozen, and dehydrated products, while the other produces only frozen foods. The company markets well over 100 processed potato items.

Caldwell has a number of sights of interest to a visitor. A large golf fairway adds an attractive greenbelt to the south side of the city. At So. Kimball and Grant Sts. one can enter the Memorial Park and view a sheltered, representative collection of antique farm implements.

Caldwell, Main St. between Sixth and Seventh Aves. in 1883.

Two log houses, moved to the park in the 1930s by the Native Daughters of Canyon County, are situated a few feet from the machinery. One cabin was built in 1864 by the three Johnston brothers, Dave, Dennis and Tom, bachelor ranchers who shared the cabin for fifty-two years. Pioneers recalled them as hospitable, immaculate housekeepers. (The Johnstons are buried together in the Canyon Hill graveyard.)

The other cabin also dates from 1864. It was built by Robert, John and Alex McKenzie near Middleton, with cottonwood logs and fitted with wood pegs. Alice McKenzie was born in the cabin.

From the park drive north on East Kimball Ave. to Main St. and northwest on Main one block to Seventh Ave.

388

The Union Pacific depot, visible on the right at the foot of So. Seventh Ave., was built in 1906-1907, a rather elaborate Queen Anne style building, even though much of its former decoration has been removed.

The Saratoga Hotel, built in 1903-1904 on the corner at 624 Main St., is a local landmark. The four-story structure was erected by the well-known pioneer merchant Howard Sebree, who established a chain of hardware and farm implement stores along the Utah and Northern and OSL railroad lines. From Dillon, Montana, he sent his son to Caldwell to open a branch store, then in 1888 decided to move there himself.

The architect of the Idanha Hotel in Boise also designed the Saratoga, and at one time it also had octagonal turrets at each end

Caldwell flood in February, 1910.

of its Seventh Ave. facade, along with a massive canopy over the Main St. entrance. Sebree became the president of the Stock Growers and Traders' Bank and mayor of the town. (It was in room 19 of this hotel that Harry Orchard lodged while plotting the assassination of ex-governor Frank Steunenberg [see I-84, Boise].)

The ground floor of the hotel is now occupied by the altogether unusual Saratoga Restaurant; its interior is a thesaurus of curios.

Continue on Main St. one block to So. Fifth Ave., turn northeast one block across the railroad tracks and southeast onto Albany Street.

The house at 823 Albany St. was built in 1890 by local contractors for William Isaacs, a sheep rancher, just before his marriage. The *Caldwell Tribune* called it "the finest house in town."

One block east from Albany at 816 Belmont St., on a lava-rock foundation, is a two-story, frame house that was built in 1890 by a Presbyterian minister, William Boone, founder and president (1891 to 1936) of the College of Idaho.

The two-story house at 904 Belmont St. was built for John Johnson in the same year as the Boone House. With its octagonal corner turrets, wraparound porch, and toothed shingles, it is the best example of Queen Anne architecture in town.

To visit the oldest college in the state, take Tenth Ave. southwest six blocks to Cleveland Blvd. and follow Cleveland southeast ten blocks to the **College of Idaho** campus.

In 1891 this private college held its first classes in the Presbyterian Church at 901 Albany St., moved to an Academy building at Albany St. and Eleventh Ave., then in 1910 moved to the present campus.

The college, accredited since 1922, is a four-year, coeducational institution with nonsectarian instruction in the liberal arts. Masters degree programs are offered in education and counseling; enrollment is about 800. Two members of its original eight-man faculty became governors of the state.

The **Evans Gem and Mineral Collection,** the finest one in the state, is on display in the Boone science building on campus. The collection was assembled by Glen and Ruth Evans who made and sold fishing flies for a living, but collected rocks as an avocation and in twenty-five years gathered one of the larger private collections in the Northwest.

Combining their pursuit of bright and unusual materials for their fly-fishing business with a search for rocks and gems, the Evans managed to collect over 5,000 specimens from more than 100 countries. Many of the rocks were obtained by trading, but the couple also collected on their own in forty-two countries. Glen preferred to finish the minerals in spherical shapes because that form shows a rock from every angle. Ruth specialized in making facets and cabochons. She served on the College of Idaho board of trustees for fifteen years, and it was her idea to give the collection to the Boone science center.

Housed in two rooms, every item labeled, and displayed in fifty-three glass cases, the Evans collection is more colorful than a basket of Easter eggs.

Interstate 84 continues southeast 6.3 miles to **Nampa,** a town that got its start in 1883 when the Oregon Short Line put the name on its station house and water tank on the site. The derivation is rather vague, though local historians attribute it to "nambe," or "nambuh," Shoshone words for "foot" or "moccasin print."

In 1887, Gardner Lane, a Boston millionaire and vice-president of the Union Pacific, was persuaded by J. A. McGee and Alexander Duffes to build a branch line of the railroad from Nampa to Boise and to finance extension of the Ridenbaugh Canal from the Boise region to the Nampa area. Duffes homesteaded 160 acres bisected by the tracks, and platted the townsite. Nampa became a regional railroad center.

Col. William Dewey (see Highway 78, Dewey) became interested in the site in 1896, after Boise businessmen reneged on an agreement to provide right-of-way and land for a hotel at the terminus of a railroad that he had promised to build to the mines at Silver City. Dewey left Boise madder than a bull in bumblebees and vowed to make cheatgrass grow in the city's streets.

In Nampa he bought about 2,000 lots from Alex Duffes and began construction of a majestic hotel called the Dewey Palace. Work on the eighty-one-room hotel with four stories, 200 feet long and 40 feet wide, began in June, 1901. A pair of verandahs ran the length of the facade, and at each end was a cupola tower sheeted with copper that could be seen in Caldwell – "just to enable residents of that place to keep Nampa in mind." The Dewey Palace Hotel cost $243,000. The interior had ceiling frescos and oak paneling, and the facility included a banquet hall, ballroom, bowling alley, billiard room, bar, barber shop and laundry; it had its own well and water tank, an electric generator, elevators, lights, steam heat, and hot water. Col. Dewey and his family occupied an apartment suite in the hotel.

The grand opening in February, 1903, was attended by 2,000 persons including Senator Borah, the governor, and fifty-nine members of the legislature. Three months later William Dewey was dead at age seventy-nine. The hotel closed in 1956 and was demolished in 1963.

As for the railroad, Dewey, like Schubert, had started something he could not finish. The Boise, Nampa and Owyhee Railroad never got past Murphy, a distance of thirty miles.

The Oregon Short Line business in Nampa, however, grew so rapidly that in 1903 a new depot was opened at the north end of Twelfth Ave. At a cost of $35,000, it was the finest depot in the state. The structure, which is regarded as Idaho's outstanding

example of Baroque revival architecture, now contains the
Canyon County Historical Museum. (To see the U.P. depot
that replaced this one in 1925, turn northwest to 1211 First St.
North.)

*Dewey Palace Hotel
in Nampa.*

*Col. Dewey, wife
Isabel (right) and
daughter, Marie
(center), in their
hotel suite in 1903.
Dewey had five
children.*

Northwest Nazarene College, founded in 1913, is located in
Nampa on Twelfth Ave. Rd. at East Dewey Ave. Since 1937 the

school has offered a four-year accredited curriculum. It is an institution of the Church of the Nazarene and serves all western states other than California. The four-acre campus includes twenty buildings.

Hay harvest in 1915 between Nampa and Caldwell.

Nampa sugar beet refinery.

The largest beet sugar plant in the U.S. is located on the northwest utskirts of Nampa, visible on the north side of I-84. Amalgamated ugar Co., headquartered in Utah, built the factory in 1942.

During the fall, the plant slices and diffuses sugar beets twenty-ur hours a day; the juice is piped into holding tanks and is later refined into White Satin sugar, which is temporarily stored in silos. Pulp from the beets is mixed with molasses, dried, and sold to farmers as livestock feed.

Though sugar beets are a relatively temperamental crop, requiring intensive cultivation and vulnerable to leafhoppers and nematodes, Idaho usually ranks third in production among the states.

Fourteen miles east of Nampa, I-84 enters the outskirts of **Boise.** As early as 1811 the area was visited by fur companies, and according to Peter Skene Ogden's journal, his French-Canadian trappers had applied the name Boissie ("wooded") to the river by 1824. Washington Irving's *The Adventures of Captain Bonneville* popularized the name.

After the Ward and Otter party massacres, in which forty-six emigrants were killed along the Oregon Trail between the Boise and Snake Rivers in a half-dozen years (1854-1860), General George Wright, commander of the Department of the Pacific, recommended that the U.S. Army establish a fort in the region. The Civil War delayed implementation of his proposal, but in January, 1863, the Secretary of War authorized the new post.

Commander of the Oregon Department, Benjamin Alvord dispatched Major Pinckney Lugenbeel from Fort Vancouver, Washington Territory, to select a site "some forty miles east of the old fort up the Boise River." (Old Fort Boise, a Hudson's Bay Company post on the Snake River, was abandoned in 1854 – see Highway 95, Parma.)

Major Lugenbeel chose a site (on Fort St.) near the intersection of the Oregon Trail with the road between the Owyhee and Boise Basin mines; moreover, the location had the necessary grass, water, wood and stone. On the Fourth of July, 1863, with three companies of infantry and one of cavalry, Lugenbeel set to work building quarters for five companies. He built a mule-driven sawmill on Cottonwood Creek, got a lime kiln underway, and opened a sandstone quarry at Table Rock. His greatest problem was the lure of the Boise Basin mines – fifty-odd men deserted within the first few months.

As soon as news of Lugenbeel's selection spread through the valley, eight men met in Tom Davis' cabin on the Boise River and laid out a townsite between his homestead and the new fort. The main street ran parallel to the river for three-quarters of a mile, with five blocks on each side, and each block had an alleyway dividing its twelve lots. By donating choice lots to prospective businessmen the founders attracted fresh settlers.

394

Additionally, in a deft political maneuver aided by Governor Caleb Lyon, whom the historian H. H. Bancroft called "a revolving light on the coast of scampdom," the new settlement managed to swipe the territorial capital from Lewiston in 1864, at the second meeting of the legislature (see Highway 12, Lewiston).

Boise City in 1866.

By the end of the 1860s Boise had over 400 buildings and about 1,000 inhabitants. The population during the early years had more ups and downs than a gold scales – reflecting the fortunes of the mines – but as Boise's agricultural base grew, it became decreasingly dependent upon the mining camps. In 1887 a branch line of the Oregon Short Line arrived from Nampa and provided a needed outlet for produce. Production was given a real boost in 1908 with the completion of the Diversion Dam and the New York Canal (see Highway 21); by 1910 Ada County had 1,500 irrigated farms and a farm population of 11,500.

In 1961 the legislature repealed Boise's charter in order that the city could expand its boundaries. Offices for numerous federal agencies are now located here, as well as corporate headquarters for businesses such as Morrison-Knudsen Co., Boise Cascade, J. R. Simplot, Ore-Ida, Albertsons, and Trus Joist.

Though twice as large as any other Idaho city, Boise meets Cyril Connolly's criterion, however, that "no city should be too large to walk out of in a morning."

The tour suggested here is only one corner of the blanket, but it conveys a fair sense of the city's diversity. It is arranged for a visitor approaching Boise on Interstate 84, East; travelers on I-84, West, should take the Franklin-West Boise Exit (No. 49) that merges with Main St. Passengers from the municipal airport enter the city via Vista Ave. and Capitol Blvd., which intersects with Main St. three blocks southeast of the Idanha Hotel, where the description begins. (The twenty-two mile route can be reduced to fifteen miles if the trip to Table Rock is eliminated.)

Main St. in Boise, between Sixth and Seventh Sts., in the 1880s.

Follow the city-center signs as Interstate 84 divides at Exit 49, on the outskirts of Boise. The left, or north lanes, lead downtown. Business Route I-84 joins Fairview Ave., which becomes Main St. at Sixteenth St.

The Chateau-style **Idanha Hotel** on the northeast corner of Main and Tenth Sts. is a local landmark. Opening on New Year's Day, 1901, the hotel was the first six-story building in the state, and contained Idaho's first elevator. Designed by a Scotch architect at a cost of $125,000, it contained 103 rooms. Among its important guests were Theodore Roosevelt and Ethel Barrymore. In the 1970s preservationists rescued the Idanha from an urban renewal project. Refurbished, it continues to provide rooms decorated with a certain nostalgic elegance.

In mid-block at 908 Main St. is **The Book Shop,** the best bookstore in Idaho.

396

Two blocks farther east, at Capitol Blvd., stands the tallest building in the state, the 267-foot **Idaho First National Bank.** It was completed in 1978 by a subsidiary of Morrison-Knudsen Co. Idaho First, established in 1864, began in a building just one block away. The bank's administrative offices occupy about 60 percent of the available space.

Angled to avoid direct sunlight, and ventilated with a computer-controlled system, the building allegedly uses one-third less energy than others its size.

Hardware store fire at 745 Main St. in 1899.

The **Egyptian** (Ada) **Theater** is located on the northwest corner of Main and Capitol; it is the best example of Egyptian revival architecture in the Northwest. Inspired by the "Egyptomania" resulting from the discovery of Tutankhamen's tomb in 1922, as well as by Grauman's Egyptian Theater in Los Angeles, the building was designed by the Boise architect Frederick Hummel and erected in 1926-1927 for $160,000. This structure was also threatened by redevelopment, but was saved through civic concern. The theater has a working pipe organ that was used to furnish sirens, horns, bird calls and music for silent films.

Continue east on Main to Third and Second Sts. The grounds on the left encompass the **U.S. Assay Office,** a National Historic Landmark. Authorized by the federal government in 1869 and opened in 1872, it was one of the more important buildings in the state.

HISTORICAL SITE

During the 1860s miners in Silver City and Boise Basin were annoyed by the cost and inconvenience of shipping their bullion to distant mints. Considerable pressure was exerted to establish a U.S. mint in Idaho Territory, but Congress selected The Dalles, Oregon, as the new location, then abandoned that plan upon completion of the transcontinental railroad, on the theory that gold and silver could now be shipped with ease. Idaho had to settle for a federal assay office.

The site was donated by Alexander Rossi, who served briefly as the first assayer at a salary of $1,800 a year. Nearly cubical, the building cost $73,000; its sandstone walls are two feet thick, and heavy bars covered the windows. The first floor contained the assayer's offices, vaults, safes, and melting rooms; the second floor served as living quarters for the chief assayer, and the basement held the guard's room, as well as supplies and fuel.

Principal business of the assay office was the evaluation of gold and silver in order that miners could price their product; value was determined by the percentage of precious metals in selected samples. For deposits weighing less than five ounces, the assay charge was 50¢, and for $1.00 the office would ascertain the value of a prospector's ore samples.

By 1888 the Boise Assay Office was willing to purchase all bullion or dust containing over 500 parts gold, and paid for it in "coin or exchange." Gold was valued at the established legal price; silver, at the market price. A small charge for melting and refining was deducted from the value of the lot, and when sufficient metal accumulated in mint bars, it was shipped to a U.S. mint for coinage. From 1895 to 1906 deposits averaged over $1.5 million annually. The staff increased to eleven men.

From the beginning of World War I, however, business declined steadily. In June, 1933, the government closed the Boise Assay Office, along with those of Helena and Salt Lake City, and closed the mint at Carson City as well.

The U.S. Forest Service acquired the building as headquarters for the Boise and Payette National Forests. At that time the iron bars were removed from the windows, and six new openings were made in the rear wall. In 1972 the historic structure was given to the state, its care entrusted to the Idaho Historical Society.

Open weekdays from 9:00 A.M. to 5:00 P.M., a room on the ground floor of the assay office contains the Henry and Fumiko Fujii collection of western rocks – a rockhound's delight.

The Alfred and Victoria Eoff mansion can be seen on the left, at 140 Main St., just past the assay office. It was designed by J. F. Tourtellotte in 1897 and cost its owner, a banker, $10,000. In 1908-1909, it served James Brady as the governor's mansion. (Carriage block and hitching post are visible on the Second St.-side.)

The Colonial revival house next door, at 110 Main St., was built in 1903-1904. Its owner, Timothy Regan, held interests in the Oro Fino and Golden Chariot mines at Silver City. The interior is paneled with oak, birch, maple, and sycamore.

Three blocks farther east, Main St. merges with **Warm Springs Ave.** During the two decades spanning the turn of the century the avenue became known as the most prestigious residential area of Boise. A geothermal well was developed in 1890, near the penitentiary at the eastern end of the street. Flowing at 800,000 gallons a day, the 170 degree F. water was used to establish a natatorium, and to heat residences along the Avenue. Pumps eventually increased the flow to 1.2 million gallons, and nine miles of pipe served the residential area at a charge of $3.00 a month for large houses. The system still heats about 200 homes.

A trolley line was installed on Warm Springs Ave. out to the natatorium, and substantial houses were built eastward along the tracks. Representing a wide range of architectural styles, the houses have been well preserved by appreciative owners.

The largest building on the Avenue, the Warm Springs Center, at the corner of Warm Springs and Bruce St., was formerly the Childrens' Home. Cynthia Mann donated the block in 1920; Tourtellotte & Co. designed the structure, and women's groups and the state legislature supported it. The home cared for abused and orphaned children. In addition to school rooms, it contained kitchen, dining hall, dormitories, and infirmary. A private group now owns the center and uses it to assist disturbed children and their families.

One block east, on the left at the corner of 904 Warm Springs and Elm St., stands the Queen Anne style house of Joseph Kinney. He owned a local saloon and occupied the house in 1904.

The attractive, English country-house, screened by trees at 929 Warm Springs, was designed by the Spokane architect Kirtland Cutter in 1925. It was built for C. C. Anderson, owner of the Golden Rule store on Main St., a mercantile enterprise that he expanded into a chain of twenty-one stores in five western states.

Just east of the Anderson house, on the same side of the street at 1009 Warm Springs, is the Mission-style residence built in 1911 for William Regan, son of Timothy Regan. The son was a director of the Boise Artesian Water Co.; he and his wife raised seven children in this house before selling it in 1939.

The three-story **Moore-Cunningham mansion** (Laura Cunningham was Moore's daughter), on the southeast corner at Warm Springs and Walnut Ave., is among the more admired residences in the city. Designed in 1891 by James King, a Boise architect from West Virginia, for $17,000, the French Chateau style structure contains fourteen rooms, some of them paneled with cherry, oak, and redwood. A founder of the Idaho First National Bank, C. W. Moore was also president of the water company, and his was the first house in the country to be heated by natural hot water. (The five-acre arboretum behind the house was donated to the city by Laura Cunningham.)

One block farther north on the right at 1205 Warm Springs, stands a fifteen-room, Georgian revival house built in 1901 for R. M. Davidson, a mining millionaire from Butte, Montana. The granite came from a nearby quarry owned by the architect. Seven Davidson children were raised in the house, which cost $15,000.

In 1896 a Boise attorney, Selden Kingsbury, contracted for the house at 1225 Warm Springs with the same architect responsible for the Moore-Cunningham mansion. The sandstone was quarried and dressed by an English sculptor and his two young sons.

At 1308 Warm Springs, on the left two doors from the corner of the next block, is a fine example of Georgian revival architecture. It was created in 1906 for Lindley Cox, a partner in a Boise land development firm.

The attractive Jacob Wagner house, on the same side of the street at 1420 Warm Springs, was built in 1894 for $1,500, in the Queen Anne style. In 1977 it was moved to this location when threatened by the expansion of St. Luke's Hospital about a dozen blocks west of here.

The four-story Natatorium was located four blocks farther east, just south of the Trolley House at 1821 Warm Springs. Built in 1892, with twin six-story towers and an enclosed 125-foot long swimming pool beneath eighty-foot curved, wooden arches, it was the most spectacular building in the city. Patrons arrived by trolley and could rent a swim suit, towel, and dressing room for 25¢.

With the pool covered, the site served half a dozen governors as the inaugural ballroom. White City amusement park developed alongside the Nat and provided diversions such as a miniature railway, Ferris wheel, movie theater, skating rink, and an ostrich farm. The Nat was torn down in 1934 after severe wind damage.

Continue 0.4 miles east on Warm Springs and turn left onto Penitentiary Road. The **Old Idaho Penitentiary,** the most fascinating tourist attraction in the city, and aside from Alcatraz, the most informative prison tour in the West, is located at the north end of this street. In 1974, six months after it closed, this outpost of the past was added to the National Register of Historic Places and converted to a public exhibit, largely through the foresight of Arthur Hart, director of the Idaho Historical Society.

The cornerstone for the penitentiary was laid on July 4, 1870; the *Idaho Tri-Weekly Statesman* commented, "A general attendance of every age and sex is requested to view an edifice that may someday be their home – and not even the wisest knows how soon." In 1872 the first prisoners were admitted.

Warm Springs Natatorium.

State Penitentiary in Boise.

401

Open from 1:00 P.M. to 4:00 P.M. daily, the complex provides a self-guided tour that includes the maximum-security building, the 1950 cellhouse, solitary confinement cells, – and outside, the women's ward. A slide show precedes the tour.

Tales of some of the convicts are revealed in a display room next to the entrance; many, such as those of Lady Bluebeard and Harry Orchard, are interesting; others, such as those of Tambiago, Diamondfield Jack, and an eleven year-old boy who served nine years, are poignant.

A **museum of electricity** in Idaho, as well as an outstanding **transportation museum** are also housed on the grounds.

The tour leaflet is sufficiently detailed to require no supplement here. Three incidents involving the prison, however, can be clarified.

Two riots occurred during the last years of the penitentiary. The first took place in August, 1971, when daytime temperatures exceeded 100 degrees F. Two buildings were burned at a cost of $25,000.

The second riot occurred on the evening of March 7, 1973, while the warden met with the inmate council to hear complaints about the transfer of a prisoner to another penitentiary; fires broke out in four buildings. The Boise fire department, with four trucks and forty firemen, controlled the flames after two hours, but damages amounted to $100,000.

Another event of interest, mentioned near the east wall of the compound, involved the attempted escape of three prisoners. In June, 1973, they chipped through the concrete floor of a storage building and began a tunnel intended to surface beyond the wall twenty-five feet away. Working evenings and weekends with a shovel, hoe, and spikes, the men carried the dirt in gunny sacks to the fire-gutted ruins and dispersed it. Guards eventually detected the new soil, and with surveillance and rollcalls uncovered the culprits when the tunnel was about half completed.

A short hike up the trail to Table Rock, northeast of the prison, leads to the site where convicts confined to "hard labor" quarried sandstone for the penitentiary walls, as well as for other state institutions.

The resplendent Queen Anne mansion across the street from the prison entrance is the **Bishops' House.** Built in 1889, and enlarged with a third story in the 1890s, it was designed by James

402

King, who also drew the plans for the Moore and Kingsbury houses noted on Warm Springs Ave.

Rt. Rev. Daniel Tuttle was the first Episcopal bishop of the missionary district of Idaho (1866-1886). In 1903 he became Presiding Bishop of the Protestant Episcopal Church in America, a position he held until his death in 1923.

The house was remodeled and expanded by Bishop Funsten (1899-1918) for his wife and five daughters. Among the guests alleged to have used its upstairs rooms were "Buffalo Bill" Cody, the singer Marian Anderson, and Senator William Borah.

Threatened with destruction in 1974, the house was preserved by an extensive, voluntary community effort, and was moved from Idaho and Second Sts. to its present location in 1976. (Telephone wires on Warm Springs Ave. had to be removed.) It is now leased from the Idaho Historical Society by Friends of the Bishops' House, a non-profit corporation that opens the facility for public and private functions.

Return west on Warm Springs Ave. to Broadway, turn left onto Myrtle St. The six-story building on the east side of Broadway at Myrtle is the **Morrison-Knudsen Co. headquarters,** built in 1969-1970.

Morris Knudsen, a Danish immigrant and Nebraska farmer, came to Idaho in 1905 to work on the New York Canal with a team of horses and a fresno scraper. On the project the fifty year-old Knudsen met twenty-seven year-old Harry Morrison, who had started as a timekeeper on the Minidoka Dam on the Snake River, and was now a concrete superintendent for the Reclamation Service – the two hit it off like finger and thumb. In 1912, with $600 in capital, a few horses and scrapers, and a dozen wheelbarrows, they decided to form their own construction company.

Their first job was a subcontract for $14,000 worth of work on a pump plant near Grand View, Idaho; they lost $1,200 but gained experience. For several years the firm built irrigation canals, logging roads and railways, then incorporated in 1923, when the gross revenues for the year reached the million dollar mark for the first time.

During World War II Morrison-Knudsen Co. built airfields, storage depots, and ships; it expanded into foreign construction – an effort that now includes over sixty countries. M-K Co. built the locks and channels on the St. Lawrence Seaway, the Distant Early Warning System, Minuteman missile silos, the Manned Spacecraft Center, and over 100 major dams. (Those in Idaho include Deadwood,

403

Cascade, Cabinet Gorge, C. J. Strike, Anderson, the Hells Canyon complex, and Teton.)

Although Morris Knudsen died in 1943, and Harry Morrison in 1971, their company has fulfilled contracts for heavy construction worth billions of dollars and has become one of the largest engineering-construction firms in the U.S.

Continue on East Myrtle 0.3 miles, then turn left on Third St. into **Julia Davis Park,** the oldest park in the city. In 1862 Tom Davis planted a thousand apple trees on this tract, and he and his wife often gave the fruit to emigrants on the nearby Oregon Trail. In 1907, after Julia's death, Davis gave the river-front acreage to the city as a memorial.

The 110-acre campus of **Boise State Univ.** is located on the south side of the park and the Boise River. BSU began as a private junior college in 1932. It opened with eight faculty members and seventy students under the wings of the Protestant Episcopal Church, and though accredited in 1933 by an inspection team from the Univ. of Idaho, church financial support was withdrawn because of the Depression in 1934.

Boise Junior College (now BSU) in the early 1940s.

With community aid Boise Junior College survived until 1939, when the state legislature passed an enabling act that allowed formation of tax-supported junior college districts.

Following the decision the city decided to locate the college on the old municipal airport, and in 1940 BJC moved to its present campus from St. Margaret's on Idaho St. In 1965 the legislature expanded the school's curriculum to that of a four-year college, and nine years later it was given university status. The campus now has the largest enrollment in the state.

Follow Julia Davis Dr. past the Boise Zoo 0.3 miles to the **State Historical Museum.** Established in 1950, and expanded substantially in 1982, the museum contains informative displays presented imaginatively. After a walk through exhibits that remind one that the old days were as inconvenient as they were picturesque, and that one is indebted, in the words of Lisel Mueller, "to the poor who didn't know they were poor, and to the brave who didn't know they were brave," return to the museum parking area.

From the west side of the museum turn right on Capitol Blvd. When built in 1924-1925, the Union Pacific depot visible at the southwest end of the Blvd. was considered the finest example of Spanish Colonial architecture in the state. A Salt Lake City firm constructed the building from local sandstone.

In 1883, confident the Oregon Short Line had to come through their city anyway, the Boise townspeople refused a request by the

Arrival of the first train at the Oregon Short Line depot in 1925.

railroad for a right-of-way subsidy of $30,000. Instead, the railroad went through Nampa, and for forty years Boise suffered the indignity of a "stub" line. In 1922 the city gave the OSL a right-of-way and $400,000 for the honor of a main line, which arrived in April, 1925. (In 1936 the OSL name was merged into Union Pacific.)

405

Drive northeast eight blocks on Capitol Blvd. to the **State Capitol Building,** an imitation of the national capitol, but nevertheless worth a visit.

The central section, built in a standard neo-classical pattern, was erected between 1905 and 1912. Sandstone from the quarry at Table Rock was laid over a steel framework to form the 208-foot dome. In 1919-1920 the east and west wings were added for the Senate and House, which brought the cost of the building to $2 million.

Large green and white Corinthian columns grace the rotunda; made from scagliola, a mixture of marble dust, gypsum and glue, they were built by Italian craftsmen brought to Boise for the job. Four types of marble, from Alaska, Georgia, Vermont, and Italy, have been used for the interior.

First floor of the Capitol rotunda under construction in 1906.

The ground floor contains a mineral display and various state agency and trade association exhibits. A glass case on the second floor holds a gilded equestian statue of George Washington. Known as the Charles Ostner statue, it was carved from pine over a four-year period by an Austrian immigrant, who first modeled the piece in snow, while working as a miner in the Florence Basin.

To obtain Washington's likeness, Ostner used a U.S. postage stamp. He gave the statue to Idaho Territory in 1869; it stood outside on the capitol grounds for sixty-five years before it was restored and brought indoors. The legislature granted the sculptor $2,500 for his effort.

Trees planted by a half-dozen presidents landscape the capitol lawn, as does a small Douglas fir that was carried to the moon on an Apollo flight.

Across Jefferson St. from the main entrance to the capitol is a small wedge of grass known as **Steunenberg Park.** Events leading to the erection of the Steunenberg memorial statue there involve the most intriguing trial in the history of the state, and one of the more unusual cases in the annals of American jurisprudence. Here is a shorthand version of the story.

A graduate of Iowa State College, Frank Steunenberg was a printer and compositor before he moved to Caldwell with his younger brother in 1887 and purchased the *Caldwell Tribune*. Steunenberg was a delegate to the Idaho Constitutional Convention in 1889, then in 1890 was chosen as a Democratic representative to the state congress. In 1896, after two terms on the Caldwell Board of Trustees, he was elected as the youngest governor of Idaho by the largest margin ever given a candidate for the office, 80 percent.

As the following incidents show, Steunenberg had uncommon character. On the ground that it is "useless adornment," he refused to wear a tie, even when conferring with the President. In another situation, on receiving prompt service in a railroad dining car, which he believed was occasioned by the sight of his diamond ring, he removed the ring and never again wore it in public.

Governor Steunenberg held office in a clamorous period. Because of the Panic of 1893, all but 10 percent of the purchase contracts for Idaho school lands were in default. Moreover, the Idaho National Guard was off in the Philippines fighting the Spanish-American War; the sheep and cattle ranchers of southern Idaho had their hands on their holsters half of the time, and the mine labor war erupted in the Coeur d'Alene valley (see Highway 4, Gem, and I-90, Kellogg).

The governor, though sympathetic to unions and a union man himself, felt compelled in May, 1899, to declare martial law in the

Coeur d'Alene district. Aware that Bunker Hill Co. had violated state laws, he was also concerned that those responsible for violence be prosecuted. In 1900, when a Congressional inquiry investigated the use of federal troops in Shoshone County, the Governor had to testify for a month in Washington, D.C. The majority report concluded that the government's actions had been proper.

After his second term, Governor Steunenberg stepped down from office and backed the candidacy of his successor, Frank Hunt. Steunenberg resisted William Borah's efforts to get him to run for Congress. "Politics is a dirty business," he remarked.

The ex-governor returned to his affairs in Caldwell, which included the Commercial Bank and the organization of the Barber Lumber Co. Five years later, on the evening of December 30, 1905, as he opened the gate in front of his house, he triggered a dynamite bomb that took his life. As his brother carried him into the house, Steunenburg said, "They finally got me, John, it's the Coeur d'Alene. I can't live." Twenty minutes later, he died.

The Caldwell police were not long in arresting Harry Orchard, alias Albert Horsley, a man whose activities at the Saratoga Hotel had aroused suspicions. Plaster, acid, and fishline found in his room, in addition to dynamite and burglar tools located in Orchard's luggage at the railroad depot, provided sufficient proof of his guilt.

Three weeks later, while awaiting trial in the state penitentiary at Boise, Orchard was approached by James McParland, a Pinkerton Agency detective who had destroyed the "Molly McGuires," a terrorist miners' organization in Pennsylvania, by acting as a stool pigeon. Convinced that Stuenenberg's death was the result of a conspiracy by the Western Federation of Miners, McParland held sessions with the murderer, and after pointing out that the state would undoubtedly hang him, used artful flattery and promises of special consideration to obtain a confession from Orchard that implicated the "inner circle" of the WFM. (Though his guilt is questionable, Orchard also confessed to seventeen other murders.)

Keeping the confession secret, McParland went to Colorado, and in complicity with the state governor, kidnapped the officers of the WFM, Charles Moyer and Bill Haywood, and their advisor, George Pettibone, on a special train back to Idaho, where the men were imprisoned in the state penitentiary. (The U.S. Supreme Court later ruled that although the seizure had been illegal, once the men were in Idaho's custody, there was no legal remedy.)

In the prosecutor's estimate, Big Bill Haywood was the most-wanted of the defendants. Born in a Salt Lake City boarding house in 1869; he went to work in the mines of Humboldt County,

Nevada, before he was old enough to vote. From Nevada he drifted north to Silver City, Idaho, and got a job in the Blaine mine pushing an ore car to support his family. His hand was crushed in an accident with one of the cars, but in 1898 he was elected to represent the Silver City Miners' Union at the WFM convention held in Salt Lake City. Elected secretary-treasurer of the WFM at the meeting, he moved to Denver. Haywood became a symbol of the working class – in the words of John Dos Passos, "... the wants of all the workers were his wants, he was the spokesman of the West, of the cowboys and the lumberjacks and the harvesthands and the miners." In 1906, while sitting in the Ada County jail (where the defendants had been transferred), Haywood was nominated on the Socialist Party ticket for governor of Colorado and received 16,000 votes.

As lawyers began to circle around the case, President Theodore Roosevelt became indirectly involved. Embroiled in a feud with E. H Harriman at the time, the President released a letter to the press that attacked Harriman's attitude as that of a man "at least as undesirable a citizen as Debs, or Moyer, or Haywood." Labor groups assailed his characterization, and while Roosevelt made no further comment concerning the case, he was kept informed of the trial developments through personal communication with Senator William Borah, and by letters from Governor Frank Gooding. (Gooding informed the President that the state had infiltrated the defense counsel's staff with a secret Pinkerton agent who was so trusted that he was used to poll the jury!) As an expression of support, Roosevelt sent his Secretary of War to Idaho to campaign for Gooding's re-election.

Haywood's was the first case to be tried, a trial that was the focus of national attention for two months. Clarence Darrow, counsel for the defense, opened with the statement, "Every illegitimate child born west of the Mississippi has been wrapped in its swaddling clothes, hurried to Denver, and laid on the doorstep of the WFM."

Chief prosecutor was James Hawley, a most able attorney, who had, incidentally, suggested the organization of the WFM to its founders a few years earlier. William Borah, about to begin an illustrious career in the U.S. Senate, served as assistant prosecutor.

Orchard's testimony was convincing, but his confession was obtained under impeachable circumstances, and his only corroborating witness retracted his confession before the trial. In the end, the all-male jury deliberated twenty hours, then delivered a verdict of not-guilty.

The trial was significant enough to deserve some footnotes. That Darrow and Borah attained subsequent fame is well known; Hawley became governor of the state (1911-1912); Pettibone was acquitted; Moyer was released without trial. Haywood, continually involved in labor strife, was convicted in 1917 under the wartime Espionage Act (along with ninty-four other IWW members), and after two years in Leavenworth, while awaiting decision on a new trial, jumped bail and fled to Russia, where he died in 1928. At his request, half of his ashes were buried in the wall of the Kremlin, and the other half in the Waldheim Cemetery at Chicago, alongside the remains of the Haymarket anarchists.

The Haywood trial: (left to right) Harry Orchard, Leon Whitzen, Peter Breen, Clarence Darrow, Haywood's mother, and Bill Haywood. (Hawley and Borah had their backs to the camera.)

Harry Orchard was sentenced to hang, but the sentence was commuted to life imprisonment in the state penitentiary. He became a Seventh-day Adventist, repented his crimes and in 1922 sought parole. Senator Frank Gooding, James Hawley, and the family of Frank Steunenberg wrote letters in support of his application. A brother, Charles Steunenberg, however, wrote the *Idaho Statesman* to protest the release, and his letter sparked an outcry sizable enough to deny the pardon. Orchard died in prison in 1954 at eighty-eight. He is buried in Morris Hill cemetery at Boise, where Hawley's grave is also located.

410

Since none of the figures in the case ever changed his story, many questions linger.

The statue that memorializes Frank Stuenenberg carries its own curious story. In 1927 an association of thirteen men granted a commission of $12,500 to the sculptor Gilbert Riswold for the effigy.

Riswold was born in South Dakota, and as a youngster made fence-post sculptures around the family homestead. At eighteen he entered Chicago Art Institute. While there, he attended a summer art colony where he met a girl named Anna, and two years later, without even a street address, he went to the west-side of Chicago

View from the Capitol dome of Steunenberg park and statue in the early 1930s.

and began looking for her.

Anna had a dream; in the morning she told her sister, "The redhead is in town." Riswold, walking the streets the next day, saw Anna's sister looking out a window, and recognizing the family resemblance, knocked on the door. Five years later, when the sculptor received his first commission, he and Anna were married.

Riswold cast the figure of Stephen Douglas that stands in front of the capitol building in Springfield, Illinois, and he had worked on the Mormon Battalion Monument in Temple Square, Salt Lake City, for nine years when he learned of the Idaho competition for the Steunenberg Memorial. He won the award in May, 1927; the statue was unveiled in December of the same year.

Shortly after the piece was finished, Riswold suffered a stroke; he died in 1938, without ever having recovered his health. Anna, still living in San Diego in 1982, was unable to attend the dedication of the Steunenberg statue – it was the only work of her husband that she never saw.

On the north side of the Capitol, across State St. is the two-story hall of the Grand Army of the Republic, built in 1892, saved by an act of the legislature in the 1960s, added to the National Register, and now used as the Garrett Photography studio.

Boise Barracks (Fort Boise) in about 1870.

From the Capitol turn left (northwest) on Jefferson St. one-half block then right on Eighth St. The sandstone structure on the right, at Eighth and State Sts., is **St. Michael's Episcopal Cathedral,** built in 1899-1902 from designs provided by the national Episcopal Church; its stained-glass window on the east wall is from the Tiffany Studios of N.Y. In 1949 the Memorial Peace Tower was added.

Three blocks farther north, at Eighth and Hays Sts., **St. John's Cathedral** occupies the northwest corner. Designed in the Romanesque style at a cost of $246,000 in 1906-1920, it is the Catholic cathedral for the Boise Diocese.

Turn right onto Hays St. for three blocks to Fort St., and veer northeast across Fort St. into the Veterans Administration Hospital grounds. This sixty-eight acre reserve is the location of **Fort Boise,** selected in 1863 by Major Lugenbeel, as mentioned earlier.

Abandoned in 1912, the post was used at times by the National Guard until 1919, when the Public Health Service obtained it for tubercular patients and World War I veterans. In 1938 the Veterans Administration acquired the site.

Follow the drive on the left through an 0.3 mile loop around the knoll and back to the Fort St. entrance. Most of the buildings are numbered. Number 34, a two-story, brick structure, was the cavalry barn, where the 9th U.S. Cavalry stabled its seventy-eight horses.

Officers' row is situated along the top of the knoll. Number 45 was the commanding officer's home the year before the fort was

Table Rock quarry.

abandoned; the interior has been modernized. Number 23B was built in 1905. Number 1, with sandstone walls two feet thick, was built in the mid-1860s, which makes it among the oldest residences in the city. General George Crook lived in the house during the Bannock War of 1878.

Follow the drive down from the knoll past Number 6 on the right, the Quartermaster's office and storehouse built in 1864. Its sandstone blocks were mortared with adobe.

Turn left on Fort St., past the log cabin built in 1863 by a soldier at the fort, John O'Farrell, for his seventeen year-old bride, and after five blocks turn left on Reserve St. Follow it through the curve to the right onto Shaw Mountain Rd. 1.3 miles, where the pavement gives way to gravel for the last 2.0 miles to the top of **Table Rock.** The summit provides an excellent view of the Boise River valley.

Return downhill to Fort St., make a right turn, and follow it north seven blocks back to Hays St., then left to the John Daly mansion on the southwest side of the street at 1015 West Hays. This Colonial revival residence is the work of the same architectural firm that designed the State Capitol, and its Corinthian columns echo those in front of the capitol.

Turn left on No. Eleventh past the **United Methodist Church** that occupies the west block. Built in 1958-1960 of Arizona flagstone for $2 million, this modern Gothic church is known as the "Cathedral of the Rockies." The inside of the thirty-foot stained glass windows behind the pulpit is finished with an unique flowed-gold technique.

Continue south one block to the **Bush mansion** on the corner at 1020 Franklin St. John Bush was a pioneer freighter, owner of the Central Hotel, and president of the Capital State Bank. In 1892 he contracted for this house at a cost of $6,000. At one time the mansion was nearly destroyed for a church parking lot.

Turn left on Franklin one block, right another block on North Tenth, and right on West State. The **Congregation Beth Israel Synagogue** is on the northwest corner at West State and Eleventh St. The Moorish revival style temple was built in 1895, and is the oldest synagogue west of the Mississippi River still used by its original congregation. The Falk brothers, early influential merchants of the community, and Moses Alexander, mayor of Boise and America's first Jewish governor (1915-1918), were founders of the congregation. In 1981 the synagogue was completely restored.

Drive northwest two blocks to Thirteenth St. The five-story building visible one block south of State St. is the corporate headquarters for **Boise Cascade Corp.**

The company was formed in 1947 through the merger of two small lumber companies, Boise Payette Lumber of Boise, and Cascade Lumber of Yakima, Washington. About half of Boise Cascade's timber needs are provided by its own lands comprising 7.3 million acres, of which only 200,000 are in Idaho. Expanding rapidly in the 1960s, the firm encountered problems in the 1970s because of its diversification and returned to its primary businesses: paper and packaging materials, lumber, plywood, and other building materials.

In 1978 the company completed a five-year, $1.1 billion capital spending program, and began a $2.3 billion program for the period 1979-1983. About 50 percent of those investments were in paper operations, as the company shifted its emphasis to printing-

414

quality grades of paper. (The *National Geographic* is printed on coated paper produced at the Boise Cascade mill in Maine.)

The building, which occupies the entire block, was designed by Skidmore, Owings and Merrill of San Francisco. Begun in 1969 and completed in 1972, the five floors of office space are linked by horizontal bridges above an interior landscaped plaza illuminated by skylights.

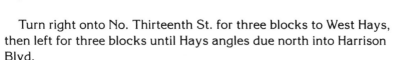

Turn right onto No. Thirteenth St. for three blocks to West Hays, then left for three blocks until Hays angles due north into Harrison Blvd.

In the 1890s **Harrison Blvd.** was designed on the north end of town to rival Warm Springs Ave. to the southeast. The double-street with a landscaped median is patterned after those of some European cities; its name commemorates President Benjamin Harrison's visit to Boise in 1891.

Follow Harrison four blocks to Eastman St. The three-story, Queen Anne house on the northwest corner was built in 1906 for the Eugene Looney family, sheep ranchers who owned the entire block, much of which was a prune orchard. In 1957 the Robert Hansbergers bought the house from one of the Looney daughters.

Detour one block east of Harrison St. on Eastman to 1301 West Sixteenth, to see a beautifully restored house built in 1906 for Lewis Heaston. Its square corner tower and corner porch entry are characteristic of the Queen Anne style, and the house resembles the Tourtellotte design on the corner one block east. Until 1980 no resident had ever occupied the Heaston house longer than seven years.

Return to Harrison Blvd. and continue north to Brumback St. The house on the northwest corner at 1403 Harrison was built in 1906 for Arthur and Mary Golden of Rocky Bar and Atlanta in South Boise Basin. Mr. Golden worked for the Falk Wholesale Co. in Boise.

Drive nine blocks farther north on Harrison to Hill Rd., then return south on Harrison to Sixteenth St. (En route, one can visit the governor's house, five blocks west of Harrison on Irene at 1805 No. Twenty-first St.)

To continue east of Boise on I-84 follow the signs south on Sixteenth St., and west on Main St., back to the Interstate.

Nine miles southeast of Boise, one can see remnants of the Oregon Trail. Take the Kuna Rd.-Black Creek Rd. (Exit 64) turnoff. Drive north 2.4 miles to the sign and left 1.0 miles to **Bonneville Point.** At the end of the gravel road a shelter provides several

415

interpretive signs, as well as a view of the Boise River Valley from the same vantage enjoyed by Captain Bonneville's men in 1833.

To see the Oregon Trail at its intersection with the gravel road, continue north one mile past the Bonneville Point branch road then return to I-84.

Sagebrush stem about fifty years old. Growth rings in sage provide accurate information about rainfall patterns in areas where no records have been kept.

Most of the highway between Boise and Mountain Home is as straight as fencewire and as flat as a trivet. Tourists may find the fifty-mile stretch "annoyingly monochrome," to use Mark Twain's phrase, but many westerners find a certain enchanting monotony in the sage desert of southern Idaho. Even Susan Ward, an eastern transplant in the *Angle of Repose,* finally wrote her Massachusetts friend, "As moonlight unto sunlight is that desert sage to other greens." On the theory that a monotony of something is preferable to a monotony of nothing, herewith a few words about the ubiquitous *Artemisia tridentata* – "tall sage." (Artemisia is remembered for the monument that she erected to her husband-King, Mausolus; *tridentata* for the three-lobed leaf tips). Tall sagebrush, like other desert plants, has adapted to its semi-arid environment: small leaves covered with gray hairs impede the

416

drying effect of sun and wind; shallow, widely dispersed roots absorb water before it can evaporate, and fallen leaves release a toxic compound that limits the growth of competing flora. The minute yellow flowers of sage, produced in early fall, are wind-pollinated. Tall sage is hardy – though Idaho bushes seldom live longer than eighty years, in the Southwest some over 200 years old have been found.

Settlers soon learned sage was not forage for cattle, and only poor forage for sheep, but they also discovered it flourished in stands ten feet high where the land was fertile and slightly alkaline, a guide to the choicest reclamation sites.

In less desirable areas several efforts were made to turn the prolific plant to commercial advantage. An Emmett farmer succeeded in grafting gooseberry and currant stock to sagebrush roots. From 1907 to 1910 a company in Shoshone made sagebrush shampoo and hair tonic from the oil boiled out of tridentata leaves, and in 1910 Chemical Products Co. of Chicago announced plans for a Nevada enterprise that would distill wood alcohol and acetic acid from sage at a profit of $15 a cord. The state donated 275,000 acres to the company, but the project faded faster than a mirage.

Mountain Home, thirty-one miles southeast of Bonneville Pt., had its genesis in the OSL railroad. In 1882 a construction tent-town on the location was called Tutville. Lots at the townsite sold for $25. By 1899 the town had four general stores, three churches, two hotels, a brick schoolhouse and a number of shops and saloons. Two newspapers were published weekly. The location was a shipping point for over one million pounds of wool annually.

The name of the town was derived from the mountain home-station of the driver on the Holladay stage line from Kelton to Boise (see Highway 20, Rattlesnake Station). With the arrival of the OSL and the expiration of the mail contracts for the stage lines, the post office/roadhouse shifted south to the railroad tracks here.

In 1891 Mountain Home took the seat of Elmore County away from Rocky Bar. At present a farm and ranch town, its mainstay in meager years is the Mountain Home Air Force Base, located ten miles west of town (see Highway 67).

Mountain Home has the highest annual mean temperature of any town in the state.

St. James Episcopal Church, built in 1900, is a charming Gothic revival structure located at 305 No. Third St. East. The white stucco interior is lit by simple stained glass windows.

417

A different, indigenous construction can be seen on West Second North, west of Main St.: the Pedro Anchustegui pelota court built in 1908 of lava rock. Pelota (or jai alai) is a Spanish national game, somewhat like handball, except that a long, curved wicker basket is strapped to the player's arm. This court has been used by Basques, who were drawn to Mountain Home by its livestock operations. Boise retains an indoor court, but this is the best outdoor one in the state.

Freighters in Mountain Home, 1884.

Mountain Home a few years later.

418

A pair of volcanic crater rings can be visited a short distance west of town. Take No. Main St. to Third West St., drive north and turn west onto Frontage Road parallel to I-84. Drive 5.4 miles to Cinder Butte Rd. Turn south across the railroad tracks and cattleguard onto Cinder Butte Rd., and after sixty feet turn left on the dirt track. Follow it 2.7 miles in a southwesterly curve up the rim of the craters.

The **Crater Rings** are twin circular depressions formed about 1.4 million years ago in the basalt of the Bruneau Formation. Slightly less than one-half mile across, they are about 200 feet deep, and 400 yards apart.

Geologists indicate the rimrock flows spread south over a 100 square-mile area. A vent formed at the site of the larger of the two crater rings and extruded a lava cone estimated to have been 150 feet high. The cone collapsed, then reformed. When the vent became blocked, pressure was released explosively over a 1½-square-mile area. Sudden lowering of the gas pressure, and possibly a simultaneous withdrawal of magma, removed support in the area of the craters, and the inward collapse formed the pits.

Interstate 84 travels northeast around Mountain Home and southeast 25.5 miles to Glenns Ferry. Three miles east of Hammett, and three miles west of Glenns Ferry, the highway passes below retaining walls forty feet high and several thousand feet long. Built in 2½ years, between 1977 and 1979, their cost accounted for half of this $6.5 million project.

The Reinforced Earth structure is a design conceived by a French architect-engineer, and was first used in 1966 in the Pyrenees Mountains. The panels are pre-cast concrete seven inches thick, connected with overlapped slip joints. Metal reinforcement strips are bolted to the rear of the panels and extend horizontally into compacted backfill.

The reinforced wall evened the highway grade and eliminated the need to move the canal on the north side of the road and the railroad tracks on the south side. (Foundation and form work for similar concrete walls would have doubled the expense.)

Gustavus Glenn, for whom **Glenns Ferry** is named, started a ferry on the Snake River in 1863 to accelerate freight traffic on the stage line from Kelton to Boise. His boat, eighteen feet wide and sixty feet long, could hold two wagons. The Glenn brothers owned freight teams on the road, and their ferry cut twenty miles from the former route to Three-Island Crossing. The Toano Rd. from Humbolt Wells in Nevada also crossed here.

419

INTERSTATE
IDAHO
84

The townsite was platted in 1871, just downstream from the old ferry. In 1908 the first bridge was built across the river here.

To visit **Three-Island Crossing State Park** take Exit 120 (Business 84) 0.5 miles southeast into Glenns Ferry, turn south on Commercial Street 0.5 miles to the state park sign, and follow the paved road west 0.8 miles to the park entrance. The visitors center contains photographs and information helpful in understanding the importance of this crossing on the Oregon Trail.

Actually, there were two different crossings in the area: Three-Island Ford one mile farther downstream, and Two-Island Crossing at the south edge of the park. Emigrants who used Two-Island crossed to the tail of the southern-most island, advanced to the head of that island, and then crossed to the head of the middle island, before wading the rest of the distance. The crossing is about 350 yards wide and six to eight feet deep. Scars from the wagon wheels can still be seen on the south hillside.

In September, 1844, Edward Parrish, who crossed here, wrote in his diary, *We crossed the river safely after noon today and camped on a fine bed of grass within site of the ford. The river is rapid and the water middling low. The bottom is gravel of the prettiest kind and the water is clear. In consequence of two islands, side by side, we had to cross three streams.*

Those who decided they would rather remain on the south shore all the way to Fort Boise often regretted the decision. In 1843 Overton Johnson, having attempted the crossing and finding it too deep, continued on the south-alternate and commented, "This is, perhaps, the most rugged desert and dreary country between the Western borders of the United States and the shores of the Pacific. It is nothing less than a wild, rocky, barren wilderness, of wrecked and ruined Nature, a vast field of volcanic desolation."

In 1971 the 513-acre park, with fifty campsites, was established. At times buffalo and longhorn cattle are exhibited in the enclosed pasture at the southeast corner of the park.

Malad Gorge State Park, 26.6 miles east of Glenns Ferry, is worth a stop. Take the Tuttle exit, drive 200 yards south to the park entrance, and follow the short, paved road to the parking area. (No campsites are available here.) Established in 1979, the 652-acre park provides a spectacular view of the Malad River in its canyon, which is 250 feet deep. A steel footbridge spans the gorge just below a sixty-foot waterfall that spews out into the Devil's Washbowl.

420

The river, sometimes called the shortest in the world because it is only 2.5 miles long, emanates from the aquifer of the Snake River Plains and loses itself in the Snake just downstream.

Three-Island Crossing on the Snake River.

Devil's Washbowl.

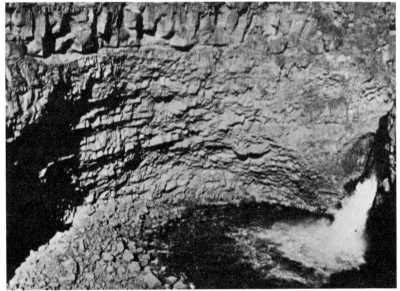

Burley is 42.8 miles southeast of Malad State Park. An agrarian town located in the center of the Minidoka southside irrigation tract, it was named in 1904 for David Burley, general passenger agent for the U.P. railroad. Mr. Burley, who was employed on the line between the townsite and Chicago, persuaded several parties to migrate west and farm potato land. The townsite, incorporated in 1906, is about three miles east of the Starrhs Ferry crossing that operated on the Snake River.

Burley in 1908.

Freighters haul a turbine for the Reclamation Service dam at Minidoka through Burley in 1909.

Burley, the seat of Cassia County since 1918, is blessed with numerous shady streets, where bungalow-style houses predominate. The **Cassia County Museum,** with its pioneer village, farm machinery, stagecoach and railroad car, is located at Main St., and Highland Ave.

A city park is located at East Main and Normal Sts., and Scholers Park is situated on the south shore of the Snake River.

Distinct **traces of the Oregon Trail** can be seen eleven miles west of Burley. From the downtown intersection of Overland Ave. and Main St. drive five miles west on Main, which becomes U.S. 30. At the Y leave U.S. 30 and continue west 5.5 miles on the Milner Rd. before turning north across the railroad tracks 0.3 miles to the BLM interpretive site near the river.

North of Burley Interstate 84 continues east 13.8 miles to a junction with I-86, then cleaves southeast 53.8 miles to the Utah border, six miles north of Snowville.

U.S. Interstate Highway 86 from a junction with I-84 east of Burley, easterly to a junction with I-15 in Pocatello. Route length: 64.4 miles.

Highway 86 curves northeast along the southern skirt of the Snake River Plain from I-84 to Pocatello. The plain is a basalt bed several thousand feet deep, composed of numerous lava flows extruded during the last few million years. The flows erupted from fissure, or vent, volcanoes located along north-south faultlines, and the lava plain is sixty miles wide (north-south), and 300 miles long (east-west). The porous lava absorbs all would-be tributaries on the north side of the Snake River from Twin Falls to Idaho Falls.

The north-south trending mountain ranges visible south of the Interstate, from its origin at I-84 until it reaches American Falls, consist of sedimentary rocks deposited in shallow seas 600 to 225 million years ago. The westernmost formation is the Sublette Range; east of it are the Deep Creek Mountains.

The exit for **Register Rock,** inside Massacre Rocks State Park, is on the north side of the highway, 31.2 miles from I-84.

A short paved road leads to a picnic area and a large, sheltered basalt boulder that was used as an autograph book by emigrants on the Oregon Trail. The names are incised and daubed; some are as early as 1849.

Return to the highway and continue east 2.5 miles to headquarters for **Massacre Rocks State Park,** on the north side of the road. The 556-acre park has a small museum, fifty campsites, and restrooms with showers.

Although Massacre Rocks is on the Oregon Trail, the lurid name was actually fogged-up in 1927 by American Falls businessmen who hoped to arouse tourism. The killings which took place in this vicinity occurred about four miles east of the Rocks.

INTERSTATE
IDAHO
86

On August 9, 1862, three separate emigrant trains, totaling fifty-two wagons, groped west along the trail from American Falls. The three parties were spaced over a stretch of five miles. In late afternoon a messenger stunned the rear train with news that the two ahead of it had been ambushed. The best description of the event is contained in a letter written the following day by John Hilman, a member of the last train:

On Saturday about 5 p.m. I was riding ahead of the train a mile or so, in search of grass and a camping place at which we might remain over Sunday. On looking up the road ahead of me I saw a horseman coming toward me in a hasty manner.

The first thing he said to me was, "My God, John, the Indians have massacred a train and robbed them of all they had, and they are only a short distance from us." I at once became conscious of our extreme danger and turned back to inform the train and bring up the wagons which were lagging behind and I expected an attack to be made at any moment. Learning that two ox teams were ahead of us and going to camp at or near the battlefield we pushed on to overtake them.

In an hours driving we came to the place where the horrible scene took place, but found the Indians had run off the stock, taking provisions, clothing, etc., of the train, but left the wagons, which the ox trains ahead of us had taken and gone on, in pursuit of grass. I found quite a quantity of blood, and fragments of such things as immigrants usually carry with them and it was evident that the Indians had done their hellish deeds in a hasty manner and left.

We pushed on endeavoring to overtake them, but only got a short distance on account of the darkness, and were obliged to camp on the very ground where the Indians had, a few hours previous, made a ring with their pandemonium like shouts, and red with the blood of innocent men and women. We at once put out a strong picked guard on the surrounding hills, got a hasty supper in the dark, staked our mules in the sage brush and hoped the night would be a short one.

Nothing happening, we pushed on at daybreak for the ox teams and grass, which we found in camp five miles distant, and here we camped during the day.

I found three men killed and several wounded, one woman mortally wounded, and the wagons which the Indians had left.

All were buried here but the affair did not end here.

Some thirty men from the two ox trains and the trains attacked the previous day, started out in pursuit of the Indians and their stock. After traveling some seven miles in the direction in which the

424

Indians went they came suddenly upon them and a fight immediately commenced. At the first fire the white men ran and the red men pursued, and after a running fight of some three miles the Indians ceased their pursuit.

In this fight three of the whites were killed and five severely wounded, one I think mortally. After we learned the fate of the last party the greatest excitement prevailed in camp and a small party went to their assistance to recover the dead and wounded, one of which was not found and one had been scalped, the first scalped man I ever saw. Late in the evening both parties returned and two more ox trains came into camp, making now some two hundred wagons and 400 men and 300 women and children.

This morning we all started together after burying the dead, and came 13 miles to Raft River, where we are all encamped for the day, and where I am writing this.

The five victims were buried about fifty feet west of Massacre Rocks. The woman died three days later and was buried at Raft River.

The gap between the Rocks was widened in 1958 to accommodate highway improvements.

North of the highway, three miles east of Massacre Rocks State Park, a lava flow from the Cedar Butte eruption, less than 100,000 years ago, poured over a twenty-square-mile area and dammed the Snake River. It formed **American Falls Lake,** which impounded the river east for forty miles, almost to Blackfoot. Remnants of the flow are visible as rimrock on the north side of the river and highway east for seven miles from Register Rock.

Interstate Highway 86 continues northeast from Massacre Rocks ten miles to American Falls (see Highway 39), and 17.9 miles to the interchange with Highway 30.

The large factories south of the highway, four miles west of Pocatello, are the J. R. Simplot and FMC phosphate fertilizer plants.

The **Simplot** operation is supplied by the Gay mine of the Fort Hall reservation and by the Conda mine (see Highway 34, Conda). Five types of solid (dry) fertilizers are manufactured here, along with five types of liquid fertilizer. Operations began in 1944; they continue twenty-four hours a day, seven days a week.

The **FMC** factory is the largest elemental-phosphorous plant in the world. It, too, is supplied with ore from the Gay mine, under an agreement with Simplot.

425

FMC traces its beginning to 1883 when a small company began selling pressure pumps to orchardists in the Santa Clara Valley of California. In 1929 Bean Spray Pump Co. changed its name to Food Machinery Corp. Now headquartered in Chicago, FMC has sales in excess of $3.5 billion and nearly an equal amount employed as assets.

I-86 travels 3.6 miles east through Chubbuck to U.S. Highway 91, or 0.4 miles farther to I-15 in Pocatello (see I-15, Pocatello).

State Highway 89 from the Idaho-Utah state line south of Fish Haven, northerly via Fish Haven, St. Charles, Bloomington, Ovid, Montpelier, and Geneva to the Idaho-Wyoming state line north of Geneva. Route length: 44.2 miles.

Highway 89 travels north for twenty miles through **Bear Lake Valley,** a basin in the Wasatch Range. After Donald McKenzie and his band of North West trappers discovered and named (Black) **Bear Lake** and valley, it was used extensively, along with Cache

Bear Lake (looking east).

Valley to the south, by the early mountain men. Some of the more impressive names in the fur trade left their moccasin tracks along the shores of the lake: William Ashley, Jedediah Smith, David

Jackson, Bill Sublette, Peter Skene Ogden, Jim Bridger, John Weber, Eph Logan, and Benjamin Bonneville.

The lake itself, visible along the east side of the highway, is about twenty miles long and seven miles wide. At one time, probably when prehistoric Lake Bonneville was at its highest, Bear Lake filled the entire valley; there are shoremarks thirty-three feet above the present highwater level.

The lake's elevation is 5,923 feet, and it usually freezes in the winter. Greatest depth, 208 feet, is along the faultline on the eastern shore. Its morning glory color is the result of large quantities of soluble carbonates.

Fish Haven, three miles north of the Utah border, was a summer campsite for Shoshone Indians.

At the mouth of the creek, which flows through the village into Bear Lake, two Mormon pioneers netted 1,800 pounds of fish in one day.

During the early 1900s a substantial commercial fishery operated on Bear Lake. Set lines, seines and large-mesh gill nets were used. A fisherman from Sweden moved to the area; he obtained nets with a

Bonneville cisco.

finer mesh from his homeland and introduced an effective method of catching smaller fish, particularly the **Bonneville cisco** – a fish found nowhere else.

The silvery cisco feeds on zooplankton; its size seldom exceeds seven inches, its weight two ounces. The fish, known as the Bear Lake sardine, spawn in January and February in shallow water along two miles of eastern shores. It always schools in a counter-clockwise circular motion. Fishermen are allowed a fifty-fish limit. If the lake is frozen, dip-nets are used through a hole in the ice; if there is open water, the fish are captured by wading into the schools with a net.

Two other species of whitefish, new to science, were discovered here in 1915; both still inhabit the lake. The Utah cutthroat, or bluenose trout, reported in 1912, is now extinct. Kokanee, rainbow, brown and lake trout, carp and yellow perch have been introduced to the lake.

Idaho and Utah outlawed commercial fishing in the 1920s.

After another 4.5 miles, Highway 89 enters the town of **St. Charles,** named for the Mormon apostle Charles Rich, who led the colonization of the Bear Lake Valley, in the belief it was part of Utah. St. Charles was settled from the north in 1864, when pioneers with ox-drawn wagons came down from Soda Springs and began a commercial garden on the site surveyed by Joseph Rich. Their cabins were built from quaking aspen.

The town is the birthplace of **Gutzon Borglum,** sculptor, born in 1867. His family moved a year later, but their cabin has been preserved. Borglum was a friend of Auguste Rodin, and is best known for the faces he carved at Mount Rushmore.

One mile north of the St. Charles city center, turn east off Highway 89 to **Bear Lake State Park.** The fifty-two-acre park is located on the north shore, about three miles from the highway. It has picnic tables, and a beach for swimming, but no campsites.

The area north of the road is **Bear Lake National Wildlife Refuge.** The road follows the sandbar, or dike, that divides Dingle Marsh and Mud Lake on the north, from Bear Lake on the south. The dike accreted from sand carried by wind and waves for centuries.

Established in 1968 on 17,600 acres of public land, the refuge is a major nesting area for Great Basin Canada Geese, as well as for sandhill cranes, and mallards, pintails, widgeon, and teal. Other waterfowl frequent the refuge: herons, egrets, terns, rails, ibis, bitterns, grebes, avocets, and white pelicans. One can view the eastern edge of the refuge by car; turn north on the road at the east end of the dike, and drive toward Dingle. Refuge headquarters is in Montpelier.

428

The Lifton pumping station of the Utah Power and Light's **Bear River-Bear Lake project** is situated on the south side of the dike road, four miles from the highway. This plant is part of the most ingenious irrigation scheme in the state.

The Bear River originates on the east side of the Wasatch Mountains in Utah, travels north into Wyoming and then curves south in a tight muleshoe through Idaho and back into Utah and the Great Salt Lake. The toe of the shoe is Soda Springs, forty miles northwest of the Lifton pumps. (Though the river was a tributary of the lake in prehistoric times, it now comes no closer than eight miles.)

Prior to 1900 the lake's natural outlet at the north end meandered through Dingle Swamp to the Bear River, sixteen miles north. In 1909 Telluride Power Co. began to construct works that would divert the Bear River into Mud Lake and Bear Lake for irrigation storage and power. The natural outlet through Dingle Swamp was closed, and north-south inlet and outlet canals were excavated between the river and the lake.

Utah Power and Light Co. was organized in 1912 and subsumed numerous companies, including Telluride. The new company continued the work on the Bear River-Bear Lake project and completed it in 1918; downstream power plants were finished in 1928.

Bear Lake is now a storage reservoir for the Bear River's spring flood. Runoff is diverted from the river near Dingle (south of Montpelier) to Mud Lake and Bear Lake. As irrigation demand increases during the summer, the water is released north through the twelve-mile long outlet canal back into the river just west of Montpelier. The water then runs through four power plants as it flows from its release point south to Utah and the Great Salt Lake.

The Lifton pumping station has two gates through which water can move by gravity flow either north or south, and five pumps which can lift 1,500 cfs into the outlet canal when Bear Lake is too low for gravity flow north. Since the pumps have a maximum lift capability of twenty-one feet, that is the limit of lake-level variation; however, annual fluctuation averages 3½ feet.

The Bear River control project is coordinated among three states through the Bear River Commission.

The **Bear Lake Hot Springs** is 2.8 miles east of the Lifton pump plant, on the south side of the road. The springs are piped into an indoor pool, where the water is held at about seventy-five degrees. Campsites are available.

On the outskirts of St. Charles, 0.1 miles north of the Bear Lake State Park road, is the west turn for the road that leads to Minnetonka Cave. Follow the paved road ten miles west up St. Charles Creek through St. Charles Canyon, to the largest developed limestone cave in the state.

Minnetonka Cave was discovered in 1907 by a resident of St. Charles who was hunting grouse in the mountains. After a number of formations were vandalized, the Forest Service decided to regulate access. A WPA project built a trail from the road to the cave (elev. 7,700), and poured concrete steps inside the entrance. It has been open to the public since 1947.

Minnetonka is open from June 15 through Labor Day, seven days a week. The tour, through rooms of stalactites, stalagmites, and helictites, covers a half-mile and requires an hour. A jacket is recommended because the interior is as cold as an earthworm.

Three USFS campgrounds are within a few minutes of the cave.

Stalagmites in Minnetonka Cave.

430

Highway 89 continues north from St. Charles, past well-kept farms. It is 4.5 miles to **Bloomington.**

In 1864 the town was laid out by Charles Rich and his eldest son, Joseph; they platted the site into ten-acre parcels and subdivided each into ten lots. The streets, with typical Mormon foresight, were set forty-four yards wide.

At a community meeting, men, according to age, drew the numbered lots; five-acre farms were distributed in the same manner. By fall there were forty cabins on the flat, but it was four years before a harvest of sufficient bounty suggested the town's name. Bloomington incorporated in 1910.

From the town center, take the road that leads west to Bloomington Canyon in the Cache National Forest. After 8.4 miles the road forks. The left branch goes to Bloomington Lake campground. Take the right fork 0.4 miles to the **giant Engelmann spruce** tree. It is 21⅔ feet in circumference, and 107 feet high. "Except during the nine months before he draws his first breath, no man manages his affairs as well as a tree does."

Paris is three miles north of Bloomington. This little agricultural community is among the more engaging small towns in Idaho.

The town was the first Mormon settlement in the Bear Lake Valley. The Homestead Act of 1862 jeopardized the Mormon hold on the Salt Lake Basin. To preclude Gentile settlers from taking up lands immediately north of Logan, Brigham Young dispatched Charles Rich in 1863 to colonize the Bear Lake Valley.

Charles Coulson Rich was a "steam engine in trousers." He had left his job as a teacher in Illinois to learn about Mormonism in Independence, Missouri; in 1832 he was baptized into the LDS Church. Rich traveled as a missionary before settling in Nauvoo. He married six women and fathered hard – they bore him fifty-one children.

When the anti-Mormon riots began, Rich and his families joined the 1846 western migration and arrived in the Salt Lake valley the following year. There he became a member of the Council of Fifty, the first governing body of the Utah settlements. He was dispatched by Brigham Young to the San Bernardino colony, where he worked "to do the will of God as it is laid upon me and my brethren." From California, Rich was sent on a mission to Europe and Scandinavia to recruit converts among the skilled craftsmen needed for the survival of the Mormon colonies. He returned from the mission only to receive Brigham's call to settle the Bear Lake Valley.

431

Undaunted, Rich gathered about forty emigrants and traveled north through Cache Valley to Franklin, and then scouted ahead through Emigration Canyon to Bear Lake country. He chose the present site after receiving permission from the Shoshone chief Washakie to settle in the north end of the valley in return for a portion of the crops produced, an agreement subsequently violated by the pioneers. The rest of the party arrived with their eleven wagons a few days later. (A typical cabin that sheltered two couples through the first winter has been preserved on the west side of South Main St.)

The following spring nearly 700 Saints came to the valley with their wagons and household goods. Rich brought a surveyor, Frederick Perris, who platted the townsite. The village plan had precedents; it was a model of Joseph Smith's plat for the City of Zion, and similar to the layout used for San Bernardino. Perris' name, though altered now, was given to the community.

In May, 1864, Brigham Young and his entourage visited Paris at Rich's request. At a public meeting, where he gave Rich civil and religious authority, Brigham stated that lots should be assigned within one block at a time rather than drawn at random.

In 1869 David Kimball succeeded Charles Rich as president of the Bear Lake Stake, which was the first stake outside Utah. He brought another hundred settlers with him, many of whom were English.

The first flour mill was built on Paris Creek in 1865, a mile west of Main St. A planing and shingle mill was established in 1870, which produced much of the wood for the beautiful frame houses, and gave Paris an appearance so different from the stone houses of Franklin and the brick ones of Oakley.

In 1882 a small church-operated telephone company was formed and provided service to St. Charles and Bloomington, part of a warning system for polygamists, who were harassed by federal agents. In 1902 the Electric Light Co. brought power to the town from a plant three miles up Paris Canyon.

When the Oregon Short Line went through Montpelier, Paris lost its economic command of Bear Lake Valley, but a branch line was built from Montpelier, and a bright yellow depot occupied the intersection at Center and Second East Sts.

Paris contains a remarkable architectural legacy. The dominant building is on the east side of Main St., the **Bear Lake Stake Tabernacle.** (A Mormon stake includes a group of local congregations known as wards, and the stake tabernacle is a regional community center.)

432

The Bear Lake Saints had been eager to erect their tabernacle, but waited several years, at the request of the president of the LDS Church, until the Logan Temple was completed.

While awaiting Church approval, the local Mormons sledded red sandstone to the construction site from a quarry eighteen miles south of town, on the east edge of Bear Lake. During the winter the stone was hauled across the ice on the lake and piled at the tabernacle grounds. Under ideal conditions a sleigh could make one trip in a day.

US 89

Bear Lake Tabernacle, front and rear.

In 1884 the First Presidency approved construction and sent a church architect, Joseph Young, a son of Brigham Young, to design the building. His plan was expansive: a Romanesque revival style church, 127 feet long, and seventy-three feet wide, with an eighty-foot tower, and seating capacity for 3,000.

Concrete footings were dug eight feet deep and six feet wide, the floor joists were set on one-foot centers. Stone cutting and carving was done by a family of Swiss masons. All of the wood was furnished by the local forests. Saints from neighboring towns camped in tents for a week at a time to help with construction. It was a four-year effort that cost $50,000. The result speaks for itself.

The interior has an intricate wooden ceiling, and the main floor slopes to the front of the church in order to give the congregation a better view.

An English architectural principle states that buildings should have "commodity, firmness, and delight." This tabernacle meets the maxim. It is open for tours during the summer, and is listed on the National Register of Historic Places.

433

Until 1979 the octagonal Paris dance hall, with its tent-shaped roof, occupied the southwest corner of the tabernacle block. It, too, was a remarkable building, built in 1913, with a floor consisting of four-inch wide boards joined in octagonal, concentric patterns, and supported beneath by springs which allowed the floor to bounce with the dance rhythms. It was the only such pavilion in the state, and despite vehement local objections, LDS authorities in Salt Lake ordered the hall demolished because it "detracted" from the tabernacle.

Drive south on Main St., and turn left on East First South two blocks to South Second East to begin a short tour of the town's charming wooden houses.

Turn left on South Second East, then left on Center St. Note the Bear Lake County courthouse on the northeast corner of Center and Main. This classic, two-story building was built in 1884-1885 for $8,100. The building was forty-six feet square, but two additions have altered it. The roof had a widow's walk, which served as a town lookout during the anti-polygamy raids of the late 1880s.

Continue west on Center, across Main St., to 58 Center St. This two-story, Queen Anne house with the octagonal corner porch, was built in 1890 by J. R. Shepherd, owner of the Paris Mercantile Co.

Drive west to the intersection with North First West and turn right. There are several cottages of interest on this street.

After observing these homes, turn around and drive south on North First West, across Center St., to South First West. This block held five identical three-room log cabins used by the wives of Charles Rich (the sixth wife resided in Salt Lake). When one wife died in 1879, Rich replaced the log cabins with four adobe brick houses. Though covered with modern siding, they can still be seen, the oldest brick structures in Paris.

Turn left on West Second South, back to Main St.

(The drive up Paris Canyon to Paris ice cave west of town is toil without remuneration.)

Ovid is another townsite settled by Mormon emigrants in 1864, four miles north of Paris. The location was selected because of its well-watered meadows. Most of the first families were Scandinavian.

The town may have been named for Ovid, New York, though some claim Ovid was Joseph Rich's favorite poet.

434

In 1872 Ovid established the first curfew in Bear Lake Valley. Children had to be off the streets by 9:00 P.M., and all unescorted women were to be indoors by 10:00 P.M.

Highway 89 swings northeast 4.8 miles to Montpelier (see Highway 30, Montpelier), doglegs 1.3 miles through town, and continues east through Montpelier Canyon over Geneva Summit (6,922 elev.), 13.7 miles to **Geneva.**

Geneva was settled by dairy farmers in 1878, but was not named until twenty years later, presumably for the Swiss city.

The highway ends 0.3 miles farther east, at an intersection with Highway 61.

Interstate 90 from the Idaho-Washington state line west of Post Falls easterly via Post Falls, Coeur d'Alene, Kellogg, Wallace and Mullan to the Idaho-Montana state line at Lookout Pass. Route length: 84.2 miles.

The town of **Post Falls** is located on U.S. Interstate 90, twenty-eight miles from Spokane and seven miles from the city of Coeur d'Alene, at eastbound Exit 5 or westbound Exit 6. Post Falls contains two sights worth the short detour required to view them.

To reach the first point of interest from Exit 5 or 6, turn north on Spokane St., then west on Seltice Way for about 100 yards. Make a left turn on a gravel lane and park just short of the railroad tracks, which are 100 yards from the curve. Climb over the locked fence-gate and follow the path that parallels the railroad tracks south, for 175 yards. On the left, against the rock face, notice a pine-board shed built to protect a unique pictograph-deed painted on the granite. The written conveyance can be viewed through a screen at the front of the enclosure. The red figure of a man on horseback is obscure, but the coyote leading a family group is easily discerned, as are the incised letters of Frederick Post's name and the date of the agreement.

Post, a German emigrant, arrived in Idaho from Illinois in 1871. That year he purchased a site by a waterfall (now Post Falls) on the Spokane River from Andrew Seltice (a.k.a. Saltese), a chief of the Coeur d'Alene tribe. This pictograph is the contract between the two men.

When Post's title to the land was questioned by the federal government in 1889, Chief Seltice signed a statement, filed as a continuation of the abstract of title, and the conveyance was recognized by an Act of Congress, signed by President Cleveland.

435

Mr. Post established a sawmill alongside the waterfall. To visit that site, return to Spokane St. and drive south to Fourth Ave. Turn right on Fourth and take the left gravel road at the fork, cross the railroad tracks and curve left to a parking spot next to the dam. This area was the heart of the 298 acres for which Post paid Seltice $500.

Post dammed all three channels of the river here with log barriers that raised the natural forty-foot fall by about four feet. He built a combination saw and grist mill and offered to sell the property to the U.S. Army for $2,000 when construction of Fort Sherman began at present-day Coeur d'Alene. The Army built its own mill so Frederick sold the land and 87 percent of the water power rights to R. K. Neill in 1900 for $25,000.

Frederick Post promoted his business interests in Spokane, as well as in the town that bears his name. He built a three-story wooden hotel with fifty-four rooms in Post Falls in the belief that steamboats from Coeur d'Alene Lake would come down the river to his landing, but the hotel and sawmill burned and Post's dream went unrealized. F. E. Post died in 1908, survived by his wife and six daughters.

It was Neill's acquisition that gave this damsite additional significance. He and some associates intended to construct a new dam, along with a power station and transmission lines, to provide electricity to the Coeur d'Alene mining district. At that time, the mines were still dependent on energy produced by wood or coal-fired steam boilers, as well as local hydroprojects that were made inoperable by winter temperatures.

A high-voltage transmission line of such size and distance was still a novel enterprise in 1901. Since there was a 142-mile line in California, and a 105-mile line for Utah mines at the time, Neill sought design assistance for the system from General Electric and Westinghouse. Both firms refused to help him because they had a vested interest in protecting the fledgling Washington Water Power Company. So Neill and his associates had to sell their interests to WPP Co.

WWP's general manager visited Charles Steinmetz, General Electric's resident genius on alternating current, and Steinmetz went over the plans and pronounced them feasible. The WWP Company signed delivery contracts with six Coeur d'Alene mining companies and in the summer of 1902 began construction of the 100-mile, 60,000-volt, transmission line with three strands of copper wire strung along thirty-five foot cedar poles.

Linemen worked mostly at night so that power could be transmitted during the day. They hung iron chains across the wires

436

to short circuit any electricity that might be fed into the line accidentally. The route chosen went through the meadows and marshes south of Coeur d'Alene Lake, crossing near the mouth of the St. Joe River, along the lakeshore, then up the Coeur d'Alene River and its south fork to Wallace, where service began in September, 1903. Six substations were built in the Coeur d'Alene valley to step down power for each mine. It became the second line known to transmit 60,000 volts.

Initially, power was transmitted from the WWP Company's plant at Spokane Falls, as the first Post Falls turbine did not begin to operate until 1906.

There are three dams at the Post Falls site, and the one next to the road blocks the river's north channel. No private vehicles are allowed through the WWP gate, but a short walk north down the road will reveal the powerhouse and mid-channel dam. The powerhouse contains five generators that produce a total of 15,000 k.w. The dam has a fifty-six-foot head and peak release occurs in the spring. Coeur d'Alene Lake, which serves as a reservoir, can be raised as much as twelve feet.

Incidentally, the original 1903 line was replaced by a 115,000 volt line in 1926, and a second new line, with the same voltage, was energized in 1930. These lines can be seen on both sides of the highway as one travels past Cataldo Mission on U.S. 90.

Post Falls at present is the site of a considerable forest products industry.

East of Post Falls, the **Spokane River** can be seen flowing west along the south side of the highway. It heads at Coeur d'Alene Lake, draining 4,300 square miles of northern Idaho. The river runs 225 miles to its confluence with the Columbia at Grand Coulee, Washington.

Basalt and glacial deposits overlie granitic and Precambrian rocks in this area. Cliffs along the south side of the river show the effects of a much higher flow.

More than most towns, water conditioned the settlement of **Coeur d'Alene city.**

The location was part of 4 million acres that belonged to the aboriginal Coeur d'Alenes. Father Pierre De Smet, the Jesuit missionary, visited a band of the tribe in 1842 – perhaps at the site of the present city. He received an effusive welcome, and Christianity was to have a major effect on the history of the tribe.

437

Lieutenant John Mullan and his "road crew" were in the area at times from 1859-1861, laboring on the predecessor to Highway 90 (see Mullan Tree). Part of the Mullan Road, rerouted in 1861, has been incorporated in Sherman Ave., which runs through the town's business district.

When General William Tecumseh Sherman came west over the Mullan route in 1877 (the year of the Nez Perce War, and the year following the battle of Little Big Horn) he was making an inspection tour of possible sites for several forts that could be used to control the Indians. He chose the beautiful and strategic spot on the north shore of Coeur d'Alene Lake, at the head of the Spokane River. Congress ratified his choise and set aside 999 acres for a military reservation at the location now occupied by the city park and North Idaho College (at the foot of Garden Ave.).

Fort Sherman (note tipis in foreground).

Camp Coeur d'Alene was pitched in April, 1878, and became Fort Coeur d'Alene a year later. A steam-powered circular sawmill was hauled in to produce the lumber for more than fifty buildings.

Four military companies were usually stationed at the fort, bringing the number of men there to approximately 250. The winters must have knocked the bottom out of the thermometer. An 1880 fort requisition requested 23 heating stoves, 110 caps, 82 gauntlets, and buffalo coats.

By 1883, when General Sherman paid a return visit, a Report of Inspection reveals in addition to company barracks buildings and

438

officers quarters, the grounds included a chapel, library, and bakery, blacksmith, carpenter and plumber shops, two ice houses, a recreation hall, and stables for 100 head of stock.

Pioneers began to settle around the fort; many of them survived by providing services and supplies to the military installation.

Kootenai County was one of the first counties to be established after Idaho became a Territory. Some of the settlers, at this point, attempted to set up a county organization, but it took three meetings in the region in order to get the required fifty signatures. Then the newly appointed auditor-assessor moved his store – and consequently the county seat – to Rathdrum, which was experiencing a boom induced by the arrival of the Northern Pacific railroad. (It was 1908 before Coeur d'Alene could muster the votes necessary to recapture the county offices.) But nearly a thousand

Soldiers from the fort ice-boating on Coeur d'Alene Lake.

people had moved to the area by the time General Sherman retired in 1887, and at that time the fort was renamed in his honor.

The sawmill at Fort Sherman, as it came to be known, was used to construct a sternwheel steamer in 1880 that functioned as a patrol and supply launch on the lake. Named the *Amelia Wheaton,* it was designed and built by a Norwegian, C. P. Sorenson. The machinery was shipped from Portland. Sorenson was designated captain of this eighty-six-foot "first lady" of Coeur d'Alene Lake steamboating.

The discovery of gold, silver, and lead in the Coeur d'Alene district in 1883-1885 brought a flood of miners into the region. The

439

Army used the *Amelia* to transport prospectors from Fort Sherman to Cataldo Mission at the head of navigation on the Coeur d'Alene River.

When Tony Tubbs began to subdivide his homestead, Coeur d'Alene had the semblance of a town. The next year a post office was established. D. C. Corbin extended a branch line from the Northern Pacific to the edge of the lake, and the community of Coeur d'Alene was incorporated in 1887.

Corbin bought the 120-foot steamer *Coeur d'Alene,* and a small prop-driven vessel *General Sherman,* as freight links across the lake to connect the terminals of his railroads from Coeur d'Alene City and from Cataldo Mission to Wallace. In addition, he built a larger workhorse in 1887: the *Kootenai.* She was equipped to break ten inches of ice, but was not always successful in that endeavor. Corbin eventually sold the steamboats, along with the railroad, to the Northern Pacific.

Coeur d'Alene in 1893.

C. L. Sorenson and Pete Johnson built the famous *Georgie Oakes* in 1890. With a 100-ton capacity, this sternwheeler plowed the lake with passengers and freight until 1917. (Capt. William Gray, the most renowned of western steamboat pilots, who took the *Norma* through Hells Canyon of the Snake in 1891, was the *Georgie's* pilot for two years on the lake.) The old steamboat was burned on the Fourth of July, 1927, as part of a waterfront fireworks celebration.

As the Oregon Railroad and Navigation Co. completed its line through Harrison to the Coeur d'Alene mining district, and ore

Electric train and steamboat at Coeur d'Alene dock.

Steamboat "Idaho" at Coeur d'Alene.

production stabilized, a ten-year hiatus on boat building occurred. Then the emphasis on lake boating shifted from freight to passengers.

At the turn of the century, just prior to the age of the automobile, "holiday excursions" became very popular. People by the hundreds, and then by the thousands, from Lewiston, Moscow, Palouse, Spokane, and Walla Walla began making tourist outings: they could take the excursion train to Coeur d'Alene and the excursion boats across the lake. It was a fashionable way to escape the summer heat, and residents of Spokane could make the round-trip in one day.

The boats offered delectable meals, the passengers could visit the Old Mission at Cataldo, feed the fish in the Coeur d'Alene and St. Joe Rivers, and dance to the music of a shipboard band on the way back. As many as 2,500 customers would often crowd the Coeur d'Alene docks on a Sunday morning.

Swank new boats were built to accommodate the tourists. The 100-foot *Spokane* had staterooms and a smoking room on her lower deck and cabins on her upper deck. The *Colfax* was built by Sorenson and Johnson as her sister-ship: slightly larger and luxuriously appointed.

Joseph C. White, a local booster, and J. and H. Spaulding, father and son, became partners and launched the *Idaho* – the largest steamer of its day. The *Idaho* had twin sidewheels, was 197 feet in length, with a twenty-foot beam. She was capable of carrying 1,000 passengers. The ship became the most popular boat on the lake, taking business away from the *Spokane* and *Colfax*. A fierce rivalry smoldered.

White and the Spauldings painted cardinal bands around the smokestacks of their steamers. The company became known as the Red Collar Line, and eventually bought out the owners of the *Spokane* and the *Colfax*. Then, despite a purported covenant not to compete, the sellers organized the White Star Navigation Co. and went back into business. The rivalry crackled into a feud.

White Star built the *Boneta,* a ninety-six-foot sternwheeler that proved better adapted for freight hauls than passenger excursions. It was just as well: Red Collar's *Idaho* rammed the *Boneta* and sank her on the St. Joe River.

The White Star raised the ship and she returned to service as a freighter. The company added the remodeled *Georgie Oakes* and the new, mettlesome, two-deck, 130-foot steamer *Flyer* to its fleet. For the next thirty years the *Flyer* was the most admired boat on the water.

The war of the Red and the White was fanned by competition for passengers as they disembarked from the electric trains at the Coeur d'Alene dock. The boats jostled each other for position and vied for the first departure. Occasionally there were races between boats, comparable to the famous races on the Mississippi River.

J. C. White finally felt compelled to buy out his competition for a second time. He effectively monopolized commercial boating on the lake, and during its peak years (1908-1913) Red Collar had a fifty-boat fleet.

442

INTERSTATE
IDAHO
90

Swimmers at Coeur d'Alene Lake in the 1890s.

Wreck of the Boneta on the St. Joe River.

Then once again, the commercial emphasis of Coeur d'Alene underwent a major transformation. Fort Sherman had been abandoned in 1900 after the troops had been dispatched to the Spanish-American War. The federal government set aside forty acres of the site for a cemetery and a park, then auctioned the balance in 1905. A timber company bought the largest portion.

443

Lumber was to dominate the community's economy for the next thirty years.

In 1910 Coeur d'Alene had a population that fluctuated between 12,000 and 20,000. Congress had decided the Indians still possessed some land worth taking, so under the cloak of the Dawes Severalty Act, 219,000 acres of the Coeur d'Alene reservation were opened for settlement by homestead. Acreage was apportioned through a lottery conducted by the General Land Office. Over 100,000 hopefuls registered for the drawing held in town. The names of the 1,350 winners were drawn August 9-12.

The same month, large numbers of settlers and loggers were

The steamboat "Rustler."

"Georgie Oakes" (left) and "Flyer" (right) in 1911.

displaced by the Great Idaho Fire, which consumed several hundred thousand acres in the St. Joe and Coeur d'Alene valleys, taking lives, homes and jobs. Refugees thronged the lakeside community.

The population declined, however, once the Chicago, Milwaukee and St. Paul Railroad established a branch connection with Spokane later that year. Avery, St. Joe, and St. Maries now had an alternate route to Washington and Montana.

Blackwell Lumber Co. bought a site with a mill, on the west side of the Spokane River where it leaves the lake, in 1909. It became one of the largest lumber manufacturing plants in the region. The operation weathered two floods and the Depression before closing in

"Idaho" on the lake, she was 147-feet long, with twin sidewheels.

Steamboats at Coeur d'Alene. "Georgie Oakes" (left). "Queen" (center forward). "Spokane" (center rear). "Idaho" rear.

445

1937. The old Blackwell log canal can still be seen, north of Highway 95, as that road approaches the west end of the Spokane River bridge.

Edward Rutledge and his lifetime friend, Fred Weyerhaeuser, purchased Northern Pacific land grant white pine stands and state timber stands (109,000 acres) and opened a sawmill on the north end of the lake, just east of the city center, in 1915-1916. The mill produced 666 million board feet by 1930 – but the company did not pay a single dividend. Potlatch Forests (now Potlatch Corporation) took over the operation, and after ten years it began to show consistent profits. This sawmill, which produced the lumber for Farragut Naval Training Base, still functions on the same site, and has probably produced more board-feet than any other mill in the district. The mill is visible from the highway on the east edge of town.

Potlatch Forests also acquired the Red Collar Line, which had been reduced to receivership by railroads, highways, and the Depression, and used it as a log towing concern for many years.

The present town of Coeur d'Alene offers an agreeable retrospect of its colorful past:

Begin with the **Museum of North Idaho,** 115 Northwest Blvd., on the edge of the city park. The museum has an impressive display of enlarged photographs of the lake's steamboat era. There is a wonderful brass sign, by the wheel of the old *Flyer,* with a message for lumberjacks: "No Calk Shoes Allowed On Upper Deck. Ask Purser For Slippers." (Most loggers preferred to stay below and visit with the crew.)

A collection of logging tools and an exhibit of logging photographs recollect a breed of men who were hard as Arkansas flint.

Hung on one wall is a huge wooden sign that was displayed yearly, until 1968, in a store window for the Coeur d'Alene Forest Festival. The text is worth quoting:

Hearye saw dogger, peavy swingers and all other sons of sawdust in this pine-shaded city.

Whereas the economy of Coeur d'Alene, mythical home of Paul Bunyan, is as dependent on the forest as barkbeetles, woodpeckers and chainsaws, and whereas the money of this community grows with trees and not on trees, and whereas trees form the texture of our skylines, the substance of our homes, and the sustenance of our economy, be it lumber, tourists or kilowatt:

Be It Therefore Resolved that the week of June –– shall be designated Forest Festival Week and that all citizens shall don the

446

attire of lumberjacks, shall inform themselves of the importance of our forests, and shall remove their hobnails at all dances.

Noncomplying citizens shall be assumed to have sawdust between their ears.

Several **Fort Sherman** military buildings survive in the vicinity of the North Idaho College campus. Drive northwest on Northwest Blvd. to Mullan Rd., left on Mullan to Lincoln Way, left on West Garden Ave. for two blocks, and left on Hubbard St. one block to the Fort Chapel at the corner of Woodland Dr. The chapel was designed and built by the War Department, and though it has passed the century mark, is well preserved. Jesuits provided services at the church from 1879 to 1887. In addition to its religious purpose, it served as a school for the post.

Return north on Hubbard St. to West Garden, turn left on West Garden and in mid-block note the two old buildings on the north side of the street. The first is the Officers' Quarters, built in 1878, and next door is Barracks Co. A, little altered from its original appearance.

Make a right turn at the end of the block, and after 100 feet turn into the parking lot next to the powderhouse museum. This brick magazine houses artifacts and information concerning the fort; the fenced backyard contains a collection of logging implements, U.S. Forest Service memorabilia, and two vehicles, one of which is a 1922 gasoline-powered lumber carrier.

The museum, barracks, and officers quarters are on the campus of North Idaho College. The school began as a private junior college in downtown Coeur d'Alene in 1933, became North Idaho J. C. in 1939, moved to the Fort Sherman campus in 1949, and now offers academic transfer, vocational-technical and adult-continuing education.

Two churches, within three blocks of each other, that date from Coeur d'Alene's heyday are worth inspecting. Take Northwest Blvd. southeast downtown to Sherman Ave. and follow Sherman to Ninth St. Turn north (left) on Ninth three blocks to the corner of Indiana Ave. where St. Thomas Catholic Church is located. The church was built in 1909-1910; the brick came from Sandpoint and the sandstone from Tenino, Washington. The 168-foot spire is a city landmark.

Drive north on Ninth one block and turn west (left) on Wallace Ave. two blocks to 618 at the intersection with Seventh St. The First United Methodist Church has a stepped gabled facade, unique among Idaho churches. It was built in 1906-1908. The *Coeur d'Alene*

Journal in 1909 remarked that the north-end stained glass window which depicts an Easter scene was "easily the finest window of its kind in this part of the country."

The lake waterfront lies a few blocks south of the downtown area. Take Third St. south from Sherman Ave. 1½ blocks to a free city parking lot. From this point it is possible to make a short, enjoyable hike up **Tubbs Hill** for a view of the lake and the town. The area is part of Tony Tubb's homestead, which he subdivided in 1883. Tubbs was the town's first justice of the peace, and steward of the Bunker Hill and Sullivan mine's boardinghouse. When the hill was threatened by hotel and condominium developments in the 1960s, the community raised the money to purchase thirty-four hillside acres for open space.

In the 1980s developers, who are known locally as "the Tumors," proposed two fourteen-story condominiums on lakeshore land just north of Tubbs Hill. Townspeople established a "Save Our Shores" committee and wrote a shoreline protection initiative that would limit building heights to three stories. With over 4,000 signatures, the measure qualified for a city election, but realtor interests obtained a writ of prohibition from the Idaho Supreme Court barring the referendum until the court could decide whether a community has the right to enact zoning ordinances by initiative.

In the meantime, the city issued a building permit, but "Save Our Shores" sued the city, and the district judge ruled that the permit should be rescinded. Candidates opposed to the high-rise development won four city council positions in a 1981 election. In late 1982 the State Supreme Court had not ruled on the proposed initiative. For the moment, it appears that thoughtful citizens have managed to constrain thoughtless growth.

Coeur d'Alene Lake was formed when glaciers to the north deposited a moraine across the valley of the St. Joe River to the south. Rivers and streams were impounded by the natural dam and flooded the valley.

The lake is named for the Indian tribe, a tribe that referred to itself as "Skeetshoo." Lewis and Clark heard of the lake from Nez Perce Indians, and though Clark never saw it, he included it on his map as "Wayton Lake" – from the Nez Perce word for "lake": e-wat'-um. When the explorer David Thompson entered the region in September, 1809, he knew the Indian tribe as the Coeur d'Alene ("Awl Heart"), and since that date precedes the era of the fur trapper, it refutes stories that associate the name with Indians who were shrewd traders and would not allow a trading post on their land. Adrien Hubert Brue, a French mapmaker, labeled the lake Coeur-Pointu ("Pointed Heart") in 1833; on other early maps the spread of water appears as Sketshue Lake. While the Coeur d'Alene name won out, the reason for its application to the Indian tribe, and hence to the lake, is apparently beyond recall.

For nearly a century, the lake has served as a reservoir for the mining wastes of the Coeur d'Alene district, which have been fed into the southern half of the lake by the South Fork of the Coeur d'Alene River. The pollution has been greatly reduced, but core samples taken by researchers in the 1970s showed heavy metal concentrations deposited to a depth of almost three feet over a wide area. It is likely the effects of these wastes are yet to be fully ascertained.

Coeur d'Alene Lake at one time had a phenomenal cutthroat trout population, but the species has declined along with the water quality.

Kokanee, a small, landlocked salmon, was introduced to the lake in 1937. Early spawning kokanees (Aug.-Sept.) turn red and spawn in tributary streams. Later runs (Nov.-Dec.) attempt to spawn along the lake's beaches; these fish do not experience a coloration change like the others. The Idaho Fish and Game Department reports about 250,000 kokanee are harvested from the lake annually.

Many other species of fish have been planted in the lake. Some Coho salmon and rainbow trout are present, but the shoreline lacks the gravel that would promote reproduction.

The largest nesting population of osprey in the western United States is found along the shores of Coeur d'Alene Lake; the birds feed primarily on warm water fish in the shallow shore areas. (Shoreline inundation by the Post Falls dam may actually have increased the food supply for these birds.) Fish hawks spend spring, summer and fall on the fringes of the lake, then migrate to Mexico and Central America for the winter.

Lake Coeur d'Alene had a mail route in 1914, believed to have been the first Postal Service water route in the country. Though that mail delivery ended in 1937, it is still possible to make a commercial lake cruise. From Sherman Ave. take First St. south into the parking area at Independence Point.

449

Finney Transportation Line runs Sunday and Wednesday trips during the summer (June through Sept.) across the lake and up the St. Joe River to Big Eddy, just below the town of St. Maries. The excursion covers ninety miles and requires six hours. A chicken dinner is served on board. Shorter cruises are available during the week.

The M.V. *Mish-An-Nock* offers two-hour cruises daily, June to September, which also originate from the city dock at Independence Point. Tickets are purchased when boarding. Check locally for departure schedules.

An enterprise, just outside Coeur d'Alene, will provide any visitor with an informative experience. It is the **Idaho Panhandle National Forests' tree nursery,** situated a mile northwest of town. From Highway 95 north, exit west on Forest Service Nursery Rd. and drive west to the 220-acre site. Tours are provided April through October, from 10:00 A.M.- 2:00 P.M., Monday-Friday. If one has only a hazy idea of silvicultural science or reforestation practices, he will be astonished by a tour of this facility.

The nursery was established in 1960 on a site that has uniform, rock-free soil and good drainage; one of thirteen such nurseries in the country. Its purpose is to serve as a "seed bank" for the National Forests in Region 1, and to produce seedling trees for reforestation projects in sixteen National Forests of the Northern Region and for co-operative federal and state agencies. In addition, the center does genetic research for the Inland Empire Tree Improvement Co-operative: Universities of Idaho, Montana, and Washington, Boise-Cascade, Inland Empire Paper Co., and Burlington Northern. (A major project is the development of a blister-rust resistant white pine.)

In order to fulfill its objectives, the nursery maintains 130 acres of irrigated seed beds and fifteen 30-by-100-foot greenhouses.

Seed cones are gathered at selected sites from standing or fallen trees and squirrel caches, often by public contract. The cones arrive at the nursery in bushel sacks. They have been tagged according to forest, district, species, elevation, year, zone, habitat type, and section, township, and range.

The cones are then dried in kilns to make them release their seeds. The seeds are stored in drums at zero degree Fahrenheit while samples are tested for germination. Some seeds are X-rayed to detect insect or fungus damage; the spent cones are pulverized and used as mulch in the seedbeds.

Nursery seedbeds are planted each spring. Germination occurs within a month and seedlings are cultured for two growing seasons. For this reason, planting requests for burned-over areas and selectively logged or clearcut sites, which must be matched to seed from the same forest, district, elevation, zone etc., have to be made three years in advance.

Seedlings grown in open seedbeds are mechanically lifted in the late fall and stored for the winter in walk-in freezers, or are lifted in the spring, two weeks before they break dormancy, and are refrigerated until sent to the forests for planting.

Greenhouse stock is seeded in plastic containers in March and July. These plants are nurtured by automated equipment. The March crop is ready for planting in September-October of the same year; the July crop is ready the following spring.

All trees grown at the nursery are coniferous, and the annual productive capacity is 40 million seedlings. During peak employment periods over 400 persons work at the nursery, packaging a million trees a day for two-week intervals.

The **Mullan Tree** is located just east of the crest of Fourth of July Summit on Highway 90, but there is no sign for eastbound cars because any attempt to cross the two lanes of oncoming traffic would be illegal and extremely hazardous. Drivers headed east should go to the bottom of the hill, where they will find it possible to execute a turn-around. Traveling west on Interstate 90, the turn-off for the tree is about three miles from the foot of the summit.

A gravel side road on the north edge of the highway leads back seventy-five yards to a white marble statue of Lt. John Mullan alongside an explanatory sign. Stairs descend to a fenced twelve-foot stump. On the far side, near the base, a Y 4 can be discerned.

Here is the story behind the xyloglyph. The U.S. Army officer, Isaac Stevens, was made Governor of Washington Territory in 1853, which at that time included northern Idaho. The same year, Congress approved an appropriation bill with provisions to survey possible routes for the Northern Pacific Railroad – the first of the proposed transcontinental routes. General Stevens was given the directorship of the survey party investigating the northern route.

A preliminary survey indicated the feasibility of a route from St. Paul, Minnesota, to Puget Sound, Washington, with a branch line to Portland. The biggest problem was where to cross the Rocky Mountains, and Stevens' Pacific Railway party explored the Missoula-Coeur d'Alene route in 1853.

Stevens then delegated most of his responsibility to Lieutenant John Mullan, a topographical engineer, who was left in charge of a party with the job of selecting the wagon route between Fort Benton, Montana, and Fort Walla Walla, Washington. The road was to be built as a military undertaking, but it was expected to serve as an alternate, less arid route for western emigration, and as a right-of-way for the anticipated railroad.

Congress appropriated $30,000 in 1854 for the undertaking, and Mullan gathered information, crossing and re-crossing the Continental Divide six times. Work was delayed by the Indian War of 1858; during that year Mullan commanded a party of Nez Perce scouts and helped Colonel Wright end the hostilities.

The Lieutenant began construction at Walla Walla in the summer, 1859, with a seventy-man crew, twenty of whom were soldiers. Work proceeded rapidly to the southern end of Coeur d'Alene Lake. A forty-foot ferry was constructed to cross the St. Joe River four miles above its mouth. The men were a week getting through the marshland south of Cataldo Mission. Then the problems began.

Timber was thicker than quills on a porcupine as they went up the South Fork of the Coeur d'Alene toward St. Regis River in Montana. The soldiers refused to cut any more trees; now there were only fifty workmen. Mullan described the situation a few years later:

The standing timber was dense and the fallen timber that had accumulated for ages formed an intricate jungle well calculated to impress one with the character of impracticability.

River crossings impeded their advance but they did reach the Montana side of the Bitterroots that fall, where they wintered, before surveying the general route through to Fort Benton in the spring.

That year floods on the St. Joe persuaded Mullan that he had chosen the wrong route around Coeur d'Alene Lake. In 1861 Congress appropriated an additional $100,000 to reroute that portion of the road; during the summer, Mullan and his men built the longer new stretch. Again, they encountered densely forested terrain.

The crew celebrated the Fourth of July in the canyon which now bears that name. They had only to reach the Cataldo Mission to intersect with the road they had previously built. It was at this time that they carved the Mullan Tree blaze.

Mullan's men were another month reaching Cataldo Mission; then they had to build sixty crossings of the Coeur d'Alene River and nearly as many on the St. Regis. The winter of 1862 was the worst

452

in many decades and the men were lucky to survive – they ate their horses. Many of them decided to quit in the spring. Mullan was unable to improve the eastern portions of the 624-mile, $230,000 road to the standard he envisioned.

Unfortunately, the spring floods of 1862 destroyed substantial stretches of the road. With so many miles of trees and water, constant repairs were needed, but there was no provision for maintenance. A few emigrant wagons and some packers used the road before it was reclaimed by nature. Even though the Congressional charter issued to the Northern Pacific Railway Company adopted the Mullan-Coeur d'Alene route, the railroad finally chose a more lucrative route to the north, around Pend Oreille Lake.

However, a century later, when a direct route for U.S. Interstate 90 across northern Idaho was selected, it matched that chosen by Captain John Mullan.

The inscription on the Mullan Tree read "M. R. July 4, 1861." The M. R. stood for "Military Road," initials the Secretary of War had ordered be used to mark the road at frequent intervals.

This white pine, estimated to have been about 325 years old, lost all but its trunk to a 1962 wind storm.

Traces of the old wagon road can still be seen west and east of the tree.

Extending east from the Mullan Tree turnoff, I-90 drops to Mission Flats, the flood plain of the Coeur d'Alene River. On a knoll to the south, the cornsilk-colored outline of the **Cataldo Mission of the Sacred Heart** is visible. This is the oldest building standing in Idaho (finished seven years before the first permanent non-Indian settlement in the state) and one of Idaho's eight Registered National Landmarks. The east and west exits to the Mission are appropriately marked, with easy access to a parking lot. The eighteen-acre Mission State Park, which includes picnic facilities, is open daily 9 A.M. to 5 P.M.

During visitor hours, the center just above the parking lot is the place to acquire information that will increase one's appreciation of this site: a sound-slide show, background displays about the Coeur d'Alene tribe and the Jesuit missionaries, and pamphlets for a self-guided tour of the church and the half-mile interpretative trail. No charge.

The Old Mission is more than a remarkable building – it is the location of an enterprise that played an important role in the historical and cultural development of the Northwest.

Father Pierre De Smet, S. J., came as a missionary to the Flatheads, at their request, in 1840. He visited the Coeur d'Alene tribe in the spring of 1842, en route to Colville (Washington) for crop seed. Being a missionary, he sowed the seeds of Catholicism along the way. Since De Smet had limited time, he devised a unique way of instructing his converts:

With the help of his interpreter he translated into Indian the Lord's Prayer, the Hail Mary, the Ten Commandments, with the Acts of Faith, Hope, Charity, and Contrition. He then made his Indian pupils stand in a circle, insisting that they should always take the same places. When they were thus arranged, he would teach to one the First Commandment, to another the Second, and so on. As to prayers he made each one learn by memory a different sentence of the same prayer, so that, everyone reciting what he had memorized, the whole would be rendered. This took him about three days, and all, young and old, soon knew the commandments and the prayers by heart.

As he promised at his 1842 meeting, the Jesuit priest sent Fr. Point and Br. Huet from his mission at St. Marys, Montana to establish a mission among the Coeur d'Alene. Since the location that they chose was baptized by the rising river each spring, in 1846 they moved to this knoll, selected by Fr. De Smet.

The Vice Provincial of the Mission of the Northwest decided to make his headquarters with the Coeur d'Alenes and developed plans for a mission that included a church and nine outbuildings.

The designs for the church were drawn by Fr. Anthony Ravalli, a Renaissance man. He had entered the Jesuit novitiate in Italy at age fifteen. There he studied theology, philosophy, medicine, mathematics, natural sciences, and apprenticed himself to an artist and a mechanic. Ravalli came to America in 1844 with De Smet.

In 1850 St. Marys closed temporarily, and Fr. Ravalli was placed in charge of the Coeur d'Alene mission. He arrived with impressive plans and simple tools: broad axe, auger, ropes and pulleys, a pen knife and an improvised whip saw. The workers were untrained but enthusiastic: two Brothers and a band of Indians. The collaboration was splendid. John Ruskin advised, "when we build, let us think that we build forever." Ravalli's effort reflects the thought. Fashioned in the architectural style known in America as Greek Revival, the building is ninety feet by forty on a four-foot wide foundation. Massive hewed beams are mortised and tenoned and all structural members are secured by wooden pegs. Holes were drilled in upright timbers and rafters, horizontal dowels were inserted between the uprights, then straw and grass was woven over the

454

framework and daubed with river mud. The walls are therefore nearly a foot thick, but hollow inside. (Fr. Caruana sheeted them with clapboard in 1865.) The ceiling panels, altars, picture frames, and statues are carved from wood. Candle holders and hinges were forged on the grounds. There are no pews because the Indians, unaccustomed to such rigidity, preferred the floor. The Coeur d'Alenes must have been pleased with the structure they had erected – not simply because of its elegance, but because it was larger than any tipi or lodge they had ever visited. (Fr. Ravalli died in 1884 and is buried at St. Mary's mission.)

With the completion of the Mission in 1853, many of the Indians settled on the grounds and learned to farm. Heretofore the Coeur d'Alene had been organized in small, semi-nomadic bands and none of them had practised agriculture. When the Governor of Washington Territory visited the site, he found the Indian farmers had 100 acres enclosed and under cultivation. They grew wheat and potatoes, pastured oxen and cows.

To a large extent, the Jesuits were responsible for inculcating a tolerant attitude among the Coeur d'Alene toward the white men. Nevertheless, some members of the tribe participated in the defeat of Colonel Steptoe in 1858, which brought swift retribution from the troops of Colonel Wright. Again, the missionaries interceded, and softened the effects of a harsh and punitive treaty – which was signed "beneath a bower of branches" on the flat below the Mission.

For years, the Mission served as a hospice to travelers and miners, though not all guests were equally impressed. This from the journal of Charles Rumby, en route from St. Louis to Portland:

Monday Sept. 29, 1862 Camped at Coeur d'Alene Mission. Said place is composed of a church about forty by sixty and some twenty miserable huts surround about it. Inhabited by a few squealy squaw's children. The Old Father is aged and looks rather hard. No feed for horses here about one miles back good grass. Bought potatoes for $2.50 per bushel.

Fr. Joseph Cataldo came among the Coeur d'Alene in 1865. He learned to speak their language, founded a number of churches in the Territory, and made the Old Mission his headquarters when he became Superior of such endeavors. He was still in contact with the Indians at the age of ninety.

The Coeur d'Alene were persuaded, with great reluctance on their part, to leave the Mission area for De Smet, Idaho, in 1877. While their reservation extended from the Old Mission to the other side of Coeur d'Alene Lake, it did not include the Mission land. Nor was there now enough ground on the flat for all of them to farm.

In 1924 the Jesuit Order deeded the property to the Diocese of Boise because after their departure the church had fallen into disuse and disrepair.

Interest in restoration of the structure was aroused in 1925 by citizen groups in the Coeur d'Alene valley, in Lewiston, Moscow, Orofino, Boise and Spokane. Contributions of several thousand dollars made it possible to repair foundation and floor, walls and roof.

Cataldo Mission of the Sacred Heart. Father Ravalli designed the facade according to the mathematical principle developed by Pythagoras, known in architecture as the "Golden Section."

Column length was determined by the base diameter on a 1:6 proportion. The false gable with a monstrance motif is not characteristic of the Greek Revival style; it served to hide a roofline necessarily steeper than those built for the mild climate of Greece.

456

By the early 1970s, the Old Mission was again in need of major preservation work. This was accomplished in 1973-1975, at a cost of $310,000, as the first project of the Idaho Bicentennial Commission.

The Old Mission became a state park in 1975.

Each year, on the Feast of the Assumption (Aug. 15), a Catholic holy day, members of the Coeur d'Alene tribe return to the Cataldo Mission to hear a High Mass celebrated by the Jesuit priest who serves their tribe.

Following the Mass, the Indians feast with traditional native foods and produce a pageant about the arrival of the missionaries called, "The Coming of the Black Robes." The public is welcome.

At **Pinehurst** one encounters the South Fork of the Coeur d'Alene for the first time. This maltreated river was once an undefiled, purling stream, thick with fish. Giant cottonwoods and cedars grew along its banks.

But miners began crushing ores in the mid-1800s and used the river as a waste conduit for pulverized ore and slimes. Thousands of pounds of zinc, lead, and suspended solids and hundreds of pounds of arsenic were dumped into its waters daily for seventy years. Over 100 million tons of ore were mined in that period. In the words of the poet Wendell Berry, "the river has become the gut of greed."

Only recently, because of federal and state laws, have mining corporations established tailing impoundments, ponds and treatment plants to reduce the flow of contaminants. It is distressing that the upper six to eight feet of the valley floor are composed of old tailings and sediments that were dumped by early mine operators, and because the water table is relatively high and makes contact with the waste products, the river will probably be too toxic for fish long after the mines have exhausted their reserves.

Pinehurst marks the entrance to the western end of the Coeur d'Alene valley or the **Silver Valley** as chambers of commerce prefer to call it. Since 1884 the mines here have produced metals valued at $4 billion. Historically, that production ranks the valley among the top ten mining districts in the world. The mines at present produce approximately 47 percent of the nation's silver – a larger portion than any other state's.

The undeniable, overwhelming commercial presence in the Silver Valley has been that of the **Bunker Hill Company,** visible along the south side of Highway 90 at the outskirts of **Kellogg.** The towering smokestacks, silhouetted against the denuded slopes, mark the locations of the company's lead smelter and zinc refinery.

The story of Noah Kellogg's jackass being responsible for the discovery of the Bunker Hill lode is an Idaho legend too firmly entrenched to dispute now – but like most legends, it is probably more fable than fact.

Noah Kellogg was a carpenter, and he worked in the Murray placer goldfields, north of present Kellogg, building flumes. He was grubstaked, for a half-interest in any claim he might discover, by Dr. John Cooper and Origin Peck, of Murray, in the summer of 1885. Noah was out on the South Fork of the Coeur d'Alene for nearly a month and returned when his supplies were depleted. The men staked him again, and this time he returned in two weeks, with tools and jackass, indicating his efforts had come to nothing.

But Kellogg's name appeared as a witness on a claim filed that September on Milo Gulch, just south of present Kellogg. He had apparently fallen in with a couple of other prospectors and all had filed claims in the gulch. Perhaps there was a conspiracy to cheat Cooper and Peck. The yarn spun later reported that while looking for his jackass, Noah found the animal standing on an outcrop of mineral, staring in amazement at an ore chute glittering in the sunlight across the canyon. (In reality, the surface showing was modest: nothing more than iron-stained quartzite containing specks of galena.)

Whatever the myth, a judge at the Murray couthouse ruled in equity that Cooper and Peck were entitled to a one-fourth interest in the Bunker Hill and Sullivan claim which Kellogg, O'Rourke and Sullivan had discovered – one of the largest lead-silver deposits in the world. Prospectors swarmed into Milo Gulch and claims were laid out like cross ties on a railroad.

As the historian, John Fahey, has pointed out, Idaho Territory copied California and Nevada mining laws in 1864, including the provision for lode miners that the locator of the vein at the place where it rose nearest to the earth's surface (apex) possessed certain rights to follow its plane downward – even outside the vertical boundaries he had staked.

A federal act in 1872 required a miner to locate a piece of land on which a mineral vein actually appeared and to stake his claim over an area running lengthwise in the direction of the vein's course, and survey it with parallel lines. Thus lode claims were twenty acres: 1,500 feet long and 600 feet wide.

Strange as it may seem in retrospect, when claims were filed on Milo Gulch close to the Bunker Hill "vein," no one then perceived the true direction of the vein. All the mines on an area about 1,000 feet wide and 6,000 feet long worked the same ore, which was found in a host rock subsequently named the Revett Formation. Mineral deposits in the formation had been "pocketed" under the influence of recurrent fault movement over the ages. But it was many years before men understood the complex structure of the formation.

Early claims straddled, rather than followed, the course of the vein. For this reason, in the early years, Bunker Hill and Sullivan and the other major mines were involved in constant litigation. No mine has a shaft so bottomless as the law. Lawyers, who earn a living by the sweat of their browbeating, had struck a glory hole. Like winter nights, the suits and countersuits were long and wearisome. The Last Chance fought the Tyler for six years. The Skookum sued the Last Chance, and that case went eight times to the Court of Appeals and three times to the Supreme Court. The *Empire State – Idaho* versus *Bunker Hill and Sullivan* assumed the entangled proportions of the epic *Jarndyce v. Jarndyce* litigation in Dicken's *Bleak House.*

No mining company could afford to allow its competitor a legal triumph, lest the right to pursue ore outside the company's claim be lost. There was even a locked door between the Bunker Hill and Last Chance claims, where the miners had encountered each other underground. Many of the precedents established in the legal duels of the Coeur d'Alene district embalmed principles that still stand in mining law. The U.S. Supreme Court ruled on three cases in one day involving a claim now owned by the Bunker Hill. The entire Coeur d'Alene valley is a quilt of claims, most patented – some still disputed.

Early development of the Bunker Hill and Sullivan lode was dependent upon an outlet route for ore. The first rock was hauled by wagon to Kingston (five miles west of Kellogg), loaded on a steamer for Coeur d'Alene, then hauled to Rathdrum, where it could be delivered to the Northern Pacific railroad.

On Christmas Day, 1886, the businessman D. C. Corbin, and Sam Hauser, Governor of Montana, completed a narrow-guage railroad from the steamboat landing at Cataldo to Wardner Junction and began hauling the Bunker's stockpiled ore. By the fall of 1887, the link to Wallace had been completed. (The track crossed the South Fork of the Coeur d'Alene thirty times in twenty miles!)

That year, a mining promoter, Jim Wardner, patched together several claims, along with that of the Bunker Hill and Sullivan, and managed to sell them to one of the better known western "robber barons," Simon Gannett Reed, for $731,000. (Noah Kellogg reputedly received $150,000 and minority stock from this sale.)

Old Mission landing, Corbin's railroad, and steamboat "Coeur d'Alene."

"Amelia Wheaton" leaves the landing.

Reed hired a top mining engineer, Victor Clement, from California's Mother Lode, for $500 a month. The new general manager of the Bunker Hill and Sullivan Mining and Concentration Company promptly attempted to reduce hourly wages. The miners struck and formed the Wardner Miner's Union – first in the Coeur d'Alene district. The company backed down, but a twelve-year contest between management and labor had begun.

While Reed used political influence to get a protective tariff on Mexican lead and fought railroad freight rates, smelting charges, and litigation from adjoining claims (by bribing witnesses and

460

jurors), Clement constructed a tram and concentrator which went into operation in mid-1891. The tram was 8,900 feet long with two cables and a transport capacity of forty tons an hour. The ore was brought down to a bunker in Wardner. The 150-ton concentrator, two miles from Wardner, was the largest in the world at the time: 447 feet long and five stories high. Leffel water wheels ran the machinery. Clement also introduced compressed air drills and had over 400 men working at the mine.

When the Northern Pacific opened a connecting line from Wallace to Missoula in 1892, Bunker Hill and Sullivan concentrates were shipped to a smelter in Helena. Later, the company operated its own smelter in Tacoma.

Because of poor health, fluctuating markets, and vexatious lawsuits, Reed decided to sell in 1892, at a $15,000 loss. The investment group that purchased the mine included the California mine inspector, John Hammond, the reaper-monarch, Cyrus McCormick, and D. O. Mills and W. H. Crocker, San Francisco bankers.

Bunker Hill and Sullivan employed about 400 miners in 1899; most of them were non-union and were paid less than the $3.50 per ten-hour day rate offered by the region's other mines. In addition, Bunker Hill and Sullivan still had an interest in company stores and required permits from men who applied for work. (These permits showed past employment and any union affiliation, a carryover from labor problems at the Frisco mill in Burke Canyon seven years earlier.) Such reactionary policies on the part of management led directly to an incident only slightly less famous in the district's history than Noah Kellogg's jackass yarn.

In the spring, 1899, the Wardner Local of the Western Federation of Miners decided to force Bunker Hill's acceptance of the union, thereby eliminating the permit-blacklist. The company said it would close for twenty years before it would recognize the union, but did raise wages to the prevailing standard. The union voted to strike the Bunker Hill and Sullivan so the company rescinded the raise, stated that any employee who joined the union would be fired, and posted armed guards.

On April 29, about 300 men, two-thirds of them armed, commandeered nine cars of the Northern Pacific train at Wallace and stopped to pick up men at each town all the way to Wardner. Estimates place the crowd at 800-1,000 men by the time it began to move toward Bunker Hill. Management at the mine had heard they were coming and did not wait to see the whites of their eyes. The premises were vacated.

The men arrived at the concentrator, placed giant powder, and touched off the fuse. Then they headed back home, leaving the mill in shambles. By nightfall, the area was quiet as a played-out mine.

Governor Steunenberg, confined to a hospital bed in Boise, was notified of the event. He wired President McKinley at 11 P.M. for federal troops, and his request was immediately granted. Negro soldiers from Spokane arrived in Wardner May 2.

The Governor sent the state auditor, Bartlett Sinclair, who apparently missed out on the Bill of Rights, to the area as his representative. More federal troops arrived. On May 3 martial law was proclaimed for Shoshone County. Wholesale arrests were ordered by Sinclair: he wanted to charge 400 men with murder and arson and 700 with conspiracy. The entire male populations of Gem, Burke, and Mullan, even men as far away as Spokane, were arrested. Prisoners were put into boxcars and warehouses until a board enclosure called "the bullpen" could be erected at Wardner. Sinclair was determined to stamp out unionism because "The State cannot endure these revolutions ... and the expense of suppressing these riots." More than fifty lawyers arrived – like buzzards over a gut wagon.

The state auditor issued a proclamation to mine owners May 8 that stated, among other things, they were not to hire union men during the period of martial law. Any mining company that disregarded the directive would be closed. The proclamation appointed the Bunker Hill and Sullivan company doctor as the agent of the state to issue permits "authorizing ... (applicants) ... to seek work." Without a permit, a man was refused work and *prima facie* every man not at work at another mine on the Saturday of the explosion was disqualified from receiving a permit.

The Mine Owners Association was, of course, jubilant. It was a devastating blow to the unions. Miners were replaced with scabs and immigrants from Montana, Utah, Colorado, and Missouri. Bunker Hill and Sullivan continued the use of a similar permit for twenty years, screening applicants for employment anywhere in the Coeur d'Alene district through an employment bureau at Wallace.

By September, Bunker Hill had rebuilt its concentrator, and half its new equipment was running.

Federal reports indicate 1,100 men were in the bull pen at various times. Some were held as late as March, 1901. Winter weather was "...raw and cold. There was consequently a great deal of sickness ... several cases of pneumonia and typhoid fever." Martial law lasted until April, 1901.

462

Of the thirteen men tried in November, out of the hundreds arrested, ten were convicted of "forcible seizure of a train carrying U.S. mails" and fined $1,000 each. Nine were sentenced to twenty-two months in prison.

The union had been run through a ball mill and would be years recovering. Five years later, despite enormous increases in productivity, wage rates were no higher than they had been fifteen years earlier, though the eight-hour day was gaining gradual acceptance.

Bunker Hill and Sullivan mine crew in the 1890s.

The Bunker Hill and Sullivan Mining and Concentration Company name was changed to The Bunker Hill Co. in 1956. The head office, which had been maintained in San Francisco, was closed in 1962. In early 1968, Gulf Resources and Chemical Corporation acquired Bunker Hill as a wholly owned subsidiary.

Gulf Resources was incorporated in Delaware in 1951 as Gulf Sulphur Corp. The company is headquartered in Houston, Texas and owns coal companies (including the largest surface mine in Pennsylvania), Pend Oreille Oil and Gas Co., and a major interest in Bethlehem Copper Corp.

Robert Allen, chairman of the company from 1960 to 1980, built Gulf Resources from a small sulfur company into a $700 million diversified natural resources firm through a series of leveraged acquisitions. Bunker Hill was the largest of those assets. In 1980 it provided 66 percent of the parent company's operating profits and 50 percent of its sales.

463

In early 1981 the Hunt family of Dallas, Texas, tendered an offer of $500 million for all outstanding shares of Gulf Resources and Chemical Corporation. The offer was placed through the Placid Oil Co., a subsidiary owned by the Hunt family. The offer was refused by Gulf Resources but the Hunts acquired 11 percent of Gulf's stock.

However, by late 1981 the economic recession had severely reduced the automotive and construction markets for lead and zinc; this coupled with the plunge in the price of silver on the international market, had produced losses of $7.7 million at Bunker Hill in the first half of the year. In addition, the parent company had a heavy debt load which totaled $225 million. The Bunker Hill Company needed perhaps $100 million in capital improvements to be competitive but lacked funds for modernization. Gulf Resources preferred to devote one-third of its capital spending to oil and gas exploration.

The tenth truth of management asserts "the easiest way to make money is to stop losing it." Gulf Resources and Chemical Corp. announced in August, 1981, that it was closing the Bunker Hill Co.

The impact of the decision was felt not just in the Silver Valley, but in Coeur d'Alene and Spokane as well; it represented an end to the largest payroll in north Idaho. Washington Water Power Co. lost its largest single customer and the Union Pacific lost its biggest hauling contract in the area.

The governor of Idaho organized a committee to seek a buyer/operator for the facility, but none could be found – even after the EPA agreed to a five-year moratorium on compliance with air-quality standards at the smelter. Gulf Resources rejected an employee stock-option purchase plan.

In early 1982 a group of northern Idaho investors, headed by the potato mogul Jack Simplot, attempted to buy the Bunker Hill complex from Gulf Resources for $65 million. The Kellogg local of the United Steel Workers of America voted to accept a 25 percent reduction in pay, but the Steelworkers' president in Pittsburgh rejected the local's vote as "advisory only" and refused to accept the labor agreement proposed by the investor group, thereby ending the rescue effort.

Proceeds from the piece-meal sale of Bunker Hill's assets were used to reduce Gulf Resources debt-to-equity ratio. Loss-carryback provisions of the state and federal tax laws allowed Gulf to offset the 1981 reverses against three years of high silver prices.

Miners going underground in a skip.

Miner at the Sunshine mine uses a pneumatic mucker.

A discussion of the processes which occurred at the Bunker Hill Co. mine, smelter and refinery is included here because the evidence will remain visible for decades, and because the mining techniques used were similar to those practiced by other mines still active in the valley. (Underground tours of mines are not available in the district, not just because of safety and liability aspects, but also because production requires tight timetables for ore and equipment movements within the mine.)

465

Diamond-drilled ore samples, examined by geologists, are used to locate areas with favorable mineral occurrence. Tunnels, shafts (usually inclined at forty-five degrees), hoists, and drifts branched with crosscuts are used to gain access to the ore. Miners use drills (run by compressed air piped into the mine) and ammonium nitrate explosives to break out the ore. They use a timbered, cut and fill method to prevent cave-ins as the stope progresses. At times in the past, this method required up to 6 million board feet of fir and larch each year – timber that could not be recovered. Now, where lower grade ore is found in denser rock, the pillar stoping method is used, leaving stone columns as support.

Diesel-powered front end loaders with hydraulic lifts and rubber tires pick up the loose ore and dump it into rubber-tired, diesel trucks. The ore is then hauled to one of the shafts where skips (giant buckets holding ten-ton payloads) hoist it to the main haulage level. There diesel locomotives pull the loaded ore cars to the concentrator (often called a mill).

Over 135 miles of tunnels, crosscuts and drifts comprise the Bunker Hill mine, from which 40 million tons of ore have been removed.

The plant closest to the south side of Highway 90 was the lead smelter, first built in 1917. Lead is derived from the mineral galena. Idaho ranked second in production among the states, and Bunker Hill supplied about 15 percent of the primary lead refined in the country. Only about 20 to 25 percent of the lead smelted here came from Coeur d'Alene mines – the balance consisted of concentrates sent for custom refining and smelting from mines as distant as Australia and South America. More than half the lead produced was destined for storage batteries, so something as insignificant as a mild eastern winter could affect the output demand at Bunker Hill.

Ore brought from the mine was crushed, screened, blended, and pulverized in a ball mill. It was then pumped to lead flotation cells, where large paddles skimmed off the lead-bearing minerals. Zinc-bearing minerals were floated away separately. Both metal concentrates were thickened in settling tanks, then fed through drum filters. The tailing sand was pumped back to the mine as a slurry (45 percent solids) to refill mined areas. (About one ton of sand was piped back for every two tons of ore removed.)

The concentrates were pelletized, then flash roasted in sinter units to remove sulfur. The porous mass that results is called sinter; it was mixed with coke and fed through a blast furnace. Lead bullion was drawn off in a continuous stream, with the slag floating free.

466

The lead bullion was moved by crane in iron pots to the lead refinery for separation of metals such as copper, gold, and silver. Hard lead was cast in ton blocks or eighty-five pound pigs; corroding lead (plumber's lead) was cast in similar blocks and 100 pound pigs.

The most outstanding, or noticeable, feature of the lead smelter is its 715-foot smokestack: the taller of the two towers and the one closest to the highway. It was built in 1976 in an attempt to disperse sulfur dioxide emissions (which combine with water vapor to make sulfuric acid) and bring the plant into compliance with the National Clean Air Act.

Ore grinders in the Bunker Hill concentrator.

The column was constructed using a continuous pour slip-form method; it required 209 tons of reinforcement bar and 7,830 tons of concrete which was poured in twenty-nine working days.

The chimney was connected by a flue system to the acid plant and to the exhaust of a baghouse. Dust from the blast furnace was captured and transferred to the baghouse for filtration. Four 1,000 h.p. fans pulled the gas stream through the baghouse for cleansing before release to the stack.

Though the towers are monuments to the "pollution dilution solution," they did effectively reduce ground-level sulfur emissions in the Silver Valley. They allowed smelter operations to proceed during periods of temperature inversions which required costly curtailment in the past.

While sulfur dioxide emissions rarely exceeded established standards, the same could not be said with regard to particulate lead emissions from the smelter. The State Department of Health and Welfare voiced considerable concern in the late 1970s when it was discovered children in the Coeur d'Alene valley evinced undue lead absorption as indicated by high lead levels in their blood. The Environmental Protection Agency promulgated a health standard for lead particulates of 1.5 micrograms per cubic meter of air, averaged over quarterly periods. But even in 1981, the count at nearby Silver King school was almost ten times the permissible level. Nowhere in the west end of the valley was the count within the guidelines.

In 1977 parents of nine former Kellogg children sued the Bunker Hill Company for $20 million on the children's behalf. The plaintiffs alleged the children had suffered brain and physical damage from lead emissions from the company's smelter.

The jury trial began at the U.S. District Court in Boise in September, 1981. The children's attorneys argued that the company knew it was releasing high levels of lead at night, following a 1973 fire which damaged the baghouse where smelter gases were filtered. During a six-month period in 1973-1974, emissions equalled those of the entire previous eleven-year period. Lead concentrations in the soil increased by twelve times from early 1971 to early 1974. Lead deposits at the elementary school attended by the plaintiff children were about 160 times higher than the level considered to be safe. The company never warned Silver Valley residents about the dangerous emissions. Management had made a decision to operate without the controls and risk the consequences.

A 1974 study by the Center for Disease Control in Atlanta showed that 88 percent of 1,000 children in the Kellogg area who were tested in a survey had unsafe levels of lead in their blood.

Lawyers for Bunker Hill and Gulf Resources blamed any disabilities on a "filthy" home environment, and on drug use.

Persons in the Silver Valley were divided on the principle involved in the case. Many were more concerned with their job prospects than the health of the children. Aspects of the controversy were reminiscent of Henrick Ibsen's play, *An Enemy of the People*. More than fifty witnesses testified at the trial.

After nearly six weeks of testimony, the parties reached an out-of-court settlement that exceeded $2 million. The money was controlled by a legal guardian appointed by the court.

The buildings located farther up Government Gulch, at the base of the second stack (610 feet high) comprised the electrolytic zinc plant and fertilizer factory.

Zinc in the lead ores of the Coeur d'Alenes was regarded as a nuisance until World War I. At that time, it was produced for the war effort, but it was not until World War II, when improvements in metallurgy made possible the economical separation of zinc and lead in complex ores, that the value of zinc produced exceeded that of lead.

Bunker Hill opened its zinc refinery in 1928. Zinc concentrates, most of which came from outside the Coeur d'Alene district, were dried in roasters, fed through a ball mill, then roasted again to burn off the sulfur. The material, called calcine, was mixed with sulfuric acid, and the resultant sulfate solution was pumped through large filters, purified, and removed from solution by electrolysis. Stripped from the cathodes, the zinc was sent to a melting furnace, where it emerged 99.99 percent pure and was cast in one-ton blocks and sixty-pound slabs.

The Bunker Hill Company was the first to produce zinc and zinc alloys of such purity, and that accomplishment caused the die casting industry, which required a high quality zinc, to become the largest consumer of the metal in the U.S. Lower quality zinc is used as a galvanized protective coating on steel pipe, sheets, and wires.

Sulfuric acid units, which captured the sulfur dioxide from the lead smelter and zinc refinery stacks, provided half the material necessary to produce phosphoric acid at the Bunker Hill fertilizer plant. The sulfuric acid was mixed with ground phosphate rock brought by railroad cars to the plant.

Even a fairly inattentive tourist cannot avoid noticing the barren slopes that tarnish the Silver Valley in the Pinehurst-Kellogg stretch. While mining companies tend to blame forest fires, a cursory inspection of early photographs and newspaper accounts proves fire is not the culprit. Mines consumed prodigious amounts of timber for stopes, shafts and chutes, and as fuel to generate steam power. Bunker Hill had its own sawmill sixty-six years, and a company publication in 1966 stated, "It is estimated that there is more timber underground in the Coeur d'Alene mining district than there is standing at the present time in the entire Coeur d'Alene National Forest."

Regeneration of the once heavily forested valley has been impeded by erosion and by smelters releasing sulfur oxides for sixty years. Sulfur dioxide injures a plant's chlorophyll mechanism.

In the early Thirties, when Vardis Fisher, under the aegis of the Works Projects Administration, wrote the first Idaho guidebook, he described Kellogg: "Below it the river bottoms look like a caricature of a graveyard, and above it the denuded mountains declare the potency of lead (sic). West of Kellogg with its miracles of machinery, there is still to be seen a poisoned and dead or dying landscape."

Matters improved. In a commendable, if modest, attempt to ameliorate the situation, Gulf Resources and Chemical Corp. spent $3,000 in 1975 to build a forty-foot greenhouse in an abandoned ventilation drift within the Bunker Hill mine. There, 3,000 feet underground, beneath Super Metalarc lamps, the company grew 4,000 ponderosa, lodgepole, and Austrian pine seedlings. The underground environment was disease and insect free, and maintained a constant seventy-five degree temperature and ideal humidity. In this manner, larger seedlings could be grown at one-fourth the conventional nursery cost. Bunker Hill Co. announced a ten-year plan to revegetate 18,000 acres which have suffered from mining and smelting activities. Thousands of seedlings were planted. As with most extractive industries, however, the corporate commitment to reclamation dissolved along with its enterprise.

Kellogg, marked by exit signs, straddles the South Fork of the Coeur d'Alene, at its confluence with Milo Creek.

The town, first called "Jackass," was laid out in 1886 by the Ingall brothers and named Milo because of the creek. However, the name of the town was changed a third time in 1887 to honor Noah Kellogg, reputed discoverer of the Bunker Hill lode.

The town incorporated in 1913 and annexed the Bunker Hill area in 1956. Obviously, it was a community almost entirely dependent on the payroll of the Bunker Hill Company and was devastated by the closure of the smelter and refinery. The company normally employed about 2,000 persons at its complex.

A short drive up the hill on the southeast edge of town provides a view of the Silver Valley and the Kellogg cemetery. The graves of Noah Kellogg and True Blake, the prospectors who made two of the more consequential discoveries in the district, are elaborately marked.

To reach the community of **Wardner** from Kellogg, drive south up Division St. through Milo Gulch. Milo was Noah's deceased brother, and it was his spirit, according to Noah, that guided the prospector (or his jackass) to the bonanza.

The collection of tents and shacks in the gulch was christened "Kentuck" in October, 1885, by miners who wanted to salute the owners of the famous Golden Chest mine at nearby Murray.

Kellogg school in 1887.

Mucking contest in Kellogg (1913).

However, Washington postal authorities rejected the name, and less than a year later, following discussions at a meeting, the miners unanimously agreed to commemorate Jim Wardner, who was boosting the community and the Bunker Hill and Sullivan mine.

South Fork of the Coeur d'Alene River floods Kellogg on Christmas, 1933.

Wardner was a charming, fiddle-footed con-man. He was born in Milwaukee, Wisconsin, in 1846. He tried a lot of things once, and money went through his pockets like they had holes in the bottom as big as his pant's leg. Jim attempted open-woods hog farming in the southern California mountains, mining in Arizona and Utah, stock market speculation in San Francisco, wheat futures in Milwaukee, and the egg market in South Dakota. Perhaps his most amusing venture was "fur farming" several thousand stray black cats on an island in the San Juans, off the Washington coast, in order to market their pelts as "hood seal" in St. Louis. It worked until the keeper, tired of catching fish for his charges, fed them to each other.

Attracted to Idaho by the goldstrike at Murray, Wardner became temporarily wealthy by promoting the Bunker Hill and Sullivan mine and by selling corner lots in this community.

In the 1890s Jim traveled to mining strikes in South Africa, British Columbia (where another town bears his name), and the Klondike. He published his autobiography in 1900.

472

The buildings of Wardner are perched along the steep slopes above what remains of the creek. A fire in January, 1890, burned half the town's Main St. Available water had frozen; blasting powder was used to make a firebreak between the buildings.

Wardner in 1905.

In 1891 the town had nineteen saloons. For those who could still see at night, there was light from 350 incandescent globes electrified by a steam-driven dynamo at the Last Chance mine. The settlement's mining payroll amounted to $100,000 a month at that time.

A second disastrous fire swept the town in April, 1893, and burned eighty buildings; nearby communities sent a trainload of supplies to aid the citizens.

In 1899 Wardner was the site of the infamous "bullpen," after the demolition of the Bunker Hill and Sullivan concentrator.

The hill northeast of the gulch is Haystack Peak. It is possible to follow the dirt road that branches to the right, seven miles up to the Silverhorn ski area on Kellogg Peak, with excellent vistas of the valley below.

Take the **Big Creek** exit off Interstate 90, about 3.5 miles east of Kellogg to view the miners' memorial on the north side of the overpass. A twelve-foot steel statue by Ken Lonn, of Kellogg, stands

473

at the base of the rock bluff. This rather prosaic piece of proletarian sculpture – a miner with drill thrust skyward – masks an epical mining disaster touched by genuine courage, even heroism.

The 173 men, comprising the normal day shift, who entered the Sunshine mine (four miles south of the memorial) on May 2, 1972 had no intimation they were about to be involved in the largest U.S. hardrock mining tragedy in over fifty years. The principal operating officials of the mining company were in Coeur d'Alene at the annual stockholders' meeting. Surface and underground foremen were responsible for the activities of their own crews, but no individual had been given overall supervisory power.

Sunshine miners' memorial.

At 11:40 A.M., following their lunch, two electricians walked out of the electric shop at the 3,700-foot level inside the mine, smelled smoke and shouted a warning. Smoke was discovered coming down a nearby raise. A foreman arrived, closed a fire door near the main shaft, and attempted to locate the source of the smoke. The drift

474

and crosscuts became so clouded he had to retreat with three other men – all of them were nearly overcome by smoke inhalation in the process.

At 12:03 P.M. the No. 10 shaft foreman telephoned the mine maintenance foreman with a request to activate the stench-warning system. (This system injects ethyl mercaptan, which smells like rotten cabbage, into the compressed air lines that extend throughout the mine.) He also asked that oxygen-breathing apparatus be sent to the mine and instructed the hoistman for No. 10 shaft to prepare the cage for moving the men to the 3,100 level of the mine.

Most workmen first became aware of the fire when smoke entered their workplaces. They made their way to the No. 10 shaft station with the hope of escaping, but dense smoke at the "chippy" cage hoistroom forced the hoistman to abandon the room.

Fortunately, No. 10 shaft had a double-drum hoist. The south cage of the drum continued to operate with volunteer cagers. The first load of twelve men was hoisted to the 3,100 level at 12:10 P.M. Hoisting evacuation continued between the 5,600 to 3,100 foot-levels until 1:02 P.M., when the double-drum hoistman died at his post.

The first rescue group, with oxygen-breathing apparatus, entered the 3,100 level from the main shaft about 1:00 P.M. The four men rescued two others, but one of the rescuers, Don Beehner, gave his mask to an escaping miner in need of oxygen, only to die of monoxide poisoning himself. The man Beehner saved, Byron Schulz, had, along with Greg Dionne, voluntarily made multiple trips on the No. 10 shaft cage between the 5,000 and 3,100 levels. Other miners, such as Jim Bush, Roberto Diaz, Harvey Dionne, Paul Johnson, Ronald Stansberry, and Norman Ulrich made heroic efforts to aid their fellow workers. Some of them died in the effort. The last survivors who evacuated on May 2 reached the surface at about 1:30 P.M. – a total of eighty men.

Nearly 100 trained rescue personnel from seven other mines in the U.S. and Canada began arriving at the Sunshine mine by 2:00 P.M. the same day. At this point, the location of the fire was still unknown, though the area was assumed to be between the 3,100 and 3,700-foot levels, and between No. 10 shaft and the main or "Jewell" shaft. The first crew recovered five bodies along the 3,700 level drift and returned to the surface about 4:30 P.M. Spouses, relatives and families of the trapped miners began to gather at the Sunshine for what was to prove a dreary, long, and cruelly disappointing vigil.

The labyrinthine rescue operation required urgent solutions to a bewildering number of problems. Under Withdrawal Order No. 1, the recovery operations were subject to the U.S. Bureau of Mines' approval.

Careful and continuing assessment of the mine's ventilation system was required because fans might be forcing smoke and carbon monoxide through the mine, but changes in air flows could disturb a balance in the lower levels upon which survivors were dependent. (It was believed most men were trapped in the lower levels.)

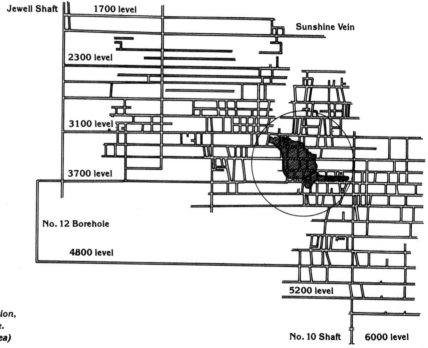

Vertical projection,
Sunshine mine.
(fire in circle area)

The rescue plan which was developed aimed at establishing fresh air and access across the 3,100 level to No. 10 hoistroom from the main shaft and the same access between the shafts at the 3,700-foot level.

Bulkheads had to be installed in order to seal old openings and to prevent leakage of contaminated air. Westinghouse Electric furnished large, inflatable bags that could be filled quickly with rigid urethane foam. New fans were installed in an attempt to increase fresh air flow; main shaft air doors had to be pressurized from the shaft side, and surface fans attempted to increase exhaust flow.

Progress toward No. 10 shaft required many seals and proceeded at an agonizing plod. Because of the delays, the Bureau of Mines attempted another approach on May 7. Two-man capsules were obtained from the Atomic Energy Commission's Nevada test site. Men were to be lowered through No. 12 borehole to the 4,800-foot level, where miners were known to have been working.

An air-powered hoist was installed at the borehole, and a closed-circuit television survey was made of its condition. Then shortly after 9:00 P.M. on May 8, the first two-man crew was lowered. They discovered that the hole contained slabs of loose rock, which could endanger their lives; so they had to scale as they went. It took crews until 7:00 A.M. on May 9 to cover the 1,100-foot distance to the 4,800 level. That evening a crew found two miners in good condition not far from the No. 10 shaft. They were hoisted up the borehole – the last survivors found in the mine.

Cave-ins on the 3,700 level, caused by the destruction of timber supports, severed compressed-air and electrical lines, and rescue efforts at that level had to be abandoned.

When an attempt was made to engage the hoist system in No. 10 shaft electrical difficulties were encountered; voltage from the Bonneville Power Administration was reduced to accommodate the hoist circuits. The first rescue crew was able to descend the No. 10 shaft the night of May 9 and began to recover bodies. Thirty-one victims were found at the 3,100 level, twenty-one at the 5,200 level, and another thirty-nine bodies at intermediate levels. By May 13 recovery was completed. The coroner issued a finding that all had died of "suffocation from carbon monoxide and smoke."

Experienced men, offered premium pay, worked to smother the fire by sealing the area with sandfill plugs and bulkheads.

The official disaster report, assembled under the Secretary of the Interior, states that "The Bureau of Mines believes that spontaneous combustion of refuse near scrap timber was the probable cause of the Sunshine mine fire." Bureau investigators believe that when air leaks around the bulkhead to an abandoned vein were closed, oxidation of waste materials near mine timbers in that vein increased to the point of combustion. The fire then burned through a urethane foam-coated bulkhead and short-circuited the mine ventilation system – high ventilating pressure forced contaminated air from the fire area into the intake airstreams on the 3,700 and 3,100-foot levels. The air returned through the 3,400 level fans and was recirculated over the fire, continually increasing the concentration of carbon monoxide. Men at the lower levels were rapidly exposed to its toxic effects.

Among the causes of the scope of the disaster the Bureau found the following factors: 1.) The stench-warning system contained about 20 percent of the necessary amount of ethyl mercaptan for the quantity of air entering the mine, and the system had never been tested. 2.) Evacuation was delayed twenty minutes while an investigation was conducted. 3.) Self-rescuers were not maintained in useable condition. 4.) The emergency escape-way system from the mine was not adequate for rapid evacuation. (Ladderways were contaminated with toxic fumes and best estimates indicated almost four hours would have been required to climb to safety under good conditions.) The mine reopened Dec. 8, 1972.

The memorial was dedicated on May 2, 1974.

Drive south on the road from the miner's memorial to an extensive tailing area on the right side of the road. Sunshine Mining Company's tailing ponds farther up the road had reached their capacity, but the Shoshone County golf course blocked northerly expansion down Big Creek.

In an agreement worked out with the Shoshone County Golf Association, Sunshine built and landscaped a new nine-hole course and clubhouse for the association, on top of the nearby mountain, at a cost of $1.4 million. The mining company then rerouted Big Creek in 1979 and constructed a new tailings pond, with a twenty-five-year life-expectancy, on the site of the old golf course.

A three mile drive up Big Creek by paved road will furnish a view of the **Sunshine mine.**

The mine was discovered by the Blake brothers, Dennis and True, who located their Yankee Boy silver claim in September, 1884. The vein was only four to six inches in width but the ore did not require concentration. Their lode was a paying producer by 1890, and the brothers worked it, with one other man, for almost twenty-five years. They shipped a gondola of ore every two months and it ranged in value from $75 to $400 a ton. True Blake, who had married Hattie Kellogg, died in 1910. Hattie moved to California, and not realizing that the ore ran deep, sold the Yankee Boy claims for less than their worth.

Lessees worked the mine for thirteen years, and when they faced bankruptcy, signed the claims over to a small Spokane firm: Sunshine Mining Co. The mine acquired the company name in 1921. New York interests provided financial help, and by 1927 profitable production was again realized. Four years later a high-grade silver vein, twenty feet wide, was discovered at 1,700 feet, and the mine

478

became the second-largest silver producer in the nation. Production peaked in 1937, with 12 million ounces of silver, but overall, the mine has become known as the largest producer of silver in the world. Sunshine completed its own silver refinery in 1981, at a cost of $6 million.

Hecla Mining Company owns 33 percent of the ore produced by Sunshine, and Silver Dollar Mining Company owns almost 10 percent. A group of Arab investors control one-third of the company's stock. The mine was the object of an unsuccessful takeover bid by the Hunt brothers of Texas when they attempted to corner the silver market in the late 1970s.

Sunshine Mining Company has also been the country's largest producer of antimony (used for storage battery grids, ceramics, plastics, and glass), with its own refinery. The company has additional income from Canadian oil and gas production.

Workings from the Crescent mine, a silver producer once owned by Bunker Hill Co., can be seen on the west side of Big Creek, just past the Sunshine. The Crescent is connected to the Bunker Hill mine by a 3½-mile tunnel.

Osburn, briefly known as Georgetown, lies on the south side of Interstate 90, four miles east of Kellogg. The town was laid out by railroad surveyors in 1887, on the Mullan Road at the mouth of Twomile Creek. Twomile Gulch led to the Murray road.

On the west end of Osburn, south of I-90 and Yellowstone Ave., but visible from the highway, is the Consolidated Silver Venture concentrator. This copper-silver mine and mill is being operated by Hecla Mining Co. under a joint venture set-up in 1980. Hecla has a 64 percent interest in the venture, and Sunshine Mining Co. owns an 11 percent interest.

After rehabilitation of the mine and concentrator in 1980, production began at the 4,000-foot level, while exploration to the 5,500-foot level was undertaken. A five-year development program is expected to cost the venturers $11 million.

About two miles east of Osburn, on the south side of the highway, along the apron of the hill, one can see surface structures associated with **Coeur d'Alene mine,** owned appropriately enough, by Coeur d'Alene Mines, a company incorporated in 1928. Offices, shop facilities, and a 450 ton-per-day concentrator were completed on the site in 1975.

The mine was brought into production by ASARCO (the American Smelting and Refining Co.) in 1976. Mining occurs at levels as deep as 4,000 feet. ASARCO has an operating agreement with Coeur d'Alene Mines, Inc. In 1981 the mine ranked fourth in the nation for silver output.

The **Galena mine,** also operated by ASARCO, is located 2.5 miles farther east than the Coeur mine, in Lake Gulch, about a mile south of the Interstate, but not visible from the highway.

The Killbuck claim, which produced the Galena mine, was discovered in 1885 by Lee George when he stopped to rest on an uprooted tree, picked up a piece of rock, broke it, and discovered galena. The mine is owned by Callahan Mining corporation, which receives 25 percent of the mine's profits under an agreement with ASARCO. The mine was brought into production in 1956, has shafts a mile deep, and is usually the second-largest U.S. silver producer. Concentrates from the Coeur and Galena mines are shipped to ASARCO smelters in Montana and Texas.

ASARCO, a corporate name frequently encountered in the Coeur d'Alene valley, has a rather intriguing pedigree. It was organized from eighteen concerns by J. P. Morgan & Co. for H. H. Rogers, John D. Rockefeller, Jr., and Leonard Lewisohn in 1899, and the corporation owned all the significant smelters in Colorado, Utah, Montana, and even in Missouri and Illinois. This smelting trust monopolized 90 percent of the U.S. lead-silver industry. There was no smelting company large enough to take all the ore large mines could produce, so ASARCO could stipulate monthly tonnage quotas and prices to mine owners. In this way, it balanced production against consumption – at a handsome profit.

The trust absorbed M. Guggenheim's Sons properties in 1901, but paid so much in stock that the five Guggenheim sons obtained control of the monopoly.

When a number of mining companies threatened to build their own smelters, the trust simply gave long-term contracts to major lead buyers, thereby making it difficult for the mine owners to locate customers for their own lead.

One mine owner-promoter persuaded John D. Rockefeller, Jr. and George Gould to finance the consolidation of several Coeur d'Alene mines in 1903; the venture was known as the Federal Mining and Smelting Company. (Rockefeller came out to inspect the mines in Gould's private railroad car.)

Federal threatened to buy or build its own smelters, which so alarmed ASARCO that M. Guggenheim's Sons formed the American Smelters Securities Co. and with its stock, in 1905, bought Federal's mines – at an inordinate price anticipated by Rockefeller – in fact,

480

he loaned them $2 million on the purchase. In 1953 Federal was merged with ASARCO, Inc.

Though mining was a relatively small activity of the original company, ASARCO has expanded its interests in this area until as much as 75 percent of the company's annual earnings before taxes have come from mining. The corporation owns or controls copper mines in Arizona, lead and zinc mines in New Mexico, Colorado, Canada and Bolivia, and silver mines in Montana and Peru. It is the largest miner and refiner of silver in the U.S. ASARCO operates smelters and refineries in seven states, is a major recycler of scrap metal, produces chemicals, and has associated company investments in Australia, England, Mexico and Peru. Corporate assets exceed $2 billion.

Silverton is a small settlement on the north side of the highway, 2.5 miles east of Osburn. It was known as West Wallace until 1941, when the present name was applied because of ore mined here.

The large, rather interesting brick structure with multiple dormers, which can be seen from the highway at Silverton, was built by Shoshone County as an infirmary in 1916-1917 at a cost of $2 million. No longer used as a hospital, it has been purchased by the U.S. Forest Service for local office space.

Wallace is the most interesting town in the Silver Valley – plan to spend some time here.

Colonel W. R. Wallace, a cousin of Lew Wallace, author of *Ben Hur,* built a cabin at the location he called Placer Center, in 1884. The site was the convergence of several creeks and two other canyon-valleys. After the customary Postal Department rebuke for a lengthy town name, the Colonel's wife, Lucy, shortened "Placer Center" by five letters and the settlement became Wallace. The community incorporated in 1888 – the first town in Shoshone County to do so. But ownership of the site was contested for five years.

Colonel Wallace used Sioux script to pay his homestead fee. The government considered that use of the script invalid and sent the Colonel a location cancellation notice in 1887, but he never informed the townspeople.

Word of the ruling reached the Wallace residents in early 1889, and people jumped property all over town, posting notices and claims everywhere. Finally, a citizen's meeting was held, and rules were adopted that recognized existing streets, and lots with established buildings. Other lots could be staked, recorded, and fenced; disputes were settled by a committee.

The Colonel was upset, understandably. He filed suit in the district court, but eventually lost the case on grounds he had been given notice of the ruling and had failed to appeal within the statutory period. He was denied the right to appeal to the Secretary of the Interior, and his petition for certiorari was also denied. The townsite patent was issued in June, 1892, and lot owners must have been delighted. As for the Colonel, he operated a steamboat on Coeur d'Alene Lake for a while, then moved to Arizona and finally to California, where he died in 1901, survived by his wife and three children.

As a headquarters for the mining supply business, people in Wallace worked like they were fighting a fire – and they did that too, soon enough. Swampy bottomland along the river was drained. Primeval, shaggy cedar trees were felled. Schoolhouse and church were built. Railroad tracks made their way up the canyons – seven train crews a day came in and out of Wallace: freight and passenger trains for Missoula, two trains on the Burke branch line, passenger and freight trains on the Osburn-Wardner narrow-gauge. Initially, ore from the various mines had to be sacked because there were not enough cars to keep it separated.

Any historian has reason to give thanks for early photographers, and Wallace was blessed with two of the best. Thomas Nathan Barnard, who as a boy studied with L. A. Huffman in Montana, set up his studio behind the Wallace Hotel in 1889, and along with his sister, Nellie Stockbridge, left a priceless visual record of life in the Silver Valley. Barnard even served as the town's fourth mayor. (Their collection of over 200,000 nitrocellulose and glass plate negatives is now housed at the University of Idaho.)

The *Wallace Press,* with an editor who had worked on the *San Francisco Chronicle,* was making an equally valuable history of the town. A stream behind the community furnished power to run the presses, and its name, Printers Creek, recalls that era.

A dam was placed in Placer Creek, south of town, and a mile-long flume was constructed to a power plant. By 1890 Wallace had 450 electric sixteen-candlepower bulbs. None of the lights had switches – they were all controlled at the electric plant – going on at 4:00 P.M. and off at 7:00 A.M., for a charge of $1.50 a month. A year later, customers had two options: lights until 11:00 P.M. or lights all night.

The Pioneer Sampling Works was operating at the mouth of Lake Gulch, 1.5 miles west of Wallace, between the U. P. and N. P. tracks. Ore from mines such as the Poorman, Black Bear, Custer and Hecla

482

was sampled there to keep the smelters honest and to establish the ore's value in New York on sample day.

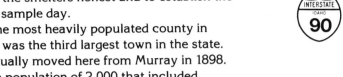

Shoshone County was the most heavily populated county in Idaho in 1890, and Wallace was the third largest town in the state. The county seat was eventually moved here from Murray in 1898. In the 1890s, Wallace had a population of 2,000 that included twenty-eight saloon keepers, ten lawyers (ten can live in a town where one cannot), five doctors, one teacher, and one preacher. Judge Angel was the justice of the peace, and he allowed prisoners a whiskey at the saloon before confinement in the jail.

There was no lack of entertainment outside the saloons: faro games, town bands and dances, prize fights, horse races, drilling contests, balloon ascensions, hunting and fishing, special trains to Coeur d'Alene Lake or Wardner on holidays. The town's baseball team was a source of special pride, though the players were humbled a bit in 1889, when they went to Spokane to play for the Idaho-Washington championship and a $1,000 purse: they lost twenty-one to one in seven innings.

Civic progress received a more serious jolt when a defective flue in one of the hotels caused a fire during the summer of 1890, and the entire business district, worth $500,000, was destroyed. Merchants set up tents and began to rebuild immediately. Local brickyards sold 400,000 bricks in one summer. (A two-story brick building at that time cost about $4,000.)

The city suffered another severe blow in August, 1910 when the Great Idaho Fire ignited the eastern end of the town and nearly 100 buildings (one-third of the town) were lost. Damage estimates exceeded a million dollars. Had it not been for the courageous efforts of many persons – switchboard operators, railroad crews, firemen – the loss would have been far greater. Following the fire, the town's water supply was so choked with dead animals and lye, that in an attempt to stave off typhoid, the mayor ordered the saloons to serve beer.

In 1981, Wallace began to cope with the rerouting of Interstate 90, which travels through the middle of town. This stretch has the only stoplight on the highway between Seattle and Boston. An elevated, highly visible route at the north end of Bank St. was chosen by the state highway department, rather than a tunnel through the mountain behind town, because it was about $38 million cheaper. Construction is expected to take five years and may require relocation of the old railroad depot.

Wallace opened the **Coeur d'Alene District Mining Museum** in 1956. Located at 511 Bank Street, it contains a collection of photographs, mineral specimens, artifacts and antiques, and instructive, life-size displays of hardrock mining techniques and tools: Ingersoll drills, the widow-maker, wiggle-tail, buzzy, Jackson drills and others.

The Wallace historic district centers on the intersection of Sixth and Bank Streets, with several buildings east and west of the corner. On the southeast corner is the Rossi Insurance building,

Wallace in 1888.
The town receives
more rainfall than
any other in the
state: 41.5 inches.

Coeur d'Alene
District Mining
Museum, Wallace.

484

built in 1892. The company paid $300,000 in claims after the 1910 fire. The chateau-style corner turret is a 1916 addition.

The White and Bender building occupies the southwest corner. This two-story, red brick edifice was constructed in 1898 from materials furnished by the Silverton brickyard. White and Bender were in the meat and grocery business.

The most picturesque building in Wallace was two blocks north on Bank Street at the railroad tracks: the Northern Pacific (now Burlington Northern) depot. The depot road was the subject of an amusing comment by the *Wallace Free Press* in winter, 1899: "We have only one abominable mud hole (in town) – Sixth St. from Northern Pacific Depot to Bank St."

The two-story stone depot with a round three-story, cone-roofed tower has a curious origin. In 1891, the Northern Pacific and its subsidiary, the Tacoma Land Company, began construction of the Tacoma Hotel in Tacoma. It was to compare favorably with the Empress Hotel in Victoria, B.C. and Chateau Frontenec in Quebec.

Construction of the Tacoma was interrupted by the Panic of 1898; doors and windows were boarded closed. Later the same year, a fire, fueled by 80,000 shingles which had been stored inside the building, left the hotel a charred ruin. After three years, the railroad company salvaged the brick facing for some new depots and sold the edifice for $34,000 to the city, which converted it to a high school that is still in use.

The buff-colored, twelve-inch long, Roman-style bricks were made in China and were imported by Northern Pacific. The railroad sent 58,000 of them to Missoula for a depot and 15,000 to Wallace. This railroad depot was constructed in 1901-1902 for $9,368. The station was closed in 1980, and highway construction in 1983 will probably require that it be moved.

Mount Pulaski, the 5,480-foot peak visible 1.5 miles southwest of Wallace, obtained its name in a manner unusual enough to be worth recounting.

Ed Pulaski, sixteen-year veteran with the U.S. Forest Service and resident of Burke Canyon, was supervising fire crews on the west fork of Placer Creek, about five miles south of Wallace, during the 1910 fire – or the "Big Blowup" as it is often called. The Big Creek fire in the St. Joe River drainage came over the hill near Striped Peak on the afternoon of August 20. The words of Pulaski's Forest Supervisor W. G. Weigle, written within a year of the event, describe what occurred:

"Mr. Pulaski, who is about forty years of age, is a man of most excellent judgment, conservative, thoroughly acquainted with the

485

Region, having prospected throughout the burned area during the last 25 years, and is considered by the old timers in the region as one of the best and safest men that could have been placed in charge of a crew of men in the hills. Mr. Pulaski was in charge of about 150 men distributed over a distance of several miles along the divide between Big Creek of the Coeur d'Alene River and Big Creek of the St. Joe River. When the danger conditions became imminent he rounded up about 40 of his men who were in the danger zone and cut off from safety on the west side of the fire where the other men were located and started with them down the mountain toward Wallace, a distance of ten miles. When he got about half way, however, he found that he was cut off by new fires. At the sight of this, his men became panic stricken, but he assured them that he would still get them to a place of safety. Being thoroughly familiar with the region, he knew of two prospect tunnels nearby, the shorter being about 50 feet in length and the longer about one hundred feet in length. Not being certain as to whether or not he could reach the largest and safest, by putting a wet gunny sack over his head, he penetrated the dense smoke to where he could see the largest tunnel, and finding it was safe he rushed back to his men and hurried them to the tunnel, getting them there just before the fire reached them. The portion of his crew with him consisted of 42 men and two horses. He got all of his men and horses inside the tunnel; except one man who had fallen a few hundred feet behind and was caught by the fire.

Pulaski ordered the men to lie face down to escape suffocation. One fellow tried to bolt outside, and the ranger drew his revolver. In his own words:

I said I would shoot the first man who tried to leave. I did not have to use my gun. Outside, the canyon was a raging furnace. The mine timbers caught fire, so I stood at the entrance and hung wet blankets over the opening, while trying to keep the flames back by filling my hat with water that was in the mine and throwing it on the burning wood.

Some of the men were in panic with fear. Some cried and some prayed. Many lost consciousness from the heat, smoke and fire gases. The wet blankets actually caught fire and we had to replace them with others that had been soaked in water. I, too, finally sank down unconscious. I don't know how long I remained in that condition, but it must have been for hours. I heard one man say, "Come outside, boys. The boss is dead." I replied: "Like heck he is."

I raised up and felt fresh air circulating through the mine as others regained consciousness. It was then 5 o'clock in the morning. When we first attempted to stand, our legs wouldn't hold us, so we dragged ourselves to the creek to ease parched throats and lips. Our disappointment was great when we found the stream filled with ashes and water too hot to drink.

Five of the men were dead when we left the mine. Finally, as the air outside became clearer, we were able to stagger to our feet and head for Wallace. We had to make our way over burning logs and through smoking debris. There were times when we were forced to crawl on hands and knees. How we got down I hardly know, as we were in terrible condition.

Shoes were burned off our feet and our clothing was in parched rags. All of us were hurt or burned. My hands were badly burned and I was blinded from trying to keep the fire from the tunnel. We all were covered with mud and ashes as we staggered to the safety of the town.

Pulaski and his crew were treated at the Wallace hospital.

Tunnel where Ed Pulaski and his crew took refuge during the Idaho Fire of 1910.

Ninemile Canyon – Murray Road (North).

The **Ninemile Canyon** road to Murray begins just past the old Northern Pacific depot in Wallace. This is an interesting drive and makes a loop that brings the driver back to Highway 90 at Kingston, just west of Kellogg. Route length: 46.7 miles.

North of Wallace 1.5 miles, on the left side of this road, is the Miners' Cemetery. Buena Vista Heights was the site of the first Wallace cemetery; this one opened five years later – "a suitable space for the silent city built by time" as the local newspaper remarked.

It is worth a stop. Near the center of the graveyard is an eight-foot granite marker that was erected by the miners' union for their members killed in the 1892 conflict at Gem. The memorial was the scene of Miners' Union Day commemorations for several years after the labor war. Since the legend has weathered and is now difficult to decipher, the inscription is printed here.

Erected by the Coeur d'Alene Miners' Union to the memory of Cummings, Hennessey and Carlson, who were killed in the cause of freedom and justice, at Gem, July 11, 1892. Dead, but their memory still lives in the hearts of their friends.

James Hennessey, aged 40 years.

Harry Cummings, aged 36 years.

Gus Carlson, aged 30 years.

Another set of shared graves, near the front lower corner of the cemetery, holds the remains of five Forest Service employees killed in the Great Idaho Fire of 1910. Eight men suffocated in the Bullion mine; their bodies were brought out days later.

The road, which is paved, travels up Ninemile Creek, then snakes up to Dobson Pass through heavy forest, before dropping down along the Beaver Creek bottoms.

At **Delta**, 11.5 miles from the cemetery, take the right fork six miles on a more or less paved surface to Murray. The drop from Kings Pass (3,319) grants a view of the ineradicable Guggenheim – given scars of a dredging operation along Prichard Creek.

On the right side of the road, at the outskirts of Murray, is a Grand Army of the Republic cemetery, begun in 1887 with the burial of a Union veteran – it is a shaded, peaceful spot for the dead to leave "the script of their bones."

Murrayville, staked in 1884, had its name adversed to **Murray** by the Postal Department in 1885. The town owes its origin, not to George Murray's claims, but to the placer discoveries of Andrew J. Prichard.

More than any other man, he was responsible for the Coeur d'Alene goldrush. He had served in the Missouri cavalry during the Civil War and came to north Idaho from Montana in the fall of 1878. After obtaining a lumber contract with a firm at Spokane Falls, he began cutting logs near Fort Coeur d'Alene. But Prichard had thoughts of founding a free-thinking religious colony in the mountains – supported by placer gold. He wrote to like-minded "liberals" whose names he obtained from the *Truthseeker* periodical.

With partners, he spent considerable time prospecting. In the fall, 1878, they discovered a promising quartz lode on the south fork of the Coeur d'Alene, near present Osburn. That lead played out, and in 1881, while examining the North Fork country, Prichard found placers at future Murray that ran as high as $42 a pan. Unable to winter there, he returned the next spring, trying to keep his find a secret. But he had to locate his claims when fellow prospectors made discoveries just below his own. Then in February, 1884, the Northern Pacific advertised the area's mining prospects in order to create business for itself, and miners swarmed into the area like honeybees after clover.

Murray emerged as the major placer center and wrested the county seat from Pierce. The town's importance diminished as interest shifted to the lead-silver lodes of the Coeur d'Alene valley. In 1909 the O.W.R. & N. Railroad reached Murray.

A dredge, owned by Guggenheim interests, was brought down from Alaska and shipped by rail from Seattle to the Silver Valley and up to Murray in 1917. Powered by electricity from Wallace, the dredge began its ten-year ravage at Dream Gulch, about a mile below Murray, and dug its way to Four Square, where bedrock eluded its thirty-foot grasp. The monster then chewed its way up to Bear Gulch, where it eventually ran out of gravel, having recovered in excess of $1 million for its owners. Over the years, the dredge was stripped of its scrap iron; the hull finally sank in a pit of its own making.

Murray retains a number of buildings worth noting. On the south side of the main street is the photogenic Masonic Lodge, a two-story, false-fronted frame structure with bracket corners, built in 1890.

On the north side of the main street, about one block east, is the Sprag Pole Inn, which contains a fascinating collection of whiskey decanters, mineral specimens, blacksmith tools, telephones and lamps. Here you can see the original grave marker of Maggie Hall Burdan, perhaps the most famous "soiled dove" in all of Idaho's mining camps; she is buried in the community's Pioneer Cemetery.

Murray, circa 1895.

Yukon Gold Dredge at Murray in 1922.

Maggie Hall emigrated from Ireland to America in 1873, and found work as a bar maid in New York. She married a man named Burdan, who proved to be a pimp and ruined her standing with "the Band of Hope." So Maggie left him and augered around the country until she heard of the gold strike on Prichard Creek.

She arrived in Murray and opened a saloon to help miners keep body and soul together. Like Murrayville, her name was docked – to Molly B'Damm.

One of the better-known tales relates how Molly would allow the local gents to assist at her bath; the amount of their assistance was directly proportional to the quantity of gold dust they sprinkled in her tub.

Molly was well-liked by the locals, however, because she was generous, tolerant, kind, and most helpful when anyone was ill.

Unfortunately, Molly contracted pneumonia in January, 1881, and died at the age of thirty-five. The town closed for her funeral.

Farther up the same side of the street is the second Shoshone County courthouse. There is a brick vault, on the east side, where the county records were kept, and the second-story doorway suggests a balcony once extended across the front of the structure. A granite block used for miners' drilling contests rests in the street in front of the building.

This is the courthouse where the case of Noah Kellogg versus his grubstakers was heard. These rooms listened to many engrossing stories. One tale certainly occasioned a risible tirade, in 1887, from the *Wallace Free Press.* The defendant had been sharing a drink with the judge and the prosecuting attorney in Burke when an Irishman flung a beer in his face. The defendant shot the fellow for his incivility. At the trial, the killer was acquitted, and the newspaper decided to list the causes for such a legal miscarriage:

First, a lawless element; second, an imbecile judge; third, a pair of unscrupulous tricky lawyers; fourth, some heavy actors who can pick a jury, intimidate witnesses and generally 'fix' things, and the piece is ready to be played. The County Courthouse ... is the Theater, the taxpayers the audience and the murderer the beneficiary.

The building is now dilapidated. No one has accepted the responsibility of restoration.

Eagle, or Eagle City, is on the paved road 3.5 miles northwest of Murray; miners filed on the ground in 1883. At that time a pair of eagles nested in a tree by the creek, and although there is no record of the type, it would have been fitting if they were golden.

491

This ephemeral town had two newspapers: the *Weekly Eagle* and *The Nugget*. Thousands of would-be miners arrived – but most found that the cake had been eaten and they could only lick the pan to tell what kind it had been. Some undiscouraged prospectors moved on up the creek to Murray.

While Eagle did not last long enough to draw flies, it did attract some unusual fellows. The town's register for the 1884 election showed one native son: Courtney Meek, born in Idaho in 1838. He was the son of the famous trapper and guide, the "merry mountain man," Joe Meek.

In addition, the Earp brothers, Wyatt, James and Warren, fresh from Tombstone, Arizona, were in Eagle in the spring, 1884. James and Wyatt purchased a saloon here for $132, called the White Elephant, and opened for business. Wyatt also purchased ten acres of placer ground for $500.

A. J. Prichard, discoverer of the ground, named Wyatt Earp as defendant in an eviction action in February, 1884 – and won his suit.

By summer's end, Eagle City was almost deserted. In December, a tent that belonged to Earp was auctioned at a sheriff's sale for nonpayment of taxes; apparently the Earps had left the diggings by that time.

Make a right turn at Eagle, drive a "Forest Service mile" (a mile and a bit) and then go left up the west fork of Eagle Creek on USFS Road 805 – it is a little less than five miles on the gravel road that crosses the creek several times, to the **Settlers Grove of Ancient Cedars**, – marked by a sign on the left shoulder of the road.

This place ranks among Idaho's more wondrous sites. Fire crews who built the 2½ mile trail through this grove of venerable cedars used considerable care to create an inconspicuous path.

The Forest Supervisor for the Idaho Panhandle National Forests, with rare and admirable foresight, requested, in a 1965 memo to district rangers, information concerning groves of outstanding trees that might be worth preserving. Settlers Grove was set aside as a result of that request – and it is a treasure comparable to some of California's redwood groves.

The tract is dominated by western red cedars, some of them thirty feet in circumference, and many of them several hundred years old. A clerestory light filters to an understory of mountain maples, bracken fern, devil's club and wild ginger. The canopy is so dense the air is always cool and moist. Associated with the cedars are western white pine, Engelmann spruce, grand fir and hemlock. Deer and elk still use the area; fish inhabit the stream.

492

It is a relatively undisturbed cedar ecosystem, much as Eugene Smalley described in 1884:

The entire region was covered with a forest growth of cedar, pine and fir, so dense as to resemble a Hindustan jungle ... there is considerable white pine, tamarack, and fir, and in places the cedar excludes all other trees and attains a surprising girth and height.

Western red cedar was a multiple-use species for the Northwest Indians: they used the woven bark for clothing, baskets and mats, the buds and twigs for medicines, and the wood for houses and canoes. Loggers found the straight-grained, rot resistant wood excellent for roofing material. Since the wood swells quickly when wet, making a leakproof surface, it was widely accepted for shakes and shingles, and their manufacture built a thriving industry in the Coeur d'Alene region.

Though resistant to rot and insects, the trees grow slowly, with 200-250 years required for a twenty-five to forty-inch diameter. The largest red cedar now known, near Forks, Washington, is 178 feet high and carries a 61-foot girth. Idaho has a cedar on the Clearwater National Forest only slightly smaller.

When the 183-acre Settlers Grove was classified as a natural botanical area in 1970, there were some unpatented mining claims with corners blazed on the trees. The Idaho Mining Association, to its perdurable shame, objected to withdrawal of the area from mineral entry.

Prichard, 2.5 miles west of Eagle, now looks like a difficult place to mail a postcard. It does, however, eulogize Andrew J., as does the creek, and a peak two miles to the east. Take the left splice at the fork and follow the Coeur d'Alene River (which heads about twenty miles to the north) along the road back to I-90.

This river, lovely until it meets the mistreated South Fork, can be floated and fished. It was given the name St. Ignatius by Fr. De Smet in 1842, but the name did not stick.

The Coeur d'Alene in this stretch was used for transportation of equipment to the Eagle-Murray mines. From Cataldo Mission, horses pulled flatboats and bateaux loaded with machinery. In this manner, by 1885, four sawmills were set up in the Prichard area. The river was also used for log drives until 1933. (Return to I-90.)

The town of **Mullan** was born in 1885, six miles from the Montana border, progeny of the Golden Hunter and Morning mines. It is named for the West Point graduate, John Mullan, who was in charge of selecting a wagon route between Fort Benton, Montana and Fort Walla Walla, Washington. (Captain Mullan died in 1909 and is buried in Annapolis, Maryland.) Three years after its origin, the settlement boasted 118 voters.

While the community awaited the arrival of the iron horse, real horses hauled two stages daily between the village and nearby Wallace. The round-trip fare was $2.50 and entitled passengers to cross the South Fork of the Coeur d'Alene twenty-two times en route.

The Northern Pacific commenced broad-gauge rail service from Missoula, Montana, to Mullan in 1891, with a line through to Wallace. (Sometimes a railroad car would break loose at the depot and go all the way downhill to Wallace "so fast it took two men to see it – one to say here she comes, the other to say there she goes.") The year the Northern arrived, Mullan had two mills and nineteen saloons. Hardrock drilling made a man drier than a dusty day.

Mullan in the 1890s (looking east).

The town's most remarkable feature in the 1890s had to be its courtroom – which was also a general store and saloon. Jurors were provided bottled ale from the cellar "in order to secure, as far as possible, a perfect administration of justice." The judge was court clerk, sometimes counsel for the prosecution, and even a creditor of some defendants. The same judge was once arrested for selling liquor from the cellar without a license.

Given the quantities of saloons in the early Silver Valley settlements, particularly at Mullan, one cannot help remembering

494

Mark Twain's droll description of the frontier process.

How solemn and beautiful is the thought that the earliest pioneer of civilization ... is never the steamboat, never the railroad, never the newspapers, never the Sabbath-School, never the missionary – but always whiskey! Such is the case. Look history over and you will see. The missionary comes after *the whiskey – I mean, he* arrives *after the whiskey has arrived. Next comes the poor immigrant with axe and hoe and rifle; next, the trader; next the miscellaneous rush; next the gambler, the desperado, the highwayman, and all their kindred in sin in both sexes; and next, the smart chap who has bought up an old grant that covers all the land; this brings in the lawyer tribe; the vigilance committee brings in the undertaker. All these interests bring the newspaper; the newspaper starts up politics and a railroad; all hands turn to and build a church and a jail – and behold civilization is established forever in the land.*

A mile east of Mullan, on the north side of I-90, notice the surface plant, hoist and mill for the **Lucky Friday mine.**

The six principal claims of the Lucky Friday group were located between 1899 and 1906 and patented in 1926. During this time the property was held by two different companies, and they explored it with shallow underground workings. Discouraged by the lack of prospects, the property remained idle from 1927 to 1938, when it was acquired by the Lucky Friday Silver-Lead Mines Company.

That company began deeper exploration. There was almost no surface expression of lead, silver or zinc, and the veins at the 1,200-foot level were small and discontinuous. But below that level, the veins showed remarkable improvement.

Over a period of almost forty years, following the first ore shipment of 500 tons in January, 1942, the net smelter returns exceeded $310 million.

The Lucky Friday expanded its hoist and water pumping capability from 1953-1957, then located sufficient reserves in 1959 to justify construction of a new 750-ton per day concentration mill. The mill produces silver-lead and zinc concentrates. These are shipped to a smelter in Helena, Montana, where final extraction of metals occurs.

In 1964 Lucky Friday Silver-Lead Mines Company was merged into Hecla Mining Company. Hecla was established in 1891. In addition to income interests from the Sunshine, Con-Sil, Coeur, Galena, and Star-Morning mines, Hecla has the Knob-Hill gold mine in Washington, and a 60 percent interest in the Sherman silver-lead mine in Colorado.

After a particularly rancorous takeover fight with Day Mines, Inc. in 1981, the latter company was merged into Hecla. At the time of the merger, Hecla had a capitalization of $227 million, and Day Mines' market capitalization was $84 million. AMAX, Inc. owned 21 percent of Hecla before the merger, and there was some speculation that the acquisition of Day's stock was meant to dilute AMAX's ownership and thereby make Hecla less attractive to AMAX as a takeover target. The merger has made Hecla the largest producer of newly-mined silver in the U.S.

The 140-foot-high headframe that dominates the view of the Lucky Friday site, north of the Interstate, was erected in mid-1980 over a new production shaft called the Silver Shaft. Its headframe contains 280 tons of steel and is topped with two twelve-foot diameter sheave wheels. The main hoist will be a double drum, 3,000 h.p. Nordberg unit with a lift capacity of 125 tons per hour.

The Silver Shaft, at 7,700 feet, will be the deepest mine shaft in the world outside of South Africa and its circular (eighteen feet in diameter), concrete lining is unique in the Coeur d'Alene district. It represents a $27 million project, expected to be completed in 1984.

Four crews, each working a forty-hour, five-day week, have excavated the shaft with the aid of a three-level platform (known as a galloway) that is suspended on cables and braced against the walls of the shaft.

The crew uses a rapid drill-blast-muck and line cycle, and averages ten to fifteen feet of depth a day. The galloway is lifted at least fifty feet before rock is blasted. Spoil is removed in buckets. Concrete, batched on the site, is pumped through a pipe to a remix pot suspended in the shaft. The lining is cast about twelve inches thick. In addition to being fireproof and nearly watertight, the concrete sleeve will result in lower maintenance costs. Upon completion, nearly 100,000 cubic yards of rock will have been excavated for the Silver Shaft, and 40,000 cubic yards of concrete will line the interior.

The Silver Shaft will provide access to the mine below the 5,000-foot level and will allow a 35 percent increase in production. Horizontal galleries, 3,000 feet long, will be driven at 200-foot intervals below the old shaft level.

At this time, the Lucky Friday employs 250 men underground, on two shifts, five days a week. The mill is also open five days a week, but operates on a twenty-four hour/three-shift basis.

U.S. Interstate 90 continues past the Lucky Friday, and after five miles, crosses **Lookout Pass** in the Bitterroot Mountains and enters Montana.

U.S. Highway 91 from the Idaho-Utah state line south of Franklin, northerly via Franklin, Preston, Pocatello, Blackfoot, Firth and Shelley to a junction with U.S. 26 and I-15 southwest of Idaho Falls. (Overlaps I-15 for 30.8 miles from Arimo to Pocatello.) Route length: 83.9 miles.

Franklin, the oldest non-Indian town in Idaho, is 1.3 miles from the Utah border, 8.3 miles north of Logan.

As fertile bottomlands and available water were preempted by settlers in the Salt Lake Valley, the Mormon empire expanded north up the Cache Valley.

In early April, 1860, at the urging of Brigham Young, five companies of emigrants headed north up the valley from Salt Lake. They selected this spot along the Cub River on April 14, and named it in honor of the Mormon apostle Franklin Richards.

The settlers placed their wagon boxes in a quadrangle 330 yards by 500 yards, then used the undercarriages to haul logs for cabins that were built in a fort-like arrangement, with the doorways facing the quad.

A communal meeting was held to distribute ten-acre lots. An irrigation ditch was grubbed from Spring Creek for vegetable gardens, and wheat, barley, oats and sugar cane were also planted.

During the first summer five children were born in the wagon boxes. Several trips were made to Salt Lake for additional supplies, and Brigham Young brought his entourage for a visit. He appointed Preston Thomas bishop of the new settement.

A log schoolhouse was notched together, the first in Idaho for white children. It had a dirt roof, straw floor, slab benches, a fireplace, and the only window glass in the colony. There were twenty pupils initially; when it rained the roof leaked so badly class was dismissed.

In 1861 a pit sawmill, or Armstrong mill as some called it, was built at Franklin, and wood was sawed for furniture, washtubs, barrels, and boards. Two years later a water-powered mill replaced it. Then Brigham Young purchased a steam sawmill in the East and shipped it West, up the Missouri to Ft. Benton, Montana, where three men brought it overland to Franklin and installed it in Maple Creek Canyon, east of the settlement. Among other feats, the mill

497

cut 300,000 board feet for the ZCMI building in Salt Lake, and railroad ties for the Utah Northern. The mill operated until 1900; the engine now rests in the Relic Hall on East Main St.

The second flour mill in the Territory (Henry Spalding's was first) was built in 1863; except for the turbine wheel and the grindstones, all of the parts were wooden. The mill was powered by water diverted from Cub River; each family received flour made from its own wheat; some of them shipped their surplus to Montana. It functioned for eighteen years. Indians frequently came to trade buckskins for a sack or two.

In 1868 the Utah legislature incorporated Franklin as a village. By treaty of 1819 the forty-second parallel formed the northern boundary of Utah, but no one knew the precise location of the line until a survey in 1872 disclosed that Franklin was in Washington Territory, which became part of Idaho in 1863. It was 1897 before the Idaho legislature issued Franklin a new charter.

The town's boom years were 1873 to 1878, when it was the terminus of the Utah Northern Railroad, which came north from Ogden. With the extension of the narrow-gauge to Preston and then on north to Pocatello, Franklin's importance diminished.

To see part of Franklin's architectural dowry, turn east off Highway 91 onto East Main St. At the corner of East Main and First St. East is the Leland Scarborough house, built in 1890.

After crossing First St. East, proceed half a block farther, to the town's Relic Hall, built in 1937. Adjacent to it is the **Relic Hall museum,** a two-story, stone store built in 1895. The cooperative store was an outgrowth of a cooperative general store organized in 1868 by Bishop Hatch. The tithing house was merged into the store in order that one enterprise could meet the commercial and welfare needs of the community.

One block farther north, at 127 East Main, stands the Lorenzo Hatch house, one of the older residences in the state. The two-story, stone structure, built in the Greek Revival style in about 1870, is in need of restoration. Hatch was appointed to succeed Preston Thomas as bishop in 1863; he was also the first mayor of Franklin, and served four terms in the Utah legislature before becoming the first Mormon elected to the Idaho territorial legislature.

In the park across the street from the Hatch house is a small, square, brick building set on a stone foundation. It was erected in 1910 as the city building for public meetings. The basement served as a jail.

Turn left at the next corner, back to Main St. at U.S. Highway 91. An historical sign and monument on the west side of the road indicate the location of the original Franklin fort.

The mile-high mountain visible just northwest of Franklin is Little Mountain, known to the settlers as Lookout Mountain, because scouts trained by the militia at Logan kept watch there for Indian bands that might threaten the village.

Seven miles northwest of Franklin is **Preston.** The area was first used as a source of wild hay, which was scythed and hauled by the settlers in Franklin. Though the winters were severe, the Preston area also served as cattle range.

The townsite was surveyed in 1888; the village incorporated in 1900, and the city in 1913. The place was called Worm Creek until 1881, when the name was switched to honor the LDS bishop William Preston.

The town was on the freight road from Corinne, Utah to Helena, Montana, during the 1870s, and on the Utah Northern Railroad after 1878.

In 1913 Franklin County was carved out of Oneida County, and Preston was voted the county seat.

Of four Congressional Medals of Honor awarded to Idaho servicemen, two were conferred on young men from Preston for heroism during World War II: one for the defense of a beach against a Japanese landing in New Guinea; the other for an attack on a pillbox in the Philippines.

The Preston post office at 55 East Oneida St. contains a painting of interest to historians: on the west wall of the lobby is a large panorama of the Battle of Bear River, done in the 1940s by a Washington artist, Elmon Fitzgerald.

To visit the Oneida Stake Academy from downtown, drive east from State St. on Second St. So. for two blocks. On the left the Preston Sr. High School, built in 1939, occupies the entire block. Turn left on East Second St. and notice the Academy building sandwiched between the high school classrooms.

The Oneida Academy was built in 1889-1894, in compliance with a recommendation by the LDS Church authorities in Salt Lake City. The anti-Mormon Idaho Test Oath of 1885 effectively prevented Mormons from serving on school boards, and in response the Church developed its own school system.

The work was supervised by a German-born stonemason; men were called on "missions" to cut and haul the stone from a quarry southeast of town. Though the labor was donated, materials cost about $20,000. The building was designed in the Romanesque revival style. It was sold by the Church to the city in 1927 for use as a public school, and was recently condemned for classroom use, but a local bond issue passed in 1975 transferred the structure to the Friends of the Academy for restoration and public use.

A pleasant fifteen-mile sidetrip can be made from downtown Preston to **Weston Canyon.**

From the intersection in mid-town, take the Dayton road west 6.6 miles. At Dayton turn south five miles on the West Side Highway to Weston, then northwest four miles on the Weston Canyon Rd.

In 1969-1970 a rockshelter visible alongside the north shoulder of the road, at the southern mouth of the canyon, was excavated by archaeologists from Idaho State Univ.

Their findings indicate that the canyon was inhabited as early as 7,000 years ago by people who hunted big game, primarily mountain sheep, and were different from the Desert culture and the Fremont culture.

One can continue northwest via the canyon twenty-two miles to a junction with I-15 north of Malad.

Highway 91 travels north and west through Preston for two miles, then west and north 3.2 miles to Battle Creek. En route, the old grade of the **Utah Northern** can be glimpsed west of the highway, as it drops to the Bear River.

The UN was built from Ogden to Franklin as a cooperative effort by the LDS church, with the intent of developing the resources of the Cache Valley from Salt Lake to Soda Springs.

Extension of the rail line north of Franklin was halted by the financial crisis of 1873. Not until the Anaconda claim was discovered at Butte, Montana in 1875, and a millsite was established, did sufficient magnetism exist to draw the rails farther north.

U.S. 91 crosses the Bear River 2.5 miles northwest of Preston. One-half mile north of the bridge, on the east edge of the highway, there is a ten-foot monument with a Mormon resume of the **Battle of Bear River.** To visit the bloodiest ground in Idaho, turn west, across the highway from the sign, on the gravel road. Follow it 300 yards to a fork; take the right branch 0.3 miles up along the

500

northeast flank of Battle Creek ravine, which overlooks the creek bottom. This almost unknown location was the scene of the worst slaughter of American Indians on record: more persons died here than at Sand Creek, or Little Big Horn, or Wounded Knee. It is one of the sadder, unwritten books of the West. The following facts have gotten out of the corral.

Brigham Young had long advocated an "easier to feed than fight" policy toward the region's Indians. In 1852 he told the Utah legislature: "Brethren, be just and quiet, firm and mild, patient and benevolent, generous and watchful in all your intercourse with them; learn their language so that you can explain matters to them and pay them the full and just reward for their labor, and treat them in all respects as you would like to be treated." Certainly an unorthodox view at the time. Nevertheless, the Saints settled on Indian lands without any recompense, and the Northern Shoshone watched the encroachment, along with its erosion of game and grassland, with growing resentment. The Mormons hoped the Indians could be taught to farm, but isolated instances of murder and depredation against whites began in the 1850s and continued into the 1860s. It is not necessary to ride over that trail again.

As a result of these attacks, in 1862 Colonel Patrick Connor and his Third California Infantry were dispatched from California to Salt Lake City to protect the Overland Mail Route.

Connor was an Irish immigrant who enlisted in the U.S. Army at age nineteen and served with General Zachary Taylor in the Mexican-American War, where he rose to the rank of captain. After the war he traveled to the California goldfields, then setted in Stockton as a businessman and headed the local militia. When he answered the state governor's call for volunteers, he was commissioned a colonel.

Colonel Patrick Connor was a pugnacious, societal anthropoid. He and his regiment had written General-in-Chief H. W. Halleck a request to "fight traitors ... and a chance to shoot seceshers," and offered to pay their own passage east to the Civil War. The request was denied; the California Volunteers were ordered to Utah instead. They went overland, east to Salt Lake City, rolling their rowels, and shooting scores of unarmed Indians en route. Connor resented his orders: "Why we were sent here is a mystery. It could not be to keep Mormondom in order, for Brigham can thoroughly annihilate us with the 5,000 to 25,000 frontiersmen always at his command."

In October, 1862, on a bluff overlooking Salt Lake Valley, Connor established Fort Douglas. He found the Saints no more to his liking than the Indians. In a communication to Major R. C. Drum, the Colonel stated:

It will be impossible for me to describe what I saw and heard in Salt Lake, so as to make you realize the enormity of Mormonism; suffice it, that I found them a community of traitors, murderers, fanatics, and whores. The people publicly rejoice at reverses to our arms (Civil War), and thank God that the American Government is gone, as they term it, while their prophet and bishops preach treason from the pulpit. The Federal officers are entirely powerless, and talk in whispers, for fear of being overheard by Brigham's spies. Brigham Young rules with despotic sway, and death by assassination is the penalty of disobedience to his commands.

In December a party of miners was attacked by a band of Indians on Bear River, and one of the men was killed. Colonel Connor began plotting a campaign against the Northern Shoshone, who were encamped for the winter on Battle Creek northwest of Franklin.

Connor decided to take the band by surprise, before it could scatter. To facilitate his strategy he ordered his infantry, consisting of about sixty soldiers, to march north to Franklin by day; he directed the cavalry of 200-250 men to ride by night. The troops hauled fifteen supply wagons and two howitzers, and the combined forces reached Franklin seven nights later. The trip had been arduous; sub-zero weather left frost-bitten soldiers in every village along the way.

The Mormons, fearful of an Indian victory, and of federal troops, were uncooperative, and Connor's departure from Franklin the night of January 28 was delayed by a lengthy quest for a guide who was willing to show them where to ford the Bear River.

The infantry departed for Battle Creek ahead of the cavalry, but they became bogged in the snow, along with the wagons and howitzers, near the location now occupied by Preston, and the cavalry proceeded to Bear River ahead of them. Smoke from the tipis revealed the Indian encampment at the mouth of Battle Creek.

Connor's cavalry massed along the south side of the river at dawn and awaited the arrival of the foot-soldiers. The Indians rode out of the brush and taunted the Volunteers with shouts (in English) across the water: "Come and get it, you California sons of bitches; we're ready for you!" The challenge was too much for Col. Connor, who ordered his cavalry, under Major McGarry, to advance across the river, before the infantry arrived.

The river was clotted with ice, and the crossing was difficult. The Indians, all Shoshone under the command of Bear Hunter, Sagwich and Sanpitch, fired across the open flat from pits screened by willow branches. After fourteen of the cavalry were killed in the first assault, McGarry had his men dismount and take cover.

Captain Hoyt reached the ford with the infantry, but the water was so treacherous that Connor had to dispatch part of the cavalry with horses for the infantry. Once the troops were consolidated on the battlefield, Col. Connor ordered Major McGarry to flank the Indian position by moving northwest across the flat and up along the northeast shoulder of the creek.

McGarry's maneuver succeeded, and the Indians were trapped in an enfilading fire as the soldiers moved down both sides of the ravine like a scythe.

When the Shoshone broke out of the canyon southwest and southeast toward the river, it was "Judgment Day come at last" – companies stationed on the flat cut them to pieces. About twenty Indians, including Sagwich, made it to the river and escaped; the rest, save 160 women and children, were shot like salmon on a riffle. In four hours the battle was over.

The settlers at Franklin had stationed messengers on horseback along the route from the battlefield to the town. (There was no settlement at Preston.) Their teams were hitched and their wagons loaded, prepared to flee in event of an Indian victory. Now that the issue was resolved in favor of the Army, they suddenly became most solicitous of the soldiers and their wounded. Cold had mauled the troops more severely than had the Indians. The Volunteers suffered twenty-two dead, fifty-three wounded, and seventy-nine disabled by frostbite. The injured were loaded in wagons and taken to town.

Some of the infantry spent the night at the battleground. Corporal Hiram Tuttle reminisced:

The night of January 29th, 1863 I never shal far get (how can I) there we camped on the Bank of Bear River with our dead dieing wounded and frozen 2 feet of snow on the ground nothing for fire but green Willows which would burn about as well as the snow oh! the groans of the frozen it seems to ring in my ears yet the poor fellows some lost their toes some a portion of their feet I worked near all night bringing water from the river to wett cloths to draw frost from their frozen limbs I had not sleep any for two nights befor it was a dreadful night to me but managed to get through the night while some never saw the morning.

Seventy Indian tipis were burned and their contents destroyed. A herd of 175 horses was confiscated; the women and children were left to fend for themselves. William Hull, who visited the site with two friends the next day, wrote:

We drove our sleigh as far as the river and rode our horses through the river. The first sight to greet us was an old Indian walking, slowly with arms folded, his head bowed in grief, lamenting the dead. He didn't speak to us, and soon left, going toward the north.

Never will I forget the scene, dead bodies were everywhere. I counted eight deep in one place and in several places they were three to five deep; all in all we counted nearly 400; two-thirds of this number being women and children.

We found two Indian women alive whose thighs had been broken by bullets. Two little boys and one little girl about three years of age were still living. The little girl was badly wounded, having eight flesh wounds in her body. They were very willing to go with us. We took them on our horses to the sleighs and made them as comfortable as possible.

Corporal Tuttle estimated the dead at "nearly 400 warriors, say nothing about squaws and young bucks that got in the way." Indian Superintendent, James Doty, reported 255 killed; the residents of Franklin who visited the grounds all counted in excess of 350 dead. (A reporter for the *Deseret News,* who visited the canyon five years later, observed, "The bleached skeletons of scores of noble red men still ornament the grounds.")

A little inaccuracy sometimes saves tons of explanation. Colonel Patrick Connor's report to General-in-Chief H. W. Halleck said, "We found 224 bodies on the field . . . How many more were killed than stated I am unable to say, as the condition of the wounded rendered their immediate removal a necessity. I was unable to examine the field." Connors added that ". . . it was not my intention to take any prisoners," and "in my march from this post no assistance was rendered by the Mormons, who seemed indisposed to divulge any information regarding the Indians and charged enormous prices for every article furnished my command."

Colonel Halleck's response was succinct:

Brig. Gen. P. E. Connor, Camp Douglas, near Salt Lake City, Utah:

I congratulate you and your command on their heroic conduct and brilliant victory on Bear River. You are this day appointed a brigadier-general.

H. W. Halleck, General-in-Chief.

Brigadier-General Connor remained in command of Camp Douglas until mustered out of the Army in June, 1866. He built a home in Stockton, Utah, and devoted himself to regional mining businesses until his death in 1891 at Salt Lake City. He is buried at Fort Douglas.

Of the Battle of Bear River, LDS Church records at the Logan Stake, made at the time, say:

We, the people of Cache Valley, looked upon the movement of Colonel Connor as intervention of the Almighty, as the Indians had been a source of great annoyance to us for a long time, causing us to stand guard over our stock and other property the most of the time since our first settlement.

In the summer of 1863 federal treaties were signed with the five main Shoshone groups.

Highway 91 bisects **Red Rock Pass** 16.5 miles northwest of Battle Creek. There is a sign on the east side of the highway that notes the location.

Red Rock Pass was cut through a sill of resistant Paleozoic shale, limestone, and dolomite, and forms a narrow gap two miles long. At one time the pass was at the shoreline of Pleistocene Lake Bonneville, 300 feet higher.

Lava flows in the vicinity of Pocatello diverted the Bear River through Lake Thatcher into Lake Bonneville. The sudden influx caused Bonneville to overflow at Red Rock. Marsh Creek Valley, immediately downstream, was flooded from wall to wall, and the rapid discharge eroded the pass to its present level.

The **Bonneville Flood,** as it is known, was catastrophic. Maximum discharge was about 15 million cfs, or about three times the average flow of the Amazon, the world's largest river. The rate of flow was approximately sixteen mph, and though peak flow lasted only a few days, voluminous discharge may have continued for at least a year. Radio-carbon dates from molluscan fossils associated with the flood debris indicate the event occurred 30,000 years ago.

Evidence of the flood was first reported by G. K. Gilbert in 1878 in the *American Journal of Science.* It was not until 1954, however, that the wide-reaching downstream effects were recognized by USGS geologists, largely as the result of J Harlan Bretz's pioneer work on the even larger Great Spokane Flood (see Highway 200, Great Spokane Flood).

Flood erosion gouged and flushed enormous quantities of boulders, known as Melon gravel, through the Snake River canyon and dropped the deposits along the river wherever the flood met relatively slack water. About half the debris may have been scoured from fourteen miles of canyon near Twin Falls.

A formula based on the relation of water velocity (the "sixth power law") to carrying capacity enables hydraulic engineers to calculate the velocity required to move boulders found in the Melon gravel. At places in the upper part of the Snake River canyon, where the width of the canyon is known, and the flood profile can be reconstructed from geological evidence, the flow velocity gives a measure of the discharge.

Evidence assembled in this manner indicates that the Bonneville Flood filled the Snake River 300 feet deep from Twin Falls west to Hells Canyon. (For more detailed information see USGS Paper No. 596, 1968.)

From Red Rock Pass the highway runs 6.9 miles northwest through **Downey,** and another 5.5 miles to an intersection with Interstate 15. Highway 91 overlaps I-15 for 30.8 miles north to the city limits of Pocatello, where it resumes in conjunction with Highway 30.

Highway 91 leaves Highway 30, 3.5 miles northwest of I-15, and moves north through Pocatello (see I-15, Pocatello) and Chubbuck for 4.6 miles, then 5.8 miles farther to Fort Hall.

The **town of Fort Hall,** headquarters for the **Shoshone-Bannock Indian Reservation,** was incorporated in 1922. Henry Hall was the oldest member of the New England firm that financed Nathaniel Wyeth's trading enterprise near here in 1834.

The Shoshone-Bannock were linguistically two distinct groups; the Bannock minority spoke a dialect of the Northern Paiute. Both groups acquired the horse and used the same environment, which extended across southern Idaho into western Wyoming, and south into Utah and Nevada. Their cultures are treated as one.

The tribes caught salmon on the Snake River below Shoshone Falls and hunted deer, antelope, mountain sheep and bear. Once horses were obtained, buffalo were pursued in Montana and Wyoming. (Some anthropologists believe the horse enabled these Indians to hunt the southeastern Idaho bison to extinction.) The Shoshone used over 100 types of seed plants; the most important was the camas.

Buffalo hunting allowed the tribes to replace their conical, grass-thatched lodges with leather tipis, and the traditional buckskin clothing of the Great Plains was adopted as well.

A mean trick of history placed the lands of these semi-nomadic tribes astride the West's most heavily traveled roads: the Oregon and California Trails, the Utah-Montana Road, and the Union Pacific railroad. The influx of emigrants and livestock thoroughly dislocated the Shoshone-Bannock culture.

After the usual problems with ratification, the Fort Hall reservation opened in 1869. The original reservation under the Treaty of Fort Bridger was 1.8 million acres, twenty-five miles wide and seventy-five miles long.

In order to encourage reservation farms, under the terms of the treaty the government was to furnish annuities, food, farm implements, irrigation and instruction. Governmental indifference, however, brought horrible hardships to the tribes; even marginal aid was never furnished. Some Indian agents were excellent administrators; others were incompetent; some Indians wanted to farm; others lacked interest, but all parties were hamstrung by the failure of Congress to fulfill its treaty obligations.

Government policy was intended to spot-weld the bands to their reservation, but promises make thin soup, and the Indians either had to leave the reserve regularly in search of food or starve.

The Treaty of 1868 gave the Shoshone-Bannock the right to visit the camas grounds near Fairfield, Idaho, to gather bulbs in the summer. Through a clerical error in Washington, D.C., Camas Prairie was changed to Kansas prairie. White farmers used this technicality to usurp the prairie for cattle and hogs. This trespass, coupled with starvation, led to the Bannock War in 1878. The three-month skirmish ended in the deaths of Buffalo Horn and Chief Egan, in different engagements.

When General George Crook visited Fort Hall to ascertain the causes of the war, he told a reporter the cause was "Hunger. Nothing but hunger. It cannot be expected that they will stay on reservations where there is no possible way to get food, and see their wives and children starve and die around them. We have taken their lands, deprived them of every means of living ..."

Matters improved slowly. In 1898 the Shoshone-Bannock tribes decided to cede 418,000 acres around and south of Pocatello to the federal government for $600,000. The agreement was ratified by Congress in 1900.

Two years later the land was opened for settlement. Lands within a five-mile limit of Pocatello were sold for cash at a public auction. The government realized a quick profit of $572,000. Under the agreement, the main roads from McCammon to American Falls, and McCammon to Blackfoot (now I-86 and I-15) were declared public highways.

In 1924 the Snake River bottomlands were purchased for the American Falls reservoir by the Bureau of Reclamation for $700,000.

Ten years later the Shoshone-Bannock tribes organized under the Indian Reorganization Act and established the Fort Hall Business Council. The council serves as the representative arm of the tribe. It negotiated agreements in 1947 and 1960 for exploitation of phosphate deposits at the Gay mine on the reservation, thirty miles northeast of Pocatello. The mine produces almost 2 million tons of ore a year, which is shipped by rail to the Simplot and FMC plants at Pocatello. This enterprise has provided the tribal income for development of agricultural lands on the reservation.

In 1972 the Fort Hall Business Council accepted a $9.3 million settlement under the Indian Claims Commission for loss of aboriginal lands. The present reservation consists of 525,000 acres; half of it is tribally owned and half of it is allotted. The Business Council is pursuing a Land Purchase Enterprise to augment tribal lands.

The tribes' chief celebration is the Festival, usually held the first week in August at Fort Hall. Two or three Sun Dances are also held each summer.

Reservation population is about 3,000.

To see the early Indian Agency buildings, turn east at the main intersection in Fort Hall, where a sign points to **Fort Hall Agency.** Cross the railroad tracks, and drive one block to Bannock St., turn right and follow Bannock one block to the stone Tribal Court building on the west side of the street. In 1896 this structure was the quartermaster building.

From the courthouse on Bannock, turn left on Pima St. one block to Yakima St., then left on Yakima. The frame building on the corner was the superintendent's quarters in 1893; and the physician's house was next door.

Return via Bannock St. to the Agency entrance and turn east on Agency Road 0.3 miles to Mission Rd.; turn right and 0.3 miles farther, on the east side of the street, is a brick Gothic Revival church. This is the **Good Shepherd Episcopal Mission** built in 1904 and still in use. The wooden building next to it was a boarding school.

In the 1870s the Methodist Episcopal Church was entrusted with religious and educational responsibility for the Shoshone-Bannock by the federal government. The Church entirely neglected its charge until the early 1900s, when it applied for a Congressional grant of 160 acres for a mission site on the Indian land. In 1967 all but twenty acres were returned to the tribe.

The site of **Wyeth's Fort Hall,** the fur trader's post and refuge for Oregon emigrants, is located on the Fort Hall reservation. It is in the Fort Hall bottoms, two miles from the west end of Sheepskin Rd., which intersects Highway 91 just north of the Fort Hall Agency. The site, however, is fenced, and permission to visit it must be obtained from the Shoshone-Bannock tribe. The request should be in writing to the Fort Hall Business Council, P.O. Box 306, Ft. Hall, 83203.

To supply trappers in the area, Fort Hall was built in 1834 by a Boston iceman-turned-trader, Nathaniel Wyeth. At the 1832 rendezvous of the Rocky Mountain Fur Co., Wyeth had agreed to bring $3,000 worth of trade goods to the 1834 rendezvous. But by the time of his arrival, the company had already been sold to Tom Fitzpatrick and Jim Bridger who then bought their supplies from William Sublette. Wyeth then continued west, constructed his fort, and opened for business:

I have built a fort on Snake, or Lewis, river which I named Fort Hall from the oldest gentleman in the concern. We manufactured a magnificent flag from unbleached sheeting, a little red flannel and a few blue patches, saluted it with damaged powder and wet it with villainous alcohol and it makes, I do assure you, a very respectable appearance amid the dry and desolate regions of Central America. Its bastions stand a terror to the skulking Indians and a beacon of safety to the fugitive hunter. It is manned by 12 men and has constantly loaded in the bastions 100 guns and rifles. After building the fort I sent messengers to the neighboring nations to induce them to come in and trade.

Fort Hall as it appeared to a member of the Cross expedition in 1849.

At nearby Fort Boise the Hudson's Bay Company, never happy with competition, undercut Wyeth's prices to drive him out of business; he lasted about as long as a rattlesnake in a cowboy's boot. In 1836 he sold to Hudson's Bay at a $30,000 loss.

The fort became a rest stop for thousands of travelers on the Oregon Trail from 1843 to 1855. In 1856 the post was abandoned, partly because of Indian difficulties, by order of the Chief Factor Dugald McTavish.

Marker at site of Old Fort Hall.

Among the better-known visitors to the fort were Thomas McKay, Capt. Bonneville, Peter Skene Ogden, Caleb Greenwood, Joe Meek, Osborne Russell, Doc Newell, Bill Craig, the Whitmans, John Mullan, and John C. Fremont.

The site is one of Idaho's eight National Historic Landmarks, but only persons who delight in getting lost and in trouble should venture into the bottomland without tribal permission. (There is a full-size replica of the fort in Ross Park at Pocatello.)

Blackfoot is on Highway 91, immediately east of I-15 and 11.6 miles from Fort Hall. The town is located at the confluence of the Blackfoot River with the Snake. In 1878 the town, first called Grove City, was named for the river, which acquired its name from a band

510

of Blackfeet encountered here by Donald McKenzie. In the same year, on Christmas Day, the Utah and Northern Railroad arrived.

In 1880 Blackfoot was considered a likely site for the transfer of the state capital from Boise, but political appointments frustrated the plan by one vote.

When Bingham County was hewed out of Oneida County in 1885, Blackfoot became the county seat. That year the legislature issued bonds for $20,000 to establish Idaho's first insane asylum at Blackfoot – until then, patients had been sent to a facility in Salem, Oregon.

In 1889 a U.S. land office was established in Blackfoot. During the first three months 300 homestead entries were processed. The land office was the registration center when the Fort Hall reservation was opened to settlement on May 7, 1907, "the Day of the Run." Several thousand sagebrush sooners staked their ground and raced for Blackfoot to file their claims.

Blackfoot's economy is based on agriculture and agricultural processing; it is the center of the largest potato-growing county in the state.

The Idaho potato variety is the russet Burbank. In 1872 Luther Burbank noticed one of his Early Rose potatoes had produced a seed ball, which was unusual for that variety. He collected twenty-three seeds from the fruit and planted them in the spring. All of the seeds produced, and one of the seedlings had tubers superior in size and number to its Early Rose parent. It proved itself the following summer, and Burbank offered it to a Massachusetts grower for $500. The grower gave him $150. Burbank accepted the money and used it to move to California, taking ten of the tubers with him to introduce the variety there. By 1906 over 6 million bushels were produced on the West Coast. He grew a half-million hybrid seedlings without producing a more successful variety.

The coat of this variety was modified by Lon Sweet, of Denver, Colorado, when he selected a sport from a Burbank and produced the netted skin of the russet Burbank, which is especially resistant to blight.

Idaho's growing conditions, with high elevation, hot days and cool nights, high soil moisture (80 percent), and light, volcanic soil produce a potato many believe is superior to all others. It is high in solids, has good texture and a pleasing flavor.

The state's potato acreage now exceeds 300,000 acres. About 70 percent of the annual crop is processed by the "convenience food" industry.

Blackfoot has several remarkable examples of period-architecture. Take East Judicial Ave. northeast to 120 So. Shilling Ave.

The semi-circular, two-story building on the northeast corner was an LDS Tabernacle, built in 1920-1921 for the Blackfoot Stake. The structure cost $78,000 and seated 1,000 persons on the main floor and 500 in the gallery. The admirable upper brickwork employs a garden-wall pattern with a diamond overlay. The oval windows have stained glass. Maple was used for the interior.

In 1959 the Blackfoot Stake spent $100,000 to convert the main dance floor into offices and meeting rooms, then built a new Stake center, and in 1980 sold the tabernacle to Bingham County as a courthouse annex and community center.

Continue north two blocks to 72 No. Shilling for a look at St. Paul's Episcopal Church, built in 1890.

Across E. Pacific, at 122 No. Shilling, is an interesting, intricate, two-story house built of brick and shingle.

Two doors farther north, at the corner of East Idaho and No. Shilling, is a lava rock house that contains the **Bingham County Historical Museum.** The house was built in 1905 for a Blackfoot businessman. It was the city's social center, then the American Legion Home from 1927 to 1974; Legionnaires placed the cannons on the lawn.

Northwest, across the street from the museum, is an unusual rusticated stone house with a turret and a pair of dormers. It was built in 1893 by Dolf Johnson for his bride but was foreclosed by its first occupant. For a time it served as a hotel. The gingerbread has been removed and the interior remodeled, but it retains considerable charm.

Return on No. Shilling via Bridge St. to Main St. and drive north on Main to West Idaho. The Oregon Short Line depot on the east side of No. Main was built in 1913 for $27,000 and still serves the Union Pacific.

Drive one block west of Main St. to 190 No. Broadway at W. Idaho. The Nuart Theatre is regarded by Dr. J. M. Neil as "the most elaborately decorated small town theatre built in Idaho." It was constructed in 1930 at a cost of $100,000, and was still being operated by the original owners fifty years later.

The Art Deco facade features maroon brick panels in warp-and-woof patterns and an elaborate white terra cotta cornice. The interior has bright, hand-painted terra cotta friezes and ornamental plaster.

512

To visit the site of the **Fort Hall military post,** established by the U.S. Army in 1870, drive northwest from the OSL depot on Main St. in Blackfoot, 0.5 miles to the county fairgrounds and Rich Lane. Turn east across the railroad tracks onto Rich Ln., follow it 7.2 miles to a cattle guard, and take the curve to the right (south) on Lincoln Creek Rd. (no sign) for 3.1 miles. The location of the post was in the flat below the west side of the road, in the semi-circle of cottonwood trees.

Fort Hall on Lincoln Creek in 1871. F.V. Hayden survey camp on the right.

In late April, 1870, Company C of the Twelfth U.S. Infantry, with ninety privates and noncomissioned officers under the command of Capt. J. Putnam, arrived on the grounds from Camp Bidwell in California. The post, established by President Grant to protect the Indians and whites from each other, operated for thirteen years. It was abandoned because the railroad gave easy access from Camp Douglas to the Fort Hall Agency.

In 1883 the Indian Department opened an industrial school in the old buildings here. It began with twenty students and had eight different superintendents in the first two years! But by 1892 there were eighty-seven students, four classrooms, a dormitory, and a 1,700-acre farm, with eighty acres under cultivation. In 1904 a new school was finally built, only a mile south of the Fort Hall Agency.

Highway 91 travels 3.2 miles through Blackfoot and then 11.8 northeast to **Firth,** a town first settled by a colony of Swedish immigrants.

Shelley is 4.8 miles northeast of Firth. It is an agricultural town similar to others in the county. John Shelley, the town founder, was the son of English Mormon parents who immigrated to Utah.

In the spring of 1885 John Shelley and two friends came north from American Fork, Utah to Iona, Idaho. John became principal of the school and then opened a general store.

He moved fifteen miles south in 1893, and the railroad delivered the lumber for a new store: the Shelley Mercantile Co. The railroad also pinned his name to the spot, which gradually became a town. John Shelley became vice-president of the town bank and donated six acres for the city park.

U.S. 91 proceeds northeast through Shelley for one mile, then at 7.3 miles intersects U.S. 26 and I-15 southwest of Idaho Falls.

U.S. Highway 93 from the Idaho-Nevada state line north to Rogerson, northerly via Hollister, Twin Falls, Shoshone, Carey, Arco, Mackay, Challis, and Salmon to the Idaho-Montana border at Lost Trail Pass. Route length: 340.8 miles.

U.S. 93 travels north from the Utah border 18.1 miles to **Rogerson.** Called Deep Creek Meadows by the first arrivals, the area was renamed Terminal City by railroad officials in 1909 because it was the end of the branch line from Twin Falls. Robert Rogerson, who also owned a hotel in Twin Falls, platted a townsite on his property next to the Terminal depot. A hotel, bank, and school were supported by the region's livestock operations; cowboys drove sheep and cattle to the rail-end stockyards from as far away as the Three Forks country,

Hollister is 8.4 miles north of Rogerson. H. L. Hollister was a settler involved in several irrigation projects in the area, often with his friend, I. B. Perrine.

Nat Soo Pah Hot Springs is three miles east of downtown Hollister; it is open during the summer and has RV spaces available.

Nine miles farther north, Highway 93 joins U.S. 30 and turns east toward Twin Falls. Two miles from the junction, on the south side of the road, is the Union School, which now contains the **Twin Falls County Historical Museum.** In addition to a gallery of photographs, the collection includes some interesting horse-powered sagegrubbers, haybalers, beetpullers, and potato-seeders – items that recall Robert Frost's couplet: "I wondered what machine of ages gone / this represented an

514

improvement on." The metal shed houses an Aultman-Taylor steam tractor and two ice wagons.

Twin Falls is three miles east of the museum. Understanding the roots of Twin Falls requires a simple grasp of the 1894 Carey Act, which was a result of a small amendment to the Sundry Civil Appropriations Bill in 1894. Intended for the reclamation of desert lands, the amendment empowered the Secretary of the Interior to grant one million acres to each state if the state caused the land to be irrigated, reclaimed, and occupied in individual 160-acre tracts within ten years of the Act's passage. Any state operating under the Act was authorized to make all contracts necessary to settle and cultivate the land.

Since they could not afford to construct the irrigation projects themselves, the states contracted with private enterprise to build the irrigation works, giving the companies the security of a lien against the reclaimed lands for the cost of the construction.

The construction company applied to the state for segregation of a development tract, showed the existence of a valid water right, and specified construction details. If the state approved the plan, the state reclamation engineer saw to it that the criteria were met within six years. The company financed its operation by mortgaging its equity or issuing bonds, and the contract stipulated that when the project was completed, it would be turned over to the water-shareowners for operation. (One acre represents one share of stock and each acre is entitled to ⅝-inch of water.)

Once satisfied that the water was available, the state advertised that the land was open to settlers. Ex-servicemen had priority in the drawing; the general public was given tracts on a first-come, first-served basis.

The state had the exclusive power to regulate water, but the construction companies were given the privilege, as a trustee, to sell water rights to the settlers in order to recover construction costs, along with a reasonable profit. In addition to the water contract, the settler had to pay the state 50¢ an acre for the land and reclaim one-eighth of his acreage within two years of his entry. If after three years the settler owned water sufficient to irrigate his 160-acres, and twenty acres were under cultivation, he received title.

In 1895 Idaho was the second state to accept the Carey Act; between 1895 and 1930, sixty-five projects were proposed to the state and over 600,000 acres were patented, which made Idaho the most successful Carey Act state. More acres were patented in one project than in all the segregations of the second-most successful state, Wyoming. The Act remains a valid federal law.

In 1900 a group of financiers, largely from Pittsburgh, filed the Twin Falls South Side proposal with the State Land Board. They planned to reclaim 244,000 acres by building a dam on the Snake River at Milner, east of Twin Falls, and diverting water through a canal along the south side of the river. The idea was fathered by I. B. Perrine, an Indiana-born Idaho settler who had developed an irrigated orchard in the shelter of the Snake River Canyon at Blue Lakes, just west of what is now Twin Falls. Perrine knew that the volcanic soil was very fertile, and he spent several years promoting the irrigation project.

Land Drawing at Twin Falls.

Grubbing sagebrush near Twin Falls.

516

In 1900 Perrine interested Stanley Milner, a wealthy Salt Lake City businessman, in the project. With help from Perrine and Milner, a mining broker with eastern connections sold the idea to Pennsylvania industrialists.

After securing bond issues in Chicago, Frank Buhl and Peter Kimberly, along with Milner and Perrine, formed the Twin Falls Land and Water Company in Utah, and contracted with Idaho to develop the South Side project under the Carey Act provisions.

In 1903 construction began on Milner Dam which was completed two years later. In 1904 the company set aside four blocks for park

Twin Falls land office, 1909.

Grubbing sagebrush with a steam tractor on the Twin Falls Tract.

purposes and platted the townsite. Water rights went for $25 an acre, and settlers flocked to the area as the Low Line Canal (ten ft. deep, eighty ft. wide) began carrying water to 60,000 acres of farmland. By 1909, when the state accepted the South Side project as complete and turned it over to the settlers' operating company, Twin Falls had bloomed like a sagebrush buttercup – it was the seat of Twin Falls County.

Important community structures sprouted around the park on Shoshone St., which forms the northwest-southeast diagonal across

Early potato digger and sorter at Twin Falls.

Muddy streets in Twin Falls, 1910.

518

the town quad. The park, between Fifth Ave. East and Sixth Ave. East, remains the location of the city's most interesting architecture.

Highway 93 enters Twin Falls from the west and becomes Addison Ave. West. Two miles inside the city limits, turn southeast on Sixth Ave. North, 0.4 miles to Shoshone Street and the city park.

It is easier to walk around the area because, like a New England commons, all the more notable buildings face the green. St. Edward's Catholic Church, distinguished by its twin seventy-five-foot towers, stands at the northeast corner of the

Loading spuds on the OSL at Twin Falls.

Twin Falls Main St. in 1920.

square. It is a splendid example of Renaissance revival architecture. Built in 1920-1921 for $60,000, the church has a remarkably embellished interior that contrasts with simple stained glass windows and a barrel vault nave. The church is usually open during the day.

The public library, near the southeast corner of the park, was built in 1939 with a $22,000 grant from the Public Works Administration and a $27,000 bond issue.

It has been remarked that "photographs are as important to the curious researcher as a taxidermist is to a hunter." From 1904 to 1934 Twin Falls and Magic Valley were fortunate to have their history recorded by a masterly photographer, Clarence E. Bisbee. Incised in the bricks above the entrance to Bisbee's studio was the aphorism "Life and art are one." Prints and 2,000 of his glass negatives are on file in the library, an invaluable record of regional change.

Rialto Theater in Twin Falls.

520

The southwest corner of the park is occupied by the Methodist Church which opened in 1909, as a dark brick structure, overshadowed in 1916 by the brown sandstone addition in a Tudor Gothic style.

At the northwest corner of the park is a third member of this distinctive congregation, the red-brick First Christian Church, completed in 1929. A Portland architect provided its neoclassical design.

The Justamere Inn, perhaps the best surviving example of Mission style architecture in southern Idaho, is located one block northwest of the park on Fourth Ave. North, at Second St. North. It was opened in 1910; built of concrete and roofed with red tile, it had thirty-three bedrooms and a large dining room. In 1979 the hotel was converted to an office building.

From the park drive southwest two blocks to Second Ave. North and follow it northwest seven blocks to West Addison. Jog north off

Twin Falls company performs Gilbert & Sullivan's operetta "Mikado" in 1912.

Addison onto Washington Street North and follow it two miles to the campus of the **College of Southern Idaho** at Falls Ave. West. Take the circle drive off Washington Street through the campus to the parking lot at the northeast end of the road.

Begun in 1965, the school is one of six junior colleges in the state; it serves nearly 5,000 students with vocational and academic instruction in an eight-county district. The beauty of the circular 240-acre campus reflects an intelligent master plan.

The entrance to the **Norman and Lilly Herrett Museum** is only a few yards northeast of the parking lot; it contains the finest anthropological collection in the state, and its story would be extraordinary anywhere.

Norman Herrett was a North Dakota schoolteacher who moved to Twin Falls during the Depression and taught shop at the local high school. He observed that his students often learned more readily from their peers than from their teachers; the fast learners were encouraged to instruct the slower ones.

When Herrett quit teaching, he opened a Twin Falls jewelry store, but he continued to share his knowledge with children. An interest in astronomy led him to build a homemade observatory and planetarium and he invited grade schools to visit them.

As the business of this teacher-turned-jeweler prospered, he gratified an interest in pre-Columbian cultures with semi-annual collecting trips to Central and South America. Rather than a narrow, in-depth collection, he amassed a widely representative one – it includes nearly 10,000 artifacts.

In 1972 the Herretts donated the collection to the College of South Idaho, which agreed to build a 24,000 sq. ft. building and hire a full-time staff for it.

Though a fund drive raised $1 million, that amount would only buy 12,000 sq. ft.; Herrett accepted the smaller space in the belief that it could be expanded later. He saw the building under construction but died in 1980 before it opened.

Inasmuch as the Herretts intended that their collection teach southern Idaho schoolchildren about the prehistoric cultures of the New World, the museum developed an innovative and diversified youth program. A children's gallery, with an exhibit that changes yearly, is staffed by teen-age guides, in accord with Herrett's learning theory. The students can work bi-weekly at the museum, one morning or afternoon; those who stay with the program through high school develop a facility for public speaking and an outstanding knowledge of anthropology and archaeology. Herrett's museum is used by two classes per day (sixty students), and is so popular that it cannot accommodate all the requests for tours.

In addition to the children's exhibit, adults will find professional, informative displays of articles from whatever geographic area is featured at the time, such as pre-Inca textiles, Snake River artifacts Mayan jade, or Peruvian pottery.

A visit to **Shoshone Falls,** the 212-foot "Niagara of the West," is not to be missed; it is only a five-mile drive from downtown Twin Falls. The best time to view it is in the spring before irrigation water is impounded upstream at Milner Dam and much of the balance is siphoned off by the Idaho Power hydroplant.

The falls were named in 1849 by Major Osborne Cross, who was leading a regiment on a military scouting expedition from Ft. Leavenworth to Ft. Vancouver. He wished to erase the name Canadian Falls, given by Hudson's Bay trappers.

Charles Walgamott visited Shoshone Falls in 1875; recognizing their scenic value, he filed on the land on both sides of the river and built a dugout shelter on the site. After the OSL railroad reached Shoshone in 1883, he operated a stage line from town to the waterfall. Accommodations for tourists were third rate. Walgamott wrote:

We found it hard to sleep 30 or 40 people with bedding for only 10 or 12. We procured 12 hammocks, each with a blanket. The tourists did not take kindly to these hammocks at a dollar a night, but my partner was a good storyteller, and every night before bedtime he would tell stories of rattlesnakes crawling into people's beds. A few stories usually created a demand for hammocks.

Walgamott sold his holdings to Charles Dewey, who built a small hotel on the south bluff; passengers took a rowboat across from the north shore. In the 1890s the U.P. railroad joined in promoting the site as a tourist attraction, and by 1911 a battery-powered train traveled from the town of Twin Falls to Shoshone Falls.

Other persons were not long in perceiving another way to exploit the falls. In 1901 Bert Perrine and H. L. Hollister attempted to harness the waterpower by tunneling up 200 feet through the rock to the brink. They ran out of money, and Shoshone Falls Power Company took over the effort three years later but failed; in 1907 its successor succeeded. The new plant produced 500 k.w., enough electricity to supply Twin Falls and Jerome. A second generator in 1909 doubled the output and expanded service to Oakley, Shoshone, and even Mountain Home.

Idaho Power Company acquired the facility in 1915 and in 1921 built the second, bigger powerplant, visible alongside the first, at the base of the falls. Output was increased to 12,000 k.w. In 1927 Idaho Power further defaced the sight with a diversion dam to store water for peak use.

*Shoshone Falls.
In 1911 the Edison
Electric Railway
brought tourists
to a hotel here.*

Only a soul that has never shuddered could view this cataract without wondering whether anyone was ever so unfortunate as to pass over the edge. The answer is "yes;" three even did so deliberately.

The regional historian Charles Walgamott wrote the story of Tom Bell in his book, *Six Decades Back.*

Bell was a Scotch miner who built a cabin at Shoshone Falls in 1878; he placer mined the back eddies along this stretch of river. In June, 1880, Bell was asked to ferry two Chinese and their supplies across the river above the falls. Apparently an oar broke in mid-stream, and despite all efforts, the men were swept to their deaths.

On March 4, 1905, the Twin Falls *Daily News* carried the following item:

Harry Wilson, a half-breed Cherokee Indian, while at Shoshone Falls Thursday, created a sensation by jumping over the falls and landing in the whirlpool below. He swam to a rock and calmly awaited the arrival of his clothing, which had been removed before making the leap. In the descent his knee struck a rock, which caused a painful, though not serious wound. The falls are 210 feet in height, and the entire distance was passed over in the descent. Mr. Wilson said he performed the feat simply to show he had the nerve.

The next person to purposely go over the falls was Al Faussett, a lumberjack from Monroe, Washington, who had more guts than one

524

At the edge of
Shoshone Falls
(note figure,
lower right).

could hang on a fence. His first experience came in Washington in
1926, when Fox Studios offered $1,500 to anyone who would run
Sunset Falls on the North Fork of the Skykomish in a canoe. The
rapid plunges 104 feet down a 275-foot-long slide. Faussett hewed a
thirty-four foot dugout from a spruce log, cowled the foredeck with
sheet metal, and announced his readiness. Fox reneged on its offer
because the craft was not a replica of an Indian canoe, but Faussett
decided to go anyway. He charged $1.00 admission and drew a
crowd of 3,000. His craft came through Sunset Falls like a brown
spear, but he emerged unscathed – fearless Faussett had found a
new career.

Over the next two years he ran four impressive falls: Eagle (40 ft.)
and Spokane (75 ft.) in Washington, and in Oregon, Oregon City (40
ft.) and Silver Creek (186 ft.). His only injuries were a concussion
and two broken ribs.

Faussett was ready for Niagara, but the difficulties and expense
of traveling to New York persuaded him to attempt Shoshone Falls
instead – furthermore, it was forty feet higher. He signed a contract
with the Twin Falls post of the American Legion for half the
proceeds to be derived from the stunt.

On July 28, 1929, ticket takers admitted 5,000 spectators to the
area overlooking the falls; 700 cars were parked on the flats, and
three grass fires enlivened the day. American Electric Company
provided radio music, and dynamite explosions kept the crowd
informed of the countdown.

Faussett's craft was an orange, canvas-covered canoe, shaped like a football. It was twelve feet long, braced with ribs of spruce and fir, stuffed with truck-tire inner tubes and excelsior. At 5:00 P.M. he slid himself into his sausage casing, zipped the canvas hatch closed, and was pushed into the current.

Al Faussett, c. 1920.

Idaho Power Company accommodated the event by interrupting its water diversion for a few minutes to raise the flow. In order to direct his craft over the south edge, Faussett had run a slender (No. 12) wire from a large boulder upstream, through a three-inch ring on his bow, and down to a man in a boat at the foot of the falls.

The boat whisked downstream with increasing speed, then snagged at the brink. Two assistants waded out with poles and poked it loose; it went over like a spent arrow.

When Faussett's torpedo resurfaced, it fell face down; two motorboats towed it to the south shore, where it was righted and the canvas knifed open. Out popped Faussett, grinning like a cat coming out of a lard pail. He suffered only a broken right hand.

Afterward, in his interview with reporters, he said, "I am certain that the nose of the boat hit a rock, from the feeling I had while inside upon landing and the resultant bounce."

The daredevil received $733 for his feat. In 1948 Faussett died of cancer in a Seattle resthome.

The third party to intentionally pitch headlong over the Shoshone Falls was twenty-one year-old Tom Rauckhorst, possessed of much nerve or very little sense – it's a race to Moot Point.

526

In September, 1974, Rauckhorst was en route to Oregon from Akron, Ohio, to visit a friend; on a whim he decided to witness Evel Knevil's rocket launch across the Snake River Canyon. He visited the falls the day before Evel's jump, and decided to make a leap of his own.

Al Faussett prepares his craft for Silver Creek Falls.

Rauckhorst had completed a few high dives, but he had no training. While looking at Shoshone Falls he suddenly announced to a handful of tourists that he was going to dive to the pool below. Of course, no one believed him.

He made his dive from the south shoulder of the falls and lost consciousness upon striking the water – he recalled awakening upside down. After resurfacing, he swam ashore and sat on the rocks for a few minutes before he climbed back to the rim, where a camper took him on a motorcycle to Twin Falls Hospital.

Doctors found that he had crushed three vertebrae and put him in a back brace. When they asked if he had any regrets, Rauckhorst replied, "I wish I knew how high it was, I would have done a different dive."

In 1882 a ferry was established about 200 yards upriver from the falls; it takes little imagination to understand why business was never brisk. In 1907 the cable broke while five persons were aboard; a passenger snubbed a cable end around a beam, and after a half hour on the verge of frying bacon with the devil, the entire party was tugged ashore.

To visit the site of **Twin Falls,** return south on 3300 East one mile to 4000 North Road (Falls Ave.), turn east for two miles to 3500 East, and north on 3500 East one mile through two curves to the overlook.

Irrigation diversions and the Idaho Power Company plant have so altered the falls in the summer that one must supplement it with a flow of imagination.

Twin Falls.

Perrine Bridge in 1927.

Return to the city of Twin Falls. Drive north out of Twin Falls on U.S. 93, 2.7 miles to **Perrine Bridge,** 475 feet above the Snake River Canyon. The view area is at the south end of the bridge on the west side of the highway.

The first span built across this chasm was opened in 1927 as the highest bridge in the world; it was built by a Seattle firm under a fifty-year franchise, granted jointly by the commissioners of Twin

Sturgeon caught near Twin Falls in 1908. Weight: 632 pounds.

Falls and Jerome Counties, that gave the company the right to operate as a toll authority. Considering the $630,000 cost, tolls were very reasonable: cars, 60¢; persons riding or walking, 5¢ each. In 1970 the two-lane Perrine Bridge was so old that it was no longer considered safe for heavy loads, and check stations were established at each end.

Preparations for its replacement were under way in 1971; two

Huge 1,500 pound sturgeon taken from Snake river near Buhl, Idaho 1911.

Sturgeon caught near Buhl; weighed on a hay scale. (Photo by Lloyd Byrne).

531

years of foundation and wall stabilization were required. The new 933-foot-long center-span arch took six months to complete and used 4,000 tons of structural steel. The bridge, which cost $8.6 million, was finished in late 1974. Its predecessor, located a few yards to the west, was dismantled for scrap.

To see the site of stuntman **Evel Knevil's canyon jump,** turn east on the first paved road at the north end of the bridge; the pavement ends, but by following the dirt track 0.5 miles one can see the earth ramp 1,600 feet across the gorge on the south side.

After a sixty-two-city press conference tour in fifteen days, Knevil's jump with Skycycle X-3 was an anticlimax. On September 8, 1974, at 3:44 P.M., nearly 20,000 persons (incuding 200 newsmen) watched the cycle, powered by 5,000 pounds of thrust, lift off the ramp at 350 m.p.h.

A malfunction caused the drogue chute to open prematurely (while the cycle was still on the ramp); before the main chute opened, the rider climbed 1,000 feet above the ramp, then the cycle with Evel in it fell to the rocks 470 feet below the rim and came to rest twenty feet from the water. Knevil suffered facial lacerations, minor bruises and major disparagement.

U.S. 93 enters **Shoshone,** 23.4 miles north of Perrine Bridge.

Shoshone may have been a double-tough town for a few years after the arrival of the railroad in the 1880s. It was a mining supply crossroads, and when Carrie Strahorn, a frontier traveler, came through, she remarked:

Ten and fifteen arrests per day were common, and there was no other jail but a hole in the ground, with guards placed around the hole. There was a fight on the streets almost every hour of the day and night. Lot jumpers were numerous, bad whiskey was unlimited, dancehalls were on every corner, guns were fired at all hours, and the loud time from gambling dens was ever vibrating through the air.

Highway 93 turns east-northeast at Shoshone and overlaps U.S. 20 to Carey and U.S. 26 from there to Arco.

Richfield is on the Little Wood River 16.1 miles east of Shoshone. The area was settled after 1907 when Magic Dam was built by the Idaho Irrigation Company as part of the Big Wood River project. A drawing was held under provisions of the Carey Act, and settlers filed on 40,000 acres; peak years for the community were 1924 to 1940.

532

The forlorn Richfield Hotel, at the corner of Main and Lincoln Streets, dates from the Carey Act ferment in the early 1900s; in the 1930s its ballroom served as the high school gymnasium.

Richfield Hotel.

First administration building at Craters of the Moon. Apollo astronauts received training in geology and map reading at the National Monument.

The highway continues through lava plains for 24.6 miles east to **Carey** – an agricultural town named in 1884 for its first postmaster.

The entrance to **Craters of the Moon,** Idaho's only National Monument, is 24.6 miles northwest of Carey, on the southeast side of the road.

In 1924 President Coolidge set aside the eighty-three square-mile area because of its outstanding geological values. The monument contains at least thirty-nine separate lava flows, some of them as recent as 250 years ago. Other features include exemplary patterns of the three types of lava, as well as cinder buttes, spatter cones, and lava tubes.

The visitors center contains informative displays, a useful prelude to the seven-mile loop-drive through the monument.

U.S. 93 continues northeast from the monument 18.7 miles to **Arco,** readily identified by the graduation dates of every high school class since 1931 enameled on Arco Rock above the town.

Arco Land Drawing, 1909.

Old Arco was located five miles south of the present townsite, at the junction of the Blackfoot-Wood River and Blackfoot-Salmon stage lines. A suspension bridge across the Big Lost River funnelled all regional traffic through the settlement every spring.

The Postal Department vetoed a request for the designation of Junction, and suggested the name of a count who was visiting Washington, D.C. at the time. The suggestion was accepted. Arco shifted four miles southeast when the stage station was moved to the Webb Springs at Big Southern Butte, then moved to its present site in 1901 when the Oregon Short Line arrived from Blackfoot and made the stage lines obsolete.

U.S. 93 travels northwest up the Big Lost River Valley 18.5 miles to the rail siding of Leslie.

A six-mile detour from Leslie leads to one of the half-dozen more spectacular gorges in the state: **Blue Jay Canyon.** Turn northeast across the railroad tracks fifty feet from the highway, curve left and follow the road for 1.8 miles to a BLM sign at an intersection. Continue in the same direction (northeast) up the alluvial fan along Pass Creek.

This startling gap in the Lost River Range has been created by the erosive power of the small creek on the relatively soft, sedimentary limestone. Douglas fir, Engelmann spruce, limber pine and a few juniper grow along the creek bottom. Local lore alleges the secluded canyon was once the refuge of moonshiners; the cliffs alone would stagger most persons.

Freight wagons at Arco in about 1915.

Mackay, rumped against the Lost River Range on the east and shadowed by the White Knob Mountains on the west, is among the more remote towns in Idaho. It is eight miles north of the Leslie siding.

In 1884-1885 the area experienced a surge of copper-mining activity in the White Knobs, and Pacific Iron Company of San Francisco built a smelter, but it was not until 1901, when the Comstock baron George Mackay paid 80 percent of the cost of a railroad branch from Blackfoot to the White Knobs, that serious development occurred. Mackay, an Irish immigrant who acquired so much wealth he did not know his worth within $20 million, built a 600-ton smelter and platted the townsite of Mackay just below it.

Mackay's mine, however, was not worth a holler in a box canyon; two years later, his company declared bankruptcy and the smelter was moved to California.

Other mines in the Alder Creek district of the White Knobs, southwest of town, succeeded in making the region Idaho's leading copper producer from 1900 to 1930.

Mackay Dam and reservoir can be seen on the west side of the highway four miles north of the town, part of the Big Lost River Project begun by an irrigation company in 1906 under the Carey Act.

The first dam was built on alluvial gravel and did not hold water any better than a cobweb does a cow. The project went through

Shay locomotive of Empire Copper Co. holding back ore cars on the mine grade in 1918.

Empire Copper Co.'s White Knob mine.

536

default twice before it was purchased at a receiver's sale by the Utah Construction Company. Utah Construction rebuilt the dam and completed the canal, but the cost ran $3.5 million for the reclamation of 8,000 acres. (After this first dam, Utah Construction became a major contractor on Hoover, Grand Coulee, American Falls and Imperial Dams).

The two-mile approach road for **Borah Peak,** at 12,662 feet the highest mountain in Idaho, is 19.8 miles northwest of Mackay Dam, on the east side of the highway. The peak was named for William Borah, Idaho's Republican Senator from 1907 until his death in 1940.

G. K. Chesterton observed, "Heights were made to be looked at, not to be looked from." For those who disagree, and are interested in making the ascent, the best time to attempt it is between July 15 and August 15, when no special equipment is needed. The main routes are from the west side, either through the canyon or along the ridge. Snow melt will normally furnish water down to 9,500 feet until mid-July. The round trip requires about eight hours, and Chesterton never saw such a view.

Nine miles farther north, the highway climbs over Willow Creek Summit (7,161 elev.) through White Knob limestone; the Pahsimeroi mountains are visible to the east.

After another ten miles, the road enters **Grand View Canyon.** The ancestor of puny Warm Springs Creek cut through a surface layer of Challis volcanics and encountered a hill of Paleozoic rock, formed about 350 million years ago. The stream gradually eroded the more resistant rock, and its course is now followed by the highway.

Challis is fourteen miles west of Grand View Canyon. The mile-high town was located in 1878 and was named after Alvah P. Challis, who helped survey the lots. The town, connected by toll road to Custer, became a trading center for the nearby mines in Stanley Basin, Yankee Fork, Loon Creek, Bayhorse, and Yellow Jacket, and the valley was a good wintering ground for pack stock and teams used by freighters.

By the mid-1960s Challis had become a cattle-ranching town with latent mineral prospects. Then in 1967, the Cyprus Mine Corportion, now a subsidiary of AMOCO (Standard Oil of Indiana), discovered a substantial molybdenum deposit on Thompson Creek forty miles southwest of town and seven miles from the Salmon River.

Cyprus announced plans for a $360 million strip mine, with a twenty-year life expectancy, and the town was suddenly as crowded as ten toes in a sock. All the problems of a boom town arose: jobseekers, trailer sites, subdivisions, school expansion, sewage treatment, expanded electric systems, and a full jail. Suspended judgment is a matter of infinite hope. As one resident remarked, "It's never safe to be nostalgic about something until you're sure it's not coming back, and I figure in twenty years the pit will be as empty as a water hole in August."

Molybdenum is used as a hardening agent in steel. The Thompson Creek pit, which will be a mile square and 1,500 feet deep, will supply about 18 percent of the world's production. Four electric shovels (each using more electricity per day than did all of pre-boom Challis) will load two dozen 170-ton Haulpack ore trucks whose loads will feed a 7,000-foot conveyer belt to the concentrator on another ridge. Several times a day semi-trucks, loaded with fifty tons of concentrate in fifty-gallon drums, will leave for the railhead in Arco.

From the east side of the highway, the **Pahsimeroi River** enters the main Salmon 17.3 miles north of Challis; it forms the boundary between Custer and Lemhi Counties.

During the winter of 1831-1832, Warren Ferris and his men from the American Fur Company camped in the Pahsimeroi Valley and killed over 100 buffalo. The valley now shelters an antelope herd.

The State Fish and Game Department operates a steelhead hatchery on the river, funded by Idaho Power Company as mitigation for losses caused by Hells Canyon Dams.

Several tungsten mines were active in Pahsimeroi Valley from the 1940s until 1959.

The road to **Cobalt** and **Leesburg** leaves the highway 35.9 miles northeast of the Pahsimeroi. The dirt-gravel road climbs twelve miles west over Williams Creek Summit (7,814 ft.) and forks after another two miles. The right fork leads ten miles up Napias Creek to Leesburg, a mining town begun in 1866 immediately after the Civil War, as its name attests.

The camp's population may have reached 3,000, and $5 million in gold was produced. Dredge dunes date from 1940-1941, though those on Moose Creek are earlier. Aside from a dozen log cabins and the gouged earth, "only the journey which memory can take will bring Leesburg to you now."

538

To return south from the ghost town, follow Napias Creek down to its confluence with Moccasin Creek, turn west 2.5 miles then south 3.0 miles to Cobalt.

The element cobalt is used as a catalyst, and as a high-temperature alloy in steel, tools and electromagnets. The U.S. has imported about 70 percent of its annual needs from Africa.

The Blackbird mine, five miles west of Cobalt, produced cobalt concentrate in 1917, closed in 1922, and reopened from 1942 until 1960, while the U.S. stockpiled the metal.

Leesburg.

In 1979 Noranda Mining Company, a Canadian-based multinational corporation, began to explore the extent of the reserves and refurbished the Blackbird mill at a cost of about $30 million. Reserves sufficient for twelve years of production exist, but development will depend on the market.

One can loop back to U.S. 93 at North Fork by traveling north down Panther Creek twenty-one miles to the Salmon River, and then eight miles east to Shoup, where the paved road follows the river seventeen miles back to the highway.

Salmon, five miles north of the Cobalt road, was a supply center for Leesburg basin. The town is situated at the forks of the Salmon and Lemhi Rivers, and in 1832 it was a winter camp for brigades of the Hudson's Bay Company, the Rocky Mountain Fur Company, and the American Fur Company – there must have been many "do 'ee hyar now" as the likes of Jim Bridger, Joe Meek, and Henry Fraeb gathered round their campfires waiting for the green-grass moon. The cavalada included Milton Sublette, Tom Fitzpatrick, Kit Carson, Captain Bonneville, and Joseph Walker.

The Salmon area developed during the mining rush of the 1860s. Colonel George L. Shoup, who had participated in the Indian massacre at Sand Creek, Colorado, helped lay out a Main Street and two cross streets that soon became the camp's business district.

Shoup owned the major mercantile in town, and in 1866 built the three-story brick building that still stands at the corner of Main and Center Streets. He was appointed the last territorial governor of Idaho, elected the State's first governor and served in the U.S. Senate from 1891 to 1901.

First house of Mr. and Mrs. George Shoup in Salmon. (George at the gate with Indians.)

Life in Salmon at present reflects its geography: cattle ranches, agriculture, logging, and tourism based on river-running, hunting and fishing. Astride the banks of the River of No Return, backdropped by the Beaverhead Mountains of the Continental Divide, it remains an historic and colorful city.

The **Lemhi County Museum** is on the east side of Main Street, on the north end of town.

U.S. 95 travels north from Salmon, along the east side of the Salmon River twenty-one miles to **North Fork.** This stretch of road parallels parts of Lewis and Clark's route in August, 1805; signs at Bird Creek and Tower Creek are helpful. (In this area Captain Clark reported sighting passenger pigeons, the first report of their presence west of the Continental Divide.)

At North Fork the Corn Creek Road follows the Salmon River thirty-two miles downstream to a campground used as a launch site for six-day river trips. (Read *River of No Return,* by Carrey and Conley.) Half of the distance is paved.

540

From North Fork the highway climbs along the forested slopes of the North Fork of the Salmon River eleven miles to **Gibbonsville.** In September, 1805, the Lewis and Clark Expedition followed this route; it was early fall and frosty nights reminded the explorers that winter's advance matched their own.

Gibbonsville was a placer-gold mining camp established in 1877 (the year Colonel John Gibbon attacked the Nez Perce encampment at Big Hole, Montana, during the Nez Perce War). Quartz lodes supported the settlement from 1880 to 1898 and yielded $2 million.

Lost Trail Pass (6,995 elev.) is fourteen miles north of Gibbonsville and marks the boundary with Montana. Missoula is ninety-two miles farther north (for a discussion of the stretch from Lost Trail to Missoula, see U.S. 12, Travelers' Rest).

U.S. Highway 95 from the Idaho-Oregon state line north of Jordan Valley, Oregon, northerly via Homedale, Wilder, Parma, Fruitland, Payette, Weiser, Midvale, Cambridge, Council, New Meadows, Riggins, White Bird, Grangeville, Cottonwood, Craigmont, Lewiston, Moscow, Plummer, Coeur d'Alene, Sandpoint, and Bonners Ferry to the Canadian boundary at Eastport. Route length: 532 miles.

Homedale is the first town encountered by travelers who enter Idaho from Oregon on northbound U.S. 95. It is thirty-three miles north of the highway's stateline entry point.

The southern alternate route of the Oregon Trail followed the south bank of the Snake River through the area that has become Homedale.

In 1898 Jacob and Ada Mussell established a ferry across the Snake at this site. Neighbors placed suggested names for the location in a hat; Homedale was the one Jake Mussell drew.

He plowed a road to nearby Roswell and contracted for another from Parma. Traffic slowly increased; in 1920 a steel bridge replaced his ferry; in 1970 the present concrete bridge was built across the old ferry site.

In 1906 the San Francisco, Idaho, and Montana Railroad Co. brought an extension from Caldwell to Homedale. The railroad was involved in land speculation; it platted a 520-acre townsite and advertised lots. Other hustlers established the Homedale Improvement Co. and the Homedale Townsite Co.

The arrival of forty Austrian immigrants in February, 1914, was a major boost for the community. The immigrant families – Marchak, Dolence, Kushlan, Miklovich, Jensenko, Demshar, Cegnar – were coal miners in Wyoming when they were gulled by promoters who promised them rich, forty-acre farms, with house, fence, and ten seeded-acres. The families, none of whom spoke English, gave their savings as down payments, and arrived by train in Homedale with two cows, two horses, and great expectations.

Their hopes were soon desolated. "You could stand at the front door," one pioneer recalled, "and there was sagebrush all around you. You could see right through the shack, and there was sagebrush again, as soon as you stepped out the back door." But exploitation of human illusion is not in itself a statutory crime; they had no recourse. "We did get a few beans that first year. I sold them for thirty-five cents."

The settlers had to haul their water in buckets. They cleared the wiry sage and dug ditches; women worked alongside the men. The Homedale folks and the storekeeper helped. "We'd have died if it wasn't for them. We had some bad times, but even the very worst times weren't as bad as they would have been if we had stayed in the Old Country, the way it is now." In 1919 the immigrants filed on the state land and paid for it a second time.

Homedale incorporated in 1920. Many of the descendants of the original forty still live and farm in the community. The area produces sugar beets, onions, potatoes and fruit.

Jump Creek Falls is the scenic attraction of the Homedale region. The easiest way to locate the waterfall is to drive south from Homedale on U.S. 95 for ten miles, turn west on Poison Creek Road and follow it 3.5 miles through five sharp bends. The pavement ends 0.5 miles after the last left turn. Continue south 2.0 miles on the gravel road. Park above the canyon entrance. Walk down the slope, scored and gashed by ORV's and dirt bikes, to Jump Creek and follow the creekbed one-quarter mile upstream. At the narrows the stream suddenly falls from a lava ledge like a ladder of glass and shatters in a large pool. In any other state, the falls would be fostered as a park.

Wilder, 3.9 miles north of the Homedale-Snake River Bridge, was platted in 1911. The town bears the name of Marshall P. Wilder, published of *The Delineator,* a popular women's magazine of the day. Wilder offered to print a favorable article if the community was named for him, and it was known briefly as Wilderia.

542

The town was nearly called Golden Gate. Investors had plans for the San Francisco, Idaho, and Montana Railroad, to reach from Butte, Montana to the "City by the Bay." Between 1904 and 1911 they built the stretch between Caldwell and Homedale. In 1911 the Oregon Short Line bought the railroad. The name "Golden Gate" survived in Wilder's first store, grade school, Baptist Church, and irrigation canal.

Jump Creek Falls.

Hops are grown in only four states, and almost all hops grown in Idaho are raised in the Wilder area. Roadside trellis poles are evident.

The crop was introduced on Wilder farmland in 1934 by the three Batt brothers: Roger, John, and Percy. The acreage in Canyon County increased from 30 to 4,000. At times, the area has the highest average yield in the country.

Hop plants are perennials; new acreage is started from root cuttings. The crop is trained on eighteen-foot trellises, and irrigated all summer; it requires a great deal of hand labor. In 1982 production costs ran $2,000 an acre.

Harvest usually begins the last week of August and requires one month. Vines are cut and stripped mechanically. Hop cones are separated from the leaves on conveyor belts, and clean hops are then dried in kilns heated by diesel-fueled blowers, at 140 degrees F. for seven hours. This reduces their moisture from 85 percent to 10 percent.

After a one-day cooling period, the hops are packed in 200-pound bales and sold to the warehouse companies. They will be blended with other hops, according to a brewer's recipe. One acre of the crop will flavor 240,000 gallons of beer.

Few farmers sell directly to breweries; most grow their hops under contracts signed several years in advance because long-term contract prices are usually better than spot prices.

The two varieties of hops most popular in Canyon County – the Talisman, and the L-8 – were developed by Dr. Ramanko, at the Parma Agricultural Experiment Station.

Parma, 8.6 miles north of Wilder on U.S. 95, was named in 1884 by Albert Fouch for the Roman colony. Fouch was a pioneer who owned ferries and bridges along the Snake River and moved to the area, from Fort Boise, to open the first store. He recalled the old fort was then headquarters for an outfit that ranged 16,000 head of horses under the care of twenty-three cowboys.

The Parma area was on the road followed by the Oregon Trail to Old Fort Boise. In 1863-1864 riverside farmers began to settle the region. The Oregon Short Line provided improved transportation in 1883, and five years later the Sebree Canal, known later as the Farmers Cooperative Ditch Co., brought irrigation for farmers who arrived from Illinois, Iowa and Nebraska.

By 1904, when the city incorporated, Parma was enjoying a boom. It had an opera house, creamery, state bank, and a four-room, brick schoolhouse. Large tracts, financed by absentee Eastern capitalists, were subdivided into small fruit farms for growing apples and prunes.

The Depression destroyed the apple market. Idaho Combination Extra Fancy and Fancy apples brought $9.00 a ton. Simultaneously, the age and size of the trees increased spraying and harvest expenses. By the end of the 1930s, the orchards were dead.

Most of the orchards were on level ground, and once problems of soil toxicity caused by repeated arboreal use of lead arsenate sprays was solved, land use shifted to row crops. The region now produces sugar beets, potatoes and onions.

Parma is the birthplace of Governor C. Ben Ross (1931-1936), and was the home of Governor H. C. Baldridge (1927-1930).

Parma.

Fort Boise, the most significant historical site on the Snake River, was located five miles from Parma.

Where Kahlar Rd. meets Highway 95, about 1.1 miles north of the Parma city limits, there is an historical information sign, twenty-five feet from the west edge of the road. To reach the fort's location, drive north from this sign one mile on U.S. 95. to the Hole Line Rd. intersection. Turn west on Hole Line and drive one mile to the stop sign at Apple Valley Rd. Cross Apple Valley Rd. and continue west 1.7 miles to the Fort Boise Wildlife Management Area. (Ignore Pitman Ln., which curves off to the right at one mile.) Just inside the management area, there is a house on the left side of the road. Proceed past the house, across the bridge, and follow the gravel 0.3 miles until it curves onto cobbles. Drive 0.2 miles farther to the lion-headed marker at the edge of the clearing, fifty feet from the river.

This is an elegiac spot: the sound of the Snake River and the gurgle of red wing blackbirds mingles with memories of Indians, Hudson's Bay trappers, and Oregon emigrants. A summary of Old Fort Boise follows.

In the summer of 1813, John Reid, employed by John Jacob Astor's Pacific Fur Company, arrived at the mouth of the Boise River. (The Boise and Owyhee Rivers enter the Snake, opposite each other, 0.3 miles upriver from this site.) Reid was in the market

HISTORICAL SITE

for Indian horses to support company plans for an overland return from the mouth of the Columbia to St. Louis in 1814. He decided to winter at the confluence of the Boise and the Snake, and built a temporary fort there.

In January, 1814, the Bannock Indians, who resented this intrusion on their salmon grounds, killed Reid and nine of his men; the post was eliminated. Madam Dorion survived with her two children, and carried word of the disaster to the rest of the Astorians at the mouth of the Columbia. The War of 1812 had already disrupted the Pacific Fur Company's plans, and before long the venture dissolved.

In 1819 Donald McKenzie, supervisor for the North West Company's Department of the Interior, decided to establish a post at the same site selected by John Reid. He, too, was defeated by Indian opposition.

At the time, Idaho was part of the Oregon country, a region open to British and American trappers and settlers under the agreement of 1818. The Hudson's Bay Company, in order to limit American penetration of the Pacific Northwest, pursued a policy of trapping out beaver west of the Rockies, and created a fur desert devoid of westward inducements. The policy worked temporarily.

After 1832 the Rocky Mountain fur trade declined, but in 1834 Thomas McKay, an independent operator associated with the HB Co., built a fort on the east bank of the Snake river, just north of Reid's site. McKay's establishment was fashioned from adobe, and after 1836 was known as Fort Boise.

Because Hudson's Bay Co. was pleased to frustrate rival traders, it agreed to cover any losses sustained by McKay while he was operating in the trapped-over region. Before long, Fort Boise was a HB Co. post. Not surprisingly, with competition eliminated and over-trapping ended, the Snake River fur trade improved. Company profits in the region rose from ₤250 in 1838, to over ₤2,400 in 1842.

Francois Payette, for whom the river and town of Payette are named, joined McKay in 1835, and was in charge of the fort for the next nine years.

Payette was a cordial host. While he was there, Fort Boise was a haven for many travelers. In 1836 the Whitmans and Spaldings reached the fort with their cart, the first wheeled conveyance in later-Idaho. John Sutter was a hunter at the post in 1838, before he went on to Sacramento and a fort of his own. The mountain men Joe Meek, William Craig, and Robert Newell visited on their way west. In 1839 a party of Oregon Trail pioneers stopped briefly. A member of the group noted: *we ware Received ... in a very polite and genteel manner and entertained Sumtuously; by our Host. he had a very fine cook and everything passed off pleasantly our table was furnished with a variety great for the mountains consisting of fowls, Ducks, Bacon, Salmon Sturgeon Buffalow & Elk and our vegitables ware Turnips Cabbag & pickled Beets all very fine table furnished with Butter & Cream with the best of Loaf Sugar, also biscuit & Bread this was our fare whilst at the Fort.*

Osborne Cross expedition drawings of Fort Boise in 1849.

Another emigrant recorded this description of the fort:

This fort ... consists of a parallelogram about one hundred feet square, surrounded by a stockade of poles about fifteen feet in height. It was entered from the west [Snake river] side. Across the

547

area north and south runs the principal building. It is constructed of logs, and contains a large dining room, a sleeping apartment and kitchen. On the north side of the area, in front of this, is the store; on the south side the dwellings of the servants; back of the main building, an outdoor oven; and in the north-east corner of the stockade is the bastion. This was Fort Boisais in 1839. Mons. Payette was erecting a neat adobe wall (12½ feet high and 400 feet long) around it. He expected soon to be able to tear away the old stockade, and before this (1843) has doubtless done so.

In 1843 the great migration along the Oregon Trail began. Every evening wagons encamped on the fort's ground, and the fatigued travelers were greeted with warmth and benevolence. When Payette retired in 1844, James Craigie succeeded him and maintained the tradition of hospitality. An English visitor at the post wrote:

Since the days of emigration Fort Boisee has been an asylum to the sick and needy, its master has always fulfilled the part of the good Samaritan. Many are the instances of his [Craigie's] charitable deeds, and many are the travelers on these plains, who survive to pray for blessings on this disinterested and generous being to whom they owe their preservation.

In 1846 the Fort Boise region became part of the United States. HB Co. retained the post in order to have a persuasive claim for compensation by the U.S. under the Oregon treaty. Local trade had diminished, and Craigie believed the post should be closed. He retired in 1852.

The following spring, floodwaters dissolved the adobe. In 1854 construction of a smaller fort began, but the Ward massacre on the Oregon Trail, about twenty miles away, spelled the end. Since Major G. O. Haller stopped at the fort on his retaliatory campaign against the local Indians, the Hudson's Bay Company men decided it was no longer safe to remain at the post, which was then abandoned.

The great flood of 1862, unequaled in a century, brought the river spooling and swirling through the grounds; the remaining ruins were whisked downstream. The Oregon-Idaho boundary survey of 1867 provides evidence that since 1868 the river has claimed 120 feet from the east bank.

The site, however, did serve as a Snake River ferry location for nearly forty years. The *Idaho Tri-Weekly Statesman* in 1864 published the following advertisement:

BOISE FERRY, ON SNAKE RIVER, AT OLD FORT BOISE

The traveling public are invited to take notice that the above ferry is now completed and furnished with good new boats and careful attendants. This ferry is located at the most eligible crossing on Snake River for travel from ... Cal., ... Oregon ... and Washington Territory. To and from Boise City and ... Idaho City, ... of which all must be convinced who once try the route. Being furnished with bouy lines, and the largest boats, it is believed to be the safest ferry on Snake River.

Proprietors
J. Keeney
John Duval
J. McLaughlin

When the steamboat *Shoshone* was built at the mouth of the Boise River in 1866, the vessel disrupted Keeney's ferry service. He had to drop his wire rope to allow the steamer navigation of the river, but within three months the *Shoshone* was laid up for want of fuel wood. In 1870 Jonathan Keeney, because of illness, sold his ferry. In 1902 the ferry was discontinued when the interstate bridge was completed at Nyssa.

The Idaho Department of Fish and Game acquired the site in 1962; it is now protected as part of a waterfowl nesting area.

Fruitland, along the Payette River, is 17.8 miles north of the Hole Line Rd. turnoff for Ft. Boise. The town, once known as Zeller's Crossing, has been a center of apple orchards since the turn of the century.

During the peak years, 1916-1930, apple and prune production supported six packing sheds and an evaporator in town. Orchardists built dirt-covered cellars to store their apples until they could pack them during the winter.

Fruit production regained importance after the 1930s as new, superior varieties were introduced and cold storage improved. Packing companies in the area now operate controlled-atmosphere storage warehouses capable of refrigerating thousands of bins of apples, as well as frozen food products.

Payette is located on a business loop off U.S. 95, 2.7 miles north of Fruitland, at the confluence of the Payette and Snake Rivers.

Though the location had a store in 1867, and in 1871 the only post office between Baker, Oregon and Boise, the town really owes its origin to a construction camp for the Oregon Short Line railroad that was situated at the mouth of the Payette in 1882. The camp was called Boomerang. Timber for railroad ties was floated down the Payette to the Boomerang sawmills.

Two brothers, A. B. and Frank Moss, who were railroad employees in charge of log drives, opened their own business, the

Merchant Mercantile, on the north side of the river, The Short Line was completed in 1884, and entrepreneurs, moving upstream from Boomerang to the Moss location, shaped the town of Payette.

In 1891 Payette incorporated. The town's name is that of the Fort Boise postmaster for the Hudson's Bay Company. Francois Payette was born on the banks of the St. Lawrence River near Montreal, youngest of six children. He seems to have had several Indian wives. While at Fort Boise, he was regarded fondly by the many travelers he assisted. One recounted:

Mr. Payette ... received us with every mark of kindness ... and introduced us immediately to the chairs, table and edibles of his apartments. He ... is a merry, fat old gentleman of fifty, who, although in the wilderness all the best years of his life, has retained tha manner of benevolence in trifles, in his mode of address, of seating you and serving you at the table, of directing your attention continually to some little matter of interest, of making you speak the French language 'parfaitement' whether you are able to do so or not, so strikingly agreeable in that mercurial people...

After his retirement in 1844, Payette went east with a Hudson's Bay brigade from Fort Walla Walla to Montreal. He drew a substantial sum in accumulated wages (L 1,535), but the remainder of his life is a mystery.

Regional water development for irrigation provided economic stability for the Payette area. In 1890 a German syndicate spent $200,000 extending the Pence-Bivens Canal, now known as the Lower Payette Canal. Farms and orchards multiplied; the Moss brothers shipped the first fruit from Payette in 1891. There are now 100,000 acres of irrigated land in the county. Water is stored in reservoirs on Little Willow Creek, and in Black Canyon on the Payette. Agriculture (livestock, field crops, fruit, dairy products) remains the area's principal source of income.

The town has several examples of uncommon architecture:

Sixth Ave. So. near Sixteenth St: The white, igloo dome, visible from Highway 95, is the Payette High School gymnasium.

The ninety-foot high, fiberglass, geodesic dome was designed by North American Rockwell in 1958, at a cost of $5 million, for a radar installation used by the USAF on Dooley Mountain, south of Baker, Oregon. The dome was listed as surplus property in 1972, and was acquired without cost by the Payette School District.

The structure was disassembled and moved to Idaho. Reassembled on a cement block foundation, it provides a 37,000 square-foot gymnasium. The interior is lit by mercury vapor lights wired to a six-ton chandelier.

550

First Ave. No. and Seventh St: Downtown Payette has a few commercial buildings that are closely linked to its past. The Coughanour blocks, two connected buildings, the oldest of which faces the railroad station on First Ave. No. at Eighth St., were built by Bill Coughanour, who came to Payette in 1885. Coughanour had managed a Boise Basin gold mine for fifteen years. He was known

U.S. Mail Service, Payette, c. 1905.

Ice house near Payette, set on fire by sparks from a passing train in 1904. Only one-quarter of the ice melted.

as "Knot Hole Billy" because he operated a sawmill south of town that made lumber from trees cut in Garden Valley. Coughanour also invested in land, cattle, and orchards. He served seven consecutive terms as Payette's mayor, and was elected to the state senate in 1896.

Second Ave. No. and Eighth St: The brick building on the corner, with twin chevrons in the facade, was the A. B. Moss Merchant Mercantile. It became the Golden Rule store in 1926 and then the Senior Citizens Center.

First Ave. and So. Ninth St. In 1904 the city engineer designed this Methodist Episcopal church. The brick and clapboard building is an adaptation of the Gothic revival style. It contains several noteworthy gothic stained glass windows. The church now houses the **Payette County Historical Society Museum.**

First Ave. and No. Tenth St: This is St. James Episcopal Church, built in 1892, of brick with a wooden steeple.

215 No. Ninth St: The First Church of Christ, Scientist, is a delightful, small structure built in 1907. The two entrances, joined under an ornamented gable with a central Gothic window, form a perfectly balanced design.

North Ninth St. and Third Ave: The Chase residence is a fifteen room, two-story brick house designed in 1890 by Campbell and Hodgson. The interior displays cut glass and golden oak. During the fifty years that the Chases lived in the house it was filled with eighteenth-century Chippendale furniture, elaborate statues, fancy lamps, pioneer photographs, Haviland dinnerware, and numerous antiques.

Mr. Chase, who died in 1936, was Payette's first depot agent; he later had mercantile and insurance interests. The Chase's daughter, Fredrica, graduated from Vassar College. She was a Carnegie assistant at the Lick Observatory in California from 1905 to 1907, and married Joseph Moore, a prominent astronomer who became director of the observatory.

U.S. 95 enters **Weiser** from the south, 12.1 miles north of Payette. On the edge of town, the highway spans the Weiser River – a river that flows south nearly 100 miles to this point, where it merges with the Snake. Weiser was named, in all probability, for Jacob Weiser, a trapper-turned-miner who made a rich strike at Baboon Gulch in Idaho's Florence Basin. In 1863 Jacob Weiser, along with Thomas Galloway and William Logan, setted where the town now stands.

552

In 1864 Reuben Olds, with two partners, obtained a franchise from the Territorial Legislature to operate a ferry across the Snake River twelve miles west of Weiser, at Farewell Bend on the Oregon Trail. The emigrants were drawn north through Weiser Valley, where they forded the Weiser River, and then, with Old's ferry, crossed the Snake for the last time. (Olds often pocketed $500 a day.)

In 1879, through chicanery involving a generous jug of Snake River redeye and a lost ballot box, Weiser swiped the county seat from its northern neighbor, Salubria.

Weiser Bridge, as the town was known initially, received a boost in 1881, when the Oregon Short Line railroad was extended through

Weiser, early view.

Driving the first spike of P&IN railroad at Weiser in May, 1899.

town en route to Huntington, Oregon. The settlement had its first shootout that year, and another in early 1882. Thomas Galloway wrote, in a letter to the editor of the *Idaho Statesman,* "All the assaults, drag-outs, knock-downs, dirk carving and pistol practice of which we have heard so much, has been intimately connected with one or the other of the whiskey mills in Weiser City."

Parade of Ringling Bros. Circus in Weiser, 1901.

An oil lamp dropped in the Weiser Hotel in 1890 kindled a fire that burned two blocks of the business district. The town was rebuilt, but business and residential growth shifted west of Weiser bridge.

At the turn of the century, two projects of major importance to the Weiser Valley were underway. The Galloway Canal would irrigate thousands of acres on the flats, and the Pacific and Idaho Northern railroad would open trade with the Seven Devils mines.

The P&IN had $8 million in capital stock, and 2,000 men were employed by contractors. The stretch through Weiser canyon was particularly difficult. Twenty miles of track, however, were laid the first year, but the rails never reached the Devils. Unlike the Galloway Ditch, the railroad did not fulfill its promise. It terminated in New Meadows.

Today Weiser, with its mild climate, supports farm, orchard, and livestock endeavors.

The liveliest time of the year here is the third week of June. The city hosts the **National Old-Time Fiddlers' Contest and**

554

Festival. Cash awards are given in several categories; elimination events during the week lead to the national championship on Saturday night.

Fiddling contests were held in Weiser as early as 1914, but the present festival was the idea of Blaine Stubblefield. Stubblefield was a fiddler and folk music collector, as well as secretary of the town's

Pythian Castle.

chamber of commerce. In 1963 the national contest was inaugurated.

Those who would not give a dollar to see an earthquake should bypass Weiser during the festival, and those who find the music irresistible will be happier than a dog with two tails – it is a fiddler's Mardi gras.

Anyone interested in late nineteenth and early-twentieth century architecture will find a banquet in Weiser – for architectural extravagance it ranks among the top four cities in the state.

This is a representative tour: Enter town on U.S. 95 from the south. Turn west on E. Commercial six blocks to E. First. Jog left, and continue on W. Commercial one block to State St. Turn south one block on State.

State St: Oregon Short Line Depot. Though the OSL arrived in Weiser in 1883, this brick depot was not built until thirteen years later. The OSL was part of the Union Pacific, and U.P. acquired Weiser's other railroad, the P&IN, in 1936.

Return to Commercial St. and drive three blocks to W. Third. Go north on W. Third one block to W. Idaho, a one-way street.

W. Idaho and 411 W. Third: Sommercamp house. A year after her husband fell to his death down a mine shaft in Silver City, Mary Sommercamp came to Weiser with her four children. In 1899 a Boise architectural firm designed this house for her. The children later established several stores in Weiser.

253 W. Idaho and W. Third: Herman Haas house. On the southeast corner, across the street from the Sommercamp residence, is a Queen Anne style house designed in 1900 by the same Boise firm that drew the Sommercamp plans. Note the stained glass windows, the octagonal east bay, and the garland freize on the round, corner tower. The house's interior woodwork has been preserved.

Mr. Haas emigrated from Germany to Oregon in 1853, when he was fourteen years-old. In 1882 he opened the first store in Weiser, and was vice-president of the first bank.

Follow W. Idaho three blocks and cross State St. On the left, four doors from the corner, is one of the more unusual buildings in the state.

30 E. Idaho St: **The Pythian Castle.** The Order Knights of Pythias was the idea, in 1864, of Justus Rathbone. Rathbone was familiar with the tale of Damon and Pythias, the subject of a popular play at the time. The two men belonged to Pythagoras' school of philosophy, which asserted man's greatest obligations were "to speak the truth and render benefits to each other." When

the king of Syracuse obtained his throne through fraud, Damon opposed him and was sentenced to death. His friend Pythias served as hostage while Damon was given liberty to bid his wife and children farewell.

Justus Rathbone conceived a fraternal order based on the principles of friendship, charity, and benevolence, that might do much to dispel the hatreds of the Civil War. President Lincoln was impressed with the organization's purpose and suggested the founder ask Congress for a charter. As a result of his request, the Knights of Pythias was the first American order chartered by an Act of Congress. In 1864 the first members took their vows in Washington, D.C., with a hand on the Bible. The organization eventually embraced 2,000 lodges. The Supreme Lodge is composed of representatives from fifty-five Grand Lodges. (Franklin Roosevelt was initiated into the order in a White House ceremony, while he was President.)

The Myrtle Lodge No. 26 was founded in 1897 by thirty Weiser businessmen. Membership reached 170 and in 1904 the Knights decided to build a new hall.

The remarkable castle was designed by Tourtellotte and Co. of Boise. Rock was quarried along the Weiser River, ten miles north of town, and six stonecutters dressed it at a lot on East Main St. The completed building cost $9,000, and the grandiose crenellated, Tudor facade is unique among Western lodge halls.

The meeting room, reached by an interior staircase, is on the second floor. The hall has been maintained in its original condition; it has an arched, pressed-tin ceiling, twenty-feet high. The facade's stained glass is best viewed from within the lodge. In its heyday Myrtle Lodge No. 26 meet weekly; now its fifty-five members meet every other week.

After viewing the castle, turn north on E. First and west on W. Main, which becomes a one-way street. Follow W. Main three blocks.

206 W. Main and W. Second: Gerwick house. James Gerwick was a sheep rancher, prune farmer, and saddle maker. In 1898 he built this outstanding Queen Anne style house on the northwest corner of W. Main. He kept the house only seven years, before moving to a ranch on Manns Creek.

Drive west another block on W. Main, turn north on W. Third to W. Court.

541 W. Third and W. Court: Colonel E. M. Heigho house. This Queen Anne style house, on the southwest corner lot, was built in 1900, for Lewis Hall, who moved from New York to Weiser as first

president of the P&IN railroad. In 1907, after Hall departed, the property was purchased by Col. Edgar Heigho. Heigho had emigrated from England in 1874 and worked for railroads from the time he was old enough to blow his own nose. He became president of the P&IN in 1910 and retired because of illness in 1919.

Travel east on W. Court for two blocks and north on W. First to W. Park.

49 W. Park and W. First: The small house with the tin roof at the southeast corner of the intersection was the residence of Walter "Big Train" Johnson while he lived in Weiser between 1906 and 1907.

There is little doubt, though perhaps enough for argument, that Walter Johnson was one of the ten best athletes ever to pick up a baseball. He was born in Kansas, but homebase was California; he was lured to Weiser by a job offer from the telephone company that included an obligation to play for the Weiser Senators, a semi-pro team. While in Weiser, Johnson pitched eighty-four consecutive scoreless innings.

His skills attracted a scout from the Washington Nationals (later Senators) who had been alerted by a letter that said, "He knows where he's throwing, because if he didn't there would be dead bodies all over Idaho." The scout signed Johnson to a $350-a-month contract, with a $100 bonus. In July, 1907, "Big Train" left the cottage on W. Park St. for the major leagues. He was nineteen years-old.

With the Washington Senators, one of baseball's worst teams, he became one of the game's greatest pitchers: he struck out 3,508 batters in twenty-one years, he was the league's strike-out leader for twelve seasons, won 416 games, had a lifetime ERA of 2.17. Johnson won thirty-two games in 1912 and thirty-six in 1913. He took Washington to the World Series in 1924 and 1925, and entered the second Series, at age thirty-seven, with twenty wins and seven losses. He was one of the first five players selected for baseball's Hall of Fame.

After retirement, Johnson ran unsuccessfully for Congress. He died in 1946.

Drive 1½ blocks east on Park St., cross State St. to E. First and go south on E. First one block to E. Liberty. Travel east on E. Liberty one block.

E. Liberty and E. Second: St. Agnes Catholic Church. This red brick church, built in 1911, has a style best described as adapted Italianate. It is worth entering to view the stained glass.

Drive north on E. Second four blocks to Hanthorne Ave.

558

1120 E. Second and Hanthorne Ave.: **Galloway residence.** As mentioned earlier, Thomas Galloway was one of the first settlers in Weiser Valley. He had come west in a wagon to Oregon, then worked as a freighter to the Cariboo and Boise Basin mines before homesteading along the Weiser River. In 1865 he built a frame house with lumber purchased in Boise Basin for $90 and hauled to Weiser.

Three years later Galloway married Mary Flournoy, and they moved to a two-room log cabin. The couple had nine children.

Tom worked as a rancher. He also labored on the Galloway Ditch to bring water to the flats west of Weiser, and served four terms in the state legislature.

Wool growers had moved into the region by 1900, and Galloway realized the ten square-miles of range where he grazed his horses would no longer support such herds. He rounded up 800 head and sold them for $15 each. The Galloways then decided to spend two-thirds of their proceeds on a new house.

A Boise firm drew the blueprints. The Weiser brickyard furnished bricks, and laid them three courses wide. The completed mansion has twelve rooms.

Thomas Galloway died in 1916, his wife ten years later. In 1966 the heirs sold the house; it is now on the National Register of Historic Places.

Return to State St. Continue north on State 0.4 miles to Indianhead Road. Turn west on Indianhead 0.6 miles to W. Seventh and Paddock Ave. Turn north on Paddock one block.

The five cement buildings along Paddock Ave., on the oval garnished with grass and trees, are sturdy mementos of one man's dream.

Edward Paddock had a heart as big as a saddle blanket and the ability to talk a cow out of her calf. He earned his way through six years of Oberlin College and New York Theological Seminary by cutting cordwood. In 1892, after twenty-three years as a minister (often in mining camps), he came to Weiser.

Rev. Paddock founded a high school, the Weiser Academy, on the site now occupied by the golf course. When he attempted to add vocational training to the college preparatory curriculum, the trustees and teachers balked.

So in 1899, at age fifty-four, Paddock decided to estabish the **Idaho Industrial Institute,** a high school for young people from rural areas who wanted an education but lacked the cash to pay for it. He wrote, "I went to work at once for the Institute and sent word into the mountains, 'If you young people want to study earnestly enough to come to Weiser, pull off your coats and grub sagebrush the rest of the time, come on and we will help you out.'"

Paddock shared his concept with Jane Slocum and Thomas Maryatt. Slocum was a lecturer and teacher from New York, an early graduate of the University of Michigan law school. She moved to Weiser, bought eighty acres and gave it to the Institute and assisted the school until her death in 1923.

Maryatt had an engineer's degree from Dartmouth. He donated eighty acres of his homestead to the Institute, and designed the campus. His untimely death in 1903 cut short his considerable contribution to the school.

"You can't teach people anything they don't want to know," said G. Bernard Shaw. In the first years of this century the school had 240 acres and forty students. But word of the unusual school traveled faster than a quirted horse. Before long, applications far exceeded vacancies. By 1915, two of the cement buildings had been erected, the land increased to 2,400 acres, and enrollment doubled. The Institute, whose name had been changed to Intermountain Institute to avoid confusion with a reform school, had the largest payroll in Washington County. Obviously, in Idaho there was a great deal young people wanted to know.

The curriculum was college preparatory, with math, science, history, language, music and art. Girls were required to take domestic science, and did kitchen work; boys took manual training and performed farm chores. An hour of recreation was mandatory. The students worked from dawn some distance into dark – lights went out at 10:00 P.M.

The Intermountain Institute inculcated Christianity without sectarianism or dogma. Discrimination by race or religion was outlawed. Even age was not a factor: a thirty-nine-year-old stagecoach driver gave up chewing tobacco in order to study at the Institute for three years. "The man who is too old to learn was probably always too old to learn."

Though Rev. Paddock spent nearly six months a year soliciting contributions from Eastern benefactors, he envisioned a school that would be self-supporting. Goods baked in the Institute's kitchen were exchanged at Weiser stores for necessities. The farm had 1,200 acres under irrigation, and fed chickens, hogs, sheep, and a prize dairy herd of Holstein-Friesian stock. Sagebrush was cut for fuel. There was a broom factory that converted homegrown straw into 2,000 brooms a year. The school had its own butcher shop, smoke house, and steam heating plant.

560

But not even this confident circle was immune to the effects of the Depression. Former patrons were unable to continue their philanthropy. The market for agricultural products collapsed. In 1933 the Intermountain Institute closed. If education, as Mark Twain remarked, "is what you must acquire without any interference from your schooling," then Paddock's vision had educated 2,000 students. (Edward P. Morgan, the nationally known newscaster, graduated from the Institute.)

For six years, the campus was as quiet as an unhatched egg. Then it was used as a vocational training site by the National Youth Administration. Because federal funding regulations required that the school be publically owned, the Institute's trustees deeded the property to the Weiser public schools, with the understanding it would revert when the project ended. The NYA was terminated by World War II, and when the school district refused to return the grounds, a lawsuit followed. The court found against the Institute's trustees; Weiser High School used the buildings until 1967.

In 1969 the Weiser School District sold the property for $32,000 to Idaho Branch, Associated General Contractors' Operating Engineers, who used the campus for a Five Crafts apprentice program. The site was sold again in 1977 to Weiser Feed and Storage. It stood empty for three years, quiet as a classroom after a hard question.

In 1979 the Historical Museum and Fiddler Hall of Fame on E. Commercial St. began looking for new quarters. The board of directors voted to acquire Hooker Hall, the administration-classroom building at the Institute. With the help of a $25,000 grant from the Department of the Interior, obtained through the Idaho Preservation Office, and the generous cooperation of Weiser Feed and Storage, the building was secured.

The board reincorporated in 1980 as the **Intermountain Cultural Center and Museum.** Labor and donations renovated Hooker Hall. The county museum occupies the first floor. Other classrooms were reopened for art, pottery, and photography workshops. The 300-seat auditorium again serves for drama, dance, and film. Paddock would be pleased.

The hall is open weekdays, and visitors are welcome.

The buildings in the oval, south to north:

The Billings Memorial Gymnasium: built in 1929 for $40,000, with a donation from Elizabeth Billings, heiress to a Northern Pacific railroad fortune. The building is believed to have been the best high school gym in the state. It contained a sixty-foot long swimming pool in the basement.

561

Slocum Hall: erected in 1909, was the boy's dormitory. Mrs. Russell Sage paid $30,000 for construction.

Hooker Hall: now houses the Intermountain Cultural Center and Museum. It held the school's offices and twenty-two classrooms. The hall was completed in 1924 at a cost of $100,000, defrayed by contributions from Fannie Hooker Forbes and Mary Hooker Dole.

Beardsley Hall: was finished in 1907; it is the oldest building on campus. The walls are sixteen inches thick. The basement was a dining hall, the first floor was the school chapel, the second and third stories were girls' dorms, and the attic was a gym. The

Idaho Inter-mountain Institute.

Students make brooms at the Institute.

562

structure burned in 1913, but the walls were undamaged and the interior was rebuilt.

Carnegie Library: was made possible by a grant in 1919 from the Carnegie Foundation. It is the only U.S. high school library funded by the Foundation. The shelves held 5,000 books, and the collection was open to the townspeople.

Return to Indianhead Road and drive 1.0 miles east to its intersection with Highway 95. The brick barn on the north side of the road was built in 1901. It marks the site of the Weiser Brick Co.

Typing class.

Debate between "Strict Constructionists" and "Progressives."

Alexander Gordon, and his son, made bricks at this location for many of Weiser's buildings. In 1922 the Gordons leased the yard to Reader and Lowe.

The ochre sand and clay pits are situated along the base of the hill, north of the barn. (One is visible from the road.) The clay was mixed with water, pugged to a certain consistency, and dried in wooden molds. The bricks were removed after they shrank, were air dried, then fired for about seven days in a kiln at 1,700 degrees F. Fire oxidized the iron in the clay and imparted the ruddy color.

Weiser had a second significant mineral deposit twelve miles east of this intersection, on the South Crane Creek Road at Nutmeg Mountain. The **Idaho Almaden quicksilver mine,** discovered by a sheepherder, was developed in 1937 and operated into the 1970s.

Cinnabar, the principal ore of mercury, was open-pit mined, and in 1939 a fifty-ton Gould rotary furnace and condensing system was installed. By 1942 85 tons of mercury had been recovered. During that period the mine was operated by the sons of President Herbert Hoover. (Hoover visited the site in 1938.)

The mine was eventually acquired by a subsidiary of El Paso Natural Gas Co. It had the largest (ninety-foot) rotary mercury kiln in the U.S. Mercury production exceeded $3.7 million. (The Almaden also produced pozzolana, a hardening agent used in the cement at Hells Canyon Dam.)

U.S. 95 travels north from Weiser to Midvale Hill, follows the general course of the Weiser River for twenty miles through hills yellow with balsamroot in the spring and tan with cheatgrass in the fall.

Highway 95 descends **Midvale Hill** to Midvale (a contraction of Middle Valley) between Weiser and Salubria Valley.

In 1963 a complex of archaeological sites was excavated on the north slope of Midvale Hill. A wealth of artifacts was recovered that indicated the people occupying the area utilized the fine-grained basalt on the summit as a source of material for flaked stone tools. All but one of the sites gave evidence of seasonal, rather than year-round, occupation.

Based on similarities of the Midvale projectile points with those from other sites, the age of the complex was placed at 3,000-5,000 years ago, with habitation discontinued about A.D. 1. The site represents the southernmost excavated manifestation of the Plateau culture.

564

The town of **Midvale** is 2.5 miles northeast of the complex. The first white settlers, the John Reed family, arrived in 1868. The Reeds built a one-room cabin on the bank of the Weiser River, established a sawmill on Pine Creek, and raised a family of eight children.

Other settlers arrived during the 1870s, but the biggest boost to the new community came in 1881 when forty emigrants with a wagon train decided to remain in the valley.

A wooden bridge was built across the Weiser River in Middle Valley in 1883. High water in the spring often washed out the dirt approach to the span. In 1896 a young couple who lived on the east side of the crossing had set a spring wedding date; when the river level rendered the bridge impassable, they stood on the bank while the minister on the west shore hollered out the ceremony. (A steel span was constructed in 1911.)

Midvale in 1920.

Ice was harvested from the river for storage in sheds here; another indication that winters were once more severe than at present. The same ice sometimes formed jams and caused floods to cover the town's roads.

The P I & N railroad tracks reached this point in 1899. In 1906 Middle Valley was condensed to Midvale.

Lambs and wool were the principal products of the Midvale region from 1905 to 1930.

Cambridge is eight miles north of Midvale, at the confluence of Highway 71 (which leads to Hells Canyon) and U.S. 95.

The community is the stepchild of an earlier town, Salubria, which was located across the Weiser River about two miles east of Cambridge. Settlers began taking homestead ranches in Salubria Valley, also known as upper Weiser Valley, in the early 1880s.

John Cuddy, who had emigrated from Ireland when he was six years old, left Boise City with E. D. Tyne in 1870, to erect a grist mill

565

on Rush Creek, five miles north of present Cambridge. Tyne sold his interest to his partner a couple of years later.

Cuddy could mill and sack nearly three tons of flour a day by himself. In addition, he ground bran and shorts to feed his 200 hogs. The mill was also used to cut lumber from the pines on his 320-acre homestead.

As the town of **Salubria** expanded, Cuddy moved his mill to the new settlement. By the 1890s it was a community with enough happenings to fill a newspaper: the *Salubria Citizen*. At the crossroads there was a bank, Hannan's saloon, and the seventeen-room Salubria Hotel. In addition, there were livery stables, blacksmith shops, mercantile, feed, and hardware shops, an Odd Fellows Hall and a two-story schoolhouse. The mail stage arrived daily from Weiser, weather permitting.

A rather insignificant disagreement during the town's development proved fatal to its growth. The P & I N railway thrust north from Weiser through Middle Valley. It was intended to serve the Seven Devil's mines and the planned route included a depot at Salubria. But Mrs. Miller, a Salubria resident, owned acreage that lay across the railroad's ambitions, and she thought she would gouge the Pacific and Idaho Northern – instead the railroad gelded the town.

This is what happened. Mose Hopper had property on the west side of the Weiser River and offered the P & I N every other lot in exchange for relocation of the route to his side of the stream. The railroad accepted his inducement, and its arrival on the far side of the river in December, 1900, meant the future of the little town with the pretty name was anything but salubrious. As Cambridge prospered, Salubria faded like an autumn leaf, then vanished.

Lewisville was the first name proposed for the new town, in honor of the railroad's president, Lewis Hall. But because the postal department rejected that selection, it was named for the community where Hall's alma mater, Harvard, is located.

Cambridge today is largely an agricultural community, dependent on cattle, dairy and hay production, along with some logging. In addition to being the location of the Washington County fairgrounds, it serves as eastern gateway to Hells Canyon. An historical museum of some interest stands on the northwest corner of Main St. and Highway 71.

To visit the site of old Salubria, take U.S. 95 east of Cambridge one mile, turn right (south) on the first paved road and follow it one mile to the Salubria Road intersection. The schoolhouse and the jail cell can still be seen, and at the east corner of the crossroads is the embedded top of the *Salubria Citizen* printing press – placed there to protect the saloon from corner-cutting freight wagons. A child used to stand on the press wheel to light the corner street lamp at evening.

Cuddy's flour mill in 1890.

Freighting wool from Salubria in 1896.

Highway 95 passes through **Indian Valley** and climbs **Mesa Hill**, thirteen miles north of Cambridge. The road cuts through what was once among the half-dozen largest fruit farms under single management in the world: Mesa Orchards Company.

The 3,333-acre ranch on which the 1,500 acre orchard was planted was purchased in 1908-1910 from homesteaders by Weiser Valley Land and Water Co. The company was the construct of Capt. Oberlin Carter, a retired army engineer, William Allison, horticulturalist, and C. E. Miesse of Chicago.

The project involved an irrigation system based on water from the Middle Fork of the Weiser River. The company agreed to construct a dam in Lost Valley (west of Tamarack) in order to protect appropriation rights of farmers downstream on the Weiser River by releasing matching flows from the reservoir when drawing on the Middle Fork for the orchard. To bring Middle Fork water to the trees, eight miles of four-foot-by-six-foot flume and two redwood inverted siphon pipes (thirty-six inches in diameter) were required.

Weiser Valley Land and Water financed the system by selling $500-per-acre shares in ten-acre blocks to Eastern and Midwestern investors. Each buyer acquired water rights in the company, and the developers contracted to care for the trees for ten years. The venture envisioned 6,000 acres of orchard with fifteen miles of fencing.

While work progressed on the flume, plantings began in 1911: eighty apple trees to an acre. Some peaches, pears and cherries were also planted. Chinese crews helped prepare the ground. Water was hauled in barrels on wagons until the irrigation system was finally completed.

Workers camped in tents on the hillsides to help with the early harvests. Within a few years, there were about fifty families living in Mesa. A half-dozen large houses had been built, as well as a dozen cottages, a bunkhouse, a machine shop with a community hall overhead, packing houses and a storage shed, along with a two-room schoolhouse, and a company cookhouse and store. In 1920 faulty wiring ignited a fire that burned the packing shed, taking the life of the manager and destroying 50,000 wooden boxes filled with apples.

The shed was rebuilt, and a 3½-mile circulating-cable tramway was added. The tram cars each carried six bushels from the sorting and grading plant to the packing shed. Eventually the Idaho Northern extended a spur line to the shed so that fruit boxes could be loaded into rail cars at the site. The tram, which crossed the old highway, operated for fourteen years.

An evaporator was installed near the packing house to process inferior fruit. Rail cars brought coke to fuel the furnaces for the dryer. Underground storage sheds were built to hold excess production for favorable market prices. In 1923 the acreage was incorporated as Mesa Orchards Co.

568

Picking season began the first week of October and generally lasted six weeks. Farmers and their families would work at the orchards for wages that carried them through the winter. Until Model T trucks took over, the fruit was hauled by teams and wagons. There was year-round work for some: thinning and pruning in the spring and summer, picking in the fall, wrap-packing, peeling and drying in the winter.

Poor weather and an unsteady fruit market put the orchard in the hands of the Western Idaho Production Credit Association in the 1930s. The orchard continued to function, and though it was slim pickings, it helped many families through the Depression. Fruit was often given to the needy. The PCA sold the acreage in 1943 to A. H. Burroughs, Jr., a relative of the founders of the calculator company.

Burroughs operated the orchard for eleven years. Because the trees were no longer prime, he introduced a cannery and made applesauce. Nearly 300 Mexican workers would help with the fall harvest, and a daily bus brought additional pickers from Weiser. The orchard had been reduced to about 700 acres, but 1945-1946 was a windfall year that brought in nearly $1 million.

Burroughs sold the land to the Bryan Ball family in 1954; they were cattle ranchers from Montana. The Balls intended to enter the fruit business, but a severe freeze struck the first year: in three days it ruined 47,000 bushel boxes of apples and 100,000 bushels that were yet to be picked. The Balls lost their enthusiasm for the fruit business. Then in 1960 Mr. Ball was killed when the roof of a storage shed collapsed on him.

Seven years later, Emma Ball sold the orchard to a rancher from Parma, Idaho, who uprooted the remaining trees in order to convert the area to a cattle pasture. The sale fell through and Mrs. Ball reacquired the property.

A mining company bought the tramway, dismantled the towers and removed cars and cable. Now Mesa is more memory than substance: footings for the dam and short sections of the flume can still be seen, but gone is the spring murmur of bees over two square miles of blossoms.

Some priceless descriptive paragraphs survive, however. Here are two of them, written in 1910 for the *Weiser American* by a real estate agent at Council, a salesman and an epic wordmonger:

When some lazy crow journeys from the fields and orchards well against the sides of eastern mountains o'er which the first faint dawn of day peeps in rosy glow toward and to Old Cuddy, whose hoary head eight thousand feet above the sea guards the valley on the west and behind which the young moon softly sinks to sleep, it fans a dozen miles of air and looks down upon twenty thousand acres of the finest Council Valley apple land, where for a full score and more years rich red apples without a single miss in each autumn's frost have ripened and mingled their fragrance with the odor of pines and not a worm has marred their beauty.

Looking down he sees an army of half a hundred thousand Jonathan, Rome Beauty, Newton, Delicious and kindred trees that one short year ago were in the nursery. He views the soil prepared and waiting to receive the almost one million young apples, peaches and pears just as soon as the gentle spring chinook shall have driven winter back into his icy vastness far beyond the northland where Peary, Cook and Eskimo gorge themselves on blubber, grow fat on greasy gum drops and dream that they had found the Pole. His roving eye perchance will penetrate the leafy bower of ancient Spitzenberg, Winesap, and Northern Spy gracing the old homestead orchard and from which season after season has been plucked fruit in perfect form and in texture flawless – the marvel of men who of such are connoisseurs and which against the world in every apple show has stood imperial, the true aristocrat of fruits.

Mesa Orchards in 1914.

The highway descends from Mesa Hill to the Middle Fork of the Weiser River, then travels straight as a wiping stick 8.9 miles to Council.

Cottonwood Creek passes through a culvert under the road 2.5 miles south of Council. The Whitney ranch was located on this creek, just east and west of the roadway; one of the buildings is still visible in a cottonwood grove. The family produced Idaho's best-known outlaw, Hugh Whitney.

One of seven children, Hugh, spent his early years at Brownlee in Hells Canyon, then the family moved to Cottonwood Creek in 1908. As teen-agers, the Whitney boys worked cattle and sheep in the area.

WANTED FOR MURDER

HUGH WHITNEY

HUGH WHITNEY

Who shot and fatally wounded Conductor William Kidd, on O.S.L. Train No. 4, June 17th, between Spencer and Dubois, Idaho, while resisting arrest by Deputy Sheriff. Also wounded three other persons in making his escape.

DESCRIPTION

Age, about 23 years; height, 5 feet, 8 inches; weight, 165 lbs.; stocky build; very dark complexion; smooth shaven; dark curley hair which comes down over forehead.

He is a sheephearder and cowboy and dresses as such always wears a handkerchief around his neck; he is an expert marksman; does not drink but smokes cigarettes; wears high heel boots with nails in end of heels.

In company with Whitney was a man supposed to be Albert F. Sesler, whose description as near as we have it is as follows:

Age, 25 years; height, 5 feet, 11 inches; weight, 150 or 155 lbs.; light complexion; thin face; inclined to be round shouldered; supposed to be ex-railroad man, but has been traveling and working with Whitney for some time near Cokeville, Wyoming.

REWARD

W. H. Bancroft, Vice-President & General Manager of the Oregon Short Line Railroad Company, issues following bulletin, dated June 18th, 1911.

"THE OREGON SHORT LINE RAILROAD COMPANY WILL PAY A REWARD OF ONE THOUSAND DOLLARS FOR THE ARREST AND CONVICTION OF THE HOLDUPS WHO YESTERDAY SHOT AND PROBABLY FATALLY WOUNDED CONDUCTOR KIDD."

(Signed) W. H. BANCROFT.

Governor of Idaho issues following reward:

"A reward of five hundred dollars each is hereby offered by the State of Idaho for the bodies, dead or alive, of the persons who wounded and killed Conductor William Kidd, in Fremont County, Idaho, on the 17th day of June, 1911. Said reward will be paid out of the Treasury of the State of Idaho.

(Signed) JAMES H. HAWLEY, Governor.

Attest: W. L. GIFFORD, Secretary of State.
Dated Boise, Idaho, June 19th, 1911, at 10 o'clock a.m.

Officers keep a close watch for parties. Arrest and notify J. F. Fisher, Sheriff, Fremont County, St. Anthony, Idaho, who holds warrant charging murder for these parties, or Joseph Jones, Chief Special Agent, O. S. L. R., Deseret News Building, Salt Lake City.

By 1910, Hugh, and his brother, Charlie, were working as herders on the Pete Olsen ranch near Cokeville, Wyoming. Though they were good workers, the foreman fired them because Hugh liked to herd sheep with his pistol and rifle, which made the whole band too jumpy. Hugh beat the foreman, who later died. The Lincoln County sheriff apprehended Hugh near Green River, Wyoming, but he escaped the next day, while awaiting transfer to Evanston for trial on a manslaughter charge.

A year later, Hugh, and his friend, Al Ross, lost several hundred dollars in a card game at Monida, Montana. They awoke the next morning broke. Necessity is the mother of contention. Hugh and Al returned to the saloon and recovered their losses at gunpoint. Charlie may have been along. In any event, the Whitneys were now wanted men.

In June, 1911, two men tried to rob the Oregon Shortline Railroad train near High Bridge, Montana. The conductor recognized Hugh Whitney, and the outlaw shot him and wounded a sheriff on the train. The robbers bailed off into the desert; Hugh made his way twenty-eight miles to Dubois, Idaho, where he bought a horse. The conductor died and Hugh was now wanted for murder.

The outlaw worked his way south, through Idaho Falls, Soda Springs, and Montpelier, to Cokeville, Wyoming, where in September, he and his brother, Charlie, robbed the First National Bank of $700. A posse was organized, but the robbers were never captured.

In June, 1952, the *Wyoming State Tribune* of Cheyenne carried a startling story. After an absence of forty-one years, Charlie Whitney had reappeared. His story was unveiled in the newspaper.

Following the Cokeville bank robbery, Hugh and Charlie had worked in a Wisconsin saddle shop for a year. Then they had labored in Minnesota and Texas until their savings were sufficient to buy ranchland near Glasgow, Montana. Their ranch work was interrupted by World War I; the brothers enlisted under assumed names and served in France. They returned to the ranch when the war was over.

After three years, they ended their partnership. Hugh married and moved to a ranch in Saskatchewan. He died there in 1951, but on his deathbed confessed his identity and absolved his brother of involvement in any crime other than the bank robbery.

Charlie had continued to ranch in Montana, where among other circumstances, he had become a friend of the governor, and had served on the school board and on the board of directors of the Glasgow State Bank. When he learned of his brother's death, he met with Governor Connor of Montana and confessed his past. The governor gave Charlie a letter that urged Wyoming's Governor Barrett to grant clemency to the ex-outlaw.

572

Whitney went to Cheyenne and appeared before the judge of the Third Judicial District. While his case was considered for ten days, he was kept in an unlocked jail cell. The bank he had robbed no longer existed, the county had been divided, and only one victim could be located. Judge Robert Christmas decided to grant a full pardon.

Charlie Whitney returned to his Montana ranch, where he died in 1955.

A railroad "wanted poster" that includes a $1,500 reward offer, and one of Hugh's pistols are on display in the Council historical museum, upstairs in the city hall on Galena St.

Council was so-named because the valley was a gathering place for diverse tribes of Indians: Nez Perce, Umatilla, and Shoshone of the Lemhi, Fort Hall and Mountain bands.

The first white settlers arrived in 1876 – the George Moser family. George found it a bountiful area; there was plentiful timber and grass, there were huckleberries and chokecherries, salmon, trout and deer, even seasonal migrations of ducks and geese.

Moser borrowed a plow from settlers in Indian Valley and cut a crude road down Mesa Hill in order to bring his wagons safely off the summit. The family built the first house in Council – of logs, with a stone fireplace.

The Moser homestead was at the intersection of the Weiser-Meadows Valley and Seven Devils trails. George and Elizabeth accommodated travelers in their second house, a two-story, frame structure. They brought in 100 head of cattle from eastern Oregon, and raised hogs and cows, selling beef, pork and butter to miners. The homesteaders made one trip a year to Boise; a round trip just to Weiser took four days.

When a grizzly bear began preying on Moser's hogs, he took his dog and went hunting; the bear found the hunter first and lacerated his legs, doing irreparable injury. Moser's dog saved his life.

Ill health took George back to Hot Springs, Arkansas, in 1894, where he died shortly after his arrival.

During the depression of the 1890s, Elizabeth Moser mortgaged the farm. In order to pay the 10 percent ($120) interest each year, she raised pigs, then drove them to the Placerville mining camp in Boise Basin and sold them to the Chinese, thus making her payments for five years and saving the ranch.

Other settlers had arrived in the Council Valley, and Marguerite Diffendaffer has made the interesting observation that the average age of the early homesteaders was forty-five. Farms with grain and alfalfa crops were made possible by a system of ditch and flume irrigation. (The grain harvest was hauled to Cuddy's mill.) The railroad arrived in 1901 and the town incorporated in 1903.

Council was originally structured around a square, but the town suffered three large fires; the worst was the last, in 1915, which began in a candy store and soon engulfed most of the businesses. Four days later, the village board passed an ordinance that new buildings had to be constructed of nonflammable materials. By that time, the community had a population of 600, and a conventional Main St. absorbed the square. The present business district of Council, including the county courthouse, sits on forty acres of the old Moser homestead.

Council, from north side of the square, in 1896. Overland Hotel on the right.

Council on Fourth of July, 1901.

574

While the mineral boom in the Seven Devils lasted, the streets of Council were crowded with miners and freighters, teams and wagons. An opera house seated 400 spectators; there were six saloons and a couple of sporting houses.

During this period, the Pomona Hotel, which stands at the corner of Main St. and Moser Ave., was built for Colonel Edgar Heigho's Washington County Land and Development Company in the summer and fall of 1910. Heigho was the president of the P & I N Railroad.

The structure cost $20,000 and is a significant example of the period's Mission style architecture. The ground floor had a lobby with fireplace, a parlor, billiard room, and dining room. There were nineteen sleeping rooms, and two bathrooms, on the second floor. A stairway from the hall leads up to the forty-four-foot tower, which afforded a pleasant partial view of the surrounding valley. The steam heating plant and cold storage were located in the basement. Renovation in the 1920s deprived the building of much of its ornamentation but it still merits inclusion on the National Register of Historic Places.

Council is now the gateway, via Hornet Creek road, to the Seven Devils country, Bear, Cuprum, and Kleinschmidt Grade down to Hells Canyon.

The best access road to the **Seven Devils Mountains** originates on the east side of Council. The route travels northwest up Hornet Creek and then north 28.3 miles to **Bear**.

From Bear, the traveler in a pickup truck can drive north 13.5 miles to **Black Lake**. The road goes through **Placer Basin**, an area of mining activity from the 1890s through the 1930s.

Black Lake was part of a 67,000-acre state game preserve from 1912 to 1935. It is now an ideal area for fisherman and backpackers. Trails leave the road-end for many of the thirty-six lakes that dot the region. The trail that leads to White Monument Peak (8,900 feet) gives a glimpse of the railroad grade, built in 1898-1899 to connect the Peacock mine with the Pacific and Idaho Northern line in Council. (In 1900 the effort was abandoned.)

For those interested in the Black Lake mine, it is located on the mountain side, well above the lake. A cable tramway carried ore buckets from the tunnel, down across the lake to the mill below. The mill was destroyed for scrap metal during World War II.

Travelers in sedans can turn left, or northwest, at the Bear Junction, and continue seven miles to a T at Indian Creek. Here it is

Views of the Huntley barn.

possible to see the remarkable **A. O. Huntley barn**, itself worth
the drive from Council. It is a board and batten, three-story
structure with a steep and fraying shingled gambrel roof. The front
transept has been lost, but the structure that remains measures
100-by-40-feet. Braced frame construction was employed.

The barn has a raised concrete foundation with a dirt-covered
cement floor where cattle were housed. Most of the original
stanchions are intact, and feed chutes run from the break in the
gambrel to the main floor. Eleven braced beams support the roof,
and the upper two stories are open for hay storage.

A. O. Huntley had a ranch where the barn is located, and in the
late 1890s he grubstaked the Caswell brothers who subsequently
discovered the Thunder Mountain gold mines in central Idaho. The
principal claims in that group were sold in 1901 to Colonel Dewey
for $100,000, and a year later another claim brought $125,000.

The proceeds furnished Huntley with the capital to improve his
ranch and herd, and to build this barn and a notable mansion.
Unfortunately, the nearby residence burned in the 1930s. Huntley
operated his ranch, and a way-station, until the agricultural
depression of the early 1920s; at that time he sold the property to
the Speropulous family, and moved to Oregon.

The structure is one of the few three-story barns that remain in
the state, and is the largest agricultural building within at least fifty
miles of the site. It is a local landmark, and though on private
property, deserves statewide appreciation.

Turn right, or northwest, at the Indian Creek T, and drive 1.5 miles
to **Cuprum**.

The settlement of Cuprum (Latin for copper) was established on
Indian Creek in 1897, midway between Kinney Point and the foot of
Kleinschmidt Grade. It had two general stores, three saloons, the
Imperial Hotel, a newspaper shop and an assay office.

The Metropolitan Trust Company of New York City had become
interested in the Blue Jacket mine and leased the property. It
financed construction of a smelter at Cuprum. The water-jacket
type smelter proved inefficient, and after two trials, was sold to the
managers of the Iron Dyke mine across the Snake River.

Cuprum is a sleepy place now, astir only because of the activities
of the Copper Queen mine.

From Cuprum, one can take a passenger car about thirteen miles
over a slow, dirt road (No. 106) to **Sheep Rock**. Persons interested
in a panorama of "America's deepest gorge" will not be

disappointed by this drive. The view from **Kinney Point** (7,126 feet) is extraordinary.

Opposite the point, on the forks of Copper Creek, is the site of **Helena**, marked by a few collapsed cabins. Helena, named for the first girl born in the camp, owed its origins to the discovery of the Peacock copper mine.

In 1899 plans were made to haul Peacock ore to a steamboat at the foot of Kleinschmidt grade. In 1897 when the steamboat plan had been scrapped, hopes were fastened on the arrival of the P & I N railroad. The railroad never appeared.

Continue to the road-end at Sheep Rock (6,847 feet). There is a short nature-trail loop out to an overlook. One can see the Snake River and portions of three states from the Rock.

It is also a lofty site for an overview of the region's geology. The Seven Devils reflect block faulting and glacial erosion. The fault blocks are elongated north-south and are characterized by steep eastern slopes and moderate western slopes. Major valleys were glaciated during the Pleistocene epoch.

The southern-most reaches of the Seven Devils region consist of younger mountains composed of tilted blocks of Columbia River basalt. Beneath the lava are older rocks: greenstones (metamorphosed lavas and sediments), limestone and intrusive igneous rocks probably related to the Idaho batholith. These older rocks are exposed at high elevations in the Seven Devil Mountains and in the lower canyons of the Snake and Salmon Rivers.

Instead of taking the Sheep Rock Rd. turnoff, one can drive 3.1 miles northeast from Cuprum, past the townsite of **Decorah**, to Landore. In 1901 miners who worked on Garnet Creek lived in Decorah. The settlement competed with Landore for trade.

Landore (land of ore), on Indian Creek, had a population of 500 between 1900 and 1905. Mines operated on ten-hour shifts, and ore was stockpiled in anticipation of the P & I N railroad's arrival. The railroad had shifted its focus from Helena to Landore. Freight wagons and a daily stage hauled from Council.

The Ladd Metal Company of Portland, Oregon, built a smelter at Landore in 1904. It was wood-fired, but not properly designed to obtain the necessary temperatures from that fuel. It was remodeled to use coke, which had to be freighted from Council. By fall, 1905, the Ladd Co. decided to cut its losses and closed the operation. The incompletion of the P & I N spur, coupled with litigation, depressed copper prices, and World War I frustrated Landore's hopes. The brick chimney that served the mill still marks the site.

Return to the T, 1.5 miles southwest of Cuprum at the Huntley barn. From this point, the driver can retrace the road to Council, or take Road No. 050 down Indian Creek and the **Kleinschmidt Grade** 7.9 miles to the Hells Canyon road, which connects with Highway 71 from Cambridge.

The base of Kleinschmidt Grade touches the Hells Canyon road about three miles north of Homestead, Oregon. The grade was built to serve as a capillary from the river to the mines of the Seven Devils.

Lake in the Seven Devils.

US 95

In 1862 Levi Allen discovered the previously mentioned Peacock copper lode. But mining in the area did not get into the ground until Albert Kleinschmidt, from Montana, purchased an interest in the Allen claims in 1885. Kleinschmidt bought three separate claims on Indian Creek. He sacked some ore and shipped it to a smelter in Anaconda, Montana, where it turned a satisfactory profit.

Kleinschmidt was now serious about the prospects for the Seven Devils area. He had made a sizeable fortune in the Montana copper strike and sensed history might repeat itself. He turned his talents and $20,000 of his money to solving the ore-transportation problem.

Albert's solution was grandiose: build a road twenty-two miles down to the Snake River from the Peacock mine, haul ore wagons to the water where a steamboat could carry their loads to a railhead at Olds Ferry or Huntington, Oregon. In 1889 he put crews to work with picks, shovels, dynamite, and horse-drawn scrappers. Some of the men made a dollar a day. They completed the road in July, 1891. It was top-hole job. When Livingston and Laney, mining geologists, examined the grade in 1920 they wrote:

This road was well located, and of all the mountain wagon roads built before the days of highway construction, this is by far the best graded road that the writers have seen in the state. It rises from about 1,500 feet in elevation at the Snake River to about 7,200 feet on the divide above Helena and there are only one or two really steep pitches in the whole of this distance, and with a little repairing, trucks could be operated over it without particular difficulty. (A passenger car used it in 1909.)

Attempts to use the steamboat *Norma* on the Snake River met with problems, and the Panic of 1893 discouraged development of the mines at that time; the ore wagons, for which the grade was built, never used it.

North of Council, U.S. Highway 95 gains elevation, passes through portions of the Payette National Forest, and through the sawmill site called **Tamarack**, reaching the community of New Meadows after twenty-four miles.

New Meadows (elevation 3,865) lies at the south end of a meadow as pretty as any in the state. It is painful to praise it here, because after 100 years of harmonious use by ranchers, a contagion of California real estate agents has plotted the valley for subdivision.

The first cabin in Meadows Valley was built at the mouth of Goose Creek (which enters the Little Salmon River), in 1864. Tom Cooper and Bill Jolly arrived in 1877 with sixty head of horses. Then in 1880, Tom Clay moved his family down from Warren's diggings, northeast of McCall.

The Pacific and Idaho Northern's rails arrived in present New Meadows in 1911; the railroad company had planned an extension to Lewiston via Grangeville, or to Missoula, but that goal was never realized. The location of the $30,000 brick depot here, visible just south of the highway on entering town, did however, cause the population to shift westward from Meadows to New Meadows.

Ore tonnage from the Seven Devils mines never materialized, and rail service from Emmett to McCall reduced passenger traffic; the railway never prospered. The train made a round trip from Weiser six days a week, and in 1930 a RT-ticket cost $3.00. A locomotive pulled a coal tender, two passenger cars, a baggage car and caboose.

In 1936 the Union Pacific acquired the P & I N for $60,000. The rail's chief client now is the Tamarack sawmill. U.P. abandoned the northern end of the line, from Tamarack to New Meadows, in 1979.

As U.S. 95 swings due north at its intersection with Highway 55 on the east end of New Meadows, note the E. M. Heigho residence on the east side of the road. It is a 2½-story Georgian revival house built of painted brick, with a metal roof.

In 1911 when the house was built, the P & I N had just reached New Meadows, and Colonel Heigho was the president and general manager of the railroad. He held the same titles with the Central Idaho Telegraph and Telephone Co., and with the Coeur d'or Development Co., which owned the New Meadows townsite. In addition, he was vice president and a director of the Weiser National Bank, and a director of the Meadows Valley Bank.

The Colonel had the house designed for his family by a Weiser architect. It had twelve rooms and a bathroom. The downstairs was furnished in the style of Louis XIV. There was a reception parlor, with Mrs. Heigho's collection of eighty-seven silver spoons on display, and a library adorned with Mr. Heigho's animal trophies. Upstairs there was a bedroom for the twin daughters, a boy's room, guest room, and servant's quarters in the attic. The basement held a heating plant, an electric water pump, laundry and coal bin. (In recent years, the house has been used as a hotel.)

The Meadows Valley Hotel was located due south of the Heigho house, across the highway intersection. The elaborate structure was built at Mr. Heigho's direction for the Washington County Land and Development Co. from July, 1910 to Feb., 1912. The hotel cost $60,000; it had forty-four furnished rooms, and the main floor included a lobby, dining room and kitchen. Almost $12,000 was spent on mahogany furniture. In 1929 the hotel burned. Only a cement curb reveals the location.

Heigho Hotel, 1913.

Highway 95 bisects **Meadows Valley** for the next ten miles. The valley contains evidence of having been a glacial lake thousands of years ago. It is now the headwaters of the Little Salmon, which joins the Main Salmon forty miles distant. For centuries the meadows provided Indians with elk, deer, fish and roots.

The hills along Meadows Valley supported heavy stands of mountain brome, bluegrass, bunchgrass and Idaho fescue. Though too high for winter range, the area provided splendid summer forage. Charles Campbell arrived in an ox-drawn covered wagon in 1879, saw the livestock potential, and established the headquarters of the Circle C ranch in 1884 on the east side of the valley. It became one of the largest cattle operations in the west; fall roundups with forty cowboys often brought over 2,000 head of stock into the meadows.

When Charlie died, his sons continued to operate the ranch. At the time the Circle C was sold, in 1973, it encompassed 29,000 acres of deeded land and 130,000 acres of leased grazing ground.

Now the valley range is in the process of summer homesite subdivision. What a clover field is to a steer, a spring to a sheep, and a mudhole to a hog – such is lovely land to a real estate agent.

Halfway across Meadows Valley by highway, is the west turnoff for **Zim's Hot Springs**. The site was homesteaded in 1889 by

John and May McGlinchey. They sold out in 1903, for $3,000, to
Henry and Daniel Yoakum.

*P&IN at New
Meadows. Tender
is the "Katherine,"
named for one of
Heigho's twin
daughters.*

The Yoakums bought the property with foresight: they believed
that the P & I N would build the railroad past their springs and that
the mud baths would be a natural spot for a resort-depot. But the
Yoakums were plagued by misfortune, the kind of fortune that
never misses.

They built a store and painted it bright yellow. The next year they
put up a two-story hotel with nine guest rooms on the second level.
Hot tubs were installed on the ground floor.

Then Henry's wife died in 1906, following a miscarriage. Henry,
unable to work and care for their seven children, had to divide the
family among relatives; broken-hearted, he died seven months later.
The railroad never came, and the store burned in 1916.

The hot springs changed hands again in 1925, for $20,000. The
buyer poured a forty-by-eight-foot concrete pool that is still in use.
He built a new dance hall, cabins, race track, baseball diamond and
bleachers. The resort thrived until the Depression; then it served as
a recreation focus for CCC boys and the local folks. Members of a
fourteen-piece band lived in the hotel for two years; the dances were
celebrated affairs.

Since World War II, the resort has had several owners; each has
remodeled and improved the place in his own way. It remains open
to the public, and the pool has been the scene of events as different
as church baptisms and smoke-jumper survival training.

The water at Zim's Springs surfaces at 149 degrees F, so hot the homesteaders used it to scald hogs. It is cooled by aeration before it fills the pool.

The **Little Salmon River** makes some scenic drops as it pours down the canyon, alongside Highway 95, all the way to the outskirts of Riggins. The river is spectacular in spring flood, but dries to a small creek by late summer. In an unsuccessful attempt to improve fish passage, the state fish and game department dynamited several of the falls in 1929.

North of Pollock 4.5 miles, and that many miles south of Riggins, is the signed turnoff for the **Rapid River fish hatchery**, located three miles up that drainage.

Idaho Power Company supports the hatchery as partial restitution for the company's destruction of chinook salmon runs that traveled through Hells Canyon of the Snake to the Weiser, Boise and Payette Rivers and up Pine Creek in Oregon.

The hatchery is operated by state fish and game personnel. It is the most successful spring chinook hatchery in the country, with a far better record than the national hatchery at Kooskia. Spawning begins around August 10-15, and more than 10 million eggs are taken at Rapid River. The summer eggs from this hatchery are used to raise a half-million smolts.

At one time, the fish and game department gave the spent fish to the public. The program was terminated because the FDA objected on grounds the salmon had been given a shot of aureomycin, a drug not cleared for human consumption in fish – even though the antibiotic has been approved for steers and hogs if there is no residue at the time of slaughter. Now the salmon are simply buried.

Shingle Creek is a northwest tributary of Rapid River, just below the hatchery. The creek is the locale of a diverting incident in Salmon River history.

The Eddys and the Splawns moved into the Salmon River country in 1886. The Eddys had seven children: John, Jim, Lewis and Newt, and three daughters whose names are not relevant to the tale. Ike and Stan Splawn were brothers, and Stan's young brother-in-law, Charley Scroggins, lived with them. Unlike the Splawns, the Eddys were cowboys and they were addicted to racehorses. Edward Hoagland has observed that "it is a short distance from what is compelling to what is compulsive," and it was the Eddys' racehorse monomania that proved their undoing.

584

The Eddy family took over the Shingle Creek area, from about two miles up the stream all the way down to the present fish hatchery. They acquired a small herd of cattle, without buying any from their neighbors.

The Splawns settled north of the Eddys, on Papoose Creek. Apparently all of the parties had less money than they could spend. What follows is a shorthand version of a rather complicated series of events.

In 1896 the Seven Devils mining boom had just gotten underway. The Nez Perce reservation lands had been opened to settlers, and the Indians were receiving land payments; they preferred gold coins to currency. Horse races were a major attraction around the state and considerable money was wagered on the outcomes. The Eddys and Splawns decided to counterfeit gold coins and disperse their product at horse races.

The cowboys brought uncommon intelligence and organization to their caper. Their parents either did or did not know about the operation. The Shingle Creek location was ideal for their private mint; production took place only during the winter, and the Rapid River access was guarded. Splawns' cabin protected the rear entrance. Visitors were about as welcome as diptheria.

Wooden molds for $5, $10, and $20 gold pieces were obtained; the $20 pieces were obviously the most popular. A special plaster was used, impressed while wet with the image of the coin to be duplicated. When the plaster cured, it was fired, then babbit was poured through a sprue into the mould. The proto-coins were subsequently dipped in a vat of chemicals mixed with a gold solution and a battery hookup allowed the counterfeiters to electroplate the pieces.

Distribution was fairly sophisticated, too. Ike Splawn lived in Lewiston with his wife and child during the summer. He handled matters in north Idaho. A well-respected gentleman near Weiser, Emmett Taylor, assisted in obtaining chemicals and technical advice from Chicago, and undoubtedly helped pass the bogus coins. The Eddys and Stan Splawn found trading the pieces at race tracks, where their horses were entered anyway, a good cover and easier than swatting flies with a broom.

Gradually, the ins and outs of rumor linked the Eddys to cattle theft and phony gold pieces. They denied and alibied, but they could not quit, any more than can a loser in a poker game.

Eventually, a part-time detective, with an interest in racehorses, William Reavis, became involved in the case because the Treasury Department had offered a $1000 reward for the arrest of the guilty

585

parties. Reavis learned the identity of the suspects from the U.S. Marshal, Eben Mounce, in Lewiston. William had the fastest horse in the territory – a little mare named Nancy Hanks. He decided to take her to Lewiston, beat one of Jim Eddy's horses, and use the mare as bait to initiate a friendship.

The plot worked, and Reavis casually hinted that he would part with a half-interest in Nancy if he could find a way to get cut in on the fake coins being circulated at racetracks. He received an invitation to visit Jim on Rapid River.

Jim Eddy (right), Frank Freleigh, brother-in-law (left), Mr. Scroggins, jockey (center).

Ike Splawn at Squaw Creek in 1916.

Before William Reavis took the stage to Grangeville, he conferred with Marshal Mounce. Once the detective got to Rapid River and headed upstream, he met with considerable hostility. Jim Eddy almost got his nose rolled up for inviting a stranger into their camp. Given the circumstances, Reavis was nervier than a busted tooth. They did not want him to stay and they did not trust him enough to let him leave – but they sure wanted his mare. So the Eddys watched the intruder constantly, and gradually over a period of three months, came to accept him. Though Reavis was never allowed to witness the manufacturing process, he did persuade them he could pass their product in Oregon.

Finally, the detective was able to get a message to the Idaho County sheriff, W. M. Williams. The ploy used to lure the Eddys and Splawn out of Shingle Creek was an arrest warrant issued by Sheriff Williams against Jim Eddy for cattle theft. Reavis urged the whole

586

clan to go to Mount Idaho to testify for Jim, because with so many witnesses he would surely be acquitted. On arrival, they were all arrested by the U.S. Marshal and the Idaho County sheriff. Ike Splawn and Emmett Taylor were apprehended separately.

The trial, in May, 1897, in Moscow required six days. The defendants were represented by competent counsel. However, Reavis had returned to Shingle Creek to help the Eddy women bury the evidence; he then dug it up, and the government had the molds, electroplating equipment, and 500 $20 gold pieces to introduce as evidence. The prosecution also had copies of Taylor's correspondence with Chicago supply houses.

Jury deliberations lasted almost eight hours. They found all defendants guilty on multiple counts. Judge James Beatty sentenced Jim and John Eddy and Emmett Taylor to sixteen years at hard labor, and handed the other defendants sentences of from two to six years.

While Reavis was a witness at the trial, someone in the town of Meadows poisoned Nancy Hanks. Rumors later circulated that the detective was shot, but they were unfounded; he returned to Enterprise, Oregon, where he ran a livery stable.

The elder Eddys sold the Shingle Creek ranch and moved to Oregon.

After release from the penitentiary, Ike and Stan Splawn returned to their homesteads on Papoose Creek.

Two and one-half miles farther north on U.S. 95 is the **Squaw Creek Road**, on the west side of the highway. Drive 1.5 miles northwest up Squaw Creek, then take the left fork southwest up Papoose Creek. Five miles up the road, and about 1.5 miles up the creek from that point, is the location of **Papoose Cave**, the largest limestone cave in Idaho, perhaps the most extensive in the Pacific Northwest.

The cave, with more than a mile of passages, was formed when water dissolved limestone that was deposited about 200 million years ago. The cavern has been mapped to a depth of more than 600 feet, ranking it among the ten deepest caves in the U.S. Exploration with an altimeter beyond the mapped area indicates the total depth is approximately 945 feet.

Unfortunately, the cave is extremely hazardous to the untrained spelunker; it is wet, cold (thirty-seven degrees F), and contains vertical obstacles ranging from fifteen to sixty-five feet. One forty-foot climb must be made through a waterfall. All of the vertical work requires ropes or ladders. Because the cave began drawing the curious public and novice cavers, a locked door was installed at the entrance. The key is available from the Forest Service for experienced parties.

Papoose Cave is one of the few in Idaho that contains a large stream in which solution and redeposition are still occurring. The cavern has some formations, but they are not abundant. Dye placed in the stream inside the cave reappeared in the Shingle Creek drainage, nearly five miles away!

Another eleven miles up Papoose Creek grade will bring the driver to **Heaven's Gate** (8,429 feet). Seven Devils Peaks are visible to the southwest and the Sheep Creek drainage can be seen to the north.

Walk up to the nearby observation tower. On a clear day, in mid-week, it is possible to see Sunday both ways. Actually, one can see portions of four states, though the Beaverhead peaks in Montana can be elusive. The road to Heaven's Gate is generally open from July 4 to October 1. There are two campgrounds.

Riggins bar was used as a camping area by Nez Perce Indians: Yellow Bull, Little White Bird, Black Elk.

In 1863 Mike Deasy stopped on the bar long enough to find traces of gold on the north end. He went on to mine at Florence and Warren, but returned a few years later to placer, while he wintered his horses on the bar. Deasy's claim was traded in 1893 to Isaac and Mary Irwin for two horses and a gold watch. Irwin moved his family of five boys down from Meadows Valley and they built the first house on the bar. Isaac was a member of the initial state legislature in Boise.

Charley Clay and his brothers, John and Bud, moved to the bar from Palouse country. For three years they worked on a ditch that would bring water from Squaw Creek to the bar so they could mine and irrigate.

Noah, Dick, and Ike Irwin and Charley Clay took homesteads on the bar. Dick and Charley donated land for the second school in 1894. Classes were attended by fourteen students taught by W. H. Palm from Meadows. The second school was located where the Idaho Bank and Trust building now stands.

At that time, the trail to the bar came up the east bank as far as Lightning Creek, where John Riggins, a native of Missouri and a blacksmith by trade, ran a ferry. The trail on the west side of the river at the ferry dock went up along the shoulder of the mountain and then dropped down to the mouth of Race Creek at the north end of later Riggins.

John's son, Richard, moved to the bar in March, 1901, with his wife Ethel. Dick Riggins had spent two years at the University of Idaho studying civil engineering, then worked as a stage driver, farmer, and freighter before settling on the location that was to bear his name.

U.S. 95 in Riggins, circa 1930.

The wagon road was pushed up river along the east bank, until in 1902 it was opposite the mouth of Race Creek. Edgar Levander had installed a new ferry at that point.

John Riggins then moved his blacksmith shop and ferry up river to the bar. Charley Clay persuaded a railroad survey crew that came down the Salmon to survey a townsite on Noah Irwin's homestead. Dick Riggins served as the town's first postmaster. His name was suggested for the town by the Post Office Department because the names offered by local people were duplicated in almost every state. Until that time, Riggins had been known as Gouge-Eye, or Clay and Irwin Bar.

In 1912 a steel bridge was built across the river on the north end of town.

Hotels, homes, stores, and churches gradually filled the bar. Riggins is still the center of a livestock industry but it is also a modern community with accommodations and services for tourists interested in the Salmon River and its backcountry.

589

Schoolmarm Peak, on the east side of the river, by the confluence with the Little Salmon, takes its name from the traditional spring class outings which hiked to the top of the 3,500-foot mountain. Preacher Mountain, 4,656 feet, on the west side of the town, is named for Mr. and Mrs. Hess and their twin boys who homesteaded the peak.

It is possible to follow the **Salmon River** (River of No Return) upstream for twenty-seven miles from Riggins. The gravel road begins at a bridge across the Little Salmon River at the south end of town, near the sawmill. The trip follows the river east along its south shore to Lake Creek bridge, eight miles from town. It then takes the north bank to Manning Bridge (seven more miles), and crosses again to the south bank and follows it to the road end at Chittam Rapid.

This trip offers an outstanding morning or afternoon drive, particularly in fair weather, but the road demands constant attention from the driver, and must be driven slowly. River outfitters use it during the summer, and hunters with stock trucks are on it in the fall. At least two-dozen people have been killed on this short stretch; in almost every instance the victim was driving too fast.

The Salmon River road was constructed by CCC crews from 1933-1939, and it was part of an effort to complete a river road from Salmon to Riggins. Fortunately, World War II disrupted the plan.

Points of interest en route:

Mile 2 **Shorts Bar**: A large, white sandbar with room for sunning and swimming.

William H. Short, for whom the bar is named, shed the snakeskin of place after place before settling along the River of No Return. Born in Massachusetts in 1833, he received a good education and learned the trade of ship carpenter. Between 1853 and 1879, he crossed the Isthmus of Panama to the California goldfields, mined in Oregon, Warren and Florence, British Columbia, Sitka, Victoria, Portland, and Santa Barbara.

In the fall of 1879, he came down to the Salmon from Florence and bought the mining claims on the bar that bears his name. Evidence of the hydraulic mining that occurred is still obvious.

Mile 8 **Lake Creek Bridge**: A mountainside on the edge of a lake up the west fork of Lake Creek slid into the lake during the summer of 1964. A wall of water came down the drainage ruining buildings and fields. It dammed the river and washed out the north abutment of the bridge.

590

The present severity of Lake Creek Rapid is a memento.

Mile 9 **Ruby Rapid**: The rapid below the road derives its name from industrial-grade garnets that can be found on the roadside shoulder and in the roadbed itself.

Mile 11 **Riggins Hot Springs**: The private residence at the east end of the suspension bridge is located on the site of the springs.

The hot spring here was well-known to the Indians before white men discovered it. The Nez Perce called it Weh-min-kesh, and scores of them gathered on the site to take advantage of the reputed medicinal properties of the spring waters. Miners, cowboys and packers came to ease their aches and ills.

Fred and Clara Riggins bought the site in 1900 from two squatters for six $20 gold pieces. Fred Riggins was twenty-nine years old when he settled with his family on Warm Springs Flat, as it was then called. All of their possessions had to be packed in over a narrow and overhung trail along the river. They planted some grain, a garden and orchard. It was several years before a survey made it possible for the Riggins to file homestead papers.

The spring served as a community bathing area from 1935-1975 but is no longer open to the public.

Mile 15 **Manning Bridge**: This bridge was built by the CCC men. Manning was working for the Corps and fell off the bluff, above the right end of the bridge, when he was returning from Riggins one evening. The old crossing was upriver, just behind the barn on the Howard place.

The area below the bridge is known as The Crevice. It is the site of a dam planned by the Army Corps of Engineers.

Mile 16 **Elkhorn Creek**: The mouth of this creek is a historically significant site along the Salmon River; it was the location of Shearer's ferry, established by Frederick and Susan Shearer during the mining boom in Florence.

Their son, George M. Shearer, was born in Winchester, Virginia, and was educated at Tuscorara Academy, Pennsylvania. He traveled to California in 1854 with his parents, returning home in 1859.

At the outbreak of the Civil War, George enlisted in General Bradley Johnston's regiment of Maryland volunteers and served the Confederate cause until captured and imprisoned in Fort Delaware.

Wounded several times in the war, he escaped from the federal prison and made his way in 1865 to Idaho. He settled at Elk Creek and rowed the ferry there for his parents. The boat was eventually replaced with a wire ferry.

591

George volunteered for the Nez Perce War in 1877; he was twice wounded in that conflict. He volunteered again, for the Sheepeater Campaign, and served under Lieutenant Catley. In 1883, he married Carrie Vollmer and they had three children. Shearer served several terms in the Idaho legislature, snowshoeing from the ferry to Boise and back – 300 miles. He was district court clerk for Idaho County at the time of his death.

Mile 20 **French Creek**: The creek that comes out of the south canyon and flows underneath the bridge was named after eight French miners.

A state bridge was completed across the river at the mouth of the creek in 1892. Construction had been delayed a year because the Salmon bridge iron was sent to Spokane and the steel for the Spokane bridge, which was fifty feet shorter, was sent mistakenly to Weiser, Idaho.

Aaron F. Parker, founder of the *Idaho County Free Press,* lobbied at the territorial legislature for appropriations which would allow construction of the bridge and road. The road allowed wagon traffic to travel from Meadows to Burgdorf or Warren, down French Creek, across the river and up through the Scott Ranch to Florence and Mount Idaho. By 1901, it was designated a state highway. In November of that year, the bridge blew down in a windstorm and the flow of traffic ceased.

There was a post office and school active in 1903-1906 at the mouth of the creek.

The bench above the road, on the downriver side of the creek, was occupied by a CCC camp in the 1930s. The buildings were dismantled by the Forest Service in 1943.

The road that sidewinders up the **French Creek grade** was built by CCC labor. It makes a steep climb to Burgdorf, twenty-three miles from the river, and then connects with the Warren Wagon Road, which travels thirty-one paved miles to McCall.

Mile 22 **Fall Creek**: The road bridges this creek, which descends 4,500 feet in five miles to its confluence with the river. In a curious twist of geography, rain that drenches the south side of the Fall Creek divide will flow into the South Fork of the Salmon (east of here) by way of Lake Creek and the Secesh River and come down the Salmon to mingle with the waters of Fall Creek, after a circuitous route of almost 100 miles.

Mile 24 **Wind River**: This stream, that flows in from the north, was called Meadow Creek on early maps. There was a trail from Florence Basin, past the Bullion mine and down to a wire bridge crossing at Carey Creek. It was naturally called the Meadow Creek

Trail, and a ferry house next to the "new" bridge is mentioned in the *Lewiston Journal.*

The Forest Service erected a modern bridge in 1961, but it collapsed as it neared completion because the anchor bolts pulled out of the stone on the south abutment. One tower and half of the bridge was salvaged. The present bridge was opened the following year.

There are two marked graves on the north flat, by the mouth of Wind River. In 1919, Neal McMeekin bought out Charles White, who owned the mining claims at the mouth of Wind River. White decided to remain until he had finished placering. In addition, he tried to take some tools and the sourdough jug. McMeekin got sore as a sore-tailed bear, arguing that he had paid for everything. White disagreed, and bang! it was "no sourdough forever" for Charlie White.

The second grave, that of Clarence Rowley, twenty-two years old, who died of exposure in 1898 on his way to the Marshall Mountain mines, lies next to White's grave at the mouth of Wind River. The crosses on the two graves were made with cement from the Wind River bridge job.

Mile 27 **Chittam Rapid**: This is the end of the road, and the take-out point for Salmon River trips that begin about seventy-five miles upriver. Power boats that service dude ranches in the canyon store fuel here.

The stretch of Highway 95, from five miles north of Riggins to White Bird Creek, twenty-eight miles distant, is the area where nine white settlers were killed by Nez Perce Indians, setting off the Nez Perce War of 1877.

Evidence of mining tunnels can be seen across the river. The placer ore was wheelbarrowed to ore chutes where it could be washed with river water. Tailing piles from placer mining activities can be detected on almost every bar on both sides of the river from this point to White Bird. The highway has obliterated a lot of the claims worked along the eastern side of the river. An item in the *Idaho County Free Press,* April, 1895, said over 100 men were rocking for gold along the river from John Day to White Bird.

Six miles north of Riggins, but about fourteen air-miles east of the highway, is Florence Basin, location of a former mining town called **Florence**.

In the summer, 1861, a party of twenty-three men, numerous enough to resist intimidation by the Nez Perce, upon whose reservation they were trespassing, stumbled onto the Florence placer ground after prospecting almost two months. Their rations had been reduced to portions of horsemeat. The men intended to keep their find a secret but "the vanity of having been entrusted with a secret is the principal cause for divulging it," and the word was soon out.

T. H. Mallory reported the earliest finds:

Miller's Creek is perhaps the richest. From the first pan of dirt washed, taken out of the first hole sunk in this creek, $25 was obtained. Miller washed out with the pan one afternoon $100. Claims were immediately staked off on this creek, and the party went to work. Each claim has since averaged, with the rocker, from $75 to $100 per day to the hand. Babboon Gulch is next richer. I have seen $75 washed out in 10 hours by one man, using the pan alone. Nasan's Gulch pays well. Five men have just cleaned up $700 the result of 10 hours work with the rocker in this gulch. Hall's Gulch, Smith's Gulch, Pioneer Gulch, and Healy's Creek will each pay at least 3 ounces to the hand.

Production had gotten underway within six weeks after discovery and a number of miners were making $100 a day. By mid-November, 350 men were working on the flat. Water was so scarce that it was recycled.

The winter of 1862 was colder than an icycle's backbone. Rockers were frozen and so were some travelers. Hardship haunted the Florence gulches. Dr. Noble left a particularly poignant observation:

On an afternoon, as I was passing one of our stores, I saw a young man with emaciated frame and ghastly countenance picking up something off a pile of snow and eating it with great relish. On stepping up to him, I found that in a famishing condition he had chanced to come on a spot or bank of snow on which some kitchen slop containing a few old cooked beans had lately been thrown out from an adjoining shanty, and these he was picking up and devouring with great avidity. I gave him five dollars, which he eagerly but thankfully clutched, went to a store, and paid it all for two and a half pounds of flour. He was a stranger without friends and wasted to a mere skeleton by want and destitution. He is now employed in packing on his back from the Mountain House, and a few days since he packed a hundred pounds of bacon on his back from there into town – more than fifteen miles, and over rough trail. One day a man called at the cabin where I stay, and in subdued tones asked, "What chance can a fellow have of getting that cow's head lying on the roof?" which he said "might do to cook when a fellow's hungry and has nothing to eat." He got it willingly. It had been lying there four months, but most of the time covered with snow.

More than 10,000 miners found their way to the basin in the spring and summer, 1862. There was not room for half of them. Along the diggings, a man could put on socks in the morning for half an hour and never find them on his own feet.

Old Florence, 1896.

It cost about $200 for a miner to travel from Portland to Lewiston. The Lewiston-Florence journey required four days. Once in camp, he found exhorbitant prices for supplies: shovels $40, kettles $10, tobacco $5 a pound, butter and tea $3 a pound, whiskey $1 a drink. But in the fall, gold was discovered in Boise Basin (120 miles south) and as the camp drained, prices plummeted and stores folded.

With so many miners, and limited but rich ground, Florence really had only one good year, 1862, when production reached $50,000 a day. She came and went like a wildflower; the Chinese picked up the petals.

Altogether, however, Florence mines yielded $10 million in gold.

Two roads lead to the basin: Nut Basin Road at Slate Creek, and the Allison Creek Road, about eleven miles up the Salmon River Road from Riggins. The trip is scarcely worthwhile, since the buildings are gone and second-growth jack pine has hidden the scars.

595

Nine miles north of Riggins is the community of **Lucile**, on the east side of the river, named for the daughter of Judge James Ailshie. His influence was helpful in getting a post office for the miners at Lucile in 1896. Lucile was a center of mining activity until 1939; it supplied the McKinley quartz-gold mine up Sheep Gulch, and the Blue Jacket and Crooks Corral mine on the Snake River side. The town was also the focus of some fierce sheep rancher versus cattleman feuds.

Frank Shield's wagon road construction camp near Lucile.

About eight miles north of Lucile is the **Foskett Memorial**, on the east side of the river, at the edge of the highway. Doctor Wilson A. Foskett was born in Warsaw, New York, in January of 1870. He graduated from Rush Medical College in Chicago and began a practice in 1897 at White Bird. There he met Loura Taylor, whom he married in 1903, and they had three children.

If ever any man was his brother's brother, it was Doc Foskett. For twenty-seven years, he traveled over Camas Prairie and along Salmon River answering calls on foot, horseback, in horse and buggy, and finally with a car. The nearest hospital was in Lewiston, so he pulled teeth, set bones, delivered babies, and performed operations under conditions contemporary doctors would find intolerable.

April 13, 1924, Doc Foskett spent the day caring for his livestock. He went to bed tired and late. He was summoned from sleep with a call to help a rancher's wife in childbirth at Riggins. Doc was up all night. He headed home, and refused to rest in Lucile because he was concerned about a young, expectant mother. Coming around the last curve in the Box Canyon, he fell asleep at the wheel and went off into the Salmon River. He was found the next morning.

The whole country was stunned by his death. River and prairie people gathered to pay their last respects; they had lost more than a doctor, they had lost a friend. A memorial was erected and when the highway was widened, a new monument was placed at the present location.

The time is over sixty years away, but Doc Foskett's memory shines like a famous poem. In the words of a pioneer western eulogy: *He did his damndest, angels could do no more.*

Slate Creek flows into the Salmon from the east side of the highway a short distance north of Dr. Foskett's memorial.

The community of Slate Creek, or Freedom, was established in 1861 and owes its name to early miners who discovered that the creek had no placer gravel.

Pack trains and cattle were wintered at Slate Creek waiting for spring so they could transport meat and supplies to Florence.

According to the *Illustrated History of North Idaho,* land at the mouth of Slate Creek was bought by Charles Silverman in 1861 from an Indian, Captain John.

Silverman's house is believed to have been one of the first on Salmon River. The *History* also reads that John Wood bought the place in the spring, 1862, paying $1000 to Silverman and Captain John. While the sum exceeded the value to an inordinate degree, he thereby acquired the lasting friendship of the Indians.

The log cabin in front of the Forest Service headquarters at Slate Creek contains an interesting display of USFS memorabilia from the district.

Behind the headquarters, just north of the fence, is an enormous black walnut tree, the largest in the state. It has a circumference of sixteen feet and a crown of over 100 feet.

Slate Creek was used as a CCC camp in the 1930s.

The highway bridges a Salmon River horseshoe bend north of Slate Creek and resumes its course along the river's east shore.

The **River of No Return** drains the largest basin within a single state outside of Alaska: 14,000 square miles of central Idaho. The headwaters of this 400-mile river are twenty miles northwest of Sun Valley, in the Sawtooth Mountains. The river joins the Snake about sixty miles from Slate Creek.

95

Ice bridges form across the Salmon during the winter, but the river seldom freezes over. Spring runoff generally peaks during the first two weeks of June. In 1974 the river flooded sections of the road between Riggins and White Bird, the highest water in over 100 years.

The Salmon is known as the "River of No Return" because pilots with wooden scows made one-way trips down its course, selling the sweepboats for scrap lumber at the trip's end and then returning overland to Salmon City. It was not until 1947 that Glen Woolridge succeeded in taking a twenty-two h.p. plywood boat upriver from Riggins to Salmon.

The U.S. Army Corps of Engineers has looked at the river with avaricious eyes for several decades. The Corps has plotted nine damsites with a combined theoretical capability of 3.5 million kilowatts. The only problem, social dislocation aside, is the fact that 35 percent of all salmon and steelhead left in the Columbia River are spawned on the headwaters of the Salmon, and the Columbia fishery is already deeply troubled by government dams stacked like tombstones from Portland to Lewiston.

SCENIC AREA

Eight miles north of Slate Creek (three miles north of Skookumchuck picnic area), there is a northwest exit from U.S. 95 that leads, after one mile, to a bridge across the Salmon River. One half-mile before the bridge, on the hillside above the road, a pipe fence can be seen next to a hackberry tree. It surrounds the graves of William Osborne, Harry Mason, Francois Chodoze, August Bacon, and Henry Moon, killed at the outbreak of the Nez Perce War. They were buried by soldiers.

If the traveler chooses to cross the bridge, he has a choice of two rewarding drives. A north (right) turn on the Canfield Road leads up to the **Doumecq** (due-mack) **and Joseph Plains**, a high plateau collared on the east and north by the Salmon River canyon and on the west by Hells Canyon. The Joseph-Doumecq is a big country, over 250 square miles, and quite isolated. The roads terminate where the country breaks off to the river canyons below. It was and is cattle country, homesteaded in the late 1800s, and dotted by a few communities such as Canfield, Joseph, Davison, Boles and Flyblow, which have since fallen into apathy. Abandoned buildings and old corrals speckle the mesa. Aside from grazing and logging, the area is substantially undisturbed by the hand of man. There are no services available on the plains, and without a map it is not difficult to get lost. With a map, an enjoyable day-trip loop can be made to **Joseph**, returning by way of Twogood Flat and Rice Creek.

598

A shorter variation of the trip can be made by following the Canfield Road about seventeen miles from the Salmon River bridge to the T at **Rice Creek**. Instead of going up on the Joseph-Doumecq, turn north (right) down Rice Creek four miles and cross the Salmon River at the mouth of **Rocky Canyon**. Continue up Rocky Canyon along Graves Creek eleven miles and reenter U.S. 95 at the town of Cottonwood.

The old **Boise Trail** infiltrated Rocky Canyon; it passed east of the Seven Devils, forded the Salmon near the present Rice Creek bridge, and went up Graves Creek and onto the Camas Prairie near Grangeville. The trail was used intensively in the 1800s, and there was a store at the mouth of Rocky Canyon in 1861.

The first road down Rocky Canyon to the river was built with pick and shovel in 1908-1909. The county improved the road in 1921. A flash flood took it out in 1948, but it was replaced in 1950 through a joint effort by the Army Corps of Engineers and the state of Idaho.

Graves Creek flows past the **Weis Rock Shelter** archaeological site, exposed by a gravel borrow-pit operation in the 1940s. Four phases of culture, each characterized by a particular set of artifact traits, were uncovered. The oldest of these phases began about 5,500 B.C. and the youngest phase ended about 1400 A.D. Nothing remains of the shelter.

The second choice available to the driver at the west end of the Salmon River bridge, a shorter alternative to the Joseph-Doumecq trek, is to turn south (left) and drive thirteen miles to **Pittsburg Landing** on the Snake River. This is a remarkable drive, though in wet weather the remarks might be expletives. In the spring, few places along the Snake are prettier than the Landing; in mid-summer the country dries out and the area is hotter than the devil's furnace.

The road climbs from Salmon River to **Pittsburg Saddle**, which affords a panorama of the Salmon and Snake River canyons, the two deepest gorges in the state (though this is not the location of their maximum depth). From the Pittsburg divide, the road drops three miles to the landing on the banks of the Snake. There is a camping area here.

The first wagon road to this location, from White Bird, over the saddle, was completed in 1900. It was referred to as a county road a year later. This route opened the gate to homesteaders, and between 1904-1915 twenty-one entries were filed in the area. Only eight went to patent; the others were rejected or relinquished. A

599

ferry bridged the river at White Bird, and another, established in 1891, was operated at Pittsburg. It was discontinued in 1933.

The history of the Pittsburg area is older than Adam. Lodge rings, petroglyphs, and artifacts found on the benches are evidence of extended use by native Americans. During the 1840-1870 period members of Toohoolhoolzote's Nez Perce band occupied the location as part of their wintering ground. One account indicates the Indians called the area "Canoe Camp."

The origin of the name Pittsburg is obscure – those who might have known its derivation are no longer alive. The name was used in March, 1864 by the Lewiston *Golden Age:*

Navigation to the mouth of Salmon River has been tested, and the opinion of experienced men, who have been up and down the river in small boats, is, that steamers can be made to run successfully to a point eighteen miles above Pittsburg Landing. The opinion of some others is that this can not be done.

LaFayette Cartee's survey map in 1867, done for the Surveyor General's Office that year, shows Pittsburgh ending with an "h" in the same manner as the Pennsylvania city.

Since the name was applied during the era of the Civil War, it is not unlikely it was given by a veteran of Shiloh, who was reminded of Pittsburg Landing in Tennessee on the Tennessee River.

The Campbell brothers of New Meadows bought the entire Pittsburg area in the early 1930s and made it part of the well-known Circle C ranch. There were sixty-one people living in the Pittsburg Landing area at that time. As with most of the private holdings along the river, this portion of the ranch was acquired by the Forest Service for the Hells Canyon National Recreation Area.

The area was used for sheep and cattle for many years. A row of Osage orange trees can be seen on the north side of the road on the upper bench. They were planted by the Henry Kurry family, cattle ranchers who arrived in 1877 and built houses from the abundant field stone.

In a field, about a mile walk from the landing, are some Indian petroglyphs and a large grinding stone. They can be found by following the road that angles northwest from the upper picnic area. The boulders are scattered among some hackberry trees on the north side of the fence within fifty feet of the road.

To enter the town of **White Bird** from U.S. 95, take the east exit before crossing the White Bird bridge. White Bird is an eponym for a Nez Perce chief.

600

A. D. Chapman, with his Umatilla Indian wife, was the first settler at White Bird Creek. As early as 1863, he was offering a boat-ferry service at the river.

The town of White Bird began to form in 1891, when S. S. Fenn established a stage station and hotel. The Fenn brothers opened the first post office. Within a few years there were three more hotels, a blacksmith shop, livery stable, grain warehouse, meat market, barbershop, and a two-room schoolhouse. A. Cooper ran a store-saloon that had a chalk line drawn across the floor; children were not allowed to cross it.

George W. Curtis established a ferry at the mouth of White Bird Creek in 1892. Six years later he sold it to his son, A. Fred Curtis, and moved his store to Riggins.

White Bird Hill on Highway 95 climbs 3,000 feet in 7.2 miles from the bridge to the summit. This stretch of highway was constructed by Morrison-Knudsen from 1965-1975. The grading cost exceeded $4 million for 6.4 miles. Some of the cuts through basalt were 300 feet deep, and a few fills 400 feet in height were required. (Catskinners, flanking each other with their equipment on forty-five degree slopes, referred to the job as the "white knuckle flight.") Altogether, the project cost $8 million. It reduced the distance between the Salmon River and the summit by five miles.

The **White Bird bridge** was designed in 1970-1972 and was completed in 1975. It is built of three steel box-section spans that are 906 feet long, and the structure contains 2.1 million pounds of steel. Most of the steel came from U.S. Steel in Gary, Indiana. The bridge cost $1.7 million.

Steel used in the bridge is the weathering type, which forms a protective film of oxide. But since the climate at White Bird is such that it would take nearly twenty years for the oxide coating to develop, the bridge was painted.

Because the crushed basalt was improperly compacted at the bridge abutments, the span moved and settled five inches; the reinforcement in the footings was damaged and required $400,000 in repairs. Bearings were also replaced.

The White Bird bridge design was awarded first prize by the American Institute of Steel Construction in 1976 for the medium span high-clearance category.

The grade climbs west of the old White Bird road, which can be seen en route to the summit, switchbacking up the slope to the east. That road was considered a remarkable engineering feat when it was completed in 1921 for $400,000, replacing a difficult, rutted

601

wagon road. It was sixteen feet wide and climbed 2,900 feet in fourteen miles. Convict labor and two steam shovels (moved on short steel rails) helped build it. The road made it possible to drive from Boise to Grangeville in thirteen hours. It was paved in 1938, and in 1974 it was placed on the National Register of Historic Places.

Old White Bird Hill grade.

Halfway up the new White Bird grade is a parking area, on the east side of the road, with an interpretive display and overview of the **White Bird Canyon battlefield**. It is worth a stop.

Several excellent histories of the Nez Perce War, and the events precedent and subsequent, have been written. The signs in the intrepretive shelter here indicate the positions of the characters involved in the June 17, 1877 tableau. Skirmishes and battles that followed this encounter are treated in other parts of this book, at the place they occurred. So the only information which would seem helpful here is a synopsis of the war and its aftermath.

Though their canyoned country buffered them against early white encroachment, the Nez Perce had a tradition of friendship with the whites from the time of Lewis and Clark.

With the discovery of gold at Pierce, Idaho, in 1860 and the establishment of Idaho Territory in 1863, the Nez Perce were pressured to revise an 1855 treaty by reducing reservation lands from 10,000 square miles to 1,200. A council was held in May, 1863, at Fort Lapwai with government and military leaders. Chief Lawyer and most of the Christian chiefs such as Timothy, Jason, and Levi, agreed to the reduction because scarcely any of their own land was affected. But Old Joseph, Toohoolhoolzote, and other headmen whose holdings would be confiscated under the new treaty angrily refused to sign it, and returned to their villages.

The government then maintained that Lawyer's signature and those of the other Clearwater chiefs bound *all* members of the Nez Perce tribe.

How specious that argument was is best revealed by a statement of Major Wood, Adjutant General, who investigated the situation for General Howard six months before the outbreak of fighting. Wood wrote:

The non-treaty Nez Perces cannot in law be regarded as bound by the treaty of 1863, and insofar as it attempts to deprive them of the right to occupancy of any land, its provisions are null and void.

For five years the treaty went unratified, promises were broken and payments forgotten. Old Joseph died, and his son, Young Joseph (Thunder Rolling from Mountain Heights) took his place with the Wallowa band in Oregon. He had promised his father that he would never sell the land of his people.

Gradually farmers and ranchers encroached on the Indian portions of the Wallowa country. Missionaries were uneasy about the effect free Indians were having on reservation Indians who practiced subsistence farming and Christianity.

Influence was exerted to confine the non-treaty Indians to the Lapwai reservation so that the treaty Nez Perce would no longer be ridiculed for having sold their freedom for an empty promise. Once all the Nez Perce were corralled at Lapwai, farmers in the Wallowa could usurp their lands with unconcern.

General Oliver Otis Howard was appointed commander of the Department of Columbia, which at the time included Idaho Territory. After listening to the complaints of settlers and missionaries, he gave Joseph and White Bird's bands one month to move onto the reservation.

The Indians moved their families and herds across the flood-swollen Snake and Salmon Rivers, and gathered near Tolo Lake on the Camas Prairie a few miles north of here.

While these non-treaty Nez Perce were enjoying their last day of freedom before entering the Lapwai reservation, three young braves from White Bird's band went up Salmon River and killed several white men for past grievances. They returned boasting of their deeds.

When Joseph and White Bird learned what had occurred, they knew there would be trouble. They moved with their people to the bottom of Lahmotta (White Bird Canyon) and braced themselves for repercussions.

General Howard got word of the murders and promptly dispatched Captain Perry with ninety-nine men to Grangeville to protect the settlers. The General also fired off a telegram to his commander in San Francisco: "Think we will make short work of it." – perhaps the most erroneous surmise in the history of western Indian warfare.

It was June 17, 1877, a year since Custer's debacle at Little Big Horn, when Captain Perry and his men went down the slopes of White Bird Canyon to meet seventy poorly armed Indians who were accompanied by 2,500 horses.

The Nez Perce hoped that explanatory discussions might allow a peaceful resolution; they rode out to meet Perry with a white flag. To the regret of many a widow and orphan, several soldiers opened fire. The Indians replied in kind. Yellow Wolf, a participant in the fight, said,

The warriors charging up the west canyon struck that flank hard. Hanging on the side of their horses where not seen, they gave the soldiers a storm of bullets. Warriors dismounted, and from hiding dropped soldiers from their saddles.

No wild horses were in this battle, as you say claimed in white man's history. Every horse carried a rider. In all there were not as many as seventy Indians in that fight.

In the meantime, our smaller party, sixteen in number, attacked the enemy's left flank. It was just like two bulldogs meeting. Those soldiers did not hold their position ten minutes. Some soldiers (citizen volunteers) on that low, rock-topped butte you see ahead there, were quickly on the run. Then the entire enemy force gave way.

We nearly headed them off. We mixed them up. I did some bow shooting. Two of my arrows struck soldiers only five steps away – one in the shoulder, the other in the breast. We did not stop to fight the wounded. We chased hard after the others.

We chased the remaining soldiers. Fought them running for several miles. We drove them back across the mountain, down to near the town they came from (Mount Idaho). Then some of the chiefs commanded, 'Let the soldiers go! We have done them enough! No Indian killed!'

The Nez Perce had routed F and H Companies, killing a third of the command without loss to themselves. In addition, they gathered a windfall of Army rifles.

Howard was stunned by the news. Fearing a general uprising, he summoned units from Alaska, Washington, Oregon, California and Georgia. Five days later he arrived at the canyon with 227 soldiers, 20 volunteers, and 175 non-soldiers, including packers and guides. The Indians simply crossed to the Salmon's south shore and awaited whatever movement the troops would make. With the help of a cable and boats, Howard began transporting his men across the river. The Nez Perce moved downriver twenty-five miles in thirty-six hours, and recrossed to the Salmon's north bank.

When General Howard reached the second ford, he realized his men were incapable of accomplishing the same feat without boats and began a reluctant withdrawal to White Bird Canyon and Grangeville. It is interesting to speculate what his thoughts were as he stared at the river, now crossed three times on his account by the Indians, without aid. Did he recall his ultimatum, which only a week earlier had forced the Wallowa band to risk their lives and property swimming the even more treacherous Snake? There was a certain justice in Howard's five-day trudge back to Grangeville, and the nettles of remorse would sting him frequently in the days ahead.

Now began a 3½-month, 1,500 mile odyessy for the Nez Perce, with battles at Cottonwood, the Clearwater, Big Hole, Camas Meadows, Canyon Creek, and finally the Bear Paw Mountains of northern Montana.

By then, the Indians were on the border of October and Canada; they paused, knowing Howard was more than "two sleeps back" and that refuge in Grandmother's Land lay only forty miles north at the "medicine line." Unknown to them, the General had telegraphed Colonel Miles to intercept them from Fort Keogh, Montana. Miles had assembled 383 soldiers, a Hotchkiss gun, a Napolean cannon and supply wagons, and rushed northwestward.

The Nez Perce bands had taken shelter in a crescent-shaped hollow along a creek. There were no trees, but ravines and coulees below the bluffs afforded some relief from the wind's cold edge. There Miles' thundering charge took them with a minute's warning and drove off the essential herd of horses. The last battle began.

Miles had planned to overrun the encampment with a three-pronged cavalry charge. He had, however, never experienced the accuracy of Nez Perce rifle fire and his baptism made him a believer. Captain Carter's charge on the edge of the village was repulsed with the loss of a third of his command. Captain Hale's K Troop was almost annihilated. When Lieutenant Eckerson rushed back to Miles and yelled, "I am the only damned man of the Seventh Cavalry who wears shoulder straps alive!", the Colonel switched from charge to siege tactics. Soldiers took shelter in depressions above the Indian camp.

Battlesmoke and snow swirled for five days. Indian messengers slipped away in darkness to seek help from Sitting Bull. In another of fate's capricious turns, the sign language of messengers was misinterpreted by the Sioux chief and aid was withheld initially in the belief that the battle was too far away. Then help was sent, but it did not arrive in time.

The fighting lasted six days. Again, Yellow Wolf left this graphic Indian version of the conflict:

But now, when I saw our remaining warriors gone, my heart grew choked and heavy. Yet the warriors and no-fighting men killed were not all. I look around.

Some were burying their dead.

A young warrior, wounded, lay on a buffalo robe dying without complaint. Children crying with cold. No fire. There could be no light. Everywhere the crying, the death wail.

My heart became fire. I joined the warriors digging rifle pits. All the rest of night we worked. Just before dawn, I went down among the shelter pits. I looked around. Children no longer crying. In deep shelter pits they were sleeping. Wrapped in a blanket, a still form lay on the buffalo robe. The young warrior was dead. I went back to my rifle pit, my blood hot for war. I felt not the cold.

Morning came, bringing the battle anew. Bullets from everywhere! A big gun throwing bursting shells. From rifle pits, warriors returned shot for shot. Wild and stormy, the cold wind was thick with snow. Air filled with smoke of powder. Flash of guns through it all. As the hidden sun traveled upward, the war did not weaken.

I felt the coming end. All for which we had suffered lost!

Thoughts came of the Wallowa where I grew up. Of tipis along the bending river. Of the blue, clear lake, wide meadows with horse and cattle herds. From the mountain forests, voices seemed calling. I felt as dreaming. Not my living self.

Howard and his troops arrived. Shelling from the cannon continued. Chief Toohoolhoolzote and Joseph's brother, Ollikot, were killed. Reluctantly, Joseph decided further resistance meant only death for the rest of his people. He decided to surrender his band. General Howard told Colonel Miles that he could have the honor of accepting Joseph's surrender.

Recently, Dr. Haruo Aoki, foremost linguist of the Nez Perce language, assembled scholarly and extremely persuasive evidence that indicates Chief Joseph's reputed "I will fight no more forever" surrender speech was never given – it was a literary concoction by Major Wood for *Harpers Magazine.*

In any event, after Chief Joseph, who could speak only for his own band, surrendered, seventy year-old Chief White Bird, who did not feel similarly bound, escaped during the night to Canada with 233 of his people.

The morning count showed 418 prisoners: 87 men, 184 women, 147 children. A large portion of the men were elderly and forty were wounded.

At the request of the Senate, General Sherman wrote a summary of this campaign which covered 1,500 miles, involving 2,000 soldiers in eighteen engagements at a cost of nearly $2 million. He concluded:

Thus has terminated one of the most extraordinary Indian wars of which there is any record. The Indians throughout displayed a courage and skill that elicited universal praise. They abstained from scalping; let captive women go free; did not commit indiscriminate murder of peaceful families, which is usual, and fought with almost scientific skill, using advance and rear guards, skirmish lines and field fortifications. Nevertheless, they would not settle down on lands set apart for them ample for their maintenance; and, when commanded by proper authority, they began resistance by murdering persons in no manner connected with their alleged grievances. They should never again be allowed to return to Oregon or to Lapwai.

When Chief Joseph surrendered his band, it was with the understanding that his people would be returned to the Idaho reservation in the spring. This belief was unfounded. They were taken to Fort Leavenworth to live along the bottomlands of the Missouri River. The Nez Perce never became acclimated to this area; nearly half suffered malaria, and twenty-one died.

They were moved again; this time to 7,000 acres of sand and sage in the Oklahoma Indian Territory. Nearly fifty of them died there. Relocated a third time within the Oklahoma reservation, the death rate continued to grow. Over a hundred children died, including Joseph's daughter.

It was scarcely their fault. In 1881, Indian Agent Thomas Jordan reported there were only 328 survivors. He said the death rate continued to be so high that "the tribe, unless something is done for them, will soon be extinct." He absolved the Nez Perce from carelessness in regard to health. "They are cleanly to a fault ... they keep their stock in good order, and are hard working, painstaking people."

607

Joseph was taken to Washington, where he pleaded the case of his people to President Hayes. Nothing changed. To his credit, General Miles, who eventually became Secretary of the Army, tried to correct the governmental injustices against the Nez Perce, but all his letters were ignored by Generals Sherman and Sheridan.

Chief White Bird died in Canada in 1882; his followers drifted back; some were killed and some were captured and deported to Oklahoma.

Public sympathy was aroused and by 1885 caused the return of Joseph and 150 of his people to the Yakima Indian's Colville Reservation in northeast Washington. Two hundred sixty-eight Nez Perce were sent to Lapwai.

Chief Joseph was allowed to visit his father's grave in the Wallowa Valley five years later. Now there were four towns in the valley. While there, he asked that a small tract be set aside for his people. The settlers replied that Joseph and his band would never be welcome.

Fifteen years later, in 1905, while sitting before his tipi on the Colville Reservation, Chief Joseph died. He is buried on that reservation.

For the traveler or history buff who wants to make a more thorough tour of the White Bird battlefield, there is a National Park Service folder available that coincides with marker posts which begin at Milepost 230 on the summit. The auto tour goes down the old White Bird grade and loops back to the parking area after covering 15.2 miles. It requires about an hour.

As Highway 95 drops from White Bird Hill toward Grangeville, **Tolo Lake** can be seen on the Camas Prairie, about four miles north. The forty-acre lake is named for a Nez Perce woman, who, in 1877, rode at night from the stockade at Slate Creek to the mining camp at Florence to request help for the homesteaders back at the "fort." A party of twenty-five miners returned to Slate Creek with her. Later, Tolo was the only Indian allowed an allotment off the reservation.

Settlers stocked the lake with carp in the 1880s; the state fish and game department planted bass there in the 1940s.

Tolo Lake is where the non-treaty Nez Perce were encamped, with scores of tipis and a thousand head of horses, when the events precipitating the War took place.

In more recent times, the lake served as an ice skating rink for persons on the prairie.

608

It is ten miles from White Bird summit to Grangeville, and entering the town from the highway is as easy as kicking off your shoes. **Grangeville** is the seat of Idaho County, largest county in the state: 5.4 million acres.

The area drew settlers and stockmen shortly after the Pierce gold rush. Aurora Shumway and John Crooks drove a herd of 3,000 cattle from The Dalles, Oregon, into the region in 1863. But after the mining boom faded, a considerable period passed before there were enough persons within twenty-five miles to get up a poker game.

In 1874 residents of the Camas Prairie persuaded Hart Spalding, son of a Lapwai missionary, to help them found Charity Grange No. 15 at nearby Mount Idaho.

The National Grange of the Patrons of Husbandry, a secret, fraternal society founded in 1867 in Washington, D.C. to advance the interests of farmers, had by 1874 grown to more than 20,000 local granges. There were 850,000 members. The Charity Grange No. 15 may have been the first grange in the Northwest.

Charity Grange Hall No. 15.

Five acres were needed as a site for the Grange Hall. Loyal Brown of Mount Idaho, who opposed the organization, refused to donate the land but John Crooks then offered a corner of his farm and the hall was built in 1876 for about $2,000. The road to it became the Main Street of a new town, which adopted its present name by one vote at the Grange's annual meeting (Mr. Brown changed his mind, but it was too late). Though national grange membership collapsed to 125,000 by 1880, Grangeville's hall remained the center of community events for nearly twenty years. (Enclosed by a stockade, it served as refuge and hospital during the Nez Perce War.)

Sister Afreda Elsensohn, noted Idaho County historian, has recorded the story that some of the city's streets were surveyed by a citizen who had a cruiser's compass and did not know enough to correct for the 23½-degree magnetic deviation; consequently those streets do not run true north and south.

Aaron Parker arrived in Grangeville in 1886, packing a hand press to begin publication of the *Idaho County Free Press.* Parker was a native of England and had been a sailor for six years before he jumped ship in San Francisco and swallowed the anchor in Idaho. The first copy of the paper was auctioned for $50, and the rest of the copies of the first issue brought $5 each as collector's items.

Before long, A. F. Parker established himself as Idaho's only active volcano. In addition, he was one of the signers of the state constitution and among the first Regents of the University of Idaho. One hundred years later, his paper continues to be published weekly.

In 1892 Grangeville began a campaign to move the county seat from Mount Idaho, but this movement did not succeed until 1902.

The town has suffered disasters usual and unusual: large fires in the business district in 1905 and 1910, and a flood down Dry Creek in 1921 that put three feet of water over Main Street and drowned the town druggist in his basement.

A large number of attractive frame residences in Grangeville date from the 1880s and 1890s. The community then had a population of

610

about 500; it prospered during the years of mining activity at Buffalo Hump and Thunder Mountain.

The most notable building in the city is at Main and State Sts., the Grangeville Savings and Trust. It was designed by James Nave, a Lewiston architect, and is the best example of his work outside

Grangeville, looking east, same period.

that city. The structure was erected in 1909, a year after the railroad reached Grangeville from Lewiston. The J. C. Penney store, within the building, has retained its pressed tin ceiling, as has the bookstore downstairs (around the corner); such ceilings have become a rarity in the state.

The First Security Bank, at Main and Meadow Sts., has an impressive antique grandfather clock on display in its lobby. The eleven foot-by-four foot clock was carved in 1822, and reached Grangeville, by way of Iowa and Washington, in the mid-1930s. It has been restored, and is exhibited through the courtesy of Walker's Jewelry.

The Alexander and Freidenrich (A & F) clothing store on Main St. has an unusual history. The store began its business in a room of the Charity Grange Hall and moved to a frame building in 1879. It is the second-oldest continuously operating mercantile firm in the state.

One other established business in town, located on the north side of Main St., merits mention: Ray Hole's Saddle Shop. Though at fifty years a mere newcomer compared to A & F, Ray Holes is the oldest saddle works under one name in the state and one of the most venerated in the West – a Ray Holes' saddle is as western as White boots or a Pendleton shirt.

Holes was born on his parents' homestead in Washington's Big Bend country in 1911; he moved to Idaho while still in his teens. Afflicted by polio when he was two years old, Ray turned to horsemanship the way some turn to athletics. He became an estimable wrangler.

As a youngster Ray Holes had worked after school in a shoe shop doing leather work by hand; now he began accepting ranch repairs; from boots to bridles – if it was leather, Ray could fix it. He made harnesses and halters, chaps and scabbards.

In 1933 a buckaroo brought him a saddle to repair; by the time he had finished, the leatherworker figured it would have been easier to have made a new saddle. He decided to build one. After botches and blunders, he got the job done. Then he went out on the Camas Prairie and round-up tested the result. The embryonic saddlemaker was fairly pleased with his product, but even more pleased when his boss ordered a copy.

When Ray returned to his ranch shop, he was fueled by the ambition to be a first-rate saddlemaker but he realized he was cinch-bound by a lack of knowledge about the craft. Rather than be snubbed up by this disability, he set out to meet old-time craftsmen who could show him what he needed to know. His quest took him through the Rockies and up into Canada.

By the time Holes returned to Grangeville in 1936, he was ready to build not only saddles, but a name for himself and his product. He had three standards: comfort, durability and beauty.

Ray made his own laminated tree forks and a modified extra-deep, semi-flat saddletree bar; he invented a type of free-swinging stirrup leathers that was welcomed by those who had to ride the Idaho backcountry. His celebrated flower-stamped designs gave the saddles a surface beauty that made them stand out like roses in a weed patch. A Ray Holes' saddle became a prized possession.

Ray finally retired in 1972 and his son Jerry took the reins. The shop's seven employees make about seventy custom riding saddles and 150 pack saddles yearly. The company gets requests from all the states, and from foreign countries as well. Buyers can expect a year's wait for their trophy. The saddlemaker's art still thrives on the Camas Prairie.

612

Driving north from Grangeville to Lewiston, one passes through an area geologically classified as the **Tri-State Uplands**. It is a gently undulating plateau of 3,000-5,000 feet, underlain by Columbia River basalt flows. The weight of the many lava flows, 2,000-3,000 feet thick, produced downwarping and further faulting of the crust. Lewiston valley occupies such a downwarped area. Craig Mountain, just south of Lewiston, is an arched or upwarped dome of Columbia River basalt, bordered by faults.

This rolling plain between Grangeville and Winchester is referred to as the **Camas Prairie** (not to be confused with the camas prairies of Fairfield and Weippe). It encompasses about 200,000 acres, bordered on the west by the Snake River and on the north and east by the Clearwater.

Much of the land is leased by farmers from the Nez Perce Indians. The area produces wheat, barley, peas, and livestock fodder. Wheat is cultivated twice a year; in the spring about 80,000 acres are seeded, leaving 20,000 in "green manure" set aside for fall planting. The average yield is fifty bushels an acre.

Barley is planted on 45,000 acres, and about one ton per acre is realized. The prairie has storage silos for about 7 million bushels of grain. Twenty thousand acres are kept in grass and alfalfa. Half that amount is planted in peas.

Fenn, seven miles northwest of Grangeville, was built in 1907 and named for two of the more remarkable achievers in the county: Stephen Fenn, and his son, Frank.

Stephen left Iowa in 1850 for the California Mother Lode, then joined the scramble to Florence Basin. He received a Presidential appointment as the first registrar for the Lewiston land office, was prosecuting attorney for Idaho County, representative in the territorial legislature for five sessions and territorial delegate to Congress from 1874 to 1878.

His son's career began at Whitman Academy in Walla Walla. He received an appointment from there to the U.S. Naval Academy, but was dismissed in 1872 for hazing a plebe.

Frank spent four years at sea, before returning to Idaho, where he taught at Fairfield, and married a sixteen-year-old girl who was one of his students.

During the Nez Perce War, Fenn became a First Lieutenant in the Idaho militia. He was at White Bird with Captain Perry and was also at the Cottonwood skirmish. Among other accomplishments, he was postmaster at Mount Idaho, lawyer in a Boise firm from 1890-1901, state chairman of the Republican Party, and a volunteer in the Spanish-American War, where he was promoted to the rank of Major.

US
95

613

In 1903 Major Fenn was appointed superintendent of all the National Forest Reserves in northern Idaho and of thirteen reserves in Montana. He served as inspector, supervisor and assistant district forester in various Idaho and Montana National Forests until 1920, when he returned to Kooskia to assist his son in the publication of a newspaper there. He died in 1927.

The town of Fenn, called Tharp until 1915, honors their name. The false-fronted Fenn store/postoffice was built in 1908.

A four-mile drive from the Fenn store leads to the townsite of **Denver**, a community that vanished when the Camas Prairie Railroad bypassed it to the west.

Drive north on the road in front of the Fenn store for 1.0 miles, turn east at the L for another 1.0 miles, then north at the T 1.5 miles, and east to the Y for 1.0 miles.

Denver was plotted on 640 acres in 1892 by a group organized as the Camas Prairie Land and Town Co. A large flour mill operated here until the 1950s; in 1898 its Prairie Rose flour was sold as far north as the Klondike. With the arrival of the railroad, buildings were torn down and moved to Fenn. Now the residents of the cemetery outnumber those of the former town.

One pathetic tale endures. The owners of the Denver drug store lost their child in a smallpox epidemic. For several years, the girl's mother refused to wash the store window where her daughter's fingerprints lingered.

Cottonwood: 12.7 miles from Grangeville. This town was named for the black cottonwood trees that grew along the creek, a species considered the largest poplar in North America. Mr. Allen opened a way station here in 1862, and many of the trees were cut to build the stage stop, Cottonwood House. The spot was at the junction of the Florence and Elk City-Warren roads.

The settlement was known as a cattle round-up center in the 1880s. It received its biggest boost in 1908, with the arrival of the railroad, but that same summer a disastrous fire began in a saloon and consumed the post office and fifty-three other buildings, causing a $250,000 loss. Only the brick German State Bank survived.

A state historical sign on the east side of the highway, one mile south of Cottonwood, indicates the nearby hill, and the location half a mile east, where the **Cottonwood skirmish** during the Nez Perce War of 1877 took place.

614

The Indians, after the White Bird battle, had recrossed the lower gorge of the Salmon River and moved up to the sage flat west of Cottonwood to camp for the night.

Captain Stephen Whipple, who had attacked Chief Looking Glass's village on the Clearwater July 1, had returned to Mount Idaho, where he received orders to proceed to an abandoned ranch at Cottonwood and await the arrival of Capt. Perry who would come from Fort Lapwai with supplies. Whipple's men arrived at the ranch and prepared a defensive position.

In the morning, the Captain sent a detachment of twelve men under Second Lieutenant Sevier Rains to scout the size and position of the Nez Perce forces. A small war party with Five Wounds and Rainbow surprised Rains' cavalrymen, shot six soldiers who were on horseback, then surrounded the others among some rocks on a hill and killed all seven.

When Whipple brought his command in search of the scouts, he was stunned to find they had been slain. He immediately retreated to the rifle pits at Cottonwood.

At dawn on the Fourth of July, Whipple's command moved toward Lapwai and met Capt. Perry eight miles down the road. By the time the two units arrived back at Cottonwood, Indians had begun to appear on the nearby hills and sporadic rifle fire was exchanged.

The next day, the Nez Perce had decided to move to the Clearwater. Since their route took them between Grangeville and Cottonwood, they dispatched fourteen warriors to screen their passage from Perry's position. The warriors' movement coincided with that of seventeen citizen volunteers from Mount Idaho who were crossing the prairie to aid Whipple at Cottonwood House. Two of the volunteers were killed as the group tried to charge past the Indian guards; the rest of them had to seek shelter in the rocks. Even after 100 years, Lew Wilmot's description of Captain Randall's death still reads like a paragraph from a movie script.

Capt. Winters sent his bugler down and asked me to get our boys and we would return to the Cottonwood House. I got up and called to the boy laying in the depression. When Curley said, 'Ben Evans is killed and Randall is wounded,' I ran down to where Randall was lying by his dead horse. He said, 'Lew, I am mortally wounded. I want some water.' I hollered to the soldiers and one brought his canteen. I lifted Randall's head and he said, 'Tell my wife –' I gave him a drink. This he threw up, and died without finishing what he wanted to say.

Though Perry could see the relief party's predicament, he refused to go to its aid. The Indians broke off the engagement when their own families had passed.

Captain Perry was later court-martialled for his inaction with regard to the "Brave Seventeen," as they came to be called, but was exonerated on grounds he acted to protect General Howard's supplies.

Cottonwood in 1898.

Cottonwood-Lewiston stage, c. 1898.

616

The **Idaho County Farm and Ranch Museum** is located at the Idaho County fairground in Cottonwood. The collection was assembled and housed by the Cottonwood Lions Club in 1967, and given to the people of the county.

The assembled implements include a replica of the original McCormick reaper, an 1887 stationary threshing machine, a 1916 Idaho Harvester, a Monitor Drill endgate seeder, and a 1920 McCormick Deering binder. There is also a photographic collection of early farming equipment on display.

The Idaho County fair is held during the last week of August. At that time, a 1912 Case steam tractor is fired up and rides are given to interested persons. The tractor, exhibited outside the museum, is fueled with straw and uses about four tanks of water a day.

A short, rewarding excursion can be made from Cottonwood. Take Front St. west out of town 2.5 miles to **St. Gertrude's Convent and the museum of the Benedictine Sisters**.

In 1903 a Cottonwood resident approached Bishop Glorieux, of Boise, with an inquiry about securing Benedictine priests from Conception Abbey in Missouri to staff the parishes of Camas Prairie. In response to a letter, the abbot made a trip to look over the situation. Lack of a railroad and the abundance of mud made him advise against establishing a Motherhouse for Benedictine Sisters, but the Benedictine Fathers arrived the following year to begin St. Michael's Priory about two miles northwest of present St. Gertrude's.

Later, the same Cottonwood citizen offered the Benedictine Sisters in Washington 100 acres if they would move to Camas Prairie. As the Sisters' community had outgrown its convent and was unable to obtain additional land there, the Superior decided in 1907 to move the community to the Cottonwood area.

The first convent and chapel were wooden, frame buildings. Construction of the large, blue porphyry stone convent and chapel began in 1919. The stone was cut locally and hauled by wagon, and nuns provided much of the labor. With its twin ninety-seven foot towers, the building cost $178,000 when completed in 1925.

The interior of the chapel, which can be viewed by visitors, has been called "the most elaborately appointed in Idaho." The ornately carved altar, along with the pillars and baldachin, was imported from Germany.

The Benedictine nuns trace their order to a twelfth century community in Switzerland. The first members to immigrate to the U.S. arrived in Oregon in 1882. The Benedictine Fathers withdrew

617

from Cottonwood in 1925; the Sisters acquired their farmland and buildings, and two years later opened a boarding and day school at St. Gertrude's. The grades and high school were included, but before long the boy's boarding facility and the grade school were discontinued.

The high school, known as St. Gertrude's Academy, was housed in a new, brick building in 1954; enrollment reached 304 students. At that time, the Sisters also staffed thirteen grammar schools in Idaho. In 1968 financial difficulties began to surface. In 1970, after forty-four years of service, St. Gertrude's Academy closed. All of the district's schools were combined as Prairie High School, and the school district purchased St. Gertrude's Academy.

St. Gertrude's chapel.

The community at St. Gertrude's convent now exceeds 100 nuns; they staff four schools and operate St. Mary's Hospital in Cottonwood and St. Benedict's Hospital in Jerome.

A fascinating museum of Idaho County lore is located next to the convent and will be opened for visitors on request at any reasonable hour. The museum began in 1931 under the inspiration and impetus of Sister M. Alfreda Elsensohn, the historian. In 1980 the collection was placed in new quarters.

The assemblage includes Brevariums from the 1600s, schoolbooks from the 1880s, the Joseph Honecker collection of bird books, Nez Perce artifacts, three cases of personal effects that belonged to Polly Bemis, the Chinese lady of Salmon River,

618

embroidered "cutwork" dresses, a trove of salt and pepper shakers, and three inventive items so wondrous that they must not be overlooked: a 1900 vacuum rug cleaner, a 1927 razor blade sharpener, and a baby bottle for twins – ask to see these pieces.

Keuterville is a 3.5 mile drive, by paved road, west of St. Gertrude's. There is a display of antique farm equipment on the left side of the road along the way, for those who might be interested.

Keuterville is the third oldest settlement on Camas Prairie; the first settlers, who were Catholics, came from Kansas in 1883. They immediately began a fund drive for a church.

One of the homesteaders placed an advertisement, in a German newspaper in St. Louis, that praised the new Catholic settlement; this publicity attracted Henry Kuther to the village. Kuther became the area's mail carrier and submitted an application to the Postal Department to establish "Kutherville" because he had no sons and feared his name would die. The department botched the name to Keuterville, but Henry fathered two boys, and thus tripled his prospects for immortality.

The first Catholic church here was roofed in 1887 and the parish was called St. Peter's. A more permanent structure, with an eighty-two-foot bell tower, was completed ten years later. Some of the faithful walked seven miles to attend services because buggies were uncommon, and Sunday was a day of rest for the horses.

The Keuterville church was destroyed by fire in 1911, but the present church replaced it by the fall of that year. For at least five years, the sermons and hymns here were in German. The bishop from Boise changed the name of the parish to Holy Cross.

Cottonwood Butte (5,732 feet) can be seen from the front steps of the church.

Ferdinand is eight miles north of Cottonwood, on U.S. 95. The town owes its survival to an engrossing scuffle.

When the Nez Perce reservation was opened to settlement in 1895, F. M. Bieker came from the area of Keuterville to establish a claim. He was not happy with his selected parcel because it lacked water, but the next day he found a map of the reservation that someone had dropped on the road; armed with it and a pocket compass, he located a better site adjacent to what is now Ferdinand. He also established claims for ten other settlers. The cost of their land was $3.75 an acre. Bieker then set up a store and had the pioneers sign a petition for a post office which was named Ferdinand, after his mother's town in southern Indiana.

95

When the Camas Prairie Railroad began building its line, Ferdinand found itself on the west side of the route. John P. Vollmer, Lewiston millionaire-banker, and a director of the Northern Pacific, used his advance information about the route to acquire land where the depots would be located. He expected to profit by the sale of town lots.

Bieker discovered Vollmer planned a town called Steunenberg one-quarter mile east of Ferdinand and the tracks. He wrote Vollmer with an offer to sell the forty acres on which Ferdinand was located if he would put the new village on the west side of the railroad. Vollmer, who would not give a duck a drink though he owned the pond, did not reply. So Bieker began selling lots to businessmen.

The surveyor arrived to plat Steunenberg, but he soon realized what would happen to the citizens of Ferdinand if he proceeded. He refused to do Vollmer's dirty work; the banker fired him. Bieker hired the surveyor to cross the tracks and plat Ferdinand instead.

Vollmer placed a notice in the *Lewiston Tribune* that the depot at Ferdinand would be located two miles farther south. Four Ferdinand businessmen then went to Vollmer and offered to move their buildings and interests to Steunenberg if he would give them free lots; the rest of the residents decided to hang and rattle.

Through political machinations that can now only be the subject of speculation, the Postal Department ordered an office opened at Steunenberg, and closed the one to the north, at Ilo, which had ten times the population. A year later the Steunenberg post office closed for lack of business.

The hotel and saloon in Vollmer's would-be town burned. He built a new store and a bank. The people across the tracks would not patronize either one. Finally, John Vollmer sold his land, and the bank and store moved west of the tracks to Ferdinand. Said Bieker:

Thus ended the townsite strife at Ferdinand and with it all hard feelings. No one had been seriously hurt although mistakes in plenty had been made on both sides. It is the competitive system, however far from the ideal it may be.

Two miles north of Ferdinand, Highway 95 passes beneath an impressive wooden trestle, the first of two that span the road between this point and Lewiston. (A high, steel trestle can be seen west of the highway, four miles north of Ferdinand.) The track supported by these bridges is part of 183 miles of line in the Camas Prairie-Lewiston vicinity jointly owned by the Burlington Northern and Union Pacific. Its traffic load on the prairie is lumber and grain.

620

The line, whose trestles can be glimpsed on the slopes of Lawyers Canyon, and whose rails can be clearly seen on the north, and then east side of the highway from Culdesac to Spalding, is known as the **Camas Prairie Railroad**, and its origin involved unusual circumstances. During the 1890s and early 1900s, Union Pacific and Northern Pacific had competed for the first rail line to Lewiston. Northern Pacific won in 1899, but by the time Union Pacific arrived in 1908, both companies were considering eastern connections through the Clearwater region, both had surveyors in the field, and both appropriated routes up the Clearwater River. Their moves and counter-moves resembled a chess game. E. H. Harriman of the Union Pacific arranged a truce in the summer, 1899, with the hope that an agreement might be reached between the companies concerning use of the area.

Termination of rail building at Culdesac in 1900 created great frustration on the part of Camas Prairie residents, who had looked forward to an easier method of marketing their crops. During the hiatus discontent was sufficient that Colonel Judson Spofford, president of Lewiston and Southeastern Electric, and Walter Hill, an engineer, surveyed a line from Lewiston to Grangeville by way of Lake Waha and Cottonwood. They planned an electric railroad and sold $400,000 worth of stock to settlers, who gave promissory notes to be voided if the rail was not built. This action apparently galvanized the N.P. and U.P.

The presidents of the two companies met on the Camas Prairie, spent the day visiting sites together, and agreed to joint construction in order to eliminate the Lewiston and Southeastern Electric. Construction resumed in 1906.

The Clearwater Shortline, a Northern Pacific subsidiary, headed the effort, and it was an expensive job because trestles, tunnels and bridges were required. Grading was completed in December, 1907, and the first work train reached Grangeville a year later.

There was not enough business for two railroads. It was another case of "pigs get fat and hogs get butchered." The Camas Prairie Railroad, a jointly-owned operating company was the answer. This mutual arrangement avoided unnecessary expense, prevented duplication of facilities and unified operations.

When the first passenger train arrived in Grangeville, December 8, 1908, 300 people were on hand to greet it, even though it steamed in past midnight.

In 1909 the Camas Prairie assumed control of the line from Riparia, Washington, to Grangeville. Under a cooperative agreement with Clearwater Timber Co. (PFI), the U.P. and N.P. built a rail line

621

from Orofino to Headquarters in 1925-1927, and it was placed under the Camas Prairie management, as was the Orofino-Stites line, acquired in 1928. The small railroad prospered, hauling loads of fruit, grain and lumber. It operated for forty years without a fatal accident, then a rear-end collision in 1951 killed three people.

By the late 1960s logs represented 50 percent of the freight moved. In the 1970-1980 period, with the opening of the Port of Lewiston, grain shipments were substantially eroded. Combined charges for shipping agricultural products by truck-barge were lower than corresponding rail rates. Another factor that hurt was the increasing tendency of farmers to ship directly from the field in order to avoid handling and elevator storage charges. Time will reveal whether the Camas Prairie line can survive.

Between Ferdinand and Craigmont, U.S. Highway 95 winds down into **Lawyers Canyon**; it is named for a Nez Perce chief, and not for those skilled in the circumvention of the law.

"Lawyer" was the name given Hallalhotsoot by the mountain men because of his argumentative disposition and general shrewdness. Lawyer was born about 1796, in the vicinity of Kamiah on the southern end of Lawyer Creek. The son of a Flathead mother and Nez Perce father, he spoke the language of both. Lawyer became chief of the treaty faction of the Nez Perce, a position he held from 1848-1872.

Hallalhotsoot, or Lawyer, was the first chief to sign the treaty of 1863 that reduced the boundaries of the Nez Perce reservation and excluded Chief Joseph's lands in the Wallowa Valley. Because of his actions, he is regarded by some Indians as a "Red Judas." He did make a trip to Washington, D.C. in 1868 to plead for fulfillment of government obligations under the 1863 agreement; while there, he met General U. S. Grant and was photographed by Matthew Brady.

Lawyer died at his home at Kamiah in 1876 and is buried in the Presbyterian cemetery there.

The canyon has served as a location for two movies: the first film, made in 1919, was *Told In the Hills,* starring Monte Blue, Ann Little and Stan Warwick; Nez Perce were given the Indian roles; the second picture, which made extensive use of the trestles, was a western called *Breakheart Pass.*

Highway 95 travels through **Craigmont** 8.5 miles north of Ferdinand. The community is quiet as an angel's wing now, but at one time it was caught between two towns that spent most of their time throwing spitballs at each other.

Chicago, Idaho, was born in 1898, one mile west of later Craigmont. It took the homesteaders four years to realize that the U.S. Postal Department was incapable of distinguishing between two like-named towns in the same country; they re-christened their town Ilo, honoring a local merchant's daughter.

After a disastrous fire in 1904, Ilo met its third crisis in devious John Vollmer, who bypassed the settlement with the Camas Prairie Railroad, a mile to the east, in order to start his own town, called, predictably enough, Vollmer. Vollmer was platted on the northeast side of the tracks.

The community of Ilo responded by moving all of its businesses and residences to the southwest side of the tracks from 1907 to 1909. The two towns were divided by the railroad's "iron curtain," and the feud that followed was hotter than a hay harvest.

The post office, housed in a brick building, had to be located on a neutral flat between the two communities. The train often stopped behind a string of box cars to shield the passengers from a view of Ilo. A salesman seen writing orders in one town had no chance of doing business in the other. In 1911, Nezperce, a town half the size of Vollmer and Ilo, won the election for the seat of Lewis County because the two rivals could not stop bickering long enough to affect the vote.

Finally, in 1920, after consolidation of the school districts, an issue which had been fought to the State Supreme Court by the citizens of Ilo, the two towns agreed on a merger. The name they chose honors Colonel William Craig, Idaho's first permanent white settler.

At a June picnic the merger was celebrated with a mock wedding: the postmaster-"minister" married Mr. Volmer to Miss Ilo, who was wrapped in red, white and blue.

The town of **Winchester** is six miles west of Craigmont and two miles off U.S. 95 from a marked exit. The highway, which used to go through the town, was shifted in 1920. The community was named at a citizens' meeting called in 1900 to establish a school district. While considering the possibilities, one fellow looked at the rifles stacked by the door and suggested they use the name of the most popular make. (A model of a Winchester big enough to slay Bunyan's blue ox is now suspended across Nez Perce Ave.)

One half mile outside town is **Winchester Lake State Park**, established in 1969 on 400 acres. The lake was created in 1909-1910 by Craig Mountain Lumber Co. The company built a sawmill near Lapwai Creek and platted the site of Winchester as a town for its employees. Needing a mill pond for its yellow pine logs, Craig Lumber dammed Lapwai Creek forming Lapwai Lake over Luke's meadows. By 1963 the mature timber had been cut and the mill was closed.

The Idaho Department of Fish and Game acquired the lake area; in 1969 the Department of Parks and Recreation assumed management and developed the site as a year-round park.

Rainbow trout are planted annually and fishermen are welcome, but power boats are not.

The lumber company had a six-mile railroad from Winchester that connected with the Camas Prairie line. The train ran twice daily with passengers and freight.

The town's hospital, hotels, school and business district burned in a series of fires from 1927-1935.

Craig Mountain Lumber Co. loading logs at Winchester.

Culdesac (nine miles north) in French means "bottom of the bag." The name was suggested by the president of the Northern Pacific, who remarked while inspecting the route of the future Camas Prairie Railroad, "This is indeed a cul de sac." (He was indeed an eastern gent.)

In 1900, at the time railroad construction was delayed, there were two towns here. One bore the name of the railroad's president, Mellen, and the other was Magnolia. The autocratic Postal Department rejected Cul-de-Sac – then reversed itself in the face of a citizens' petition and accepted the phrase written as one word. Mellen and Magnolia were conjoined in the bottom of the bag.

A native of Culdesac is responsible for the fact that there is no channel one on our television sets. Bob Olin, born in Culdesac in 1907, earned a degree in electrical engineering at the University of Idaho in 1930 and joined Potlatch Forests, Inc., where he eventually became director of telecommunications.

As a mechanical engineer in the woods, Bob perceived that the inability to communicate with a mechanic or parts warehouse at headquarters made equipment breakdowns expensive. He also realized, in the mid-1940s, that mobile radios such as those developed by the military were the solution.

To recruit support from members of the forest industry, Olin gave a demonstration at the 1947 Intermountain Logging Conference in Spokane, using two taxis with mobile radios outside the auditorium and a transmitter-receiver on the stage. The audience was convinced.

A committee was formed which drafted a petition to the FCC requesting that the channel one television frequency be deleted and reassigned to industrial use. After federal hearings in Washington, D.C., the petition was granted.

By 1949, 200 v.h.f. radio channels had been assigned to private industry, including ten clear and ten shared-use channels utilized by

Culdesac to Grangeville stage, 1906.

logging companies across the nation – and no program appears on channel one.

Four miles west of Culdesac, on U.S. 95, turn south on the paved road at **Jacques Spur**. Drive seventy-five yards, then stop on the left side of the road. Walk fifty feet up to the overgrown cemetery; it can be entered through a gap in the wire fence. On the far side of this hidden graveyard is a white stone with the words: Wm. Craig, Lt. Col., 2 Wash. Terr. Vols., Oct. 16, 1869/his wife Pah-Tis-Sah, Isabell Craig, May 8, 1886. This is the grave of a mountain man whose life is embedded in Idaho history like a bullet in a tree. William Craig has suffered undeserved anonymity, but there is space here to do little more than fire a salute.

Craig was a mountain man when the west was, in A. B. Guthrie's phrase, "wide as forever with the sky flung across." His affidavit, filed in 1855 as a settler on unsurveyed lands on Lapwai Creek, revealed he was born in (West) Virginia in 1809 and first came to the Oregon country in 1829.

The young man ran away from home to join the fur trade in St. Louis, perhaps as early as 1825. He worked for Smith, Jackson and Sublette until they sold out to the Rocky Mountain Fur Company. His closest pards were Joe Meek and Robert Newell, so he must have had a sense of humor, and he numbered Osborne Russell, Kit Carson, Jim Clyman and Warren Ferris among his friends.

When Jedediah Smith got into a scrimmage with the Blackfeet near Yellowstone, Craig was there, and he was at the Battle of Pierre's Hole, and with Joe Walker when they fought the Paiutes on the lower Humboldt. Craig lifted fur in the Three Forks country, the country of the Crows, on the Bear River, Salmon River and the headwaters of the Snake.

He joined Captain Bonneville's outfit for the spring hunt in 1833; he was at the Green River rendezvous and went to California with Walker's brigade. For two years he may have trapped on the headwaters of the Missouri. In 1836 he settled in Brown's Hole, by the Gates of Lodore on the Green River, with his friends, Meek and Newell. The men fashioned an impromptu log-mud shelter they called "Fort Davey Crockett." For almost three years they operated out of this remote basin.

By 1839 the fur trade was a gone beaver. Craig and his cronies attended the last Green River rendezvous the next summer. There he met the missionary party of Rev. Harvey Clark and agreed to escort it to Fort Hall, in what is now southern Idaho. From the fort, Newell, Meek and Craig decided to float their stick back to the Oregon country. An era was ending – wagons plodded west, and the prairie was going grass-side-under behind them.

Craig had married a Nez Perce woman, Isabell, at the 1838 rendezvous. The two of them went to Lapwai, where her father, Chief James, resided, and there they cultivated the first farm in Idaho.

626

Henry Harmon Spalding, the Presbyterian minister, was already entrenched on the banks of the Clearwater, proselytizing the Nez Perce, and he resented Craig's intrusion. He referred to the trapper as "a selfish, lawless, self-ruined scape goat from the State." The mountain man, on his part, had little use for the missionary's narrow-minded despotism. After the Whitman massacre, Craig did, however, save the lives of the Spalding family.

Col. William Craig.

The Indians held Craig in high esteem; he was welcome on their land. In 1848 he was appointed Indian Agent at Lapwai, and a short while later Governor Stevens made him a Lieutenant Colonel of

Washington Territory. He served the Governor as a valuable interpreter and negotiator with the Indians.

Craig moved his family to Fort Walla Walla for a time, where he was made first postmaster and Indian Agent for the Cayuse in 1859. But when Elias Pierce discovered gold on the Nez Perce reservation in 1860, the Indian Agent returned to his farm on Sweetwater Creek.

He established a ferry across the Clearwater, which proved to be a lucrative business, but that must have been tame doings for the likes of Craig. He died of a stroke in 1869, survived by his wife, a son and three daughters.

Bill Craig never blew his own horn, he was self-effacing and laconic; consequently he has been given little more than a marginal note in the history of the fur trade.

Craig Mountains and the town of Craigmont commemorate this mountain man's endeavors.

Proceed 3.3 miles farther down this road to **St. Joseph's Mission**, which is perched on the edge of Mission Creek, on the left, at the end of the pavement. This carefully maintained house of worship was built in 1874 at the direction of Fr. Joseph Cataldo (see Cataldo Mission) as the first Catholic mission for the Nez Perce.

Fr. Cataldo had been sent to teach at a small government school at Fort Lapwai but left to establish a church in Lewiston for a white congregation because questions were raised concerning the separation of church and state.

He eventually returned when Chief Slickpoo donated land for the mission. Whites, Nez Perce and Coeur d'Alene Indians, and even some Chinese miners made contributions to the building fund. The Jesuit Brothers planted over fifty fruit trees on the grounds, and Indians who comprised the village of Slickpoo lived in cabins across the road from the church.

The Sisters of St. Joseph began an orphanage-school in 1902, and a novitiate for nuns two years later. The school, with two dormitories, classrooms and cafeteria, operated for sixty-six years. Captain Lloyd Bucher of the hapless S.S. *Pueblo* attended this school (both his natural and adoptive parents had died).

The school was demolished by the new landowner in 1970. Mr. and Mrs. John Pfeifer bought twelve acres, along with the church, which had become dilapidated, in 1960 and restored the structure. Though private property, it is included within the Nez Perce Historical Park and is open to the public during posted hours.

Mass is still celebrated at St. Joseph's on the last Sunday in May. (From this point, return to Highway 95.)

The location of **Fort Lapwai** is one mile south of present Lapwai, a block west of the highway. Fort Lapwai was established in July, 1862, to prevent white encroachment on the Nez Perce reservation, and later, to protect the settlers as well. John Silcott was employed by the government to build a sawmill. Sewell Truax and his volunteer troops occupied the fort. In 1864 President Lincoln issued the proclamation required to establish a military reservation for the post.

Fort Lapwai was vacated for a year, then in 1866 it was garrisoned by Army regulars. The post and garrison were active during the Nez Perce War; it was from this spot that Captain David Perry, with F & H Companies, First Cavalry, was dispatched by General Howard for Mount Idaho and then White Bird. In 1884 the fort was abandoned.

The parade ground is still visible, but the north end of the site is now occupied by the North Idaho Agency of the Bureau of Indian Affairs, which moved here in 1904 from Spalding. It is the agency for the Nez Perce, Coeur d'Alene and Kutenai tribes. One building survives from 1866, quarters from Officers' Row. It is situated on the southwest side of the fort grounds. The structure had an open fireplace in each room.

Fort Lapwai.

Lapwai is one mile north of the fort, just west of U.S. 95. Most of the Indians here are descendants of the Christian Nez Perce treaty bands. There are about 2,000 members on the Nez Perce tribal roll, and the reservation's Indian population numbers about 1,600. (The tribal office is located in Lapwai.)

Lapwai was the name given the first mission among the Nez
Perce in 1836 by Henry Spalding. It is said to be the Nez Perce word
for butterfly: "lap lap," coupled with the suffix for water, "wai" –
the name suggested to the Indians by the quantities of butterflies
that gathered about Spalding's millpond.

The Nez Perce, or "Nimapu" as they call themselves, once lived
in fifty or so small, extended-family villages along the many streams
that sculpt their aboriginal territory. They hunted elk, deer,
mountain sheep and bear, and obtained trout and salmon from the
Snake, Salmon and Clearwater Rivers. The basic root-staple was
camas, but bitterroot, kouse, huckleberries, serviceberries,
chokecherries, pine nuts and black moss were also gathered.

The Nez Perce acquired horses in about 1730, discovered
selective breeding and developed the largest herds found in the
Great Basin, Plateau, or Northwest Coast culture areas. They were
renowned horsemen, traveling annually to the Great Plains for
buffalo.

The tribe wove cornhusk bags; their mountain sheep horn bows
were the envy of other western tribes, and in recent times they
produced admirable bead work.

Physically, the Nimapu were above average height and had
features of the finest Indian type. In temperament they were
courageous, trustworthy and hospitable.

Their reservation, which extends from Kooskia to Spalding, and
from Ferdinand to Lenore, now encompasses only 88,000 acres; it
once included about 10,000 square miles. The policy responsible for
this attrition has been covered in well-wrought histories. It suffices
to say here that when the treaties, more honored in the breach than
in the observance, were ratified and the Dawes Act passed, the Nez
Perce reservation was forcibly reduced.

When John Collier became head of the Bureau of Indian Affairs
under President Franklin Roosevelt, he proposed that the Bureau
"make a strong effort to rebuild the old tribal organizations" in all
tribes that were interested in such a plan. Congress passed the
legislation, and three-quarters of the Indian tribes, including the Nez
Perce, voted to set up a system of tribal government that would
hold all tribal funds and lands as common property.

In 1946 Congress passed the Indian Claims Commission Act to
hear Indian appeals against the federal government. The Nez Perce
retained legal counsel to prepare and present their claims. Those
claims alleged unconscionable consideration for lands ceded under
the 1863 treaty, trespass and mineral severance on the 1855 treaty
reservation, and a request for the value of the reduced reservation

ceded to the government in 1893. Judgments in the amount of $7,882,000 were awarded. The descendants of Chief Joseph's Wallowa band, now on the Colville (Wash.) reservation, received $800,000 for the lands taken in 1863. (Washington, D.C. lawyers took $776,000 in fees from these awards.)

Land parcels awarded two Nez Perce women under the Allotment Act of 1887 formed the major portion of the town of Lapwai, north of the fort. By 1895 a store was doing business on Main St., and more businesses had opened by the time plats were filed in 1907. The town was not incorporated, however, until 1911.

Two buildings in Lapwai are worth historical appraisal. One is the Lapwai Valley Presbyterian Church, designed by Lewiston's best architect, James Nave, under a contract granted by the Indian agent. The church is located on the northeast corner of Locust and First St. East. It was built in 1909 for $2,600. Thirty Nez Perce were converted the week the church was dedicated. Presbyterian services are still held here.

The other building is that of the First Lapwai Bank, one block west of Main St. at First St. West. The structure has been converted to a residence, and its exterior is partially re-sided, but it still carries historical interest. The old bank is one of the more unusual commercial buildings in Idaho.

At the turn of the century, the Nez Perce began to accumulate income from timber sales and rental of reservation farmland. The Indians were wary of Caucasian banks after most of their funds (perhaps $80,000) had been lost in the 1897 failure of Browne's Moscow National Bank. It was believed that Nez Perce money was being buried, and it was thought that an Indian bank might overcome this distrust.

Three Nez Perce and two white businessmen from Lapwai incorporated the bank in 1909 with $10,000 in capital, most of it provided by the Nez Perce stockholders, making the enterprise "the first institution of the kind ever organized in the U.S."

Corbett Lawyer, grandson of Chief Lawyer, was the wheelhorse of the Nez Perce owners. Corbett had attended Carlisle in Pennsylvania, and Dickenson Teacher's College, before returning to Lapwai to work for the Bureau of Indian Affairs.

The bank was erected with Indian labor and had a shingled tipi on the front-facing roof. (The tipi burned in 1930.) The institution opened in summer, 1909, with a white president, cashier and teller. It had $32,000 in deposits at the end of the second year, and $50,000 in resources in 1918.

The enterprise was voluntarily liquidated in 1927; it is reported that the last cashier disappeared with the assets.

First Lapwai Bank.

Early view of Lapwai (note tipis, left center).

Spalding, in the **Nez Perce National Historic Park**, is five miles north of Lapwai.

A delegation of three Nez Perce and a Flathead Indian went to St. Louis in 1831 to ask their "Red Hair" friend, William Clark, who was then Superintendent of Indian Affairs, for help in obtaining information about the white man's books and religion: "Big Medicine." Unfortunately, no one spoke Nez Perce in St. Louis. Clark was friendly and did what he could to summarize the story of the Bible. Two of the Nez Perce died while they were in the city, another died en route home and the Flathead never returned to the

632

Clearwater country. But the tale of the Noble Savage in search of the Word of the Lord filtered east. In 1834, zealots, like cheat grass, invaded Oregon Territory, which included Idaho. It has been remarked that "a difference of opinion is what makes horse races and missionaries," and the missionaries who arrived in the Nez Perce country differed so often among themselves that they resembled spiritual jockeys more intent on triumphing over one another than over the heathen. The banks of the Clearwater became the finish line, and the settlement of Spalding was the winner's circle.

Henry and Eliza Spalding were Presbyterian missionaries who came west with Marcus and Narcissa Whitman. The couples were incompatible, so they agreed on a division of the vineyard. While the Whitmans opened their mission at Waiilatpu, the Spaldings were escorted up the Clearwater from Fort Walla Walla by a band of Nez Perce leading twenty-five pack horses and some livestock. The year was 1836 and Henry Spalding was thirty-three years old.

The Spaldings built a two-room eighteen-by-twenty-four-foot mission house at the base of Thunder Hill on Lapwai Creek, two miles from the Clearwater. The natives supplied the couple with fish and venison until crops could be planted in the spring.

Spalding's middle name was Harmon, and no one ever wondered why it was not Harmony. To his credit, he was an indefatigible worker, and with help he built the first sawmill and grist mill, planted the first orchard, and introduced the first printing press to Idaho. His daughter was the first white child born in the state. But to his discredit, Henry Spalding was cantankerous, argumentative, and dyspeptic. He quarreled with many of the Indians and all of the non-Indians.

A school was established, and Eliza carried the burden of instruction which affected about 100 students. In the spring of 1838 the Spaldings moved down to the south bank of the Clearwater and constructed a new two-story mission/house that had four rooms on each floor and a fireplace at each end. Other buildings were gradually added.

Missionaries were sent to reinforce Spalding's efforts, but none could tolerate the bearish man for long. The mission board issued an order recalling him, then rescinded the decision. But after the Whitman massacre (fourteen victims) in November, 1847, the Spaldings were ordered to Walla Walla by the federal government. The mission was closed.

The Spaldings then settled in Oregon. Eliza died and Henry remarried. He finally received permission, in 1863, to return to

Lapwai as a teacher, where during his absence a fort had been constructed. He quarreled with Whitman's son and the Indian agent and within two years he was again dismissed.

It was 1871 before Spalding was able to persuade the mission board to reappoint him. He was now seventy. Henry preached, baptized – and squabbled. Finally, under pressure from the government, the presbytery ordered Spalding to move to Kamiah, where a second church was under construction. He went, but not without bitterness. Henry Spalding died at Lapwai in 1874 and is buried in the graveyard near the historical park headquarters, alongside his first wife, whose body was moved from Oregon in 1913.

Within the National Historical Park are several buildings and a museum worth a visit. The cemetery is down on the flat, not far from the river. Spalding's second house site is east of the cemetery about forty yards, surrounded by an iron fence. Roses grow on the twin piles of chimney rubble. A short distance southeast of the ruins is an Indian Agency building that dates from 1861-1862. The exterior has been restored. Beneath the road ramp a few yards away, is the Poor Coyote cabin, which belonged to an Indian couple and is representative of transitional housing.

The visitor can also see the Lewis and Margaret Watson store, operated from 1911 to 1964; generally, at least half of the Watson's customers were Nez Perce. The family lived in rooms adjoining the store. The interior is undoubtedly the finest period-store display in the state.

Across the road from the store is the Spalding Presbyterian church, built in the mid-1880s. For some time after Spalding's death, it had only Nez Perce pastors. The church is still used for religious services.

Park headquarters are located on the hill, in the new museum, where there are informative displays, and slide shows given in an auditorium. This museum contains one of the better exhibits of Nez Perce artifacts in the country. Summer hours are 8:00 A.M. - 6:00 P.M. and winter hours are 8:00 A.M. - 4:30 P.M..

At the bridge just northwest of Spalding, U.S. 95 merges temporarily with U.S. 12. The roads separate at the foot of Lewiston Hill.

Lewiston Hill was an impediment to commercial transportation between the river city and Moscow for many years. With the demand for better roads in the early 1900s, Lewiston businessmen sought better access to the Palouse hills. In 1914, E. M.

634

Booth, a Nez Perce County engineer, surveyed a new hill route and reported that the 9.5 mile roadbed could be built within a 4 percent grade for $50,000.

When Booth became the state highway engineer, he advanced and supported the Lewiston Hill project. C. C. Van Arsdol, an engineer who had overcome difficult railroad and irrigation routes, was retained for the job. In 1917 the road that writhed through sixty-four curves in a 2,000-foot climb was opened to traffic. Construction costs totaled $100,000.

In July, 1975, work began on the present grade. It opened in the spring, 1979; the cost, including right-of-way, was $22 million.

Near the summit, there is a left-turn lane where it is possible to exit from the highway onto Vista Road and drive 0.5 miles to a remarkable viewpoint above Lewiston and the Snake and Clearwater Rivers. There are two memorial tablets on the edge of Vista Rd.: one for the engineer, C. C. Van Arsdol; the other for a pioneer commercial pilot, Bert Zimmerly, who came to Lewiston in 1934 and organized the first airline in Idaho. He flew many errands of mercy, before being killed in a plane crash near Pullman, Washington.

Old Lewiston grade.

From the summit of Lewiston Hill, Highway 95 travels north through the **Palouse hill country** toward Moscow. The Palouse hills are the most productive soft white wheat area in the world. As farming became mechanized here, horses and mules were used with

635

multiple-hitches on the steep slopes. The larger teams used for combine harvesting consisted of sixteen to forty-four horses. The wheat farmers became dexterous teamsters. They eventually used multiple-hitch teams for plowing, harrowing and seed-drilling, as well. Visitors from farming areas in other parts of the country were incredulous when they witnessed the harvest feats performed on the Palouse with extended teams.

Harvest crew on the Palouse.

Multiple-hitch harvest team.

Headers (a modification of the reaper that cut the grain heads so they could be delivered to a thresher) were designed to be pushed by multiple teams. In this way, the horses were prevented from trampling the uncut grain on the hillsides. Push binders and combines were also developed – about one machine for every section (640 acres).

Horseless farming began in the region during the 1930s. Skeleton wheel tractors and Caterpillar tractors pensioned the horses and mules. At present, a man on a tractor can simultaneously seed and

636

fertilize 300 acres in a ten-hour day; thirty-six horses attempting the same job in the same time might cover 140 acres.

With the widespread application of commercial fertilizers and herbicides, beginning in the 1960s, yields have increased from forty bushels an acre, to eighty. The highly productive Gaines semi-dwarf strains of wheat have offset topsoil losses caused by soil pulverization. But agricultural technology cannot continue to outpace soil erosion, and soil economists believe the region faces a decline in productivity.

Genesee is 18.1 miles north of Lewiston and 1.4 miles east of U.S. 95. The area was settled by homesteaders, from 1879-1890, who chose the area for the richness of its soil.

The merchant-banker, John Vollmer, related how the town got its name when he and Mr. Stone went for a ride during the summer, 1870.

... *as we drove along, we passed down Cow Creek and through a sequestered little valley still in its natural state. Stone exclaimed, 'This reminds me of my old home, the Genesee Valley in New York state.' The suggestion was made that we so name it and from that time on it bore that name. When (Alonzo) Leland started his newspaper he always referred to this valley by the name of Genesee and so it became universally known by that appellation.*

Vollmer controlled the location of the Spokane and Palouse railroad tracks, which in 1888 connected the community with Spokane; it was a branch line of the Northern Pacific. He forced the town's principal merchants to relocate on acreage he had purchased.

The Northern Pacific had hoped to extend the tracks south to Lewiston, but Genesee remained the terminus for ten years because surveyors found that the hills north of Lewiston were too steep to provide an affordable grade. Cattle and hogs were driven to the Genesee loading chutes from as far as Grangeville and Cottonwood.

Once the railroad reached Lewiston via the Clearwater River, in 1898, Genesee faded like a rainbow. The town is now about half its former size.

At Walnut and Fir Sts., the J. P. Vollmer building still stands; it has one of the more elaborate galvanized iron facades left in Idaho. The front is a prefabricated modular facing that was manufactured by Mesker Brothers of St. Louis. To advertise its product the firm distributed about 500,000 mail order catalogs each year in the western states. Though ten similar fronts were sold in Idaho, only three survive.

Vollmer's store, which was built in 1898, housed part of his wholesale and retail grocery business. The first floor has been substantially altered to accommodate the doors of the volunteer fire department; the second story originally served as a dance hall.

Moscow is located on Highway 95, 13.5 miles north of Genesee, 31 miles from Lewiston. In addition to being the site of the state university, Moscow is blessed with a diversity of architecture that is rivaled by only two other towns in Idaho.

The city is the seat of Latah County; the only county in Idaho, and perhaps in the U.S., established by an act of Congress (1888).

The first settlers arrived in 1869. Almon Ashbury Lieuallen called the area Paradise Valley and established a post office in 1872 under that name. Because camas bulbs were abundant, and a favorite fodder of razorbacks, some nearby farmers called the valley "Hog Heaven."

Moscow in 1882.

The name Moscow was adopted in 1875, by which time Lieuallen had opened a store with a "shoebox post office" on what became the Main Street. Allegedly the source of the name was Lieuallen's belief that the problems of isolation confronting the community were comparable to those in Russia at the "time of troubles" under Ivan the Terrible. A visitor described the town in the 1880s as "just a lane between two farms with a flax field on one side and a post office on the other," but five years later the settlement had a population of 300.

638

Travel was slow, though regular stage service was established with Lewiston. Then in 1885, the Palouse and Columbia Railroad, a branch of the Oregon Railroad and Navigation Co. (Union Pacific) arrived, preceding the Northern Pacific by five years.

As soon as the city's residents outnumbered those of Lewiston, they made an effort to obtain the county seat. Though the attempt failed, Representative Fred Dubois succeeded in getting a bill through Congress carving Latah County out of Nez Perce County (Congress can modify a Territory at will). In addition, by agreeing to drop its support of a bid by north Idahoans to join Washington in statehood, Moscow was chosen as the site of the state's land grant college, the University of Idaho, in 1889.

Moscow had the advantage of being located in the heart of the fertile Palouse country. Farm crops proved to be a better, habitual bet than the one-time harvest of giant white pines upon which the communities north and east of Moscow wagered their future.

View of Moscow taken from courthouse steps in 1896. Our Savior's Lutheran Church in center foreground; University administration building in background.

Farmers and merchants did well. By 1920 Moscow was a commercial center and university town with a population of 4,000.

Moscow has an abundance of admirable architecture; examples selected here are suggestive rather than exhaustive.

Main and Fourth St.: The city's Main St. has a number of interesting older buildings. Two are located at the southwest and northwest corners of Fourth St., which is now a mall. The Skattaboe block is a two-story commercial building of the

639

Romanesque style, which has been used by telephone companies since the early 1900s. The brickwork was done by Taylor and Lauder, of Moscow, who operated their own kilns and were the most active masonry contractors of the period. They built most of the downtown brick structures and the major ones on the University campus.

On the northwest corner of Fourth and Main is the Hotel Moscow, erected in 1891-1892. The red brick, three-story building with sandstone trim is an example of the Victorian Romanesque style in American commercial architecture.

The town's first hotel was destroyed by fire in 1890, and this one was constructed on the same site by a corporation for $30,000; its owner, R. H. Barton, purchased a half-interest. The ground floor has now been adapted to commerical use. Hotel Moscow and the Skattaboe block are listed in the National Register of Historic Places.

Main and Third St.: The historic facade of David and Ely, Inc. department store has been hidden by screened aggregate panels installed in the 1950s. The building was erected in 1889 for Dernham and Kaufmann's U.S. Wholesale & Retail General Merchandise store. In 1900 it became David & Ely, and "David's" was the best-known department store in Moscow for seventy-nine years. There are plans to remove the homely panels and expose the attractive, original facade.

Main and First St.: The McConnell-McGuire Department Store, built in 1891, is located on the southeast corner of the intersection. It is a cast iron and wood beam structure with an elaborate facade which is cast iron at street level and pressed tin above. The gargoyles are wolf faces. When the department store went bankrupt, the upper floors were converted to apartments. In 1980 the building was remodeled.

The Fort Russell Historic District, just east of Main St., contains many of the more interesting houses in the city. The district includes nine blocks of brick and frame dwellings; most of them represent Victorian or early twentieth-century architecture. (For ease in touring, the houses are mentioned in street-sequence.)

110 So. Adams at Second St: The McConnell Mansion. This house is a city landmark, and as the office of the Latah County Historical Society it is open for public inspection.

William McConnell was born in Michigan, and like thousands of other young men, was drawn to California by the gold rush. He taught in Oregon for two years before coming to Idaho in 1863, where he settled on the Payette River, near Horseshoe Bend, and raised fruit and vegetables for the miners in Boise Basin. When horse thieves raided his ranch, he headed an effective vigilante committee and shortly was appointed Deputy U.S. Marshal in Boise City. He resigned after two years, returned to Oregon and in 1879 was elected president of the state senate. After a few years, McConnell was back in Idaho to open a general merchandise store in Moscow. His mansion was constructed in 1886 and the family moved in on Christmas Eve.

McConnell Mansion. McConnell's daughter, Mary, married Senator William Borah, and died in 1976 at age 105.

The financial panic of 1893 caused international difficulties, and incessant summer rains that year created local problems that gave the hard times fourteen rattles and a button. The wheat crop was lost; hopes were qualified. Farmers lost their land; McConnell lost his store, grain elevator, and warehouse. Since his wife, Louisa, had homesteaded the house they were able to hold on to it a bit longer.

During this troubled period, McConnell served as Idaho's first Senator, then as the state's third governor from 1893 to 1896. When he returned to Moscow at the end of his second term, he had to give up the house. The mansion, which had cost $6,000 to build was valued at $5,000 in 1896.

It had sat vacant for four years when Dr. W. A. Adair, a local physician, bought the place in 1901 and he kept it until his death in 1934. Then it was bought in 1940 by Frederic Church, a history professor at the University; he had lived in the house as a renter for nineteen years and owned it for twenty-six more. On his death,

641

Church willed the mansion to Latah County for community and historical club use. His niece and nephew donated the contents of the residence to the county. The interior has been partially restored and furnished with period pieces.

The general style of the house is best described as Eastlake, though it exhibits some elements of the Victorian Gothic and Queen Anne styles. It has elaborate band-sawed decoration, particularly within the gables. Supposedly, the house was designed from a plan book with ideas from the owner and a local carpenter.

221 No. Adams: The Dernham house was built about 1885 for Henry Dernham, co-owner of Dernham and Kaufmann's U.S. Wholesale and Retail General Merchandise store on Main St. in Moscow. The two-story house, with hexagonal bays and colored glass panes, is an excellent example of Queen Anne architecture.

124 No. Polk at "A" St.: The former Tom Taylor house is a wonderful 1½-story Queen Anne cottage with Eastlake trim. It has decorated vergeboards, shaped shingles and an elegant, large round window with stained glass side sections. The house was built circa 1885.

325 No. Polk at "C" St.: The Miller house, or "House of the Seven Gables," is one of the more famous in Moscow. It was built in 1908-1911 by a Portland architect for Mark Miller, owner of a local flour mill.

House of Seven Gables.

The exterior of this 2½-story, chalet-style mansion is richly decorated: exposed, curved rafters, with notched and "locked" purlins that project through wide, carved bargeboards, and stained glass in the first floor upper windows.

The interior has oak panelling, built-in bookcases, and a built-in grandfather clock in the entry hall. The second floor contained four bedrooms, though the master bedroom has now been divided. The third floor contained a ballroom with a twelve-foot ceiling, but it has been remodeled into bedrooms.

On the north side of the house was the covered porch once used by horse-drawn carriages and now converted to a garage. The servants' quarters in the rear, and the cement drive used by the carriage, can still be seen.

403 No. Polk at "C" St.: Across the street, north of the Miller house, is the Butterfield home – Moscow's sole example of Georgian Revival architecture.

Charles Butterfield built the house in 1902-1903, using the plans from his sister's house in Janesville, Wisconsin. It was the only house on the block at the time of its construction, and the truncated roof supported a widow's walk. Because of the cost, Butterfield was forced to rent apartments in the upper story.

604 "C" at No. Polk St.: East, across the street from the Butterfield residence, is a charming 1½-story frame Queen Anne house dating from the 1880s.

528 E. First at No. Polk St.: This attractive house, on a corner lot, dates from 1890 and was owned originally by the proprietor of Davids' Department Store in Moscow, Frank David. It was built by George Hallum, who for many years was the head carpenter for the University. The two-story, T-shaped house has a screened sleeping porch and a wealth of decorative shingle work.

430 "A" at Van Buren St. This house is more monument than mansion; it was sired by a silver mine.

Henry Day worked in the lumber business in California for twenty years before he brought his family to Wardner, Idaho to open a grocery store. The Days had five children. Harry, the oldest son, discovered the Hercules claim in 1889 in the Coeur d'Alene district. The family members took equal shares in the mine and labored for twelve years to put it on a paying basis.

The youngest son, Jerome, attended Gonzaga College in Spokane and then enlisted in the cadet corps at the University of Idaho. But Jerome also worked as a laborer in various mines, joined the Western Federation of Miners, and may even have been present when the Bunker Hill mill was dynamited in 1899. He was a union official and worked his way up to shift boss. Then the Hercules struck a rich vein at a secondary level. (Within twenty-five years the mine would produce $80 million worth of ore and declare dividends amounting to $20 million.) At twenty-six, in order to train himself as an assayer, Jerome enrolled at the University of Idaho as a special student in mineral chemistry.

The young Day married Lucy Mix of Moscow, and a Boston architect designed this house for them in 1902. It has been described as a "Queen Anne-going-colonial" transitional style. The sprawling two-story structure has metal crenellations and finials on the roof and beveled glass around the south entrance. Several doorways have been added since the mansion was divided into apartments.

Jerome Day Mansion.

The carriage house, with Mission-style gables, just north of the residence, was added at a later date for Jerome's sixty h.p. Stevens-Duryea auto.

Jerome Day became director of the Moscow State Bank in 1904, and its president in 1908, as well as president of the state bank at Orofino. He financed the Idaho National Harvester Co. that made grain harvesters in Moscow from 1906-1918.

Described as a "likeable, gregarious, wealthy man," Jerome was elected to three terms in the state senate as a Democrat. He quit the legislature in 1915 and from 1923-1941 made his home in Wallace and alongside Lake Coeur d'Alene. Day served on the board of

644

education, and as a regent of the University from 1933-1941. He died in Phoenix in 1941, and left a voluminous collection of Western Americana to the University of Idaho library.

For a period, the University rented this house for its president; at this writing it is owned by a geology professor at the school.

310 "A" St.: This house, built in 1878 for Judge James Forney, is reputed to be the oldest remaining dwelling in Moscow. Like Samuel Johnson's play, it is "worth seeing, but not worth going to see."

308 So. Hays at Third St.: The Mason Cornwall house is an unusual Idaho residence, a high Victorian Italianate home constructed of brick by Taylor and Lauder. They used a smooth stucco veneer over the sixteen-inch thick walls to simulate cut stone. The two-story L-shaped house had a cupola view-tower in the

Cornwall house.

center of the roof when completed in 1889. Mr. Cornwall wanted a campanile, but the builders had apparently never seen one. The cupola was removed in 1940, and red tiles replaced the metal roof shingles at that time.

Cornwall was a wealthy Moscow businessman who owned substantial acreage, as well as buildings on Main Street. After his death, his name and date were chiseled off the residence – some say by his sons, who did not get along with him.

Third and Washington St.: This handsome Renaissance-Revival styled post office building was constructed in 1909-1910 by a Michigan company for $79,000. A new federal building was completed in 1974, and this one was declared surplus. A fund drive was undertaken to convert the structure to a community center.

110 So. Jefferson at Second St.: Two blocks from the old post office is the Mission-style Moscow-Latah County public library. Carnegie libraries that still function in the state are few as fingers. This one was designed by a Boise architect in 1905-1906, and was built for $10,000.

Carnegie libraries have an interesting wellspring. Andrew Carnegie (1835-1919), born in Scotland, was the prototype of Horatio Alger. His family immigrated to an area that is now part of Pittsburgh, and the thirteen-year-old boy worked in a cotton factory for a $1.20 a week.

Andrew obtained a job as a messenger in a telegraph office and so impressed the division superintendent that he hired him as his personal clerk. Through work, friends, and investments, Carnegie became director of the Union Pacific briefly, and eventually president of Carnegie Steel Co., worth $320 million. His properties, sold to J. P. Morgan, were the genesis of U.S. Steel Corporation.

Believing that it was a disgrace to die rich, Carnegie systematically ladled out his wealth during his lifetime. Among the programs he developed to distribute a portion of his surplus was one that provided free public buildings to communities that would stock them with books and maintain them with tax funds in perpetuity.

Enterprising towns made an effort to secure such buildings; many of them have peculiar or unusual architecture because few people in the U.S. at that time had any idea of what a public library should look like or how it should function. Library service as Americans know it was in its infancy; reservoirs for cattle were far more common than reservoirs of books.

Carnegie never asked that his name be used on the libraries, and fewer than one-third did. Requirements for a grant were threefold: 1.) The city had to own the library site with clear title. 2.) The community had to guaranty a levy that would annually raise 10 percent of the amount requested. 3.) The building plans had to be submitted for approval to the Carnegie Institute.

The largesse ended in 1917 because a survey indicated that tax pledges were not being kept, but by that time the concept of public

646

libraries was generally accepted and the Carnegie Foundation felt its funds would be better employed working out problems of library service and performance.

While it lasted, the Carnegie program provided $50 million, which built over 2,000 free libraries.

101 Almon at First St.: The Almon Asbury Lieuallen residence is two blocks west of Main St. Lieuallen was a pioneer stockman in Paradise Valley and a pioneer merchant in Moscow; he named the city.

The A. A. Lieuallen house is architecturally significant as the only Mansard-roofed residence left in Moscow, and one of a few in the state that date from the 1880s.

This twelve-room house was remodeled into six apartments in 1917, and they were the first apartments in town with running water and electric stoves.

Eighth St. and Jackson St.: One block west of Main St., on a two block area, is the best concentrated collection of grain elevators in the state. Structures range in age from 1885 to 1942, from wooden buildings to those of concrete and corrugated tin over timbers. Curiously, early corrugated metal was nailed on vertically, while more recent installations reveal horizontal application.

The Union Pacific depot, built in 1885, is located nearby, at Eighth St., a half-block off Jackson St. It is among the three oldest depots in the state.

In 1887 a bill was introduced in the Territorial Legislature to establish the **University of Idaho** at Eagle Rock (now Idaho Falls). The bill was opposed by a delegate from the Moscow area, who offered an amendment changing the site to Moscow; the matter was tabled by the Senate.

Two years later, two young delegates, Willis Sweet and John Brigham, from Moscow and Genesee, wrote Council Bill No. 20 "an Act to Establish the University," while attending a legislative session in Boise. They drafted the Act in their hotel room.

When Bill No. 20 was introduced, the *Idaho Daily Statesman,* of Boise, ranted, "We have about as much use for a university in Idaho as there is for the fifth wheel of a wagon." But there was virtually no opposition to the bill in the legislature. The chairman of the Committee on Territory Affairs commented to the House that "... it would be recognized as an olive branch in the interest of peace and good-will extended by one section of the Territory to another, between which there has been long and bitter contention; and would unite the sections in the march of progress." In January, 1889, Bill No. 20 passed both houses.

647

The charter for the University of Idaho, which became part of the state constitution, provided $15,000 for site purchase and building planning. Building funds were to come from a half-mill tax for each dollar of assessed valuation of taxable property in the Territory. State funds were not immediately available, but federal Morrill-Hatch Act money for land-grant colleges with agricultural experiment stations, allowed the University to subsist.

Upon Idaho's admission to the Union, Congress set aside sections 16 and 32 of each township for the benefit of the public schools. The grant included nearly 3 million acres; 90,000 were for the agricultural college at the University, and 96,000 were for the rest of the University. Rentals, land sales, timber sales, and mineral royalties from these grant-lands are invested in an endowment fund; only the accrued interest can be used to support the institution.

The Regents purchased a twenty-acre wheatfield at Moscow for $4,000, and hired Franklin Gault, with a master's degree from Cornell College, Iowa, as the first president. His salary was $4,000 and his student body did not exceed thirty.

In March, 1906, the administration building burned. It was a major blow. Though arson was suspected, it was never proved. Classes were held in the gymnasium, the Moscow Carnegie library, the Methodist Church, and local lodge halls.

Insurance policies paid $135,000, but the new administration building, designed by the Boise architect J. Tourtellotte, cost twice that amount. In order to appease the legislature, and still obtain the needed funds, the Regents decided to build an agricultural building first, use it for interim classrooms, and finance the new administration building over three years, as state bonds were retired. In this manner, the University figuratively rose from the ashes.

As the state's land-grant institution, the University has the exclusive responsibility for instructional, research, extension, and public services in the fields of agriculture, forestry, engineering, and mining. (The Idaho Bureau of Mines and Geology, a state agency, maintains its headquarters and research facilities on the campus.) The University has the only college of law in the state; it is also the chief research center for the state, and the center for research-oriented graduate studies. The graduate school was formally organized in 1925; doctorates are offered in twenty-one study areas.

There are now about 8,000 students on the 450-acre campus. In order to increase the opportunities for knowledge, some faculty, libraries and equipment are shared for programs with Washington State University, across the state line, eight miles away.

It is worth noting here that the public return on the investment in the University has been repaid with interest sufficient to please even the most parsimonious taxpayer. In the area of agriculture alone, the University has cultivated high-yield, disease resistant varieties of wheat, barley, oats and peas, promoted specialty crops, controlled diseases and pests, increased beef production, improved dairy herds, developed systems of erosion control and water management, and experimented with vegetable oils and fodder beets that hold promise as fuel sources. The result of this research has almost incalculable value to the state. In 1974, for example, the direct-gross benefit from the new potato storage technology developed by the University of Idaho Agricultural Experiment Station at Aberdeen was estimated to be $384 million!

For a convenient entrance to the University of Idaho from Main St., take Highway 8 west to Line St., turn left across the railroad tracks, and stop at the information center on the left. Visitors can obtain a parking permit and campus map at the center, and tours are available on request.

Here are some suggestions for the tourist who wants to make a cursory walk across campus. Leave the information center and go south on Line St. four blocks. The faculty office complex (and complex it is) contains the University museum with displays that are changed periodically.

Across Line St. from the museum, on Seventh St., is the College of Mines and Earth Resources. This building has several floors of mineral and mining engineering exhibits. In the basement, there is a scale model of a portion of the Sunshine mine; the model cost $26,500 and was used by plaintiffs' attorneys in the lawsuit that followed the disastrous 1972 fire at the mine. After the trial, the model was donated to the college.

Morrill Hall, the next building south of the College of Mines, was the University's first agricultural building. A collection of fossils from nearby Miocene Lake Clarkia can be viewed in the Morrill basement.

Pine St. runs south from Morrill Hall one block to University Ave. The Life Sciences building is on the southeast corner; its third floor houses the best collection of Idaho mammal mounts in the state. Jack O'Connor's trophies, gathered over a lifetime as an outdoor-writer, are here, along with the life-mounts of the Northwest Mammal Gallery, and the Biological Sciences Bird and Mammal Collection, which contains full skeletons of elk, moose, bear, deer, cougar, etc., and study skins, skulls, and antler displays. Recently, the Jess Taylor collection was added; it includes two "grand slams" of mountain sheep, impressive Rocky Mountain ram horns from the Salmon River drainages, and deer and elk antlers in the Boone and Crockett class. (These exhibit rooms are open only during the school year.)

University of Idaho, c. 1930.

Engineering students in about 1898.

650

The Administration building can be seen one block south of the Life Science collections. The Tudor Gothic structure was erected in 1909, to replace an earlier one destroyed by fire. Its central section, with an eighty-foot clock tower, cost $260,000; the north wing was added in 1912 and the south wing was completed in 1916. Enter the

Home economics class in Ridenbaugh Hall.

Mining engineering students in 1925, members of mine rescue class.

north wing to view the Gothic auditorium with windows of stained glass.

Kibbie Dome is three blocks west of the Administration building. The enclosed stadium, best appreciated from the interior, is a remarkable feat of architectural engineering. The Trus-Dek roof system uses wood and steel arches to span 400 feet at a height of 150 feet. The stadium, used for intercollegiate football and basketball, cost $7.8 million.

For twenty miles north of Moscow, U.S. Highway 95 skirts the western flank of the Palouse Range. This is an area of rolling, asymmetrical hills with rises of twenty to eighty feet. They are dunes of loess, reshaped by wind and snow and dissected by runoff. The loess is 150 feet deep in places and rests on a thick sequence of basalt flows. The hills tend to have steep north and east facing slopes and gentle west and south-facing skirts. Occasionally, the undulations are interrupted by a higher hill of older rock, part of the pre-lava erosional surface; such peaks are called steptoes.

The loess is layered: fertile silt loam two to four feet deep on top of three feet of light brown soil and both underlain by a light yellow loess, generally fifty to seventy-five feet deep. The loess layers present a geological puzzle: what kind of wind system transported this deposit over several hundred square miles and why did it bed here? According to one theory, the glacial rock-flour, blown from a dustier, drier region (perhaps the Big Bend of the Columbia River) more than 100,000 years ago, was trapped by the moist grasslands of the Palouse region.

Prevailing winds for the area are from the southwest, and some soil is still wind-deposited. Dustfall in the hills has been calculated at 7,500 acre-pounds per year, which would require almost 25,000 years for an eighty-foot mantle of loess. The duration and strength of the prehistoric windstorms will never be known, but it is easy to imagine yellow dust clouds that turned day to night for years unnumbered.

The Palouse hills, which reach from Lewiston north almost to the southern end of Coeur d'Alene Lake, comprise a high-yield dryland wheat region because the loess has the ability to retain large quantities of water. In addition, mild winters (well above the ten degree F limit) coupled with moist springs and dry summers constitute a weather pattern favorable for soft white winter wheat. Spring wheat, however, does not do well here because it cannot attain its growth before the summer drought.

652

The original vegetation in the Palouse was tall prairie grass. The transition to forest occurred just east of Moscow. Highest yields of wheat and peas are in those areas that were originally grass. Average wheat yields are seventy-five or more bushels per acre near Moscow, but decline to only twenty-five bushels per acre twenty-five miles east of the city because soils are less fertile in the country that was once forested.

Soil Conservation Service agrologists say that erosion in the Palouse country is greater than occurs anywhere else in the U.S., because farmers pulverize the soil unnecessarily and excess rain, unabsorbed, carries off the soil. The Palouse basin, with a million acres of cropland, loses 17 million tons of soil a year; annual soil losses of twenty to thirty tons per acre are common. Unless farming systems change, according to a recent Agricultural Department study, the rates are expected to increase.

Minimum till, or no-till agriculture is recommended for the Palouse country; the wheat stubble should be left for the winter. One of the problems with such a method is that initially the yields will be lower. Farmers, with high production costs, are reluctant to adopt new, less successful methods, even though they would conserve soil.

The turnoff for **Skyline Drive** through **McCroskey State Park** is on the west side of U.S. 95, 25.5 miles north of Moscow, at the Latah-Benewah County line.

This 4,400-acre park was a valentine from Virgil McCroskey to the people of Idaho. Though it is hard to believe, the gift was resisted by citizens' groups and politicians.

During the Reconstruction Period after the Civil War, the McCroskey family, with ten children, left Tennessee to homestead in eastern Washington, near what is now the town of Steptoe.

One of those children, Virgil, went to Washington State College and received degrees in pharmacy and history. He bought a drug store in Colfax, Washington, where he worked from 1903-1920, then he ran the family farm, which he had purchased, until 1936. But most of the period from 1921-1939 Virgil spent traveling through the United States and the world.

Ivan Doig has written that "memory is the near neighborhood of dream." Two memories now fused in a dream that was to absorb the next thirty years of McCroskey's life. Virgil's mother, Mary, had died of "pioneer hardships" two years after she arrived on the Washington homestead. Virgil had visited most of the western National Parks during his travels. He decided to create a regional park in memory of his mother in particular, and pioneer women of the Northwest in general. He solicited help for the development of the ridgeline park, but when others lost interest, he worked alone.

Virgil McCroskey, bachelor, farmer-pharmacist, dreamer, stitched acres and years together like a needlepoint sampler along the 4,000-foot ridge from Mineral Peak to Huckleberry Peak. Acres, quarter sections, sections. He hired bulldozers to clear the angular road, he grubbed out view areas, picnic spots, campsites. He cajoled right-of-ways and collected deeds. Finally, in 1951, the Skyline Drive was finished. McCroskey offered it, along with 4,400 acres of woodland, to the state as a park. It was refused on grounds the parks department could not afford to maintain it, and there was public opposition as well.

But Virgil persisted. He enlisted support from Boy Scout troops, he obtained the backing of the Idaho State Lands Commission, and some legislators – and he prevailed, in 1955.

One consideration for the acceptance was that McCroskey maintain the park for fifteen years. He agreed. And after fifteen years, in 1970, at age ninety-three, Virgil McCroskey died. His legacy is Mary Minerva McCroskey State Park.

The twenty-two mile dirt road follows the ridgetop to the Idaho-Washington border. Though the shoulders of the road are forested, there are several fine views of the Palouse country. The park has a few geologic features, including a white quartz dike that strikes across the crest within 100 feet of Vista Point.

Virgil remarked that the forested, mountain park he created "... is inhabited by silent and benevolent spirits. I can work all alone in this park, where I spend most of my waking hours, and not see another human being and never be lonely."

DeSmet, just west of Highway 95, is eleven miles north of McCroskey State Park, and within the **Coeur d'Alene Indian Reservation**. The highway runs through the reservation for a distance of about thirty miles, to Rockford Bay on Coeur d'Alene Lake.

De Smet is the third location of the Jesuit's **Sacred Heart Mission**, which was founded in 1842 on the banks of the St. Joe River by Fr. Pierre De Smet. The settlement still serves as the site of a Coeur d'Alene tribal grammar school which is located beyond the poplar trees on the knoll that can be seen west of the highway.

At the time the Jesuit missionaries arrived among the Coeur d'Alene (see Cataldo Mission) the tribe was located essentially in three village-bands: one on the St. Joe River, another on the

654

Spokane River, and the third on the Coeur d'Alene River. Each band had its own sub-chief, one of whom was also recognized as the head chief of the tribe.

The Indians spoke an Interior Salishan language, closely related to the Spokane. They were primarily hunters and fishermen, but gathered camas bulbs in meadows near present Clarkia, Moscow, and De Smet. Like other Idaho Indians, they adopted the horse and thereby a peripheral involvement with the Great Plains bison hunting culture, but in most respects their life cycle resembled that of other Columbia Plateau groups. Their territory encompassed 3 million acres.

Some of the Coeur d'Alene were drawn into the Yakima Indian War and defeated Colonel Steptoe in 1858. The Governor of Idaho Territory, in 1866, recommended that the tribe be placed on a reservation. The Interior Department concurred, and President Andrew Johnson ordered that a reservation be established. An area about twenty miles-square was withdrawn from the public domain, but no effort was made to confine the Indians within its limits. It was just as well, because when the tribal members learned of the reserve's existence several years later, they summarily rejected it as too small.

In 1873 President Grant created a reservation by Executive order. It was a relatively generous tract: a wedge extending from De Smet north to Cataldo Mission, then northwest to Post Falls, and south to De Smet. But Grant's order lacked the finality and security of a Congressional treaty, and no remuneration was offered for expropriated lands. Nevertheless, Fr. Diomedi urged the Coeur d'Alene to at least protect this remnant by moving to Nilgo-Alko ("Hole in the Woods"), within the reservation boundaries. Temporary quarters were built at this site, two miles from De Smet, in 1877, but it was not until Fr. Diomedi moved the furnishings out of the Cataldo Mission the following spring, that the Indians began to erect permanent buildings at De Smet. Most of them settled within fifteen miles of the mission. In July, 1881, Fr. Cataldo laid the cornerstone for the Cathedral of the Sacred Heart, at De Smet, which served as the center of worship for almost sixty years – until 1939, when it burned, along with the mission records and several hundred precious Indian items.

Shortly after the Coeur d'Alene moved to De Smet, the Sisters of Charity of Providence opened the Convent of Mary Immaculate and began teaching girls in a grade school there. In 1881, fire destroyed part of the convent-school, but two years later, the new Providence

Academy at Sacred Heart was dedicated. The boy's school, which had been taught by priests, was merged with this grade school.

In 1889 a three-man Congressional commission appointed to deal with the Coeur d'Alenes, met with tribal leaders in De Smet. The council held discussions intermittently for several weeks, and an agreement was finally concluded whereby the Indians were allowed a reservation of 400,000 acres, while 2.3 million acres (80 percent timber land) was ceded to the federal government for $650,000. (The first government offer was $150,000.) Most of the money was distributed on a pro rata basis among tribal members; $150,000 was expended over a fifteen-year period on reservation developments.

Cathedral of the Sacred Heart at DeSmet.

The treaty was ratified in 1891. A section specified "... no part of the reservation shall ever be sold, occupied, opened to white settlement or otherwise disposed of without the consent of the Indians residing on said reservation." It might just as well have read, "Trust in God, but tie your horse."

The Dawes Severalty Act of 1887, a disastrous attempt to force Indians into white cultural patterns, was used by Congress as a cleaver to hack up tribal lands among members in severalty and pass the larger portions along as homesteads to new settlers. Each Indian was expected to choose 160 acres of agricultural or grazing land from his ancestral grounds.

The Coeur d'Alene tribal council unanimously rejected allotment and sent a delegation to Washington, D.C. The tribal representatives

656

were met in the nation's capital by the Commissioner of Indian Affairs and told to go home and select their quarter-sections before the special allotment agent did it for them.

Congressional allotment legislation made certain that the Dawes Act overrode the contradictions contained in the Treaty of 1891. The reservation was surveyed in 1905, while the Indians pulled up the stakes at night. In July, 1909, 638 residents of the reservation were each granted 160 acres. The remaining agricultural land was opened by a homestead lottery the following year.

Allotment marked the beginning of a period of social disintegration for many Indians. The agency superintendent moved

Boys' school at DeSmet.

the reservation headquarters from De Smet to Tekoa, Washington, in 1906 because he felt his family would be more comfortable there. The Tekoa agency drew Indians to the town's saloons; Coeur d'Alene problems caused by cultural displacement were exacerbated. Eventually, new headquarters were established in Plummer.

The Wheeler-Howard Act of 1934 was an admission by Congress and the Bureau of Indian Affairs that allotment was a wretched failure. The Coeur d'Alene organized under the new Act and replaced their traditional council with an elected Tribal Council – chairman of the Council supplanted the chief as political leader, and the chief's role became a ceremonial one. With new organization and leadership, the Coeur d'Alene began to revitalize their society.

657

Indicative of their accomplishments was the election of their Tribal Council chairman to the state legislature in 1966.

Coeur d'Alene reservation lands now total 69,000 acres and the tribe has 1,500 members. A tribal festival is held each year at Worley, Idaho, during the second week of July.

The proud name of the Coeur d'Alene has been given to a mountain range, National Forest, lake, river, mining district and city.

The prominent brick building with composition siding, which now occupies the hilltop, replaced the second Providence Academy, which burned in 1908. The classrooms and chapel in this building were on the second floor (above the basement), the Sisters lived on the next floor, and the attic was used by girls who boarded at the mission. About 100 students were accommodated.
(In addition to the school, the nuns operated a farm and dairy at De Smet.)

In 1978 after ninety-six years, Providence Academy closed. The Sisters returned the buildings to the tribe, and after a few years, a new grade school opened on the hillside, below the old one. It is funded by the Bureau of Indian Affairs, and has a tribal school board. High school students attend classes in Plummer.

The church, which is located next to the old school, replaced the cathedral that was destroyed by fire. It was dedicated by Bishop Kelley in 1953. The Jesuit Order still ministers to the tribe, and a priest lives in the residence alongside the church. The buildings just east of the old school are the kitchen facilities and workmens' quarters that served the Academy.

A half-mile west of the church is the De Smet cemetery; the dead "cradled in this tender acre" have been marked with a solicitude not found in any other graveyard in the state.

Tensed, one mile north of De Smet, is De Smet spelled backward by the Postal Department – almost.

Plummer Butte can be seen to the east, on the approach to **Plummer**, 12.6 miles from Tensed.

When surveying the area for the opening of the Coeur d'Alene reservation, government surveyors laid out a mile-square townsite and named it after a member of their crew. Town lots were sold at Coeur d'Alene in July, 1910, and the settlement sprouted along the tracks of the O. W. R. & N. and Milwaukee, St. Paul like goatweed after a rain.

Large stands of ponderosa, fir, cedar and tamarack surrounded Plummer, and until exhausted, furnished employment for the community. By World War I, the town had reached the shank-end of its boom.

In the early 1900s Indian ponies overpopulated the range around Plummer. There were cooperative roundups, and the animals were shipped to market by rail. The bones of those that had starved were gathered in wagons and sold for fertilizer, just as settlers sold buffalo bones collected on the plains east of the Rockies.

Worley is named for the Coeur d'Alene agency superintendent of 1909; the same one who thought he would be happier in Tekoa than De Smet, and moved the Indian agency. The Coeur d'Alene Indians hold a tribal festival here during the second week of July. The town is six miles north of Plummer, on Highway 95.

U.S. Highway 95 leaves Worley, curves around the west side of Coeur d'Alene Lake, and intersects Interstate 90, twenty-seven miles north at Coeur d'Alene city. (See I-90 for Coeur d'Alene city)

Four miles north of Coeur d'Alene, U.S. 95 enters the town of **Hayden Lake**. In a card game in 1878 Matt Heyden won the honor of naming the lake, and inadvertently, the town (now misspelled).

The lake, fringed by forest, has an irregular forty-mile shoreline and a depth of 800 feet in places. Three campgrounds are available to the public, as well as beaches for swimming, fishing and boating.

A house, with perhaps the most fascinating heritage of any in Idaho, is located 3.6 miles from Highway 95, on the shore of Hayden Lake. Turn right on Honeysuckle Road, which is the first road that intersects U.S. 95 inside the city limits. Drive 0.9 miles east on Honeysuckle to So. Hayden Lake Rd. Turn right and travel along the south side of the lake 1.7 miles to the Tobler Marina. Continue on So. Hayden another 1.0 miles to the commodious, white house that squats moodily on the rise along the right side of the road. This is the **F. Lewis Clark mansion**, and the details of its past, still within the realm of hearsay, would make an absorbing novella.

Mr. Clark came to Spokane in 1884, a year after he graduated from Harvard at the age of twenty-two. He was a native of Maine, and his father was a wealthy merchant-banker.

In Spokane, Clark bought a mill site from Frederick Post, and with F. E. Curtis, built the C & C Mill, the largest in the Northwest. It produced 600 bushels of flour a day, and the product was shipped

659

to England, and even to China. After six years, he sold his interest for a $200,000 gain; he never looked back.

With foresight, Clark shrewdly bought Spokane real estate east of the town. He spent weeks on horseback, and camped out in the hills, in order to anticipate the direction of the city's growth and to predict the avenue of roads and railroads. His land investment of $960 in 1885 was worth $1 million by 1905.

F. Lewis Clark married Winnifred Wiard in 1892, and four years later, the architect Kirkland Cutter designed their mansion in Spokane. That baronial, seven-acre estate, at West 701 Seventh in Spokane, still exists – a monument to unbridled, nineteenth-century ambition.

The Coeur d'Alene and Rossland mines engaged Clark's interest in the 1890s and early 1900s. He joined Charles Sweeny in a partnership that consolidated mining claims in Idaho's Silver Valley under the Empire State-Idaho company. Within two years, the pair had turned a $685,000 profit. The millionaire eventually traded his Coeur d'Alene interests for additional Spokane real estate.

Clark had learned to sail as a youngster in Maine. In 1907, he bought a 105-foot sailing yacht, and took it, along with a sixteen-man crew, to Europe to compete in German and Spanish regattas. The ship won cups in all the races she entered. The Clarks were feted by Kaiser Wilhelm of Germany, Prince Henry of Prussia, and King Alfonso of Spain.

The Hayden Lake villa, sometimes called Honeysuckle Lodge, was designed as a summer home for the Clarks by a Boston architect, and was finished in 1912. The house, with a warren of rooms (seven bathrooms, nine fireplaces) contains 15,000 square feet and required several years to complete. It represents a rare, early residential use of reinforced concrete in Idaho, and the structure was the most expensive house in the state at that time. An itemized assessment of the 900-acre estate, made in 1918 by the Exchange National Bank of Coeur d'Alene, revealed the following costs: home $137,800, water system $38,000, drive and retaining wall $34,500, superintendent's cottage $8,800, gate keeper's cottage $3,000, small cottage $2,100, three-room cottage $1,000, barn $2,000, garage and milk rooms $2,800, chicken run and dove cote $1,100, hothouse and heating plant $2,600, landscaping and paths $60,000, tennis court $3,000, retaining wall $11,000, garden shed, ice house, blacksmith shop and wood shed $5,600, land $72,000 – total $385,300.

The slate for the roof was imported from England, the crystal chandeliers and marble for the fireplaces came from

660

Czechoslovakia, and the wallpaper in the expansive living room was hand-painted in France. The house had a ballroom, billiard and smoking rooms, library, built-in hallway guncases, wine cellar, bank vault, and a separate heating plant for the servants' quarters when the Clarks were away.

F. Lewis Clark Mansion.

By 1910 the Clarks had begun to spend winters in California. On a stormy evening in Santa Barbara, January 16, 1914, F. Lewis Clark put his wife, Winnifred, on a train bound for San Francisco. He dismissed his chauffeur, saying he preferred to walk the mile back to his hotel. Newspapers later reported that the couple had argued before parting. F. Lewis Clark was never seen again.

When it was discovered that his hotel room had not been used during the night, a search was begun. It was the chauffeur's opinion that his employer was not equal to the walk back to his hotel. (Because he was troubled by a stomach malady, Clark employed his own physician at $12,000 a year.) Then Clark's hat was found on the beach.

Whether F. Lewis Clark slipped his moorings accidentally or deliberately was never known. The police used dynamite around the city wharf in an attempt to raise his body, but none surfaced. If Clark committed suicide, the undertow and heavy surf would have carried his body out to sea.

A large reward was offered for information concerning his disappearance. On January 29, the Los Angeles police department received a letter:

We are holding Millionaire Clark for ransom of $75,000. State in Examiner if his folks will pay it or not. He is well taken care of. Yours, The Blackmailers. Notice: Make prompt reply in the papers, as he is very anxious to get out.

Mrs. Clark requested more information, but never received any. She left San Francisco for Hayden Lake. For years the widow investigated clues that came in letters from all over the country; she never credited the suicide theory, and kept a light at night in the windows of Honeysuckle Lodge.

By 1918 the Clark fortune had suffered such reverses that the Exchange National Bank foreclosed on the villa. Mrs. Clark moved to an apartment in Spokane; the mansion there had already been sold. In failing health, she went to Massachusetts in 1940, because her only child, Theodore, lived there. She died of a heart attack two weeks after her arrival. Her estate was valued at $10,000.

The Clark house moldered gently for over twenty-five years. The Charles Lund family acquired it in 1933, but never lived in it. They used one of the cottages as a summer home. Then in 1945, in a generous gesture, they allowed the house to be converted into a Navy convalescent house. The Elks lodge provided funds to make the building habitable. One floor was remodeled into a dormitory, and the kitchen was reactivated. Naval officers from nearby Farragut training base occupied the outlying cottages.

A few years later, the house was purchased by A. B. Lafferty, owner of a tugboat fleet that pulled log brailes across Coeur d'Alene Lake. After his death, the residence was sold again, and used as a boys home for several years.

In the late 1960s the old villa was opened to the public as the Clark House Lodge. Ten bedrooms were available at rates as low as $5.00 a night. There were dining facilities and a cocktail lounge. The Lodge closed in the early 1970s.

Three partners who bought the house submitted a proposal to reopen the premises as an inn in 1978. Since the estate has dwindled to seven acres, and is now surrounded by other residences, there were neighborhood objections to the grant of a liquor license, and to the attendant increase in nighttime traffic. The inn never opened.

At the time this was written, the Clark House was owned by two partners. While the storied structure has managed to retain a certain elegiac elegance, its next chapter remains a question mark.

U.S. 95 meets Highway 52 at **Athol**, thirteen miles north of Hayden Lake. Athol had a large steam-powered sawmill in 1903; it burned in 1912. The town was reborn when nearby Farragut Naval Training Center was established in 1942. The community's name is said to be that of an Indian chief. Farragut State Park is five miles east of Highway 95 (see Highway 52).

Cocollala is the elongated lake 13.5 miles north of Athol, on the west side of the highway. The name is reportedly an Indian word meaning "cold water." (It certainly sounds like it.)

North of the lake three miles, Dufort Road intersects Highway 95, on the west side. It is a two mile drive down the road to **Round Lake State Park**.

The 142-acre park, which includes a 58-acre lake, was established in 1965; its fifty-three campsites are shaded by cedars and hemlocks, pines, fir and larch. The lake, circled by a two mile trail, is only thirty-six feet deep, so it warms sufficiently to offer comfortable swimming. Restrooms and showers are available.

Sandpoint, on Lake Pend Oreille, is 8.3 miles north of the Dufort Road-Round Lake turnoff.

U.S. 95 enters Sandpoint from the south over a bridge at the egress of the Pend Oreille River. Osprey often nest along the southwest shore.

The bridge is the fourth crossing built here. In the early 1900s the settlers on the south shore of the lake had only railroad trestle or rowboat access to the businesses of Sandpoint; most found it easier to use mail-order catalogues from Spokane.

In 1908 merchants and farmers raised $10,000 and persuaded the county commissioners to build a ferry. Then the commissioners discovered they could build a bridge, with the additional advantage of diverting traffic through town, for just $2,000 more. So the ferry plan was scuttled in favor of the bridge.

Bridge construction began before it occurred to anyone that the structure would impede boat traffic. A steel lift-bridge eighty feet long, in the middle of the channel, was added to the plans, which doubled the cost – to $50,000.

The bridge was built on 1,540 cedar pilings and was almost two miles long when completed in 1910, making it the longest wooden bridge in the world. Its novelty attracted considerable tourist traffic.

After twenty-five years the bridge was in need of replacement. Planks had been laid lengthwise instead of crosswise and the surface had developed undulations, not unlike a lake in high wind.

A second bridge was constructed in the 1930s with the help of Work Projects Administration labor. It was still regarded as the world's longest wooden bridge.

A third span replaced the earlier ones in 1956, at a location slightly east of the old one. The third bridge used fill, and concrete spans; the picturesque past was traded for a durable future. However, problems soon surfaced. Modern bridges are built with a fifty-year life expectancy, but Sandpoint needed a new one in half that time. The bridgeway had been salted for many winters to counteract surface ice. Saltwater eventually penetrated to the reinforcing bars and caused rust flakes that made the concrete deteriorate.

The latest bridge, built parallel to the previous one, is on thirty-five-foot spans and rests on pilings driven 40 to 150 feet into the lake bed. It has features which will allow expansion to four lanes if necessary.

Sandpoint Bridge.

The first commercial transaction and freight shipment by white men in Idaho was made in 1809-1810, perhaps at the site that was to become Sandpoint. Cartographer David Thompson bartered "120 or 130 skins" with the Indians living on what he referred to as the "Point of Sand" near the mouth of the Clark Fork.

Permanent settlers did not arrive in the Sandpoint area until the 1880s; it was called Pend d'Oreille and Sandy Point until the latter won acceptance. The townsite was platted in 1898 when the Great Northern railroad telegrapher, L. D. Farmin, subdivided his homestead along Sand Creek. The village incorporated two years later, and between 1880 and 1906 three major railroads brought their rails through town.

At the turn of the century, logging and milling were the area's major industries. Thomas Humbird, son of John Humbird, of Mason, Wisconsin, began sawmill operations in 1902. His father was a friend and business partner of Frederick Weyerhaeuser. Weyerhaeuser and the elder Humbird combined Northern Pacific's white pine lands on the Priest River (which Edward Rutledge had purchased) with the Sand Point Lumber Company holdings to form Humbird Lumber Co. in 1900. The Company had paid-in capital of $1 million by 1904.

Thomas Humbird was a capable manager. He ran mills in Kootenai, and Newport, Washington, as well as the one at Sandpoint. When the Sandpoint facility burned in 1907, he rebuilt it

Sandpoint in 1909.

as a two-band sawmill. Lake Pend Oreille provided ideal log storage and the logging, manufacturing, and marketing aspects of the enterprise were handled competently. It was a successful venture. When the last sawing was done in 1931, the company had produced slightly more than 2 billion board feet of lumber and had paid dividends of 430 percent. During that period, Sandpoint was also the largest shipping point for cedar poles in the west.

Settlers moved into the country after 1910 to buy cut-over stump ranches from the lumber companies at bargain prices – sometimes $1.25 an acre. When the would-be farmers cleared the land with horse teams, chains and dynamite, they were often disappointed to discover that land which grew trees would not necessarily grow crops.

Miners were also disillusioned. Though the area was only sixty miles from the famous Coeur d'Alene district, similar wealth was not discovered here. C. F. Haskill wrote in 1890:

This is great mining country ... There are prospects located everywhere; the most promising prospect I can see is that everybody will starve if they don't go to work.

The town's business district suffered three debilitating fires, but Sandpoint today is a pleasant resort town with streetscapes of interesting houses and variegated flower gardens.

The public library, at 419 North Alder St., was designed by the U.S. Treasury Department as a post office at a cost of $80,000 in 1927-1929. If reflects the California Mission style.

At the east end of Cedar St. is Idaho's only Gothic-style railroad depot. The Northern Pacific (now Burlington Northern) station, built in 1916, has gables topped with sphere-shaped stone finials. The baggage room is on the northern end, and there is an open porch for carts. The structure, which replaced an earlier one, evokes the era when railroads were the most important artery in a town's life.

Aside from the lake, the primary tourist attraction in Sandpoint should be the **Vintage Wheel Museum** at the corner of Cedar St. and Third Ave. There is free parking for visitors, and the modest admission price is a bargain.

Two men merged their lifetime collections of antique automobiles, renovated a building, and opened this museum in 1979. It includes a splendid display of regional historic photographs, a sizeable gathering of log brands from Montana, a wonderful collection of spark plugs, and an exhibit of Idaho license plates, along with a leather plate from Nebraska, issued by the Department of the Interior before states had the power to sell license plates.

The sterling collection of vehicles has, among other rigs, sleighs, an 1878 horse-drawn hearse, the Nezperce mail coach, a 1906 Case steam tractor, a 1907 International Auto Buggy, 1914 and 1923 Stanley Steamers (with boilers built to withstand four times the 600 psi operating level), a 1913 Cadillac touring car from Wallace, Idaho, a 1928 Model A Ford dump truck, a 1936 Cord with front-wheel drive, and a 1962 Rolls Royce. There are twenty-three cars in all; thirteen Fords and ten steam engines. All of the vehicles are in operating condition.

Bonner County's Historical Museum is located in an attractive, cedar-sided building at 905 Ontario St., in the lake-edge park.

Sandpoint hosts an unusual event the first week of October: the International Draft Horse Competition.

666

Highway 95 travels north from Sandpoint, flat as a carpenter's dream, along the **Purcell Trench**. Enormous ice lobes flowed through the trough from the Canadian ice fields 32,000-80,000 years ago. The **Selkirk Range** billows on the west (Priest Lake lies in the valley behind it), and the **Cabinet Mountains** indent the eastern skyline.

The origin of the trench is related to faults along both its western and eastern margins; a long, narrow block of the earth's crust has been downfaulted along the axis of the trench. The faults extend past Bonners Ferry, up the Kootenai River valley and beyond the Canadian border.

All of the area here, under 2,600 feet in elevation, was covered by part of a lake about 30 million years ago. Lava flows at the time created fossil beds to the south, where leaves from ginkgos, sequoias, magnolias, etc. suggest the climate 12 to 30 million years ago was much milder and moister in the Pend Oreille region than it is today.

The **Kalispel Indians**, sometimes called Pend d'Oreilles, occupied the territory for twenty miles north of Sandpoint. Their tribal land was not restricted to this valley, but extended into Washington and Montana as well. They are closely related to the Coeur d'Alenes and other Interior Salashan peoples.

Because no salmon spawned in the Kalispel territory, the Indians travelled to British Columbia to obtain chinook. The Kalispel did fish Lake Pend Oreille, and they used the Clark Fork route to Montana for buffalo hunts. Essentially hunters, the bands stored food in order to subsist through the winter.

Unlike most Idaho tribes, the Kalispel had limited numbers of horses because their land was too heavily forested to support large herds.

Cultural artifacts include coiled baskets, rawhide containers, horn spoons, and stone pestles. Kalispel clothing closely resembled that of the Great Plains groups. Long lodges of double lean-to construction were commonly used as winter shelters in small villages. Mat-covered, conical summer lodges were gradually replaced by bison-skin tipis after horses were acquired.

About 100 surviving members of the tribe now occupy a reserve (not a reservation) in the Usk-Cusick area of Washington, along the Pend Oreille River, about twenty miles west of the Idaho border.

The **Pack River** flows under the highway, 10.6 miles north of Sandpoint. The gravel road that goes northwest up this drainage travels through the 1967 Sundance burn. From the road end it is possible to hike three miles to Harrison Lake.

The upper Pack River area is the southern limit of Idaho's small band of mountain caribou *(Rangifer tandarus montanus)*. The herd, probably no more than thirty animals, represents the only natural band of caribou left in the lower forty-eight states. They are among the country's rarest mammals.

Caribou are members of the deer family, but unlike deer, both males and females have antlers. They are somewhat smaller than elk. The animals summer in high alpine habitat, where they forage on grasses and shrubs; they winter in moist basins where lichens, hanging from trees, provide food.

The town of **Naples** received its name from Italians working as construction crews on the Great Northern Railroad in the winter of 1892. The gandy dancers were so efficient they sometimes laid four miles of iron in a day. Jim Hill rode the first train through from St. Paul to Spokane in January, 1892. Naples is twenty-two miles from Sandpoint.

Bonners Ferry, ten miles north of Naples, straddles the banks of the Kootenai River.

The old Indian-Wild Horse Trail from Seneacquoteen came north through this area. When gold was discovered on Wild Horse Creek, British Columbia, in 1863, thousands of prospectors, conscripted by the fever, came up the trail via Walla Walla to cross the river at this point.

Not one to let an opportunity drift past, Edwin Bonner obtained an exclusive five-year franchise from the Territorial Legislature for this seven-mile stretch of river. His toll rates were $1.50 for loaded pack animals and .50 for a person on foot.

Improbable as it may sound, several camels crossed the river at Bonners Ferry, en route to the Wild Horse mines.

Arabian camels had been introduced in Texas by the U.S. Army as substitute pack animals. The officer in charge of them believed one camel was worth four good mules. They could subsist on brush, carry 1000-pound loads, travel thirty-five miles a day, and go six to ten days without water. There were two problems: mule skinners did not know how to handle the creatures, and their odor and sight stampeded any pack stock encountered on the trail.

Nonetheless, some were imported by the American Camel Company of San Francisco and sold to miners. (A safe means of shipping gold dust!) Several pack trains of five to six camels passed

668

through Pend Oreille country and up the Kootenai valley on their way to the diggings at Wild Horse.

(A miner in Montana shot one of the animals on the trail because he thought it was a moose, then had to part with his watch and mining claim to mollify the furious owner – and was thereafter known as "Camel" McNear.)

After the mining boom subsided, the settlement of Bonners Ferry looked like it might be stranded out of place and time. Richard Frey leased the ferry from Bonner in 1875, and in 1880 the first post office was named Frey, but the original name was soon reinstated.

It was the coming of the Great Northern Railroad that kept the town from going under in the 1890s. A celebration greeted the arrival of the first locomotive. The *Spokane Review* wrote:

The valley of the Kootenai now resounds with the neighing of the iron horse of civilization. Home seekers are locating along the valley and the miner is searching the crevices of the rocks and the slopes of the mountains in search for treasure. Woodmen are getting ready to fell the forest and in a few years this great valley will be alive with the hum of industry.

Dedication of the Great Northern Railroad at Bonners Ferry in 1926.

As for the ferry, Boundary County bought it in 1902 for $500. In 1906 the Spokane International Railroad bridged the river.

Bonners Ferry Lumber Co., a Wisconsin firm with Weyerhaeuser money, began operating here in 1904. The company had more problems than a rat-tailed horse tied short in fly time: driving logs down the rocky Kootenai River destroyed much of the wood, the Northern Pacific would not haul large logs through its tunnels, Canada would not permit export of the company's timber, and then in 1909, the mill burned. Though Bonners Ferry Lumber rebuilt and produced several hundred million board feet of lumber, when it closed in 1926, the company had never showed a profit.

Bonners Ferry Lumber Co.

Bonners Ferry historic district lies northwest of the new bridge that crosses the river into town. Fray's ferry post is still represented by a building on the north side of the riverbank. Adjacent to the ferry site is the Spokane International's railroad bridge, built in June, 1906. D. C. Corbin constructed this line to give Spokane businessmen access to less-expensive Canadian rail rates (see Moyie River Road). This is one of the few wooden truss bridges left in the state.

The **Boundary County Museum** is in the basement of the modern library building at Riverside and Kootenai Aves.

The tribal headquarters for about sixty **Kutenai Indians** can be visited a short distance from Bonners Ferry. Take North Main St. across the bridge, to the north side of the river, and turn left on Chinook St. Follow Chinook 0.3 miles to Kaniksu, turn left and drive 1.1 miles to the reserve. It is located on the wooded island, surrounded by shoals of grain.

670

Linguistically, the Kutenai are among the few cultures in North America that have been classified as a separate entity. They remain something of an enigma to anthropologists. Early explorers, fur traders and missionaries remarked on the distinct features of their language.

The Kutenai are a remote Algonquin group associated with no

Bonners Ferry, c. 1930.

other western tribe – buffalo hunters with a Plains Culture transferred to the forest. They have retained a system of elected chieftains to the present day. These Lower Kutenai are related to bands of Upper Kutenai living in British Columbia.

The aboriginal territory of the Kutenai was rich in fish, and they harvested great quantities of salmon, trout and sturgeon. They hunted big game in their own area and bison on the Great Plains in the summer. Members of the tribe also gathered roots and bulbs, such as camas, and collected and dried huckleberries, service berries, blackberries and chokecherries. Black moss was pounded into a bread. Because of the severity of the climate, hunting was curtailed during the winter months.

The later Kutenai lived in tipis, used bark canoes, elk-horn framed buckskin saddles, cedar bows and storage boxes, carved wooden bowls and some sun-dried pottery. Their clothing resembled that of the Plains Indians.

In 1855 a large reservation was set aside in Montana for the Flatheads. The U.S. Government then urged the Kutenai to migrate there, but only a few families were persuaded. Most of the Lower Kutenai of Bonners Ferry refused to go.

The group was not under any tribal agency, and in 1895 the federal government formalized land allotment policy. The land was divided by the Indian Council so that each family received about eighty acres. The band had its own inheritance customs at a member's death. (Tribal land now amounts to about 2,700 acres.)

In 1913 a government agricultural agent was sent to Bonners Ferry to help the Indians solve farming problems. He meddled with the land inheritance customs of the Kutenai and managed to discourage many of them from farming.

A number of Kutenai were converted to Catholicism by the Jesuits at an early date. The Indians built a log mission church on Mission Hill in 1888 and later replaced it with a frame building. By 1890 some members of the band had settled in eighteen houses in a circle around the church.

Government-built housing was made available to the Kutenai in 1931, and the church, now called St. Michaels, was moved a short distance to the center of the new homes. St. Michaels still stands, along with modern houses, as part of the communal circle.

To visit the most active wildlife refuge in the state, go back across the Bonners Ferry bridge, turn west on Riverside Road, which runs along the south bank of the Kootenai River, and follow it five miles to the 2,700-acre **Kootenai Wildlife Refuge**.

Anyone with an interest in wildfowl will find this a fascinating sanctuary. It was created in 1965, when the Bureau of Sport Fisheries and Wildlife bought the land with money received from the sale of duck stamps. Managed primarily to benefit waterfowl, in late spring and early fall it is an observer's happy hunting ground. Two hundred fifteen avian species have been identified on the refuge.

Several species of ducks use the area during breeding and migration. Mallards and golden eyes are the principal nesters; mallards and pintails are the primary migrants. Canada geese are most numerous in the fall, often numbering over 2,000. Golden eyes, wood ducks, and sora rails are common. So are ruffed grouse and pheasants. Whistling swans migrate through in the spring. Great blue herons, sandpipers, killdeer and lesser yellowlegs can be spotted along shorelines and in the marshes. On a bulletin board at headquarters, bird sightings are listed by species and quantity; a bird list is available there, as well.

Most of the refuge is comprised of lowlands that formed a part of the Kootenai River flood plain before it was diked in the mid-1920s. A dike extending thirty-seven feet above the river bed surrounds all but the timbered west edge of the acreage. Large ponds are replenished with water from creeks and the river.

Over 300 acres of grains and legumes, raised by local farmers under cooperative agreements, are left standing for feed.

The refuge is open during daylight hours and can be seen on foot or from a vehicle. A trail at refuge headquarters leads 430 yards up through tamarack and cedars to delightful Myrtle Creek Falls.

Myrtle Creek Falls.

During the peak of migration, the sight of thousands of birds lifting in a concerto against the early morning or evening sky is a spectacle not easily forgotten. It recalls Galway Kinnell's lines:

The south-going Canada geese,
At evening, coming down
In pink light over the pond, in great
Loose, always dissolving V's –
I go out into the field,
Amazed and moved, and listen
To the cold, lonely yelping
Of their tranced bodies in the sky.

Copper Creek Falls.

It is possible to drive south from the refuge 2.8 miles on Road 13, park at the Snow Creek bridge, and hike 200 yards up the trail alongside the creek to ten-foot **Snow Creek Falls**. (To go south on U.S. 95, return to Road 13, also marked USFS 417, continue south on it and re-enter Highway 95, via Deep Creek Canyon, at Naples.)

Highway 1 branches northwest from U.S. 95, 14.7 miles north of Bonners Ferry. Ten miles past this divide, on U.S. 95, is the exit to **Robinson Lake**, 0.4 miles north of the highway. This campsite has a small, dark lake encircled by a path. The area is heavily forested by trees ghosted with witch's broom.

Five miles farther north on U.S. 95 is the turnoff, on the east side of the road, for **Copper Creek Falls**. Road 2517 leaves the highway fifty yards north of a bridge across the Moyie River. The gravel road travels southeast 2.2 miles to a small sign that marks the trail on the left. An easy path leads 400 yards back to an enchanting seventy-foot waterfall.

U.S. Highway 95 leaves Idaho at **Eastport**, one mile from the Copper Creek Falls turnoff.

State Highway No. 97 from a junction with Highway 3 southeast of Harrison, northwesterly and northerly via Harrison to a junction with Interstate 90 at Wolf Lodge Bay. Route length: 35.8 miles.

Eleven miles north of St. Maries, State Highway 97 angles northwest to **Harrison** from Highway 3. The community, situated on a point by Coeur d'Alene Lake, is 7.2 miles from State Highway 3, and lies just south of the mouth of the Coeur d'Alene River.

The location was an ideal site for a sawmill but was within the Coeur d'Alene Indian reservation. New citizens, possessed of more clout than the land's original citizens, persuaded President Benjamin Harrison to withdraw a mile-wide townsite strip from the reserve in 1889 and rewarded the executive action by bestowing his name on the settlement.

Within a few years, there were several sawmills at Harrison. The railroad had arrived in 1890 and considerable Coeur d'Alene mining traffic passed through the community. By the turn of the century the town had attracted seven sawmills, four shingle mills, a dozen saloons and a redlight district.

In 1904 J. J. Pugh and Guy and Walt Russell of Russell and Pugh Lumber Co., along with Sheriff Perl Bailey and some community leaders, led a successful movement to outlaw saloons. Consequently, Harrison was dry as a kiln for many years.

One of the worst industrial fires in Coeur d'Alene history struck the town in mid-July, 1917; it consumed Grant Lumber Co. and part of the town. No effort was made to rebuild.

Steamboats moored at Harrison.

Harrison before the fire in 1917.

Today, the lumber industry, in a town where mills once produced 500,000 feet a day, has gone the way of the ivory-billed woodpecker.

676

On a gravel road along the lake, on the west edge of town, is the picturesque, two-story Victorian home that was once the Baptist Church parsonage. It has an octagonal tower and fishscale shingles.

A little farther down the same road is the building that housed the once busy, but now abandoned, laundry.

State Highway 97 continues north, along the east shore of Coeur d'Alene Lake twenty-seven miles, to join U.S. Interstate 90 about seven miles east of Coeur d'Alene city.

Less than two miles south of the intersection with I-90, is the entrance to **Mineral Ridge Scenic Area.** This 152-acre reserve, administered by the BLM, has three miles of loop trails which provide views of **Beauty Bay** and Wolf Lodge Bay. Typed information sheets along the trails give facts about forest development. The area has been logged, and the most interesting trees have been dead for decades.

Unless the visitor wants to climb 700 feet to the ridge for a pigeon's-eye view of Interstate Highway 90, it is best to take the

Beauty Bay on Coeur d'Alene Lake.

677

shorter, Silver Tip trail, just above the parking area, to a more pleasing overlook of Beauty and Wolf Lodge Bays.

Vardis Fisher, in writing about such a view of Coeur d'Alene Lake said:

The view afforded will depend on the position of the sun, for this lake is not the same at morning, noon, and evening, or when one is looking away from the sun or against it. If the wind is very gentle, the surface wears a pattern like that of fern leaves, and if the wind is a little stronger, then it is like a dappled blue pavement of glass ... There are areas where a deeper blue seems to have been poured in shadow on the blue ... or it may look as if liquid light has been spilled on the water.

Wolf Lodge Bay has become a favorite wintering area for northern bald eagles that migrate south to this region to feed on spawning kokanee, a pattern established since the fish were introduced to the lake in 1937. The eagles begin to arrive in November; their numbers peak in January, and they leave in February.

200

IDAHO

State Highway No. 200 from just north of Sandpoint, via Hope and Clark Fork to the Idaho-Montana state line near Cabinet. Route length: 33 miles.

Excellent lakescapes of **Pend Oreille** (pond-oray) are apparent on the drive from Sandpoint east around the north end of the lake on State Highway 200.

This largest of Idaho's lakes (twice the size of Coeur d'Alene) has a length of 143 miles and an extreme width of six miles. Most interesting is its great depth: 1,225 feet at one spot on the south end. An estimated 700,000 acre feet of water each year moves out of the lake, beneath Rathdrum Prairie, into the Spokane and Little Spokane Rivers.

The origin of the lake's name is clouded: George Stewart, in *Names on the Land,* points out that as a name of the Indian tribe, it does not make sense; it "is not even good French" for "ear pendants." Alexander Henry used the name "Earbob" for the Indians, though there appears to be no more evidence for that descriptive appellation than there was for "pierced nose" being given to the Nez Perce. Apparently the name was never "pendant d'oreilles" and therefore may simply have been incorrectly translated into French. The argument that the name was descriptive of the lake's shape is tenuous because it presupposes a map or an impossible overview. In 1809-1810 David Thompson referred to the body of water as "Saleesh" and "Kullyspell." In the 1860s, the name was written "Pend Oriels" and "Pend' Oreille." It seems certain the answer has now eluded us.

Pend Oreille lies in the Purcell Trench, and was formed during the Pleistocene Epoch – within the last million years. According to geologists, during the maximum glaciation of this period, the glacial ice was evidently thick enough to pass over the tops of the Selkirk and Cabinet Ranges at elevations of 6,000 feet or more. This would require a mobile ice mass with a minimum thickness of 4,500-5,000 feet in the vicinity of Sandpoint. Ice over the southern end of the lake at that time must have been 2,000 feet thick.

Carl Savage, in his *Geologic History of the Pend Oreille Lake Region,* postulates several events that resulted in the formation of the lake: 1.) Early faulting and shattering of the bedrock. 2.) Probable presence of easily eroded Cambrian limestone along the axis of the basin. 3.) Presence of easily eroded lake sediments. 4.) Erosion by two or more glacial lobes in the last 25,000 years. 5.) Damming of the south end of the lake basin by glacial debris.

Pend Oreille Lake deserves a reputation for outstanding fishing. Fourteen species of colorful game fish are found in its water: kokanee (small land-locked salmon), Kamloops, rainbow, brown, brook and hybrid trout, mountain and Lake Superior whitefish, yellow perch, black crappie, bluegill, brown bullhead, and large mouth bass. The world record Kamloops trout was hooked here in 1947, and so was a record thirty-two-pound Dolly Varden trout in 1949. (Dolly Varden was a character with pretty petticoats in Dicken's novel *Barnaby Rudge.*)

Since the lake is sometimes swept by fierce storms during the summer, boaters should be weather-vigilant.

Highway 200 follows the route of the **Northern Pacific Railway** (now Burlington Northern) around the north end of Pend Oreille Lake and up the Clark Fork. This is part of the "Big Bend," a 100-mile detour from the proposed Clearwater route, as well as from the Mullan-Coeur d'Alene road recommended by the military. The Northern Pacific chose this route over the others because of the enormous timber reserves located along its path. Congress had enlarged the land grant to alternate sections for thirty miles on each side of the track in the states, and to fifty miles in the territories. The railroad's finances were precarious, and acquisition of the timber would improve the credit of the company. (A Congressional report estimated the total land grant to the Northern Pacific exceeded 48 million acres!)

The company did most of its own work on this line, using Chinese laborers for clearing and grading. The crews worked toward each other through Idaho from Washington and Montana. Most of the work around the lake was done in the winter, 1881-1882, and snow was shoveled much of the time. Lake steamers hauled supplies to the camps.

Building the Clark Fork stretch "was by far the most difficult of the entire Northern Pacific line and much the most expensive." A roadway had to be blasted along the canyon wall above the river. Within three miles of the lake, three trestles had to be built: 2,000, 1,400 and 1,300 feet long. Then an 8,400-foot pile bridge was required to cross the arm of the lake into Sandpoint; some of the pilings were 100 feet in length.

By January, 1882, the Northern Pacific was running trains around Pend Oreille Lake, and the iron was completed to Montana in 1883.

Hope is sixteen miles from Sandpoint; a frontage road on the north side of the highway gives access to the community on the west end of town. It is a short drive down that road to a granite memorial for **David Thompson**, dedicated in 1928. Of David Thompson the world has not heard enough. This intrepid man was worthy of a cenotaph ten times taller than the one here.

Born in England to impoverished Welsh parents, David was bound to the Hudson's Bay Company as a seven-year apprentice at the age of fourteen. He was shipped to the Churchill Factory post on Hudson Bay in 1784.

Resourceful and intelligent, he quickly became a reliable wilderness man. Thompson learned trading, surveying and survival, and accomplished extensive Canadian exploration assignments for the Company west and southwest of Hudson Bay. When his term with Hudson's Bay ended, he left to join the North West Company of Montreal.

His new employer gave him important mapping assignments. He came within a few miles of identifying the source of the Mississippi River, and surveyed the shores of Lake Superior – mapped in ten months nearly 4,000 square miles. Alexander Mackenzie, no slouch himself, told Thompson in those few months he had accomplished more than the company could have expected in two years.

In 1799 David Thompson married a woman who was half Cree or Chippewa. They had five children in the west and eight more after they went east. He took his family with him on most of his travels. He was made a partner, in 1801, of the North West Company.

The new partner explored incessantly: Lake Superior, Lesser Slave Lake, Peace River country, Red Deer River, the foothills of the Rockies. He was directed to attempt crossing the Continental Divide in 1806.

Thompson reached the upper Columbia the following year, wintered near its source with the Kutenai Indians, and established a post there – the first on the upper waters of the Columbia.

Spring, 1808, found the trapper-explorer portaging from the head of the Columbia to the south-flowing Kootenai River (spelled Kootenay in Canada) with the intention of opening trade with the Flatheads, Nez Perce and Blackfeet. He came south of present Bonners Ferry before returning east, almost to Lake Superior, with his furs – at one point covering 132 miles in a single day! Then in August he came west again to the headwaters of the Columbia for the winter.

Before Thompson began his second descent of the Kootenai, he squeezed in another round-trip east with his furs. He came down the Kootenai in September, 1809, to Lake Pend Oreille, and then east, where, near this monument, he built Idaho's first white establishment: Kullyspell House. It was to serve as a trading center for the Kalispels, Flatheads, Spokans, and Coeur d'Alenes. In late September Thompson explored the Pend Oreille River to a point west of present Newport, Washington. Leaving a supply of trading goods at Kullyspell House, he went up the Clark Fork and wintered in Montana, near Thompson Falls, where he built another post.

In April he came back down Clark Fork with twenty-eight packs of pelts, visited Kullyspell, then went up the Kootenai and back across the Rockies to deliver the season's fur harvest to the company post. The man moved like he had a posse on his tail.

Thompson had to detour around the Blackfeet in 1810, through what is now Jasper National Park, because they were furious that he had given rifles to their enemies. In his absence, his men had abandoned Kullyspell House because of the marauding Blackfeet. In July, 1811, he took a cedar canoe, paddled by four Indians and five French Canadians, downriver from Kettle Falls to the mouth of the Columbia. Thompson returned up the Columbia, making another round-trip east in two months. He spent the winter, 1811-1812, in Montana and again came down the Clark Fork in March – his last trip before going east with the furs.

The explorer-surveyor now went to Montreal and worked two years on a ten-by-six-foot map of all the western lands he had examined. It was hung in the dining hall of the North West Company's post at Fort William, where only company partners and employees were allowed to see it, lest the hard-won information be seen by the eager eyes of the Hudson's Bay Company.

David Thompson and his family then settled near Montreal, where he surveyed the international boundary between Canada and the U.S. for ten years, employed by the British Boundary Commission.

Thompson suffered in his last years. His eyesight failed, he had to sell his scientific instruments and even pawn his coat. He managed to write the fascinating narrative of his explorations, but it was never published in his lifetime. (Washington Irving tried to buy it, but offered insufficient money and recognition.) David Thompson died at age eighty-seven, and was buried in an unmarked grave in Montreal's Mount Royal cemetery.

This great man might never have been given his just accolade had it not been for a geologist working in the west during the 1880s for the Geological Survey of Canada. He was impressed with the accuracy and detail of the maps he was using and his curiosity about their origin led him to discover Thompson's journals, notebooks, and map in Toronto. Through his efforts, David Thompson's journal was finally published in 1916.

The location of **Kullyspell House** was reestablished in 1923 with the aid of a blind eighty-year-old Indian who had seen the two stone chimneys as a boy. Following his instructions, the overgrown, jumbled rocks were found. The location is on private land on Memaloose Point, and therefore no marker indicates the exact site.

Settlement of Hope began in 1882 during construction of the Northern Pacific railroad. The town is said to have been named for a veterinary surgeon, Dr. Hope, who treated the horses of the railroad contractors.

The town was platted in 1896, partially burned in 1900, rebuilt, and incorporated in 1903. At the turn of the century it had about 800 residents.

Memaloose Point, or the Hope Peninsula, fingers out into the lake on the south side of the highway. It supports the David Thompson Game Preserve.

On the end of the promontory is an Indian petroglyph occupying an area eighteen feet in length and from two to seven feet in height, that contains twenty-eight figures, most of which appear to be stylized bear tracks. Other representations include projectile points, a mountain goat, and two sets of circles.

There are similar inscriptions on the rocks of Memaloose Island – just offshore from the point, and on Cottage Island, as well. Their age and meaning are unknown.

Vardis Fisher claims the islands were used for platform burials by the Pend Oreille Indians.

Dedication of David Thompson Monument at Hope, Sept., 1928.

The mouth of the **Clark Fork River** can be seen where it disembogues in Lake Pend Oreille about eight miles east of Hope. This sleepy site is the locale of "the greatest flood documented by man" – the so-called **Spokane Flood**. Geologists agree that this unprecedented event occurred 18,000-20,000 years ago during the Great Ice Age. (In 1962 the first radio-carbon dating of this flooding was derived from carbonaceous material at the Wanapum dam site and gave a maximum limiting date of 32,000 years ago.) The deluge left its mark along a course extending 550 miles – from western Montana to the Pacific Ocean.

Although glaciation had begun in the northern hemisphere at least 2 million years earlier, glacial history leading to the flood began approximately 100,000 years ago. At that time, glaciers were sliding southward from enormous ice fields in southern British Columbia, following the major south-trending valleys which led into Washington, Idaho and Montana. Such glaciers crept down the Pend Oreille and Priest River valleys, and the Purcell Trench (which in places confines the Kootenai River).

According to geologists, the Purcell ice lobe scoured its way into a basin that now holds Pend Oreille Lake and moved from there southwestward across Rathdrum Prairie and Spokane valley to the eastern outskirts of the area now occupied by the city of Spokane.

The southern movement of the Purcell lobe effectively staunched the flow of the Clark Fork River with a dam of glacial ice. The dam, near the mouth of the Clark Fork, was buttressed by the cliffs at the north end of the Bitterroot Range, on the south side of the river. The Clark Fork valley was obstructed by a wall of ice nearly 2,000 feet high.

Meltwater from other glaciers behind the dam formed **Glacial Lake Missoula** – covering at its highest level an area of about 3,000 square miles and containing an estimated 500 cubic miles of water: half the volume of Lake Michigan. (Traces of the ancient shoreline can be clearly seen on Sentinel Mountain at Missoula, Montana, where the lake was about 950 feet deep.)

Eventually, the water realized any lake's only hope: overflow. The breach undoubtedly widened rapidly, undercutting the sides until the dam collapsed. Within a relatively short time – perhaps only a day or two – the water of this natural reservoir was released.

The deluge was cataclysmic – unmatched by any flood known. The avalanche could only go south and southwestward. Current velocities in the Clark Fork Canyon narrows are calculated to have reached forty-five mph. The maximum rate of flow is estimated to have been 386 million cubic feet per second, or about ten times the combined flow of all the rivers of the world. (For comparison, the rate of flow for the world's largest river, the Amazon, is 6 million c.f.s., and for the Columbia River is 255,000 c.f.s.)

The inundation that thundered out of the mouth of the Clark Fork valley roared through Pend Oreille Lake, mauled Rathdrum Prairie and debouched into the Spokane valley. One arm of the tidal wave swept down Coeur d'Alene Lake and surged across the divide between Lake and Rock Creeks. But most of the water raced down the Spokane valley; its prodigious volume, velocity, and turbulence provided the erosional energy required to obliterate the loess which covered the lava flows and carved the channeled scablands of eastern Washington.

The duration of the flood is unknown, but a reasonable guess by geologists says the crest was short-lived – perhaps lasting less than two days. At Wallula Gap, Washington, just south of the confluence of the Snake with the Columbia, where all the floodwaters from the lava fields had to pass, it is estimated that it took a month from the time the dam was breached until the scabland streams returned to normal flows.

Geologists have found some evidence that the Purcell lobe advanced and blocked the Clark Fork River at least four times, but the large lake creating the great flood was formed about 18,000 years ago.

Indications of the Spokane Flood were first remarked in the early 1920s by J Harlen Bretz, a geologist from the University of Chicago. His theory was dismissed by the U.S. Geological Survey, on grounds that catastrophic causes must never be invoked as long as any gradualist alternative exists, but detailed studies by many geologists working over the area for more than fifty years have pieced together sufficient evidence to vindicate Bretz's concept. Earlier geologists, including Bretz, who worked at ground level could not see the evidence that is now obvious in good aerial photographs. Bretz lived to see the acceptance of his theory of catastrophic geological change. Even planetary geologists found the channelway features of Mars best interpreted by Bretz's hypothesis. In November, 1979, at the annual meeting of the Geological Society of America, J Harlen Bretz, age ninety-five, was given the profession's premier award, the Penrose Medal.

Though the best confirmation of the Great Spokane Flood is visible from the air, there is an excellent display of giant ripple marks that can be seen on the south side of Marble Pass, Montana, less than a mile east of State Highway 28, between Perma and Camas Hot Springs. South of the pass, a wall of water at least 800 feet high deposited ridge after ridge of coarse gravel in great dunes. They cover an area of six square miles, measure twenty to thirty feet in height and from 200 to 300 feet apart. Some of the ridges are nearly two miles long. Huge boulders bear percussion chips made as they collided with one another while suspended in the flood water.

People are usually curious whether early man may have witnessed the deluge, but the question cannot be answered with certainty. The earliest known evidence of man in Idaho, determined by Carbon 14 analysis of charcoal from a site considerably farther south of the ice dam, dates 14,000 years ago. So there is no definite proof man was living in the Pacific Northwest at the time of the flood.

Cabinet Gorge was given its name by French trappers – it was suggested by the recesses in the rock walls along the Clark Fork River. The peaks of the Cabinet mountains were sculptured by alpine glaciers as recently as 12,000 years ago.

Clark Fork River eroded Cabinet Gorge through the mildly metamorphosed sedimentary rocks (hardened mudstones) of a formation which is part of the Belt Series. In the area southeast of Hope, one can see the best exposures of these formations which began accumulating 1.6 billion years ago. The river here was probably superimposed across the bedrock as it eroded through layers of sediment deposited in Glacial Lake Missoula.

Beetop Mountain and **Scotchman Peak** (6,390 ft.) are on the left between East Hope and Clark Fork town.

The Clark Fork River has had more names than Istanbul: Bitterroot, Deer Lodge, Hell Gate, Missoula, Silverbow. All of these names were eliminated in favor of Clark Fork by the Board on Geographic Names in 1921.

In June, 1870, two small steamboats, the *Cabinet* and the *Missoula*, property of the Oregon and Montana Transportation Co., a subsidiary of the Oregon Steam Navigation Co., descended the rapids of the Clark Fork to Lake Pend Oreille.

Glacially eroded grooves and striated surfaces, evidence of ice-lobe passage, occur on the bedrock above the cliffs at Denton curves, east of Hope.

686

The town of **Clark Fork** had lead-silver mines that were active from 1913-1943. A fifty-ton concentrator operated here. Nearly $2.5 million was realized from 24 million pounds of lead and one million ounces of silver.

East of the community of Clark Fork, 7.5 miles, a Washington Water Power billboard extolling the merits of private utilities (which WWP Co. just happens to be), signals the turnoff for a half-mile drive down to the **Cabinet Gorge Dam** viewpoint.

This dam was another of the Defense Program construction hustles. In one of the quickest approvals on record, the Federal Power Commission licensed the $47 million Washington Water Power Company project in January, 1951. Ebasco Services, Inc., a New York firm, was the designer and supervisor; Morrison-Knudsen was the prime contractor.

Washington Water Power purchased the site from Northern Pacific Railway, which owned ten miles of the reservoir shoreline. Seven miles of Northern Pacific track and five miles of state highway had to be relocated.

Since the dam is only a half mile west of the Montana border, the Montana legislature had to pass a special bill authorizing water storage in that state for use in Idaho.

The Clark Fork River, which glided below the 350-foot walls of the Z-shaped gorge, posed a special problem: its flow varied from a late-summer low of 5,000 cubic feet per second to a record spring high of 190,000 c.f.s. This meant that if the concrete for the spillway was not completed in one season, the spring flood could wash out the upstream cofferdam and overtop the dam site, carrying away ten months of work. Performance schedules were critical.

Diversion of the river was accomplished by using thirty-two tons of dynamite to slide 50,000 cubic yards of rock into the narrow canyon from the southern gorge-wall. The spectacular blast was felt in Sandpoint, thirty miles away. The water was shunted through a pair of tunnels, each 1,000 feet long, which had been driven through the rock of the right abutment. Cofferdams were installed above and below the construction site, and a half-million cubic yards of rock were excavated. Work went on around the clock, as 1,500 men labored at the enterprise.

The race was won in April, 1952, when concrete reached the level of the spillway. The first of four 50,000 k.v. generators went on line in September of the same year.

The true-arch dam is 208 feet high and about 600 feet long. Its strength lies in the thrust its bow exerts on the canyon walls, because nowhere is the dam more than forty feet thick. It impounds water 105 feet above a river that was ninety-five feet deep. The reservoir has a length of twenty-four miles. Transmission lines connected to the power grid run from Noxon (Montana) to Spokane.

The company claims the dam was completed in half the time and at half the cost of federal estimates.

One mile beyond the Cabinet dam site, Highway 200 arrives at the Montana state line as abruptly as the end of a book.

Epilogue

I am in daily touch with the past without living there. I suspect that the only present we can really live in – the only enduring present – is one that makes connections: horizontally to other people living now elsewhere under other circumstances; vertically down to the dead and up to the unborn, down to history and up with endeavor. In the Middle Ages most people lived only on the timeless and vertical plane of religion, seasonal change an endless circle: the same round between heaven and hell. Now most people live only on the horizontal, and our time is space: miles and numbers, quantities and travel. The enduring present lives at the point where these lines cross.

Donald Hall

690

692

Photographic Credits

All photographs are from the Idaho Historical Society collection except the following:

Pages 1, Conley; 3, Army Corps of Engrs.; 6, Dept of Commerce; 21-22, USFS; 23, Weyerhaeuser Co.; 32, Conley; 45, Dept. of Comm.; 50, Weyerhaeuser Co.; 52, Army Corps of Engrs.; 58, Weyerhaeuser Co.; 59, Conley; 78, Ore. Hist. Soc.; 87, Potlatch Corp.; 120 Dept. of Comm.; 131, Conley; 141, Duane Garrett; 144, Union Pacific; 154, Conley; 155, Dept. of Comm.; 165, Ernie Day; 197, Conley; 201, BLM; 212, Conley; 222, Air National Guard; 243, Ore. Hist. Soc.; 248, Boyd Norton; 264, Dept. of Comm.; 276, Conley; 277, Ernie Day; 289, St. Parks and Rec.; 293, 297, Conley; 307, Dept. of Comm.; 318-319, BLM; 336, Jerry Hughes; 345, Henri Cartier Bresson, Magnum Photos; 349, Ore. Hist. Soc.; 357, Ernie Day; 360, Conley; 411, Ore. Hist. Soc.; 416, USFS; 421, Dept. of Comm.; 426-427, Dept. of Comm.; 430, USFS; 438-445, Museum of No. Ida.; 456, Conley; 465, Idaho Statesman; 467, Dept. of Comm.; 474, Conley; 487, USFS; 516-520, Bisbee Collection, Twin Falls Library; 526-527, Ore. Hist. Soc.; 531, Lloyd Byrne; 543, Conley; 555, Duane Garrett; 562-563, Intermtn. Cult. Ctr.; 576, Larry Hill; 579, Dept. of Comm.; 586, John Carrey; 589, Ore. Hist. Soc.; 627, Ore. Hist. Soc.; 656-657, Crosby Library, Gonzaga Univ., 673-674, Conley; 677, Dept. of Comm.

Cover photo: Larry Hill (Road to Redfish Lake).
Rear cover: BLM (top), Duane Garrett,(bottom).

Events Calendar

Date	Place	Event
JANUARY		
1st Week	Bayview	FISHING DERBY.
3rd Week	Priest Lake	WINTER CARNIVAL.
	Sandpoint· Schweitzer	WINTER SKI CARNIVAL. Snow sculpture, parade.
	Kellogg	SILVER VALLEY WINTER FESTIVAL.
Last Week	Busterback Ranch S. of Stanley	BUSTERBACK STAMPEDE. Cross-country ski race.
FEBRUARY		
1st Week	Pierce	WINTER CARNIVAL.
1st Week	Preston	KANGANARK MUSHERS PRESTON SLED DOG RACE.
1st Week	Boise	CRANSTON CUP JUNIOR SKIING.
	McCall	WINTER CARNIVAL.
2nd Week	Kamiah	LINCOLN'S BIRTHDAY CELEBRATION. Indian Games and War Dances.
2nd Week	Lava Hot Springs	WINTER CARNIVAL.
Mid-February	Priest Lake	NW CHAMPIONSHIP DOG SLED RACES.
MARCH		
1st Week	Boise	BOISE SPORTS AND RV SHOW.
	Twin Falls	MAGIC VALLEY GEM SHOW.
1st Week	Idaho Falls	ANNUAL TOUR OF ARTISTS HOMES AND STUDIOS.
Last Week	Boise	BOISE HOME AND GARDEN SHOW.
	Busterback Ranch S. of Stanley	SPRING ROUNDUP. Party and fun day on cross-country skis.
Last Week	Pocatello	IDAHO STATE CHAMPION CUTTER AND CHARIOT RACES.
APRIL		
1st Week	Coeur d'Alene	COIN AND ANTIQUE SHOW.
Last Week	Weiser	ANNUAL SPRING SHOW AND SALE. Art show.
Last Weekend	Idaho Falls	GEM AND MINERAL ROCK SHOW.
	Idaho Falls	ANNUAL SPRING ART SHOW.
Last Sunday	Arco	ATOM BUSTER BREAKFAST.
MAY		
1st Week	Riggins	SALMON RIVER RODEO.
	Sandpoint	KAMLOOPS AND KOKANEE WEEK. Fishing Derby.
1st Week	Boise	MUSIC WEEK. Citywide music programs.

698

2nd Week	Payette	SPRING FAIR.
Mid-May	Payette	APPLE BLOSSOM FESTIVAL AND BOOMERANG DAYS. Parade, barbecue, carnival.
Mid-May	Coeur d'Alene	LAKE COEUR D'ALENE DAYS FESTIVAL. Boat parade, logging festival.
	Parma	FORT BOISE DAYS. Contests, parade.
Late May	Priest Lake	SPRING FESTIVAL AND FLOTILLA.
Last Saturday	Kendrick	LOCUST BLOSSOM FESTIVAL
Last Week	Council	ADAMS COUNTY LITTLE BRITCHES RODEO.

JUNE

1st Week	Kamiah	KAMIAH RODEO.
1st Week	Massacre Rocks	TRAPPER RENDEZVOUS.
	Rigby	JEFFERSON COUNTY STAMPEDE.
	Blackfoot	BLACKFOOT ANNUAL RODEO.
1st Week	Weiser	HELLS CANYON RODEO.
	Weiser	EXPERIMENTAL AIRCRAFT FLY-IN.
	Buhl	LITTLE BUCKAROO RODEO.
	Meridian	PANCAKE FEED AND DAIRY SHOW.
2nd Week	Cambridge	HELLS CANYON ART AND HOBBY SHOW.
Mid-June	Ketchum	INTERNATIONAL FASCHING FESTIVAL.
3rd Week	Weiser	NATIONAL OLD TIME FIDDLERS CONTEST AND FESTIVAL. National fiddle competition, parade, jam sessions.
	Emmett	CHERRY BLOSSOM FESTIVAL AND SQUAW BUTTE ROCKHOUND SHOW.
3rd Week	Mackay	ANNUAL MACKAY RODEO.
	Aberdeen	ABERDEEN DAYS. Homemakers fair, contests, breakfast and barbecue supper.
Last Saturday	Craigmont	JUNE PICNIC. Parade, street sports, noon buffalo barbecue.
Last Week June to Mid-July	Craigmont	TALMAKS ANNUAL CAMP MEETING. Religious revival for Nez Perce Tribe.
Last Week	Sun Valley	SHOSHONE INDIAN TRAP SHOOT.
Last Saturday	Rupert	RUPERT JAMBOREE. Chuckwagon feed, specialty acts, dancing.

JULY

1st Week	Sandpoint	GAY 90'S ARTS AND CRAFTS.
	Nordman	FRONTIER DAYS. Carnival, lumberjack competition, buffalo barbecue.
	Grangeville	BORDER DAYS. Amateur rodeo, barbecue.
	Sandpoint	LIONS CLUB CELEBRATION. Parade, carnival.
	Winchester	WINCHESTER DAYS. Parade, fiddlers contest, museum.
1st Week	Rexburg	WHOOPEE DAYS. Parade, rodeo, black powder shoot, barbecue.
	Driggs	ALL GIRLS RODEO.

699

	Salmon	SALMON RIVER DAYS. Parade, water can contests, breakfast, demolition derby.
	Montpelier	BEAR LAKE MONSTER FESTIVAL AND 4TH OF JULY. Old fashioned games, picnic.
1st Week	Rexburg	ARTS AND CRAFTS SHOW.
	Caldwell	4TH OF JULY CELEBRATION.
	Marsing	OLD FASHION 4th of JULY.
	Buhl	SAGEBRUSH DAYS. Rodeo, parade, barbecue.
	Council	FOURTH OF JULY. Porcupine races.
	Stanley	PANCAKE BREAKFAST.
	Rupert	4TH OF JULY. Three night rodeo.
	Cascade	THUNDER MOUNTAIN DAYS. Buckaroo breakfast, parade, barbecue.
1st Weekend after 4th	McCall	SQUARE AND ROUND DANCE FUNSTITUTE. Dancing and workshops.
2nd Week	Worley	WHAA-LAA-DAYS. Indian games and war dance contest.
2nd Week	Weiser	HELLS CANYON RODEO.
	Idaho City	IDAHO CITY ARTS FESTIVAL. Artists, music and theater groups.
	Caldwell	LITTLE BRITCHES RODEO.
2nd & 4th Week	Pocatello	"SUN DANCE" War Dances and Indian games.
Mid-July	Bonners Ferry	KOOTENAI RIVER DAYS. Free pancake breakfast, rodeo, lumberjack competition.
	Priest River	PRIEST RIVER LOGGERS CELEBRATION. Lumberjack competition, parade.
Mid-July	Sun Valley	TRAIL CREEK CABIN BASQUE BENEFIT. Weight lifting, wood chopping. Oinkari Dancers.
3rd Week	Nampa	SNAKE RIVER STAMPEDE.
	Stanley	MOUNTAIN MAMAS ARTS AND CRAFTS FAIR.
4th Week	Caldwell	CANYON COUNTY 4-H AND FFA FAIR.
	Boise	ANNUAL DRUM AND BUGLE CORPS. Championships.
Last Full Week	Hailey	RAY NELSON INVITATIONAL. LITTLE LEAGUE TOURNEY.
Last Week	Boise	BASQUE PICNIC AND STREET DANCE.
	Boise	BASQUE HOLIDAY DANCE.
Last Week	Harrison	OLD TIMER'S CELEBRATION. Theater revue, melodrama, dance, parade.
	Kooskia	KOOSKIA DAYS. Parade, old time fiddlers jamboree.
	Sandpoint	LIONS CLUB BARBECUE.
	Moscow	IDAHO STATE SQUARE AND ROUND DANCE FESTIVAL.
	Plummer	INDIAN DAYS AND PLUMMER FESTIVAL. Parade, street games, races.

| Last Week | Lava Hot Springs | ANNUAL MOUNTAIN MAN RENDEZVOUS. |
| | Preston | PRESTON FAMOUS NIGHT RODEO. |

AUGUST

1st Week	Coeur d'Alene	ANNUAL FESTIVAL OF ARTS.
	Deary	FRIENDSHIP FESTIVAL. Cowboy breakfast, loggers and fiddlers contests.
	Hayden Lake	BARBECUE DAY. Fireman's water barrel fight, games, races.
	Pierce	1860 DAYS. Longhorn barbecue, lumberjack competition.
	Coeur d'Alene	ART ON THE GREEN.
1st Week	Driggs	PIERRE'S HOLE RENDEZVOUS. Melodrama, barbecue, parade, fiddle and black powder contests, rodeo.
Early August	Island Park	ISLAND PARK RODEO.
	Idaho Falls	WAR BONNET ROUNDUP. Idaho's oldest rodeo.
1st Week	Sun Valley	SUN VALLEY ARTS FESTIVAL.
Early August	McCall	ANNUAL WATER CARNIVAL AND REGATTA.
	Boise	I.O.N. YOUTH APPALOOSA HORSE SHOW.
2nd Week	Mackay	ANNUAL MACKAY ALL GIRLS RODEO.
2nd Week	Lapwai	PI-NEE-WAU-DAYS. War dance, exhibits, music, Indian games.
Mid-August	Cataldo	YEARLY PILGRIMAGE TO OLD CATALDO. Coeur d'Alene Indians.
	Winchester	MUD SPRINGS CAMP. Indian games, feast.
Mid-August	Fort Hall	SHOSHONE-BANNOCK INDIAN FESTIVAL AND RODEO.
	Pocatello	FRONTIER DAYS RODEO.
Mid-August	Burley	CASSIA COUNTY RODEO. Country Western jamboree.
	Homedale	OWYHEE COUNTY RODEO.
3rd Week	Caldwell	CALDWELL NIGHT RODEO.
Last Week	Boise	WESTERN IDAHO FAIR.
Last Week	Rexburg	MADISON COUNTY RODEO.
	Salmon	LEMHI COUNTY RODEO.

SEPTEMBER

Labor Day Weekend	Riggins	RAFT RACE AND BARBECUE.
1st Monday	St. Maries	BENEWAH COUNTY FAIR and Paul Bunyan Days.
1st Week	Blackfoot	EASTERN IDAHO STATE FAIR.
1st Saturday	Garden Valley	PAYETTE RIVER CATTLEMEN'S ANNUAL BARBECUE.
1st Weekend	Filer	TWIN FALLS COUNTY RODEO.
Labor Day Weekend	Ketchum	WAGON DAYS.

701

1st Saturday	Kamiah	BARBECUE DAY. Cowboy breakfast, sports, parade, barbecue.
Mid-September	Coeur d'Alene	NO. IDAHO FAIR & RODEO.
2nd Week	Mountain Home	AIR FORCE APPRECIATION DAY. Parade, carnival, noon barbecue.
	BOISE	ARTS AND CRAFTS FESTIVAL.
Mid-September	Lewiston	LEWISTON ROUNDUP. Cowboy breakfast, rodeo.
3rd Week	Orofino	LUMBERJACK DAYS.
Last Week	Shelley	IDAHO ANNUAL SPUD DAY. Parade, baked potatoes, fishing derby.

OCTOBER

1st Week	Sandpoint	ALL BONNER COUNTY BAZAAR.
	Sandpoint	DRAFT HORSE INTERNATIONAL SHOW.
2nd Week	Mountain Home	SAILING REGATTA C.J. STRIKE RESERVOIR.
Thanksgiving Weekend	Coeur d'Alene	Winterfest Art Show.
Last Week	Coeur d'Alene	ARTS AND CRAFTS FAIR.
Last Weekend	Riggins	FIDDLERS JAMBOREE. Jam sessions.
Last Weekend	Fort Hall	SHOSHONE-BANNOCK INDIAN DAY. War dances, Indian games and rodeo.

NOVEMBER

Mid-November	Boise	BASQUE CARNIVAL AND BAZAAR.
Late-November	Twin Falls	SAINT ANDREWS ANNUAL DINNER. Scottish dinner.

DECEMBER

Mid-December	Boise	HANDEL'S MESSIAH. Christmas concert at St. John's Cathedral.
	Boise	CATHEDRAL OF THE ROCKIES. Christmas concert.
3rd Week	Boise	ANNUAL BASQUE SHEEPHERDERS BALL.

Mileage Chart

	BLACKFOOT	BOISE	BURLEY	COEUR d'ALENE	GRANGEVILLE	IDAHO FALLS	JEROME	LEWISTON	POCATELLO	SALMON	SANDPOINT	SHOSHONE	TWIN FALLS
ABERDEEN	39	225	69	529	423	64	110	494	39	224	547	122	104
ALBION	100	178	18	561	376	126	63	447	81	286	606	75	57
AMERICAN FALLS	44	210	55	535	408	70	96	480	25	230	553	108	89
ARCO	59	189	140	443	388	67	101	459	81	138	461	83	111
ASHTON	80	303	178	487	*470	54	215	*515	103	183	505	196	212
BLACKFOOT	—	248	98	492	446	26	138	518	23	187	510	142	132
BOISE	248	—	160	384	198	257	116	270	234	328	429	117	130
BONNERS FERRY	537	462	621	78	263	510	578	192	559	349	33	570	591
BUHL	148	119	54	503	317	174	29	389	129	263	548	42	16
BURLEY	98	160	—	543	358	124	45	429	79	278	588	57	39
CALDWELL	272	26	183	389	203	281	140	275	258	352	434	141	153
COEUR d'ALENE	492	384	543	—	186	466	500	115	515	305	45	501	513
DRIGGS	100	323	197	508	*490	74	235	*536	123	203	526	216	232
DUBOIS	76	266	173	431	*423	50	178	*469	99	136	449	159	187
EMMETT	278	30	190	379	193	287	146	264	264	358	424	147	160
GOODING	159	102	66	486	301	167	22	372	141	238	531	17	36
GRANGEVILLE	446	198	358	186	—	*449	314	72	432	*287	231	315	328
HAILEY	135	142	100	493	340	144	62	411	158	188	511	43	71
IDAHO FALLS	26	257	124	466	*449	—	165	*494	50	161	484	150	158
JEROME	138	116	45	500	314	165	—	386	120	240	545	19	15
LAVA HOT SPRINGS	57	269	114	*548	467	83	154	539	35	244	566	167	148
LEWISTON	518	270	429	115	72	*494	386	—	504	*333	160	387	399
McCALL	355	107	267	277	91	364	223	162	341	*378	322	224	237
MALAD	79	276	120	570	474	105	161	545	57	266	588	173	155
MONTPELIER	110	322	167	602	521	137	208	592	88	297	620	220	201
MOSCOW	*544	299	459	84	101	*518	415	30	534	*357	130	416	429
MOUNTAIN HOME	206	44	117	428	242	214	73	313	192	285	473	74	87
NAMPA	264	20	176	397	211	273	132	282	250	344	442	133	146
NEW MEADOWS	368	119	279	265	79	376	235	150	354	*366	310	236	249
OROFINO	*478	254	413	150	56	*452	370	42	488	*291	195	371	383
PAYETTE	304	57	215	356	170	313	172	242	290	383	401	173	185
POCATELLO	23	234	79	515	432	50	120	504	—	210	533	132	113
PRESTON	91	303	147	582	501	117	188	572	68	277	600	200	182
REXBURG	54	276	151	461	*444	28	188	*489	77	156	479	169	186
RIGBY	41	271	138	464	*446	15	179	*492	64	159	482	165	173
RUPERT	93	165	9	549	363	119	50	434	74	279	594	62	44
ST. ANTHONY	66	288	163	473	*456	40	200	*501	89	168	491	182	198
SALMON	187	328	278	305	*287	161	240	*333	210	—	323	221	249
SANDPOINT	510	429	588	45	231	484	545	160	533	323	—	544	558
SHOSHONE	142	117	57	501	315	150	19	387	132	221	544	—	28
STANLEY	192	214	173	420	*403	200	135	*448	214	115	438	116	144
SUN VALLEY	148	154	113	482	353	157	75	424	170	177	500	56	84
TWIN FALLS	132	130	39	513	328	158	15	399	113	249	558	28	—
WALLACE	443	412	534	49	214	417	495	157	466	256	94	477	504
WEISER	318	71	229	342	156	326	185	228	304	397	387	186	199
MISSOULA, MT	326	*369	416	166	*171	300	378	*216	348	138	184	359	387
PORTLAND, OR	675	428	586	369	404	684	543	333	661	*665	412	544	556
SALT LAKE CITY, UT	180	343	186	671	541	206	228	613	157	366	689	240	222
SPOKANE, WA	521	383	543	29	185	495	499	114	543	333	72	500	513
W. YELLOWSTONE	135	357	232	435	*440	109	269	*485	158	237	453	251	267

*Via Lolo, Montana – U.S. 12

Colophon

This book was set in Korinna on an Autologic APS-5 by Bonnie Robinson, Judy Hambley, Kurt Reuter, and Freda Cenarrusa of B&J Typesetting Co., Boise, Idaho.

Korinna was designed in 1904 by Berthold in Germany, and revised in 1977 by Ed Benguiat for International Typeface Corporation.

Book design is by Roger and Julie Sliker of Ada, Michigan.